YEAR BY YEAR
A VISUAL CHRONICLE

UPDATED AND EXPANDED

With a Foreword by Stan Lee and
Afterword by Joe Quesada

LONDON, NEW YORK,
MELBOURNE, MUNICH, AND DELHI

Editors Catherine Saunders, Heather Scott, Julia March, Alastair Dougall
Project Editor Elizabeth Dowsett
Designers Hanna Ländin, Ron Stobbart, Lisa Crowe, Jill Clark, Mark Richards, Dan Bunyan, Dynamo Ltd
Senior Designers Nathan Martin, Robert Perry
Creative Technical Support Adam Brackenbury
Managing Editor Laura Gilbert
Design Manager Maxine Pedliham
Brand Manager Lisa Lanzarini
Publishing Manager Julie Ferris
Category Publisher Simon Beecroft
Production Controller Amy Bennett
Production Editors Siu Chan, Sean Daly
Pre-Production Producer Rebecca Fallowfield

First published in Great Britain in 2008 by
Dorling Kindersley Limited,
80 Strand, London, WC2R 0RL.
This edition, 2013.

4 6 8 10 9 7 5 3
008-187360-Sep/2013

A CIP catalogue record for this book is available from the British Library

ISBN: 978-1-40937-888-4

Colour reproduction by Media Development and Printing Ltd, UK.
Printed and bound by Hung Hing, China

Discover more at
www.dk.com

YEAR BY YEAR
A VISUAL CHRONICLE

UPDATED AND EXPANDED

CONTENTS

27
OUR OWN LITTLE
A PROPOSAL! AT
DON'T FAINT,
--- WE MUST

the SEA BEAUTY
NAMORA
LET NONE ESCAPE ALIVE!
IF ONLY THERE WAS SOMEONE WHO COULD HELP US!
SENTINEL OF THE SPACEWAYS
THE SILVER SURFER
AVENGERS
HIS NAME IS... YELLOWJACKET
AMAZING FANTASY
INTRODUCING SPIDER MAN
THOUGH THE WORLD MAY MOCK PETER PARKER, THE TIMID TEEN AGER...
X-MEN
AT LAST!! THE X-MEN COME FACE-TO-FACE WITH "the BROTHERHOOD of EVIL MUTANTS"
WAR ADVENTURES ON THE BATTLEFIELD
"SLAUGHTER ON...
CAPT. SAVAGE AND HIS LEATHERNECK RAIDERS
THOR
STRACZYNSKI COIPEL MORALES MARTIN
MARVEL SUPER-HEROES FEATURING: CAPTAIN MARVEL
"THE COMING OF CAPTAIN MARVEL!"
ALL NEW! NEVER SEEN BEFORE!
PLUS: FIVE ALL-TIME GREATS FROM THE GOLDEN AGE!
THE BLACK KNIGHT! THE DESTROYER! CAPTAIN AMERICA! THE HUMAN TORCH! THE SUB-MARINER!
STARRING FEDERAL AGENT CLARK MASON
HULK
IN SAVAGE COMBAT WITH THE CRYPTO-MAN
ON THE CITY STREETS, DEATH IS WAITING!
I POSSESS... THE POWER!
MAKE MINE MARVEL!

FOREWORD

Hi, Heroes!
Believe it or not, there was once a world without Marvel Comics!

Mighty Marvel was originally known as Timely Comics. Timely published all sorts of titles: westerns, comedy, romance, animation, monsters—you name it, we did it.

Then came that fateful day in 1962 when we gave a grateful human race the first issue of *The Fantastic Four*. It was so successful that we immediately followed with *The Uncanny X-Men*, *The Incredible Hulk*, and *The Amazing Spider-Man*. (You can see, I'm particularly partial to adjectives.)

As our sales went through the roof, our success proved to be the death knell of Timely Comics. I decided then and there that we needed a new name to reflect the growing popularity of our expanding Super Hero line.

And so—I dreamed up "Marvel Comics." I loved that name because it lent itself to slogans and catch-phrases like: "Make Mine Marvel!," "Marvel Marches On!," and "Welcome to the Marvel Age of Comics!"

It seemed that nothing could stop us. Before long we had added such titles as *Iron Man*, *Daredevil*, *Dr. Strange*, *Sgt. Fury And His Howling Commandos*, later followed by *Nick Fury, Agent of SHIELD*.

We also introduced such off-beat characters as The Silver Surfer, Ant Man, The Inhumans, The Watcher, Galactus, The Punisher—gosh, I could go on and on.

But I must confess that I have a particularly warm spot in my heart for our villains. Charismatic as the heroes may be, their victories over the super-powered bad guys give them their greatest glory. After all, who has not thrilled to the titanic threats of such evil-mongers as Dr. Doom, The Green Goblin, The Abomination, Magneto, The Vulture, Bullseye, The Dread Dormammu, The Super Skrulls, The Mole Man, The Kingpin, The Scorpion, Dragon Man, Kraven the Hunter—and those are just the tip of the Marvel mountain of menace.

Still, even though I dreamt up all the quaintly capricious characters I've been telling you about, chances are they'd never have become so successful if not for the incredible contributions of the superbly talented artists with whom I worked.

You see, I merely gave a brief outline of each story to artists like Jack Kirby and Steve Ditko, to mention just two of our major stars. With outline in hand, they would then draw the actual strip without any further instructions from me. When finished, the illustrated pages would be returned to me and I would add all the dialogue, captions, and occasional sound effects. It was truly a collaborative effort consisting of three elements: 1) My original story. 2) The artist's illustrated interpretation of that story. 3) The dialogue which fleshed out the story and gave the characters their personality.

Everything we've done has been for just one purpose—to guarantee you hours of reading enjoyment. I fervently hope we've succeeded.

Excelsior!

Stan Lee

AUG.
NO. 1
10¢
LET NONE ESCAPE ALIVE!
IF ONLY THERE WAS SOMEONE WHO COULD HELP US!
APPROVED BY THE COMICS CODE AUTHORITY
IND.
4
MAR.
THE X-MEN
-TO-FACE WITH
UTANTS"
AMAZING FANTASY
12¢
THOUGH THE WORLD MAY MOCK PETER PARKER,
INTRODUCING
SPIDER MAN
APPROVED BY THE COMICS CODE AUTHORITY
MC
15
AUG
WAR ADVENT
ATLAS
MARVEL
VARIANT EDITION
1
STRACZYNSKI
COIPEL
MORALES
MARTIN

INTRODUCTION

Hoo-Ha!
That was my first reaction when I heard that my fabulous friends at dashing DK were planning to assemble a history of Marvel Comics—a veritable month by month, year by year chronology that would list the major events (and lots of the minor ones) of the most captivating comic book company of all time!

The titanic tome would start at the very beginning of the company we now know as Marvel Comics, and take us on a wondrous ride back through time to when it was called Timely Comics (1939–1950) and then Atlas Comics (1951–1961). We would journey through the Golden Age of Comics (1938–1955), the Silver Age (1956–1969), the Bronze Age (1970–1979), and through to the Modern Age of Comics (1980–the present).

Of course, my enthusiasm came to an abrupt halt once I realized that those cunning con artists at dastardly DK wanted me to work on the blasted thing. That would require hours of digging through old comics (hey, could be fun), researching old newspaper and magazine articles (sounds interesting), and rummaging through my own rather malfunctioning memory (a total waste of time!). A project as prodigious as this would require more than mere facts! It would demand personal observations, anecdotes, and educated insights into what may have inspired certain creations. (What the heck did Stan Lee have for dinner the night before he wrote "The Threat of Tim Boo Ba" for *Journey Into Mystery*?!?)

But wait! Already I could foresee a problem. We would have to base the entire chronology on the cover dates that appeared on the actual comic books—and that would be CRAZY! Here's a secret: a cover date on a comic book bears no relationship to reality. Let's say Banana Man first debuted in a September-dated comic. The truth is, he had really been created months earlier. As one who has produced a fair number of these four-color fantasies (well, they only had four colors when I started, as opposed to the thousands available now) I know that for a September-dated comic, the writer submits his part in January. The penciller illustrates the job in February. It is scripted, inked, lettered, colored, and edited in March. In the old days, it then took three months for a comic to be printed and distributed. (It takes only one now.)

However, here's the really wacky part—a book with a cover date of September would usually go on sale in June. (In the 1940s and 1950s, that cover date might have even been October or November.) Comic book dates weren't supposed to tell you when they went *on* sale. Their job was to tell the person who ran the newsstand when to take them *off* sale, when they could safely be removed from the old spinner racks (remember them?) and returned to the company.

Bah! As long as we keep this secret between you and me, no one else will ever realize how ridiculous it is to base this chronology on cover dates!

I'm through rambling. It's time to turn the page and enjoy the wonderment that awaits!

Face front, True Believer!

Tom DeFalco

1939

IN THE BEGINNING

The modern American comic book, as we know it today, began to take form in 1929 and gathered momentum in the mid-1930s. However, it was in 1938 that the comic book became truly popular. That was the year in which Detective Comics' *Action Comics* #1 was published, featuring the first appearance of Jerry Siegel and Joe Shuster's creation Superman, the first of the Super Heroes.

Action Comics was so successful that other publishers wanted to produce comic books and Super Heroes of their own. One of these men was Martin Goodman, a publisher of pulp magazines. In 1936, he released *Ka-Zar*, the first of his pulp magazines based on a continuing character. A white man turned lord of an African jungle, Ka-Zar was in the tradition of Edgar Rice Burroughs's Tarzan. In 1938, Goodman started a science fiction magazine with a title that would serve him well in the future: *Marvel Science Stories*, which later became *Marvel Tales*.

In 1939, Frank Torpey, the sales manager of a company called Funnies, Inc., persuaded Goodman to start publishing comics. Goodman called his comic book line Timely Publications, and his first comic book, which had a cover date of October, 1939, had a familiar name: *Marvel Comics* #1.

OCTOBER

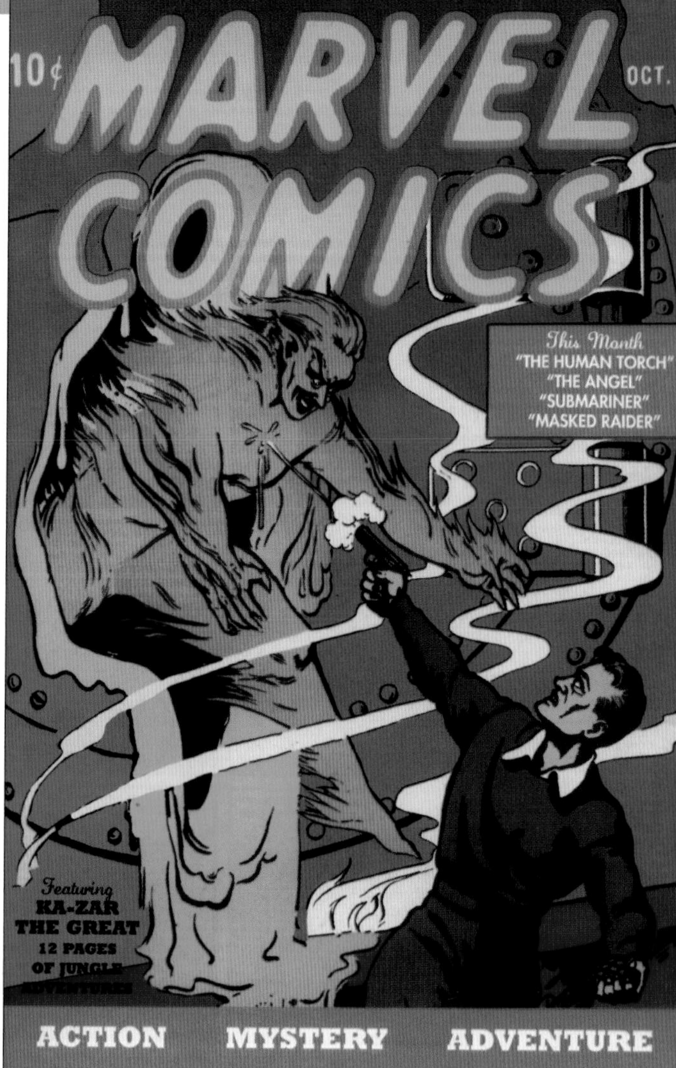

A SUPER HERO START

"Something went wrong with my figurings somewhere. Everytime this robot the Human Torch contacts oxygen in the air he bursts into flame!"

• *Marvel Comics* #1

The first issue of *Marvel Comics* introduced a pair of characters who would become two of Timely's greatest stars of the Golden Age of Comics, the period from 1938 through the 1940s. The original Human Torch and the Sub-Mariner were both Super Heroes, but they were far from being imitations of Siegel and Shuster's Superman. They were like modern elementals: the Torch, who literally burst into flame, embodied fire, and the Sub-Mariner, the prince of an underwater kingdom, represented water.

More importantly, neither the Torch nor the Sub-Mariner were conventional heroic figures. The misnamed Human Torch was not truly human, but an android—a robot in human form—who initially ran amok after escaping his creator in his first story. Magazine illustrator Frank R. Paul made the Torch look like a truly frightening menace on the cover of *Marvel Comics* #1. The Sub-Mariner was not only half-human, he was also an active enemy of the human race. The Torch and Sub-Mariner foreshadowed the path that Marvel would take in the 1960s, presenting Super Heroes who were outsiders in "normal" society.

Among the many other characters introduced in *Marvel Comics* #1 was the company's first Western hero, the Masked Raider, who was created by writer/artist Al Anders. Meanwhile, the original Ka-Zar, who had featured in Martin Goodman's pulp magazine, made his comics debut. This jungle hero, whose real name was David Rand, would go on to inspire the creation of Kevin Plunder, Marvel's present day Ka-Zar.

OCTOBER

NAMOR THE SUB-MARINER

"Here is the Sub-Mariner! An ultra man of the deep... lives on land and in the sea... flies in the air... has the strength of a thousand men."

• *Marvel Comics* #1

Writer/artist Bill Everett originally created Namor the Sub-Mariner in 1939 for an eight page title called *Motion Picture Funnies Weekly*. Produced by Funnies, Inc., this black-and-white magazine was intended to be handed out in movie theaters, but this idea fell through. So when Funnies, Inc. packaged *Marvel Comics* #1 for Martin Goodman, Everett added four pages to his story, which finally saw print in color.

Namor ("Roman" spelled backwards) was the grandson of Thakorr, the ruler of a vast undersea empire in the Antarctic. Everett referred to Namor's water-breathing race as "sub-mariners." Later, they would be called Atlanteans, a blue-skinned offshoot of humanity who originally founded their nation on the ruins of sunken Atlantis.

Namor, however, was different from other sub-mariners, being half human. His father was Captain Leonard McKenzie, an Antarctic explorer, who encountered Princess Fen, Thakorr's daughter. They fell in love, but McKenzie's expedition was wiped out by Atlanteans who came after Fen. (McKenzie would turn up alive decades later.) Fen bore McKenzie's son, Namor, who had the same skin color as his father, could breathe in and out of water, and possessed vast superhuman strength. He could even fly using small wings on his ankles.

When humans in diving suits appeared near his kingdom, Thakorr assumed that they were advance scouts for an invasion and ordered Namor to attack New York City. Amazingly, in the year that World War II began, Bill Everett created a series that enabled readers to understand the point of view of a character with his own moral code who regarded America as the enemy.

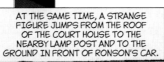

OCTOBER

THE HUMAN TORCH
by CARL BURGOS

THE ORIGINAL HUMAN TORCH

• *Marvel Comics* #1

Conceived by writer/artist Carl Burgos, the original Torch inspired the creation of Johnny Storm, the Human Torch of the Fantastic Four. When Professor Phineas T. Horton displayed his most important creation, the Human Torch, the android burst into flame. Surprisingly, he was unharmed. In a bid to control the Torch, Horton entrapped him, but he escaped, wreaking havoc. The Torch later learned to control his flame power and became a crime-fighting Super Hero.

AT THE SAME TIME, A STRANGE FIGURE JUMPS FROM THE ROOF OF THE COURT HOUSE TO THE NEARBY LAMP POST AND TO THE GROUND IN FRONT OF RONSON'S CAR.

THE FIRST ANGEL

• *Marvel Comics* #1

One of Timely's leading stars was the crime-fighter known as the Angel, who made his debut in November and would appear in over one hundred stories during the comics' Golden Age. He was created by writer/artist Paul Gustavson, who took inspiration from author Leslie Charteris's fictional adventurer called the Saint. The Angel, whose real name was Tom Hallaway, wore a superheroic costume, although he had no superhuman abilities. He later received the "mystic cape of Mercury," which allowed him to fly. Over twenty years later, editor Stan Lee and artist Jack Kirby would reuse the name "Angel" for the winged member of their original X-Men.

Martin Goodman hired writer/artist Joe Simon to be Timely's first Editor-in-Chief in late 1939.

Ka-Zar first appeared in the self-titled pulp magazine in October, 1936.

MEANWHILE IN 1939...

VICTORY FOR GENERAL FRANCO
The Spanish Civil War comes to an end when the last Republican forces surrender to General Francisco Franco's Nationalist forces.

MOLOTOV-RIBBENTROP PACT
Amidst a sense of coming war in Europe, Germany and the USSR sign a non-aggression pact. The agreement also states how the two nations would divide other European countries between themselves.

WORLD WAR II BEGINS
Hitler's invasion of Poland on September 1 is quickly followed by a declaration of war from Britain and France.

THE MANHATTAN PROJECT
Albert Einstein writes to President Roosevelt about the possibility of developing an atomic bomb. His letter leads to the Manhattan Project, an initiative between the US, Canada, and Britain to develop the first nuclear bomb.

SCIENCE FICTION CONVENTION
The First World Science Fiction Convention is held over three days in New York.

THE FIRST FROZEN PRECOOKED MEALS ON SALE
Birds Eye creates the first precooked meals to be sold frozen.

AND AT THE MOVIES...
Gone with the Wind, *epic, fiery, melodrama set in the Civil War South, with Clark Gable and Vivien Leigh;* Stagecoach, *this western dispatches a disparate group of frontier archetypes into dangerous "Injun" territory;* The Wizard of Oz, *technicolor musical fantasy in which Judy Garland's Dorothy seeks her safe return from Oz by following the Yellow Brick Road.*

The Sub-Mariner
HERE IS THE SUB-MARINER! --AN ULTRA-MAN OF THE DEEP...LIVES ON LAND AND IN THE SEA...FLIES IN THE AIR...HAS THE STRENGTH OF A THOUSAND MEN...IS A YOUTH OF DYNAMIC PERSONALITY...QUICK THOUGHT AND FAST ACTION...FROM WHENCE DOES HE COME. AND WHAT IS HIS MISSION?
BY Bill Everett

A SALVAGE SHIP'S DIVER COMES UP ~

THE DIVING PLATFORM IS HOISTED, AND SWUNG TO THE DECK OF THE SALVAGE SHIP S.S. RECOVERY"--

HOW DO YOU FEEL, NELSON?
OKAY, CHIEF - BUT KINDA PUZZLED. THERE'S SUMP'N SCREWY ABOUT THAT WRECK -
SOME TIME LATER, THE DIVER, ROD NELSON, STEPS FROM THE DECOMPRESSION CHAMBER, AND IS ASKED WHAT HE FOUND ON THE BOTTOM -

I FOUND THE SAFE IN THE MAIN SALOON, ALL RIGHT, BUT IT LOOKS LIKE SOMEBODY GOT HERE BEFORE WE DID - THE SAFE'S EMPTY! THEN, TOO, IT LOOKS LIKE WHOEVER RIFLED IT HASN'T BEEN GONE LONG - THERE WAS A KNIFE ON THE DECK, AND IT HADN'T EVEN RUSTED -

THAT'S STRANGE, NELSON - THERE'S BEEN NO REPORT OF ANY OTHER SALVAGE SHIP IN THESE WATERS FOR THREE YEARS -WE OURSELVES HAVE BEEN CRUISING HERE FOR A WEEK, AND WE'VE SEEN NO SIGN OF LIFE AT ALL.

WELL, THERE'S ONLY ONE THING TO DO - I'LL HAVE TO SEND YOU DOWN AGAIN WITH CARLEY, TO SEE WHAT EVIDENCE YOU CAN PICK UP - THEY MAY HAVE LEFT SOMETHING BY WHICH WE CAN IDENTIFY THEM.

OKAY - SEND CARLEY AHEAD - I'LL BE WITH YOU IN A MINUTE ....

ALL, SET, CARLEY ? I'LL DROP THE ACETYLENE TORCH AS SOON AS YOU HIT BOTTOM
AND SO CARLEY SETTLES BENEATH THE SURFACE, LITTLE KNOWING THE PHENOMENA HE AND NELSON ARE ABOUT TO WITNESS -

SAY, ROD, DID YOU LEAVE THAT SIDE HATCH OPEN ? OR WAS IT SPRUNG IN THE WRECK ?
NO - IT WAS CLOSED WHEN I WAS DOWN BEFORE - THERE'S SOMETHING UNCANNY ABOUT THIS -
ON THE SEA BOTTOM THEY CONVERSE BY TELEPHONE ~

NAMOR SURFACES

In these ominous opening pages to the Sub-Mariner's debut in Marvel Comics *#1 (Oct., 1939), divers descended beneath the ocean depths, never to return. Thinking them to be robots, the Sub-Mariner killed the divers and then wrecked their ship. Upon discovering that the divers were humans, the undersea emperor Thakorr sent the Sub-Mariner to attack the surface world to deter further invaders of his realm. This first Sub-Mariner story was given a special flavor of mystery and excitement by the stylized draughtsmanship of the character's creator, Bill Everett.*

1940s

The story of Marvel Comics began with an amazing burst of creativity. When Timely published its first comic, *Marvel Comics* #1, in 1939, America was still suffering from the Great Depression and Europe was engulfed by World War II. American pop culture responded with a new sort of hero: the Super Hero, an individual who could take on the great threats that menaced the world. In the three years from 1939 to 1941, the first great Marvel Super Heroes appeared: the Sub-Mariner, the original Human Torch, and Captain America. Once America entered World War II, Joe Simon and Jack Kirby's *Captain America Comics* sold nearly one million copies per issue. Yet, once the war was over, tastes radically changed. Timely pursued one new trend after another: funny animals, teen comedy, crime, westerns, and romance. Within a decade, Super Heroes had fallen into oblivion, and the comic book industry was on the brink of disaster. Meanwhile, a teenage office assistant named Stanley Lieber had become Marvel's Editor-in-Chief. This was Stan Lee, the man who would one day revolutionize and reenergize Super Hero comics...

I HAVE RETURNED FROM AN ADVENTUROUS TRIP! MANY THINGS HAVE I TO TELL YOU!

1940

SIMON, LEE, AND KIRBY

Initially relying on Funnies, Inc. to produce comics for him, Timely publisher Martin Goodman gradually formed his own staff. By the end of 1940 Timely had employed three of the most important figures in Marvel's—and comics'—history.

First, in the fall of 1939, Goodman hired writer/artist Joe Simon away from Funnies, Inc. to work as Timely's Editor-in-Chief. In 1940, Simon was joined on staff by his collaborator, artist Jack Kirby. Working closely together on both writing and art, Simon and Kirby devised a new, dynamic style of visual storytelling for the comic book medium. Toward the end of 1940, Simon and Kirby got an assistant, the teenage cousin of Goodman's wife. Who could have imagined that young Stanley Lieber would become world-famous as Marvel writer, Editor-in-Chief, and publisher Stan Lee?

JANUARY

MASTER OF COVER ART

• *Marvel Mystery Comics* #3

With its second issue *Marvel Comics* was renamed *Marvel Mystery Comics*. Issue #3, along with the new Timely comic *Daring Mystery Comics* #1 (Feb.), bore the company's first covers by artist Alex Schomburg. Born in Puerto Rico in 1905, Schomburg became the principal Timely cover artist of the 1940s. Stan Lee later said that, "Alex Schomburg was to comic books what Norman Rockwell was to *The Saturday Evening Post*."

JANUARY

BETTY DEAN DEBUTS

• *Marvel Mystery Comics* #3

When the Sub-Mariner attacked New York City, policewoman Betty Dean undertook a courageous scheme to capture him. Betty pretended to be drowning and, when Namor investigated, she pointed a gun at him, intending to take him to the authorities. Despite this initial clash, Betty later became Namor's friend and ally.

M Joe Simon created, wrote, and drew the adventure strip "The Fiery Mask" in *Daring Mystery Comics* #1.

FEBRUARY

NAMOR VS. NAZIS

• *Marvel Mystery Comics* #4

Although the US would not enter World War II until 1941, Timely began its own war on Nazi Germany. Policewoman Betty Dean managed to persuade Namor that the Nazis were his enemies and so the Sub-Mariner battled a German U-boat in this issue.

JUNE

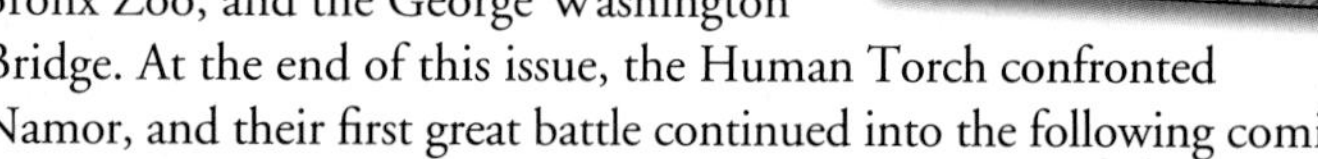

THE START OF THE MARVEL UNIVERSE

• *Marvel Mystery Comics* #8

By revealing that Namor and the Torch existed in the same fictional world, the crossover story in this issue began to establish the concept of the Marvel Universe. Waging a one-man war on the United States, the Sub-Mariner destroyed the top of the Empire State Building, the Bronx Zoo, and the George Washington Bridge. At the end of this issue, the Human Torch confronted Namor, and their first great battle continued into the following comic.

AUGUST

THIN MAN AND BLACK WIDOW

• *Mystic Comics* #4

This issue introduced Bruce Dickson, alias the Thin Man, a Super Hero who was endowed by a lost civilization with the power to flatten and stretch his body. Black Widow also debuted, slaying evildoers to send their souls to her master, Satan.

FIRST EPONYMOUS HERO

• *Red Raven Comics* #1

The first Timely hero to become the title hero of his own comic book was the Red Raven, created by Joe Simon and artist Louis Cazeneuve. Unfortunately, *Red Raven Comics* was not successful and did not see a second issue.

M *Red Raven Comics* #1 also featured "Mercury In The 20th Century," a story drawn by Jack Kirby about the Roman God.

FALL

TORCH MEETS TORO

"Toro—henceforth you shall be known as... Toro, the flame kid—there'll be a fortune in it for all of us."

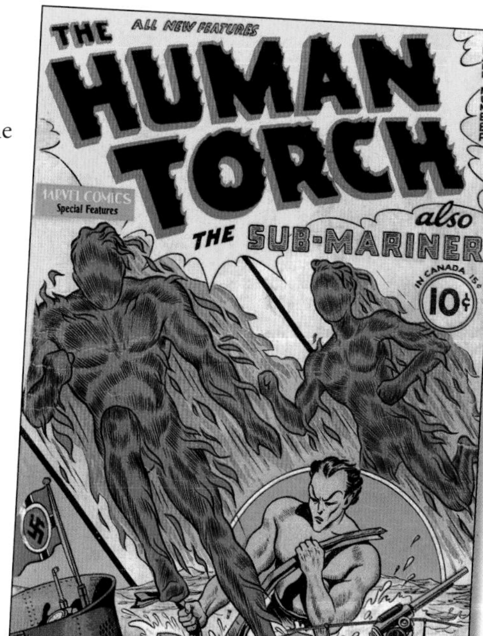

• *The Human Torch* #2

When *Red Raven Comics* proved unsuccessful, Timely changed the title and the lead character but continued the numbering. Thus, the first issue of *The Human Torch* was numbered as issue two.

In the 1940s, it became a popular trend to give a Super Hero a teenage sidekick. It was presumed that comics' young readers would identify with the boy sidekick. Thus, they could imagine themselves vicariously going on adventures with the lead hero, who became a father figure to his young sidekick. Since the original Human Torch was actually an artificially constructed android, giving him a "son" would further humanize him.

Hence, in *The Human Torch* #2, the Torch found Toro, a boy performing in a circus as a "fire-eater," who was somehow immune to flames. When the Torch came near the boy, Toro burst into flame, while remaining unharmed. The Torch realized that Toro had the same super-powers as himself and he mentored Toro in the use of his powers. Together they became a crime-fighting team.

Toro's real name was Thomas Raymond. In later decades Marvel would solve the mystery of how Toro acquired his super-powers by establishing that he was a mutant, making him one of the first mutants to appear in a Marvel (then Timely) comic.

Toro remained the Torch's sidekick until 1948, when he was supplanted by Sun Girl. Toro teamed with the Torch when the latter's series was briefly revived in April, 1954. The adult Toro perished heroically in battling his mentor's enemy, the Mad Thinker, in *Sub-Mariner* #14 (June, 1969).

STAN THE BOY

Starting in late 1940, editor Joe Simon and artist Jack Kirby had their own kid sidekick: seventeen-year-old Stanley Martin Lieber. At first Stan was merely a gofer, performing mundane chores and errands.

Stan dreamed of becoming a writer, and Simon gave him the opportunity. In this era, society looked down on comic books, and, Stan later said, "I felt someday I'd be writing The Great American Novel and I didn't want to use my real name on these silly little comics." So he tried various pseudonyms, settling on "Stan Lee." Ironically, it was comics that made him famous, and Stanley Lieber eventually legally changed his name to Stan Lee.

MEANWHILE IN 1940...

FIRST AFRICAN-AMERICAN ON A POSTAGE STAMP

The educator and leader of the African-American community, Booker T. Washington, is the first black man to be honored on a US postage stamp.

NEW PRIME MINISTER IN BRITAIN

In Britain, Winston Churchill faces the challenges of leading a country at war when he becomes Prime Minister after Neville Chamberlain resigns.

NYLON STOCKINGS ON SALE

The first nylon stockings go on sale in New York. They are so popular that more than 780,000 pairs are sold on the first day.

OPERATION DYNAMO AT DUNKIRK

350,000 British, French, and Belgian troops are evacuated from Dunkirk by boat when they become encircled by German forces.

THE BATTLE OF BRITAIN

The Royal Air Force and the Luftwaffe battle in the skies over Britain. In mid-September, Hitler postpones his invasion due to heavy losses.

A SECOND FILM FROM DISNEY

RKO distributes Pinocchio, *Walt Disney's second full-length animated film, which follows the success of Disney's first movie,* Snow White and the Seven Dwarfs, *released in 1937.*

AND AT THE MOVIES...

The Grapes Of Wrath, *America's Depression-era, dustbowl tragedy is vividly recreated in John Ford's adaptation of John Steinbeck's novel of dispossessed farmers trekking to California;* His Girl Friday, *Howard Hawks's frantic, theatrical comedy features the fastest dialogue ever filmed in this newsroom-centred battle of the sexes;* Rebecca, *Hitchcock's tense, atmospheric adaptation of Daphne Du Maurier's tale of a woman haunted by the spirit of her new husband's dead wife.*

SEPTEMBER

THE FIRST MARVEL BOY

• *Daring Mystery Comics* #6

Editor Joe Simon and artist Jack Kirby only did one story about Martin Burns, alias the Super Hero Marvel Boy, but it was memorable. Marvel Boy battled spies serving a foreign dictator named "Hiller," but it was clear that the villains were really the Nazis.

Simon and Kirby created the original Marvel Boy (shown here), whose name was reused in 1950 by a Super Hero created by writer Stan Lee and artist Russ Heath.

NOVEMBER

BEHOLD THE VISION

• *Marvel Mystery Comics* #13

Another creation by the team of editor Joe Simon and artist Jack Kirby was the original Vision. Also known as Aarkus, Vision was an eerie, green-skinned being from another dimension, who could appear out of smoke to battle criminals on Earth. Aarkus inspired writer Roy Thomas and artist John Buscema to create the modern android Vision, who first appeared in *The Avengers* #57 (Oct., 1968).

ALSO...

THE KING OF COMICS

The most important and influential artist in the history of Marvel Comics, Jack Kirby was born as Jacob Kurtzberg in 1917 and grew up on Manhattan's Lower East Side. As a boy he belonged to the Suffolk Street Gang, the inspiration for the Yancy Street Gang in *Fantastic Four*. A self-taught artist, Kirby became an assistant animator on *Popeye* cartoons at the Max Fleischer Studio. Later Kirby worked on comics for the great cartoonist Will Eisner at the legendary Eisner-Iger studio. Kirby first met Joe Simon when they both worked for Fox Comics and Kirby followed Simon to Timely; they would remain a creative team for nearly two decades.

LOOK AT CAP GO TO WORK ON THOSE SPIES!

1941

HEROES VERSUS HITLER

In 1941, isolationists in the United States put up considerable resistance to becoming involved in what they saw as Europe's war. However, Timely publisher Martin Goodman and the team of editor Joe Simon and artist Jack Kirby believed that the Nazis were a worldwide threat. Timely characters such as the Sub-Mariner were already combatting the Nazis. Simon and Kirby decided to create another hero who was their response to totalitarian tyranny abroad. On the cover of *Captain America Comics* #1, they portrayed their new creation, Captain America, dressed in a uniform bearing the colors, stars, and stripes of the American flag, and punching Adolf Hitler in the jaw.

Cap was not the first patriotically themed Super Hero, but he would become the most enduring. He was also Timely's most popular hero, with nearly a million copies of his comic sold per month.

SPRING

NAMOR VS. NAZIS

• *The Sub-Mariner* #1

One of Timely's stars, Namor the Sub-Mariner, became the title character of his own comic book in the spring. Alex Schomburg's powerful cover significantly showed Namor employing his incredible strength to overturn a German submarine full of Nazi soldiers.

M Jeff Mace, the costumed hero called the Patriot, was created by writer Ray Gill and artist Bill Everett in *The Human Torch* #4.

MARCH

STARS AND STRIPES

"We shall call you Captain America, son! Because, like you—America shall gain the strength and the will to safeguard our shores!"

• *Captain America Comics* #1

In March, Captain America made his patriotic debut. A frail youth named Steve Rogers was determined to join the army and serve his country in these perilous times. Rogers was declared unfit for service and rejected, but his fervor impressed an army officer and Rogers was offered the opportunity to become part of a secret experiment. Professor Reinstein administered his "super-soldier serum" to the youth, which transformed Rogers into a physically perfect human being. Realizing that Reinstein's plan to create an army of American "super-soldiers" could work, a Nazi secret agent shot the professor dead. Rogers quickly overpowered the assassin. But the secret of the serum died with Reinstein, and Steve Rogers would be the only one of his kind.

The government turned Rogers into their special costumed agent, Captain America, who represented traditional American ideals and the will to fight for them. Originally he carried a triangular shield, which was soon replaced by a round shield that proved to be indestructible. Steve Rogers was now in the army. When army mascot Bucky Barnes discovered that Private Rogers was secretly Captain America, the Captain made Bucky his costumed sidekick.

Writer Joe Simon and artist Jack Kirby established virtually all of this in their origin story in the first issue of *Captain America Comics*. They would produce the first ten issues of the comic before leaving the company after a falling out with publisher Martin Goodman. In March, 1964, artist Jack Kirby and writer Stan Lee would revive Captain America for a new generation of readers in *The Avengers* #4.

THE RED SKULL

• *Captain America Comics* #1

Since Captain America represented the spirit of American liberty and democracy, then inevitably his archenemy would be the embodiment of oppression and totalitarianism. In *Captain America Comics* #1 editor Joe Simon, artist Jack Kirby, and scripter Ed Herron introduced that enemy: the Red Skull, a Nazi mastermind who wore a blood-red death's-head mask. (Actually, the Red Skull in issue #1 was unmasked as an impostor; the real Red Skull turned up in issue #7 in October.) The first great Marvel Super Villain, the Red Skull continued to menace humanity decades after the fall of Nazi Germany. Not even apparent—or actual—death stopped the Red Skull for long.

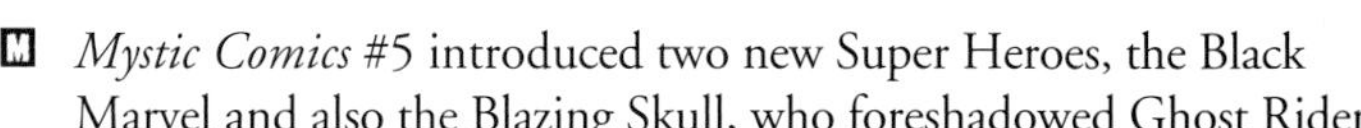

M *Mystic Comics* #5 introduced two new Super Heroes, the Black Marvel and also the Blazing Skull, who foreshadowed Ghost Rider.

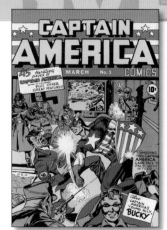

DARING NEW HEROES

• *Daring Mystery Comics* #7

This issue introduced Elton Morrow, who became the superheroic Blue Diamond with diamond-hard skin. Bill Everett, creator of the Sub-Mariner, came up with another seagoing Super Hero, Lt. Peter Noble, alias the Fin.

MAY

STAN LEE'S FIRST STORY

• *Captain America Comics* #3

Joe Simon and Jack Kirby's assistant Stanley Lieber wrote his first story for Timely, a text story called "Captain America Foils the Traitor's Revenge." It was also his first Super Hero story, and the first work he signed using his new pen name of Stan Lee.

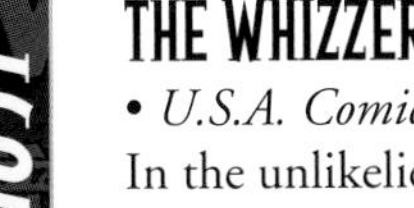

SUMMER

THE TEAMS OF SUMMER

• *Young Allies Comics* #1

Super Hero sidekicks Bucky and Toro teamed up with kids named Jeff, Knuckles, Tubby, and Whitewash as the Young Allies in this issue. Created by Joe Simon and Jack Kirby in a text story in *Captain America Comics* #4, they were originally called the Sentinels of Liberty.

In *All Winners Comics* #1 Captain America, the Human Torch, the Sub-Mariner, the Angel, and the Black Marvel teamed up.

AUGUST

THE WHIZZER

• *U.S.A. Comics* #1

In the unlikeliest of origin stories, the blood of a mongoose endowed Bob Frank with the ability to move at superhuman speed. He became the costumed Super Hero called the Whizzer, who later joined the All Winners Squad and married his superheroic colleague Miss America. First drawn by Al Avison, the Golden Age Whizzer would go on to inspire the names of super-speedsters in both the Squadron Supreme and Squadron Sinister.

Captain America Comics #5 included Stan Lee's first actual comics story entitled "'Headline' Hunter, Foreign Correspondent."

JACK FROST

• *U.S.A. Comics* #1

Jack Frost, who debuted in this issue, was one of the first heroes co-created by writer Stan Lee. Frost could generate intense cold, and freeze water vapor in the air into solid ice. Both his powers and his appearance resembled those of a later Stan Lee co-creation, Iceman of the X-Men.

FALL

THE GREAT FLOOD

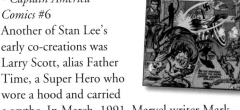

• *The Human Torch* #5

As many as a dozen comics writers and artists congregated in artist Bill Everett's apartment for a weekend to create this classic sixty-page story featuring the greatest battle between the Human Torch and the Sub-Mariner. It also represented the pinnacle of the Sub-Mariner's war against the human race. Aptly titled "The World Faces Destruction," it climaxed when Namor unleashed "the great anti-American blitz:" a "mammoth tidal wave" that flooded and devastated Manhattan!

FATHER TIME

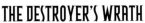

• *Captain America Comics* #6

Another of Stan Lee's early co-creations was Larry Scott, alias Father Time, a Super Hero who wore a hood and carried a scythe. In March, 1991, Marvel writer Mark Gruenwald reused the name "Father Time" for a member of the Elders of the Universe.

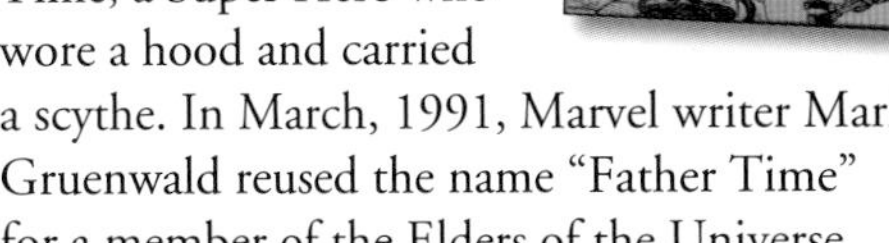

THE DESTROYER'S WRATH

• *Mystic Comics* #6

The most significant and successful of Stan Lee's early co-creations was the Destroyer. First drawn by Jack Binder, the Destroyer was reporter Kevin Marlow, who was accused of spying in Nazi Germany and imprisoned in a concentration camp. There, a scientist gave Marlow a serum that enhanced his physical abilities. Escaping, Marlow assumed the costumed identity of the Destroyer, wearing an inhuman mask and a death's-head insignia, to combat the Nazis.

STAN THE MAN

When Editor-in-Chief Joe Simon and artist Jack Kirby left Timely in late 1941, the only person left on staff to step up to the job of Editor-in-Chief was Stan Lee, who was still only eighteen years old! But, except for his wartime stint in the army, Stan Lee would remain Marvel's Editor-in-Chief until 1972.

MEANWHILE IN 1941...

US PROGRAM TO AID THE ALLIES
President Roosevelt signs into law the Lend-Lease Act, under which the US will lend war material to countries fighting against Nazi Germany.

PEARL HARBOR
The US enters the war after the its fleet is attacked at Pearl Harbor by Japanese warplanes.

ENIGMA MACHINE IN ALLIED HANDS
HMS Bulldog *captures the Enigma cryptography machine aboard the German submarine U-110, which leads to the decryption of German communications.*

OPERATION BARBAROSSA
Germany invades Russia, obliterating the Nazi-Soviet non-aggression pact of August, 1939.

PLUTONIUM DISCOVERED
Scientists at the University of Berkeley discover the radioactive element Plutonium.

GARBO RETIRES
Actress Greta Garbo, star of Anna Karenina *and* Grand Hotel, *retires at age thirty-six.*

FIRST AMERICAN FM RADIO STATION
W47NV goes on the airways in Nashville, Tennessee. It becomes WSM-FM, the first commercial FM radio station to be granted license in the US.

AND AT THE MOVIES...
Citizen Kane, *Orson Welles's biopic of a vainglorious newspaper magnate uses innovative narrative and cinematography;* The Maltese Falcon, *dialogue-driven film noir features Humphrey Bogart as a cynical PI drawn into a hunt for a priceless statuette;* Dumbo, *Disney tale of the reunion of a clumsy, readily ridiculed baby circus elephant with his "imprisoned" mother.*

YOU DON'T STAND A CHANCE AGAINST CAPTAIN AMERICA.

1942

TIMELY GOES TO WAR

Japan attacked the United States naval base at Pearl Harbor, Hawaii, on December 7, 1941. Various key people in Timely's comics would soon enter the armed services, including Editor-in-Chief Stan Lee, the Human Torch's creator Carl Burgos, and the Sub-Mariner's creator Bill Everett. Joe Simon and Jack Kirby had already left Timely, and they would end up in the military as well. The day after the Pearl Harbor attack, another Timely contributor enlisted, joining the Army Air Corps. This was Mickey Spillane, who had been doing two-page text stories for Timely, and would become world famous for his novels featuring detective Mike Hammer. Despite these changes to the staff, Timely still managed to produce some significant titles in 1942.

JANUARY

CITIZEN V

• *Daring Mystery Comics* #8

A lieutenant in the British army, John Watkins was seemingly killed by machine gun fire from a German warplane. After miraculously surviving, Watkins agreed to go behind enemy lines to fight the Germans and thus to inspire the conquered people of Europe to rise against them. Watkins adopted the masked identity of Citizen V after the "V for Victory" sign. The 1990s' comic *Thunderbolts* would establish that Watkins had a number of successors as Citizen V.

APRIL

COMEDY IN COMICS

• *Joker Comics* #1

Recognizing the potential market for humor comics, Timely publisher Martin Goodman launched Joker Comics, which, as its name suggested, featured only comedy. The first issue marked the debut of the popular series Powerhouse Pepper by legendary cartoonist Basil Wolverton. Powerhouse Pepper was a competent boxer, if slightly dimwitted. This issue also featured Marmaduke Snood Jr., alias Stuporman, whom writer/artist Harry Douglas had created in *Daring Mystery Comics* #6 (Sept., 1940). Stuporman was one of the first Super Hero parody series, preceding Marvel's *Not Brand Echh* by over two decades.

M *Daring Mystery Comics* became the humor series *Comedy Comics* with issue #9.

JULY

ZIGGY PIG AND SILLY SEAL

"Meet me 'n' all my pals in Krazy Komics every month! Be seein' ya!"

• *Krazy Komics* #1

In the 1940s, animated cartoons featuring comical animals were shown in movie theaters before the main feature films. Timely publisher Martin Goodman decided to capitalize on the popularity of these cartoons by moving his comics company into the genre of funny animals.

The cover for the first issue of Krazy Komics *spotlighted Toughy Cat, but Ziggy Pig and Silly Seal would become Timely's best-known funny animals.*

Two of Timely's biggest funny animal stars were Ziggy Pig and Silly Seal, who made their debuts as a team in this issue. Artist Al Jaffee created Ziggy first, though it was editor Stan Lee who came up with his name. Later, Lee asked Jaffee to devise another funny animal character. Realizing that he hadn't seen a talking seal in animated cartoons yet, Jaffee invented Silly Seal. Lee suggested giving Silly a friend, and so Jaffee paired him with Ziggy Pig. As in such classic comedy duos as Laurel and Hardy or Abbott and Costello, one member of the team—Ziggy Pig—was the leader or straight man, and the other—Silly Seal—was the lovable but dumber stooge. Ziggy Pig was frequently seen wearing a black and yellow sweater with a large "Z" on the front while Silly Seal was seen with a striped toboggan cap and scarf. The anthropomorphic pair regularly found themselves contending against another character, Toughy Cat, who became their primary antagonist.

The funny duo were cover stars of all eight issues of *Animated Funny Comic-Tunes* (1944–1946) and in January, 1944, they got their own comic, *Ziggy Pig and Silly Seal Comics*, which lasted until September, 1949.

After his time at Timely ended, Ziggy and Silly artist Al Jaffee worked with editor Harvey Kurtzman on the early *MAD* magazine.

WINTER

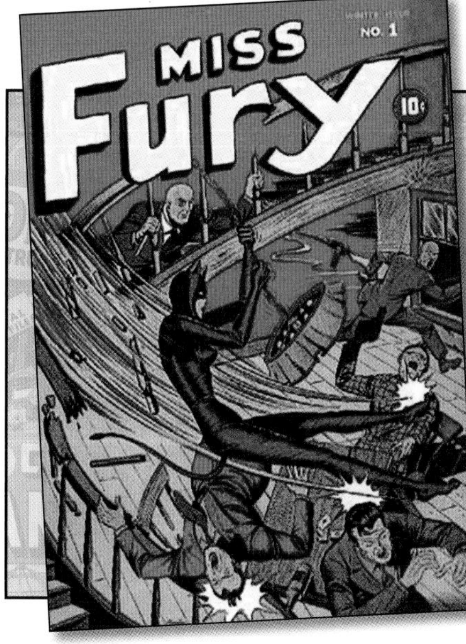

MISS FURY DEBUTS

• *Miss Fury* #1

It was quite rare for a woman to draw an adventure series, either in comic strips or in comic books. But in 1941, cartoonist Tarpé Mills created a newspaper strip about socialite Marla Drake. Drake was the crime-fighter originally called the Black Fury but soon renamed Miss Fury. Mills's heroine had no super-powers and wore a daringly skintight costume in her adventures. During the war, Miss Fury often battled Axis agents. Timely reprinted the "Miss Fury" Sunday newspaper strips in comic book format, beginning with this issue in Winter, 1942, and ending with issue #8 in the winter of 1945–46.

ALSO...

SUPER HEROES AND SILLIES

In 1942, Timely's Super Hero comics were still going strong with comedy titles also coming into their own.

Timely's first comic, *Marvel Comics*, had changed its name in December, 1939, becoming *Marvel Mystery Comics*. This series would continue through the 1940s, ending with issue #92 in June, 1949.

Captain America Comics, which had only begun the previous year, would also run through the 1940s, coming to an end with issue #75 in February, 1950. Other Timely heroes would often appear in this comic, including the Sub-Mariner in issue #20 (Nov., 1942).

War was still a common focus, as depicted in May's *U.S.A. Comics* #4, whose cover featured Major Liberty fighting Japanese officers and a disk in the top right corner that stated "Remember Pearl Harbor."

On the comedy front, *Daring Mystery Comics* had been renamed Comedy Comics in April, 1942, while Martin Goodman licensed the rights to do comics based on the Terrytoons animations, beginning with *Terry-Toons Comics* #1 in October.

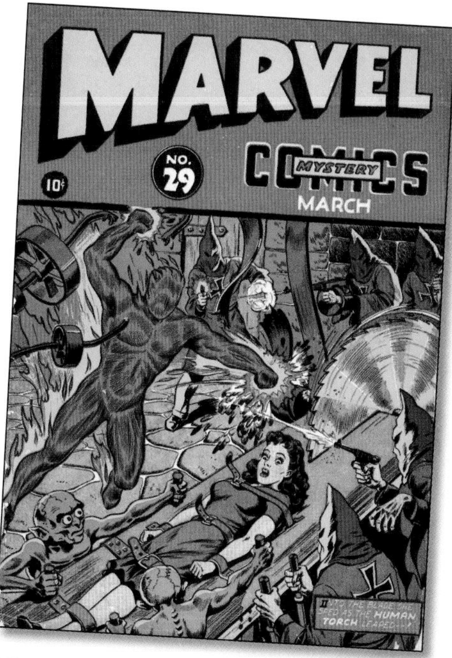

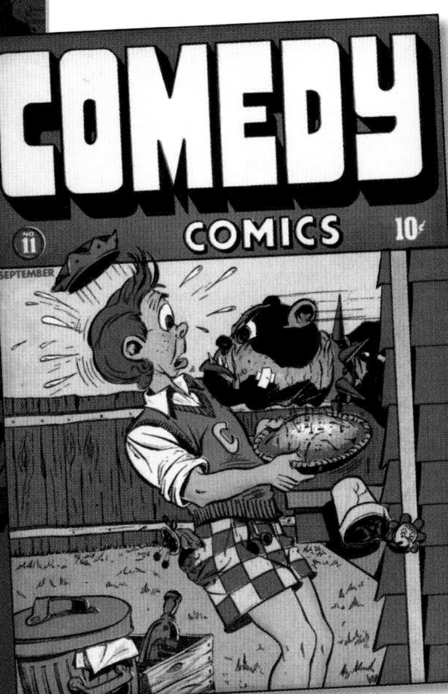

VINCE FAGO BECOMES EDITOR

The only interruption in Stan Lee's long, three decade service as Editor-in-Chief came when he volunteered to enter the army in 1942, now that the United States had entered World War II. Since funny animals were the new trend in comics, artist Vince Fago, who had worked with Lee on Ziggy Pig and Silly Seal, took over from Lee as Editor-in-Chief.

MEANWHILE IN 1942...

THE "FINAL SOLUTION" PLOTTED

At the Wannsee conference in Berlin, senior Nazis plan the "final solution"—the deportation and extermination of the European Jews.

FIRST US TROOPS ARRIVE IN EUROPE

Several thousand infantry troops of the US Army land in Northern Ireland to face the war in Europe.

THE VOICE OF AMERICA SPEAKS

The first radio piece on The Voice of America *broadcasts. Its aim is to send propaganda to the areas of the world under German occupation.*

PENICILLIN: A NEW WONDER DRUG

The first patient is successfully treated for streptococcal septicemia with penicillin. The new drug proves invaluable in the war effort for treating soldiers with bacterial infections.

BATTLE OF EL ALAMEIN

After weeks of battle, Allied forces break the Axis line at El Alamein, forcing the German and Italian troops into retreat. In response, Prime Minister Churchill says, "This is not the end. It is not even the beginning of the end. But it is perhaps, the end of the beginning."

"T-SHIRT" IS BORN

The US Navy designs a new short-sleeved garment to be worn under shirts. After the war it takes off among civilians as the "T-shirt."

FIRST "GOLD RECORD"

Record label RCA Victor sprays a record of the hit song Chattanooga Choo-choo *gold after it has sold a million copies.*

DREAMS OF A WHITE CHRISTMAS

Bing Crosby has a musical hit with White Christmas, *when it appears in the movie* Holiday Inn.

WAR IN THE PACIFIC

In early 1942 the war in the Pacific was not going well with America losing Guam, Hong Kong, Wake, Singapore, and the Philippines, but in late 1942 the US started to turn around the war with major offences at Midway and The Coral Sea.

MALTA GETS GEORGE CROSS FOR BRAVERY

The island of Malta in the Mediterranean gets awarded the George Cross medal for bravery, which is usually reserved for individuals. It was getting, on average, seven bombing raids a day.

AND AT THE MOVIES...

Casablanca, *Michael Curtiz's perfectly cast, bittersweet, romantic masterpiece, set around Rick's Café Américain, packs a mighty punch;* Bambi, *Disney's animal animation about an orphaned deer who learns to survive hostile hunters and a forest fire.*

COMEDY COMICS
NO. 9
APRIL
10¢
A RIOT OF FUN
GRRRR-!
GRRRR!
CRUNCH!
GRRRR!

Comedy Comics #9 ***(April, 1942)***
Timely's Daring Mystery Comics *turned into* Comedy Comics *with issue #9.* Comedy Comics *#9 and* Joker Comics *#1, which had the same cover date, were Timely's first humor comics and both used caricatured human characters. This issue of* Comedy Comics *featured Basil Wolverton's science fiction comedy strip "Splash Morgan," and backup stories starring Super Heroes, including Ben Thompson's Citizen V, Bill Everett's The Fin, and the Silver Scorpion.*

1943

DIVERSE DIRECTIONS

Even though their creators were in the armed forces, Timely's leading Super Heroes—Captain America, the original Human Torch, and the Sub-Mariner—were still going strong. Not only did they star in their own comic books, but all three also appeared in the first five issues of the new *All Select Comics* series that Timely launched in the Fall. Somewhat lesser lights, the Destroyer and the Whizzer, also turned up in this comic and it marked the final appearance of the original Black Widow.

From 1939 through 1941, there had been an explosion of creativity in the new Super Hero genre at Timely. But in 1943 the principal creators responsible for that explosion were in the armed services. While Stan Lee was gone, Vince Fago was Timely's Editor-in-Chief. No new significant Super Hero characters were being created. *Kid Komics*, starring writer Otto Binder's hero Captain Wonder, for example, lasted merely two issues.

Instead, Timely was diversifying its line, attempting to attract other audiences. Super Rabbit was a super-powered funny animal, and Miss America was a Super Hero designed for young female readers.

JANUARY

BASIL WOLVERTON'S BOXER

• *Powerhouse Pepper Comics* #1

Having debuted the year before in *Joker Comics* #1, cartoonist Basil Wolverton's Powerhouse Pepper won his own comic book, although it was suspended after one issue. Powerhouse would continue to appear in other comics until his own series was revived in Spring, 1948. A boxer with superhuman strength, Powerhouse was not particularly smart but had a heart of gold. His stories were comedies notable for their combination of slapstick with rhyming and alliterative dialogue. Powerhouse's writer/artist, Basil Wolverton, was best remembered for his comically grotesque characters, and most notoriously designed Lena the Hyena for cartoonist Al Capp's *Li'l Abner* strip.

FEBRUARY

CAPTAIN WONDER

• *Kid Komics* #1

In Captain Wonder's origin story by writer Otto Binder and artist Frank Giacoia, Professor Jordan had "the strength of a grasshopper and the spine of a jellyfish" until he was exposed to the fumes of his own experimental "Wonder Fluid." This endowed him with the strength of twelve men, and, as Captain Wonder, he soon saved his town from the Super Villain called Mister Death. But the Captain's series ended with the next issue of *Kid Komics*.

Captain Wonder clobbered a stereotypically portrayed Japanese officer in artist Syd Shores's cover for Kid Komics *#1.*

MARCH

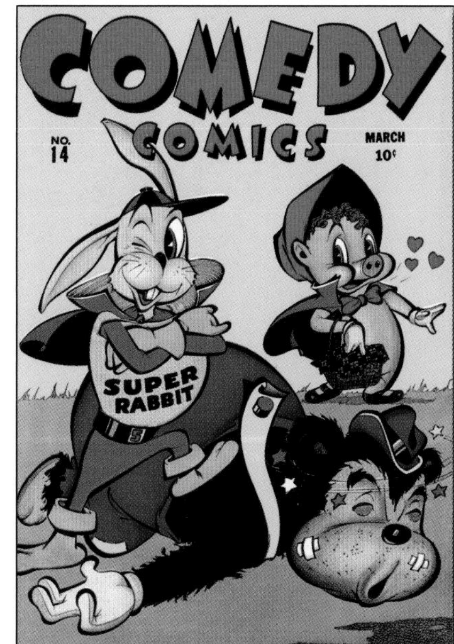

SUPER RABBIT

"Have no fear! Super Rabbit's here!"

• *Comedy Comics* #14

It was inevitable that the success of comic book Super Heroes would lead to Super Hero parodies. It also made sense that, if Super Heroes and funny animals were both successful, some creators would try to fuse them together.

But why were there so many super-powered rabbits? In late 1942, Fawcett's comics line introduced Hoppy the Marvel Bunny. Then Super Rabbit, created by cartoonist Ernie Hart, made his first appearance in issue #14 of the Timely series *Comedy Comics*. A month later, Bugs Bunny appeared in theaters in animation director Chuck Jones's cartoon *Super-Rabbit*. Nobody knew why but rabbits sure were popular!

Timely's Super Rabbit was really a meek little rabbit named Waffles, who was sometimes portrayed as a reporter (as if parodying Detective Comics' Clark Kent) and other times as a shoeshine boy (anticipating the later animated animal Super Hero Underdog from Charlton Comics). However, by rubbing his magic ring, Waffles could transform into the larger, more robust Super Rabbit. Living in a world of funny animals, Super Rabbit fought animals who were crooks, and even animals who were Nazis!

Not only did Super Rabbit remain the hero featured on the covers of *Comedy Comics*, he was one of Timely's leading characters in the 1940s. He appeared in many other Timely humor comics as well, including *Krazy Comics*, *Comic Capers*, *Illustrated Funny Comic-Tunes*, and *All Surprise Comics*. Super Rabbit even outlasted other Timely Golden Age stars, since his last story appeared as late as February, 1952, in *It's A Duck's Life*.

Six months after his debut in Comedy Comics *#14, Super Rabbit hopped into a tale in the premiere issue of* All Surprise Comics.

MEANWHILE IN 1943...

THE PENTAGON OPENS

The new headquarters of the US Department of Defense opens in Arlington, Virginia. The five-sided building becomes such a symbol of the US military that its name becomes synonymous with the Department itself.

GERMAN SURRENDER AT STALINGRAD

After nearly six months battling door-to-door for control of Stalingrad and more than 1.5 million dead, Nazi soldiers surrender to Soviet troops, in a significant turning point of World War II.

EISENHOWER APPOINTED

General Dwight Eisenhower is selected to command the allied armies in Europe. This role includes responsibility for the future successful invasion of France and Germany.

AND AT THE MOVIES...

I Walked with a Zombie, *Jacques Tourneur's Caribbean-set horror film about a nurse discovering that her catatonic patient is really a zombie;* The Ox-bow Incident, *William A. Wellman's western makes an impassioned plea for rule of law in this true tale of a mob lynching of three innocents;* For Whom The Bell Tolls, *romantic drama based on Ernest Hemingway's novel set against the Spanish Civil War.*

FALL

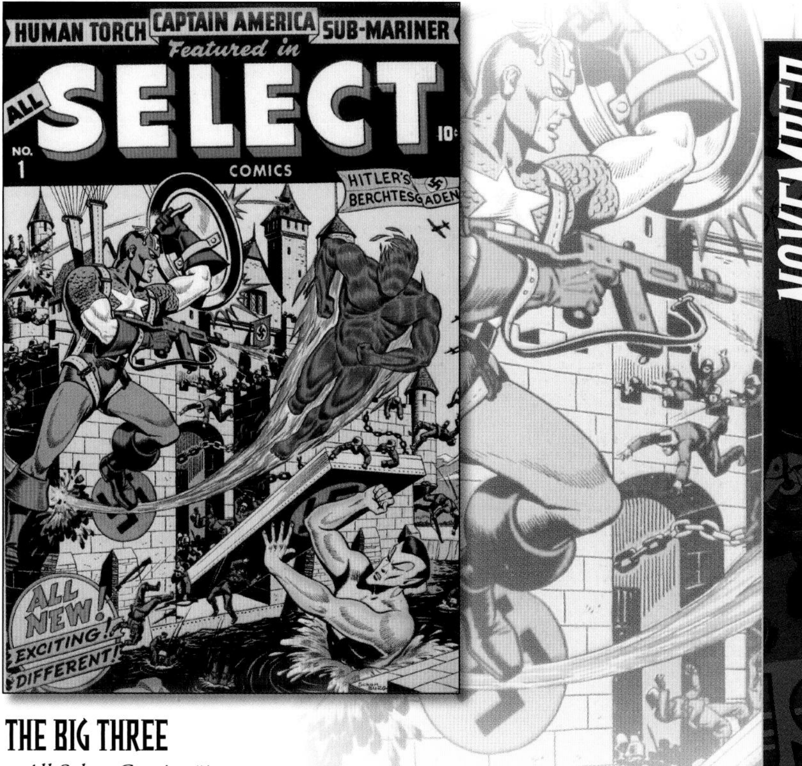

THE BIG THREE

• *All Select Comics* #1

Despite all featuring on this characteristically dynamic cover by artist Alex Schomburg, Captain America, the Human Torch, and the Sub-Mariner did not appear in the same story in this first issue of *All Select Comics*. Instead, as in *All Winners Comics*, which premiered in Summer, 1941, each of Timely's top three Super Heroes appeared in separate stories. Not until after the war would editor Stan Lee team them up in a comics adventure.

NOVEMBER

MISS AMERICA

• *Marvel Mystery Comics* #49

The famed Miss America beauty pageant began in 1921. Twenty-two years later and Timely created their own Miss America. The similarity between this new hero and the beauty pageants was in name only: Miss America's creators, writer Otto Binder and artist Al Gabriele, actually intended their new character to be a female counterpart to Captain America. Born in Washington, D.C., teenage heiress Madeline Joyce was struck by lightning while tinkering with an experimental device. As a result, she gained the ability to fly (as well as super-strength in her first stories), and became the costumed crime-fighter Miss America. Since the original Black Widow, who had debuted in July, 1940, worked for the devil, Miss America was Timely's first true super-powered heroine.

HURRY, SKIDSY--OR YOU'LL MISS YOUR TRAIN!!

1944

THE FIRST MARVEL MOVIE

Maybe surprisingly, the first Marvel-based movie was made as early as 1944. Republic Pictures' *Captain America* movie serial was released in fifteen installments, beginning in February, 1944, and was the last Super Hero serial that the company would release. For Republic Pictures at that time it was a major undertaking, being the most expensive movie serial that the studio had ever produced. It would be twenty-two years until Marvel heroes were adapted to the screen once more, in the *Marvel Super Heroes* television series of 1966. Coincidentally, this series also adapted comic stories into multi-part serials, featuring Cap, the Hulk, Iron Man, Thor, and the Sub-Mariner.

In the comics' world, Timely took further strides toward winning girl readers as well as boys. The company quickly changed course with its experiment to create a female Super Hero. Timely began to introduce new humorous but more realistic series about girls who were thought to be more like the readers they hoped to attract. They changed *Miss America Comics* to feature a new teen heroine, Patsy Walker, and Miss America was eventually dropped entirely from her own magazine. Patsy Walker would go on to star in a range of comics over the next twenty years.

JANUARY

THE OTHER BIG THREE

• *Ziggy Pig And Silly Seal Comics* #1

Timely's three leading funny animal stars became title characters of their own comic books in 1944, beginning with *Ziggy Pig And Silly Seal Comics* in January. It lasted six issues, concluding in September, 1946. The *Super Rabbit* comic outlasted *Ziggy Pig And Silly Seal Comics*, running fourteen issues from February, 1944, until November, 1948.

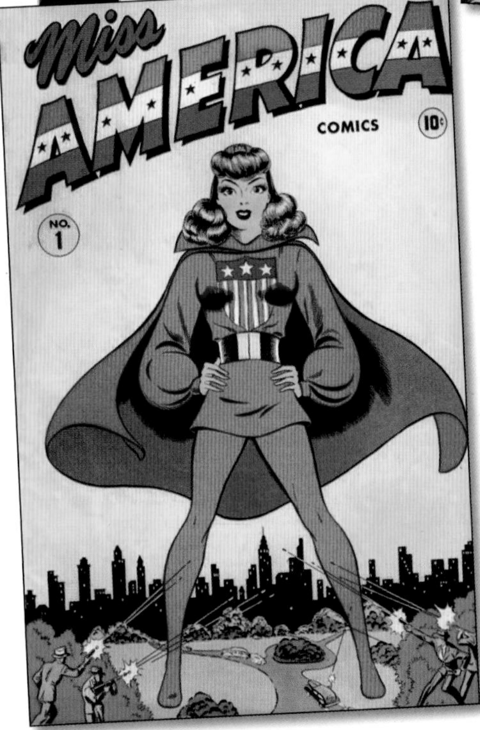

MISS AMERICA

• *Miss America Comics* #1

With her debut in November, 1943, Miss America swiftly became the title character of her own comic book. By the second issue, however, the comic had been retitled *Miss America Magazine*, and the comic art of a blonde woman had been replaced with a photograph of a brunette model wearing Miss America's costume. After that issue, the magazine changed direction and started to focus instead on subjects aimed at girls like fashion and cooking.

FEBRUARY

THE POPULARITY OF MOVIE SERIALS

From the silent movie era into the 1950s, many theaters showed weekly movie serials. These were lengthy adventure stories that were divided into weekly installments. Each installment, except for the concluding chapter, ended with a cliffhanger on which the hero or another character was seen in perilous danger. These movie serials would go on to inspire such movie hits as George Lucas and Steven Spielberg's *Indiana Jones*. Both Lucas and Spielberg have said that they were influenced by the movie serials they watched as children.

Hollywood's Republic Pictures was the leading producer of Saturday afternoon movie serials in the 1940s. In 1944, Republic brought the first Marvel character to the screen with its fifteen-part *Captain America* serial. Captain America was played by the obscure actor Dick Purcell, but the villain, Dr. Cyrus Maldor, alias the Scarab, was portrayed by Lionel Atwill, a celebrated character actor of the period. John English, who often worked on movie serials, and Elmer Clifton, famous for his westerns, were the directors.

MARCH

HAPPY DAYS

• *Gay Comics* #1

The first issue of this happy comic cheered readers with work by cartoonists Harvey Kurtzman and Basil Wolverton. As well as *Gay Comics,* Wolverton also worked on the character Tessie The Typist, who received her own comic in the summer of 1944.

FALL

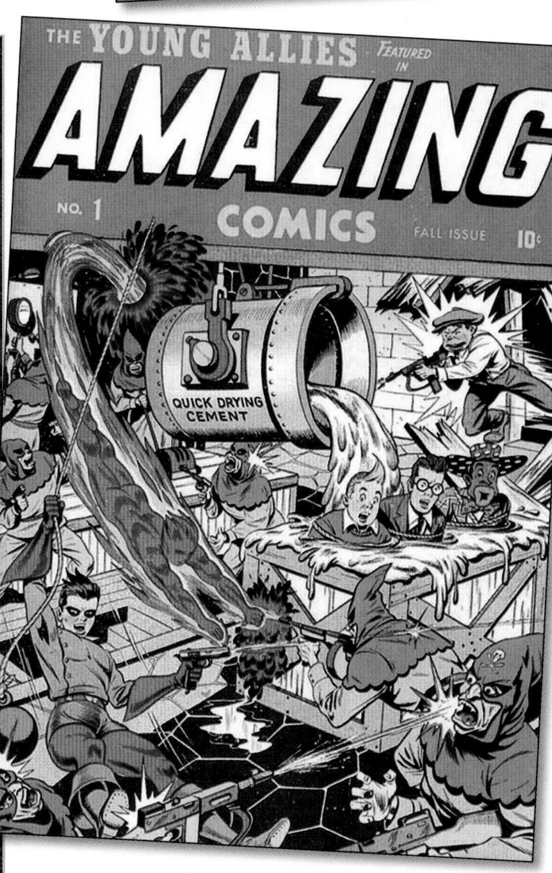

NAME CHANGES

The latter half of the year saw many Super Hero comics renamed. Timely revived *Daring Mystery Comics* as *Daring Comics* with issue #9 (Fall) and *Mystic Comics* with issue #1 of the second volume (Oct.). *Amazing Comics* became *Complete Comics* with issue #2 (Winter) and starred the Destroyer, Whizzer, and Young Allies.

FALL

FUNNIES FEATURE

• *Comic Capers* #1

Responding to the popularity of the funny animal genre, Timely launched two titles. Super Rabbit starred in the first issues of *Comic Capers* and *Ideal Comics*. Also in June, *Krazy Komics* became *Animated Funny Tunes*.

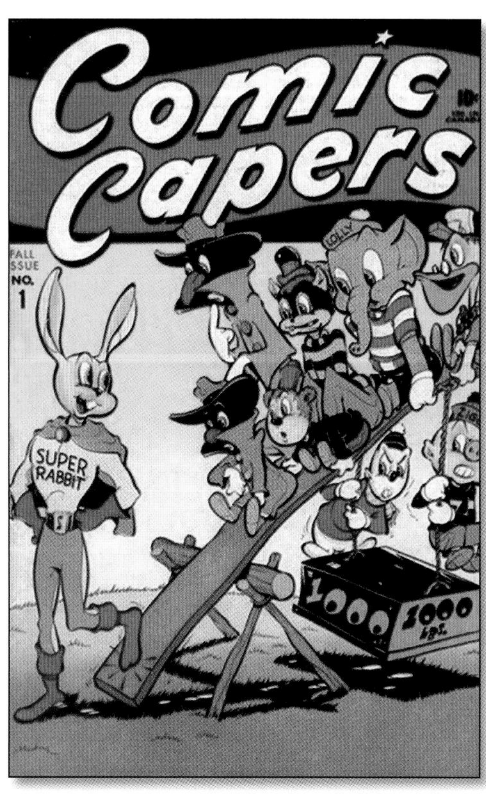

NOVEMBER

MISS AMERICA AND PATSY WALKER

• *Miss America Magazine* #2

The second issue of *Miss America* introduced the character who would steal the show from the heroine. Created by cartoonist Ruth Atkinson and possibly also by Stan Lee, perky redhead Patsy Walker became Marvel's leading teen humor star for the next two decades. Patsy's boyfriend (and future husband) Buzz Baxter and her best friend Hedy Wolfe also debuted in *Miss America Magazine* #2. Miss America herself soon vanished from her own magazine, and Patsy took over as its new star. In 1976, writer Roy Thomas revived Miss America as a member of the Liberty Legion.

MEANWHILE IN 1944...

SIEGE OF LENINGRAD ENDS

One of the longest sieges in modern history is finally over after 900 days, but not before 1.2 million civilians die of starvation.

D-DAY LANDINGS

Operation Overlord: 155,000 Allied troops land on the beaches of northern France. The Battle of Normandy begins as Allied forces fight to liberate France.

PARIS LIBERATED

The German commander in Paris surrenders to Allied forces and Charles de Gaulle declares the Fourth Republic of France.

DNA DISCOVERED

Scientists discover the instructions of the building blocks of life. They announce that genetic information is carried by DNA—deoxyribonucleic acid—although there is still little understanding of how it works.

THE LEAD PIPING IN THE DRAWING ROOM...

Anthony Pratt invents and files a patent for the murder mystery "whodunnit" board game, Clue (or Cluedo), to the pleasure of generations of detectives.

AND AT THE MOVIES...

Double Indemnity, *this hard-boiled film noir, featuring Barbara Stanwyck's definitive femme fatale, crackles with wit and stifled suspicion;* Henry V, *Laurence Olivier's stirring, stylized wartime propaganda presents a masterful cinematic adaptation of Shakespeare's patriotic drama of victory against overwhelming odds;* Meet Me In St. Louis, *Vincente Minnelli blends music, melodrama, and Judy Garland in this musical.*

Miss America was portrayed by model Dolores Conlon on the cover of Miss America Magazine *#2.*

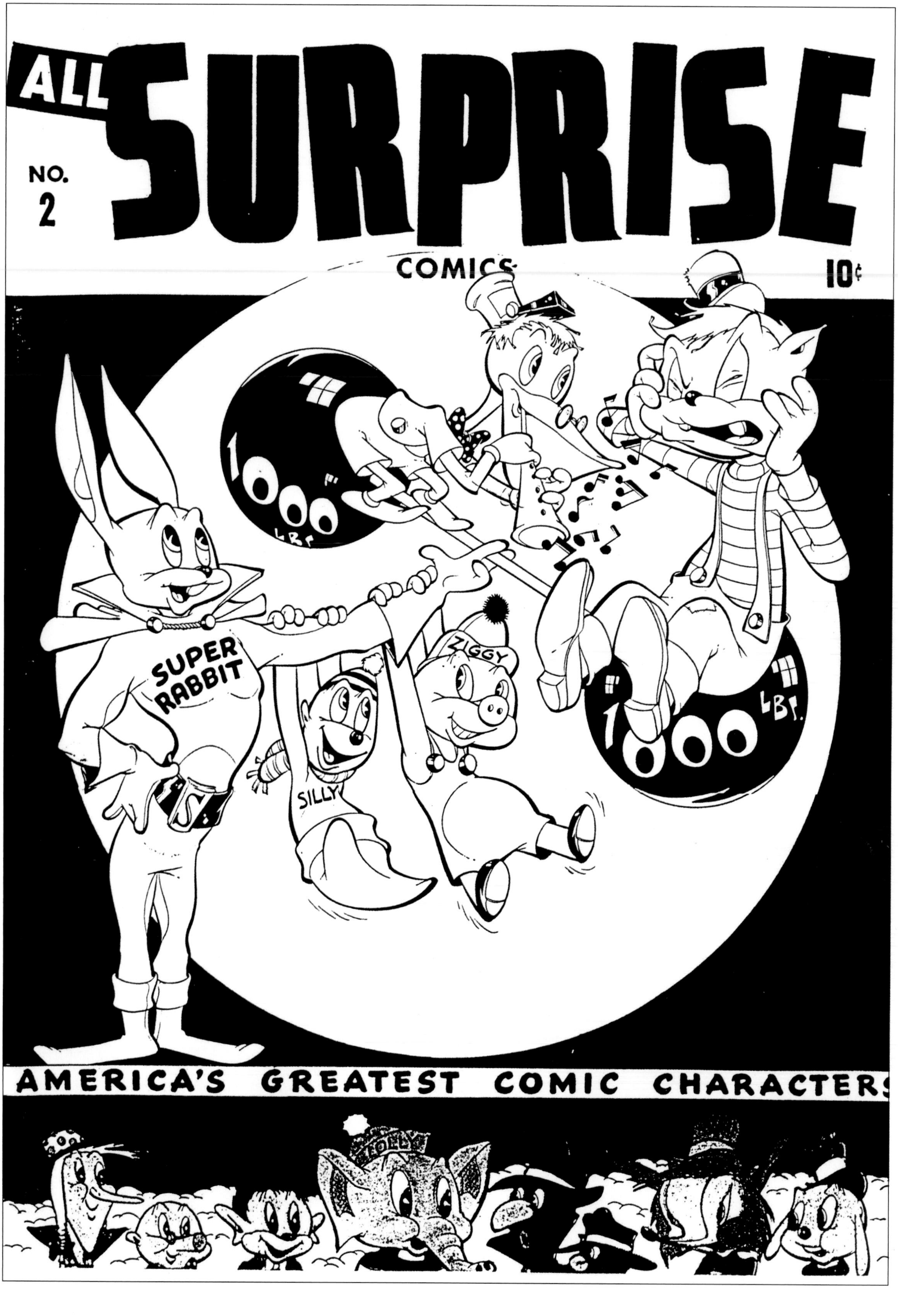

ALL SURPRISE COMICS

NO. 2

10¢

1000 LBS.

SUPER RABBIT

ZIGGY

SILLY

1000 LBS.

AMERICA'S GREATEST COMIC CHARACTERS

All Surprise Comics #2 *(Winter, 1944)*
An extremely rare example of Timely original cover artwork. This page shows the cover in its inked form; the opposite page shows the final, colored result.

ALL SURPRISE

NO. 2

COMICS

10¢

1000 LBS.

SUPER RABBIT

ZIGGY

SILLY

1000 LBS.

AMERICA'S GREATEST COMIC CHARACTERS

ll Surprise Comics
2 (Winter, 1944)
uper Rabbit, one of the rst funny animal ersions of a Super Hero, as the star of All urprise Comics. *This sue's cover featured Super abbit, the ubiquitous iggy Pig and Silly Seal, nd the Terrytoons team f Gandy Goose and ourpuss.*

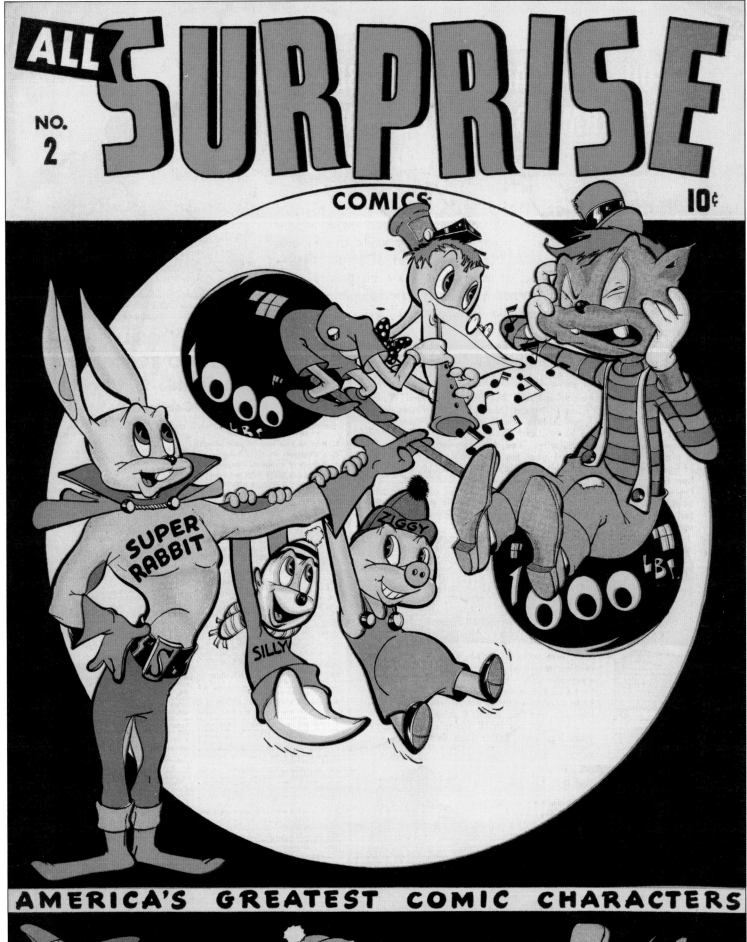

1945

CHANGING AUDIENCES

In 1945, the Super Hero genre was not even a decade old. Yet already Super Hero comics sales were in decline. Only a year after his movie serial, even one of Captain America's showcases, *U.S.A. Comics*, was cancelled. As Super Hero sales fell in the mid-1940s, comic book readers at the time might well have wondered if Super Heroes were merely a short-lived fad. How could this be?

One reason was that World War II ended in 1945. A considerable portion of the comics audience in the war years was not children but young members of the armed forces. With the war over, these young veterans returned home, where their attention turned to starting careers and families. Back then comic books were perceived as children's entertainment, to be left behind when one truly became an adult.

By 1945, Timely was actively pursuing a new, responsive audience for comic books: young girls. This was the year that the company's new heroine, teenager Patsy Walker, got her own comic book after her brief apprenticeship in a backup feature in *Miss America Magazine* #2 (Nov., 1944). Another new character, Millie the Model, debuted in her own comic. Millie and Patsy would become two of Marvel's greatest successes from the 1940s into the 1960s.

SPRING

GUYS AND DOLLS

• *Georgie Comics* #1

Timely did not just build teen humor comics series around female characters like Patsy Walker, Millie the Model and Nellie the Nurse. The *Georgie Comics* series featured an adolescent boy who, bedazzled and befuddled by the beautiful girls around him, constantly found himself in awkward—and humorous—situations.

SEPTEMBER

Hunting rabbits on the cover of his first issue, Dopey Duck demonstrated the reason for his first name.

FUNNY ANIMAL CLASS OF 1945

• *Animated Movie-Tunes* #1

Timely's new comic *Animated Movie-Tunes* was misnamed, since its lead characters—Timely's talking animal stars, Super Rabbit, Ziggy Pig, and Silly Seal—had never appeared in animated cartoons. Presumably Timely wanted to persuade its young readers that its funny animals were just as good as the ones they saw in movie theaters. Dopey Duck also received his own short-lived comic book in the summer and *Funny Frolics* also began in this season.

FALL

U.S.A. COMICS ENDS

• *U.S.A. Comics* #17

It may have been an ominous sign for the Timely Super Heroes when *U.S.A. Comics* was cancelled with issue #17. The comic regularly starred Captain America, and had introduced other Super Heroes including the Whizzer, Jack Frost, The Defender, and Captain Terror.

WINTER

MILLIE THE MODEL DEBUTS

"Here comes the blonde bombshell!"

• *Millie The Model* #1

There were only three comics that were published continually from Timely's Golden Age of the 1940s into Marvel's Silver Age of the 1960s: *Millie The Model*, *Patsy Walker*, and *Kid Colt, Outlaw*. Of these three, *Millie The Model* ran the longest, with a continuous run of 207 issues spanning the nearly three decade period from Winter, 1945, to December, 1972.

Millie was a model at Hanover Agency, where she met her boyfriend, Clicker, who was a photographer there. Her adventures often involved her best friend, Toni Turner, and her friendly nemesis and fellow model Chili Storm.

Millie The Model was created by cartoonist Ruth Atkinson, who drew the stories in the first issue. Mike Sekowsky, who later worked on DC Comics' *Justice League Of America*, took over as principal *Millie The Model* artist after the first issue. With issue #18 Dan DeCarlo began a ten-year stint as artist, running from June, 1949, to issue #93 in November, 1959. During this period, DeCarlo established the look of the series. DeCarlo was succeeded on *Millie The Model* by writer Stan Lee and penciller Stan Goldberg, who brought the title into the 1960s. From 1963, *Millie The Model* became a more serious romance and adventure series before reverting to its original humorous tone. Later, readers were invited to submit their own fashion designs to the comic, in the hope that the artists would use them in the book.

There were also numerous spinoff series, including *A Date With Millie*, *Life With Millie*, *Mad About Millie*, and *Modeling With Millie*. Even after Millie's own series came to an end, she continued to make occasional guest appearances in other Marvel titles, such as *The Defenders*. In 1985, she appeared in Trina Robbins's *Misty* as the title character's aunt.

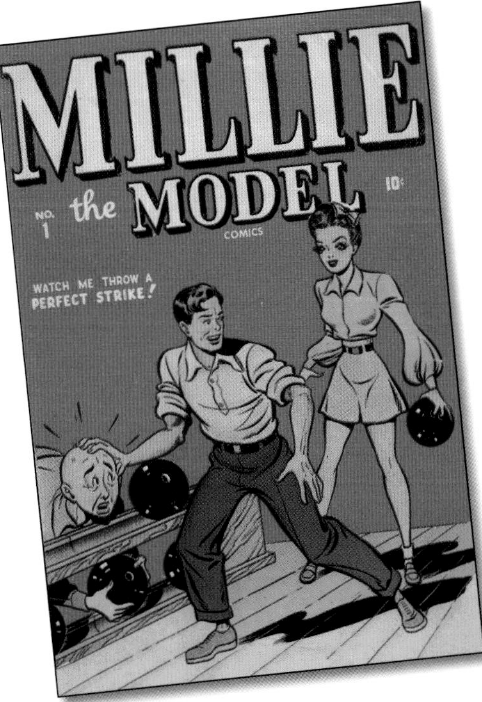

ALSO...

PATSY THE STAR

• *Patsy Walker* #1

After debuting in *Miss America Magazine* #2 (Nov., 1944), Patsy Walker became the star of her own comic book a year later. Patsy's earliest stories were drawn by her creator Ruth Atkinson and Mike Sekowsky drew the cover for *Patsy Walker*'s debut issue. Later artists included Al Hartley and future *MAD* magazine contributor Al Jaffee. Patsy would win two more regular series in the 1950s: *Patsy And Hedy* in 1952 and *Patsy And Her Pals* in 1953. Even after the original *Patsy Walker* comic ended in February, 1962, its heroine kept going, eventually completing a transition into Super Hero comics as the costumed Hellcat in 1976.

LEAD NURSE

• *Nellie The Nurse* #1

Like *Tessie The Typist* and *Millie The Model*, *Nellie The Nurse* was yet a Timely title that featured young career women with alliterative names. *Millie The Model* lasted the longest by far, perhaps because she had a more glamorous career than the other two. Though *Nellie The Nurse* was a humor series, it appeared to be the first comic book series to portray a nurse in a lead role. Stan Lee co-created *Nellie The Nurse*, and Mike Sekowsky drew the first issue's cover.

STAN LEE RETURNS

With the end of World War II in 1945, Stan Lee returned to his former position as Timely's Editor-in-Chief. He found a line of comics that had greatly changed in only three years, with new emphasis on comics aimed at girls, with female lead characters and girl-friendly topics.

MEANWHILE IN 1945...

A FOURTH TERM FOR FDR
Franklin D. Roosevelt is sworn in as President for an unprecedented fourth term.

AUSCHWITZ LIBERATED
The Red Army uncovers the horrors of the Nazi concentration camps when they reach Auschwitz and Birkenau in Poland.

YALTA CONFERENCE
The "Big Three"—Roosevelt, Churchill, and Stalin—meet to discuss plans for the continuing conflict and the governance of post-war Germany.

ROOSEVELT'S SUDDEN DEATH
President Roosevelt dies suddenly of a cerebral hemorrhage and is succeeded by Harry S. Truman.

V-E DAY
The Allies celebrate Victory in Europe Day when Nazi Germany surrenders, bringing an end to the war in Europe.

POTSDAM CONFERENCE
Truman, Atlee, and Stalin meet to decide how to administer defeated Nazi Germany and manage post-war Europe.

US USES THE ATOMIC BOMB
The US detonates atomic bombs on the Japanese cities of Hiroshima and Nagasaki in a bid to bring Japanese surrender to a rapid conclusion.

AND AT THE MOVIES...
Brief Encounter, *David Lean's finely crafted, stiff-upper-lip romantic melodrama about a doomed affair set around a railway station;* The Lost Weekend, *Billy Wilder's film about alcoholism, presents Ray Milland as a desperate writer on a downward trajectory.*

1946

A NEW TEAM SPIRIT

By 1946, Timely had stopped introducing new Super Heroes. The public had been more receptive toward the genre during World War II, when the whole world was in peril. But in the aftermath of the war, the readership had changed and it wanted comparatively realistic comics stories, like teen comedies. Even the popularity of the funny animal comics seemed to be fading.

Nonetheless, 1946 was a landmark year in the evolution of the Marvel Super Hero. It was then that the company first organized its leading Super Heroes into a team—the All Winners Squad. Although that team lasted for only two appearances in the 1940s, it helped inspire writer Roy Thomas's Invaders in the 1970s, which presented Captain America, the original Human Torch, and the Sub-Mariner as a World War II band of allies. The All Winners Squad was also a forerunner of the Avengers in the 1960s.

In asking editor Stan Lee to create the All Winners Squad, publisher Martin Goodman was taking an important step forward. In the future, team books like *Fantastic Four* and *The X-Men* would present opportunities for a large cast of characters with different personalities to interact with one another amid dynamic action sequences that played to Marvel's strengths.

FALL

Willie Comics *was a title about the adventures of a teenage boy.*

NAMES IN FLUX

Funny animal comics were beginning to be revamped into teen humor titles. *Kid Komics* turned into Ziggy Pig and Silly Seal's *Kid Movie Komics* in Summer, 1946, before becoming *Rusty Comics* in April, 1947. *Animated Movie-Tunes* became *Movie Tunes Comics* in Fall, before turning into *Frankie* with issue #4 in December, 1946. And also in Fall, Super Rabbit's *Ideal Comics* became *Willie Comics* with issue #5.

FIRST SUPER HERO TEAM

"See the Human Torch, Captain America, and Sub-Mariner battle the world's most fearful villain in a complete, sizzling, action thriller!"

• *All Winners Comics* #19

Artist Alex Schomburg had long been creating covers combining Captain America, the Human Torch and the Sub-Mariner for *All Select Comics*, and DC Comics had been teaming up its top heroes in the Justice Society of America since 1940. Finally, editor Stan Lee introduced Timely's first proper Super Hero team in a multi-part serial in the pages of *All Winners Comics* #19. The members included not only Captain America and Bucky, the Human Torch and Toro, and the Sub-Mariner, but also the Whizzer and Miss America. Appropriately, the team was named the All Winners Squad. (Stan Lee later said that he would not have come up with the idea for the All Winners Squad himself, and that it must have been publisher Martin Goodman's idea.)

Lee assigned the story to writer Bill Finger, the unofficial co-creator of DC Comics' Batman. The seven chapters of this saga, The Crime of the Ages, were divided among pencillers Vince Alascia, Al Avison, Bob Powell, and Syd Shores.

The story's principal villain was Isbisa, who plotted to steal an atomic bomb in an attempt to conquer the world. Appearing only once in the 1940s, Isbisa would later return as a flashback in the Super Hero team comic *Giant-Size Avengers* #1 (Aug., 1974), and then in *Vision And The Scarlet Witch* #2 (Dec., 1982) and *The Sensational She-Hulk* #30 (Aug., 1991). The All Winners Squad was not the commercial blockbuster it should have been. The team appeared only one more time in issue #21 in the Winter. Not even this landmark team-up, it seemed, could reverse the falling fortunes of Timely's Super Heroes.

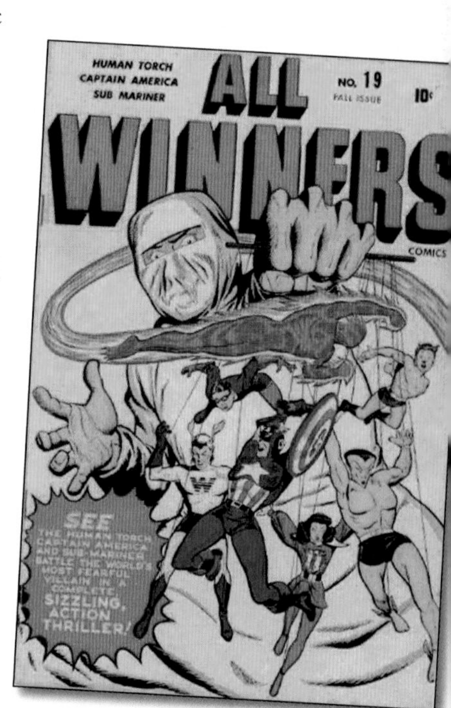

FALL

ENTER THE BLONDE PHANTOM

• *All Select Comics* #11
Secretary Louise Grant was in love with her boss, private detective Mark Mason. To help him solve his cases, she secretly adopted the glamorous secret identity of the Blonde Phantom, wearing a black domino mask and a long, red evening gown. Carrying a gun and adept at hand-to-hand combat, the Blonde Phantom was more dangerous than she might have first appeared. Created by Stan Lee and artist Syd Shores, she was a Timely character squarely aimed at female readers.

M Timely started its *Mighty Mouse* comic in Fall. Mighty Mouse had far more impact on the public than another Timely funny animal, Super Rabbit.

OCTOBER

END OF THE YOUNG ALLIES

• *Young Allies Comics* #20
Beginning in Summer, 1941, Joe Simon and Jack Kirby's *Young Allies Comics* was Timely's first experiment with a Super Hero team, since two of the members of the young team were costumed heroes Bucky and Toro. But in October, the title was cancelled with issue #20.

WINTER

BLONDE PHANTOM'S SUCCESS

• *Blonde Phantom Comics* #12
In Winter, *All Select Comics* was retitled *Blonde Phantom* with issue #12, only one issue after the Blonde Phantom had made her debut. She continued to appear for the rest of the 1940s in *All Winners Comics*, *Blackstone The Magician*, *Marvel Mystery Comics*, *The Sea Beauty Namora*, *Sub-Mariner Comics,* and *Sun Girl*, as well as *Blonde Phantom* itself, which ended in March, 1949. In *The Sensational She-Hulk* #2 (June, 1989), writer/artist John Byrne brought back an older Louise Grant Mason, who had married her detective boss Mark Mason, and subsequently restored her youth using technology from the underground realm of Subterranea.

WINTER

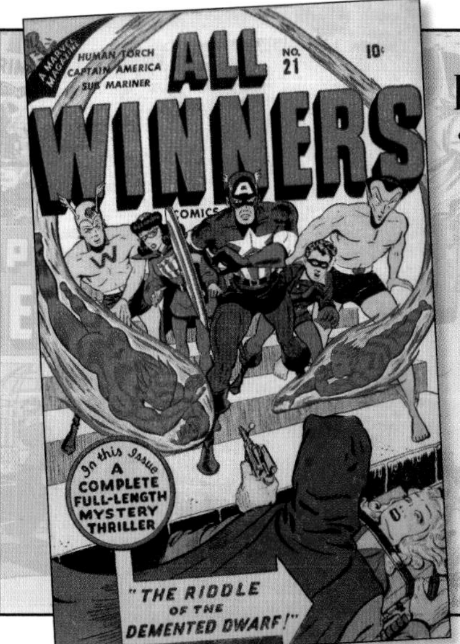

ALL WINNERS' FAREWELL

• *All Winners Comics* #21
For this issue, Otto Binder wrote "Menace of the Future World," the second adventure of the All Winners Squad, which would prove to be their last in the Golden Age of Comics. This time there were two new major villains: Future Man, a time traveler from 1,000,000 A.D., and his partner, the glamorous criminal mastermind Madame Death. The All Winners Squad thwarted these villains' attempts to use Future Man's advanced technology to conquer the Earth.

ALSO...

HARVEY KURTZMAN

Harvey Kurtzman was one of the most innovative and influential figures in the history of American comics. After serving in the US Army in World War II, Kurtzman began freelancing for Timely. Between 1946 and 1949 he created his first important work in comics—the humor strip, "Hey Look!," which appeared in various Timely comics over this period as a one-page or even half-page filler.

Editor Stan Lee gave Kurtzman free rein to do whatever he wanted in writing and drawing the "Hey Look!" strips. As a result, Kurtzman used the strips as a sort of experimental comics laboratory, developing his distinctive visual style and satiric brand of humor.

Though created in 1946, Kurtzman's first "Hey Look!" was not actually published until it appeared in Timely's *Jeanie Comics* #17, cover-dated January, 1948. But later "Hey Look!" strips had already begun appearing in various Timely titles starting with *Joker Comics* #23, cover-dated June, 1946. Over the course of three years Kurtzman produced roughly 150 "Hey Look!" strips.

In 1949, Kurtzman went to work for EC Comics, where he became the editor and chief creative force behind the classic series *Two-Fisted Tales* and *Frontline Combat*. In 1952, Kurtzman became the original editor of EC's new humor magazine *MAD*, and, through his writing and layouts for the art, shaped *MAD*'s satiric sensibility.

In 1990, Kurtzman published his final comic book for Marvel, entitled *Harvey Kurtzman's Strange Adventures*.

GENE COLAN COMES TO MARVEL

In 1946, Stan Lee hired young artist Gene Colan to work as a staff penciller at Timely. With his beautiful illustrative style, Colan would later go on to become one of Marvel's greatest artists, memorably working on *Daredevil*, *The Invincible Iron Man,* and *Sub-Mariner* in the 1960s and *Doctor Strange*, *Howard The Duck,* and *The Tomb Of Dracula* in the 1970s.

MEANWHILE IN 1946...

SPACE TRAVEL A POSSIBILITY

In Project Diana, radar waves are bounced off the Moon, measuring the exact distance between the Earth and the Moon. The discovery that communication is possible beyond the Earth opens the possibility of space exploration.

INDEPENDENCE FOR THE PHILIPPINES

The Philippines are declared a Republic when they are granted full independence after centuries of Western dominance.

A MELTED BAR OF CANDY LEADS TO THE MICROWAVE

Dr. Percy Spencer notices that a candy bar in his pocket melts while he is testing a magnetron. This discovery leads him to invent the microwave oven.

FIRST "SOAP OPERA" ON TV

Faraway Hill—*the story of a New York widow who moves to a small town—debuts on the DuMont Television Network. It is widely regarded as the first television soap opera.*

AND AT THE MOVIES...

It's A Wonderful Life, *Frank Capra's uplifting, sentimental fantasy has James Stewart's suicidal character shown a world bereft of his good deeds;* Great Expectations, *David Lean directed this marvelously acted, highly atmospheric version of Dickens's classic tale.*

OUTA MY WAY... SUCKER!

1947

A TIMELY IDENTITY CRISIS

Timely had made its name with Super Hero comics in 1939. But by 1947 did Timely even have a name any more? As the Timely tag had not caught on, the insignia no longer appeared on its comics. Publisher Martin Goodman had experimented with a new corner logo "A Marvel Magazine," which appeared on the cover of *Blonde Phantom* #12 in Winter, 1946. Later Goodman tried a circular cover symbol reading "Marvel Comic." But he dropped that, too. Of course, in the early 1960s, Goodman's comics line would adopt the name "Marvel" permanently. But by the late 1940s, his line of comics no longer had a name. The situation would not change until Goodman began calling them Atlas Comics in December, 1951, after his newsstand magazine distribution company.

The comics line's lack of a public name mirrored its loss of a strong artistic identity. Captain America, the Human Torch, and the Sub-Mariner had been distinctly different from the Super Heroes at other companies. But now that the former Timely was moving away from its classic heroes, just what made its comics different from the competition? In a creative slump, Goodman's nameless comics line was following new trends, such as crime comics, rather than creating them.

APRIL

TEEN COMICS BOOM

Only a year ago, *All Winners Comics* had featured the two classic adventures of the All Winners Squad in issues #19 (Fall, 1946) and #21 (Winter, 1946). Now, with the missing issue #20, *All Winners Comics* became *All Teen Comics*, featuring Patsy Walker, Georgie, and Willie. Other comics also branched into the teen humor genre. *The Human Torch* turned into *Junior Miss* and two of Super Rabbit's vehicles, *Comedy Comics* and *Krazy Komics*, became *Margie Comics* and *Cindy Comics*.

Comics readers still flocked to humor books about teenagers and dating, while Super Hero fantasies continued their decline.

MAY

NAMORA, THE FEMALE SUB-MARINER

"In this issue, a full-length action thriller: 'The Coming of Namora!'"

• *Marvel Mystery Comics* #82

On returning to the Atlantean community in the Antarctic, Namor the Sub-Mariner discovered that it had been attacked by a band of criminals from the surface world. In the original story in *Marvel Comics* #1 (Oct., 1939), the criminals had wiped out the Atlanteans; in this retelling, Namor and his cousin, Aquaria Nautica Neptunia, teamed up and vowed to take vengeance on those who had killed her father. Aquaria changed her name to Namora and since Namor meant "Avenging Son," she was now the Avenging Daughter. From then on Namora became the Sub-Mariner's companion in his Golden Age adventures.

Like Namor, Namora was the daughter of a surface human and an Atlantean. She too had pink skin and superhuman strength and could breathe in the air or underwater. For a time she also had wings on her heels that enabled her to fly.

Namora was created by artists Ken Bald (who later drew the newspaper comic strip "Dark Shadows") and Syd Shores, but the Sub-Mariner's own creator, Bill Everett, later drew many of Namora's solo adventures.

In the 1970s, Everett would establish that Namora was murdered by the evil Llyra, but had given birth to a daughter, Namorita, who would become the Sub-Mariner's protégée. Writer/artist John Byrne would further reveal that Namorita was really an altered clone of Namora rather than her child. In January, 2007, Namora turned up alive and part of a new Marvel team. This Super Hero team was named the Agents of Atlas, after Marvel's company name in 1951.

Like the Sub-Mariner, Namora had to immerse herself in water from time to time to maintain her powers.

JULY

THE ASBESTOS LADY

• *Captain America Comics* #63

Apart from the Red Skull there were few Timely Super Villains created in the 1940s, and even fewer who were memorable. One exception was the Human Torch's foe, the Asbestos Lady. Finding an obvious defense against the Torch's powers, she wore a flameproof asbestos costume, and carried a gun that fired bullets containing asbestos, plus a flame-thrower. The following May, in *The Human Torch* #30, the Torch met another adversary called the Hyena.

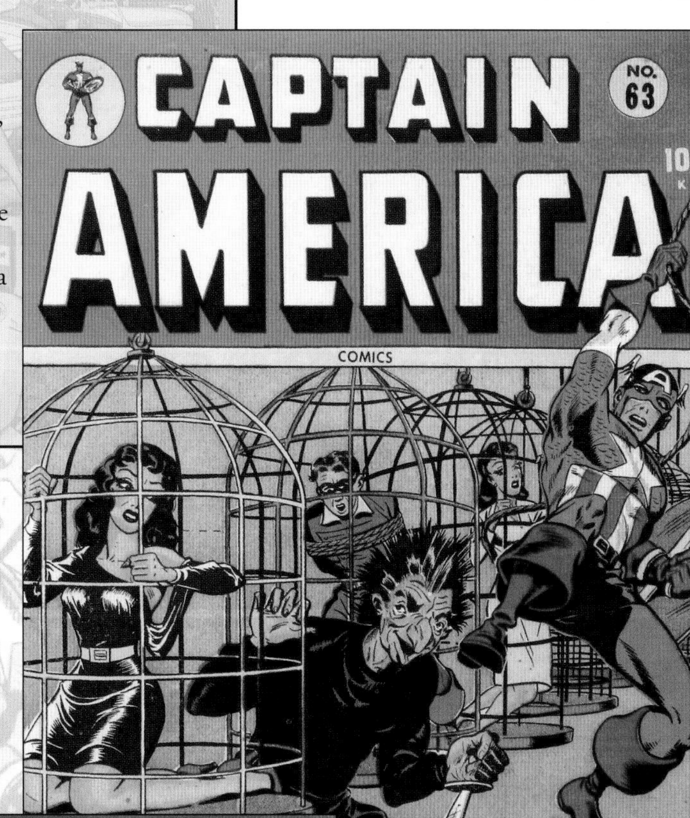

AUGUST

Timely's deal with Terrytoons came to an end with *Terry-Toons Comics* #59. Mighty Mouse would reappear on the Marvel list in October, 1990.

FALL

CRIME COMICS

• *Official True Crime Cases Comics* #24

A new trend in comic books was crime comics, which focused not on the lawmen but on the lawbreakers. *Sub-Mariner Comics* was retitled *Official True Crime Cases Comics* with issue #24, and even *Wacky Duck* became the crime series *Justice* with issue #7.

MEANWHILE IN 1947...

"COLD WAR"

Bernard Baruch, an advisor to President Truman, coins the term "Cold War" in a speech to Congress to describe the emerging conflict between the USSR and its World War II allies.

A NEW ERA FOR INDIA AND PAKISTAN

After a long struggle, India gains independence from the British Empire. Pakistan splits from India, but clashes over the region of Kashmir launch the Indo-Pakistan war.

A CIA FOR THE USA

The National Security Act is passed, which creates the CIA—Central Intelligence Agency—a government agency tasked with coordinating the intelligence effort in the new, post-World War II world.

AIRPLANE BREAKS SOUND BARRIER

Chuck Yeager, an American test pilot, becomes the first person to travel faster than the speed of sound in a Bell X1 rocket plane.

A ROYAL WEDDING

Her Royal Highness, Princess Elizabeth, who is first in line to the British throne, marries Philip Mountbatten at Westminster Abbey in London. He becomes the Duke of Edinburgh.

"HOLLYWOOD 10" BLACKLISTED

As the McCarthy era of Communist paranoia takes off, the US film industry blacklists ten screenwriters and producers amidst allegations that they are Communist sympathizers.

IS THE TRUTH OUT THERE?

Reports of a strange object crashing into the New Mexico desert are later refuted by officials at Roswell Army Air Field, who say that the object recovered was actually a weather balloon.

MARSHALL PLAN

US Secretary of State George C. Marshall introduces a plan for the US to aid Europe's recovery after World War II.

BUGS BUNNY STARS

Looney Tunes' Bugs Bunny and Cecil Turtle star in Rabbit Transit, *which pits the two characters against each other in a race in the manner of Aesop's* The Tortoise and the Hare *fable.*

AND AT THE MOVIES...

Crossfire, *Edward Dmytryk's tense, nocturnal, expressionist thriller is the first Hollywood film to tackle racial bigotry;* Brighton Rock, *British film noir about rival racketeers in Brighton's underworld revolves around Richard Attenborough's menacing, baby-faced Pinkie;* Gentleman's Agreement, *director Elia Kazan's drama about a journalist, played by Gregory Peck, who pretends to be Jewish in order to research anti-Semitism in New York City.*

NO. 6 SEPT.
ZIGGY PIG
SILLY SEAL
COMICS
10¢

Ziggy Pig And Silly Seal Comics ***#6 (Sept., 1946)***
Created by future MAD *magazine artist Al Jaffee, Ziggy Pig and Silly Seal were two of Timely's most popular characters. They appeared in such series as* Animated Funny Comic-Tunes *and* Silly Tunes *(both of whose titles seemed inspired by Warner Brothers'* Looney Tunes*),* All-Surprise Comics, Comic Capers, *and* Krazy Komics. *Yet Ziggy and Silly's fame lasted a mere half decade: Having debuted in 1942, they virtually vanished after 1947. This sixth and final issue of* Ziggy Pig And Silly Seal Comics *featured a fine example of the "infinity cover," with the characters staring at their own images on a cover theoretically* ad infinitum.

THERE IS SOMEONE TO HELP YOU-- NAMORA IS HERE!

1948

TIMELY'S BULLPEN

Despite the creative slump of 1947, Martin Goodman's comics company was bursting with activity in the late 1940s. Although Super Heroes and funny animals had faded, the company had moved into genres such as crime, romance, and westerns that were proving popular. In 1948, Stan Lee even experimented with producing female Super Hero titles aimed at girls, including *Sun Girl*, *The Sea Beauty Namora*, and *Venus*.

Formerly based in Manhattan's McGraw-Hill Building, Timely had moved to the fourteenth floor of the Empire State Building during World War II. There, in the late 1940s, Stan Lee presided over a large staff of artists, who worked alongside each other in one large room. Among them were Carl Burgos, John Buscema, Gene Colan, Dan DeCarlo, Mike Sekowsky, and the artists' supervisor, Syd Shores. In baseball, relief pitchers practise in an area called the "bullpen." So too the artists' room in the Goodman offices became known as the "Bullpen." The original Bullpen did not last but in the 1960s, Stan Lee revived the term "Bullpen," even though artists then worked at home. The term "Bullpen" now refers to the community of editors, writers, artists, and other staffers who collaborate in producing Marvel comics.

SPRING

A COMICS CRIME WAVE

• *Lawbreakers Always Lose!* #1

By the late 1940s, crime comics had become a hot trend, and were flying off newsstands everywhere. Though invariably condemning crime, the new wave of comics frequently made criminals the protagonists, and, to add to the excitement, many of the stories were supposedly based on real life cases. In 1948, Timely launched two new crime comics, *Crimefighters* (April, 1948) and *Lawbreakers Always Lose!* (Spring, 1948).

Basil Wolverton's *Powerhouse Pepper* comic book resumed with issue #2.

MARCH

MARVEL GOES WEST

• *Two-Gun Kid* #1

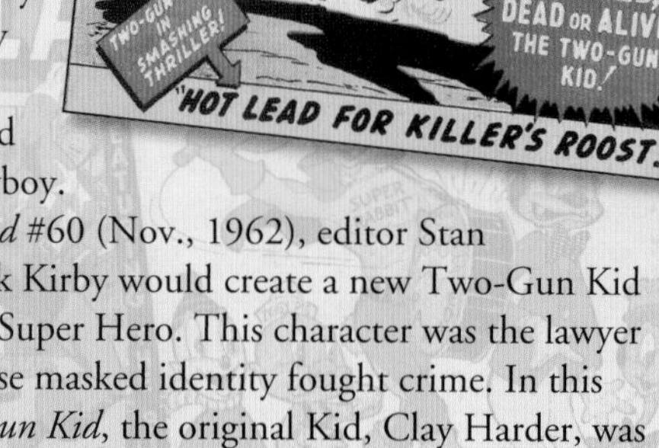

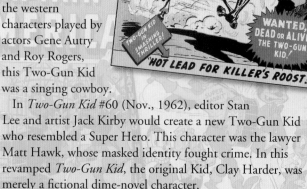

In this, Marvel's first western comic book, Clay Harder starred as the original Two-Gun Kid and was drawn by Syd Shores. Harder, who had been wrongly accused of murder, wandered through the Old West, using his prowess as a gunslinger to battle wrongdoers. Like the western characters played by actors Gene Autry and Roy Rogers, this Two-Gun Kid was a singing cowboy.

In *Two-Gun Kid* #60 (Nov., 1962), editor Stan Lee and artist Jack Kirby would create a new Two-Gun Kid who resembled a Super Hero. This character was the lawyer Matt Hawk, whose masked identity fought crime. In this revamped *Two-Gun Kid*, the original Kid, Clay Harder, was merely a fictional dime-novel character.

SUN GIRL DEBUTS

• *Sun Girl* #1

In a further attempt to appeal to girls, Timely introduced Sun Girl in her own comic. She also temporarily replaced Toro as the Human Torch's sidekick in the same way that, when Bucky was hospitalized, the Super Hero Golden Girl became Cap's new crime-fighting partner.

First drawn by Ken Bald, Sun Girl starred in her own three-issue comic book and with the Human Torch in The Human Torch *#32–35.*

AUGUST

OUTLAW HERO OF THE WEST

"Hold 'em off, Kid! I'm comin'!"

• *Kid Colt, Hero Of The West* #1

In the nineteenth-century American West, rancher Dan Colt thought that his son Blaine was a coward. In fact, Blaine had trained himself to be an expert with a gun, but he knew he had a hair-trigger temper. He was so quick on the draw that he feared he might kill someone in a flash of anger.

Indeed, after head of the Ranchers Protection Association Lash Larribee shot Dan Colt dead, the enraged Blaine confronted Larribee, outdrew, and killed him. Accused of murder (just like the original Two-Gun Kid and the later Rawhide Kid), Blaine roamed through the Old West as Kid Colt, a fugitive continually seeking to redeem his reputation by battling criminals.

Kid Colt foreshadowed the success Marvel would later have in portraying Super Heroes who were outsiders or even were accused of being criminals. His first issue was titled *Kid Colt, Hero Of The West*, but with the third issue in December, 1948, it became, and remained, *Kid Colt, Outlaw*.

Editor Stan Lee wrote numerous *Kid Colt, Outlaw* stories, and Jack Keller drew the character for many years. Other *Kid Colt, Outlaw* artists included Jack Kirby, Dick Ayers, Gene Colan, Reed Crandall, Russ Heath, Joe Kubert, and Joe Maneely.

The *Kid Colt, Outlaw* comic book was the longest running western comic book series ever. It ran from 1948 to 1968, and was then revived in 1969, although most of the stories from 1966 onwards were reprints. *Kid Colt, Outlaw* finally ended its thirty-one-year run in April, 1979.

The character was subsequently revived in the four-issue series *Blaze Of Glory* (2000) and the one-off *The Mighty Marvel Westerns: Kid Colt And The Arizona Girl* (Sept., 2006).

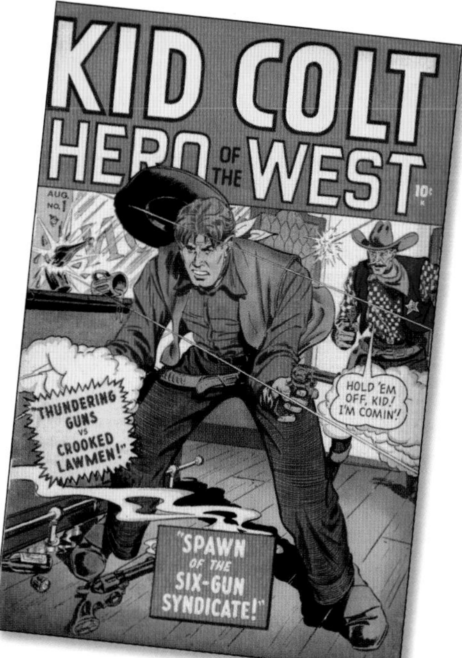

AUGUST

THE GODDESS OF LOVE DEBUTS

• *Venus* #1

In her first comic, Venus, the Roman Goddess of Love, left her home on the planet Venus to live among mortals on twentieth-century Earth. Adopting the name Victoria Starr, she became a reporter for *Beauty* magazine. Initially humorous in tone, *Venus* eventually became a fantasy adventure series. Not only did Olympian Gods appear, but so did the Norse Gods Thor and Loki. Timely's character Venus was most closely associated with artist Bill Everett, who wrote and drew her in the 1950s and revived her in *The Sub-Mariner* in the 1970s. A mythological naiad who claimed to be the Venus of the 1940s later joined a new team, the Agents of Atlas.

NAMORA GETS HER OWN TITLE

• *The Sea Beauty Namora* #1

The Sub-Mariner's cousin Namora won her own comic book series, appealingly titled *The Sea Beauty Namora*. Even though Sub-Mariner creator Bill Everett wrote and drew many of the stories, the series expired after only three issues.

SEPTEMBER

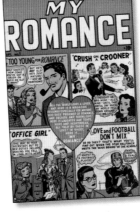

TIMELY IN LOVE

• *My Romance* #1

The romance comics genre had recently been established, and was proving popular with readers. Timely swiftly plunged into the new genre, starting with *My Romance* #1 in September.

NOT SO FUNNY ANY MORE

• *Super Rabbit* #14

Super Rabbit was cancelled with its fourteenth issue and the character made his last appearance in *It's A Duck's Life!* #11 (Feb., 1952). Fellow animals Ziggy Pig and Silly Seal had made their final Golden Age appearance in *Silly Tunes* #7 (Apr., 1947).

JOHN BUSCEMA JOINS TIMELY

After answering a newspaper ad, John Buscema was hired by editor Stan Lee to be a staff artist. He would become one of the best known Marvel artists, remembered for his work on *The Avengers*, *Fantastic Four*, *The Silver Surfer*, *The Mighty Thor*, and especially *Conan The Barbarian*.

Timely's many new western comics in 1948 included *Annie Oakley*, *Tex Morgan*, *Tex Taylor*, and *Wild West*.

MEANWHILE IN 1948...

THE BERLIN BLOCKADE BEGINS

The blockade of Berlin begins when the USSR cuts off all road and rail links to West Berlin with the intention of starving the western part of the city into surrender.

GHANDI ASSASSINATED

Indian pacifist and campaigner, Mahatma Ghandi, is shot dead by Hindu militant Nathuram Godse.

A DECLARATION OF HUMAN RIGHTS

The General Assembly of the UN adopts an international Universal Declaration of Human Rights, which guarantees peoples of the world certain basic rights.

AND AT THE MOVIES...

The Naked City, *influential documentary-style thriller shot on location in New York, tells the story of a murder;* The Red Shoes, *Michael Powell and Emeric Pressburger's luminously handled account of a ballerina torn between romance and her career captures all the magic of theatrical performance.*

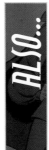

1949

THE GATHERING STORM

By the end of the decade, the public reaction to comics was starting to become negative. Not only were comic books criticized as subliterary junk, but they were blamed as one of the causes of juvenile delinquency. After house-to-house comic book collections, the books were publicly burned in communities throughout America. The leading crusader against comics was a psychiatrist named Dr. Fredric Wertham, who first wrote about them in the *Saturday Review Of Literature* in 1948.

Marvel ran an editorial in its May, 1949, comics that specifically mentioned Dr. Wertham and the *Saturday Review*. The editorial pointed out that, "Since almost all kids of any kind read comics, naturally some of the delinquents read comics too." So, it continued, "why not give the comics credit for the good influence they have been on these millions of healthy, normal kids, instead of just blaming them for our handful of delinquents?" The editorial was signed, "The Editors, Marvel Comic Group."

If only the threat could have been tamed so easily. In the 1950s, Dr. Wertham would continue his anti-comics campaign, Congress would investigate comic books, and the American comic industry would face its darkest period.

MARCH

HUMAN TORCH FLAMES OUT

• *The Human Torch* #35

The original Human Torch made his final appearance in his own comic book with issue #35 but would return in the anthology comic *Young Men* in December, 1953. The Blonde Phantom also lost her own comic in March with issue #22 though a Modern Age Blonde Phantom returned in the 1980s.

LOVE COMICS EXPLOSION

Spotting a popular trend, Marvel deluged the market with romance comics. Beginning in March with the retitling of issue #4 of *My Romance* to *My Own Romance*, new romance titles included *Actual Romances* #1 (Oct.); *Cupid* #1 (Dec.); *Faithful* #1 (Nov.); *Love Adventures* #1, *Love Dramas* #1, and *Love Secrets* #1 (all Oct.); *Love Trails* #1 (Dec.); *Molly Manton's Romances* #1 (Sept.); *My Diary* #1 (Dec.); *My Love* #1 (July); *Our Love* #1 (Sept.); *Romance Tales* (starting with issue #7 in Oct.); and *Young Hearts* #1 (Nov.).

MAY

HOLDING A TORCH

• *Love Tales* #36

In the 1940s, Timely would launch a new comic book while continuing the numbering of a previous one. Thus *The Human Torch* ended with issue #35, and two months later the new romance comic *Love Tales* commenced with issue #36. *Love Tales* ran for eight years, ending with issue #75 in September, 1957. Even more oddly, Marvel would revive *The Human Torch* comic book in April, 1954, starting with issue #36, but it was cancelled permanently with issue #38 in August.

In 1975, it was revealed that the android body of the Torch was converted into the second Vision. The resurrected original Torch and the Vision later existed simultaneously as separate beings.

FORSAKING FANTASY

• *Lovers* #23

What could better demonstrate the change in comics readers' tastes than the title switchover from *Blonde Phantom* #22 to *Lovers* #23? The cover of issue #23 featured a photo of two ordinary kids on a date, sharing a milkshake.

JUNE

DECARLO MEETS MILLIE

• *Millie The Model* #18

Future *Archie* artist Dan DeCarlo began his ten-year run on *Millie The Model* with issue #18. DeCarlo was known for his distinctive style in drawing women, combining cartooniness and genuine sexiness, whether in cartoons for men's magazines or in portraying Archie's girlfriends, Betty and Veronica. From issues #18–93 (June, 1949–Nov., 1959), DeCarlo wrote and drew *Millie The Model,* defining the visual appearance of the characters.

JUNE

FULL CIRCLE

• *Sub-Mariner Comics* #32

Appropriately Bill Everett's Namor the Sub-Mariner closed out his Golden Age career by returning to his beginnings. Namor had debuted with his origin story, written and drawn by Bill Everett in *Marvel Comics* #1 ten years before. This final issue of the 1940s *Sub-Mariner Comics* series presented Everett's new retelling of that same story. With issue #33 in August, Marvel launched yet another romance comic, *Best Love.*

Marvel Mystery Comics #92 was the final issue under that name.

AUGUST

FIRST MARVEL TALES

• *Marvel Tales* #93

Timely's first comic was titled *Marvel Comics,* which became *Marvel Mystery Comics* with issue #2. With issue #93 it became *Marvel Tales* and would run under that title until August, 1957. In 1964, *Marvel Tales* was revived for a reprint series.

OCTOBER

MIXING GENRES

Unlikely as the pairing might seem, Marvel combined westerns and romance, beginning with *Cowboy Romances* #1 in October, and followed by *Romances Of The West* #1 (Nov., 1949), *Rangeland Love* #1 (Dec., 1949), and also *Western Life Romances* #1 (Dec., 1949).

OCTOBER

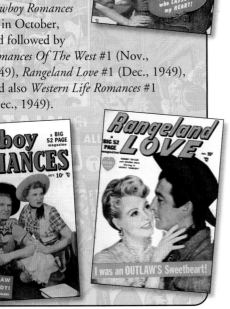

THE END OF THE SUPER HEROES

"The Red Skull strikes again!"

• *Captain America's Weird Tales* #74

The end of the road had come for the first wave of Marvel Super Heroes. Even Timely's Big Three of Captain America, the Human Torch, and the Sub-Mariner were facing the ax. It was only ten years since the Torch and Namor had debuted, riding the new Super Hero genre's extraordinary wave of popularity. However, by 1949, that popularity had sunk so low that Marvel turned *Captain America Comics* into a horror series, *Captain America's Weird Tales,* with issue #74. Not only did the comic cover's "Weird Tales" logo dwarf Captain America's name, but the cover art hid the Captain's face from the readers. The uncharacteristic story inside featured Captain America literally descending into hell, where he battled the Red Skull.

In the final issue of *Captain America's Weird Tales* (#75, Feb., 1950), Captain America's name still featured on the front cover, but Cap himself did not appear on the cover or in the interior art! It was an utterly ignominious end for the greatest Timely hero of the Golden Age.

Captain America had been the last survivor of the Big Three: *The Human Torch* and *Sub-Mariner Comics* had both ended in the first half of 1949.

It would take a radical rethinking of the Super Hero concept, not only to make Super Heroes popular again, but to make them appeal to an older, more sophisticated audience. But in 1949, Stan Lee's Marvel Super Hero revolution lay twelve years in the future.

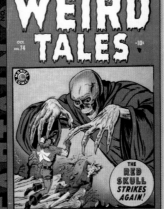

The Red Skull dominated on the front cover of Captain America's Weird Tales.

MEANWHILE IN 1949...

BERLIN BLOCKADE LIFTED
After 318 days, the USSR abandons its blockade of West Berlin. The rail and road supply routes through the Soviet-controlled zone of Germany resume.

THE ATOMIC ARMS RACE BEGINS
The USSR shocks America when it tests its first atomic bomb. The design is based on the bomb that the US dropped on Nagasaki in 1945.

TWO NEW GERMAN COUNTRIES
The British, French, and American sectors are merged together to create the Federal Republic of Germany. Soon after, the Soviet zone is declared the German Democratic Republic.

CHINA TURNS "RED"
After victory in the Chinese Civil War, Communist leader Mao Ze Dong announces the establishment of the People's Republic of China.

AND AT THE MOVIES...
The Third Man, *Carol Reed's atmospheric, Graham Greene-scripted, noir thriller about black marketeers set in a corrupt, postwar Vienna;* On The Town, *three sailors on twenty-four-hour leave hit New York in search of fun and romance in this exuberant, ambitious musical featuring Gene Kelly.*

DECEMBER

STILL FURTHER WEST

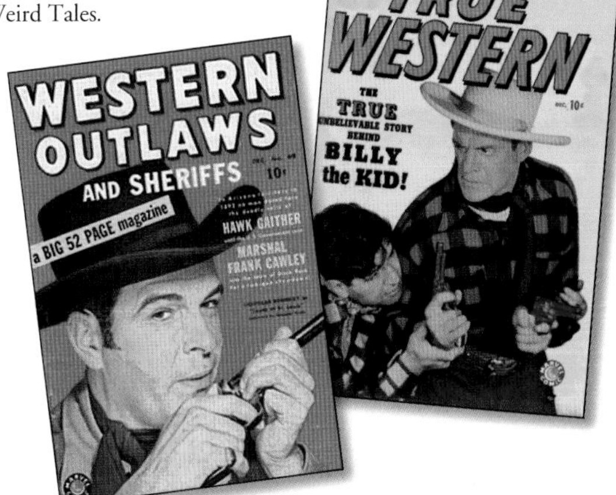

Kid Colt and the Two-Gun Kid both appeared in the two issues of *Best Western,* which began its numbering with #58 (June, 1949). In issue #60, the series was descriptively retitled *Western Outlaws And Sheriffs.* Also in December, *True Western* #1 debuted, featuring real life outlaw Billy the Kid.

ALSO...

MARVEL MISCELLANY

Among the many other comics that Marvel produced in 1949 were *Little Lenny* and *Little Lizzie* (both in June); *Casey: Crime Photographer* (Aug.); *Wonder Duck* #1 (Sept.); *Blaze The Wonder Collie* (beginning with issue #2 in Oct.); *Girl Comics* #1 (Oct.); *Film Funnies* #1 (Nov.); *Sport Stars* #1 (Nov.); and *Man Comics* #1 (Dec.). *Blaze Carson* gave way to *Rex Hart* with issue #6 (Aug.), and *Willie Comics* turned into *Li'l Willie Comics* with issue #20 (July).

Ideal: A Classical Comic #1 ***(July, 1948)***
In 1948, Timely began publishing Ideal: A Classical Comic, *which ran comics stories based on historical figures. The first issue featured Antony and Cleopatra, the third issue had Joan of Arc on the cover, while Richard the Lionhearted starred in the fourth. Timely may have been seeking to placate parents and educators who regarded comic books as trash unfit for young readers.* Ideal: A Classical Comic *lasted only four issues before turning into a romance comic entitled* Ideal: Love And Romance.

1950s

The 1950s would prove to be one of the most tumultuous decades for the comic book industry, and for Timely. The end of World War II meant the end of paper rationing, which led to more publishers pushing more product onto the newsstands of the nation. Consequently, the racks were choked with product. Additionally, the rise of television as a mass-medium and its popularity among children would prove a formidable competitor for the attention of the readership—especially since television was beamed into the household for free. And a series of well-intentioned but ultimately destructive investigations into the nature of the comic book business would leave the entire field crippled.

1950

THE WINDS OF CHANGE

The Super Hero fad that had fueled sales during World War II had tapered off, with all but the most popular costumed crimefighters headed for literary limbo, and the rush was on to find and exploit the next big trend. Timely founder and publisher Martin Goodman had proceeded with caution during World War II, due to paper rationing, and maximized profit on every title that used up a portion of his paper allocation. With paper rationing lifted at the start of the 1950s, Goodman now led the charge, determined to acquire a dominant position on the sales racks. More concerned with selling paper than content, Goodman's strategy in 1950 was to seek out a successful trend—be it westerns, romances, or horror—flood the market with it, pocket the profit, and then move on when the trend went bust. In this manner, Timely would become a dominant presence throughout the 1950s, and a gadfly to other publishers, especially those innovators who were starting trends, rather than simply exploiting them.

JANUARY

PROSPECTING FOR TRENDS

• *Cowgirl Romances* #28

In January, *Jeanie Comics* transformed into *Cowgirl Romances* in an attempt to cross-pollinate western and romance audiences. Martin Goodman's experience, as a publisher who began with lurid pulp magazines in the early 1930s, told him that the title was a strong reason why readers bought a magazine. As such, he was constantly experimenting with his line of titles, renaming some (even when the contents remained pretty much the same) and replacing others when he thought he smelled a new trend. In the same vein, in June *Cowboy Romances* became *Young Men*, and *True Western* became *True Adventures* #3 (May) an then *Men's Adventures* #4 (August). In this way, Timely gyrated through the year, constantly prospecting for a newsprint gold mine, and eliminating titles or concepts that did not measure up. This remained the pattern throughout most of the 1950s.

FEBRUARY

CAPTAIN AMERICA COMICS CANCELED

• *Captain America's Weird Tales* #75

The final issue of *Captain America Comics* (recently retitled *Captain America's Weird Tales*) carried a February date. Unlike the previous issues, which featured the fervent, patriotic adventures of Cap, this comic didn't have a single appearance of its star-spangled namesake! Instead, behind its shock-promising cover (illustrated by a young Gene Colan, who fifteen years later would be an important figure in the burgeoning Marvel line), the book contained four generic mystery-horror stories. This was a short-lived attempt to jump on the bandwagon of horror comics, a growing segment of the marketplace. It was a seemingly permanent farewell to the character who had been Timely's best-selling and most popular Super Hero during the war years, and an indicator of the horror trend that what was to come in the months ahead.

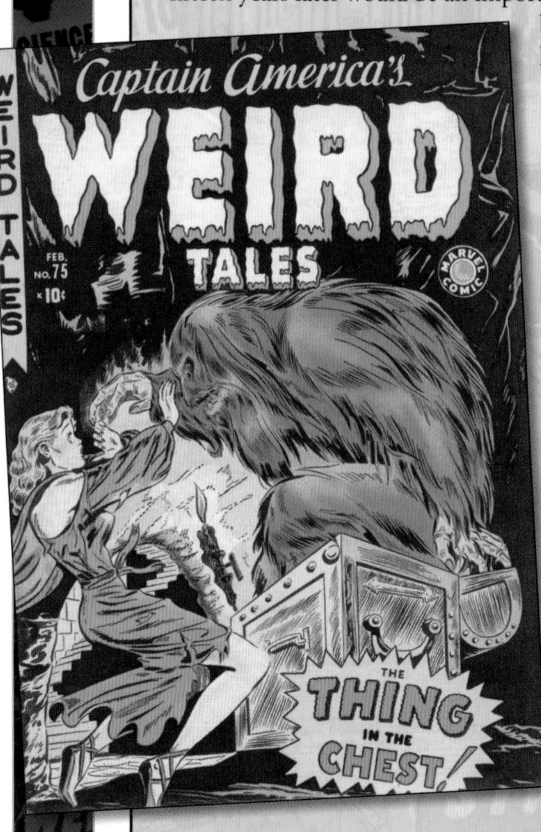

As interest in Super Heroes died off, publishers moved into more profitable genres, such as horror.

MAY

TITLE ROULETTE

• *Cindy Smith* #39

With issue #39, *Cindy Comics* became *Cindy Smith*, which itself became *Crime Can't Win* two issues later in September, with no change to the numbering. Retitling a magazine, rather than canceling it, was common for two reasons. Firstly, to secure mailing permits for subscription copies, a publisher had to pay a fee for each title. By continuing the numbering of a failed book with a new title, Martin Goodman was often able to avoid having to pay this fee a second time. Secondly, in this time of fierce competitiveness, retailers were more likely to stock a title with the appearance of a successful track record, so a higher issue-number was more likely to guarantee that your comic book would be seen and purchased than one with #1 on the cover.

There was little loyalty to any concept or approach. So if Cindy *did not work as a teen humor strip, it was given a facelift and turned into an out-and-out romance title.*

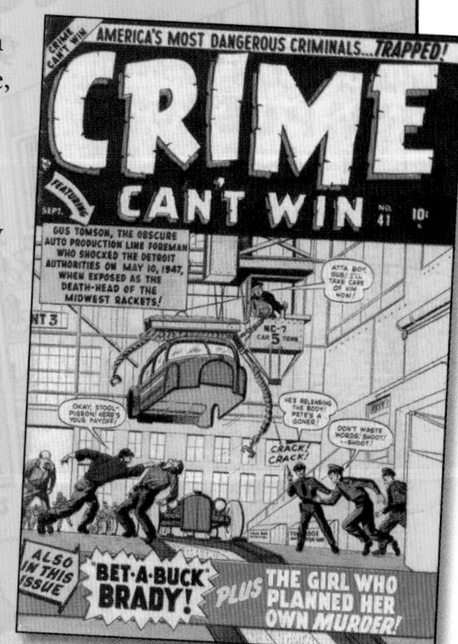

Crime Can't Win *was an attempt to jump onto the bandwagon started by Lev Gleason's popular* Crime Does Not Pay *series, featuring supposedly true and lurid tales of gangsters and crime bosses.*

DECEMBER

THE APACHE KID RIDES!

• *Apache Kid* #53

One of Timely's more durable characters, the Apache Kid, had made his first appearance in *Two-Gun Western* #5 in November, 1950, and December heralded his own title, *Apache Kid* #53 (the numbering continued from *Reno Browne, Hollywood's Greatest Cowgirl*). The Apache Kid was Alan Krandal, who had been adopted and raised by the Apache chief Red Hawk after his parents were killed. Returning to white man's society with the name Aloysius Kare, he would assume his Native American attire and war paint as the Apache Kid to battle threats to both his homes. Unlike many western series of the era, *Apache Kid* generally depicted Native American culture with respect, and differentiated between the different tribes of indigenous Americans. While the series ended in January, 1952, it was resurrected for a brief period in 1955 and 1956, and went on to be reprinted in the 1970s. The Apache Kid himself returned in the 2002 *Apache Skies* limited series in Marvel's adult MAX line.

FLYING SAUCER SUPER HERO

• *Marvel Boy #1*

Timely's first costumed character of the 1950s appeared in *Marvel Boy* #1, an attempt to marry the Super Hero genre with the growing interest in flying saucers. Its Russ Heath-illustrated origin story told of how Professor Grayson was fearful that world war would soon engulf the planet. He built a rocket ship to carry himself and his infant son away from strife-torn Earth. Arriving on Uranus, they were taken in by the small native population, under whose tutelage the boy, Robert Grayson, achieved both mental and physical perfection. Armed with a pair of wristbands that could project light bursts to blind his foes, Robert returned to Earth as Marvel Boy, charged with protecting both his natural and adopted homes from threats from outer space. Taking a job as an insurance claims investigator, Marvel Boy patrolled the nation, encountering threats from beyond the stars, from strange supernatural creatures, and from corrupt and criminal earthmen.

Given that the series debuted in its own title and with a #1 issue, rather than transitioning from another series on the publishing schedule, it appears that there was a good deal of faith in Marvel Boy. And while he wouldn't catch on immediately, Marvel Boy would later become an important element in the Marvel Age, returning as a villain in *Fantastic Four* #164 (November, 1975), begetting the cosmic hero Quasar, and later reappearing as a member of the Agents of Atlas, more than fifty years after his debut.

MEANWHILE IN 1950...

"WE WILL HAVE H-BOMB"

Following recent Soviet atomic bomb tests, the nuclear arms race steps up a gear as President Truman announces plans to develop a hydrogen bomb. It is expected to be 100 to 1,000 times more powerful than those dropped on Hiroshima and Nagasaki.

US TROOPS SENT TO KOREA

The Cold War takes on a more international perspective when President Truman sends air and naval troops to South Korea's defense after North Korean forces march into their territory.

MCCARTHY WARNS AGAINST COMMUNISTS

Senator Joseph McCarthy makes claims against alleged communists in the US administration, fueling anti-communist suspicions during the tensions of the Cold War.

LINK FOUND BETWEEN SMOKING AND LUNG CANCER

Morton Levin publishes the first major study linking smoking with lung cancer.

MEET SNOOPY

A new comic strip is launched: Peanuts *by Charles Schultz becomes a world phenomenon running in more than 2,400 newspapers and reaching millions of readers in 68 countries.*

AND AT THE MOVIES...

Sunset Boulevard, *an exposé of Hollywood features Gloria Swanson's forgotten silent-movie star among a gallery of self-deceivers;* All About Eve, *a dark tale of showbusiness stars Bette Davis as an ageing actress ruthlessly undermined by an ambitious stalker.*

1951

WAR ON THE NEWSSTANDS!

The escalation of the Korean War in 1951 gave publishers their latest trend: war comics. Those with a Korean War focus or an anti-communist agenda became all the rage. And no outfit produced them in greater quantity than Timely. Also in 1951, the popularity of weird horror comics grew. Weird though they were, these stories often had literary merit and featured excellent artwork by the finest illustrators. A sly sense of humor, at once chest-thumping and self-deprecating, added an element of satire to what might otherwise have been nothing more than gruesome horror stories. Stan Lee would use a similar approach to characterize Marvel a decade later. The weird horror comics also began to credit their artists, making them celebrities to their fans and a selling point—another trend that Lee would use in the Marvel Age.

MARCH

A TIME FOR WAR

• *Battle* #1

Publisher Martin Goodman's first war-themed series, *War Comics*, had debuted in December, 1950, and it was joined in March, 1951 by *Battle*. These two series would form the spine of Timely's war-themed publishing efforts, and would continue uninterrupted until 1957.

In addition, Goodman transitioned *Young Men* and *Man Comics* into war titles. They began with stories devoted to draft-dodging and the need for America's young adults to join the service and do their duty to their country, and eventually expanded into full-fledged exploits of servicemen and soldiers—*Young Men* even became *Young Men On The Battlefield* in December. Such themes were presented in stark black-and-white terms of little sophistication; Americans were the good guys and the Reds, be they communist Chinese or Russians, were the enemy. No shades of grey were necessary, or desired.

M *Mystic* #1—cover-billed as "The Most Eerie Stories Ever Told!"—begins.

M *Spy Fighters* #1 continued the war comic trend by devoting most of its space to tales of undercover American agents outwitting morally corrupt communist hordes.

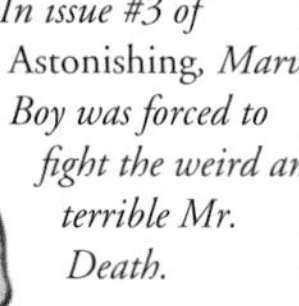

In issue #3 of Astonishing, *Marvel Boy was forced to fight the weird and terrible Mr. Death.*

APRIL

MARVEL BOY DEFEATED BY WEIRD-HORROR!

• *Astonishing* #3

The increasingly popular trend for horror wrote the final chapter for Marvel Boy, the first costumed hero of the decade. With issue #3, *Marvel Boy* became *Astonishing*, and while the headband-wearing teen would continue to headline for three more issues, his adversaries grew progressively darker and more sinister. Artist Bill Everett, the originator of the Sub-Mariner, took over the series, pitting the boy from Uranus against ghastly and gruesome opponents. Marvel Boy's final story featured in the comic's sixth issue, but *Astonishing* would continue on without him, serving up the same weird and horrific stories that filled *Strange Tales* and *Mystic* until 1957.

A STRANGE DEBUT

• *Strange Tales* #1

In response to the horror bandwagon, Timely launched two perennial titles. March had seen the debut of *Mystic*, but more significant was *Strange Tales* #1, which would become the longest-running series to enter the Marvel Age and would eventually serve as home to the Human Torch, Doctor Strange, and Nick Fury, Agent of SHIELD. For its first ten years, however, it showcased a diverse collection of short shock-horror tales. Yet, the contents of *Strange Tales* and *Mystic* were utterly interchangeable, with only an often-used blurb on the splash panel indicating which series it eventually saw print in—"One of the strangest tales ever told!" for *Strange Tales* and "One of the world's most mystic tales" in *Mystic*.

Strange Tales *followed the typical anthology format of featuring multiple short suspense stories in each issue. In this regard, it was no different from any of the other horror comics in the Timely line.*

More Super Hero than soldier, Combat Kelly set the mold for the later Sgt. Fury by meeting the Nazi onslaught head on with a wisecrack and his fists.

THE FIRST WAR HERO

• *Combat Kelly* #1

Inspired by war movies of the John Wayne variety, Timely released *Combat Kelly*, its first war title devoted to a single character. Not all that dissimilar to Sgt. Fury, who would debut a decade later, Kelly was a combat-happy infantryman, characterized by his two-fisted tough-guy approach to warfare. Supported by his comedy-relief sidekick "Cookie" Novak, Kelly wisecracked and knuckle-dusted his way through the conflict, making short work of the enemy. As other soldiers often commented, it was as though "Kelly's trying to win the war all by himself!" *Combat Kelly* would outlast the Korean War and run through 1957, returning in June, 1970, in *Combat Kelly And His Deadly Dozen* for a short-term tour of duty against the Nazis in World War II.

A NEW LOGO

In December, publisher Martin Goodman abandoned his distributor Kable News and launched his own distribution network, Atlas. An Atlas emblem began to appear on the Timely covers, uniting them visually under the same publishing house. This logo would become a fixture, and the name Atlas, while never formally adopted by the publishing side of the company, was used in common parlance. In 1963, when the time came to give the Super Hero line a name, editor Stan Lee wanted to call it the Atlas Comics Group, but was overruled by Goodman, who felt that Marvel Comics Group would be stronger.

MEANWHILE IN 1951...

PEACE TREATY SIGNED WITH JAPAN

World War II officially ends when forty-nine countries sign the Treaty of Peace with Japan in San Francisco. As a result of negotiations, American troops are allowed to be stationed in Japan.

SEVERE FLOODS HIT THE MIDWEST

Heavy rain causes a major catastrophe in Kansas and Missouri, leaving devastation across two important agricultural and industrial states. Nearly one billion dollars are lost and twenty-eight people die in the worst floods in the area since 1844.

NATIONAL MONUMENT UNVEILED

The George Washington Carver National Monument in Joplin, Missouri, is the first national monument created in honor of an African American. Born into slavery, Carver was well-respected in farming for such inventions as the Jesup Wagon, a mobile school that brought education to farmers.

FIRST VIDEOTAPE RECORDER

Charles P. Ginsburg of Ampex Corporation develops the technology to convert live images from television into electronic impulses and then save them on magnetic tape: the Videotape Recorder (VTR) is born.

NEW TERM: "ROCK 'N' ROLL"

Alan Freed, a DJ at Cleveland radio station WJW, coins a new term—"Rock 'n' Roll"—for the black rhythm and blues music that is increasingly popular on the airwaves.

TEEN ANGST AND REBELLION

The anti-materialistic literary movement—the "Beat generation"—gathers pace with the publication of J.D. Salinger's Catcher in the Rye, *sparking controversy for its offensive language and depiction of sex and teenage defiance.*

SUGAR RAY BEATS LA MOTTA

Previously a welterweight, Sugar Ray Robinson, now a middleweight, defeats the Bronx Bull, Jake La Motta, in the thirteenth round.

9TH STREET SHOW OPENS

A ground-breaking art show opens with abstract expressionist paintings by post-war artists of the avant-garde New York School.

AND AT THE MOVIES...

Rashomon, *Akira Kurosawa's virtuoso film set in medieval Japan has four people tell different versions of the same violent incident;* An American In Paris, *an infectiously romantic, left-bank musical about a penniless artist who scorns a rich woman's patronage for true love based on George Gershwin's symphonic composition;* The African Queen, *charming Hollywood entertainment about the unlikely love affair between a crude steamer captain and a priggish missionary fatefully thrown together.*

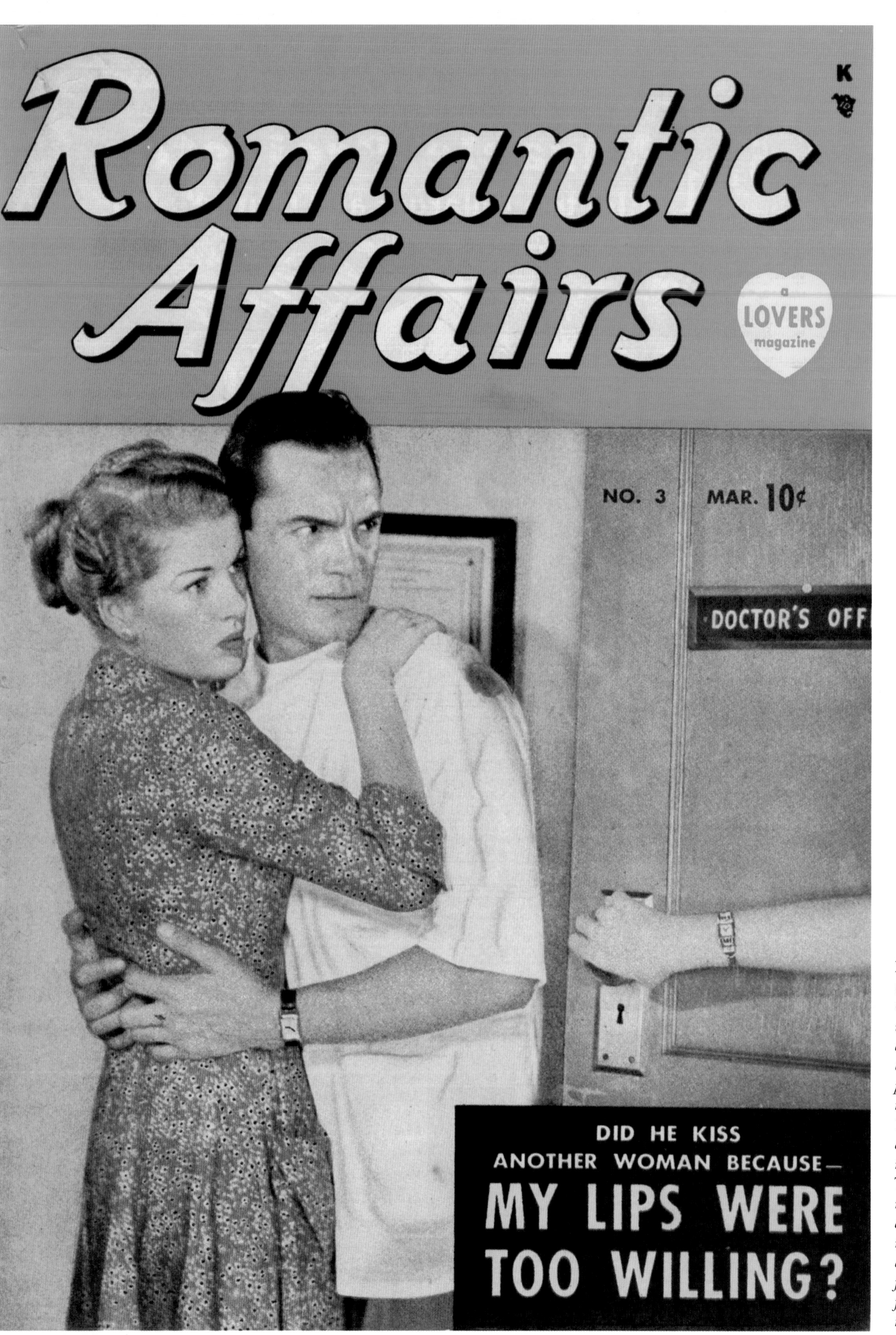

Romantic Affairs ***#3 (March, 1950)***
One of the strategies used on the romance covers to try to attract buyers was to use photographs, rather than line drawings. This made these comics closely resemble their newsstand relatives, the True Love *fiction magazines. Often, the companies would draft members of their editorial staff or freelance artists to pose for these covers, rather than professional models.*

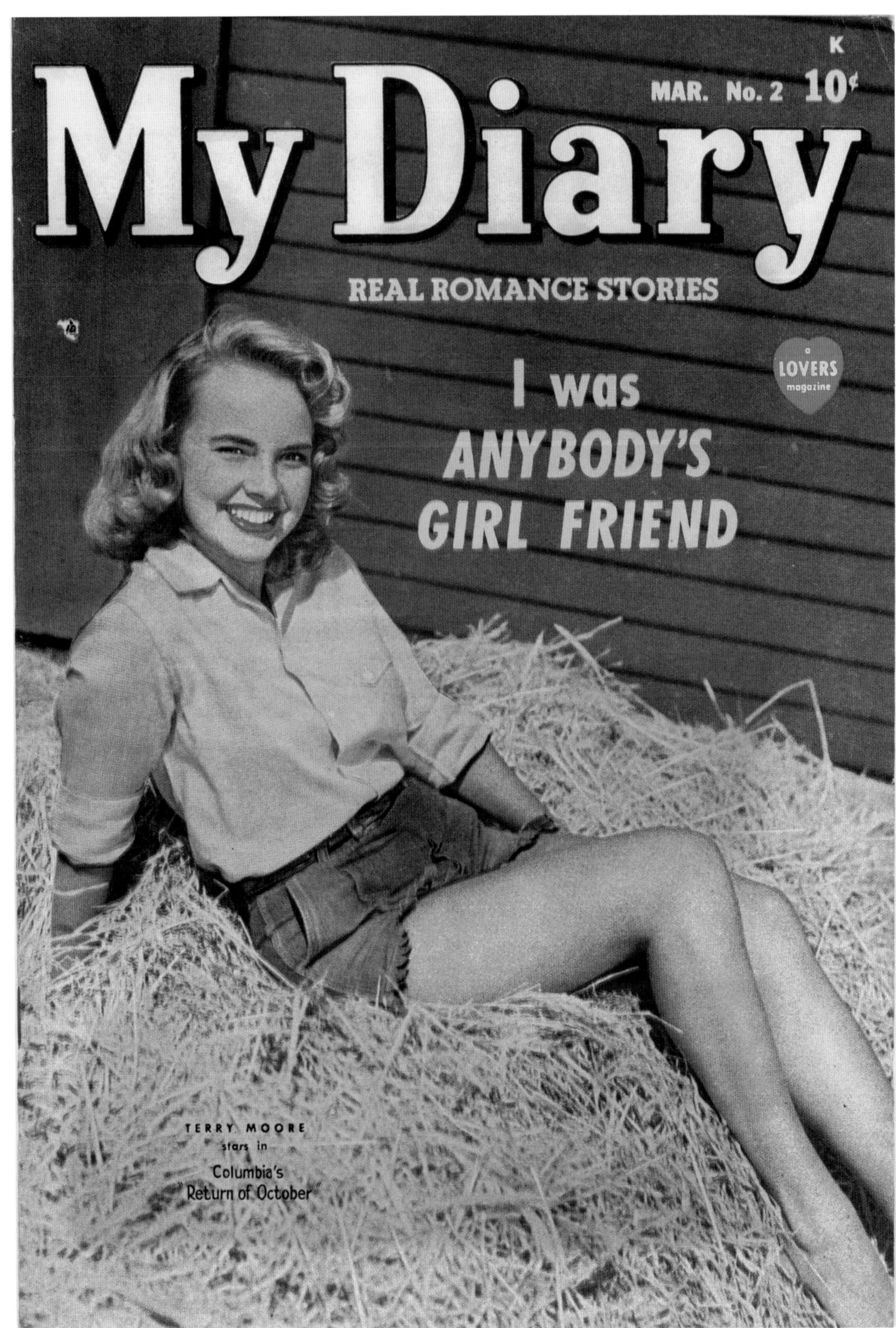

My Diary ***#2***
(March, 1950)
The covers of most romance comics promised thrills much more salacious than what was actually delivered, as in the case of this issue's blurb, "I Was Anybody's Girl Friend." Covers often promised that the stories within were true, but that was almost always a lie.

1952 ATLAS CONQUERS ALL

Although nobody working in Martin Goodman's pulp factory would realize it at the time, 1952 would prove to be the year of Atlas' greatest sustained growth. In control of his own distribution and with no outside forces limiting the number of titles he could release, Goodman ramped up production. He flooded the marketplace with almost 400 releases over the year, an all-time high that would not again be equaled until the speculator boom of the 1990s, when an influx of consumers trying to invest in what they saw as collectibles caused a gold rush run of additional titles to be published. Atlas shouldered its way onto the newsstands of America, establishing a strong and lasting presence through sheer numbers, rather than reader loyalty. Atlas wasn't anybody's favorite comic book company necessarily, but just about anybody reading comic books in 1952 was reading Atlas.

Most of these series would be discontinued after only a handful of issues, but this kind of focused and sustained bombardment of material is what allowed Goodman and Atlas to flourish, often at the expense of more innovative competitors. Martin Goodman must have been feeling very good about the future in 1952.

JANUARY

WAR VICTORIES

The Korean War continued to be good for business, and Atlas launched a number of new books in an attempt to secure a stronghold in the market. Beginning with *War Adventures* in January, other titles followed including *Battle Action* in February; *War Combat* in March; *Battlefield*, *Men In Action*, and *War Action* al in April; and *Battlefront* and *Combat* in June. None of these series featured continuing characters, but instead contained a diverse assortment of one-off war stories, often illustrated beautifully. The sheer number of stories being produced virtually guaranteed a repetition of themes, and the overly simplistic depiction of life on th battlefield tended to glamorize combat, making it seem like a game.

Spy Cases and *Spy Fighters* also jumped onto the war trend by transitioning most of their space to tales of undercover American agents outwitting the dim and morally-corrupt communists. Most of the titles in the Atlas line were issued bimonthly to insure a good sell-through by maintaining a position on the racks longer. So, it mu have felt like a full-fledged invasion at every corner candy store.

APRIL

VENUS DESCENDING

• *Venus* #19

Martin Goodman was always ready to discontinue a title if there was any indication that sales were slowing but occasionally there was a series that defied extermination and that tried to adapt to the trends in order to remain viable. *Venus* was such a magazine. The book starred the Greek goddess, who had descended from the heavens and fallen in love with Whitney Hammond, the publisher of *Beauty* magazine. Venus worked for the magazine as a model and copywriter while her colleagues were oblivious that she was the mythological figure This set-up remained in place for the life of *Venus*, but the tone of Venus' adventures and the content of her stories changed wildly.

Venus was created in August, 1948, as part of a sustained effort by Atlas to appeal to girls. The other two series featuring female heroes that had been launched in the same year—*Sun Girl* and *Namora*—had both quickly faded away. *Venus* survived by changing its stripes, first by mimicking the teen comedy craze, and then becoming an all-out romance title, with painted covers in the style of the romance novels that were taking the country by storm. Within a few issues, the title had become fantasy and science fiction. When writer-artist Bill Everett took over *Venus* with its thirteenth issue, he went all-out towards making it a shock-horror series. However, none of these changes did more than stave off cancellation of *Venus* for a few months and the magazine ended in April.

The character of Venus woul return in the Marvel Age in Sub-Mariner, Champions, *and* Agents of Atlas.

JUNE

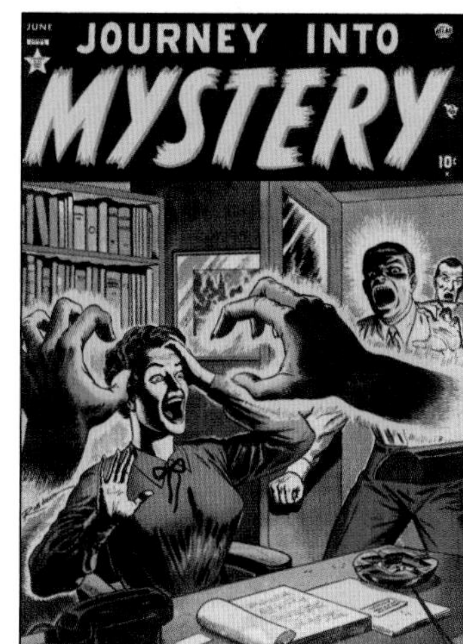

A LONG JOURNEY BEGINS

• *Journey Into Mystery* #1

From a historical perspective, the most important title that Atlas released in 1952 was the first issue of *Journey Into Mystery*. Another shock-horror title virtually identical to *Strange Tales* and *Mystic*, *Journey Into Mystery* would become another Atlas perennial, surviving through the near-end of Atlas in 1957 to become the birthplace of the mighty Thor in August, 1962. The series was retitled *Thor* in March, 1966, and in that form continues to the present day.

The most striking feature of the first issue, however, was the absolute lack of cover copy. Typically, Atlas covers carried at least one if not several blurbs extolling the virtues of the stories contained in that issue—a policy Stan Lee would resume when the Marvel Age got up and running in the early 1960s. But in this rare instance, artist Russ Heath's compelling cover artwork was allowed to exist on its own. This gave the first issue a certain air of sophistication. By the second issue, however, it was back to business as usual.

MEANWHILE IN 1952...

A NEW QUEEN FOR BRITAIN

His Majesty, King George VI, dies in his sleep, aged fifty-six, bringing an end to his sixteen-year reign. He is succeeded by his twenty-five-year-old daughter, Her Majesty Queen Elizabeth II.

FIRST H-BOMB TEST

The world's first H-bomb is detonated on the Pacific island of Eniwetok. This operation, code-named Ivy Mike, marks a significant step forward for the United States in the arms race against the USSR.

ANNE FRANK'S DIARY PUBLISHES

The voice of an ordinary young girl reveals the human tragedy behind the horrors of the Jewish Holocaust in Europe.

EVA PERON DIES

The First Lady of Argentina dies at the age of thirty-three from ovarian cancer. During Juan Peron's presidential reign, Evita (as she was known) championed women's rights and was adored by the descamisados or shirtless poor.

DISCOVER *THE POWER OF POSITIVE THINKING*

Norman Vincent Peale's self-help book publishes, outlining the theory of positive thinking and its uses.

FIRST DIET SOFT DRINK

Kirsch Beverages sell a diet ginger ale as the first "No-Cal Beverage."

AND AT THE MOVIES...

High Noon, *real-time western, about a lone marshal resolved to defend his town against a vengeful gang, presents a powerful allegory of McCarthyism;* Singin' In The Rain, *bittersweet musical comedy parodies Hollywood's transition to the talkies with lively tunes and choreography immortalized by Gene Kelly;* The Bad And The Beautiful, *Vincente Minnelli's tragicomic take on the Hollywood system charts the rise and fall of a megalomaniac movie tycoon.*

ALSO PUBLISHED

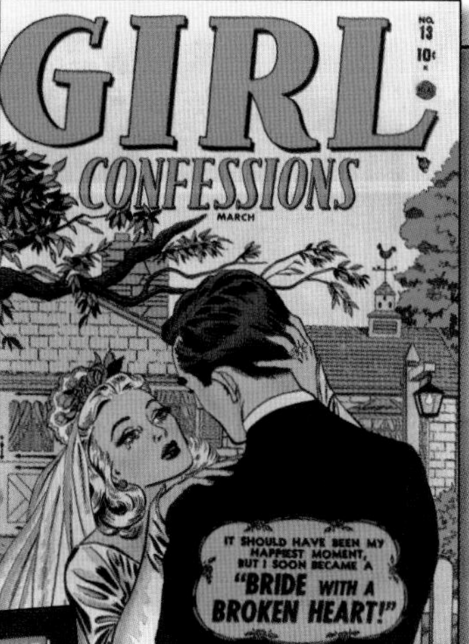

Girl Confessions *#13 (March)* Girl Confessions *picked up the numbering from* Girl Comics, *but placed its emphasis on tearful tales of heartbreak.*

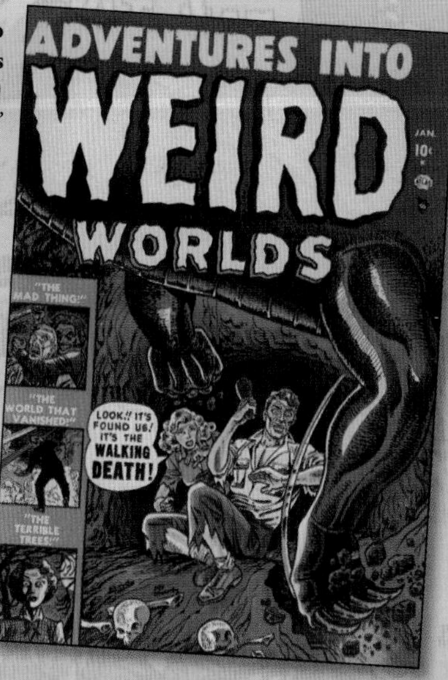

Adventures Into Weird Worlds *#1 (Jan.)* *With "Weird" becoming something of a buzzword in the world of comics, Atlas launched* Adventures Into Weird Worlds *in 1952.*

Crime Exposed *#14 (June)* Crime Exposed *ended its two-year run of sensationalistic stories of gangsters and hoodlums in issue #14.*

BEST OF THE REST

An overview of Atlas' output in 1952 shows a diverse and growing line-up, covering virtually every conceivable reader's taste. In addition to the proliferation of war series, there were romance titles (*Girl Confessions, Love Adventures, Love Romances, Love Tales, Lovers, My Own Romance, True Secrets*); horror books (*Adventures Into Weird Worlds, Astonishing, Journey Into Unknown Worlds, Marvel Tales, Mystery Tales, Spellbound, Suspense, Uncanny Tales*); crime comics (*All-True Crime, Amazing Detective Cases, Crime Can't Win, Crime Cases, Crime Exposed, Justice*); westerns (*Kid Colt, Outlaw, Texas Kid, Two Gun Western, Western Outlaws And Sheriffs, Wild Western*); teen comedy (*Georgie, Millie The Model, Nellie The Nurse, Patsy Walker*); radio tie-ins (*My Friend Irma*), sports (*Sports Action*); and even funny animal humor (*It's A Duck's Life*). And while none of it was particularly intended to stand the test of time, it was all entertaining.

Despite the threat posed by the advent and rise of TV as a mass medium, comic book circulations were up, and the majority of children between the ages of eight and twelve regularly read and purchased comic magazines. This young audience, which made up the backbone of comic book buyers, was perceived as not being terribly discerning in their tastes, so by flooding the marketplace with titles in every genre, Atlas pushed the competition off the newsstand racks and positioned itself excellently to claim a lion's share of those sales.

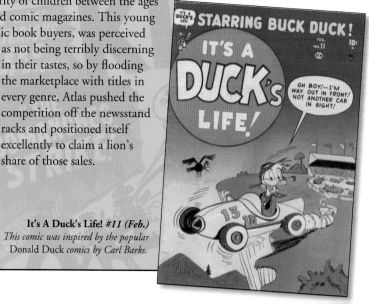

Two Gun Western *#14 (June)* *This comic featured all of Atlas' favorite cowboys.*

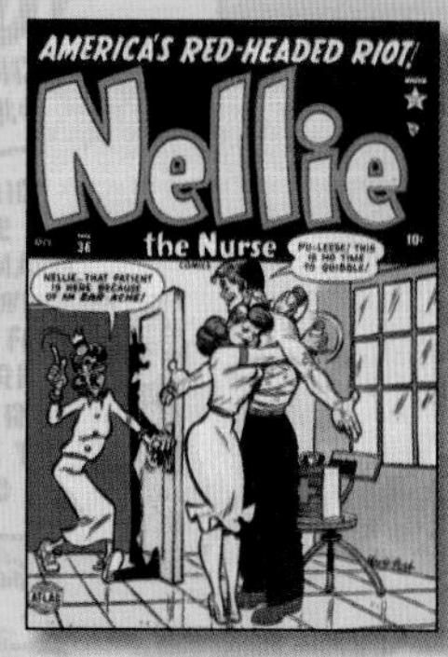

Nellie The Nurse *#36 (Oct.)* Nellie *would return for a single issue in 1957.*

Sports Action *#14 (Sept.)* *Sport didn't translate well into the static medium of comics.*

It's A Duck's Life! *#11 (Feb.)* *This comic was inspired by the popular* Donald Duck *comics by Carl Barks.*

1953

PORTENTS OF DOOM

As the 1950s wore on, the tide of popular opinion turned against comic books. The horror genre had produced stories of increasing violence and gore which many viewed as distasteful. More articles were appearing in publications such as *Reader's Digest* decrying comic magazines and their publishers, saying that they were bad for children and ruined young eyes. The most avid anti-comics crusader, a child psychiatrist named Frederic Wertham, had a book scheduled to come out in 1954 entitled *Seduction of the Innocent*, which claimed that reading comic books turned children into juvenile delinquents. Excerpts from the book were running in various parents' magazines, intended to drum up sales and interest.

The comic book publishers argued that their comic stories encouraged reading and that their audience was intelligent enough to distinguish between fantasy and reality. Pro-comic book/anti-Wertham editorials appeared in Timely books as early as 1948. However, public opinion wasn't with the comic book industry. If something was not done soon, the US government might very well descend upon comic books.

APRIL

FIRING BACK AT THE CRITICS

• *Suspense* #29

BIG SUSPENSE-PACKED PAGES
SUSPENSE
ON SALE EVERY MONTH!
WHAT STRANGE TERRORS ARE SEEN...
BY THE LIGHT OF THE MOON!
"THE RAVING MANIAC"
"MAN BEHIND THE BLINDS!"

Inspired by the threat to his livelihood from Frederic Wertham's comments, editor Stan Lee, together with artist Joe Maneely, parodied the psychiatrist, in a four-page story appearing in *Suspense* #29 entitled "The Raving Maniac." In it, a thinly disguised representation of Wertham accosted editor Lee at the Atlas offices, claiming that the horror stories Lee was publishing were vile, irresponsible, and harmful. Lee coolly turned aside his visitor's criticisms one by one, and in a twist ending doctors arrived to take the Wertham stand-in back to the insane asylum from which he had escaped. It was no doubt a satisfying story for Lee to pen, but it did nothing to change the direction events were heading in.

MAY

CLEANING UP COMICS

• *Man Comics* #26

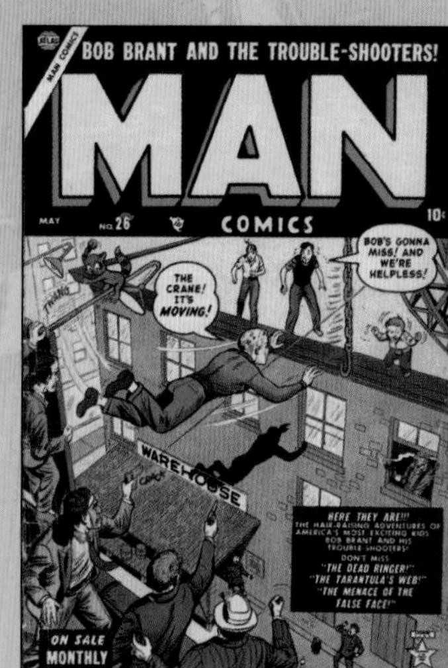

With public opinion turning against horror comic books, the race was on to find cleaner, socially acceptable reading trends. While not abandoning the horror and crime titles completely, Atlas looked for other genres that might prove as profitable. The end of the Korean War later in the year signaled a downturn in the fortunes of war comics. Atlas began to cull its line, and, with this issue, transitioned *Man Comics* into a vehicle for Bob Brant and the Trouble-Shooters, adventurous teens in the mold of the Little Wise Guys from Lev Gleason's *Daredevil Comics*. However, this move did not capture the dimes of readers, and the series was discontinued two issues later.

POPULAR PATSY

• *Patsy And Her Pals* #1

With the proliferation of teen humor titles, Atlas decided to expand teen-humor heroine Patsy Walker's world even further by publishing *Patsy And Her Pals*. Patsy was a popular character, already headlining in two titles by 1953—*Patsy Walker* and *Patsy And Hedy*—as well as being the lead feature in *Miss America*. Atlas also introduced a new teen girl character in *Wendy Parker*, though this magazine's sales were so sluggish that by January, 1954, they had to cover-bill "Patsy Walker—In This Issue!" in order to keep readers interested.

JUNE

THE WAR IS OVER

• *Young Men* #21

Young Men On The Battlefield was losing readers now that the Korean War was nearing an end. So, in an attempt to find a more successful subject, the comic reverted to its original title—*Young Men*—and ran stories of auto racing, starring Flash Foster and his High-Gear Hot Shots. But, like the introduction of Bob Brant in *Man Comics*, this move did not stave off the defection of readers, and Foster's adventures only lasted three issues.

JULY

JUNGLE JAPES

• *Lorna The Jungle Queen* #1

Jungle girls were always popular with the comic-reading public, so Atlas brought out *Lorna, The Jungle Queen* to romp around the underbrush. The illustrations of scantily clad beauties in fur attire were guaranteed to garner attention from a slightly older audience looking for titillation.

M *Homer Hooper* #1, another teen hero comic, began in July but only lasted until December.

AUGUST

THE HIGH ROAD

• *Bible Tales For Young Folk* #1

In August, Atlas tried a new tack, publishing *Bible Tales For Young Folk*. This was a tentative step into a publishing arena that was dominated by *Classics Illustrated*, an Elliot Publishing series of comic book adaptations of classic literature. However, *Bible Tales For Young Folk* would end a mere six months later.

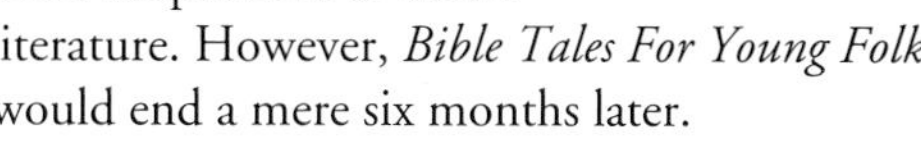

SEPTEMBER

ADVENTURES IN OUTER SPACE

• *Speed Carter, Spaceman* #1

With the popularity of TV programs like *Space Patrol*, Atlas introduced *Speed Carter, Spaceman*, which was devoted to interplanetary adventure. Martin Goodman hedged his bets by styling the cover after popular sci-fi magazines and featuring minimal copy. But Speed Carter crashed on takeoff, and only lasted six issues.

DECEMBER

ZANY HUMOR

• *Crazy* #1

One new trend that was proving popular was humor publications. EC Comics launched *MAD* magazine, which lampooned anything and everything. The satire of *MAD* grabbed readers, but many other humor titles filled magazine racks. In this vein, Atlas produced *Crazy* (billed as "Man! Dig This Crazy Little Mixed-Up Mag!"). It died a quick death, lasting seven issues, but would return in February, 1973.

RETURN OF THE HEROES

• *Young Men* #24

Television had an influence on several aspects of the Atlas line. Over the airwaves, the brand new *Adventures of Superman* program had introduced an entirely new generation of potential customers to DC's Man of Steel.

Martin Goodman decreed that the most popular costumed champions from the Timely era would live again. And so, the cover of *Young Men* #24 proclaimed, "Look! He's back from the dead! It's the HUMAN TORCH!" In a departure from the established wisdom of the time, which said that comic book readership turned over every three or four years, *Young Men* #24 took great pains to explain the disappearance of the Torch, his sidekick Toro, and his allies Captain America and the Sub-Mariner for the past five years—the Torch had been overpowered by criminals and imprisoned on an atomic testing range; Toro, who had similar powers to the Human Torch, had been brainwashed by the communists; Captain America had retired to live as a schoolteacher once the Nazi hordes were overcome; and the Sub-Mariner had returned to Antarctica, having grown tired of human companionship. But now, they were all back, and in the thick of the fight.

MEANWHILE IN 1953...

THE WAR IN KOREA IS OVER

After three years of fighting and over two million lives lost, an armistice is signed marking the end of conflict in Korea, the US's first "unpopular war."

MEN ON TOP OF THE WORLD

In a Super Hero display of strength and determination, Edmund Hillary and Tenzing Norgay are the first people to conquer the highest point on Earth when they reach the summit of Mount Everest.

THE NAME'S BOND...

Casino Royale *is published. It is the first appearance of James Bond, Ian Fleming's secret agent, code named 007.*

THE RISE OF "TEENAGERS"

With the rise of youth culture, a new market called teenagers emerges. With their purchasing power, they start to make an impact on society with their style and values. Seeds of youth rebellion also grow at the movies with films like The Wild One, *starring Marlon Brando.*

AND AT THE MOVIES...

Peter Pan, *Walt Disney's animated version of J.M. Barrie's classic story about the boy who never grew up;* Shane, *a stranger arrives, protects the homesteaders from a murderous cattle baron, and departs, in this western.*

EVERY STYLE, EVERY SUBJECT

The 1950s were a decade full of diversity for Atlas and for the industry as a whole. Comic book publishers attempted titles spread across the widest possible number of genres in an attempt to find a sales hit. Westerns, war comics, romance titles, humor books, adventure tales, suspense and horror, television adaptations, true crime, science fiction—no idea, no approach seemed too crazy to attempt. This scattershot approach to publishing resulted in very few continuing characters of any note, and the presumptions of the editors—that readers demanded multiple stories in every comic book title, and that those readers were primarily very young children—led to a lack of sophistication or depth in these offerings. For all the wide range of styles and subject matters, one comic book read pretty much the same as any other.

NU! NU! STOP! STOP!
CLOSE-UP
DON'T YOU REALIZE WHAT THAT CREATURE IS? IT'S NOTHING HUMAN! IT'S... IT'S A LORELEI!
YES... YES, YOU ARE RIGHT, KARL... I--I DON'T KNOW WHAT CAME OVER ME!
NOW WHAT DO YOU SAY, MAN? DO I WIN MY BET OR DON'T I?
WAS ONE OF THOSE TYPICAL MEDITERRANEAN VILLAGES!
SOME WOULD SAY T
INHABITANTS, AND AS FORBIDDING...
GENE COLAN
TOMORROW G. I. TROOPS WILL COME THROUGH THESE WOODS TO STRIKE AT THE REDS! THE PURPOSE OF THIS PATROL IS TO SCOUT CONDITIONS OF TERRAIN AND ENEMY STRENGTH...
BUT LET'S TAKE A CLOSE LOOK AT STAN! THAT'S A 35 MM COMBAT MOVIE CAMERA HE'S CARRYING...
AND A MUSETTE BAG
SPARE FILM...
BLAM
RINGO KID
GROCERIES
LIVERY
HERMAN BROS. FURS & HIDES
DOCTOR'S OFFICE
THE WHOLE TOWN'S WATCHIN'... GOOD, IT'LL MAKE MY JOB EASIER!
HORROR
TERRIFYING MYSTERY FROM A WEIRD WORLD.
WONDER WHO THAT TALL STRANGER WAS?
SILVER
BLAST REVERE
IN THE DAYS OF THE FIRST ROCKET
HE'S BLACKED OUT... AND I'M UNDER STRICT ORDERS NOT TO TOUCH THE CONTROLS! WELL... THIS IS THE END!
YOU'VE GOT TO HANDLE THE SHIP, BLAST! YOU'RE THE ONLY ONE THAT KNOWS HOW!
BLAST REVERE'S DILEMMA!
9820
DURING THE EARLY DAYS OF THE ROCKET AGE, THE MOST DARING AND RECKLESS OF ALL THE JUNIOR ROCKET-MEN, WAS YOUNG BLAST REVERE, LATER THE DIGNIFIED AND SEDATE CHIEF OF ALL GALAXY, BUT NOW CALLED...
FOR PETE'S SAKE! WHAT'S THE MATTER WITH THOSE GUYS DOWN THERE? I'M HANDLING THE SHIP OKAY! WHAT'RE THEY WORRIED ABOUT?
YEAH... WH... WHA... WHAT?
HE'S A SCREWLOOSE! HE'S OFF THE BEAM! HE'LL KILL US ALL! ORDER THAT YOUNG SCAMP TO COME DOWN!
CALLING REVERE! CALLING REVERE! TAKE YOUR SHIP DOWN! THAT'S AN ORDER!

1954

SUMMER OF SUPER HEROES

Martin Goodman must have received some promising reports concerning *Young Men* #24, because as 1954 got underway, the company spearheaded a revival of its Super Hero line. However, the initial reports must have been wrong, as all but one of these titles would be axed before the year was out—the Marvel Age of Super Heroes would have to wait another seven years.

Otherwise, it was business as usual as new titles were introduced and old titles cycled out in the search for newsstand gold. There were new westerns (*Western Outlaws*, *Arrowhead*), *MAD*-style humor publications (*Riot*, *Wild*), jungle comics (*Jungle Tales*, *Jungle Action*), military series (*Navy Action*, *Marines In Battle*), adventure and crime titles (*Police Action*, *Spy Thrillers*), and romance books (*Girls' Life*). Atlas even produced *3-D Tales Of The West* and *3-D Action*, each with two pairs of 3-D glasses, in case the reader lost one!

But the tide of public opinion continued to turn against comics. Debate about comics' dangerous influence on children reached fever pitch with the publication of Frederic Wertham's *Seduction of the Innocent*. The Senate Subcommittee on Juvenile Deliquency began an investigation into the issue, which would have a devastating effect on the comic book industry by the end of the year.

FEBRUARY

THE BIG THREE

• *Young Men* #25

Young Men continued to be the flagship of the Super Hero movement into 1954. Each issue contained a story about Captain America, the Sub-Mariner, and the Human Torch (who was cover-featured as he had the most "eye-appeal" on the racks). Atlas did not skimp when it came to talent for illustrating these features. After an initial outing by Russ Heath, the Human Torch strip was illustrated by either the Torch's creator Carl Burgos, or up-and-coming young artist Dick Ayers. Captain America became the province of John Romita, whose Milton Caniff-inspired artwork gave the feature a compelling realism. (A decade later, when he returned to work for Marvel, Romita would be complimented by some for the work "his father" did on Captain America in the 1950s.) Most impressive artistically, the Sub-Mariner revival was given over to the hero's originator Bill Everett, who had matured as an illustrator and a storyteller in the fifteen years since Namor first crested the waves.

The one drawback to the Super Hero adventures produced in this period was the writing. Potboiler stories were the norm. With only six to ten pages to work with, there was not a lot of room for character development. The heroes tended to be cardboard, square-jawed good guys, and the villains all irredeemably nasty. There was little to speak of in terms of the heroes' personal lives: Cap may have spent his days as schoolteacher Steve Rogers, but he was so rarely seen in that role that it seemed like something he did to mark time between shield-slinging rather than an active career choice. While competently produced, there was nothing groundbreaking here and *Young Men* ended in June after only five Super Hero-filled issues.

APRIL

THE SUB-MARINER GOES SOLO

• *Sub-Mariner* #33

After his popularity in *Young Men*, the Sub-Mariner was given back his own title, resuming the numbering from 1949. Artist Bill Everett brought his fevered imagination to the series. In addition to the undersea champion's contemporary adventures, Everett produced short stories detailing events in the young Prince Namor's development, including when he first discovered that he could survive out of water and the first time he met a person from the surface world.

The stories of the Sub-Mariner were the best of the Super Hero adventures of the time, but a certain raison d'être was missing. Namor would get involved in situations through the summons of his human friend Betty Dean, not because of any drive of his own. He was missing the motivation that had first characterized him, and so drifted from one adventure to the next without any direction.

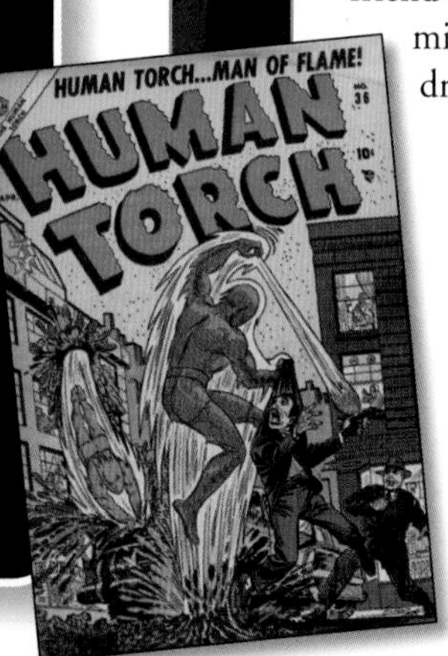

THE HUMAN TORCH REIGNITES

• *The Human Torch* #36

Having ended in March, 1949, The Human Torch's title was resumed with issue #36. The Torch and his partner, Toro, battled costumed criminals, alien beings from beyond the galaxy, and communists. But the stories were wooden and the Torch's tricks using his flame became repetitive. It swiftly became a series with limited appeal, despite consistently good artwork from Dick Ayers and the Torch's creator, Carl Burgos.

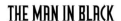

MAY

CAPTAIN AMERICA STRIKES AGAIN

• *Captain America* #76

Like his fellow Super Heroes, the Human Torch and the Sub-Mariner the month before, in May, Captain America returned to his own title, resuming the series that had finished in February, 1950.

As in the past, Cap and his young sidekick, Bucky, stood sentinel against the enemies of the nation. But where in his prime Cap had the backdrop of World War II and the Nazi menace to provide him with both context and an endless stream of evil antagonists, he fared less well against the Cold War of the mid-fifties. About the best he could manage in most cases was simplistic red-baiting. Even the Red Skull, once the most vicious and terrifying proponent of National Socialism, was recast awkwardly as a communist agent. Also limiting was the length of the stories. The prevailing wisdom of the period indicated that buyers wanted multiple stories in every magazine. This meant that three or four truncated Cap stories would be featured in every issue, the short page counts preventing any interesting conflicts or situations from being properly developed.

Men's Adventures #27 switched from a shock-horror anthology to a *Young Men*-style Super Hero sampler, but was cancelled after only two Super Hero outings.

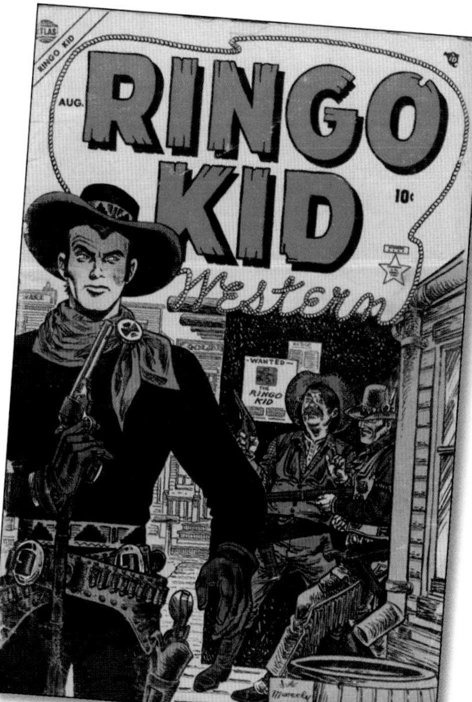

AUGUST

THE MAN IN BLACK

• *Ringo Kid Western* #1

Having debuted the previous year in the back pages of *Wild Western* #26 (February, 1953), the Ringo Kid grew popular enough to be granted his own series. This black-garbed plains-drifter was the son of a Caucasian father and a Comanche mother, and grew up an outcast because of his mixed heritage. Upon reaching adulthood, he set out with his Comanche sidekick, Dull Knife, to tame the West. The Ringo Kid's adventures weren't really all that different from those of the many other Atlas cowboys of the era, but his jet-black attire gave him a visual distinctiveness that set him apart.

SEPTEMBER

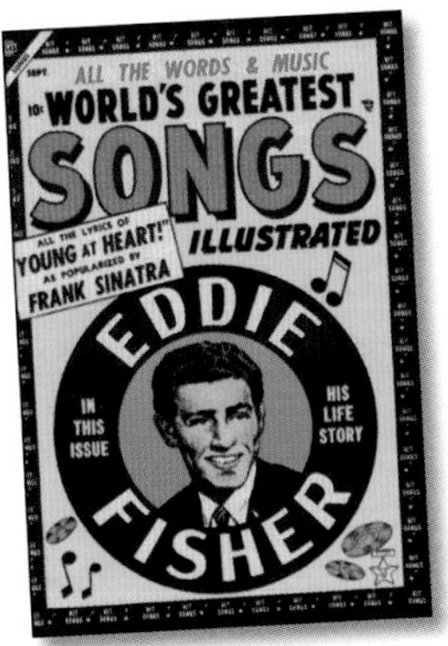

A COLLECTION OF SONGS

• *World's Greatest Songs Illustrated* #1

Perhaps the most bizarre release from Atlas in 1954—and perhaps the entire decade—was *World's Greatest Songs Illustrated*, which turned the lyrics from popular tunes by the likes of Frank Sinatra and Eddie Fisher into illustrated stories, while at the same time providing tips and advice for would-be songwriters. The only issue published included a text page soliciting comments from the readership, but anybody who wrote in with a review or a tune of their own would have been sadly disappointed when no follow-up ever appeared.

AN OUTLAW FOR JUSTICE

• *Outlaw Kid* #1

One of the more memorable Atlas western strips debuted in September. Illustrated by famed comic book artist and eventual animation designer Doug Wildey, the Outlaw Kid was Lance Temple, a prairie lawyer who had promised his blind father that he would never use a gun. But when the law of the courts proved inadequate, he would don a mask and mete out six-gun justice as the Outlaw Kid.

PUBLIC UPROAR OVER COMICS

• *Seduction of the Innocent* by Frederic Wertham

In 1954, psychiatrist Frederic Wertham's condemnatory book, *Sedution of the Innocent*, became a best seller, and set off a firestorm of controversy and complaint from concerned parents nationwide, who were suddenly worried about what their children were reading. Organized protests and boycotts of outlets selling comic books became routine, as did mass comic book burnings—local children were urged to bring their illicit funnybooks to a local church or schoolyard, where a communal pyre would be lit to destroy the alleged filth. Things got so bad that Estes Kefauver's Senate Subcommittee on Juvenile Delinquency spent two days hearing testimony on the material in comic magazines and their influences on juvenile crime, with Frederic Wertham as a star witness. While these hearings ended inconclusively, the writing was on the wall. If the industry was going to prevent the United States government from enforcing regulatory oversight upon it, it was going to have to start policing itself.

MEANWHILE IN 1954...

FOUR-MINUTE-MILE MAN BREAKS WORLD RECORD

Roger Bannister breaks the world record and becomes the only person ever to run a mile in less than four minutes. He finishes in 3 minutes and 59.4 seconds, beating the previous record of 4 minutes and 1.3 seconds held by Gunder Hägg of Sweden.

COLOR TELEVISIONS ON SALE

The first commercial color television is available and costs $1,000, nearly four months of the average salary. However, most programming is still broadcast in black and white.

THE WORLD'S FIRST NUCLEAR POWER STATION

Obninsk in the USSR is the first nuclear power station to create electricity for a power grid.

AMERICA TESTS H-BOMB

Nuclear testing is carried out at Bikini Atoll in the Pacific Ocean. The H-Bomb was 600 times as powerful as the Hiroshima bomb.

BOEING 707'S MAIDEN FLIGHT

The four-engined Boeing 707 travels from Seattle on its first flight. The aircraft can carry 219 passengers and achieve a top speed of 600 mph (966 kph).

CENSORSHIP FOR COMICS

The Comics Code Authority is set up as a result of public concern about the inappropriate contents of comics. Comic creators are subject to rules forbidding "excessive violence," "lurid, unsavory, gruesome illustrations," and vampires, werewolves, ghouls, and zombies. Comics are no longer allowed "terror" or "horror" in their titles, "in every instance good shall triumph over evil," and comics must not disrespect authority.

NO MORE RACIAL SEGREGATION IN SCHOOLS

The US Supreme Court rules that segregation of children in public schools based solely on race is unconstitutional. This landmark decision leads to the lengthy and troubled process of desegregation of public schools.

ROCK AROUND THE CLOCK

Universally recognized as the original "rock 'n' roll" song, Rock Around the Clock *is recorded by Bill Haley and His Comets.*

AND AT THE MOVIES...

On The Waterfront, *Elia Kazan's hard-hitting social realist melodrama, set amidst New York City's docks, showcases the Method acting style;* Rear Window, *Alfred Hitchcock's voyeuristic murder mystery centers around James Stewart as a photojournalist confined to his room by a broken leg;* 20,000 Leagues Under the Sea, *Disney adaptation, starring Kirk Douglas and James Mason, of Jules Verne's seafaring novel about an encounter with a giant sea creature.*

1955

THE COMICS CODE CHANGES THE GAME

In 1955, in an act of self-defense against the negative publicity about the dangerous effects of comics on children, publishers banded together as the Comics Magazine Association of America and formed the Comics Code Authority (CCA). The CCA would review upcoming releases, enforce an agreed-upon code of ethics, and reject or revise material as deemed necessary to insure good taste. Comics that passed through this censorship crucible were permitted to carry the stamp of the CCA on their covers. The public relations campaign was so thorough that titles without the seal often did not reach the newsstands, but were returned or pulped, unopened.

The Code was a hardship to some. In 1955, EC Comics, whose titles featured words, such as "Weird" and "Horror," that were banned by the Code, went out of business as a result. However, the Code had an upside for Atlas. The demise of other publishers meant less competition on the racks and it freed up top talent. While the Code wrote an end to most shock-horror titles, Atlas' books survived by toning down content, and stressing twist endings and weird atmospheres rather than outright horror. The few romance comics became more chaste, with the couple often turning away from the camera when they kissed.

MARCH

A KID COWBOY WITH STAYING POWER

• *Rawhide Kid* #1

One of the most durable western characters, the Rawhide Kid, was a generic cowboy who was not terribly successful when he first appeared but possessed remarkable staying power. Rawhide's series lasted until the Atlas upheaval of 1957. The series was then revived and revamped in August, 1960, in part due to the popularity of the *Rawhide* television series, and it benefitted from being the first solo character series worked on by Stan Lee and Jack Kirby. In April, 2003, a Marvel MAX adult-oriented limited series revealed that the Kid was gay.

Western titles were the most affected by the Comics Code of 1955. One of the provisos of the Code stated that nobody in a comic could shoot another person. This resulted in absurd gunfights issue after issue, in which the hero would shoot his opponent in a hundred indirect ways; for example, by shooting ropes out of chandeliers to drop them on the bad guys, or using the sound of the firearms to spook horses to stampede down on the villains.

APRIL

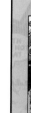

A TYPICAL DUMB BLONDE

• *My Girl Pearl* #1

Stan Lee apparently had a soft spot for *My Girl Pearl*, a series he originated with artist Dan DeCarlo, who would go on to create *Josie And The Pussycats* and *Sabrina The Teen-Age Witch* for Archie Comics. Pearl was the stereotypical dumb blonde, and Lee delighted in the opportunity to wheel out story after story based on Pearl's inability to comprehend what was going on around her. *My Girl Pearl* ran for four issues, returned for a two-issue encore in July, 1957, and came back for five issues in August, 1960.

DELLA VISION ON TELEVISION

• *Della Vision* #1

Television was still a new and novel concept in 1955 and publisher Martin Goodman tried to tap into its popularity—and also limit the threat it posed to comics—with the introduction of *Della Vision*, a television queen in the mold of the popular Marvel character Patsy Walker. But, unlike Patsy, Della was off the air in a mere three issues, and was replaced by Patty Powers, queen of the silver screen.

MAY

YE OLDE KNIGHT OF CAMELOT

• *Black Knight* #1

One of the best-remembered but short-lived series of the period, *Black Knight* followed the adventures of Sir Percy of Scandia, who under cover of darkness would don enchanted armor provided to him by Merlin the Magician and defend Camelot from the avaricious plans of Mordred the Evil. Stan Lee originated the character and wrote at least the first issue, using the olde English that would one day characterize Thor. The dramatic artwork was primarily by artist Joe Maneely in what was the closest he had come to a proper Super Hero strip. Though the series ended in April, 1956, the character found new life as both a villain and a hero in the 1960s.

JULY

TELEVISION TIE-IN

Atlas was beginning to tone down their shock-horror titles in the wake of the upheaval caused by the Comics Code Authority. However, it was clear that publisher Martin Goodman would need to continue to develop other trends that Atlas could use.

One area Atlas looked toward was television. Inroads were being made into overall readership numbers by television, so choosing to publish a comic of a TV show seemed the obvious solution. Atlas opted for a popular children's show called *The Adventures Of Pinky Lee*, and the first issue carried a coverdate of July. The series ended after five issues.

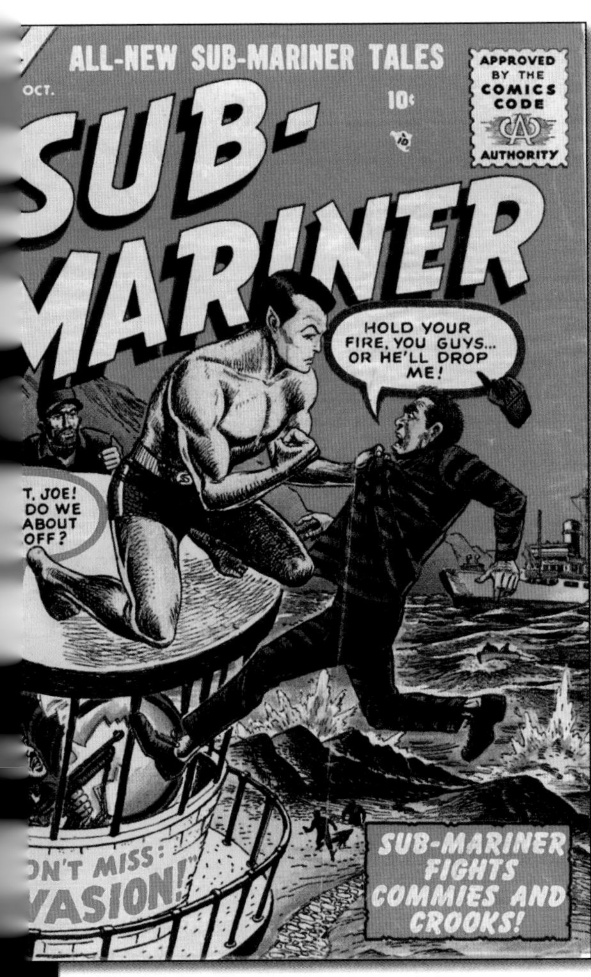

ALL-NEW SUB-MARINER TALES
OCT.
10¢
APPROVED BY THE COMICS CODE AUTHORITY
SUB-MARINER
HOLD YOUR FIRE, YOU GUYS... OR HE'LL DROP ME!
T, JOE! DO WE ABOUT OFF?
ON'T MISS VASION!
SUB-MARINER FIGHTS COMMIES AND CROOKS!

OCTOBER

FAREWELL TO NAMOR

• *Sub-Mariner* #42

Martin Goodman had been in talks with television executives about turning Namor's adventures into a live-action TV series, reportedly to star actor Richard Egan. However, negotiations wound up going nowhere, and, as a result, *Sub-Mariner's* extended lease on life came to an end with issue #42. This would be the last pre-Marvel appearance of a Golden Age hero. Ironically, the title of the last story in the final issue was, "When The Light Goes Out."

NOVEMBER

IRVING FORBUSH

• *SNAFU* #1

November saw the birth of a character who would cast a long shadow into the Marvel Age—Irving Forbush. Forbush appeared in Marvel's satirical magazine *SNAFU* (a military term meaning Situation Normal: All Fouled Up) whose first issue posed the rhetorical question: "Irving Forbush—Man or Myth?" Irving Forbush was *SNAFU's* mascot, as Alfred E. Neuman was *MAD* magazine's mascot. Forbush's name stuck in Stan Lee's mind long after *SNAFU's* three issues had departed the sales racks—when he began writing promotional text for the new Marvel books in the 1960s, Lee began to name-drop Irving once again on the letters pages and in Stan's Soapbox column. Irving Forbush became a running in-joke and was eventually incarnated in *Not Brand Echh* (Aug., 1967) as Forbush-Man, a longjohn-wearing parody of a Marvel hero.

A REAL-LIFE COWBOY SUCCESS STORY

• *Wyatt Earp* #1

In addition to the Rawhide Kid, Atlas introduced another of its most popular and long-lasting western characters in 1955. *Wyatt Earp* featured fictionalized adventures of the historic lawman. *Wyatt Earp* was helped considerably by the unaffiliated television series starring Hugh O'Brian in the title role and the comic became Atlas' best-selling western of the 1950s.

MEANWHILE IN 1955...

ROSA PARKS REFUSES TO GIVE UP HER SEAT

An unknown seamstress breaks with tradition and refuses to give up her bus seat to a white passenger in Montgomery, Alabama. In reaction to her arrest, Martin Luther King Jr. calls for a black boycott of buses in Montgomery, which lasts over a year, until the desegregation of buses. Rosa Parks' defiance is the trigger for the modern civil rights movement.

WARSAW PACT SIGNED

Russia, Poland, East Germany, and the other members of the Eastern Bloc sign a treaty creating a military alliance of socialist states in reaction to the potential threat from NATO, created in 1949.

CHURCHILL RESIGNS

Sir Winston Churchill resigns as Prime Minister of the United Kingdom. Churchill led Britain through World War II and this was his second period in his office.

ALBERT EINSTEIN DIES

Best known for his theory of relativity, Albert Einstein also campaigned to prevent the use of the atomic bomb. He was aged seventy-six at the time of his death.

FIRST DISNEYLAND OPENS

Just outside Los Angeles a new world opens across the drawbridge of Sleeping Beauty's castle. The "Magic Kingdom," set in 160 acres, is made up of five "lands" full of rides.

JAMES DEAN DIES IN A CAR CRASH

The twenty-four-year-old Hollywood star and icon of the rebellious youth of America dies behind the wheel of his sports car.

FIRST POLIO VACCINE

Jonas Salk invents the world's first vaccine against polio, a disease that in 1949 affected 43,000 Americans alone. Salk's vaccine and one invented by Sabin in 1957 protect against the illness to the extent that in 1994 polio is announced eradicated in all the Americas.

HOVERCRAFT THEORY TESTED

Christopher Cockerell successfully tests his hypothesis using two cans and a hair-dryer, which leads him to create the world's first hovercraft.

AND AT THE MOVIES...

Rebel Without a Cause, *Nicholas Ray's gripping treatment of teenage delinquency and a troubled father-son relationship introduces James Dean as the ultimate iconic rebel;* Bad Day At Black Rock, *western noir starring Spencer Tracy as a one-armed stranger confronted by a hostile town with something to hide;* The Ladykillers, *deliciously black English comedy of manners about a gang of thieves who hide out in a genteel old lady's home.*

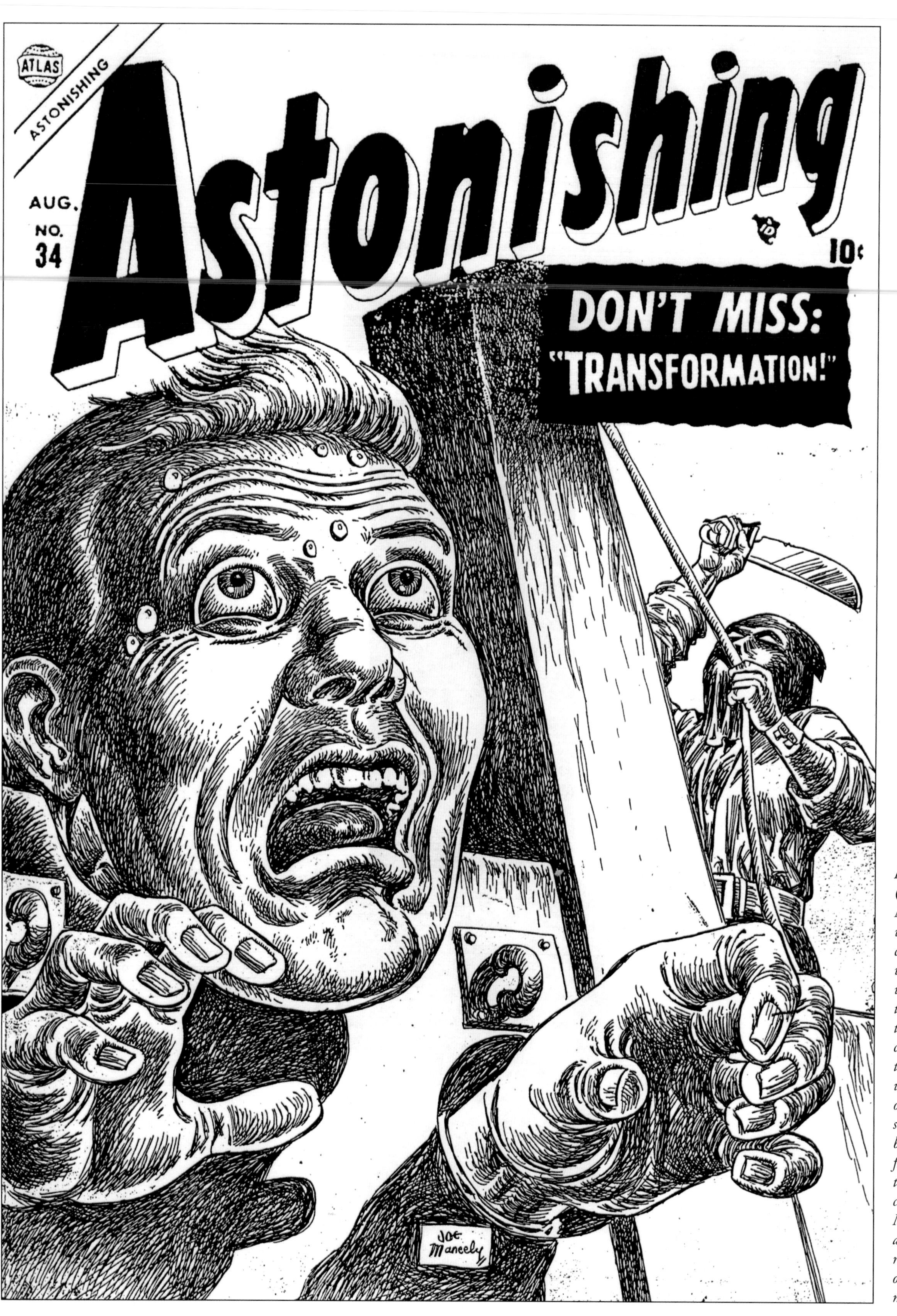

Astonishing ***#34, (August, 1954)***
Many of the artists who worked in comics in this period would often do more work on an image than would ever see the light of day. The crude printing meant that the finest lines would often close up or disappear, or simply be smothered by the coloring on the final comic book. But this did not stop craftsmen such as Joe Maneely from going all-out in their rendering, for their own satisfaction if nothing else.

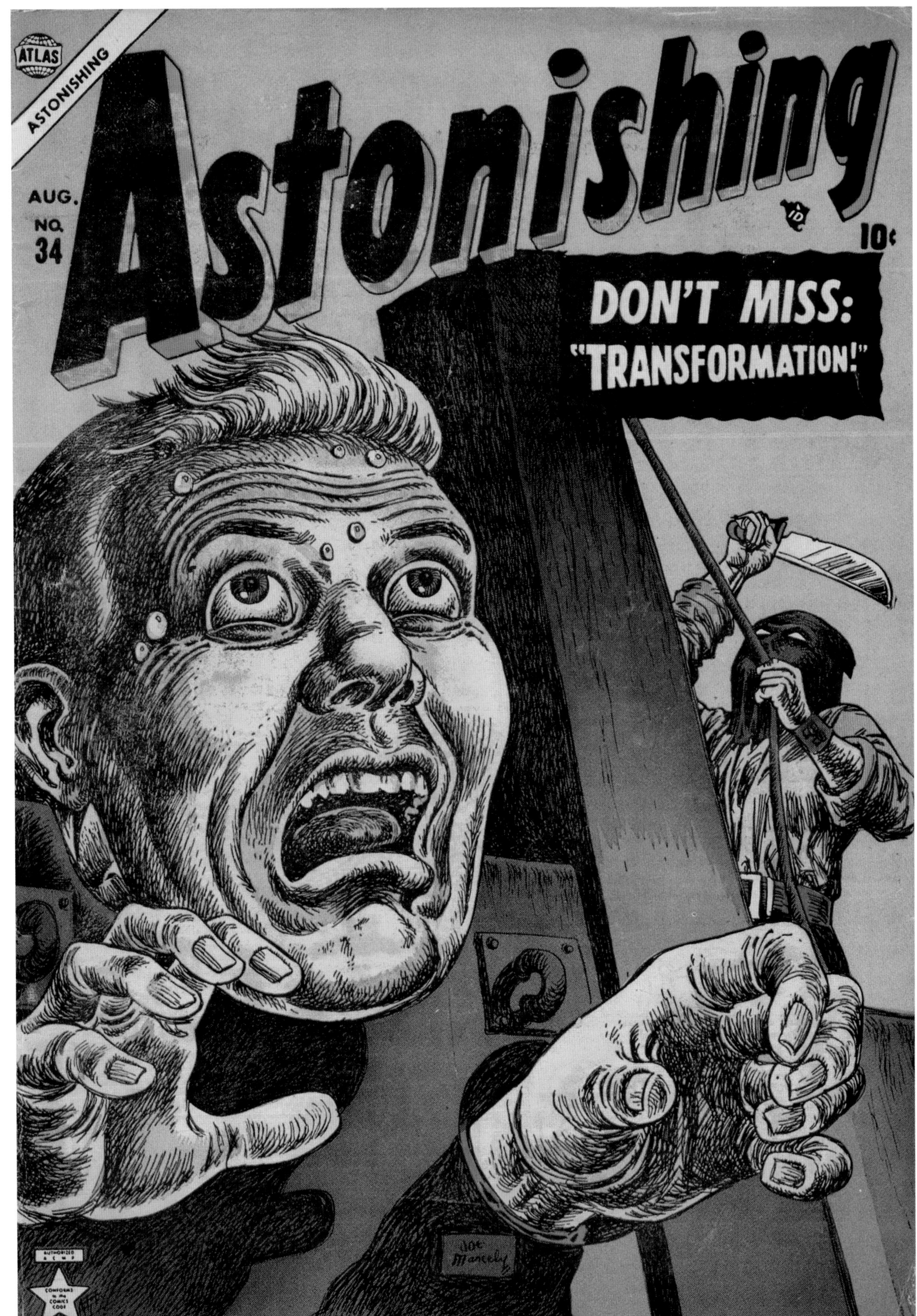

Astonishing #34, (August, 1954)
The colored illustration on this issue of Astonishing *is relatively restrained for the period. There is no gore to be seen, and the impact of the image is made by the evocation of terror on the face of the soon-to-be-executed prisoner. Even the blade of the guillotine is out of the shot.*

1956

THE GOING GETS TOUGH

As 1956 began, the after-effects of the Senate witch hunts and the negative public perception of comics' effect on children continued to have an impact on comic book sales—not to mention the growing competition posed by television. Throughout the comic book industry, both long-time and fast-buck publishers alike quit and moved into other far more profitable and diverse lines of endeavor.

At Atlas, business continued more or less as usual, with no particular trend coming to the forefront as a cash cow. Publisher Martin Goodman did manage to take advantage of the turmoil by reducing page rates for his artists as a cost-saving measure. Freelancers of the period speak of a pattern, where they would bring in a completed job to editor Stan Lee and be given a follow-up assignment, but at a rate that was two dollars less than the previous assignment. This practice continued throughout the year, with some artists ending 1956 receiving half as much money for their work as they had when the year began. As a result, a mass exodus from the comic book business began among the creative community, as artists looked for more stable employment elsewhere, often within the advertising business.

APRIL

LOST AND FOUND

• *Mystery Tales* #40

When it first saw print, *Mystery Tales* #40 was just another insignificant issue of the generic shock-suspense series, unnoteworthy in every way save for featuring some of the earliest published work of Steve Ditko, who would go on to co-create Spider-Man. But five decades later, this issue would gain prominence and notoriety when it was featured on an episode of the popular television series *Lost* that aired in May, 2008.

MAY

INSPIRED BY PLANET EARTH

• *World Of Fantasy* #1

Undersea explorer Jacques Cousteau first came to prominence with his initial documentary on the ocean depths, *The World Of Science*, in 1956. Capitalizing on the publicity surrounding Cousteau's documentary, Martin Goodman released a trio of "World" series of his own—*World Of Suspense* in April, *World Of Fantasy* in May, and *World Of Mystery* in June. Other than their tenuous connection to Cousteau's picture, the three titles were otherwise undistinguished, their contents matching both each other and any other random issue of *Strange Tales* or *Journey Into Mystery*. Of the three, *World Of Fantasy* proved the most durable, lasting nineteen issues and surviving the Atlas collapse of 1957. *World Of Suspense* and *World Of Mystery*, however, both came to an end in July, 1957.

AUGUST

OUR MAN BARKER

• *Sergeant Barney Barker* #1

In 1956 Atlas released *Sergeant Barney Barker*, a comic about the adventures of an unscrupulous but lovable army sergeant who always had personal gain foremost in his mind. Every issue of the comic carried the tagline, "Even With Barker…We Won The War!" *Sergeant Barney Barker* lasted only three installments, but featured some humorous artwork by war comics veteran John Severin, who would go on to be a mainstay of the satirical *Cracked* magazine.

OCTOBER

PERIL FROM THE ORIENT

• *Yellow Claw* #1

One of the most memorable titles of the year was itself a throwback to years gone by. *Yellow Claw* #1 introduced the eponymous Asian Super Villain, inspired perhaps by the fiends from the "yellow peril" novels of the 1930s, including master criminal Fu Manchu (then the subject of a successful TV serial). The first issue of *Yellow Claw* was written by Al Feldstein, the writer and editor behind much of the success of the EC comics line, and eventually the editor and mastermind of *MAD* magazine. Workhorse Joe Maneely provided the atmospheric artwork. Like so many other series of the period, *Yellow Claw* met its end within a scant four issues but it would go on to have a significant impact in the Marvel books to come with Yellow Claw himself eventually becoming a recurring villain in the Marvel Universe, particularly bedeviling Nick Fury, Agent of SHIELD, and Captain America in the 1960s and 1970s. His supporting cast would also reappear, including his nemesis, FBI agent Jimmy Woo.

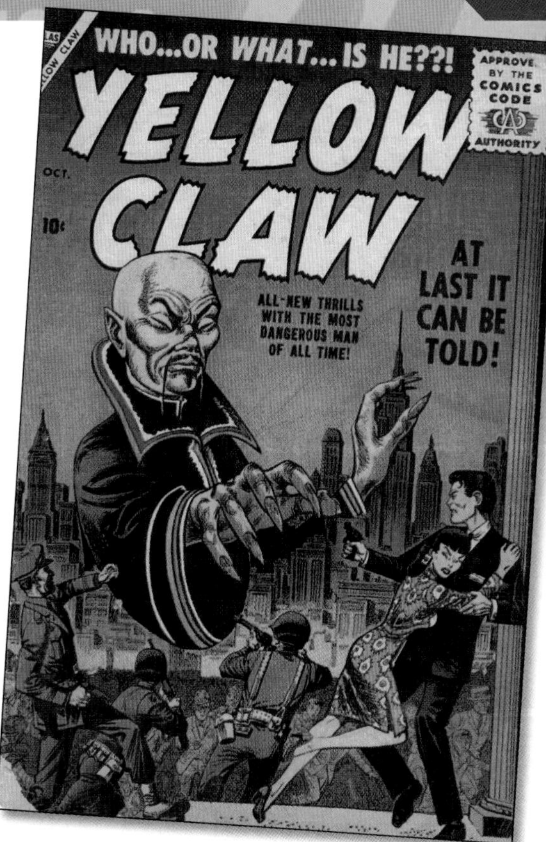

Yellow Claw *was the first Atlas series to headline a villain rather than a hero.*

DECEMBER

A KING IN DISGUISE

• *Yellow Claw* #2

The second issue of *Yellow Claw* signaled the return of artist Jack "King" Kirby. After creating Captain America in March, 1941, Kirby and his collaborator Joe Simon left Timely in a dispute with Martin Goodman over promised royalties. Since then, the Simon & Kirby team had moved from company to company, blazing a trail of success throughout the industry. But by 1956, the downturn in the business had brought an end to the team's own publishing endeavor, Mainline Publications, and Joe Simon had left the industry to seek out work in advertising. Driven to support his family, Kirby looked for work wherever he could get it, which brought him to Atlas' doorstep again toward the end of 1956. In addition to being a supremely fast artist, Kirby was also a prolific idea man, and in the last three issues of *Yellow Claw* he showcased wild science fiction ideas such as a miniaturized army, an electrified alien from beyond the stars, living shadows, and a titanic, robotic god-totem. It is quite possible that Kirby wrote the stories himself, too. While *Yellow Claw* failed, Kirby's contributions would become invaluable in steering the company through the turmoil to come.

ALSO...

SETTING THE SCENE FOR THE MARVEL SUPER HERO REVOLUTION

Atlas's attempt to revive and revitalize the Super Hero genre in 1954 had not really taken off. After a promising start, sales had fallen and the year ended with most of the revived Super Hero titles being axed: it seemed the era of Super Heroes might be over. But by 1956, events were transpiring in the comic book industry that would pave the way for the Marvel Super Hero revolution of the 1960s.

Sales of titles by other publishers proved that readers were not tired of Super Heroes, but wanted something new. Complete overhauls, rather simple resurrections of old favorites, were enthusiastically received, especially when characters were given a modern 1950s sheen and a flavor steeped in science fiction. This began what became known as the Silver Age of Comics, a Super Hero renaissance that would lead inexorably to the beginning of the Marvel Age. Within a few years, Atlas would take this idea to a new level by creating brand new Super Heroes, characters that would resonate with a new generation of comics readers and reflect the spirit of the times.

MEANWHILE IN 1956...

SPIES SURFACE IN USSR

Guy Burgess and Donald Maclean—two of the "Cambridge spies," who passed information to the Soviets—resurface in the Soviet Union. The revelations that British agents were working for the USSR send shock waves through the paranoia-era of the Cold War.

UPRISING IN HUNGARY FAILS

Hungarians revolt against their pro-Soviet government, but the USSR sends in troops to crush the rebellion, sending a clear message to the world that the Kremlin still rules the Warsaw Pact with an iron fist.

SUEZ CRISIS LEADS TO PETROL RATIONING

Egypt takes control of the Suez Canal, sparking international condemnation and the subsequent Suez Crisis. Israel invades Egypt, and Britain and France bomb Egypt to force the reopening of the canal.

ELVIS RELEASES HIS FIRST HIT

After entering the US music charts for the first time earlier this year with Heartbreak Hotel, *Elvis Presley hits the big time. But his style of dancing causes controversy and it is suggested that he only appears from the waist up on television.*

A NEW ART MOVEMENT POPS UP

Artists Richard Hamilton, John McHale, and John Voelcker submit Just What is it that Makes Today's Home so Different, so Appealing? *to the* This is Tomorrow *exhibition in London. It is one of the first pieces to be considered "pop art:" works that draw on mass culture, like comics and advertising, for their inspiration.*

5MB FOR THE FIRST HARD DRIVE

IBM creates the world's first computer hard disk drive, which has a capacity of five megabytes.

BOGEY DIES

Screen tough guy Humphrey Bogart dies at the age of fifty-seven. He appeared in such classic films as Casablanca *and* The Big Sleep *and won the Best Actor Academy Award for* The African Queen *in 1952.*

ACTRESS MARRIES PLAYWRIGHT

Actress and icon Marilyn Monroe marries playwright Arthur Miller in a civil ceremony in White Plains, New York.

AND AT THE MOVIES...

The Searchers, *John Wayne's tormented racist veteran obsessively tracks down the Indians who abducted his niece in John Ford's western;* Written On The Wind, *Douglas Sirk's daring and subversive melodrama addresses the fatal connections between sex, money, and power in this sophisticated soap opera;* Invasion Of The Body Snatchers, *a small American town is gradually taken over by an alien presence in this paranoid sci-fi allegory of McCarthyism.*

NO MATTER WHERE I TURN, I'M TRAPPED!

1957

FALL OF ATLAS, RISE OF MARVEL

The year that everything ended for Atlas Comics was 1957, though nobody realized it at the outset. Despite the exodus of artistic talent from Atlas in 1956, at the start of 1957 everything was business as usual, with publisher Martin Goodman's outfit continuing to publish around sixty titles, cycling in new concepts as new ideas struck, and culling those books not pulling their weight. However, before the year was out, Atlas would be a crippled shell of itself, clinging to life at the whim of its strongest competitor, and forced to contract its publishing line to the point of insignificance. The Atlas name would also be a casualty. Martin Goodman's comic book publishing venture would finish out the year with only a small handful of titles, without a name or brand identity, and seemingly without much of a future.

JANUARY

ATLAS GOES AMERICAN

At the end of 1956, Martin Goodman shut down his in-house distribution system, and signed a deal with American News to distribute the Atlas line, the effects of which were first seen going in to 1957. (The Atlas name and globe would be kept to promote line unity.) The advantage of such a deal was the fact that American owned 1,500 retail outlets, as well as a distribution network of 100,000 accounts, and could guarantee that Atlas' titles got onto the racks. With all but the cleanest companies still having difficulties due to the Senate hearings, this seemed like a good bet. Goodman stood to make more money through increased circulation, and he could eliminate the overhead of running a distribution wing himself. In reality, however, this deal would almost mean the end of Atlas.

MAY

DISTRIBUTION DOWNFALL

Working with distributor American News should have helped Atlas. Unfortunately for Martin Goodman, American News had its own problems. For the past few years, some of its biggest sellers had been deserting the firm, switching to independent distribution channels. Additionally, American found itself under investigation for running a monopoly (as it controlled distribution, wholesale, and retail accounts) and restraint of trade, not to mention allegations of mob connections. When American's largest remaining client, Dell, chose not to renew their contract, and subsequently sued American for restraint of trade, it was clear what would happen. In May, 1957, American announced that it was closing its Wholesale Periodical Division, leaving a number of publishers without the means to distribute—including Atlas.

Goodman's entire operation of men's magazines and paperback books was imperiled, not merely his comic book division. As he scrambled to make a new deal to get his product to market, he instructed editor Stan Lee to cease buying new work, for the duration. Freelance artists such as John Romita, Joe Sinnott, and Dick Ayers were instructed to turn in whatever they had completed of their current jobs, and told that there would be no more assignments forthcoming. (Production man and sometimes-letterer Morrie Kuramoto was known to exclaim "Shades of '57!" whenever something horrible occurred in the business from that day forward.) Many creators were forced to leave the field entirely, seeking out work elsewhere in order to make ends meet.

SEPTEMBER

THE LAST RESORT

With Atlas in a dire situation, Martin Goodman was forced to turn to the last place anybody would have expected. He struck a bargain with Independent News (IND.), the distribution arm of National Periodical Publications, better known today as DC Comics. The ten-year deal with IND. allowed Goodman to resume his operation, but there were some very strict restrictions on what and how much he could publish—restrictions that were onerous to a binge-and-purge publisher such as Goodman. IND. was concerned about Goodman's history of flooding the market with titles in a given genre if he sensed a hit. So, chief among these restrictions, IND. limited his output to only eight releases a month. In order to maximize his profit potential, Goodman chose to produce sixteen bimonthly titles.

OCTOBER

THE KILL LIST

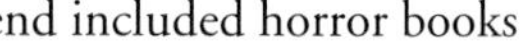

The IND. restriction meant the end of between sixty and seventy titles—80% of Atlas' output. Also eliminated was the Atlas name and globe, to be replaced on covers by the small IND. which identified a publication distributed by Independent news. Those series which met an untimely end included horror books (*Adventure Into Mystery, Astonishing, Journey Into Unknown Worlds, Marvel Tales*—the successor title to Timely's first release, *Marvel Mystery Comics—Mystery Tales, Mystic, Mystical Tales, Spellbound, Strange Stories Of Suspense, Strange Tales Of The Unusual, Uncanny Tales, World Of Mystery, World Of Suspense*), crime comics (*Caught, Tales Of Justice*), romance titles

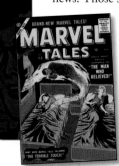

(*Lovers*, *Love Tales*, *My Love Story*, *Stories Of Romance*, *The Romances Of Nurse Helen Grant*, *True Tales Of Love*), war series (*Battle Action*, *Battle Front*, *Battle Ground*, *Combat Casey*, *Combat Kelly*, *G.I. Tales*, *Marines At War*, *Marines In Action*, *Navy Action*, *Navy Tales*, *War Comics*), westerns (*Black Rider*, *Kid Slade Gunfighter*, *Outlaw Kid*, *Quick-Trigger Western*, *Rawhide Kid*, *Ringo Kid Western*, *Six-Gun Western*, *The Kid From Dodge City*, *The Kid From Texas*, *Two-Gun Western*, *Western Kid*, *Western Outlaws*, *Western Trails*, *Wild Western*), jungle titles (*Jann Of The Jungle*, *Lorna The Jungle Girl*), and comedy series (*A Date With Millie*, *Dippy Duck*, *Melvin The Monster*, *My Girl Pearl*, *Patsy And Her Pals*, *Sherry The Showgirl*, *Showgirls*, *Willie The Wise-Guy*). Material prepared for these titles would be sprinkled through the surviving books for more than a year to come, as the unused inventory was burned off.

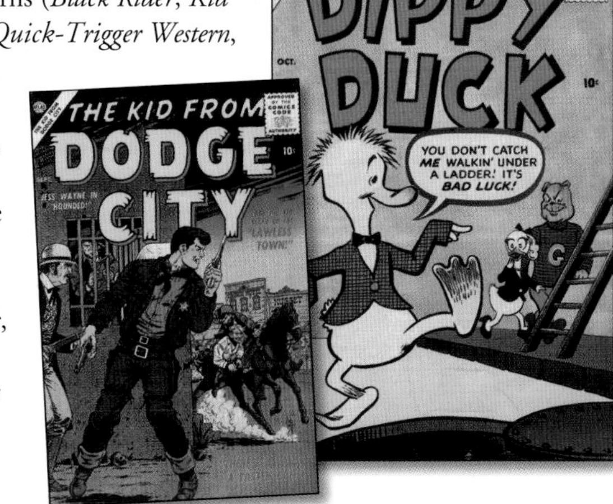

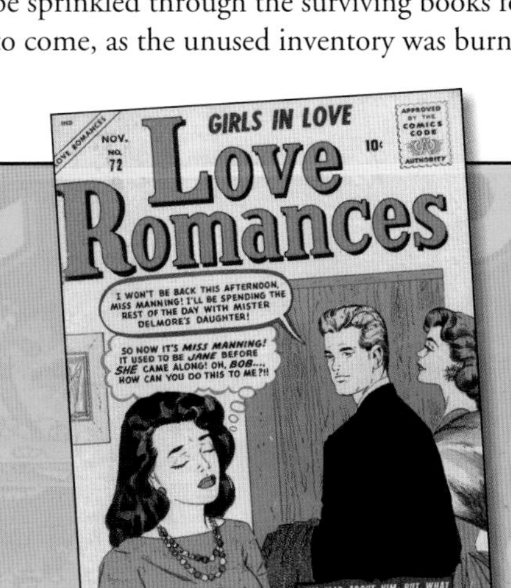

THE SWEET SIXTEEN

By November, Martin Goodman and Stan Lee were left with just sixteen titles on which to rebuild their line and turn a profit. They had pared down the list of releases to their most profitable titles across a number of different genres: *Battle*, *Gunsmoke Western*, *Homer, The Happy Ghost*, *Kid Colt, Outlaw*, *Love Romances*, *Marines In Battle*, *Millie The Model*, *Miss America*, *My Own Romance*, *Navy Combat*, *Patsy Walker*, *Patsy And Hedy*, *Strange Tales*, *Two-Gun Kid*, *World Of Fantasy*, and *Wyatt Earp*. Production on new material for these books geared up slowly as the backlog of existing material was exhausted. But even so, only a small fraction of the total number of creators employed at Atlas at the beginning of the year would be able to get work. And now, in order to try out a new idea, Goodman would have to ax an existing title in his tiny line-without-a-name due to the restrictions imposed by IND. Goodman and Lee could no longer get bigger. So, they would have to get better instead.

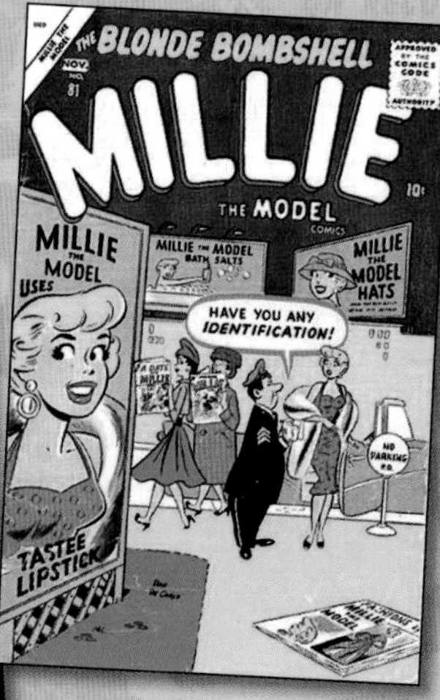

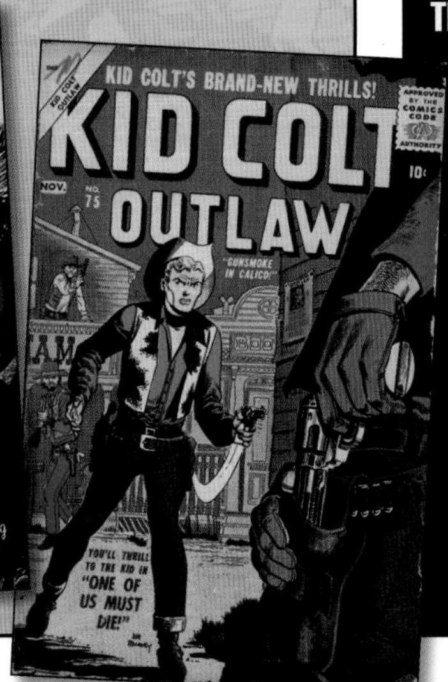

MEANWHILE IN 1957...

THE SPACE RACE BEGINS
The USSR launches Sputnik 1, *the first man-made satellite to orbit the Earth.*

WAVE OF DECOLONIZATION IN AFRICA
Ghana becomes the first British colony in Africa to win independence, marking the beginning of a rapid period of decolonization.

FIRST NUCLEAR POWER PLANT IN THE US
The US opens Shippingport Atomic Power Station in Pennsylvania, the first in the country to produce electricity.

LITTLE ROCK CRISIS
A group of nine African-American students enrol at Little Rock Central High School but are prevented from entering the school. After intervention from President Eisenhower, the group are permitted to attend the school.

THE "BABY BOOM" PEAKS
The birthrate that has been growing in the US and UK since the end of World War II spikes at a record high in 1957 before declining gradually until a drop in 1964.

THE ERA OF THE "BEATNIKS"
The term "beatnik" takes hold to refer to the "beat generation," a movement of writers, whose work forms an undercurrent against the mainstream postwar desire for a reassuringly planned order. The literature pushes the boundaries and helps to liberalize what can be published in the US.

ON THE ROAD PUBLISHES
Viking Press releases Jack Kerouac's novel, a stream of consciousness, considered a prime example of the beatnik generation of literature

THE CAT IN THE HAT PUBLISHES
Dr. Seuss' first book about the mischievous cat is published in an attempt to create more interesting and entertaining reading material for early readers.

UNPRECEDENTED VIOLENCE ON THE STAGE
The musical play West Side Story *crashes onto Broadway with a bold new musical and dance style, and places the story of Romeo and Juliet in contemporary New York.*

AND AT THE MOVIES...
Twelve Angry Men, *compelling courtroom drama in which a jury are persuaded not to find the defendant guilty by one doubting member;* The Seventh Seal, *Ingmar Bergman's medieval fable, in which a black-robed Death is challenged to a game of chess;* The Bridge On The River Kwai, *wartime film set in a Burmese POW camp about a British CO compelled to protect "his" bridge.*

Marvin Mouse ***#1 (Sept., 1957)***
A comic book artist in the 1950s needed to be a jack-of-all-trades, able to illustrate any subject matter that a publisher might want. So it was that Bill Everett, creator of the Sub-Mariner and illustrator of some of the most hallucinatory and disturbing horror stories in the history of comics found himself working on the one-and-only issue of Marvin Mouse *with writer Stan Lee.*

MARVIN MOUSE
MARVIN
MOUSE
SEPT.
APPROVED BY THE COMICS CODE AUTHORITY
10¢
I WANT *THAT* ONE!

JELLY BEANS 1¢
Bill Everett

KAREN, YOU LITTLE FOOL! IT'S YOU! DON'T YOU SEE? IT'S ALWAYS BEEN YOU FOR ME!

1958

A YEAR OF REBUILDING

After the dramatic upheaval of 1957, stability began to return to Martin Goodman's comic line. For a couple of months it had looked as though editor Stan Lee himself might be out of a job if the comic book division shut down for good. Now, Stan could devote himself to trying to make something of the slim pickings with which he had been left. As the stack of inventory was gradually used, production on Goodman's line of titles began to slowly gear up again. After years of running to stay in place, needing to fill the pages of as many as sixty releases a month and not being able to devote much attention to any of them, Lee now found himself in a position to be selective. While he had always done a certain amount of writing for the company, the reduction of the line meant that Lee was able to write virtually everything himself. Any writing that Lee could not do was turned over to one or two trusted freelancers, most often Lee's younger brother, Larry Lieber. So, in 1958, given the limited number of assignments to be given out, Lee was able to assemble a tight-knit team of his best artists.

THE ARTISTS BEHIND THE DRAWINGS

JOE MANEELY

As Stan Lee was bringing together a team of illustrators, one artist would no longer be available to join the group. Joe Maneely died in June, aged only thirty-two, falling between the cars of a moving train while making his way home. Maneely was both quick and versatile and one of Lee's favorite collaborators—the pair had attempted vainly to get a newspaper strip off the ground in the late 1950s and Maneely produced the lion's share of covers and stories for the Atlas line during its time of greatest production. He was adept at everything from westerns and war comics to kids comedy and funny animals—he could switch from one to the other with ease. Maneely was also the artist to whom Lee would turn when he needed to instruct other, younger artists in how to tell a story visually—John Romita has spoken of the day he spent visiting with Maneely in his studio, at Lee's request, and how much he learned from the man in that one sitting. The passing of Maneely was especially a loss to Marvel as, had he lived, he would no doubt have been one of Lee's major collaborators during the Super Hero revival.

JACK KIRBY

With the loss of Joe Maneely, Stan Lee began leaning more heavily on the services of Jack Kirby. A street-smart virtuoso in the art of comic book storytelling, Kirby was also lightning fast, capable of turning out multiple complete issues in a single month. He was also an able story man, who had years of plotting experience. As a matter of expediency, Lee and Kirby began experimenting with a different way of producing their stories. Rather than typing out a complete script for a given feature, with copy and art direction all spelled out, Lee began giving Kirby and his other artists looser outlines that were the broad strokes of what the story would be about. Kirby would draw the tale to its requisite number of pages and return the penciled artwork to Lee, who would then write the final copy for the story. This allowed Lee to eliminate the parts of the job that were most tedious to him, while making the dialoguing of a story even more interesting, like a puzzle to be solved. This "Marvel method" of producing stories would not become standard for a number of months, but it was one of the key secrets to why the Marvel Super Hero comics were more visual-centered and action-oriented than those of the competition.

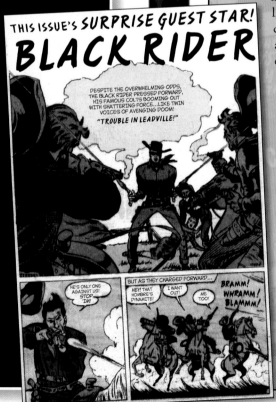

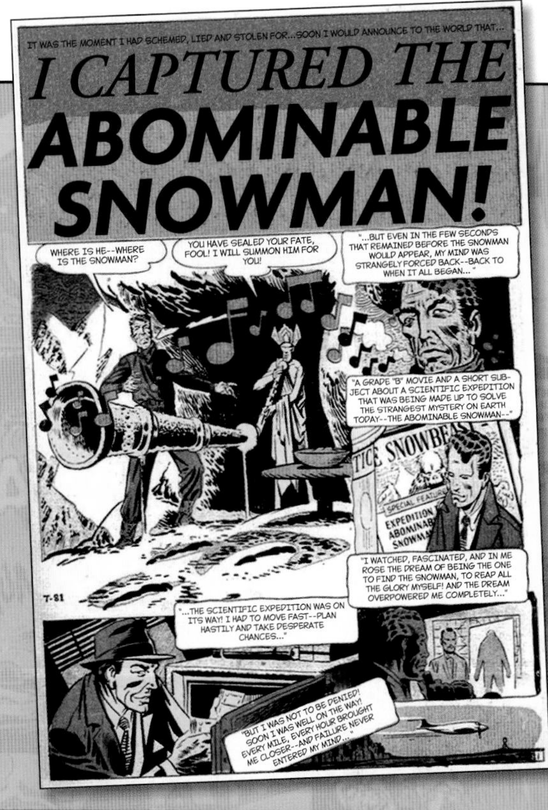

STEVE DITKO

In addition to Jack Kirby, another artist who began to come to the fore as a valued collaborator was Steve Ditko. Ditko had been one of a dozen artists producing stories for Atlas' weird-mystery titles, such as *Mystery Tales*, but the implosion of the company coincided with a leap in his storytelling abilities. His stylized, atmospheric, paranoiac artwork was the antithesis of Kirby's power-packed pencils, but within that sensitivity lay an intriguing design sense and a subtle identification with the little guy. Ditko's work conveyed a feeling of anxiety regardless of the subject matter he was illustrating. He could make even the most idyllic situation seem sinister just in the manner in which the pages were composed. Together, Stan Lee and Ditko began producing a series of short five-page shock ending stories, in the tradition of short story author O. Henry or the soon-to-be-launched *Twilight Zone* television series, for comics such as *Journey Into Mystery* and *Strange Tales*.

MEANWHILE IN 1958...

A SPACE AGENCY FOR THE US

NASA—the North American Space Agency—is formed "for the benefit of all," marking the American government's commitment to the Space Age.

US SATELLITE IN ORBIT

Following the 1957 Soviet satellite Sputnik 1, *the US races to get its own satellite into space.* Explorer 1 *is launched from Cape Canaveral.*

ANTI-NUCLEAR CAMPAIGNS

Alongside the rise of nuclear activity for military and energy purposes, an opposition movement also swells. In Britain, CND is formed and places itself at the forefront of the peace movement.

FIRST TRANSATLANTIC PASSENGER FLIGHTS

The first jet passenger service flies across the Atlantic from New York to London.

ELVIS JOINS THE ARMY

Elvis Presley is inducted into the US army as Private no. 53310761. He completes training in Texas and is then posted to Friedberg, Germany.

AND AT THE MOVIES...

Touch Of Evil, *Orson Welles' film noir tackles corruption and conscience against the backdrop of a sleazy border town;* Vertigo, *Alfred Hitchcock's intricately plotted thriller features a retired, acrophobic police cop drawn into a murder plot involving a female double.*

NOVEMBER

Journey Into Mystery *became the longest-running series to emerge from the 1950s, lasting in one form or another until issue #521 in 1998.*

FROM BATTLE TO MYSTERY

• *Journey Into Mystery* #49

From a publishing standpoint, 1958 was solid, with only one or two minor changes to the post-Atlas line-up of sixteen titles. It was the military titles that flagged first. In November, *Marines In Battle* ended in favor of a revival of *Journey Into Mystery*, one of Martin Goodman's steadiest mystery titles, which returned to the schedule after an absence of just over a year.

DECEMBER

STRANGE WORLDS SETS THE STYLE

• *Strange Worlds* #1

Martin Goodman was inspired by the sudden interest in technology and science fiction that the space race had generated since the Russians launched the first unmanned satellite, *Sputnik 1*. So, Goodman metamorphosed *Navy Combat* into *Strange Worlds*, the first entirely new title in the post-Atlas line. With a cover by Jack Kirby and a lead story about flying saucers, *Strange Worlds*, while short-lived, was a step in the direction that the company would move in next. The marriage of science fiction themes with tales of incredible monsters were in the vein of those that were beginning to show up on drive-in movie screens and seemed likely to be able to capture the attention and the dimes of young readers.

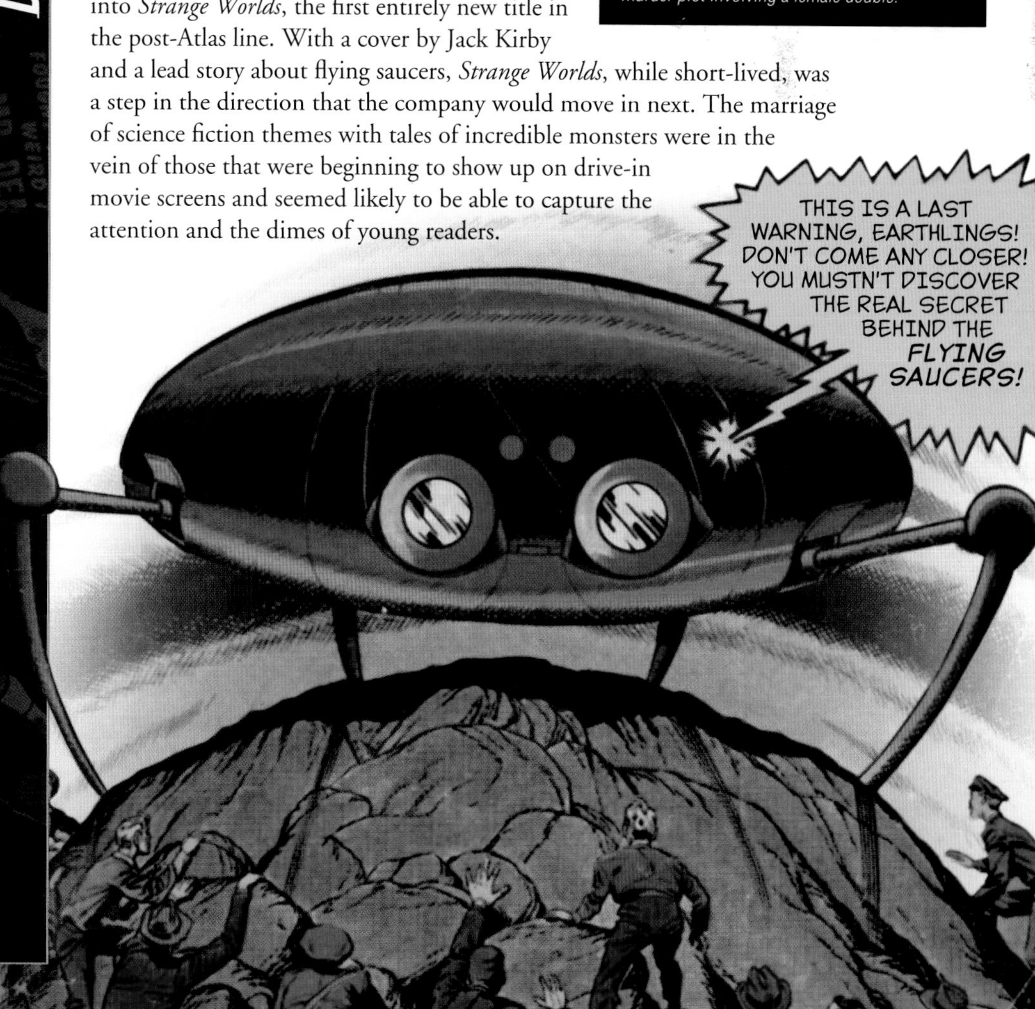

THIS IS A LAST WARNING, EARTHLINGS! DON'T COME ANY CLOSER! YOU MUSTN'T DISCOVER THE REAL SECRET BEHIND THE FLYING SAUCERS!

MIGHT AS WELL BE THROWING DAISIES AT IT!

1959

MARVEL BULLPEN COMES TOGETHER

In the final year of the decade, publisher Martin Goodman's post-Atlas comic book company ramped back up to full, if somewhat curtailed, production. By this point, editor Stan Lee had assembled a small but steady pool of creative talent to produce the company's output, in addition to himself. This group of artists included Jack Kirby, Steve Ditko, Don Heck, Larry Lieber, Paul Reinman, Stan Goldberg, Al Hartley, and Dick Ayers, all of whom would become principle early players in the birth of the Marvel Super Hero line in the 1960s. There would still be occasional jobs for other creators along the way, but the nucleus for what would, six years later, be known as the Marvel Bullpen had been formed.

As the decade closed, Goodman and Lee were once again on track, producing a variety of features. None of them were especially outstanding, but all of them were commercial enough to turn a profit for the nameless comic book group, which continued to click along. It was no longer an industry giant due to its sheer volume, but instead was a bottom-feeder, eking out a modest living at the outer edges of the field. It was, perhaps, the least-assuming comic book company going into the 1960s and the one that readers and retailers had the least expectations for.

JANUARY

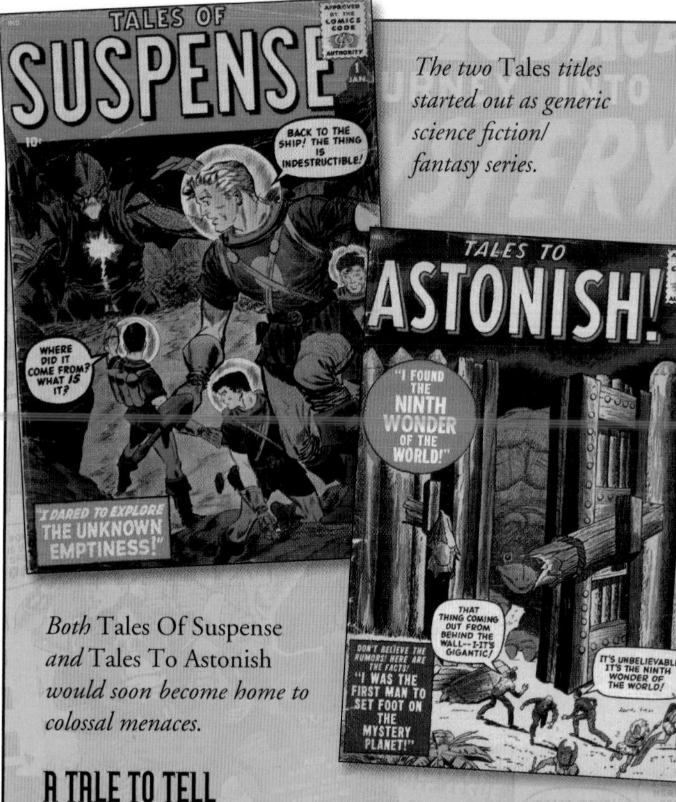

The two Tales *titles started out as generic science fiction/ fantasy series.*

Both Tales Of Suspense *and* Tales To Astonish *would soon become home to colossal menaces.*

A TALE TO TELL

• *Tales Of Suspense* #1 and *Tales To Astonish* #1

January saw the birth of two titles that would each have a place of importance in the coming age—*Tales Of Suspense* and *Tales To Astonish*. In November, 1958, continuing to chase the trend that revived *Journey Into Mystery* in the same month and created *Strange Worlds* in December, Martin Goodman ended *Homer, The Happy Ghost* and *Miss America*. He replaced them with these two new weird-mystery titles with an emphasis on science fiction in the new year. *Tales Of Suspense* would one day be the birthplace of Iron Man and *Tales To Astonish* eventually became the home of three important Marvel characters—Ant-Man, the Hulk, and Sub-Mariner.

SEPTEMBER

MONSTERS ON THE PROWL

• *Journey Into Mystery* #54

While *Tales Of Suspense* and *Tales To Astonish* began as generic catch-all science fiction anthologies, before the end of 1959 a format began to emerge that would carry over to *Journey Into Mystery* and the other sci-fi titles in the line.

Inspired by the success of giant monster movies such as the import *Godzilla* and *Them!*, Stan Lee began leading off each of these comics' issues with a saga featuring a new colossal-sized menace, most often illustrated by Jack Kirby. These monsters would frequently feature short, vowel-filled names such as Goom, Googam, Xom, Monstro, Fin Fang Foom, or Groot, and would menace humankind until they were undone by the efforts of some unassuming person, either a scientist or a bystander lacking in self-confidence. While not terribly sophisticated (and a little repetitive when read one after another), these stories excelled in visual excitement. Page after page was filled with the creature of the

SEPTEMBER

issue bloodlessly causing carnage and terror as it strode the planet, inexorably drawing nearer to its own undoing. Each story usually featured a twist ending. Kirby was second to none when it came to depicting power on the comic book page, and for all their formulaic sameness, these stories were among the most visceral and exciting comics then being produced.

Journey Into Mystery #54 was among the earliest releases to cover-feature such a creature. However, while the cover was drawn by Jack Kirby, the story of Monstro on the insides was illustrated by Steve Ditko.

THE DEVELOPMENT OF STEVE DITKO

The second and third story slots in fantasy magazines, such as *Tales Of Suspense* and *Tales To Astonish*, would typically be filled by short weird-fantasy stories drawn by artists such as Don Heck, Paul Reinman, and Larry Lieber. These stories tended to be simple potboilers, wherein an unscrupulous character would get his comeuppance in some fantasy manner, or a deserving sort would get his moment of glory. The final story in each issue, however, was inevitably produced by Stan Lee and artist Steve Ditko, a five-page feature with a twist ending. Ditko opened the tales with his beautiful symbolic splash pages (like the one below), aided by the stylish lettering of Artie Simek and Sam Rosen. These functioned almost as movie posters and revealed a keen sense of design and an ability to capture the imagination with a single image. Ditko wasn't the flashiest artist in the roster, but he was proving to be the most sophisticated.

OCTOBER

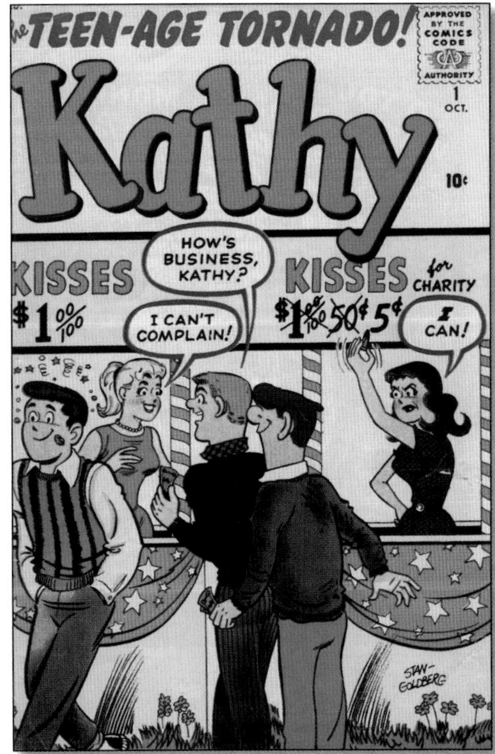

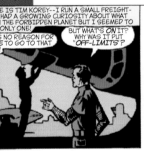

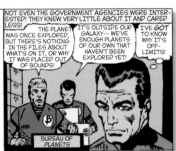

GIRLS, GIRLS, GIRLS!

• *Kathy* #1 and *A Date With Millie* #1

In October, publisher Martin Goodman eliminated *Strange Worlds* and *World Of Fantasy* in favor of two new series. *Kathy*, cover-blurbed as "The Teen-Age Tornado," was a feminine take on the formula of lighthearted comedy centring around the school and social life of its teenaged protagonist. The second title released in this month, *A Date With Millie*, was a spin-off of the *Millie The Model* comic. Both comics featured four or five short stories an issue, each one largely a vehicle for simple verbal and visual gags. But in these pages, Stan Lee honed his skills at establishing characterization through dialogue, and his particular talent for a witty phrase or a well-timed bon mot. Eventually, Lee would apply this style to his Super Hero writing, making the Marvel heroes among the wittiest and most personable to ever appear.

In the chaos of the post-Atlas reorganization, Lee's favorite teen humor artist Dan DeCarlo had been snatched up by Archie Comics. However, in DeCarlo's absence, Stan Goldberg rose to the occasion, drawing the majority of both *Kathy* and *A Date With Millie*, while inheriting *Millie The Model* as well.

MEANWHILE IN 1959...

THE DAY THE MUSIC DIES

Three rock 'n' roll musicians—Buddy Holly, Ritchie Valens, and J.P. "The Big Bopper" Richardson—are killed when their airplane crashes in Iowa.

REVOLUTION IN CUBA

Following a military uprising in Cuba that overthrows Fulgencio Batista, Fidel Castro is sworn in as Prime Minister.

TWO NEW STATES FOR THE US

President Eisenhower signs the bill to legally grant Statehood to Alaska and Hawaii, making them the 49th and 50th American states.

THE FIRST ANIMALS RETURN SAFELY FROM SPACE

NASA launches two chimpanzees into space and then recovers them from the Atlantic.

VIETNAM WAR CLAIMS FIRST AMERICAN DEATHS

Master Sergeant Charles Ovnand and US Army Major Dale R. Buis become the first two Americans killed in action in the Vietnam War. The pair are killed at Bien Hoa, near Saigon.

BARBIE STEPS OUT

The adult-bodied fashion doll makes her debut at the American International Toy Fair in New York, wearing a black and white zebra-striped swimming costume. Barbie is one of the first toys to have a marketing strategy based on television advertising and Mattel sells 350,000 dolls in the first year of production.

FIRST VIEWS OF THE EARTH FROM SPACE

People on Earth are able to see how their planet looks from space when the first photographs and then the first television images are sent back from space.

FIRST TRANSPACIFIC PASSENGER FLIGHT

Following the first transatlantic passenger flight in 1958, Qantas airline launches the first transpacific passenger jet service from Sydney to San Francisco.

COPY THAT

Twenty-two years after the patent was filed, the first office photocopier—the Xerox 914—is commercially available.

AND AT THE MOVIES...

Ben-Hur, *this epic, starring Charlton Heston as the chariot-racing ex-slave, was the most expensive film of the 1950s;* Some Like It Hot, *Billy Wilder's classic comedy about cross-dressing jazz musicians on the run, stumbling upon a radiant Marilyn Monroe, possesses the perfect blend of wit and chemistry;* Sleeping Beauty, *Disney's sixteenth animated feature based on the classic fairy tale by Charles Perrault uses music adapted from the 1890 ballet by Tchaikovsky.*

Two-Gun Kid *#42 (June, 1958)*
Joe Maneely was one of the fastest and most versatile artists of the period, and he likely would have gone on to become a major creative force for Marvel had he not died in 1958. Maneely would typically do most of his drawing straight in ink, only putting down the roughest of guidelines in pencil before diving in with brush and pen.

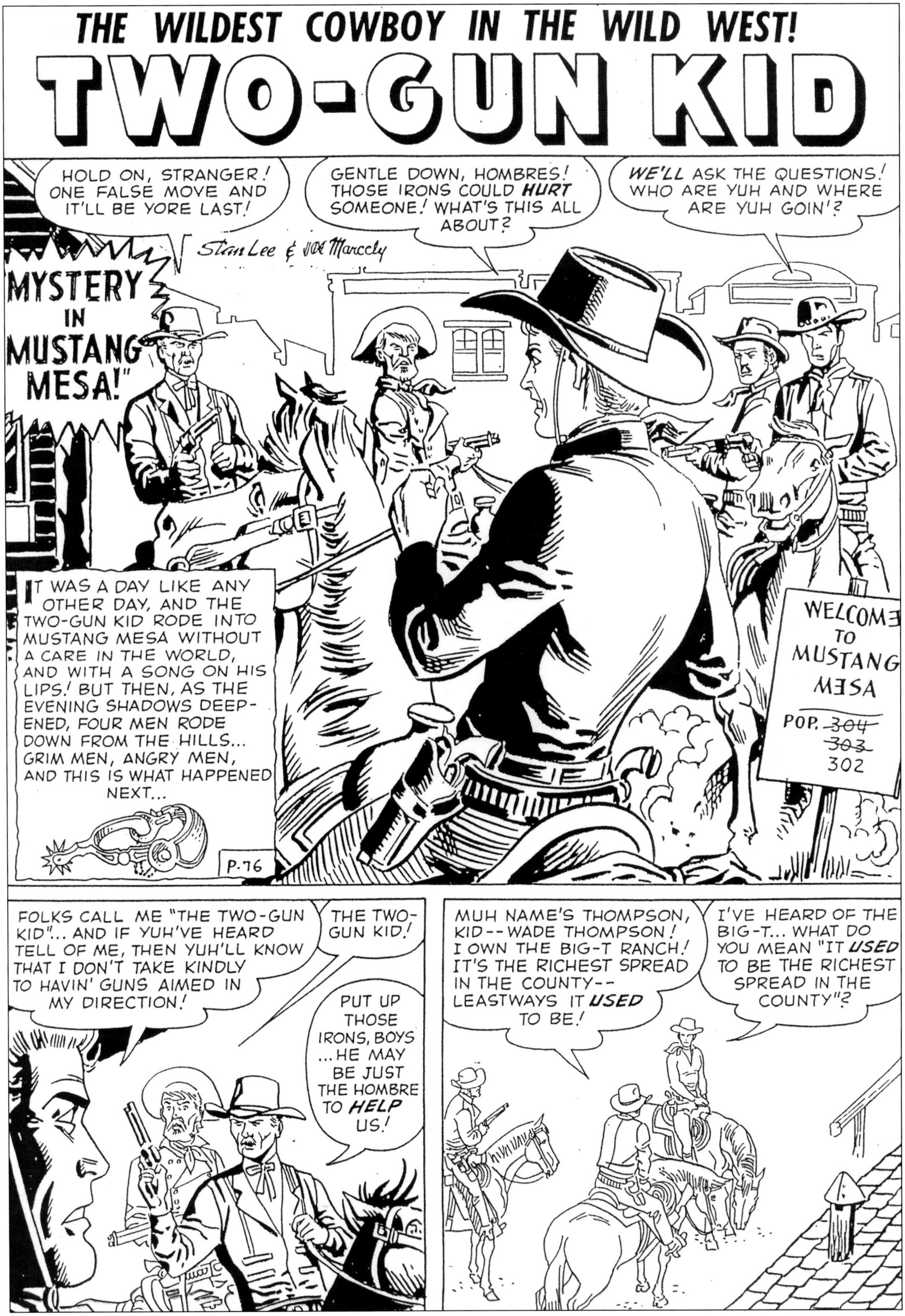

THE WILDEST COWBOY IN THE WILD WEST!

TWO-GUN KID

HOLD ON, STRANGER! ONE FALSE MOVE AND IT'LL BE YORE LAST!

GENTLE DOWN, HOMBRES! THOSE IRONS COULD **HURT** SOMEONE! WHAT'S THIS ALL ABOUT?

WE'LL ASK THE QUESTIONS! WHO ARE YUH AND WHERE ARE YUH GOIN'?

Stan Lee & Joe Maneely

"MYSTERY IN MUSTANG MESA!"

IT WAS A DAY LIKE ANY OTHER DAY, AND THE TWO-GUN KID RODE INTO MUSTANG MESA WITHOUT A CARE IN THE WORLD, AND WITH A SONG ON HIS LIPS! BUT THEN, AS THE EVENING SHADOWS DEEPENED, FOUR MEN RODE DOWN FROM THE HILLS... GRIM MEN, ANGRY MEN, AND THIS IS WHAT HAPPENED NEXT...

WELCOME TO MUSTANG MESA

POP. ~~304~~ ~~303~~ 302

P. 76

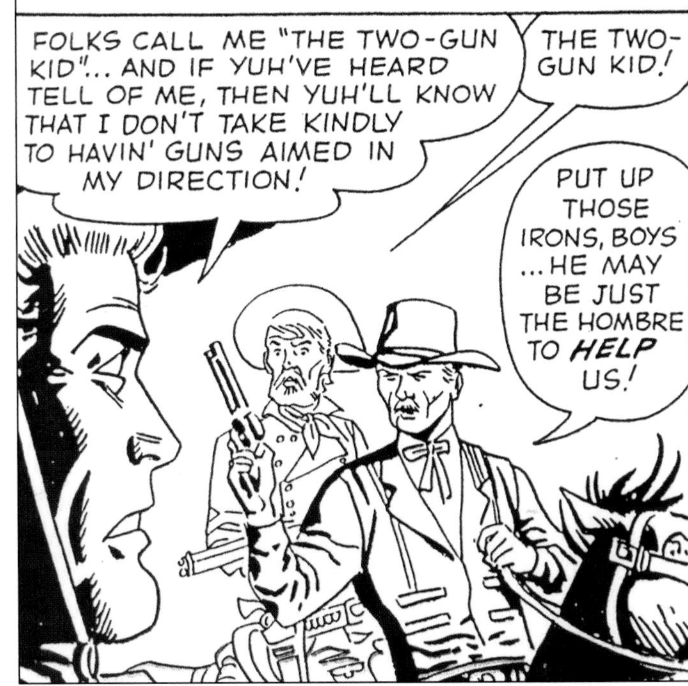

Two-Gun Kid #42 (June, 1958)

It was unusual in the 1950s for artists to be allowed to sign their work, and rare for a writer. One of the exceptions was Stan Lee who, as editor as well as writer, could approve this. Stan tended to sign everything he wrote, and often included the artist's name as well, in this case Joe Maneely. Other artists would try to sneak their name into the background and hope that the publisher would not notice it.

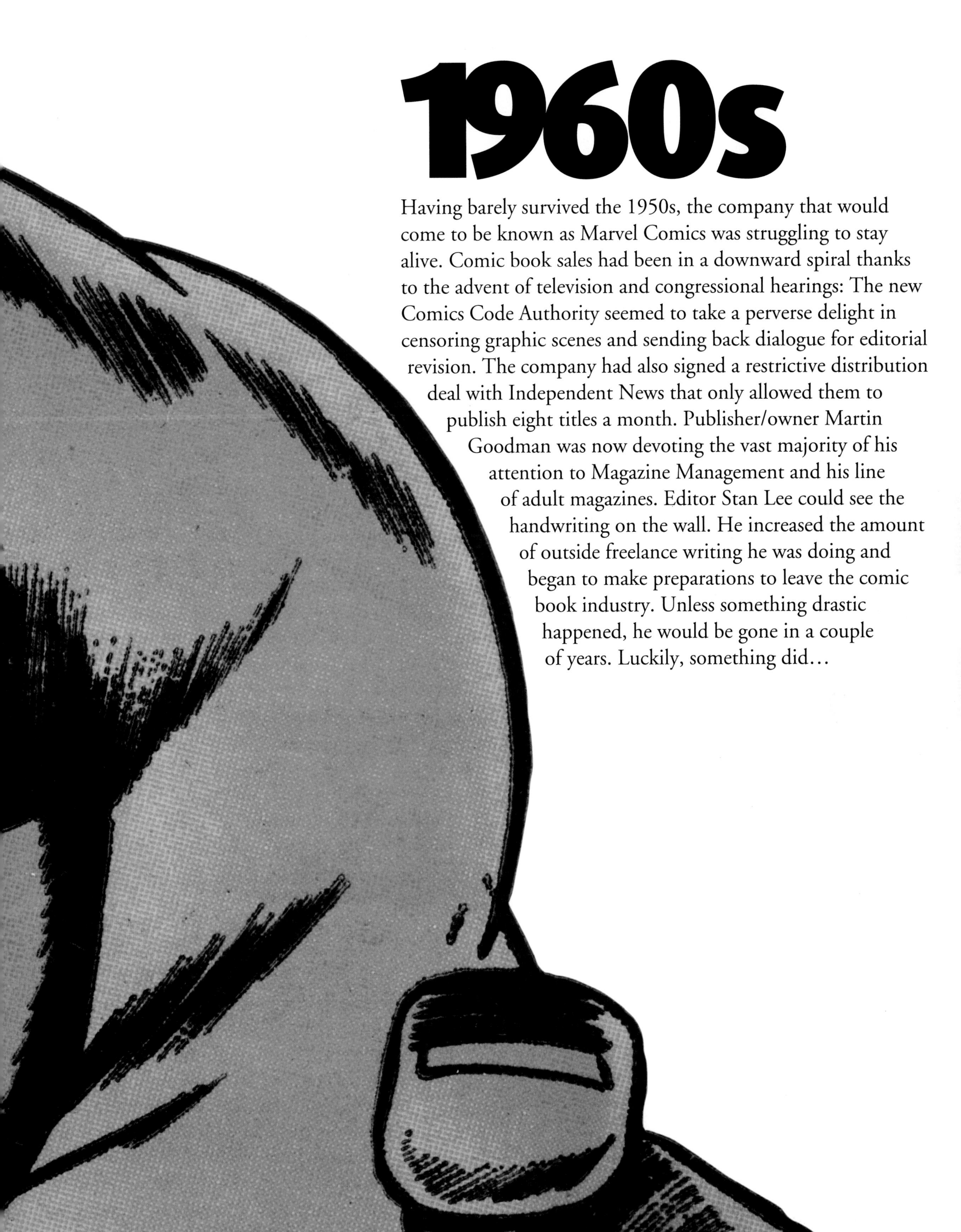

1960s

Having barely survived the 1950s, the company that would come to be known as Marvel Comics was struggling to stay alive. Comic book sales had been in a downward spiral thanks to the advent of television and congressional hearings: The new Comics Code Authority seemed to take a perverse delight in censoring graphic scenes and sending back dialogue for editorial revision. The company had also signed a restrictive distribution deal with Independent News that only allowed them to publish eight titles a month. Publisher/owner Martin Goodman was now devoting the vast majority of his attention to Magazine Management and his line of adult magazines. Editor Stan Lee could see the handwriting on the wall. He increased the amount of outside freelance writing he was doing and began to make preparations to leave the comic book industry. Unless something drastic happened, he would be gone in a couple of years. Luckily, something did…

IT'S *THE RAWHIDE KID*! WHAT'S *HE* DOING IN TOWN?

YOU ***KNOW*** HIS REPUTATION! THERE'S GONNA BE GUNPLAY FOR SURE!

1960

WHEN THE DECADE DAWNED

Martin Goodman's publishing philosophy into 1960 continued as before—to follow the trends! If westerns were hot, publish more westerns. If romance was selling, do more romance. At the start of 1960, he was publishing five teenage/humor comics (*Millie The Model*, *A Date With Millie*, *Kathy*, *Patsy Walker*, and *Patsy And Hedy*), four westerns (*Gunsmoke Western*, *Kid Colt, Outlaw*, *Two-Gun Kid*, and *Wyatt Earp*), four monster/suspense titles (*Journey Into Mystery*, *Strange Tales*, *Tales To Astonish*, and *Tales Of Suspense*), two romances (*Love Romances* and *My Own Romance*), and one war title (*Battle*). Distributed by Independent News, Goodman was limited to eight titles a month, although this began to loosen toward the end of the year.

By 1960, the company that would call itself Marvel had dropped the umbrella name of Atlas Comics from its covers. However, because of tax laws that favored small publishing houses, Goodman used different corporate entities to print his comics, for example *Kid Colt, Outlaw* was published by Leading Magazine Corp., *Battle* by Male Publishing Corp., and *Strange Tales* by Vista Publications, Inc.

On the creative front, Stan Lee was the company's editor and most prolific writer. He was also the art director and assigned most of the adventure covers to artist Jack Kirby.

JUNE

THE FINAL *BATTLE*

• *Battle* #70

After being published for a little over nine years, *Battle* ended its run with its seventieth issue. An anthology title that usually contained stories from assorted wars and conflicts, *Battle* had featured the artwork of many legendary comic book artists like Jack Davis, Bernie Krigstein, Carl Burgos, John Severin, Joe Kubert, Bob Powell, Al Williamson, and Jack Kirby.

IN THIS ISSUE: "FACE-TO-FACE WITH THE ENEMY!"

Decreasing sales must have convinced owner/publisher Martin Goodman that war comics had run their course because *Battle* #70 was the last war-related title that Marvel published until *Sgt. Fury And His Howling Commandos* appeared in 1963.

M Although westerns like *Kid Colt, Outlaw* and *Two-Gun Kid* were still selling, *Wyatt Earp* was cancelled after issue #29 to make room for a new title, which was chosen to be *Rawhide Kid*.

AUGUST

A NEW RAWHIDE KID

• *Rawhide Kid* #17

In many ways, the Marvel Age of comics—the creative frenzy at Marvel that began in the early 1960s—started with *Rawhide Kid* #17. Needing a new western to fill the space of the recently cancelled *Wyatt Earp*, editor Stan Lee decided to recycle an old title. He selected artist Jack Kirby to illustrate the new feature, a decision that would prove pivotal to setting the tone of all the Super Hero comics that were destined to follow. *Rawhide Kid* was the first time Lee and Kirby worked together to redevelop a previous character from the ground up.

The original *Rawhide Kid* was published from March 1955 to September 1957 and featured a wandering gunfighter who wore a rawhide vest, but Lee and Kirby chose to update the concept. Since *Kid Colt, Outlaw* seemed to be the company's most popular western hero, the new Rawhide also became an outlaw. Kirby designed a short, red-haired eighteen-year-old who dressed all in black, except for white gloves and a yellow hat.

No one knows exactly who contributed what to the new *Rawhide Kid*, but given that Lee had a writing credit and that Kirby and his inker Dick Ayers signed the work together, it would seem that Lee began the series by writing full scripts that told Kirby what to draw in each panel. However, because Lee and Ayers' first shared credit appears in issue #24 (indicating simply that the story is by both of them), it is likely that Lee developed his system of working "Marvel-style", whereby the artist worked from a brief story outline or a conversation, while working on *Rawhide Kid*.

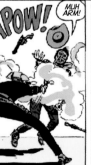

AND THEN THE LEGEND WAS BORN! FOR, BEFORE HAWK COULD SQUEEZE HIS TRIGGER WHILE HE ALREADY HAD HIS COLT IN HIS HAND AIMED AT JOHNNY BART, THE YOUNG AVENGER DREW! IN ONE IMPOSSIBLY FAST MOTION, HE HAD HIS GUN, AIMED HIS GUN, AND FIRED HIS GUN!!!
KAPOW!
MUH ARM!

AS THE WEAPON WENT SPINNING OUT OF HAWK'S INJURED GUNHAND, JOHNNY BART CAUGHT A GLIMPSE OF THE OTHER GUNMAN IN THE MIRROR, ABOUT TO SHOOT HIM FROM BEHIND!
NOT THIS TIME, SPADE!

AUGUST

A NEW TEENAGE HUMOR COMIC

• *My Girl Pearl* #7

At this time, Marvel jumped from genre to genre in reaction to the market. To replace *Battle*, Stan Lee revived *My Girl Pearl*, a teenage humor strip, last seen in 1957. The first issues had been drawn by Dan DeCarlo, but this issue was pencilled by Stan Goldberg. Both artists later achieved fame with Archie Comics.

SEPTEMBER

A CHANGE OF TITLE

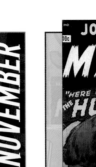

• *Teen-Age Romance* #77

Called *My Own Romance* until its issue #76, the title was renamed *Teen-Age Romance* with issue #77. *My Own Romance* had featured so called "true" romance stories that were billed as "as told to" Stan Lee and had included artwork by such comic book greats as Matt Baker, Jay Scott Pike, Don Heck, Dick Giordano, and Vincent Colletta. *Teen-Age Romance* continued in the same vein but was primarily drawn by Colletta.

Johnny Clay, also known as Johnny Bart, was an orphan raised by former gunslinger Ben Bart on a ranch near Rawhide, Texas.

OCTOBER

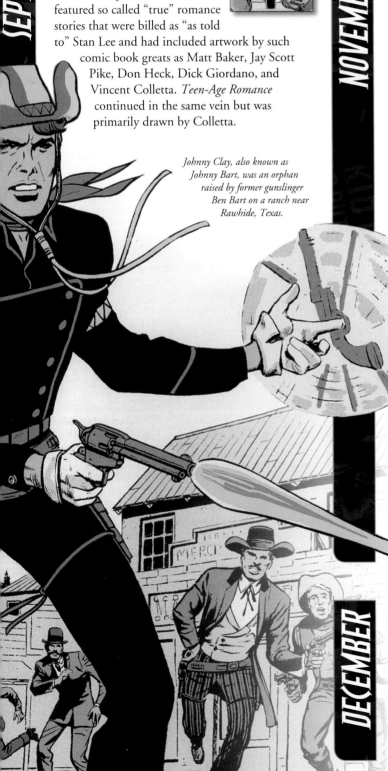

LONGER CHAPTERS

• *Rawhide Kid* #18

Beginning with *Rawhide Kid #18*, Lee and Kirby started following the formula that they had established in their monster/suspense titles, whereby they produced longer lead stories that were broken into separate chapters.

NOVEMBER

THE FIRST HULK

• *Journey Into Mystery* #62

A typical Marvel monster/suspense title of its day, *Journey Into Mystery* had a thirteen-page lead story written by Stan Lee and drawn by Jack Kirby, with two five-page backup stories drawn by Don Heck and Steve Ditko. The lead story of issue #62, "I Was A Slave Of The Living Hulk!", introduced a giant monster called the Hulk—similar in name only to the future Hulk. An alien who hypnotized the Earth's entire population, he proved popular enough to return in *Journey Into Mystery* #66 and was renamed Xemnu the Titan when he fought the Defenders and his better known namesake in *Marvel Feature* #3 (June, 1972).

DECEMBER

A NEW TITLE FOR MILLIE

• *Life With Millie* #8

Previously *A Date With Millie*, this title was renamed in an attempt to follow trends. The style of stories and the creative team of editor Stan Lee and artist Stan Goldberg remained the same.

MEANWHILE IN 1960...

STUDENTS DEMONSTRATE AGAINST SEGREGATION

As part of the wider civil rights movement, one thousand black students stage a sit-in on the old Confederate Capital steps in Montgomery, Alabama. They pray and sing national anthem songs in opposition to educational segregation.

JOURNEY TO THE DEEP

Jacques Piccard and Don Walsh become the only people ever to descend to the Mariana Trench, the deepest part of any ocean on Earth.

HOLLYWOOD WALK OF FAME

The first five-pointed star is laid in the pavement in Hollywood in the name of film actress Joanne Woodward.

THE LASER BEAMS INTO HISTORY

Theodore Maiman demonstrates the first operating laser, opening the door to a future of DVDs, barcodes, laser printers, and a wide range of medical and industrial procedures. At the time, however, it is described as "a solution in need of a problem."

NEW WAVE JAZZ

Saxophonist John Coltrane forms his own quartet and becomes the voice of the new wave jazz movement.

TO KILL A MOCKINGBIRD PUBLISHES

Harper Lee's story of Scout and her brother Jem captures the tensions, tolerances, and prejudices of life for black and white Americans living in the Deep South in the 1930s.

AIR TRAVEL GOES SUPERSONIC

Concorde makes its first supersonic flight.

A CELEBRITY INTERRACIAL WEDDING

Entertainer Sammy Davis, Jr. marries the Swedish actress May Brit, although interracial marriage is still illegal in most US states.

FIRST PARALYMPICS

The first Paralympics are held in Rome a couple of weeks after the Summer Olympics. Four hundred athletes with spinal injuries from twenty-three countries compete in eight events.

AND AT THE MOVIES...

Psycho, *a classic Hitchcock horror film featuring a lonely motel keeper and one guest;* Ocean's Eleven, *in which a gang plan a heist of Las Vegas casinos;* Spartacus, *Kirk Douglas plays the inspirational leader of the doomed slave revolt against the Roman Empire in Stanley Kubrick's epic biopic;* The Magnificent Seven, *a Western set in Mexico about gunmen who protect a village from bandits;* Village of the Damned, *a science fiction film where small children with strange powers take over a village.*

I SHALL CRUSH YOU LIKE AN INSECT!! FOR I AM *FIN FANG FOOM!*

1961

THE REBIRTH OF THE SUPER HERO

Monster/suspense titles moved to the forefront in 1961, surpassing the once popular teenage/humor comic genre. As a result *Tales Of Suspense* quickly became a monthly, and *Kid Colt, Outlaw* reverted to bimonthly status. The distributor, Independent News, had loosened its restrictions, so Marvel was able to publish nine to twelve titles a month. Consequently, a fourth monthly monster/suspense title, *Amazing Adventures*, launched in June. However, publisher/owner Martin Goodman saw a new trend on the horizon: Super Heroes were making a comeback.

According to comic book legend, he was playing golf with an unnamed executive, who mentioned that Super Heroes were selling well for DC Comics, especially a comic that starred the Justice League team. So, Goodman immediately told editor Stan Lee to produce a team of Super Heroes for Marvel. Goodman probably expected Lee to follow DC's lead, merely recycling and updating Super Heroes from the 1940s. Lee, however, took a different approach, which began with the Fantastic Four...

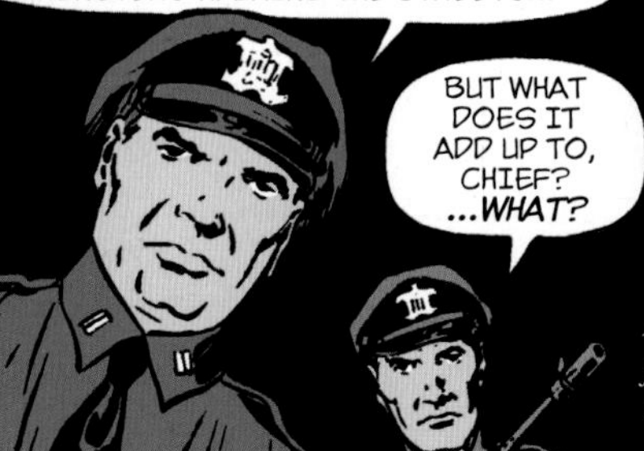

I DON'T KNOW HOW TO EXPLAIN IT, BUT THERE'S SOMETHING WEIRD HAPPENING IN CENTRAL CITY! THOSE WORDS IN THE SKY... THOSE SCATTERED REPORTS OF MONSTERS WALKING THE STREETS...
BUT WHAT DOES IT ADD UP TO, CHIEF? ...WHAT?

At first, the Fantastic Four were met with fear and suspicion. Rumors of an alien invasion began to circulate.

JUNE

DR. DROOM

• *Amazing Adventures* #1

A master of the dark and mystical world of black magic, Dr. Droom was reintroduced during the Marvel Age, in the backup "I Am The Fantastic Dr. Droom!" In an origin story similar to the future Dr. Strange's, the doctor went to Tibet to treat an ailing lama. After a series of challenges, he was chosen to succeed the lama because of his courage and unwavering devotion to duty. In a politically incorrect scene that would never be permitted today, Droom was transformed from Caucasian to Asian so he could continue the lama's work. Dr. Droom was later renamed Dr. Druid when he reappeared in the 1970s.

On the outside, *Amazing Adventures* was a new monthly monster/suspense title, that appeared to follow Marvel's standard formula: issue one featured a thirteen-page giant-monster story by the artists Jack Kirby and Dick Ayers. Two five-page backups followed: one drawn by Steve Ditko and one by Kirby. (Lee's name does not appear until "The Fourth Man!" in issue #6.) No writer was credited with Dr. Droom's story, but it read more like the work of Lee's brother Larry Lieber than either Lee or Kirby.

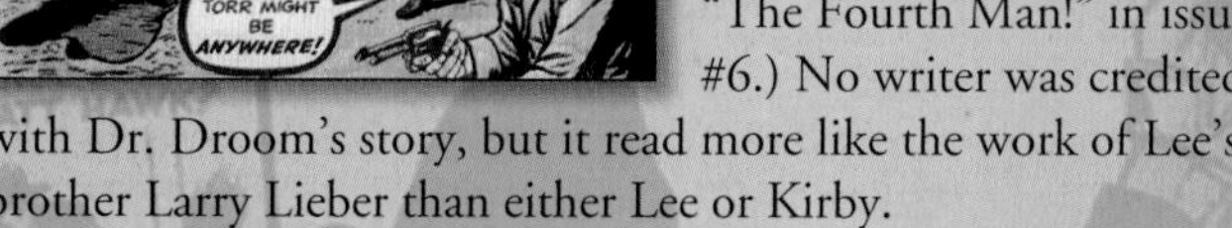

MIXING GENRES

• *Rawhide Kid* #22

Hoping to attract the readers of the better selling monster/suspense titles, Lee and Kirby mixed genres in *Rawhide Kid* #22. The outlaw fought a monster—a living totem pole—who was more appropriate to *Tales Of Suspense* than a western title.

OCTOBER

FIN FANG FOOM

• *Strange Tales* #89

Standing nearly fifteen stories high, Fin Fang Foom was a dragon who referenced monsters like Rodan and Godzilla of Japanese movie fame. Stan Lee also once mentioned *Chu Chin Chow*, a musical comedy roughly based on *Ali Baba And The 40 Thieves*, as an inspiration for the creature's name.

Fin Fang Foom had been sleeping for centuries in a cavern beneath the Great Wall of China. Chan Liuchow, a student of ancient Chinese history, awakened him in *Strange Tales* #89 and used him to discourage Communist China from invading the island of Taiwan. The dragon proved so popular that he was later brought back to battle both Iron Man and the mighty Thor. Fin Fang Foom also appeared as a recurring villain in the 1990s on the animated *Iron Man* television series and *The Invincible Iron Man* animated movie in 2007.

NOVEMBER

A NEW BREED OF SUPER HERO

"Together we have more power than any humans have ever possessed!"

• *The Fantastic Four* #1

After working in comic books for twenty-two years, Stan Lee was primed to do something different when Martin Goodman asked him to produce a new team of Super Heroes. Instead of bringing back the likes of Captain America or the Sub-Mariner, Lee decided to create the type of super-team that he would enjoy reading about. At this time, the typical Super Hero was an infallible paragon of virtue, who zealously guarded his secret identity and had a girlfriend that was usually in love with his alter ego. Lee and Kirby wanted their new heroes to be real people who argued among themselves, made mistakes, and had feet of clay. They wouldn't wear colorful costumes or bother to keep their real identities a secret. They wouldn't live in a mansion or have a secret headquarters and the hero and heroine would already be in love when the series started. One of the members would be a hotheaded teenager who was an updated version of the Human Torch. Another would be an ugly, antisocial, easily enraged monster—someone who looked more like a villain than a hero. Lee and Kirby tossed around ideas before Lee wrote a two-page outline for the first issue. Since monster/suspense titles were still the top sellers, *The Fantastic Four* #1 featured a giant bug-eyed monster on the cover and numerous other creatures inside. This meant it looked far more like a monster/suspense title than a Super Hero book and the characters, with their everyday personalities, certainly didn't talk or behave like typical Super Heroes.

MEANWHILE IN 1961...

JFK IS YOUNGEST PRESIDENT
John Fitzgerald Kennedy is sworn in as the 35th President of the United States at the age of 43.

USSR PUT FIRST MAN IN SPACE
Yuri Gagarin is the first man to go into space. He returns after a 108-minute flight in orbit.

BAY OF PIGS INVASION
Cuban exiles, backed by Washington, invade Cuba but do not succeed in overthrowing Fidel Castro's government.

JFK SENDS HELP TO VIETNAM
President Kennedy sends equipment, advisors, and support to help the South Vietnamese government in their fight against the Viet Cong.

AND AT THE MOVIES...
West Side Story, *an update of* Romeo and Juliet *to 1950s New York gangs;* Breakfast At Tiffany's, *stylish romcom with an elegant Audrey Hepburn.*

DECEMBER

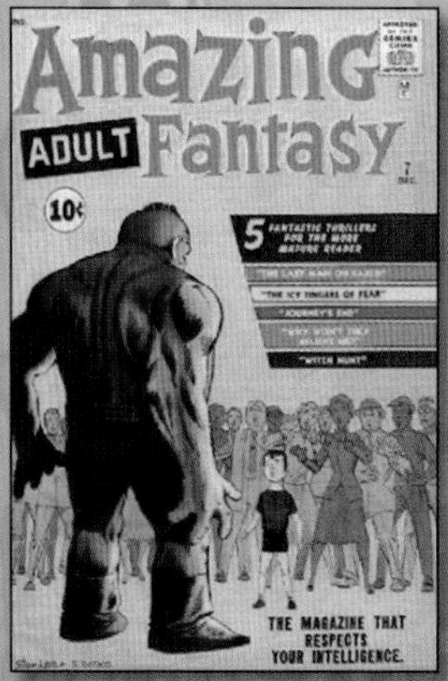

TARGETING OLDER READERS

• *Amazing Adult Fantasy* #7

With its seventh issue, *Amazing Adventures* became *Amazing Adult Fantasy*, but this move proved to be more than the usual Marvel name change. Having just created a new type of Super Hero title in *The Fantastic Four*, Stan Lee tried the same thing with monster/suspense comics. He envisioned a comic aimed at older readers and even included a contents page to make it appear more like a conventional magazine. Since screenwriter Rod Serling's *Twilight Zone* was gaining popularity and critical acclaim on television, Lee believed there was a market for intelligent fantasy and science fiction stories. This title also established the way Stan Lee and Steve Ditko would later work together on *The Amazing Spider-Man*: Lee would discuss his plot ideas with Ditko, who would then lay out the story, drawing it panel by panel, accompanied with rough dialogue to explain what was happening. Lee would later write the finished dialogue, adding additional explanations, ideas, or characterization.

M Because Super Heroes were now selling, *Rawhide Kid* #25 set the Kid against the Bat, a masked gunman.

The Fantastic Four ***#1 (Nov., 1961) by Stan Lee and Jack Kirby.***
The space race between the United States and the Soviet Union was on everyone's mind in the early 1960s and was a great starting point for Stan Lee and Jack Kirby's new super-team. Desperate to beat "the Reds" into space, Reed Richards built his own spacecraft. Unfortunately, he failed to include proper shielding and cosmic rays transformed him and his crew into the Fantastic Four.

HIGHER AND HIGHER, LIKE A SILVER BULLET, ROARS THE SLEEK SPACE CRAFT...
WE HAD TO DO IT!! WE HAD TO BE THE FIRST!
BUT WE'RE REACHING THE COSMIC STORM AREA... HANG ON!
RAK TAC TAC TAC TAC
HEAR THAT?? IT'S THE COSMIC RAYS!! I--I WARNED YOU ABOUT 'EM!!
THEY'RE PENETRATING THE SHIP!! OUR SHIELDING ISN'T STRONG ENOUGH!!
BUT I DON'T FEEL ANYTHING.
NATURALLY! THEY'RE ONLY RAYS OF LIGHT! YOU CAN'T FEEL 'EM-- BUT THEY'LL AFFECT YOU JUST THE SAME!

MY HEAD!! IT--IT'S POUNDING AS THOUGH IT'S ABOUT TO BURST!!
BEN WAS RIGHT!! WE SHOULD HAVE WAITED... SHOULD HAVE GOTTEN HEAVIER SHIELDING!

JOHNNY! WHAT IS IT? WHAT'S HAPPENING TO YOU?
I DON'T KNOW, SIS! MY BODY FEELS HOT--LIKE IT'S ON FIRE!! I-I FEEL LIKE I'M BURNING UP!!
UGH!! LISTEN TO ME...

...SOMEBODY ELSE TAKE TH
CONTROLS... I CAN'T HANDLE THE SHIP ANY MORE! MY--MY ARMS ARE HEAVY--TOO HEAVY--CAN'T MOVE--TOO HEAVY--GOT TO LIE DOWN--CAN'T MOVE!!
BEN!

1962

THE SIXTIES START SWINGING

A dramatic turning point in the story of Marvel Comics came in 1962. Until this time, most of the profits had been generated by monster/suspense comics. The company was only producing five monthly titles as the year began and the bimonthlies were all teenage/humor comics, westerns, romances, and one Super Hero comic—*The Fantastic Four*. But change was in the air. DC Comics were continuing to introduce new Super Hero titles and the genre was gaining in popularity.

It did not take long for editor Stan Lee to realize that *The Fantastic Four* was a hit. Though it took nine months for the sales figures of the comics on the mass market newsstands to be finalized, the flurry of fan letters all pointed to the FF's explosive popularity. Before this point, Marvel rarely received fan letters and most complained about spelling and production errors. After the release of *The Fantastic Four #1* (Nov., 1961), the deluge of fan mail focused on characters and their actions. The readers also bombarded Lee with demands, most frequently for another Super Hero title. Lee was happy to comply, but he wanted each new character to be as innovative as the FF had been. If he had to do Super Heroes again, Lee was determined that, once again, he would do them his way.

JANUARY

HANK PYM

• *Tales To Astonish* #27

The first appearance of Dr. Henry "Hank" Pym in a Marvel monster/suspense title was an inauspicious beginning for a man destined to become one of Marvel's most popular Super Heroes and founder of the Avengers. Created by Stan Lee and artist Jack Kirby, Pym appeared in one of the comic's four stories, "The Man In The Ant Hill." Pym invented a shrinking potion and was reduced to the size of an insect. This character was possibly inspired by the 1957 sci-fi movie *The Incredible Shrinking Man*. In later comics, Pym would jump to the other end of the size spectrum, becoming Giant-Man and Goliath.

The Skrulls used their shape-shifting abilities to make it seem that the Fantastic Four had perpetrated a series of terrible crimes.

THE SKRULLS

• *The Fantastic Four* #2

The second issue of the increasingly popular *The Fantastic Four* introduced the shapeshifting Skrulls, created by Stan Lee and Jack Kirby. These bug-eyed creatures were leaders of an interstellar empire and could take on the image and shape of any person, animal, or object. Like the 1956 sci-fi movie *The Invasion Of The Body Snatchers*, Lee and Kirby tapped into a fear that gripped the US at this time: the fear that Russian spies were infiltrating society and walking secretly among the population. The Skrulls could have appeared in any of Marvel's monster/suspense titles, but it was in *Fantastic Four* that Reed Richards stopped them from invading Earth by showing them pictures of its most powerful defenders, clipped from the pages of Marvel Comics' own *Strange Tales* and *Journey Into Mystery*.

MARCH

COSTUMES, HEADQUARTERS, AND THE FANTASTI-CAR

• *The Fantastic Four* #3

Stan Lee and Jack Kirby had received demands from readers who wanted the Fantastic Four to be a more traditional super-team, rather than ordinary people with super powers. So, they decided to show a cut-away diagram of the FF's "secret headquarters" and revealed that the FF traveled in a special flying car, which could separate into four vehicles. This issue also disclosed Sue Storm's costumes for her teammates. Early designs included masks, but Lee decided against them since the team had already revealed their identities. However, not everything was rosy in the FF world.
Tired of being bossed around, the Human Torch quit the team but would return one issue later.

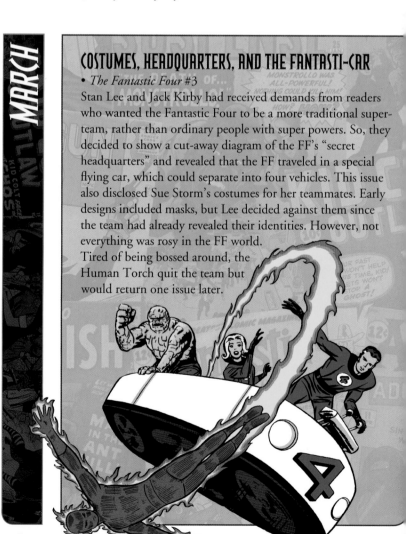

MARCH

MIRACLE MAN

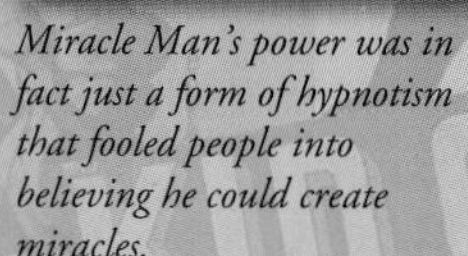

Miracle Man's power was in fact just a form of hypnotism that fooled people into believing he could create miracles.

• *The Fantastic Four* #3

The Fantastic Four's constant foe, Miracle Man burst onto the scene in "The Menace Of The Miracle Man" story in the third issue of *The Fantastic Four*. He was a master hypnotist who could create realistic illusions on a grand scale. These included growing to gigantic size, appearing to be stronger than the Thing, and even seeming to bring a giant-sized exhibit of a monster from Mars to life. However, Miracle Man was later defeated when he lost his powers after being temporarily blinded by the Human Torch and was finally shot dead by the criminal exterminator, Scourge.

- The bimonthly *Teen-Age Romance* ended with #86 to make room for *The Incredible Hulk* comic.
- The cover of *The Fantastic Four* #3 proclaimed that it was "The Greatest Comic Magazine In The World!"

A selfless act by Dr. Banner turned the scientist into a super-strong menace to society.

MAY

THE HULK

"Half-man, half-monster, the mighty Hulk thunders out of the night to take his place among the most amazing characters of all time!"

The cover artwork for the Incredible Hulk *#1 was pencilled by Jack Kirby and inked by George Roussos.*

• *The Incredible Hulk* #1

Billed as "The Strangest Man Of All Time," the Hulk made his debut mid-way through the year. In May, Stan Lee still didn't know how well *Fantastic Four #1* had sold, but this didn't stop him from working on a second super-title. Based on their collaboration on *The Fantastic Four*, Lee worked with Jack Kirby. Instead of a team that fought traditional Marvel monsters however, Lee decided that this time he wanted to feature a monster as the hero. He and Jack Kirby mixed the legend of Frankenstein's monster with *Dr. Jekyll And Mr. Hyde* and added a dash of Cold War paranoia. The result was a scrawny weakling of a scientist who became a super-strong, hulking brute. That description also provided Lee with the character's name—the Hulk!

This feeble scientist, Dr. Bruce Banner, designed an experimental new G-Bomb that was based on gamma radiation. Moments before the bomb was set to detonate, Banner realized that a teenager had entered the test area. After ordering his assistant Igor to stop the countdown, Banner raced out to warn the boy. Igor, of course, proved to be a Russian spy and ignored Banner's instructions. Though he managed to save the boy, Banner was bathed in the full force of the gamma rays when the bomb exploded. As a result of this contamination, Banner transformed into the Hulk whenever the night fell and returned to being human with the rising sun.

The Hulk was originally gray but color technology at the time meant that gray could not be produced consistently so it was decided to use the more reliable—and, ultimately, iconic—green.

Like *The Fantastic Four*, *The Incredible Hulk* #1 was also broken into multiple chapters with each splash page signed by Lee and Kirby. This was done to make casual readers who flipped through the comics on the newsstands think the issue contained a few different stories.

- Betty Ross (Banner's longtime girlfriend and, eventually, his wife) and General "Thunderbolt" Ross also debuted in *The Incredible Hulk* #1.
- Having learned from *The Fantastic Four* #1, Lee used *The Incredible Hulk* #1 to ask readers to write to the editor with their opinions.

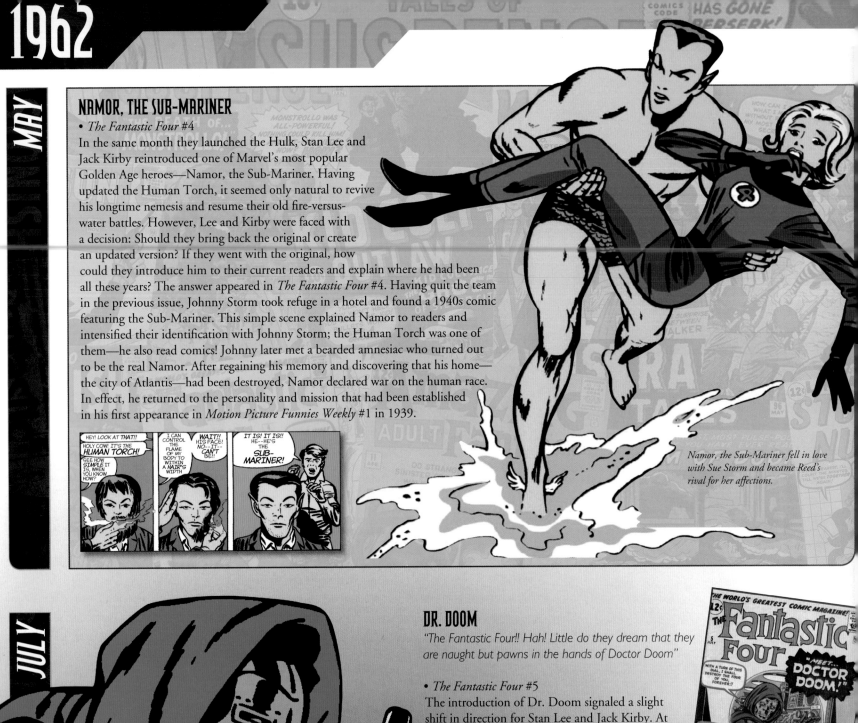

MAY

NAMOR, THE SUB-MARINER

• *The Fantastic Four* #4

In the same month they launched the Hulk, Stan Lee and Jack Kirby reintroduced one of Marvel's most popular Golden Age heroes—Namor, the Sub-Mariner. Having updated the Human Torch, it seemed only natural to revive his longtime nemesis and resume their old fire-versus-water battles. However, Lee and Kirby were faced with a decision: Should they bring back the original or create an updated version? If they went with the original, how could they introduce him to their current readers and explain where he had been all these years? The answer appeared in *The Fantastic Four* #4. Having quit the team in the previous issue, Johnny Storm took refuge in a hotel and found a 1940s comic featuring the Sub-Mariner. This simple scene explained Namor to readers and intensified their identification with Johnny Storm; the Human Torch was one of them—he also read comics! Johnny later met a bearded amnesiac who turned out to be the real Namor. After regaining his memory and discovering that his home—the city of Atlantis—had been destroyed, Namor declared war on the human race. In effect, he returned to the personality and mission that had been established in his first appearance in *Motion Picture Funnies Weekly* #1 in 1939.

Namor, the Sub-Mariner fell in love with Sue Storm and became Reed's rival for her affections.

JULY

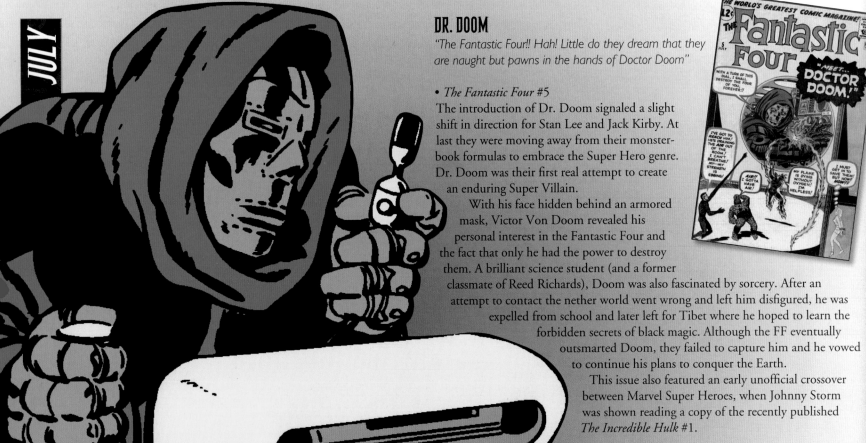

DR. DOOM

"The Fantastic Four!! Hah! Little do they dream that they are naught but pawns in the hands of Doctor Doom"

• *The Fantastic Four* #5

The introduction of Dr. Doom signaled a slight shift in direction for Stan Lee and Jack Kirby. At last they were moving away from their monster-book formulas to embrace the Super Hero genre. Dr. Doom was their first real attempt to create an enduring Super Villain.

With his face hidden behind an armored mask, Victor Von Doom revealed his personal interest in the Fantastic Four and the fact that only he had the power to destroy them. A brilliant science student (and a former classmate of Reed Richards), Doom was also fascinated by sorcery. After an attempt to contact the nether world went wrong and left him disfigured, he was expelled from school and later left for Tibet where he hoped to learn the forbidden secrets of black magic. Although the FF eventually outsmarted Doom, they failed to capture him and he vowed to continue his plans to conquer the Earth.

This issue also featured an early unofficial crossover between Marvel Super Heroes, when Johnny Storm was shown reading a copy of the recently published *The Incredible Hulk* #1.

Since Reed Richards had once questioned his calculations, Dr. Doom became obsessed with the need to prove that Mr. Fantastic was his mental inferior.

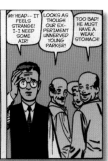

THE FIRST APPEARANCE OF SPIDER-MAN

"It's the spider! It has to be! Somehow—in some miraculous way, his bite transferred his own power—to me!"

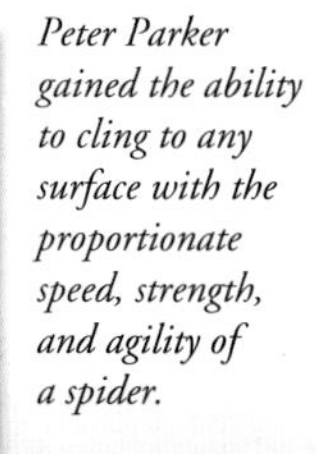

Peter Parker gained the ability to cling to any surface with the proportionate speed, strength, and agility of a spider.

• *Amazing Fantasy* #15

As sales of Super Hero comics rose, the monster/suspense titles began to suffer and *Amazing Adult Fantasy* became the first casualty. Since Marvel was still restricted to the number of titles it could publish, *Amazing Adult Fantasy* had to end so that *The Fantastic Four* could come out monthly. So, realizing that he had nothing to lose in the last issue—renamed *Amazing Fantasy* with issue #15—Stan Lee decided to try another take on the traditional Super Hero. Instead of being someone else's sidekick, Lee's new hero would be a teenager. He would be blessed with amazing super powers and cursed with typical teenage problems. While most Super Heroes led perfect lives, this new character would worry about money, suffer disappointments, get injured, be ignored by women, and lose as many battles as he won.

In his youth, Lee had been a fan of a pulp magazine called *The Spider, Master of Men*. It featured a crime-fighter in a slouch hat who wore a ring that left the image of a spider on the face of anyone he punched. Deciding that his new character would have spider-like powers, Lee commissioned Jack Kirby to work on the first story. Unfortunately, Kirby's version of Spidey's alter ego Peter Parker proved too heroic, handsome, and muscular for Lee's everyman hero. Lee turned to Steve Ditko, the regular artist on *Amazing Adult Fantasy*, who designed a skinny, awkward teenager with glasses. However, while he did not get the assignment to draw Spider-Man, Jack Kirby drew the cover for *Amazing Fantasy* #15.

Raised by his Uncle Ben and Aunt May, Peter Parker was a shy honor student. He was popular with his teachers, but was ridiculed by his classmates and ignored by girls. In his origin story, he attended a science exhibit, was bitten by a radioactive spider, and gained his amazing spider-like powers. Unlike most Super Heroes, Peter didn't immediately don a costume and begin patrolling the city. Instead, he tried to cash in on his new powers by entering a wrestling contest and later appearing on television. He was well on his way to fame and success when he deliberately allowed a fleeing burglar to escape the police. However, when his beloved uncle was later murdered by the very same burglar, Peter learned that, "with great power there must also come—great responsibility!"

Although Stan Lee has always claimed that *Amazing Fantasy* #15 was slated to be the title's last issue, the final caption of Spider-Man's origin story reads, "Be sure to see the next issue of *Amazing Fantasy*—for further amazing exploits of America's most different new teen-age idol—Spiderman!" Interestingly, the character's name is spelled both "Spiderman" and "Spider-Man" in his origin story.

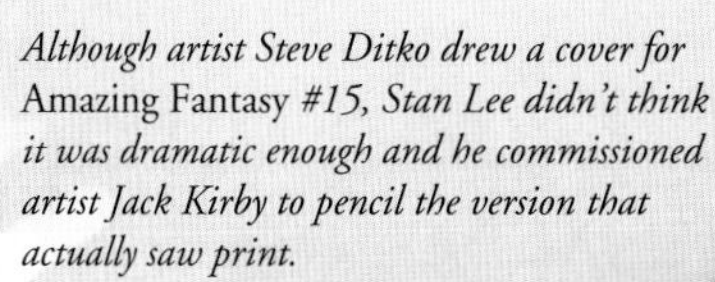

Although artist Steve Ditko drew a cover for Amazing Fantasy *#15, Stan Lee didn't think it was dramatic enough and he commissioned artist Jack Kirby to pencil the version that actually saw print.*

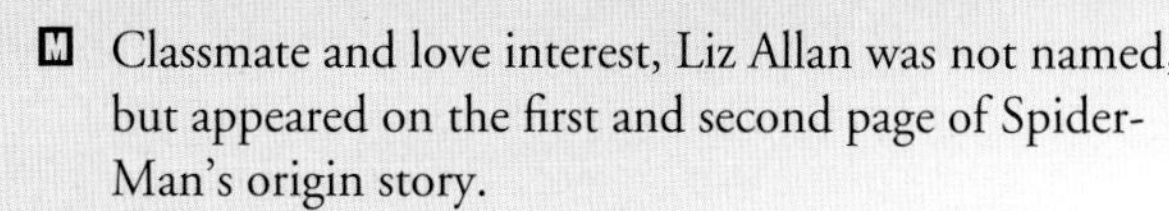

- Classmate and love interest, Liz Allan was not named, but appeared on the first and second page of Spider-Man's origin story.
- The class bully Flash Thompson and Peter's Aunt May also appeared in the first story.

As the God of Thunder Thor was the Lord of the Storm: wind, rain, lightning, and thunder heeded his summons an obeyed his commands when he stamped the handle of his enchante hammer twice upon the ground.

AUGUST

THOR DEBUT

"Whosoever holds this hammer, if he be worthy, shall possess the power of THOR."

• *Journey Into Mystery* #83

Shortly after he started work on Spider-Man, Stan Lee began on his next idea. He wanted to create someone who was stronger than the Hulk and more powerful than the entire Fantastic Four. An interviewer had described the new Marvel Super Heroes as "contemporary mythology" and this concept inspired Lee. He had always been fascinated by the legends of the Norse Gods and realized that he could use those tales as the basis for his new series centered on the mighty Thor. Unfortunately, Lee had two problems: his growing workload prevented him from actually writing the new series and he had to find somewhere to put it. For the first problem he turned to his younger brother Larry Lieber, a writer and an artist, who had contributed to many Marvel stories over the years. Unlike Lee who preferred to give his artists an outline, Lieber wrote full scripts that described the action and dialogue for every panel in the story. The heroic and glamorous style that had made artist Jack Kirby wrong for Spider-Man was perfect for the qualities of Thor. As for where to put the new series, the cancellation of *Amazing Adult Fantasy* allowed Lee to increase *The Fantastic Four*'s frequency and then launch a new bimonthly title. Realizing that monster books were on their way out, Lee eventually decided to make Thor the lead feature of *Journey Into Mystery* #83.

THE LEGEND HAS COME TRUE! BY THE WILL OF THE GODS, I AM ALIVE! I AM INVINCIBLE! I AM--THOR!!!

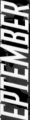

Trained in the Asgardian arts of war, Thor was a true warrior-born who possessed superhuman strength and was utterly fearless in battle.

SEPTEMBER

THE ANT-MAN RETURNS

• *Tales To Astonish* #35

Having created a living god in Thor, Stan Lee now created the complete opposite. He resurrected an earlier concept and the cover of *Tales To Astonish* #35 proudly proclaimed, "You'll gasp in amazement at the return of the Ant-Man!" Hank Pym, the reckless scientist from *Tales To Astonish* #27 (Jan., 1962), was back. After his experiences, Pym had a growing fascination with ants, and later devised a cybernetic helmet to communicate with them and a protective costume to shield him from accidental stings or bites.

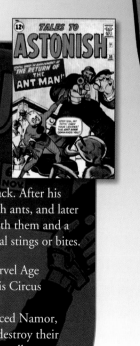

- *The Incredible Hulk* #3 featured the first Marvel Age appearance of the all-new Ringmaster and his Circus of Crime, who briefly captured the Hulk.
- In *The Fantastic Four* #6, Dr. Doom convinced Namor, the Sub-Mariner to join forces with him to destroy their mutual enemies, but he later betrayed his new ally.

OCTOBER

LOKI AND THE GODS OF ASGARD

• *Journey Into Mystery* #85

This story, penned by Larry Lieber, began at the point where Loki, Thor's half-brother and the God of Mischief, had been trapped within a tree until someone shed a tear for him. Causing a leaf to strike the God Heimdall in the eye, Loki got his tear and set out after Thor, against whom he had a virulent grudge. Thor's alter ego, Don Blake, recalled the legends about the wicked God Loki, but he didn't recognize him when they first met. Loki employed magic to battle Thor, but was eventually defeated and returned to Asgard, the home of the Norse Gods connected to the Earth by the Rainbow Bridge called Bifrost.

- The Norse Gods Odin, Balder, and Tyr also made their first appearances in *Journey Into Mystery* #85, although only in a single panel with their backs to the readers.
- The most popular member of the FF, the Human Torch, began a series of solo adventures in *Strange Tales* #101, written by Larry Lieber and drawn by Jack Kirby.

NOVEMBER

THE WIZARD DEBUTS

• *Strange Tales* #102

The Wizard had a humble beginning in a story written by Larry Lieber and drawn by Jack Kirby for *Strange Tales* #102. One of the smartest men in the world, the Wizard was a great inventor and escape artist who became jealous of the Human Torch's fame and so decided to prove his superiority. Defeated, he joined forces with Paste Pot Pete, another of the Torch's enemies, who later changed his name to the Trapster. This partnership eventually led to the formation of the Frightful Four, the evil counterpart to the Fantastic Four. Although the members of the Frightful Four have changed over the years, they continue to present the FF with some of its deadliest challenges.

The Wizard challenged the Human Torch because he was bored with his other accomplishments and needed a new challenge.

- *Journey Into Mystery* #86 was the first time Thor called upon chief God Odin's help and was the time-traveling Zarrko's debut.

A NEW TWO-GUN KID

• *Two-Gun Kid* #60

Since Stan Lee still had room on the publishing schedule for another bimonthly title and both *Kid Colt, Outlaw* and *Rawhide Kid* were maintaining their sales, he decided to try his hand at another western. As with *Rawhide Kid*, Lee and Jack Kirby built a new character around an old title. The new *Two-Gun Kid* followed on from issue #59, which had ended in April 1961, but this new comic combined the traditional western with the Super Hero genre. In *Two-Gun Kid* #60, attorney Matt Hawk obtained the skills to become the masked crime-fighter. This issue also introduced the Kid's love interest, Nancy Carter, and his mentor, Ben Dancer.

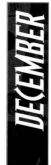

NOVEMBER

THE PUPPET MASTER AND ALICIA MASTERS

• *The Fantastic Four* #8

The Puppet Master (who was later revealed to be Phillip Masters) and his stepdaughter Alicia were introduced in *The Fantastic Four* #8. The Puppet Master discovered that he could control anyone's mind by making a replica of them with his special radioactive clay. He used his blind stepdaughter Alicia in a plot to destroy the Fantastic Four, but the young sculptress soon fell in love with the Thing. Determined to break up the romance, Masters allied himself with the Super Villain Mad Thinker, but the Puppet Master eventually reconciled with Alicia and gave up crime.

The Puppet Master made Alicia impersonate Sue because she resembled her.

DECEMBER

EGGHEAD

• *Tales To Astonish* #38

Hank Pym's greatest enemy first appeared in *Tales To Astonish* #38 in a story by Larry Lieber and Jack Kirby. A super-genius, Egghead turned to crime to eliminate his perpetual boredom. He often employed gadgetry of his own invention and he became obsessed with destroying Ant-Man. Misunderstanding Ant-Man's relationship with his ants, Egghead tried to lead an insect insurrection against Ant-Man, but it backfired on him. He was finally killed when the Avenger Hawkeye caused a gun to explode in his face.

- *Strange Tales Annual* #1 went on sale, featuring assorted old suspense stories.

MEANWHILE IN 1962...

NUCLEAR STANDOFF COOLS

The Cuban Missile Crisis steps down a gear when the USSR agrees to dismantle the missiles based in Cuba and the USA promises to lift its blockade and not invade Cuba.

FIRST BLACK STUDENT AT THE UNIVERSITY OF MISSISSIPPI

After violent clashes and two dead, James Meredith is admitted to the University of Mississippi. But, due to the threat of violence, he is accompanied by Federal Marshals.

FIRST TRANSATLANTIC TELEVISION TRANSMISSION

The first transatlantic television transmission is made via the Telstar satellite: worldwide television and cable networks are now a reality.

A CAN OF TOMATO SOUP

An exhibition in West Hollywood features Warhol's iconic Campbell's soup canvasses. Campbell's Soup Company sends him cases of tomato soup, with their admiration (although they decline to buy a print).

MARILYN MONROE DIES

Film star Marilyn Monroe is found dead in her home after taking an overdose of sleeping pills.

CHEESE & ONION POTATO CHIPS

Golden Wonder is the first food manufacturer to add flavor to potato chips when it introduces a cheese and onion variety.

AND AT THE MOVIES...

Lawrence of Arabia, *David Lean's epic desert blockbuster about the eccentric British officer's guerrilla campaign;* The Manchurian Candidate, *John Frankenheimer's deft political thriller has a Korean POW return to the US as a brainwashed assassin;* To Kill A Mockingbird, *Robert Mulligan's adaptation of Harper Lee's novel sees Gregory Peck's idealistic lawyer defending a black man accused of raping a white woman.*

I HAVEN'T EXACTLY GOT ANY SUPER POWERS BUT I CAN WIGGLE MY EARS REAL GOOD!

1963

THE MARVEL AGE OF COMICS

Super Heroes had accomplished the one goal their villainous counterparts had always failed to—they had conquered the universe! The Marvel Universe! Three monster/suspense titles had already surrendered to the invasion of Super Heroes and the final one, *Tales Of Suspense*, fell with issue #39 in March with the introduction of the invincible Iron Man as its lead feature.

Believing in the importance of fan mail, Stan Lee introduced Marvel's first letters page in March. Although his secretary Flo Steinberg actually wrote most of the answers, Lee used them to establish himself as the voice of Marvel and they even took center stage in a story in *The Fantastic Four* #11. Two issues later, the letters page was expanded and included the first "special announcements" section, which began by thanking readers for their support, declaring the results of a poll against adding new members to the FF, a reminder to pick up Iron Man in *Tales Of Suspense*, and a mention that the Sub-Mariner would return. This section would eventually become the popular "Bullpens Bulletins" feature that would appear in every Marvel comic.

In May, the company finally decided to establish a new brand name and began to call itself Marvel Comics, a name that Lee had often tried to use in the past. It also introduced its unifying now-legendary Marvel corner box on all its covers.

JANUARY

TYRANNUS

• *The Incredible Hulk* #5

Tyrannus was a former Roman Emperor who ruled the underground kingdom of Subterranea and employed a Fountain of Youth that made him virtually immortal. His character was inspired by Ayesha, the immortal female protagonist of H. Rider Haggard's novel *She*. At first, his main interest was in conquering the world, though he would later spend most of the 1970s embroiled in battles with the almost blind but powerful Mole Man for control of Subterranea.

SO! THE DREADED HULK LIES HELPLESS AS A BABE! REST, YOU NEED? YOU SHALL GET NONE HERE! ON YOUR FEET--SLAVE!

Having kidnapped Betty Ross to lure the Hulk to his caverns within the center of Earth, Tyrannus used powerful volcanic gas to subdue and imprison the green goliath.

FICTION OR REALITY?

• *The Fantastic Four* #10

Having previously established that the Human Torch read comic books (May, 1962), Stan Lee and Jack Kirby continued to blur reality and fiction by appearing as themselves in this issue.

FEBRUARY

IMPOSSIBLE MAN DEBUT

• *The Fantastic Four* #11

An alien with the power to morph into any shape or substance he desired, the Impossible Man was hated by readers at first because he was not a serious menace. However, he became popular when writer Roy Thomas exploited the character for comedy by having him visit the Marvel offices in *The Fantastic Four* #176 (Nov., 1976).

CASH? WHAT A STRANGE WORD! WHAT IS CASH?
SAY, ARE YOU TRYIN' TO PULL OUR LEG, PIN-HEAD?
CASH IS WHAT THEY KEEP IN BANKS, MISTER! JUST GO TO A BANK AND ASK FOR SOME! THEY LOVE TO GIVE IT AWAY!

This issue also introduced Willie Lumpkin, the FF's mailman, who was based on a newspaper comic strip that Stan Lee had produced with artist Dan DeCarlo.

MARCH

IRON MAN DEBUT

"You are not facing a wounded, dying man now—or an aged, gentle professor! This is Iron Man who opposes you and all you stand for!"

• *Tales Of Suspense* #39

Set against the background of the Vietnam War, Iron Man signaled the end of Marvel's monster/suspense line when he debuted in *Tales Of Suspense* #39. Stan Lee wanted his new hero to be a wealthy businessman, following the tradition of the pampered playboy that went as far back as the Scarlet Pimpernel. Like Batman's alter ego Bruce Wayne, Tony Stark would be a handsome, successful, and moneyed businessman. However, Stark would also have a terrible secret. The accident that led to his becoming Iron Man also injured his heart. He needed his armored chest plate to stay alive.

Lee discussed the general outline for Iron Man with Larry Lieber, who later wrote a full script for the origin story. Don Heck, an artist who had contributed to many western and monster stories over the years, designed the new character. Since Jack Kirby was the regular cover artist for *Tales Of Suspense*, he did the first cover.

In his first story, Tony Stark was a millionaire industrialist who designed weapons for the United States Army, but his heart became severely damaged when he was captured by Communists. With the help of another prisoner—who later sacrificed himself to save him—Stark designed his life-saving Iron Man armor and in doing so became a nearly unstoppable juggernaut.

Like the Hulk, Iron Man's armor was first colored gray, but printing concerns led it to be converted to golden yellow for his second appearance.

MARCH

THE TEEN BRIGADE FORMS

• *The Incredible Hulk* #6

Kid gangs had been appearing since silent films and were a staple of comics in the 1940s. The Teen Brigade was a network of teenagers formed by Rick Jones. They used ham radios to contact each other whenever anyone needed help and they played a major role in bringing together the Avengers in *The Avengers* #1 (Sept., 1963).

SPIDER-MAN GETS HIS OWN TITLE

• *The Amazing Spider-Man* #1

Thanks to a flood of fan mail, Spider-Man was awarded his own title six months after his first appearance. *Amazing Spider-Man* began as a bimonthly title, but was quickly promoted to a monthly.

The Amazing Spider-Man #1 introduced J. Jonah Jameson, the blustery editor/publisher of the *Daily Bugle*. With his skill at manipulating the media, tendency toward hyperbole, and tightness with a dollar, Jameson was a character that Steve Ditko modeled after his own editor/collaborator, Stan Lee. Jameson first appeared hunched over a typewriter—a sight familiar to anyone who ever worked with Lee. Since the *Daily Bugle* was heavily dependent on pictures, Jameson's crusade against Spider-Man ironically led him to hire a freelance photographer, a high school student named Peter Parker.

J. Jonah Jameson was suspicious of anyone who concealed his identity behind a mask and he didn't believe in vigilante justice. He also didn't believe that anyone could be a hero every day of the week.

THE CHAMELEON DEBUTS

• *The Amazing Spider-Man* #1

Like the silent film star Lon Chaney Sr., the Chameleon was a "man of a thousand faces." A professional criminal, he originally used makeup to change his appearance, but he then had his skin surgically altered so he could take on any appearance at will.

M *Hulk* was not selling well so it was cancelled to make room for *The Amazing Spider-Man*.

M The month the Hulk's title ended, he guest-starred in *The Fantastic Four* #12.

1963

APRIL

THE RED GHOST AND HIS APES ARE ZAPPED

• *The Fantastic Four* #13

With the Cold War's space race dominating the news, Stan Lee and Jack Kirby mixed real world events with comic book fantasy in *The Fantastic Four* #13. Inspired by movies like *King Kong* and *Mighty Joe Young*, apes had become a comic book staple. Familiar with the Fantastic Four's origin, Ivan Kragoff—the Red Ghost—trained a crew of apes to pilot a space ship. Determined to reach the moon before America, he deliberately exposed himself and them to cosmic rays so that they could develop superpowers and become counterparts to the Fantastic Four.

THE WATCHER APPEARS

• *The Fantastic Four* #13

The Fantastic Four #13 also introduced the all-powerful, all-seeing Watcher. A virtually immortal extraterrestrial who observed the phenomena of the universe, Uatu the Watcher lived in the mysterious Blue Area of the Moon, an abandoned alien city that still contained enough atmosphere for the Fantastic Four to breathe. This character served as the inspiration for the Watchers who later observed the battling immortals on the television series *Highlander* and also the Watchers who performed the same function for vampire hunters in the television series *Buffy The Vampire Slayer*.

MAY

A NEW WAR COMIC

• *Sgt. Fury And His Howling Commandos* #1

Convinced that Marvel's personality-driven stories combined with action-oriented artwork could sell any type of comic, Stan Lee somehow persuaded publisher Martin Goodman to try yet another war comic. It was presented as being by "the talented team that brings you the famous Fantastic Four!" Jack Kirby designed the characters and drew the first seven issues and Lee employed the same kind of witty dialogue and outrageous action as the Super Hero titles. The Howling Commandos were seven misfits stationed in England under the command of Captain "Happy Sam" Sawyer who regularly assigned them to missions listed as "impossible" or "suicide." This issue also introduced "Dum-Dum" Dugan and Gabriel Jones, who later joined Fury when he starred in *Nick Fury, Agent of SHIELD*.

KEEP MOVIN', YOU LUNKHEADS!! NOBODY LIVES FOREVER! SO GIT THE LEAD OUT AND FOLLOW ME! WE GOT US A WAR TO WIN!

MAY

THE VULTURE SWOOPS

• *The Amazing Spider-Man* #2

"He strikes from above—silently and without warning! For he is the Vulture!" Adrian Toomes was an inventor who created an electromagnetic harness that enabled him to fly. Betrayed by his business partner, he then turned to crime. Introduced in the lead story of *The Amazing Spider-Man* #2 and created by Stan Lee and Steve Ditko, the Vulture was the first in a long line of animal-inspired Super Villains that were destined to battle everyone's favorite web-swinger.

THE TERRIBLE TINKERER APPEARS

• *The Amazing Spider-Man* #2

Phineas Mason, aka the Tinkerer, appeared to be a harmless old man who ran a small repair shop. But, he was actually a genius who specialized in creating advanced gadgetry for the criminal underworld. He has continued to menace the webhead over the years since his first appearance.

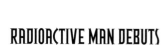

Working with movie stunt men, the Tinkerer disguised himself and his gang as aliens in an elaborate plot to blackmail the government.

JUNE

RADIOACTIVE MAN DEBUTS

• *Journey Into Mystery* #93

Radioactive Man was created when Dr. Chen Lu deliberately exposed himself to radiation. He wanted to gain enough power to punish Thor for stopping an invasion of India by the People's Republic of China. Radioactive Man later joined the original Masters of Evil and the Thunderbolts.

THE MAD THINKER DEBUTS

• *The Fantastic Four* #15

With his fabulous brain and infallible computers, the man called the Mad Thinker believed he could seize control of New York City and declare it an independent nation with himself as its ruler. While mad scientists were nothing new, Stan Lee and Jack Kirby gave their new creation the ability to predict events down to the exact second. The Thinker eventually allowed himself to be imprisoned and he continues to run his criminal operations from behind bars.

Using Reed Richards' notes, the Mad Thinker created a living android who possessed incredible strength.

JULY

THE WONDROUS WASP

• *Tales To Astonish* #44

Destined to marry and later divorce Hank Pym, Janet Van Dyne made her debut as the Wasp in *Tales To Astonish* #44. Based on a story idea by Stan Lee and a script by H.E. Huntley, the Wasp was designed and drawn by Jack Kirby. H.E. Huntley was actually the pen name of Ernie Hart, the writer and artist best know for creating Timely Comics' Super Rabbit. Aside from being the Ant-Man/Giant-Man's partner, the Wasp also became a charter member of the Avengers and was even chair of the group during the 1980s.

DR. OCTOPUS

• *The Amazing Spider-Man* #3

Created by Stan Lee and Steve Ditko, Dr. Octopus shared many traits with Peter Parker. They were both shy, both interested in science, and both had trouble relating to women. They also both gained amazing powers from a scientific accident involving radiation, which led to them coming out of their shells and deciding that no one was going to push them around anymore. Otto Octavius even looked like a grown up Peter Parker. Lee and Ditko intended Otto to be the man Peter might have become if he hadn't been raised with a sense of responsibility. Dr. Octopus was also the first Super Villain to defeat Spider-Man on their first encounter.

The Human Torch guest-starred in *The Amazing Spider-Man* #3 and it was his speech to the students of Midtown High that inspired Peter Parker to face his fears and challenge Dr. Octopus to a second battle despite his defeat the first time.

DR. STRANGE

• *Strange Tales* #110

The sales of *Strange Tales* had dramatically increased with the addition of the Human Torch as its lead feature. Aside from the Torch, the magazine continued to carry two five-page mystery/suspense stories. If one Super Hero feature improved sales, Stan Lee wondered, what would two do?

Lee was a fan of a radio drama called *Chandu The Magician* when he was a child, and so he decided that his new Super Hero feature would star a magician. Since Lee was enjoying his collaboration with Steve Ditko on *The Amazing Spider-Man*, he decided to assign the new feature to Ditko, who usually handled at least one of the backups in *Strange Tales*. They discussed Lee's ideas for the character and the general direction for the first story. Ditko designed the look of Dr. Strange and visually laid out the story without a written plot or script.

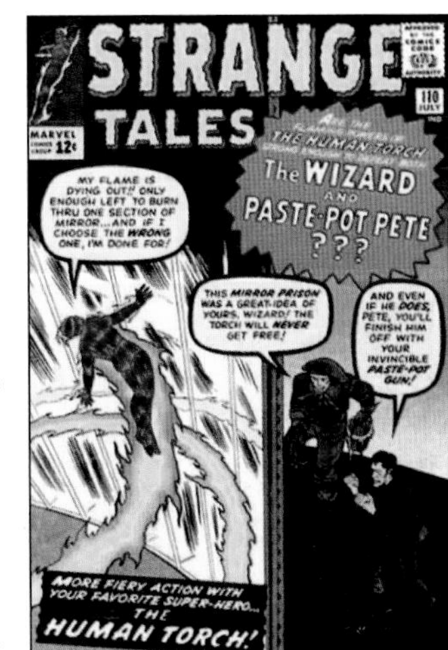

When Dr. Strange first appeared in *Strange Tales* #110, it was only clear that he dabbled in black magic and had the ability to project his consciousness into an astral form that could leave his physical body. It wasn't until *Strange Tales* #115 (Dec., 1963) that readers learned that he had been a surgeon who lost the ability to operate after suffering terrible nerve damage in a car accident. Like Dr. Droom before him, Strange went to Tibet where an ancient mystic taught him the secrets of sorcery.

- The Ancient One, Dr. Strange's mentor, and Wong, his loyal manservant, were also introduced in *Strange Tales* #110.
- Nightmare, the ruler of his own Nightmare World within the Dream Dimension, also debuted in *Strange Tales* #110.

KALA, QUEEN OF THE NETHERWORLD DEBUTS

• *Tales Of Suspense* #43

Inspired by Ayesha, the immortal female protagonist of H. Rider Haggard's novel *She*, the character of Kala was the queen of an underground kingdom. She later achieved fame when she battled both the Roman Emperor Tyrannus and the scientist Super Villain Mole Man for control of Subterranea.

AUGUST

BARON MORDO

• *Strange Tales* #111

Dr. Strange's archenemy, Baron Mordo was introduced in *Strange Tales* #111. A former student of the Ancient One, Mordo was eventually banished for using sorcery to gain personal power.

He has often allied himself with other magical entities like the dreaded Dormammu in his attempts to destroy Dr. Strange.

SEPTEMBER

THE AVENGERS ARE FORMED

"And thus is born one of the greatest Super Hero teams of all time! Powerful! Unpredictable! Brought together by a strange quirk of fate, the Avengers are on the march, and a new dimension is added to the Marvel Galaxy of Stars!"

• *The Avengers* #1

The Marvel Super Heroes were growing in popularity and so were their sales. The rising profits convinced Independent News—the company that distributed Marvel's comics—to allow another expansion. Instead of being held at nine to eleven titles per month, Marvel could now produce ten to fourteen, so Stan Lee was told to add two new bimonthly Super Hero books.

The first title was a no-brainer. As soon as Marvel began to produce solo Super Heroes, the readers demanded to see these heroes team-up with each other. They wanted Spider-Man to meet Ant-Man and Thor to visit Iron Man. It had been Martin Goodman's conversation about Justice League Of America that had originally sparked the rebirth of Super Heroes at Marvel, so Lee realized he could give the readers what they wanted by simply doing his own version of the JLA. This title would also provide him with a regular home for the Hulk, whose own comic had been canceled. Jack Kirby was the logical choice to pencil the new series. He had already drawn all of the characters, although some only on covers. Also, Lee knew that he only had to give Kirby a few rough story ideas and that Kirby could easily plot the panel-by-panel action by himself. Filled with some wonderful visual action, *The Avengers* #1 has a very simple story: the Norse God Loki tricked the Hulk into going on a rampage. In response, Rick Jones and his Teen Brigade tried to contact the Fantastic Four for help. However, Loki redirected the radio signal so Thor would hear it, in the expectation that he would battle Loki. But Iron Man, Ant-Man, and the Wasp also responded. The heroes eventually learned about Loki's involvement and united with the Hulk to form the Avengers.

Although the Hulk joined the team at the end of The Avengers *#1, by the end of the second issue he had quit and teamed up with the Sub-Mariner. In issue #3, he battled against his former teammates.*

BLIZZARD DEBUTS

• *Tales Of Suspense* #45

Iron Man's longtime enemy—Blizzard—was called Jack Frost when he first appeared in *Tales Of Suspense* #45. Covered in ice and with the ability to project intense cold, snow, and ice, he also appeared in the same month as Iceman in *X-Men* #1.

SEPTEMBER

BUT WHEN I WAS YOUNG, NORMAL PEOPLE FEARED ME, DISTRUSTED ME, I REALIZED THE HUMAN RACE IS NOT YET READY TO ACCEPT THOSE WITH EXTRA POWERS! SO I DECIDED TO BUILD A HAVEN... A SCHOOL FOR X-MEN!

Professor Charles Xavier was one of the most powerful telepaths in the world and he believed that mutants could coexist peacefully with mankind.

THE X-MEN GATHER TOGETHER

"Never within the memory of man, was there a 'class' such as this! Never was there a 'teacher' such as Professor X! And never were there 'students' such as the... 'X-Men'."

• *The X-Men* #1

Stan Lee still needed another new bimonthly Super Hero title. All of his previous heroes had gained their powers from outside events: Spider-Man had been bitten by a radioactive spider, the Fantastic Four had been exposed to cosmic rays, and Iron Man had been injured and taken prisoner. Lee wanted to find a new source of super-powers. The answer was obvious. What if his new heroes were simply born with their powers?

Lee immediately called in Jack Kirby and they began to discuss the new series. Roughly based on Charles Darwin's theory of evolution, the two men reasoned that the human race was destined to evolve. What if it evolved through a series of mutations? What if humanity feared and hated all mutants: both the good and the bad? What if these mutants gained their amazing powers with the onset of puberty? Knowing that most teenagers felt like freaks and outsiders, Lee and Kirby pushed the metaphor by setting the series in a school for "gifted students."

Lee wanted to call the new series *The Mutants*, but publisher Martin Goodman vetoed the idea. He didn't think kids would know what a mutant was. Since his new characters would be born with an extra power, Lee eventually settled on the *The X-Men*.

The X-Men #1 introduced the world to Professor Charles Xavier and his teenage students: Cyclops, Beast, Angel, Iceman, and Marvel Girl. Magneto, the master of magnetism and future leader of the evil mutants, also appeared.

Magneto believed that humans had lost the evolutionary race and that mutants were destined to rule the Earth.

The X-Men #1 also revealed a version of the Danger Room, a place that could computer generate any surroundings imaginable, in which the X-Men could practice their skills. This room enabled Lee and Kirby to establish visually how the X-Men's powers worked.

THE SANDMAN APPEARS

• *The Amazing Spider-Man* #4

Beginning his crime career in *The Amazing Spider-Man* #4, the Sandman was able to transform all or part of his body into a sand-like material and form any shape. He later moved up to battling the Fantastic Four and became a charter member of the Frightful Four, but then a near-death experience made him renounce crime through the 1980s and 1990s. He even became a crime-fighter with Silver Sable's Wild Pack and a probationary member of the Avengers before returning to his old ways in the 2000s.

Sandman could alter his density, making himself as soft and pliant as a pile of loose sand or as hard and solid as a rock.

- Betty Brant—J. Jonah Jameson's secretary and Peter Parker's first real girlfriend—debuted in *The Amazing Spider-Man* #4.
- Super-Skrull was first sent by the Skrull Emperor to destroy the world's greatest super-team in *Fantastic Four* #20.

"TALES OF ASGARD"

• *Journey Into Mystery* #97

Believing that two Super Hero strips in a comic would sell better than one (the same logic that had led to the creation of Dr. Strange), Stan Lee began "Tales Of Asgard" in *Journey Into Mystery* #97. These backup stories originally began with updated versions of Norse mythology, but later switched to the adventures of a younger Thor and his friends in Asgard.

- The Plantman, who was able to control all plant life and make human duplicates out of plants, first appeared in *Strange Tales* #113.

NOVEMBER

ANT-MAN BECOMES GIANT-MAN

• *Tales To Astonish* #49

Realizing that an insect-sized hero with the strength of a regular human paled in comparison to his other superstars, Stan Lee drastically increased Ant-Man's powers so he could grow to giant-size proportions.

MOLECULE MAN IS CREATED

• *The Fantastic Four* #20.

Owen Reece, a clumsy lab assistant, became Molecule Man when he inadvertently gained the power to control and reshape matter at the molecular level. He later figured prominently in the twelve-issue, 1980s series *Secret Wars*.

THE LIZARD MEETS SPIDEY

• *The Amazing Spider-Man* #6

Half-man! Half-reptile! The Lizard presented a unique problem to our friendly webhead from the moment they first met. As Dr. Curtis Connors, he was a loving family man who was both friend and mentor to Peter Parker. But as the Lizard, he was a savage beast with the sole intention of destroying humanity so that reptiles could inherit the Earth.

A FAKE CAPTAIN AMERICA

• *Strange Tales* #114

As the Human Torch had been instrumental in bringing back the Sub-Mariner in *The Fantastic Four* #4 (May, 1962), it seemed only natural that he would also help usher in Captain America. Unfortunately, this Cap proved to be an imposter, a skilled acrobat that the Torch had fought in *Strange Tales* #106 (March, 1963).

DECEMBER

THE HATE-MONGER ARRIVES

• *Fantastic Four* #21

A bigot and terrorist, the Hate-Monger employed an army of storm troopers and used a weapon called the Hate Ray, which spread hatred among all those it targeted.

Nick Fury also featured in this issue. Having been promoted to Colonel, he foreshadowed his future as an agent of SHIELD, when he enlisted the Fantastic Four in his struggle against the Hate-Monger.

THE SUB-MARINER IS CROWNED KING

• *Fantastic Four Annual* #1

The Sub-Mariner was finally reunited with his undersea people and crowned King of Atlantis. This issue also introduced his future wife, Lady Dorma, and his future enemy, the warlord Krang.

MEANWHILE IN 1963...

JFK ASSASSINATED

America reels at the fatal shooting of President Kennedy as he sat in an open car on his way to a political festival in Dallas, Texas. Lyndon B. Johnson is sworn in as the thirty-sixth President.

MARTIN LUTHER KING: "I HAVE A DREAM"

At a civil rights demonstration of two-hundred thousand people in Washington, the Reverend Martin Luther King addresses the crowds, sharing his ambitions for black and white Americans to exist harmoniously as equals.

FIRST WOMAN IN SPACE

In the next stage of the space race, Lieutenant Valentina Tereshkova follows in the footsteps of fellow Russian Yuri Gagarin and is the first woman to orbit the earth.

SUPERHUMAN FEAT FOR RUNNER

US athlete Bob Hayes sets a world record for running 100 yards (91.44 meters), completing the distance in 9.1 seconds.

ALCATRAZ CLOSES

The Alcatraz Island federal penitentiary in San Francisco Bay—known as "The Rock"—closes after twenty-nine years of housing prisoners, including Robert Stroud, nicknamed the "Birdman of Alcatraz", and Al Capone.

WHAAM!

Roy Lichtenstein paints Whaam!*, a classic of the pop art movement, which takes direct inspiration from the art of comic books.* Whaam! *shows a fighter plane shooting down an enemy aircraft, accompanied by the onomatopoetic wording "Whaam!"*

THE SMILEY FACE APPEARS

The cultural icon, the yellow smiley face, has modest beginnings when it is created by The State Mutual Life Assurance Company to boost employee morale and to encourage smiling when dealing with customers.

THE FEMININE MYSTIQUE PUBLISHES

Betty Friedan's ground-breaking work about women's place in society ignites the Second Wave of feminism.

A ZIP CODE FOR EVERY ADDRESS IN THE US

The five-digit codes take effect across America.

AND AT THE MOVIES...

The Pink Panther, *Blake Edwards' classic farce with Peter Sellers as the bumbling, stumbling Inspector Clouseau trying to catch a notorious thief;* The Great Escape, *a thrilling war film set in a German POW camp with an all-star cast, including Steve McQueen;* Cleopatra, *an expensive exercise in costume drama that nearly bankrupted the studio and imperial love-in between Richard Burton and Elizabeth Taylor.*

AS HIS FIRST TV SPECTACULAR ENDS, PETER PARKER BREATHES THE FIRST SWEET SCENT OF FAME AND SUCCESS!
I'M FROM LIFE! WE'LL PAY ANY PRICE FOR A PICTURE SPREAD!
SIGN WITH ME! I'LL PUT YOU IN THE MOVIES!
WAIT! WE WANT AN INTERVIEW!
SEE MY AGENT, BOYS! I'M BUSY!

WHEW! RID OF 'EM AT LAST!
HEY! WHAT'S GOIN' ON??
STOP! THIEF! STO
HIM! IF HE MAKES IT TO THE ELEVATOR HE'LL GET AWAY!

MADE IT!

I'M SAFE NOW! THAT COP CAN NEVER GET DOWN TO THE LOBBY AS FAST AS I CAN IN THIS HIGH-SPEED EX-PRESS ELEVATOR. LUCKY THAT GOON IN A COSTUME DIDN'T STOP ME!

WHAT'S WITH YOU, MISTER?? ALL YOU HADDA DO WAS TRIP HIM, OR HOLD HIM JUST FOR A MINUTE!
SORRY, PAL! THAT YOUR JOB! I'M TH
BEING PUSHED ARO
--BY ANYONE! FRO
NOW ON I JUST LO
OUT FOR NUMBER O
--THAT MEANS M

I OUGHTTA RUN YOU IN--
SAVE YOUR BREATH, BUDDY! I'VE GOT THINGS TO DO!

AND, A FEW HOURS LATER...
PETER, YOU KNOW THAT MICROSCOPE YOU'VE ALWAYS WANTED? YOUR UNCLE AND I BOUGHT IT FOR YOU THIS AFTERNOON!
GOSH THAT'S TERRIFIC!

YOU'RE THE GREATEST FAMILY ANY FELLA EVER HAD!
THEY'RE THE ONLY O
WHO'VE EVER BEEN K
TO ME! I'LL SEE TO
THAT THEY'RE ALWA
HAPPY, BUT THE RE
OF THE WORLD CAN
HANG FOR ALL I CA

Amazing Fantasy #15 (Aug. 1962) written by Stan Lee, art by Steve Ditko.
Whether by accident or design, Stan Lee and Steve Ditko struck gold when they created Peter Parker. Like many of the readers, Peter was insecure around women, faced high-school bullies, and felt like an outsider. He was considered a nerd by his peers and he hated being "pushed around" by authority figures. In his origin story, Spider-Man experienced every emotion—from fear when he was first bitten by the spider, to elation when he discovered his powers, and then to crippling guilt when he realized that his lack of responsibility in stopping a fleeing burglar had resulted in the death of his beloved Uncle Ben.

THE DAYS THAT FOLLOW, THE SPIDERMAN BECOMES THE SENSATION OF THE NATION!
RMAN SLATED
EW TV SERIES!
Chronicle
ERMAN WINS
WBIZ AWARD!
The VIEWER
ERMAN PLAYS
ACKED HOUSE!
Daily Voice
HO IS THE
IDERMAN?

ONE EVENING AS PETER
ER RETURNS HOME FROM
RSONAL APPEARANCE...

A POLICE CAR! IN FRONT OF OUR HOUSE! WHAT CAN BE WRONG??

BAD NEWS, SON--YOUR UNCLE HAS BEEN SHOT--MURDERED!
UNCLE BEN --DEAD! NO! NO! IT CAN'T BE!

WHO DID IT?? WHO SHOT HIM??
IT WAS A BURGLAR--YOUR UNCLE SURPRISED HIM! BUT DON'T WORRY, LAD WE'VE GOT HIM TRAPPED! HE'S IN THE OLD ACME WAREHOUSE AT THE WATERFRONT! WE'LL GET HIM!

'RE AUNT IS
XT DOOR--
NEIGHBORS
E LOOKING
FTER HER!
WAIT--
I'VE GOT TO GO! I'VE GOT TO GET HIM!

I KNOW THE OLD ACME WAREHOUSE! IT'S BEEN DE-SERTED FOR YEARS! A KILLER COULD HOLD OFF AN ARMY IN THAT GLOOMY OLD PLACE!

BUT HE WON'T HOLD OFF--SPIDERMAN!

AS FOR WHO I AM, YOU CAN
JUST CALL ME... DAREDEVIL!!

1964

MARVEL COMICS IN HYPERDRIVE

From the moment the company officially declared itself Marvel Comics in May 1963, Stan Lee kicked into hyperbole overdrive. He began to promote the "Marvel Universe" and to refer to the "Marvel Age of Comics." His style of creating stories was even dubbed the "Marvel Style"—he discussed plots with the artists, who had the responsibility of fleshing out the action as they drew the artwork, before he wrote the dialogue. He presented the company like a secret society, an organization that only catered to the most discerning comic book readers. (Although, of course, anyone with access to a newsstand and twelve cents could join.) He also used slogans like, "Face Front, True Believer!," "Make Mine Marvel!," and "Excelsior!" on covers and in the letters pages of the comics. Readers followed his lead and used the same slogans whenever they contacted the company.

Although Marvel was fully committed to Super Heroes, it still published five teenage/humor comics, three westerns, and a war title.

Aside from scripting most of the comics, Lee also found time to write two black-and-white magazines—*You Don't Say* and *Monsters To Laugh With*—for Marvel publisher/owner Martin Goodman's Magazine Management division, which both consisted of still photos with funny lines of dialogue.

JANUARY

THE BLOB APPEARS

• *The X-Men* #3

What's more powerful: an immovable object or an irresistible force? Stan Lee and Jack Kirby attempted to answer this question when they created the Blob. Immovable and virtually indestructible, Fred J. Dukes earned his living as a sideshow freak in a traveling circus until he discovered he was a mutant. He refused X-Men membership and tried to destroy the uncanny teenagers. He later joined Magneto's Brotherhood of Evil Mutants but ultimately tried to redeem himself by signing on with the government's Freedom Force.

The Blob was practically impossible to injure. His skin could not be punctured and his body was able to absorb the impact of anything smaller than a bazooka shell.

BARON VON STRUCKER

• *Sgt. Fury And His Howling Commandos* #5

Modeled after the Aryan Superman, Baron Wolfgang Von Strucker was the leader of the Nazi Death-Head Squad, who challenged Nick Fury to a duel in *Sgt. Fury And His Howling Commandos* #5. The Baron would go on to form his Blitzkrieg Squad, the Nazi counterpart to the Howling Commandos, and would later regularly battle Fury's security organization SHIELD as the leader of the evil group HYDRA.

When they first met, Strucker challenged Fury to a personal duel, but drugged him to guarantee victory.

FEBRUARY

ELECTRO DEBUTS

• *The Amazing Spider-Man* #9

The Master of Electricity surged on the scene in *The Amazing Spider-Man* #9 as a menace so powerful that even Spider-Man's strength was useless against him. Max Dillon suffered from an inferiority complex and bolstered his low ego by using his newfound electrical powers to become the ultimate bully. He was a founding member of the Sinister Six and even served a brief stint with the Frightful Four.

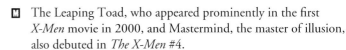

MANDARIN DEBUT

• *Tales Of Suspense* #50

Deep within the Valley of Spirits in the People's Republic of China stands the mysterious Palace of the Star Dragon, the home and headquarters of the most evil genius of all—the Mandarin! Following the tradition of Sax Rohmer's Dr. Fu Manchu and Atlas' own Yellow Claw, the Mandarin first appeared in *Tales Of Suspense* #50 in a story written by Stan Lee and illustrated by Don Heck. The Asian counterpart to Tony Stark's Iron Man, the Mandarin's goal was to conquer the world using advanced technology. He also possessed ten rings of extraterrestrial origin that granted him fantastic powers.

- "The Return Of Zarrko, The Tomorrow Man" in *Journey Into Mystery* #101 was the first time a thirteen-page lead story did not conclude but was continued in the following issue.

THE SCARLET WITCH AND QUICKSILVER

• *The X-Men* #4

Having already created a few reluctant Super Heroes like Spider-Man and the Thing, Stan Lee and Jack Kirby decided to try their hands at a pair of reluctant Super Villains when they created the Scarlet Witch and Quicksilver in *The X-Men* #4. Pietro Maximoff (Quicksilver) was a mutant born with super-speed and his twin sister Wanda (the Scarlet Witch) had the ability to cast hex bolts that altered probability and caused weird incidents, like objects suddenly falling apart, flying across a room, or bursting into flames.

The twins started out as members of Magneto's original Brotherhood of Evil Mutants, but eventually followed their true natures and joined the Avengers. They were also surprised to learn that Magneto was their father in *The Avengers* #185-187 (July-Aug., 1979).

THE ENFORCERS

• *The Amazing Spider-Man* #10

Rather than have Spider-Man battle the usual faceless thugs, Stan Lee and Steve Ditko introduced the Enforcers in *The Amazing Spider-Man* #10. The super-strong Ox, the rope-swinging Montana, and the agile martial artist Fancy Dan were hired muscle who went on to work for the Green Goblin, the Kingpin of Crime, the mysterious crime lord known as the Big Man, and for other assorted crime bosses. This issue also introduced Frederick Foswell, a *Daily Bugle* reporter, who was later revealed to be the Big Man.

MARCH

- The Leaping Toad, who appeared prominently in the first *X-Men* movie in 2000, and Mastermind, the master of illusion, also debuted in *The X-Men* #4.
- Featuring a two-part battle with the Hulk, *Fantastic Four* #24 contained the first twenty-two-page Marvel comic story that extended beyond a single issue.

CAPTAIN AMERICA IS BACK

"Step forward Captain America! Your rightful place is here... among the Avengers."

• *The Avengers* #4

"Captain America lives again!" announced the cover of *The Avengers* #4. A mere five months after his imposter had appeared in *Strange Tales* #114, the real Cap was back. Because it normally takes three to four months to prepare a comic book for publication, the decision to bring the real Cap back would have been made soon after *Strange Tales* #114 published and was probably influenced by the very positive deluge of fan mail. Since Jack Kirby had co-created Cap with his then-partner Joe Simon, and Stan Lee's first published work was a text story in *Captain America Comics* #3 (May, 1941), both men had a personal stake in the character.

Completely ignoring his brief 1950s' resurrection in the Atlas Comics, Cap was found frozen in ice where he had been since the death of his partner Bucky Barnes at the end of World War II. During the story, Cap was confronted by the Sub-Mariner. Although they had both been members of the All-Winners Squad from the 1940s, neither character seemed to recognize the other.

Cap's greatest power was his ability to find a way to triumph in the face of overwhelming odds.

APRIL

THE BLACK WIDOW

YOU SENT FOR ME, COMRADE LEADER?

• *Tales Of Suspense* #52

Natasha Alianovna Romanova, aka the Black Widow, was a Russian spy assigned to capture American industrialist Tony Stark (the Iron Man's alter ego). Her story was plotted by Stan Lee, written by N. Korok (the pen name of former Timely and Atlas writer/artist Don Rico), and drawn by Don Heck. A Marvel-version of the famous Mata Hari, the Black Widow was also a highly skilled gymnast and master of the martial arts. During the course of her career, Natasha romanced both Hawkeye and Daredevil, defected to the West, joined SHIELD, formed the Champions super-team, and even served as an Avenger. She clashed with Yelena Belova, a younger super-spy, who also called herself the Black Widow.

APRIL

THE ENCHANTRESS DEBUTS

• *Journey Into Mystery* #103

Amora, the Norse version of the Roman Goddess of love, Venus, had long desired to conquer the heart of the mighty Thor and leapt at the chance in *Journey Into Mystery* #103. An enthrallingly beautiful woman who was also an accomplished sorceress, the Enchantress often teamed-up with the Executioner, who was hopelessly in love with her. Although she joined Baron Zemo's Masters of Evil, her ultimate—but unfulfilled—goal was always to marry Thor and rule Asgard, the home of the Norse Gods, at Thor's side.

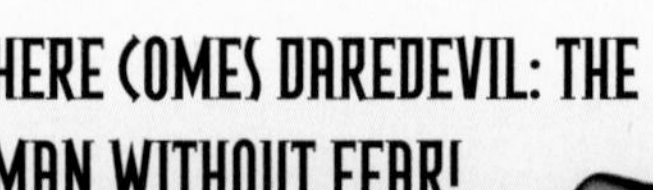

HERE COMES DAREDEVIL: THE MAN WITHOUT FEAR!

"Whenever I don this costume, I'll no longer be Matt Murdock! But I'll need a new name! What if the kids in the old neighborhood could see me now!! The kids who taunted me... called me 'Daredevil'! Wait! That's it!!"

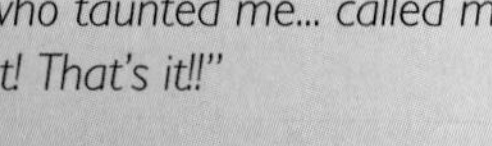

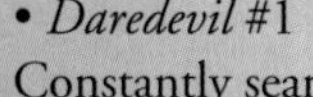

• *Daredevil* #1

Constantly searching for new ways to twist the Super Hero formula, Stan Lee had already introduced a number of characters who possessed great powers combined with a weakness or two to keep them in check. He decided to reverse this process and start with a character who had a great weakness: a Super Hero whose powers only served to compensate for a pre-existing handicap. Matt Murdock would be blind, but would possess heightened senses that allowed him to function as well as anyone else. Years of training would make him a gifted gymnast and fighter. A dedication to justice would lead him into becoming a costumed hero. Stan Lee chose the name Daredevil because it evoked swashbucklers and circus daredevils, and he assigned Bill Everett, the creator of the Sub-Mariner, to design and draw *Daredevil* #1.

This issue also introduced Franklin "Foggy" Nelson, Murdock's college roommate and best friend. They attended Columbia University and then Harvard Law School together. The two formed their own private law practice after graduating. In the movie *Daredevil* (2003), Foggy was played by Jon Favreau who later directed *Iron Man* (2008).

MY NAME IS KAREN PAGE, MR. MURDOCK! I HOPE YOU'LL BE PLEASED WITH ME!
HER VOICE IS LIKE MUSIC! FROM THE SOUND, SHE'S FIVE-FEET-FOUR, YOUNG. AND I KNOW SHE'S LOVELY!

Matt and Foggy's first secretary was Karen Page. They were both immediately attracted to her, but when she chose Matt, Foggy nobly stepped aside.

Usually disguised as Murdock's cane, Daredevil's billy club separated into two parts which could be used as fighting batons.

April

THE EXECUTIONER DEBUT

• *Journey Into Mystery* #103

The son of an Asgardian Goddess and a Storm Giant, Skurge, aka the Executioner, was a massive misfit and one of Asgard's deadliest warriors. His love for the Enchantress led him to battle Thor in *Journey Into Mystery* #103 and he later become a member of the original Masters of Evil just to be near her. However, Skurge eventually regained his honor when he sacrificed himself to save Thor from being trapped in the land of the dead in *Thor* #362 (Dec., 1985).

YOU HAVEN'T BEATEN ME YET! I CAN STILL CUT THROUGH SUB-SPACE ITSELF. PUTTING EVEN YOU IN ANOTHER UNIVERSE FROM WHICH YOU SHALL NEVER ESCAPE!

July

THE GREEN GOBLIN APPEARS

• *The Amazing Spider-Man* #14

When the Green Goblin soared into the webhead's life, Stan Lee and Steve Ditko didn't bother to discuss his secret identity. They just knew they had an interesting character to add to Spider-Man's growing gallery of villains and figured that they could solve the mystery when the time came. There is evidence that Ditko had always intended the Goblin to be Norman Osborn, who appears as a background character in *The Amazing Spider-Man* #23 (April, 1965) and is introduced as Harry Osborn's father in issue #37 (June, 1966). However, his origin as the Green Goblin wasn't revealed until issue #40 (Sep., 1966). He was one of Spider-Man's most popular foes and even featured in the first Spider-Man movie in 2002.

THE MASTERS OF EVIL UNITE

• *The Avengers* #6

The Masters of Evil, the Avengers' evil counterparts, launched their first attack in *The Avengers* #6. The team originally consisted of the Mysterious Melter (*Tales Of Suspense* #47), the Black Knight (*Tales To Astonish* #52), Radioactive Man (*Journey Into Mystery* #93), and Baron Zemo, a never-before-seen Captain America villain. Although Zemo was a new creation, he claimed the credit for the death of Bucky Barnes and the events that led to Captain America's icy imprisonment in *The Avengers* #4.

SORRY, THEY GOT AWAY, ZEMO! THEY WERE JUST TOO FAST FOR US!
WE'D BETTER PICK UP THEIR TRAIL BEFORE THEY FIND A SOLUTION FOR ADHESIVE X!!
A SOLUTION FOR ADHESIVE X!! I NEVER THOUGHT OF THAT! IF ANYONE CAN FIND IT, THE AVENGERS CAN! AND, IF I CAN STEAL IT FROM THEM... !!

August

KRAVEN THE HUNTER

• *The Amazing Spider-Man* #15

Kraven was a cross between Tarzan and famous wild-animal hunters like Clive Beatty and Frank Buck. His real name was Sergei Kravinoff and he was the half-brother of the Chameleon. Kraven tested his skills in the most dangerous game of all when he first challenged Spider-Man.

August

... AND INSTEAD, THE GREY GARGOYLE SHALL MAKE HIS FIRST PUBLIC APPEARANCE AS I GO TO THE PLACE WHERE I SAW THOR FLY WITH THE STONE TAXI DRIVER!

THE GREY GARGOYLE STRIKES

Journey Into Mystery #107

An airliner arrived from France and the ground crew was startled to discover that all of the passengers and crew had been transformed into stone! French chemist Paul Duval became the Grey Gargoyle, one of Thor's most powerful foes when he gained the power to temporarily convert human flesh into solid rock, like a modern day Medusa.

September

KANG, THE CONQUEROR!

• *The Avengers* #8

Time travel had fascinated writers of speculative fiction ever since H.G. Wells wrote *The Time Machine*, so Stan Lee and Jack Kirby introduced their own master of time in *The Avengers* #8. Previously introduced in *Fantastic Four* #19 (Oct., 1963) as Rama-Tut, Kang was a time traveler from an alternate future who assumed his new name when he challenged the Avengers. In *The Avengers* #10, Lee and Dick Ayers created another master of time called Immortus. Time travel can be very confusing and writer Roy Thomas later revealed that Immortus was actually another of Kang's identities, along with a third called the Scarlet Centurion. For years, Kang believed he was related to Dr. Doom, but writer John Byrne eventually explained that he was actually descended from Reed Richards.

- Dr. Octopus, the Vulture, Electro, Sandman, Kraven, and Mysterio pooled their powers against the wall-crawler in *The Amazing Spider-Man Annual* #1.
- As readers flocked to Marvel's Super Heroes, Lee reprinted the origins of some of his most popular characters like Spider-Man, the Fantastic Four, and the Hulk in *Marvel Tales Annual* #1.

SO, LET IRON MAN... AND EVERY COSTUMED ADVENTURER LOOK TO HIS LAURELS!! FOR HAWKEYE IS ABOUT TO MAKE THEM ALL LOOK SICK!

HAWKEYE APPEARS

• *Tales Of Suspense* #57

An orphan who ran away to join a traveling carnival, Clint Barton was mentored by Jacques Duquesne, the man destined to be the Swordsman. Barton studied archery until he became the world's greatest marksman and was later inspired by Iron Man to become the Super Hero Hawkeye. After designing a costume for himself, he stopped a jewelry store robbery, but a case of mistaken identity led the police to assume he was part of the gang. The Black Widow saved him from capture but also tricked him into fighting Iron Man. Hawkeye later cleared his name and even became an Avenger. He even set up and led the team's West Coast branch.

OCTOBER

A NEW HULK SERIES

• *Tales To Astonish* #60

Still restricted to publishing a limited number of titles, Stan Lee had a problem. He had created a number of Super Heroes who didn't have their own magazines and readers were demanding to see more of them. Remembering how he had added Dr. Strange to *Strange Tales* and "Tales of Asgard" to *Journey Into Mystery*, he decided to produce two regular Super Hero stories together in one title. The first of these split books was *Tales To Astonish* #60. As well as featuring Giant-Man, it introduced a new series—The Incredible Hulk—starring the famous character.

OCTOBER

SIMON WILLIAMS BECOMES WONDER MAN

• *The Avengers* #9

Created to infiltrate and destroy the Avengers, Wonder Man ultimately sacrificed himself to save them. In a vain attempt to compete with Stark Industries, businessman Simon Williams drove his company into bankruptcy in *The Avengers* #9. Desperate to get revenge on Tony Stark (aka Iron Man), Williams allowed Baron Zemo to transform him into a living engine of destruction. As Wonder Man, he was given the strength of Giant-Man and fists that could equal the power of Thor's unstoppable hammer, however, he later repented and aided the Avengers against Zemo. A side effect of his transformation caused him to fall into a coma-like sleep that made him appear dead. He was eventually resurrected in the 1970s and formally joined the Avengers team.

Thanks to Baron Zemo, Wonder Man's entire body became saturated with ionic energy that prevented him from ageing and made him virtually immortal.

NOVEMBER

THE DREAD DORMAMMU

• *Strange Tales* #126

Dormammu was a demon-like, extradimensional entity with an almost unlimited hunger for power. He first battled Dr. Strange in *Strange Tales* #126. Having conquered countless magical dimensions, Dormammu was determined to add the Earth's plane of reality to his empire and often returned to threaten humankind.

Unlike human sorcerers, who could only manipulate the magical energy that surrounded them, Dormammu could produce a seemingly endless supply of his own magical energy.

- Clea, Dr. Strange's longtime girlfriend from the Dark Dimension, debuted in *Strange Tales* #126.
- *Fantastic Four Annual* #2 revealed that Dr. Doom had been a college classmate of Reed Richards, who had tried to dissuade Doom from the experiment that scarred his face.

A NEW SERIES FOR CAPTAIN AMERICA

• *Tales Of Suspense* #59

After guest-starring in the Iron Man story in *Tales Of Suspense* #58, Captain America was awarded his own regular series by Stan Lee in a split book. The series began with a ten-page story in *Tales Of Suspense* #59.

ACTUALLY, IT WAS ONCE THE RESIDENCE OF MULTI-MILLIONAIRE ANTHONY STARK, BUT HE DONATED IT TO THE WORLD'S MIGHTIEST FIGHTING TEAM AS A PUBLIC SERVICE...
BEFORE I LEAVE FOR THE EVENING, SIR, I THOUGHT YOU MIGHT LIKE SOME FRESHLY BREWED COFFEE!

Tales Of Suspense *#59 also presented Edwin Jarvis for the first time, the longtime butler of the Avengers.*

DECEMBER

CAPTAIN AMERICA MEETS SGT. FURY

• *Sgt. Fury And His Howling Commandos* #13

This issue featured the Howlers in an untold tale of World War II that guest-starred Captain America and his teenage partner Bucky Barnes.

After sneaking into occupied Europe, Cap joined Fury and the Howlers to destroy a giant tunnel under the English Channel that the Nazis were secretly building to invade Britain.

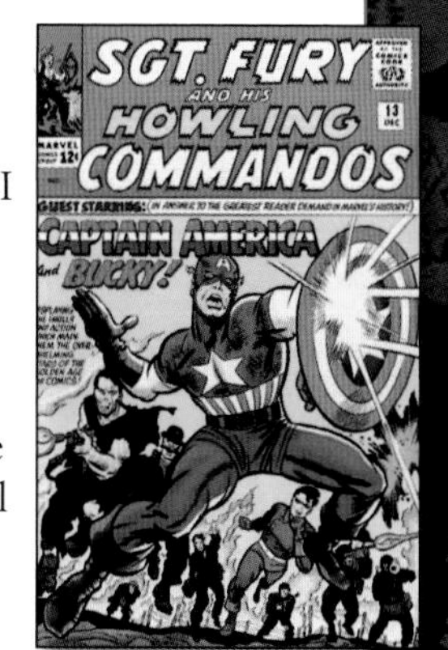

DECEMBER

THE LEADER

• *Tales To Astonish* #62

Since the Hulk was a creature of strength, it seemed only natural that he should have an enemy whose greatest power was his mind. Created by Stan Lee and Steve Ditko for *Tales To Astonish* #62, the Leader was once Samuel Sterns, a simple laborer. Like the Hulk, an accident involving gamma radiation transformed him, but rather than his body, it was his brain that was mutated, so he possessed a super-intellect. The Leader came to believe that his superior brain entitled him to rule the Earth. He often battled the Hulk to achieve his goal until he eventually evolved into a higher form of life that was composed entirely of mental energy.

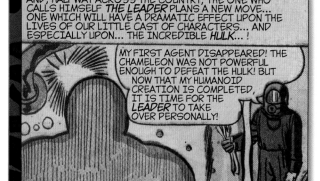

AND, HALFWAY ACROSS THE COUNTRY, THE ONE WHO CALLS HIMSELF THE LEADER PLANS A NEW MOVE... ONE WHICH WILL HAVE A DRAMATIC EFFECT UPON THE LIVES OF OUR LITTLE CAST OF CHARACTERS... AND ESPECIALLY UPON... THE INCREDIBLE HULK... !
MY FIRST AGENT DISAPPEARED! THE CHAMELEON WAS NOT POWERFUL ENOUGH TO DEFEAT THE HULK! BUT NOW THAT MY HUMANOID CREATION IS COMPLETED, IT IS TIME FOR THE LEADER TO TAKE OVER PERSONALLY!

The Leader was a super-genius who could remember everything he had ever seen, experienced, or read and he used this knowledge to create highly advanced technology.

THE M.M.M.S. IS REVEALED

• *Fantastic Four* #33

Having tantalized readers with the mystery initials "M.M.M.S." in the previous month's letters page, the first item in the Special Announcement Section of *Fantastic Four* #33 declared that Marvel Comics had officially formed a fan club that would be called "The Merry Marvel Marching Society." For a mere dollar, a member would receive a large membership pin, an official recording of the voices of Stan Lee and the rest of the Bullpen, a "nutty" new Marvel notepad, a "magniloquent" Marvel mini-book, a "mind-snapping" Marvel pencil, a "majestic" M.M.M.S. certificate, and a "munificent" membership card. The Marvel Age of Comics had truly arrived!

MEANWHILE IN 1964...

NELSON MANDELA SENTENCED TO LIFE FOR TREASON

In South Africa, civil rights activist Nelson Mandela is incarcerated in Robben Island prison, off Cape Town, and becomes a symbol of the resistance movement against apartheid.

JOHNSON SIGNS THE SWEEPING CIVIL RIGHTS ACT

The most sweeping piece of civil rights law in the history of America comes into effect, prohibiting racial discrimination in employment, public places, and union membership and provides federal government with the powers to enforce desegregation.

FIRST MAJOR STUDENT ANTI-WAR DEMONSTRATION

In New York up to one thousand students march through Times Square in protest to the Vietnam War. 700 also demonstrate in San Francisco.

FIRST PICTURES OF THE MOON

US satellite, Range 7, captures the first close-up pictures of the surface of the moon.

"SMOKING MAY BE HARMFUL"

In the first such announcement from the US government, the Surgeon General, Luther Leonidas Terry, states that smoking may be dangerous to people's health.

CAMPBELL REACHES RECORD SPEED

Racer Donald Campbell breaks the world water speed record, traveling at 276.33 miles (444.71 km) per hour across Lake Dumbleyung in Perth, Western Australia. This follows his world record for the fastest speed on land.

G.I. JOE IS HERE TO PLAY

Building on the success of Barbie, Hasbro launches the world's first action figure: a line of World War II-themed G.I. Joe dolls, one for each of the four branches of the American armed forces.

FIRST US STATE LOTTERY

Sweepstake tickets for the first US State lottery go on sale in New Hampshire.

HIPPIE FASHIONS

The hippy era brings a distinctive fashion style, with bell-bottom jeans, long, full skirts and fabrics with tie-dye, paisley, and batik prints.

AND AT THE MOVIES...

Dr. Strangelove or: How I Learned to Stop Worrying and Love the Bomb, *Stanley Kubrick's black cold-war comedy on nuclear annihilation that features Peter Sellers in a memorable triple role;* Mary Poppins, *Disney's supercalifragilistic musical about a nanny who brings a little magic into the lives of a banker's family;* Goldfinger, *the third 007 film;* Viva Las Vegas, *an Elvis Presley musical;* A Shot in the Dark, *the second film in the Pink Panther series.*

A SHORT TIME LATER...
MAGNETO'S ISLE IS INDEED WELL HIDDEN! EVEN WITH DIRECTIONS IT WAS HARD TO FIND!

SUB-MARINER!! I KNEW YOU'D COME! I AM MAGNETO!! THIS IS MY ISLAND!
SILENCE!
NONE SPEAK IN THE PRESENCE OF ROYALTY WITHOUT FIRST BEING RECOGNIZED!!

BEFORE WE TALK, I SHALL SCOUT THIS ISLE AND MAKE SURE I HAVE NOT ENTERED SOME SORT OF HIDDEN TRAP!!
ALL I HEARD ABOUT HIM IS TRUE! HE IS EVERY INCH A MONARCH!
AND HE'S SURE OF HIS STRENGTH!

BUT I MUST FIND A WAY TO INFLUENCE HIM... TO CONTROL HIM!

LET MY SISTER GO, MAGNETO, OR BY THUNDER, I'LL...!

SHE'S IN NO DANGER,

IT'S ALL RIGHT,

HE'LL BE PUTTY IN OUR HANDS!

OUR LIVES!*
* X-MEN #4...EDITOR.

EVERYTHING ON THIS ISLE IS POWERED BY MAGNETISM!
HOW NOBLE HE LOOKS...HOW SLIM, YET MUSCULAR! HE'S FASCINATING!

WHY WOULD SOMEONE SO FINE, SO MASTERFUL, WANT TO ALLY HIMSELF WITH THE EVIL MAGNETO?? WELL, IT IS NOT FOR ME TO QUESTION!
I'LL APPROACH HIM...TAP HIM ON THE SHOULDER, AND THEN...OH, NO! I CARELESSLY MADE A GESTURE! IT WILL CAUSE MY HEX POWER TO OPERATE!!

I FEEL LIKE A LIVING DYNAMO! I'VE BECOME ALL MUSCLE! I CAN LICK ANYBODY!

1965

SUPERHUMAN SOAP OPERAS

Drawing on the movie serials of his youth, Stan Lee began to produce multipart sagas in the split books *Tales Of Suspense* and *Tales To Astonish*. He also used his skills from writing romance comics to create Super Hero soap operas. Each hero had a love life filled with complications: Thor's father didn't approve of him dating a mortal and Tony Stark secretly loved Pepper Potts, but so did his loyal chauffeur.

During this period Lee frequently referred to his main rival—the company that would become DC Comics—as "Brand X," a name he had once used for Marvel. He also regularly handed out the legendary Marvel No-Prize to fans who wrote or did something that especially pleased him. The fan would receive absolutely nothing: Lee mailed the winners empty envelopes which said, "Congratulations! This envelope contains a genuine Marvel Comics NO-PRIZE which you have just won! Handle with care!" In August, Lee introduced the Merry Marvel Bullpen Page, which contained ads for the M.M.M.S. fan club and the first Marvel T-shirts. In December this page became the *Bullpen Bulletins*, with gossip and The Mighty Marvel Checklist of the comics currently on sale. These early *Bullpen* pages were customized so the one in *Fantastic Four* featured FF images and the one in *The Amazing Spider-Man* showed Spidey and the Green Goblin.

JANUARY

ANOTHER ENEMY FOR SPIDER-MAN

• *The Amazing Spider-Man* #20

Since scorpions prey on spiders, it seemed only natural that Stan Lee and Steve Ditko introduced one as a foe in *The Amazing Spider-Man* #20. *Daily Bugle* editor J. Jonah Jameson funded an experiment by Dr. Farley Stillwell that transformed Mac Gargan into the Scorpion. Although bigger, stronger, and far more powerful than Spider-Man, Gargan paid a terrible price for his strength: as his powers increased, his sanity slipped away. Later, in his search for domination, he temporarily merged with the symbiote Venom to become even more powerful.

As well as great strength, Gargan possessed a mechanical tail that hit with the force of a pi driver. It could also propel him through the air and fire destructive blasts of energy.

FEBRUARY

COUNT NEFARIA AND THE MAGGIA

• *The Avengers* #13

Europe's wealthiest nobleman, Count Nefaria, had a terrible secret: he was also the most powerful crimelord on Earth. Created by Stan Lee and Don Heck, Nefaria secretly ran the worldwide criminal organization called the Maggia, using his vast fortune to gain super-strength, lightning-like speed, invulnerability, and the power to project lasers from his eyes. His later exploits included framing the Avengers for treason and battling the X-Men.

To defeat the Avengers, Count Nefaria moved to America and brought his European castle with him.

FEBRUARY

DRAGON MAN DEBUT

• *Fantastic Four* #35

The fire-breathing monster known as Dragon Man first took wing in *Fantastic Four* #35. Stan Lee and Jack Kirby modeled him after both Frankenstein and King Kong. Dragon Man was an artificial creature created in a laboratory who was often drawn to beautiful and sensitive women. He possessed the intelligence of a dog and was often used as a pawn by other Super Villains.

- Also in *Fantastic Four* #35, Reed Richards finally proposed to Sue Storm while visiting his alma mater State University.

ROMANTIC TWISTS

• *Journey Into Mystery* #113

Forbidden by his father to date the mortal Jane Foster, Dr. Don Blake finally told her that he was secretly Thor in *Journey Into Mystery* #113. However, Jane thought Don had gone temporarily mad and did not believe him. She did not accept the truth until *Journey Into Mystery* #124 (Jan., 1966).

- Super Heroes had become so hot that even the Rawhide Kid battled costumed villains, like the Masked Maverick in *Rawhide Kid* #44.

THE CLASSICS REPEATED FOR NEW FANS

• *Marvel Collectors' Item Classics* #1

Realizing that many of his new readers had missed his early stories, Stan Lee began publishing *Marvel Collectors' Item Classics*. The first sixty-eight-paged issue reprinted *Fantastic Four* #2 (Jan., 1962), *The Amazing Spider-Man* #3 (July, 1962), the Ant-Man story from *Tales To Astonish* #36 (Oct., 1962), and a "Tales Of Asgard" story from *Journey Into Mystery* #97 (Oct., 1963).

MARCH

DAREDEVIL GOES RED

• *Daredevil* #7

Daredevil traded in his original yellow, red, and black costume for the much sleeker all-red one that he still wears today when he faced Namor, the Sub-Mariner in one of the greatest Marvel super-battles of all time. Clearly outmatched by Namor, Daredevil still proved he was the man without fear.

ABSORBING MAN DEBUTS

• *Journey Into Mystery* #114

"The stronger I am, the sooner I die!" screamed the cover of *Journey Into Mystery* #114. Once Loki gave "Crusher" Creel the power to absorb the physical properties of anything he touched, the criminal became more than a match for the God of Thunder. Absorbing Man also took on the Hulk and fought the entire Avengers to a standstill. The only time he was truly conquered was when he met and fell in love with the Super Villainess Titania during the *Secret Wars* limited series (1984). They became partners in crime and later marriage, although they eventually divorced.

- In a swinging sixties story, the Human Torch and the Thing take their girlfriends to a Beatles concert in *Strange Tales* #130.
- Based on the original story from *Captain America Comics* #1 (March, 1941), Lee and Kirby updated Cap's origin in *Tales Of Suspense* #63. The next month Cap began a World War II series.

MARCH

THE FRIGHTFUL FOUR FORMS

• *Fantastic Four* #36

The Wizard struck back at the Fantastic Four, fueled by his jealousy of Reed Richards' fame and still furious for the defeats he had suffered at the hands of the Human Torch. He gathered together his former partner the Trapster, along with the Sandman and Medusa to form the Frightful Four. Of all the enemies that the FF has fought, the Frightful Four have come the closest to defeating them.

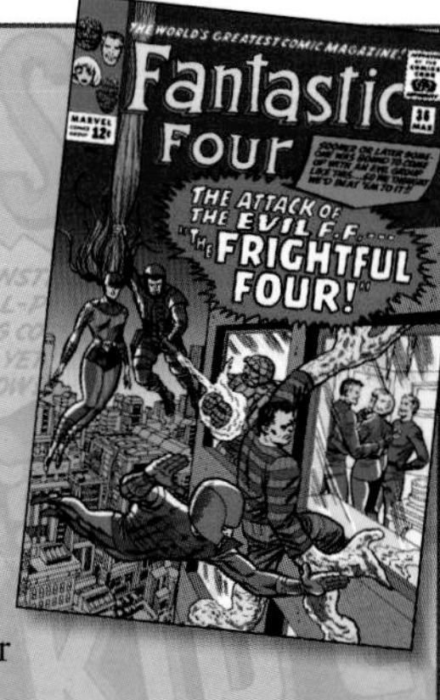

MEDUSA DEBUTS

• *Fantastic Four* #36

Like her namesake from Greek mythology, Medusa had living hair that obeyed her every wish. She was first introduced in *Fantastic Four* #36, but it later became clear that she was a member of the Royal Family of the Inhumans and engaged to their leader, Black Bolt. During the course of her career, she served as a replacement member of the FF, even though she once belonged to their evil counterparts, the Frightful Four. She eventually married Black Bolt and became ruler of the Inhumans.

Medusa's hair possessed superhuman strength. It was about six feet long and could stretch to at least twice that length.

KA-ZAR IS REVIVED

• *The X-Men* #10

Originally created for pulp magazines, and then used in *Marvel Comics* #1 (Oct., 1939), Ka-Zar the Great was brought up by tigers. Although he followed the long tradition of humans raised by beasts that extends all the way back to Romulus and Remus, the mythical founders of Rome, Ka-Zar also bore a striking resemblance to Edgar Rice Burroughs' character Tarzan, who was also an English Lord. When Stan Lee and Jack Kirby revived the character, they also paid homage to another of Burroughs' ideas: The dinosaur-filled Savage Land is based on Burroughs' *Savage Pellucidar*.

Ka-Zar was raised by a sabertoothed tiger, rather than apes, like Tarzan.

MAY

THE STRANGER FROM OUTER SPACE

• *The X-Men* #11

A seemingly all-powerful extraterrestrial, the Stranger was more suited to the pre-Super Hero days of *Strange Tales* and *Journey Into Mystery* than *The X-Men.* Created by Stan Lee and Jack Kirby, he was mistaken for a mutant when he first appeared. The Stranger feared that mankind and its growing mutant population could eventually become a threat to the entire galaxy. Like the Watcher before him, the Stranger correctly predicted that the Earth would soon play a pivotal role in the universe as it encountered other alien races and cosmic entities.

THE OLD ORDER CHANGETH

• *The Avengers* #16

Stan Lee had slowly become a victim of his own success. He had created a universe where characters from one title often guest-starred in another. The readers loved it, but they also wanted to know the proper order to read all these appearances. Since *The Avengers* featured characters that regularly appeared in other comics, Lee was constantly receiving letters demanding to know, "If Thor is in the middle of a multi-part epic in *Journey Into Mystery*, how can he be fighting so-in-so in this month's *The Avengers*?" Lee's solution was as elegant as it was revolutionary: he decided to change the super-team's line-up in *The Avengers* #16. He replaced Thor, Iron Man, Giant-Man, and the Wasp with Hawkeye, Quicksilver, and the Scarlet Witch. Only Captain America—whose other series was set in World War II—remained to lead the new team. No Super Hero team in the history of comic books had ever gone through such a massive overhaul. A new precedent had been set! The Avengers line-up continued to change and evolve over the years.

- Lady Pamela Hawley, Nick Fury's first true love, was killed during the London Blitz in *Sgt. Fury And His Howling Commandos* #18.
- The Two-Gun Kid arrived too late to help his friend Jim Bowie and the other doomed defenders of the Alamo in *Two-Gun Kid* #75.

JUNE

THE STILT-MAN

• *Daredevil* #8

Equipped with a revolutionary new hydraulic system and an armored suit, the Stilt-Man sprang into action in *Daredevil* #8. Created by Stan Lee and Wally Wood, his limited powers made him a joke among other criminals, even though he managed to defeat Spider-Man on more than one occasion.

JUNE

MARY JANE WATSON

• *The Amazing Spider-Man* #25

Ever had a well-meaning relative send you on a blind date with someone with a "good" personality? Peter Parker's Aunt May had been trying to do just that. Fearing his aunt's taste and already involved with Betty Brant, Peter had no interest in Mary Jane Watson, the niece of his aunt's neighbor. After months of hearing about her, she finally appeared in issue #25 of *The Amazing Spider-Man.* Stan Lee and Steve Ditko allowed Betty Brant and Liz Allan to see her, but they blocked the reader's view with a strategically placed plant. Betty thought Mary Jane looked like a movie star, but readers didn't get to judge for themselves until issue #42. Although Ditko introduced her, he never actually got a chance to draw or design her. That honor was reserved for John Romita Sr who later took over the series. Romita modeled Mary Jane after the actress Ann-Margret from the movie *Bye Bye Birdie* (1963). Mary Jane's outgoing personality struck an immediate chord with readers and they demanded she became Peter's girlfriend. Although Lee preferred the more reserved Gwen Stacy, after an off-and-on relationship for many years, Mary Jane and Peter were married in *The Amazing Spider-Man Annual* #21 (1987). But a recent deal with the extradimensional demon Mephisto to save Aunt May's life meant that the marriage was erased from everyone's memory.

JULY

THE JUGGERNAUT

• *The X-Men* #12

Having introduced an immovable object with the Blob, Stan Lee, Jack Kirby, and the legendary penciller Alex Toth tried their hands at an irresistible force when the Juggernaut trudged into *The X-Men* #12. With a temper like his biblical namesake, Cain Marko was a bully who tormented his younger stepbrother, Charles Xavier. Marko found a mystical ruby in Korea, which transformed him into an unstoppable engine of destruction. With the aid of Black Tom Cassidy—whom he met in prison—the Juggernaut often battled the X-Men, but eventually gave up his criminal ways and redeemed himself by joining the group of his former enemies.

The Juggernaut was not a mutant but gained his powers by magic.

THE CRIME-MASTER

• *The Amazing Spider-Man* #26

Though he challenged the Green Goblin for control of the underworld when he first appeared in *The Amazing Spider-Man* #26, the man known as the Crime-Master was killed by police the following month. *Daily Bugle* reporter Frederick Foswell later revealed that the Crime-Master was actually Nick "Lucky Lobo" Lewis, who had previously appeared in issue #23.

JULY

THE DESTROYER APPEARS

• *Journey Into Mystery* #118

The same month that they introduced the Juggernaut in *X-Men*, Lee and Kirby created another indestructible force. Hidden in a grotesque temple lay the ultimate weapon from a bygone age. An armored figure, built by the Gods to defend the Earth from cosmic threats, the Destroyer possessed incalculable power. All it needed was the intelligence of a sentient being to animate it. Thanks to Loki, it fell into the hands of an evil hunter named Buck Franklin who attempted to destroy Thor. It was later animated by various of the Asgardian gods like Loki, Lady Sif, Thor, and even Odin himself.

AUGUST

SHIELD DEBUT

"A human weapon is needed to smash the entire HYDRA network! A man... who'll devote his life to it... a man like you, Fury!... Your entire life qualifies you for this job."

• *Strange Tales* #135

Stan Lee had dropped Thor and others from the Avengers because of readers' confusion about them being in two different places at once each month. For the same reason he decided to remove the Human Torch from *Strange Tales*, which left a gap. The spy genre had been growing in popularity ever since the first James Bond film *Dr. No* (1962) and the advent of television's *The Man From U.N.C.L.E.* Having already established Nick Fury as a CIA agent in *Fantastic Four* #21, Lee had the right man for the job. With Jack Kirby providing the artwork and more than a few wild ideas, Fury was made the director of the Supreme Headquarters International Espionage Law-enforcement Division (SHIELD). Employing Tony Stark to design high-tech gadgetry that would have made even James Bond blush, SHIELD was responsible for worldwide security and answered to the United Nations. Like Captain America, Fury regularly appeared in two different series, but they were set in different time periods: he battled with SHIELD in *Strange Tales* in the present day and fought in World War II in *Sgt. Fury And His Howling Commandos*.

Strange Tales #135 also introduced Fury's flying car and Life Model Decoys, robots that perfectly mimicked particular humans. This issue was also the first time readers met SHIELD's evil counterpart HYDRA, a subversive organization dedicated to world domination.

SHIELD was an international organization in membership, scope, and jurisdiction.

AUGUST

THE COMING OF THE SWORDSMAN

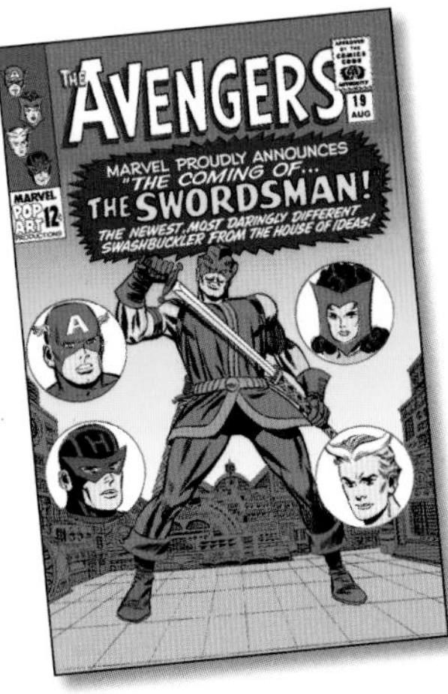

• *The Avengers* #19

Hawkeye's first mentor, Jacques Duquesne, was a master swordsman and carnival performer who turned to a life of crime. Created by Stan Lee and artist Don Heck, the Swordsman tried to join the Earth's mightiest Super Heroes, but after being refused, he began working for the criminal mastermind, the Mandarin. He later fell in love with a martial artist called Mantis and died while battling Kang to save her.

THE SUB-MARINER REPLACES GIANT-MAN

• *Tales To Astonish* #70

Prince Namor replaced Giant-Man as the lead feature in *Tales To Astonish* #70. The Sub-Mariner series was written by Stan Lee and drawn by Gene Colan, who was using the pen name Adam Austin at the time.

THOR'S "WARRIORS THREE"

• *Journey Into Mystery* #119

Inspired by the adventures of Alexandre Dumas' *D'Artagnan and the Three Musketeers*, Stan Lee and Jack Kirby revealed that Thor also had three inseparable companions. Armed with a battle mace, Hogun the Grim came from an unnamed land in the Asgardian dimension and rarely smiled. Fandral the Dashing was the swashbuckler known for his flamboyant personality and skill with the ladies. Volstagg was an older warrior who bragged better than he fought and volunteered for missions to get away from his nagging wife and houseful of children.

SEPTEMBER

MOLTEN MAN

• *The Amazing Spider-Man* #28

In the origin story of Molten Man, two men collaborated on the same invention. One did most of the work. The other, Mark Raxton, came up with the idea, supplied the money to produce it, and then stole it for himself before it had even been tested. In the scuffle that ensued he became covered in the liquid and absorbed the super-strong powers of Molten Man. Scripted by Stan Lee, "The Menace Of The Molten Man" was plotted and drawn by Steve Ditko. Molten Man's alter ego, Mark Raxton, was later revealed to be the stepbrother of Peter Parker's friend Liz Allan and ultimately he gave up his life of crime.

It was also in *The Amazing Spider-Man* #28 that Peter Parker graduated from Midtown High school.

HERCULES AND THE GODS OF OLYMPUS

• *Journey Into Mystery Annual* #1

While battling a pack of Storm Giants, the mighty Thor accidentally crashed through a mystical barrier and found himself in Olympus, the home of the Greek gods. Thor later encountered Hercules on a bridge that was only wide enough for one. A fight erupted when neither god would allow the other to cross first, although they would later become close friends. Hercules lived for the thrill of battle, and loved bestowing the "gift" of combat on both his friends and foes. He would eventually journey to Earth and join such super-teams as the Avengers, the Champions, and the Defenders. This issue also introduced Zeus, the all-powerful monarch of Olympus and the father of Hercules.

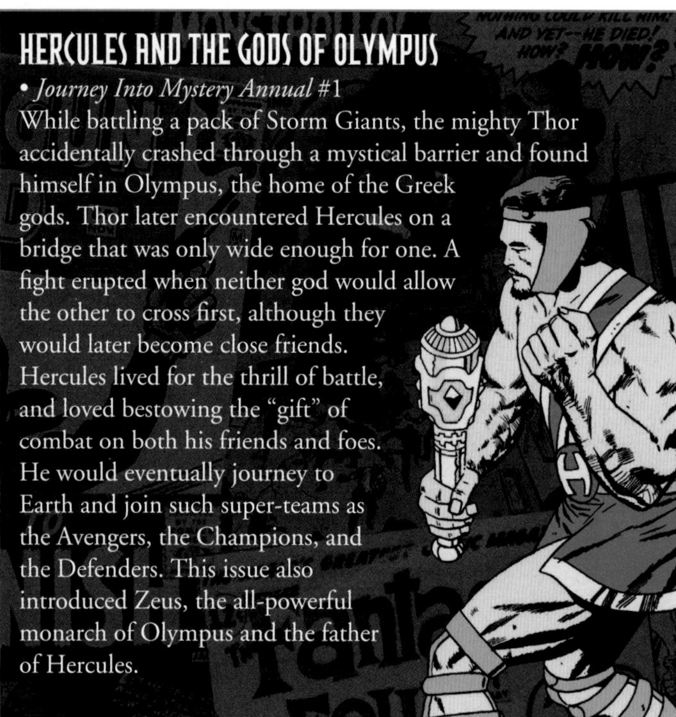

OCTOBER

POWER MAN DEBUT

• *The Avengers* #21

Stan Lee never let a good gimmick go to waste. He and Don Heck brought back the machine responsible for creating Wonder Man to produce a brand new Super Villain in *The Avengers* #21. Erik Josten had been a mercenary employed by Baron Zemo, who, after Zemo's death in *The Avengers* #15, joined up with the Asgardian goddess Enchantress and became Power Man. However, Josten seemed to have a problem hanging on to names. After losing "Power Man" to Luke Cage, he grew to a giant size and became Goliath. Later, when the second Baron Zemo formed the Thunderbolts, Josten started calling himself Atlas.

NOVEMBER

FANTASTIC WEDDING

• *Fantastic Four Annual* #3

Having seen them together as a couple since *Fantastic Four* #1, the fans couldn't wait for the wedding of Sue Storm and Reed Richards. Hyped as "The world's most colossal collection of costumed characters, crazily cavorting and capering in continual combat," the sixty-eight page annual contained a twenty-three page lead story and reprints from *Fantastic Four* #6 and #11. It guest-starred over twenty Marvel Super Heroes and an even larger number of Super Villains. Even Stan Lee and Jack Kirby tried to attend the festivities, but were denied entrance by Nick Fury because they didn't have invitations.

QNAX APPEARS

• *Tales To Astonish* #73

Bred to be the ultimate fighting machine, Qnax first battled the Hulk in *Tales To Astonish* #73. The extraterrestrial later traveled the galaxy as a gladiator, helped the Hulk defeat a monstrous creature called the Galaxy Master, and attempted to liberate his planet Xantares from its evil rulers, the Council of Elders.

SENTINELS DEBUT

• *The X-Men* #14

Both Stan Lee and Jack Kirby had served in World War II and were familiar with the Nazi military organization called the Schutzstaffel, or, as it was better known, the SS. This elite military unit rounded up political prisoners and sent them off to the concentration camps. There can be little doubt that Lee and Kirby had the SS in mind when they introduced the Sentinels in *The X-Men* #14. Designed and built by Dr. Bolivar Trask, the original Sentinels were heavily armed robots that stood about twenty feet tall. Their mission was to protect humanity's genetic purity by capturing and subduing all mutants.

The original Sentinels came to believe that they could only guarantee humankind's safety by ruling the world.

THE SLEEPERS WAKE UP

• *Tales Of Suspense* #72

After a series of stories set in World War II, *Tales Of Suspense* #72 signaled a major change in direction for Captain America. His adventures now occurred in the present day. To make the transition easier, Stan Lee and Jack Kirby began the first new tale with Cap recalling his final battle with the Nazi agent Red Skull during the war and remembering that his enemy had planted Sleepers—giant robots—that were set to awaken in 1965.

GWEN STACY DEBUTS

• *The Amazing Spider-Man* #31

Gwen Stacy, the platinum blonde ex-beauty queen of Standard High, met Peter Parker on his first day of college in this issue. Worried about his aunt's failing health, Peter didn't really notice her at first and they danced around each other for nearly thirty issues before actually starting to date. The relationship grew increasingly more serious, but was destined to end in tragedy. Gwen was kidnapped by the original Green Goblin and—despite Spider-Man's best efforts to save her—was hurled off the George Washington Bridge in New York in *The Amazing Spider-Man* #121 (June, 1973).

HARRY OSBORN DEBUTS

• *The Amazing Spider-Man* #31

The same issue that introduced Gwen Stacy established Spider-Man's greatest enemy, who was also his best friend. Another graduate of Standard High, Harry Osborn was the son of the rich industrialist Norman Osborn, who secretly led a life of crime as the Green Goblin. Peter and Harry became friends over time and even shared an apartment together. After his father was killed during a battle with Spider-Man, Harry discovered Peter's secret identity and sought revenge as the new Green Goblin. Harry eventually married Peter's former high school friend Liz Allan. They had a son whom they named after Harry's father. For years, Harry was torn between his friendship for Peter and his hatred of Spider-Man. He ultimately chose to sacrifice himself to save Peter's life in *The Spectacular Spider-Man* #200 (May, 1993).

DECEMBER

THE INHUMANS

• *Fantastic Four* #45

Reed and Sue Richards spent their honeymoon encountering the Inhumans, a lost race that diverged from humankind 25,000 years ago and became genetically enhanced. The previous issue had re-introduced Medusa from the Frightful Four when she was on the run from a creature called Gorgon who had the ability to create destructive tremors with his massive hooves. Issue #44 also revealed Medusa and Gorgon to be Inhumans. In issue #45, the Human Torch met the rest of the Inhuman royal family: Crystal (an elemental), her pet Lockjaw (a teleporter), Karnac (a super-martial artist with the ability to perceive an object or person's weakness), Triton (a sea creature), and Black Bolt, their powerful leader.

Mistaking the Human Torch for another Inhuman, Crystal invited him to meet her family, but Medusa immediately recognized her former enemy.

PRINCESS RAVONNA DEBUTS

• *The Avengers* #23

Princess Ravonna, the woman who stole Kang's heart, first appeared in *The Avengers* #23. Kang had almost conquered the entire Earth in one possible future timeline. The last land to resist him was ruled by Princess Ravonna and he soon fell in love with her. A former henchman kidnapped her and Kang had to join with his enemies, the Avengers, to save her. Although he failed in that particular timeline, he tried to be reunited with her in other alternate futures.

M "Whom Can I Turn To?" in *Modeling With Millie* #44 was the first Marvel story scripted by Roy Thomas, the man who was destined to succeed Stan Lee as the company's editor.

MEANWHILE IN 1965...

MALCOLM X SHOT DEAD
Black-nationalist leader Malcolm X is assassinated while giving a speech at a rally in Harlem.

FIRST AMERICAN WALKS IN SPACE
Edward Higgins White II, the pilot of Gemini 4, *takes the first American spacewalk.*

BEATLE-MANIA SWEEPS THE US
The Beatles arrive in New York. Their appearance on the Ed Sullivan Show *launches John, Paul, Ringo, and George across America.*

CIVIL RIGHTS MARCH OF 25,000 IN ALABAMA
A month of civil rights protests culminates in a march of twenty-five thousand to Capitol in Montgomery, led by Martin Luther King. Because of bomb attacks, the marchers are given the protection of three thousand troops.

US SOLDIERS IN VIETNAM
The role of US troops in Vietnam has shifted from supporting the South Vietnamese in their struggle against the Viet Cong, to a military offensive. By the end of the year there are 190,000 American soldiers in Vietnam.

FIRST "TEACH-IN" HELD
As part of the growing anti-war movement, teachers at the University of Michigan stage a new type of non-violent protest against the Vietnam War. This event is copied at thirty-five campuses across the country.

JOHNSON'S "GREAT SOCIETY"
President Johnson announces his package of social welfare programs, under the banner of the "Great Society."

BOB DYLAN "GOES ELECTRIC"
The folk singer causes outrage at the Newport Folk Festival in Rhode Island with his legendary first "plugged-in" set, which marks his transition from folk to rock.

FREEZE-DRIED COFFEE BEANS
Nescafé Gold Blend goes on sale and is the first freeze-dried instant coffee.

ROLLING STONES RISE
A new British band emerges in the US as the "anti-Beatles," offering a more aggressive style of music from their fellow British band.

AND AT THE MOVIES...
The Sound of Music, *Robert Wise's feelgood, alpine musical about a governess who brings music into the lives of the Von Trapps;* Doctor Zhivago, *David Lean's revolutionary Russian epic, adapted from Boris Pasternak's novel about a poet-doctor's frustrated love for beautiful Lara;* Thunderball, *the most successful film in the Bond franchise;* Repulsion, *Roman Polanski's hallucinatory psychological chiller vividly portrays the disintegration of a lonely woman's fragile mind.*

NOW I SHALL LEARN FOR CER
WHO IS THE POWER BEHIND MO
AHHH ... AN IMAGE BEGINS TO
EVEN AS I SPEAK! IT IS MOR
AND BEHIND HIM ... BEHIND HI
I SEE ...

THE ARTIST STEVE DITKO

Artist Steve Ditko entered the comic book industry in 1953 and three years later started freelancing for Martin Goodman's Atlas Comics, where he first met Stan Lee. Ditko was a master at drawing facial expressions and hand gestures. He could envision realistic cityscapes as easily as weird, surrealist fantasy worlds—which was clearly shown in both the Spider-Man and Dr. Strange stories, the most famous features he co-created with Stan Lee, like this Dr. Strange example from *Strange Tales* #135 (Aug., 1965).

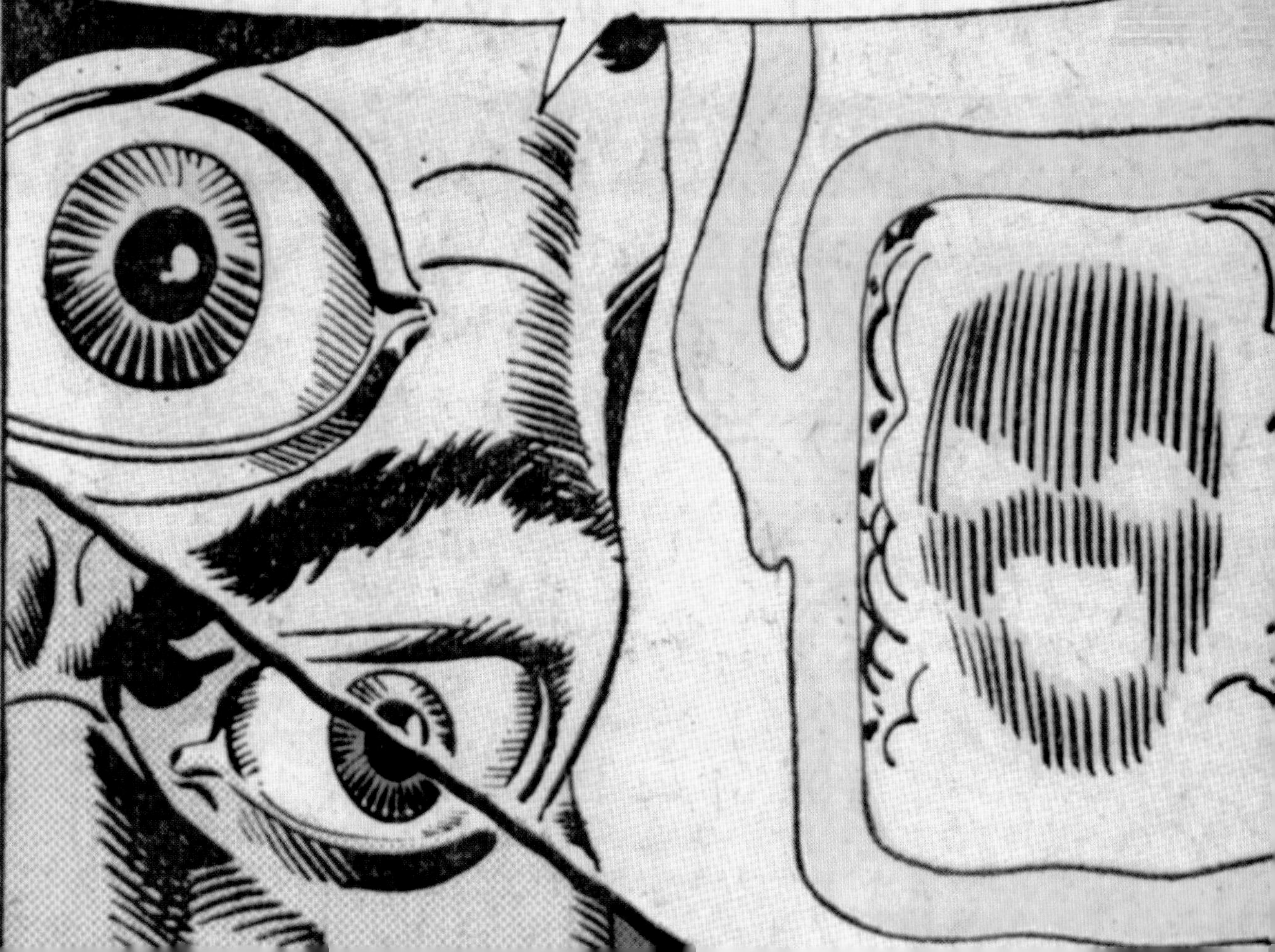
THE DREAD DORMAMMU!! OF COURSE! NOW THERE CAN BE NO DOUBT! I SUSPECTED AS MUCH! BUT NOW I HAVE THE POSITIVE PROOF! I KNOW THAT ONLY A POWER FROM ANOTHER WORLD COULD BE GREATER THAN THAT OF MINE!

IT'S TIME FER US TA SAVE HUMANITY AGAIN!

1966

MARVEL IN THE MAINSTREAM

News of the Marvel Age of Comics had begun to reach the general public by 1966. Newspapers like the *Chicago Daily News* and the *New York Herald Tribune* published features on the company. Stan Lee was interviewed by personalities like Tom Dunn and Mike Wallace and the Dow-Jones' *National Observer* reported that Marvel was selling 33 million comics a year.

Marvel was all the rage and celebrities like movie director Federico Fellini and singer Peter Asher from folk duo *Peter and Gordon* visited the Marvel offices, claiming to be major fans. Trying to cash in on the new comic book craze, other publishers attempted to copy the Marvel style and began churning out Super Heroes. Lee lumped this competition together, referring to it all as "Brand Echh." Marvel also began to license its characters: Marvel-themed plastic model hobby kits, hats, Halloween costumes, trading cards, and board games all appeared.

In the March *Bullpen Bulletins*, Lee shared the glory with Jack "King" Kirby, "Dazzling" Don Heck, and "Darlin'" Dick Ayers, saying he only had to, "give them the germ of an idea and they make up all the details as they go along, drawing and plotting out the story." Lee also welcomed writers Roy Thomas and Denny O'Neil, and artists John Romita, Frank Giacoia, and Werner Roth into the growing Marvel Bullpen.

JANUARY

THE PLUNDERER

• *Daredevil* #12

Playing off the ever-popular Cain and Abel scenario, Stan Lee created Lord Parnival Plunder, the brother of Lord Kevin Plunder (later revealed to be Ka-Zar). The story was plotted and laid out by Jack Kirby with finished artwork by John Romita. Having stolen his brother's title and estates, Parnival took on the identity of the Plunderer and employed a weapon made from vibranium, a metal that emitted vibrations capable of destroying all other metals.

FEBRUARY

THE FIXER AND MENTALLO

• *Strange Tales* #141

Stan Lee and Jack Kirby's character Paul Ebersol predated Microsoft founder Bill Gates in *Strange Tales* #141. Ebersol, aka the Fixer, was technical wizard, a science geek who was a genius when it came to creating advanced hardware. He was originally paired with Mentallo, a mutant with the ability to read minds and project thoughts. The Fixer later changed his name to Techno when he joined Baron Zemo's Thunderbolts.

SGT. FURY'S EYE PATCH

• *Sgt. Fury And His Howling Commandos* #27

To explain why the present-day Nick Fury, Agent of SHIELD, wore an eye patch, Stan Lee and Dick Ayers told the story of how he had been injured during a mission in World War II. During an encounter with Nazi soldiers, a grenade exploded, damaging his left eye. Although an operation could have saved the eye, it would have put him out of action for the remainder of the war and Fury could not bear to leave the Howlers, so he adopted the eye patch.

SO! THE SILENT ONE DARES RETURN FROM EXILE! THIS TIME BLACK BOLT HAS GONE TOO FAR!!

MAXIMUS

• *Fantastic Four* #47

Another variation on the Cain-and-Abel theme was the story of brothers Maximus and Black Bolt of the Inhumans. Introduced in *Fantastic Four* #47 by Stan Lee and Jack Kirby, Maximus had always desired his older brother's throne and tried to enlist the alien race called the Kree against him. However, Maximus lost his sanity after being exposed to Black Bolt's sonic scream. No longer hampered by rational thought, he routinely devised advanced weapons and complicated strategies to seize the reins of power.

- Stan Lee and artist Don Heck gave Dr. Doom a unique reason for attacking Cap's new team in *The Avengers* #25: to practice for his next battle with the Fantastic Four.
- Although Ka-Zar had been introduced nearly a year earlier, he was revealed to be Lord Kevin Plunder in *Daredevil* #13.
- Since guest-stars were so popular, Larry Lieber teamed up Kid Colt with Rawhide in *Rawhide Kid* #50.

BATROC THE LEAPER

• *Tales Of Suspense* #75

Conceived as a French version of Captain America, Georges Batroc first appeared in *Tales Of Suspense* #75. He claimed to be the world's greatest mercenary and a master of Savate, the French art of kickboxing. A former member of the French Foreign Legion, he had the ability to leap greatest distances and was an expert at hand-to-hand combat. He led an ever-changing band of mercenaries that he called Batroc's Brigade.

SHARON CARTER

• *Tales Of Suspense* #75

Sharon Carter became an agent of SHIELD after she was inspired by an older relative who had been in the French Resistance and had known Captain America in World War II. Code-named Agent 13, she specialized in undercover work. She and Captain America were often paired together and eventually fell in love.

Unfortunately, their work kept getting in the way and they were always breaking up for long periods of time. At one point, Sharon was assigned to serve as Cap's liaison officer and she is believed to have killed him while under the control of Dr. Faustus and the Red Skull.

GALACTUS AND A NEW STRUCTURE FOR STORYTELLING

"Galactus, who drains entire planets of their elements, and leaves them dry, unable to support life!"

• *Fantastic Four* #48

Although sales continued to rise, Stan Lee expected Super Heroes would eventually lose their popularity. It had happened before and would happen again. So, as he had nothing to lose, Lee decided to go for broke and tried to create the ultimate Super Villain. He and Jack Kirby had already introduced good and bad gods in their Norse and Olympian pantheons. What if there was someone even more powerful than Odin? Someone even Zeus feared? A being so incredibly powerful that he needed to consume the energy from living planets to survive? Lee discussed this germ of an idea with Jack Kirby who then plotted out Marvel's first true cosmic epic. The Super Villain Galactus first appeared on the last page of *Fantastic Four* #48 and announced that the Earth was doomed. While the idea of introducing the main villain on the final page had been used before, and as recently as the previous month's *The X-Men* #17, this particular cliffhanger was so powerful that it permanently changed the structure of comic book storytelling. To this day, multipart stories are constructed to follow the formula established by *Fantastic Four* #48. Although the "Galactus Trilogy" extends over three issues, it actually begins at the bottom of page 7 of *Fantastic Four* #48 and concludes on page 13 of *Fantastic Four* #50.

MARCH

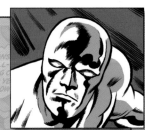

THE SILVER SURFER

"The Silver Surfer, zooming along the starways like a living comet—with the freedom and abandon of the wind itself!"

The Surfer was actually Norrin Radd, an extraterrestrial who had agreed to serve Galactus in order to save his own planet from destruction.

• *Fantastic Four* #48

Stan Lee may have started the creative discussion that culminated in Galactus, but the inclusion of the Silver Surfer in *Fantastic Four* #48 was pure Jack Kirby. Kirby realized that a being like Galactus required an equally impressive herald; someone to scout the way and make sure everything was ready for his arrival. Lee was immediately taken with the way Kirby drew the Surfer and contributed a formal, almost Shakespearian speech pattern and personality. When he arrived, the Surfer was astonished to learn that humans consume food. He experienced beauty and pity for the first time and these emotions forced him to turn against his master to save the Earth. Galactus eventually relented, but punished the Surfer by establishing an impenetrable barrier that effectively imprisoned him on Earth until *The Silver Surfer* Vol. 3, #1 (July, 1987).

M Since *Journey Into Mystery* had become devoted to the Thunder God, its name changed with *The Mighty Thor* #126.

M Believing that the Hulk was finally dead and that it was time to divulge the truth, Rick Jones told the world that, "Bruce Banner is the Hulk!" in *Tales To Astonish* #77.

Galactus stood over twenty-eight feet high and possessed a level of cosmic power beyond human comprehension.

1966

APRIL

PLUTO

• *The Mighty Thor* #127

Stan Lee and Jack Kirby were in a playful mood when they introduced Pluto, the Olympian God of the Netherworld, as a sleazy Hollywood producer in *The Mighty Thor* #127. Promising fame and fortune, Pluto tricked Hercules into signing a contract that condemned him for all eternity. At this time Marvel had recently negotiated a deal to license some of its characters to television, so this story line could have been inspired by Lee and Kirby's own experiences.

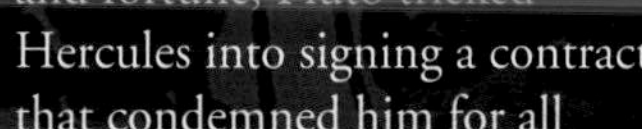

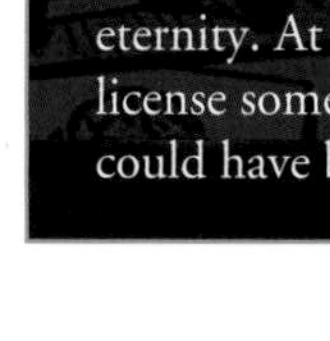

MAY

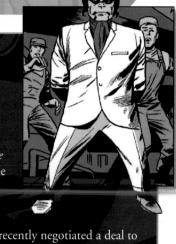

THE LOOTER

• *The Amazing Spider-Man* #36

Norton G. Fester believed he was a scientific genius, despite the fact that he had consistently failed the subject in school.

As dumb luck would have it, Fester accidentally stumbled upon a meteor that gave him super-strength and launched his bumbling career in crime. A lovable loser whose very incompetence made him popular with the readers, Fester didn't even bother to name himself during his first appearance. He later took on the name Meteor Man, but eventually changed it to the Looter.

A NEW ARTIST FOR SPIDEY

• *Daredevil* #16

Sensing that Steve Ditko was preparing to leave *The Amazing Spider-Man*, Stan Lee decided to use *Daredevil* #16 and #17 to test John Romita's ability to draw the webhead, Aunt May, and J. Jonah Jameson. Issue #16 also featured the first appearance of the Masked Marauder, Daredevil's longtime foe.

THE COLLECTOR

• *The Avengers* #28

In the 1940s and 1950s, comics were often discarded. They were read, traded, passed around the neighborhood, and gathered in paper drives during World War II. Stan Lee noticed that his current readers actually seemed to be saving their comics and many even hunted down missed issues. Possibly inspired by this new behavior, Stan Lee and Don Heck created the Collector, a powerful extraterrestrial who collected interesting life forms, particularly Super Heroes.

BRINNG!
AH! MY ELECTRONIC WARNING ALARM!
YOUR FELLOW AVENGERS ARE HERE--TO BE ADDED TO MY EVER-GROWING COLLECTION!

M *The X-Men* #20 revealed how Professor Xavier lost the use of his legs: while fighting the Hell-Lord Lucifer, he was lured into a trap and buried beneath a concrete slab.

JUNE

THE GOLDEN AGE LIVES AGAIN!

• *Fantasy Masterpieces* #3

Originally featuring early Marvel monster/suspense tales from the 1950s and 1960s, *Fantasy Masterpieces* began to reprint Super Hero comics from the 1940s with its third issue, starting with stories from *Captain America Comics* #1.

WYATT WINGFOOT

• *Fantastic Four* #51

Roughly based on the Native American athlete Jim Thorpe, Wyatt Wingfoot casually sauntered into Johnny Storm's life in *Fantastic Four* #51. The two became best friends and college roommates, and Wyatt joined the Fantastic Four on many of their adventures. He met and began a long romance with Jennifer Walters/the She-Hulk when she briefly replaced the Thing on the team.

A NEW AGENT OF SHIELD

• *Tales Of Suspense* #78

After months of offering his services to SHIELD, Captain America received a surprise visit from Nick Fury in *Tales Of Suspense* #78. The two old army buddies soon found themselves fighting a group of subversive scientists who called themselves AIM (Advanced Idea Mechanics) and aimed to take control of the world's governments using their advanced technology creations.

JULY

THE RED SKULL RETURNS

"Phases one and two have been completed! Now we are ready for phase three--the final destruction of Captain America!"

• *Tales Of Suspense* #79

Stan Lee and Jack Kirby decided to resurrect the original Red Skull in this issue, after having featured him in Cap's recent World War II series in *Tales of Suspense* and having reprinted his stories from the 1940s in *Fantasy Masterpieces*. Johann Shmidt was an orphan, who was working as a bellhop when he was discovered by Adolf Hitler. The Nazi leader transformed Shmidt into the ultimate terrorist and personally supervised his training. The American Government learned of the Red Skull and responded with the "super-soldier" program that created Captain America. Cap and the Skull battled all through World War II.

In this ten-page story, readers learned how Red Skull had survived the war: during the fall of Berlin, he was seemingly killed by a cave-in within Hitler's bunker, but an experimental gas had actually put him in a state of suspended animation. Having been awakened, the Skull renewed his war with Cap and repeatedly tried to conquer the world. He built a worldwide terrorist organization and has often led a group of former Nazis called the Exiles.

The Red Skull was totally ruthless, an expert at various forms of hand-to-hand combat, and a superb marksman. He often employed his "dust of death", which transformed his victim's head into an emaciated red skull.

JULY

BLACK PANTHER DEBUT

"And now, let the Fantastic Four come! The Black Panther will greet them... as they have never been greeted before!"

• *Fantastic Four* #52

After nearly a decade of nonviolent protests and marches, by 1966 the Civil Rights movement had made significant gains for people of color in the United States. Congress finally passed the Voting Rights Act of 1965, guaranteeing basic civil rights for all Americans, regardless of race. Stan Lee wanted to do his part by creating the first black Super Hero. Lee discussed his ideas with Jack Kirby and the result was seen in *Fantastic Four* #52.

Instead of following the usual clichés, the Black Panther was a brilliant scientist who was also the hereditary ruler of the highly advanced and prosperous African nation, Wakanda. He was an Olympic-level athlete and the equal of Captain America in hand-to-hand combat. Using his physical skills and weapons that he had invented, the Panther managed to temporarily defeat each individual member of the Fantastic Four when they first met.

The Black Panther was the title bestowed upon the ruling tribal chief of the African nation of Wakanda.

The Black Panther was an immediate hit with Marvel's readers. Unfortunately, a few months after *Fantastic Four* #52 appeared, activists Huey P. Newton and Bobby Seal formed a highly controversial political action group called the Black Panthers. Whether or not Lee was aware of this group at the time is anyone's guess, but the character's name was briefly changed to the Black Leopard, perhaps to distance him from the real-life Panthers. However, in the 1970s when the Black Panther got his own title, he reclaimed his original name.

The Black Panther, T'Challa, possessed exceptional night vision and developed a combat style that incorporated acrobatics and many cat-like stances and moves.

GLADIATOR

• *Daredevil* #18

When Stan Lee and John Romita created the Gladiator, they were poking fun at all the other publishers who had started to imitate the Marvel style of Super Hero comics. The Gladiator, aka Melvin Potter, owned a small costume shop. He hated Super Heroes, and believed that their only appeal was their colorful costumes. He figured he could become just as famous by designing the right costume with powerful weapons.

BOOMERANG

• *Tales To Astonish* #81

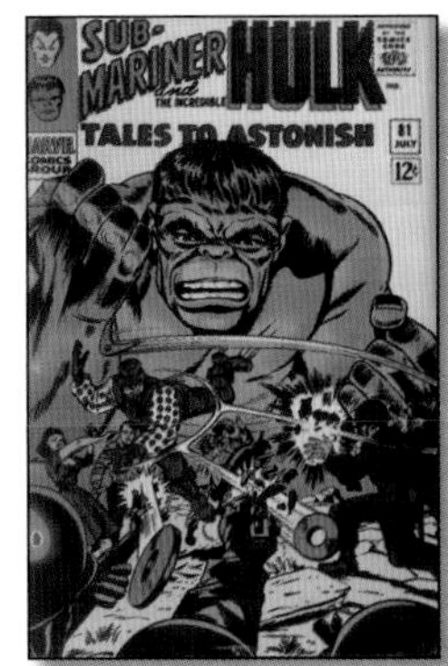

A former Australian baseball player, Fred Myers was known for his incredible accuracy. After being thrown out of baseball for taking bribes, he began a life of crime using his specialized boomerangs. He later worked for Justin Hammer, for the Secret Empire criminal organization, and was a founding member of the Sinister Syndicate.

LANCER BOOKS

Lancer Books, a well-known publisher of mass-market paperbacks, licensed the rights for four books that reprinted the adventures of the Fantastic Four, Spider-Man, Daredevil, and Dr. Strange. These black-and-white books printed the comic pages sideways, like newspaper comic strips, and were Marvel's first real attempt to move from the comic racks to the book stores.

AUGUST

THE OLD BULLPEN CHANGETH

• *The Amazing Spider-Man* #39

The July *Bullpen Bulletins* announced that Steve Ditko was leaving Marvel and that his final issues were *The Amazing Spider-Man* #38 and the Dr. Strange story in *Strange Tales* #146. To this day, no one really knows why Ditko quit. Bullpen sources reported he was unhappy with the way Lee scripted some of his plots, using a tongue-in-cheek approach to stories that Ditko wanted handled seriously. It is also known that Ditko often objected to Lee's use of sound effects. Some said he quit because he thought Peter Parker should cease being a loser once he entered college. All anyone knows for certain is that the two men had rarely talked in months. Ditko would plot the stories without consulting Lee and drop off the pencilled artwork for him to script. According to Lee, he learned of Ditko's departure from production supervisor Sol Brodsky—Ditko hadn't told his former collaborator that he was leaving.

Lee immediately assigned John Romita to *The Amazing Spider-Man* #39. Although he had worked for Lee in the 1950s, Romita had spent nearly ten years drawing romance titles for DC Comics and had a more traditional approach to visual storytelling than Ditko. He also drew handsome men and prettier women. Romita's work on *The Amazing Spider-Man* really clicked with readers and sales dramatically increased. Fearing that the change in artists might cost him readers, Lee finally solved the long-running mystery of the Green Goblin by revealing he was actually Norman Osborn in issue #40 (Sept., 1966). And as if that wasn't enough, the Goblin also discovered that Spider-Man was Peter Parker and captured him.

AUGUST

KLAW
• *Fantastic Four* #53

The man who would murder the Black Panther's father was introduced in *Fantastic Four* #53. Ulysses Klaw was a physicist who devised a weapon that could transform sound waves into solid objects that obeyed his commands. All he needed was a supply of vibranium, a special metal found in the Black Panther's African nation of Wakanda, which he eventually succeeding in stealing and used to leave the Panther an orphan. His criminal exploits have led to many battles with both the Panther and the Fantastic Four.

SEPTEMBER

SONS OF THE SERPENT
• *The Avengers* #32

Stan Lee and Don Heck introduced the villainous group Sons of the Serpent in *The Avengers* #32. Possibly modeled on the notorious Ku Klux Klan—a secret organization known for advocating white supremacy—the Sons of the Serpent hated anyone who wasn't born in America or shared their beliefs. The Avengers stood against them because "whenever the deadly poison of bigotry touches us, the flames of freedom burn a little dimmer."

THE ORIGIN OF THE GREEN GOBLIN
• *The Amazing Spider-Man* #40

During the course of *The Amazing Spider-Man* #40, readers finally learned how accidental exposure to an experimental chemical had increased Norman Osborn's strength and worn away his sanity, turning the ambitious businessman into a deadly super-criminal.

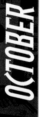

ORIGIN OF THE HOWLING COMMANDOS
• *Sgt. Fury And His Howling Commandos* #34

The origin of the Howling Commandos was detailed in *Sgt. Fury And His Howling Commandos* #34. While helping to train British Commandos in low-level parachuting techniques, Nick Fury and his childhood friend Red Hargrove caught the eye of Lieutenant Sam Sawyer. He recruited them for a mission in Holland where they eventually met Dum-Dum Dugan and battled Nazi agents. After Red was killed during the attack on Pearl Harbor, Sawyer assigned Fury to lead an elite group of Army Rangers that eventually became the Howlers.

SEPTEMBER

EGO THE LIVING PLANET
• *The Mighty Thor* #132

Constantly trying to outdo themselves, Stan Lee and Jack Kirby came up with a truly unique super-menace when they created Ego the living planet. Ego was a self-aware planet that had been formed around the time of the Big Bang and lived in a mysterious region of space known as the Black Galaxy. Roughly the size of Earth's moon, it was able to generate armies of non-living warriors from its own mass and use them to conquer its enemies.

Ego could control its entire mass and often shaped itself to resemble a gigantic face with which it addressed powerful beings.

Publisher Martin Goodman made a deal with the company Gantray-Lawrence to produce an animated television show calle *Marvel Super Heroes*. Starring Captain America, Hulk, Iron Mar Thor, and the Sub-Mariner, this was the first time the new Marv characters appeared on television.

OCTOBER

THE SUPER-ADAPTOID
• *Tales Of Suspense* #82

Stan Lee and Jack Kirby conceived the ultimate menace to pit against Captain America when they introduced the Adaptoid. The Adaptoid was a synthetic life-form created by the scientists of AIM (Advanced Idea Mechanics). Powered by a sliver of the all-powerful Cosmic Cube, he was the ultimate weapon against super-human foes. He could assume the physical skills and properties of anyone within his vicinity and eventually took on the powers of all the Avengers, but even that wasn't enough to defeat Captain America.

OCTOBER

THE RHINO

• *The Amazing Spider-Man* #41

The first original Super Villain produced by the new Spider-Man team of Stan Lee and John Romita was the Rhino, who seemed to be an unstoppable force. Like the Juggernaut, he possessed the steady, relentless speed of an onrushing freight train. Nearly as strong as the Hulk, the Rhino was practically invulnerable in his protective rhinoceros hide.

Aleksei Sytsevich was a poor Russian immigrant who worked as an enforcer for some local gangsters until he was transformed into the Rhino.

COMIC SUPPORT

• *Marvel Super Heroes* #1

To help support the new animated television show, Martin Goodman told Stan Lee to produce a comic called *Marvel Super Heroes*. The first issue contained reprints of *Daredevil* #1 and an early battle between the Golden Age Human Torch and the Sub-Mariner. The title later replaced *Fantasy Masterpieces* and restarted with issue #12.

NOVEMBER

PETER PARKER HITS THE JACKPOT

• *The Amazing Spider-Man* #42

After teasing the readers for more than two years, Stan Lee finally allowed Peter Parker to meet Mary Jane Watson. She was originally portrayed as a gorgeous, empty-headed party girl, but we later learned that this persona hid a far more complex woman. Her parents were always moving so Mary Jane had become an extrovert in order to make new friends quickly. She knew almost from the beginning that Peter was Spider-Man as she had witnessed him sneaking out of his aunt's house one night. She was afraid of getting involved with him, but unfortunately, the attraction proved too great. Mary Jane eventually fell in love with Peter and they later married in *The Amazing Spider-Man Annual* #21 (1987).

FACE IT, TIGER...
YOU JUST HIT THE JACKPOT!

NOVEMBER

THE HUMAN TORCH VS THE HUMAN TORCH

• *Fantastic Four Annual* #4

Having already introduced the original Human Torch—from the Golden Age of comics—to modern readers through various reprints, Stan Lee and Jack Kirby brought him back in *Fantastic Four Annual* #4 in a story that featured a prolonged battle with his modern-day namesake.

THE LIVING LASER

• *The Avengers* #34

Never one to pass up a good gimmick, Stan Lee must have become aware of the growing use of lasers in commercial enterprises because he and Don Heck introduced the Living Laser, a technician who attached lasers to his wrists. Although he possessed a powerful weapon, the Living Laser usually worked as a mercenary for the likes of the Mandarin, Batroc's Brigade, the Lethal Legion, and even the Masters of Evil. Later, an attempt to increase his powers backfired and transformed him into a sentient being made entirely of light.

SPIDER-MAN TRIES TO JOIN THE AVENGERS

• *The Amazing Spider-Man Annual* #3

The Avengers extended an invitation to Spider-Man in *The Amazing Spider-Man Annual* #3. To join them, all he had to do was pass an initiation test, which was to find and defeat the Hulk. However, when the Hulk transformed into Bruce Banner during their fight, Spidey felt sorry for him and refused to complete his mission. The webhead did succeed in joining the Avengers in the 1980s and the New Avengers in 2006.

Spider-Man assumed the Avengers wanted to punish the Hulk and didn't realize that they actually intended to help him.

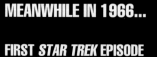

MEANWHILE IN 1966...

FIRST *STAR TREK* EPISODE BROADCAST

The fascination with science fiction is fueled with a new series about "space… the final frontier" and becomes a worldwide television phenomenon.

CBS: *PSYCHO* "TOO VIOLENT"

The broadcaster pulls out of plans to televise Hitchcock's movie Psycho *amid fears that it is too violent for home viewing.*

THE MINI SKIRT IS ON THE UP

The short skirt cut well above the knee, popularized by model Jean Shrimpton, hits the US and becomes an instant craze.

TIME MAGAZINE REPORTS ON "SWINGING LONDON"

The magazine's cover story reveals a London dominated by youth and 1960s popular culture: Mary Quant's fashions, the Rolling Stones' music, an explosion of discotheques, and liberal politics.

SHOOTING SPREE AT TEXAS UNIVERSITY

America is left reeling after the first major shooting rampage on an education campus. Charles Whitman kills fourteen and wounds dozens more as he fires from the observation deck of the university's tower.

BUILDING BLOCKS OF LIFE DISCOVERED

American biochemists Marshall Nirenberg and Har Khorana finish deciphering DNA, the genetic code common to all living organisms.

WOMEN'S MOVEMENT

A group of women, including Betty Friedan, found the National Organization for Women (NOW). It is the largest women's rights group in American and it aims to put an end to sexual discrimination through political lobbying, litigation, and public demonstrations.

THE FIRST "ACID TEST" PARTY

The first of Ken Kesey's psychedelic parties that celebrate LSD is held in San Francisco. These counterculture parties contribute to the transition from the beat generation to the hippie movement.

AND AT THE MOVIES...

Batman, *the first full-length adaptation of the DC Comics character;* A Man for All Seasons, *a portrait of the life of Sir Thomas More;* The Good, the Bad, and the Ugly, *Sergio Leone's third spaghetti western, with its legendary three-way shoot-out, confirms his reputation and Clint Eastwood's charisma;* Thunderbirds Are Go, *the first movie based on the television series;* Fahrenheit 451, *a depiction of a dystopian future where independent thought is outlawed;* Dr. Seuss' How the Grinch Stole Christmas, *a classic adaptation of the book.*

THE BEST COURSE OF ACTION IS TO USE MY UNIVERSAL BEAM BLASTER!

1967

A GROWING LEAGUE OF FRANTIC FANS

In the first *Bullpen Bulletins* of 1967, Stan Lee gave an insight into the lead time needed to produce comics. He explained that he was writing this on July 14, 1966: the comic would go on sale in October and be cover-dated January 1967.

Marvel was now publishing fourteen to eighteen titles a month. *Stars And Stripes*, the newspaper for the US military, did a feature story on the company and more than one hundred college campuses formed their own chapters of the Merry Marvel Marching Society. Members of the M.M.M.S. began to receive the *Merry Marvel Messenger*, a free newspaper that was an expanded version of the *Bullpen Bulletins* and included news, biographies of the staff, and previews of upcoming publications.

Mark Evanier—who would go on to write comics and television programs—wrote suggesting that the M.M.M.S. have officers: anyone who bought a Marvel comic was entitled to the rank of RFO (Real Frantic One) and a published letter in a Marvel comic elevated him or her to QNS (Quite 'Nuff Sayer) status.

The June *Bullpen Bulletins* featured the first *Stan's Soapbox*. Stan Lee began it by explaining the Marvel Philosophy, which was basically to produce stories exciting enough to entertain him and his creative team.

JANUARY

BANSHEE DEBUTS

• *The X-Men* #28

Writer Roy Thomas wanted to introduce mutants from other countries into the X-Men. His first attempt was Banshee. The character was originally a woman, but Stan Lee told Thomas to make her a man because he didn't think it would look good for the X-Men to gang up on a single Super Villainess. Drawn by Werner Roth, Banshee was a former Irish Interpol agent who eventually joined the X-Men and later left to oversee Xavier's Academy, which taught the young mutants of Generation X.

M *The X-Men* #28 also introduced Factor Three, a top secret subversive organization inspired by James Bond's SPECTRE and *The Man From U.N.C.L.E.*'s THRUSH.

LADY SIF IS INTRODUCED

• *The Mighty Thor* #136

Although a blonde Goddess named Lady Sif had already appeared in the "Tales Of Asgard" story in *Journey Into Mystery* #101 (Feb., 1964), the more recognizable, raven-haired Asgardian warrior-Goddess finally showed up in *The Mighty Thor* #136. Thor used to bounce Sif, the sister of the God Heimdall, on his knee. Because the Gods of Asgard are virtually immortal and take longer to grow older, Sif eventually became Thor's contemporary. They fell in love while still adolescents, but parted when Sif was sent to train as a warrior. They were reunited shortly after Thor ended his relationship with his nurse Jane Foster.

AS A YOUNG GIRL--SILENTLY WATCHING YOU GALLOP INTO BATTLE, I HAVE LOVED YOU, SON OF ODIN! I HAVE LOVED YOUR SPIRIT, YOUR STRENGTH--YOUR MATCHLESS COURAGE--AS ONLY A CHILD CAN LOVE!
BUT, NOW YOU HAVE CHANGED! AN AURA OF SORROW PERVADES YOUR MANNER--!
AY! EVEN A GOD MAY KNOW THE PANGS OF DESPAIR!

Lady Sif was a master swordswoman who possessed an enchanted sword that opened a dimensional pathway between Asgard and Earth.

FEBRUARY

AWW, DON'T BE FORMAL, BUDDY, YOU CAN CALL ME MISTER MURDOCK!
MATTHEW SAID YOU WANTED TO SEE ME--SO FEAST YOUR EYES, KIDDIES!
HEARD ANY GOOD STORIES LATELY?
HOW ABOUT SOME BAD ONES?

MATT MURDOCK'S TWIN BROTHER

• *Daredevil* #25

Matt Murdock decided to introduce his legal partner and his secretary to his identical twin brother when they began to suspect he was Daredevil. Unfortunately, he didn't actually have one. So, Matt pretended to be his own twin, who was a glibber and more enthusiastic party boy.

However, Matt soon found himself competing with "Mike" for Karen Page's attentions and juggling three identities proved too much so he faked Mike's death in issue #41.

M A failed toy inventor, Vincent Patillo, aka Leap-Frog, tried to use jumping coils for crime in *Daredevil* #25. This was not successful, but his son went on to be the Super Hero Frog-Man.

FEBRUARY

THE GHOST RIDER APPEARS

• *The Ghost Rider* #1

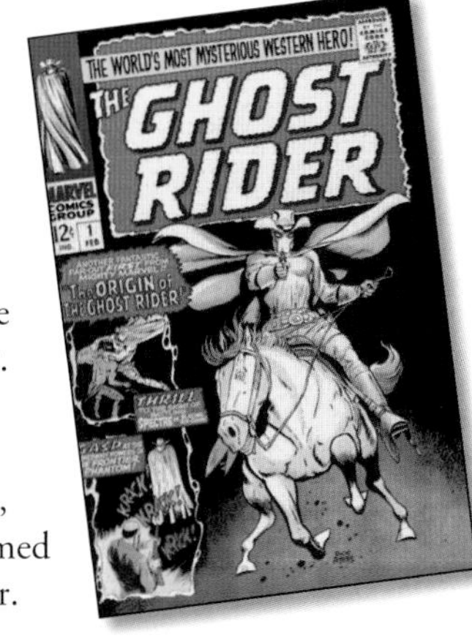

Ghost Rider had been produced by another publisher in the 1950s, but when the trademark fell into the public domain, Marvel created their own version. Carter Slade was a teacher who donned a costume to fight for law and order in the Old West. After he was killed, his brother Lincoln assumed the identity and changed his name to the Phantom Rider. In the 2000s, Lincoln's descendent Hamilton Slade roamed the plains as a modern-day Phantom Rider.

THE INHUMANS BREAK FREE

• *Fantastic Four* #59

After being trapped by an impenetrable force-field in the city of Attilan since *Fantastic Four* #48 (March, 1966), the Inhumans freed themselves when Black Bolt's sonic scream shattered the Great Barrier.

THE FIRST APPEARANCE OF ULIK

• *The Mighty Thor* #137

As powerful as Thor himself, Ulik first trudged on to the scene in *The Mighty Thor* #137. The strongest and fiercest of all the Rock Trolls, Ulik lived with his monstrous race in the caverns beneath Asgard. Time and again, he sought to defeat Thor. He also led his people against the armies of Asgard and, on a few occasions, even tried to invade the Earth.

Ulik was powerful enough to shrug off a direct blow from Thor without any apparent injury.

MARCH

SHOCK WAVES FOR SPIDER-MAN

• *The Amazing Spider-Man* #46

Everyone's favorite web-slinger was first jolted by the sinister Shocker in *The Amazing Spider-Man* #46. Created by Stan Lee and artist John Romita, Herman Schultz was a former safe-cracker who attempted to invent a device that could shake safe doors loose. His vibro-shock gauntlets proved a lot more powerful than he imagined, so he designed a foam-lined costume to protect himself and became a one-man crime wave.

In the same issue, Peter Parker finally moved out of Aunt May's house and into an apartment he shared with Harry Osborn.

M "In our midst... an immortal!" Following Thor's lead, Hercules also joined the "Earth's Mightiest Heroes" in *The Avengers* #38.

APRIL

EMIL BLONSKY BECOMES THE ABOMINATION

• *The Amazing Spider-Man* #47

Stan Lee needed a villain who could stand up to the Hulk. Someone stronger and more powerful. Working with artist Gil Kane, he proudly presented the Abomination. Emil Blonsky was a Russian spy who found Bruce Banner's gamma-radiation equipment and used it to become a bigger, stronger, and far more intelligent version of the Hulk. Although he towered over his smaller adversary, the Abomination could never defeat the Hulk for long—the Hulk was just too stubborn to ever admit defeat and his strength grew in direct proportion to his anger. Blonsky lived in New York's sewers for a time and later murdered Banner's wife, Betty.

AN IRON MAN WANNABE

• *The X-Men* #31

Imitation is said to be the highest form of flattery, but it also has its drawbacks. Writer Roy Thomas and artist Werner Roth took their own shot at all Marvel's imitators when they introduced Cobalt Man. Trying to model himself on Iron Man, Ralph Roberts built his own armored suit, but he soon learned that he wasn't as good as the original.

PRINCE BYRRAH RETURNS

• *Tales To Astonish* #90

Originally introduced in the Golden Age of comics, Namor's old enemy—Prince Byrrah—finally returned to comics in *Tales To Astonish* #90, courtesy of Stan Lee and the prince's original creator, writer/artist Bill Everett.

MAY

A NEW VULTURE

• *The Amazing Spider-Man* #48

Stan Lee thought that whenever Spider-Man battled the Vulture, he looked like a bully picking on a senior citizen. He discussed the problem with artist John Romita and they decided to create a new, younger Vulture. Convinced he was dying, Adrian Toomes—the original Vulture—told Blackie Drago where to find the Vulture wings so that he could take up where Toomes had left off. Unfortunately, readers didn't like the new Vulture and Lee received enough letters to convince him to bring back the original in *The Amazing Spider-Man* #63 (Aug., 1968).

THE LEADER OF HYDRA IS REVEALED

• *Strange Tales* #156

After battling HYDRA for nearly two years, Nick Fury learned in *Strange Tales* #156 that its mysterious leader was his old World War II enemy, Baron Von Strucker.

THE FIRST APPEARANCE OF BLASTAAR

• *Fantastic Four* #62

An inhabitant of the mysterious anti-matter universe called the Negative Zone, Blastaar could generate blasts of concussive force from his fingertips. A ruthless monarch whose people overthrew him and set him adrift in space, he accidentally discovered Reed Richards' portal to Earth in *Fantastic Four* #62. Blastaar often battled Annihilus for control of the Negative Zone and also tried to conquer the Earth.

Blastaar possessed superhuman strength. He could survive in airless space and go weeks without nourishment.

THE GROWING MAN DEBUTS

• *The Mighty Thor* #140

How do you defeat a foe who grows larger and more powerful every time you strike him? That was the question that Stan Lee and Jack Kirby posed when they created the Growing Man. A robot designed by Kang the Conqueror, Growing Man grew to giant proportions with every blow of Thor's enchanted hammer and would have eventually grown large enough to sink a continent if Thor hadn't trapped him within his magical vortex.

JUNE

THE LIVING TRIBUNAL JUDGES

• *Strange Tales* #157

Dr. Strange first incurred the wrath of the Living Tribunal in *Strange Tales* #157 when he unleashed an ancient evil upon the universe. The Tribunal was an extra-dimensional being of incalculable power who had existed since the dawn of the universe. Its sacred duty was to preserve the cosmic balance between good and evil. It had three separate faces, which represented equity, vengeance, and necessity, and it could only pass final judgment when all three were in agreement.

JULY

WILSON FISK, THE KINGPIN OF CRIME

"Instead of many rival gangs operating haphazardly throughout the city... Instead of countless crooks acting alone, without a chance agains the police... The underworld will now be run like a business... and the chairman of the board will be... the Kingpin!"

• *The Amazing Spider-Man* #50

Stan Lee wanted to create a new kind of crime boss. Someone who treated crime as if it were a business. Someone who would act like the Chairman of the Board of a mighty corporation. The boss of all the other crime bosses. He pitched this idea to artist John Romita and it was Wilson Fisk who emerged in *The Amazing Spider-Man* #50.

Predating Mario Puzo's novel *The Godfather* by two years, Fisk was a man of many contrasts. He was both a ruthless criminal and a man who worshipped his wife, a heartless killer and a dedicated father. After moving up the ranks of organized crime, Fisk had seized control of the New York underworld and began to exert his power over the city when it looked like Spider-Man had retired from crime-fighting. Spider-Man returned and they battled frequently until the Kingpin's wife convinced him to retire. Fisk later returned to crime and focused on Daredevil, eventually learning Matt Murdock's secret identity and attempting to ruin him. Fisk lost and regained his criminal empire many times over the years, but he always returned stronger than ever.

A lifelong body builder, Wilson Fisk possessed excellent hand-to-hand fighting skills and was very agile for a man of his size.

JULY

THE "SPIDER-MAN NO MORE" STORY

• *The Amazing Spider-Man* #50

The famous "Spider-Man No More!" story line appeared in *The Amazing Spider-Man* #50. Frustrated that being Spider-Man had only caused him unhappiness, Peter Parker discarded his costume and quit web-spinning. A version of this story also appeared in the 2004 movie *Spider-Man 2*.

THE SINISTER SENTRY IS DISCOVERED

• *Fantastic Four* #64

Stan Lee and Jack Kirby's *Fantastic Four* #64 predated the best-selling book *Chariots of the Gods? Unsolved Mysteries of the Past* by almost a year. Written by Erich von Däniken, the book theorized that extraterrestrials had visited some ancient civilizations and seemed like gods to them. In *Fantastic Four* #64, two archeologists followed the trail of an ancient civilization and discovered a giant alien robot still living in the ruins. Left behind by the space-traveling Kree, Inter-Galactic Sentry 459 immediately attempted to protect his outpost.

Like the previously introduced Skrulls, the Kree were destined to play a major role in the Marvel Universe. Ruled by a vast consciousness called the Supreme Intelligence, they would launch galactic wars against the Skrulls and the Shi'ar. They would also routinely attempt to conquer or destroy the Earth, sending agents like Ronan the Accuser, Dr. Minerva, and Captain Mar-Vell.

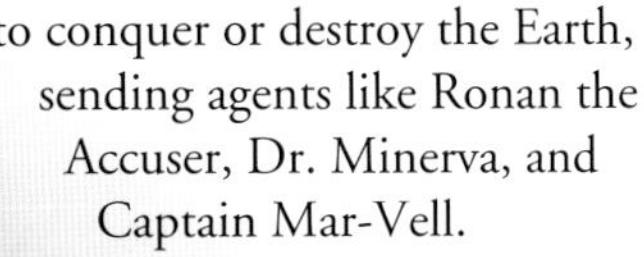

Built by the Kree, the Sentry robots stood guard over military stations and strategic scientific outposts.

AUGUST

THE CHANGELING DEBUTS

• *The X-Men* #35

The Changeling first appeared in *The X-Men* #35 as a brooding figure in the shadows. Readers later learned that he could assume anyone's appearance. As second-in-command of the mysterious Factor Three, he tried the X-Men for crimes against their fellow mutants in *The X-Men* #37 (Oct., 1967). But he later turned against Factor Three when he learned of their plan to eliminate all life on Earth. To make up for his crimes, he secretly agreed to help Professor Xavier by impersonating him.

JOE ROBERTSON IS PROMOTED

• *The Amazing Spider-Man* #51

Joe "Robbie" Robertson was originally hired to assist the *Daily Bugle* Editor-in-Chief, J. Jonah Jameson. He made his first appearance in *The Amazing Spider-Man* #51, when he became the City Editor.

Artist John Romita had planned for Robertson to have a cauliflower ear and be an ex-boxer, but Stan Lee vetoed those ideas. Robertson's quiet demeanor and open mind when it came to Spider-Man was a refreshing contrast to Jameson's loud tirades against the wall-crawler.

RED GUARDIAN IS KILLED

• *The Avengers* #43

Alexi Shostakov, the former husband of the Black Widow, was chosen by the KGB to become the Soviet Union's answer to Captain America, codenamed Red Guardian. He was killed while on a mission to China in *The Avengers* #43, but his costumed identity was later assumed by others.

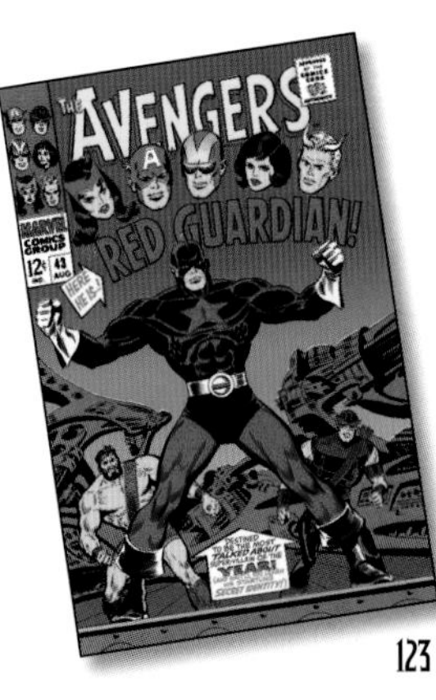

August

MARVEL GOES "MAD"

• *Not Brand Echh* #1

Based on Stan Lee's playful term for his distinguished competition, Marvel launched a new humor comic called *Not Brand Echh*. Although officially copyrighted as *Brand Echh* for its first four issues, *Not Brand Echh* was a parody comic book that followed in the humorous tradition of *MAD Magazine*, which had also begun life as a comic book. It ran for thirteen issues and poked fun at both Marvel and its competition.

Not Brand Echh *satirized many different heroes and villains of all the major comic book companies—including Marvel—and pointed out their foibles, behaviors, and melodramatic dialogue.*

September

WARLOCK IS BORN

• *Fantastic Four* #66

Adam Warlock was an artificial being created by scientists to be the first of an invincible army. Simply referred to as "Him" in his early appearances, Warlock later rebelled against his creators in *Fantastic Four* #66 (Sept., 1967) and left to explore space. He encountered the High Evolutionary, a being able to evolve genetic matter, who gave him his Soul Gem—a gem that could project beams of concussive force and absorb souls. He often battled the Titan called Thanos, who once mortally wounded him, forcing him to retreat into his Soul Gem, where he stayed for many years.

FREDERICK FOSWELL DIES

• *The Amazing Spider-Man* #52

The *Daily Bugle* reporter Frederick Foswell—who had been the criminal leader the Big Man and also the police informant called Patch—lost his life in *The Amazing Spider-Man* #52 for daring to challenge Wilson Fisk, the Kingpin of Crime.

- *The Avengers King-Size Special* #1 contained a forty-nine-page story with the old and the New Avengers, billed as: "The biggest continuous action epic ever in the Marvel Age of Comics!"
- Electro assembled the Emissaries of Evil group to get revenge on Daredevil in *Daredevil Annual* #1 by Stan Lee and Gene Colan.

September

SPIDER-MAN AND THE FANTASTIC FOUR COME TO LIFE

Marvel continued to branch into the world of television with two new series, featuring their popular characters. The first animated television series to star everyone's favorite webhead was simply called *Spider-Man* and it ran until 1970. It premiered on the American Broadcasting Company (ABC) and was originally produced by Grantray-Lawrence, the animation company behind the *Marvel Super Heroes* show. Animator Ralph Bakshi, who was better known for films like *Fritz the Cat* (1972) and *Lord of the Rings* (1978), took over production in 1968.

Produced by Hanna-Barbera Productions, *Fantastic Four* appeared on ABC from 1967 to 1970 along with *Spider-Man*. Former Marvel artist Alex Toth helped design the characters for animation and the show featured such villains as Dr. Doom, the Red Ghost, and Galactus. Since Namor was currently appearing in the syndicated *Marvel Super Heroes*, Triton of the Inhumans was substituted for him when the show adapted the story from *Fantastic Four* #4 in which Namor was found by Johnny Storm (May, 1962).

October

THE YELLOW CLAW RETURNS

• *Strange Tales* #161

This issue featured the first Marvel Age appearance of the Yellow Claw. Loosely based on the character Dr. Fu Manchu from Sax Rohmer's series of novels, the Claw had starred in his own Atlas Comic during the 1950s, but in 1967 he returned to renew his attempts at conquering the world.

MODOK DEBUTS

• *Tales of Suspense* #94

MODOK, the "Mental Organism Designed Only for Killing," could use his brain to control or destroy anyone. Created by Stan Lee and Jack Kirby, MODOK was used as a guinea pig for a human/computer hybrid by the subversive organization called AIM. He eventually seized control of AIM, but was later ousted. In 2007, he formed MODOK'S 11, a team of Super Villains, including Puma, Mentallo, Armadillo, Chameleon, Nightshade, Living Laser, Rocket Racer, and the Spot.

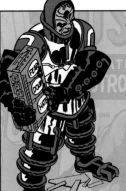

THE PSYCHO-MAN APPEARS

• *Fantastic Four Annual* #5

Stan Lee and Jack Kirby designed a new Super Villain who could control emotions. The Psycho-Man tried to expand his territory to include the Earth and later created his own version of the Hate-Monger—an android that spread terrorism and bigotry through New York City using pamphlets that had been treated with chemicals that incited hatred.

BATTLING MAGNETO

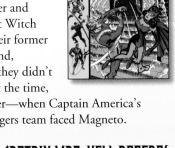

• *The Avengers* #47

Quicksilver and the Scarlet Witch battled their former leader—and, although they didn't know it at the time, their father—when Captain America's new Avengers team faced Magneto.

CAPTAIN MAR-VELL APPEARS

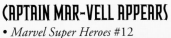

• *Marvel Super Heroes* #12

Captain Mar-Vell was a Kree warrior sent to spy on the Earth, by Stan Lee and artist Gene Colan. Mar-Vell came to admire mankind and soon found himself protecting them. Later, he became trapped in the Negative Zone and had to become physically bonded with Rick Jones in order to escape. After being named the "Protector of the Universe," he discovered he was dying of cancer. In 2008, a shift in time opened, transporting a younger Mar-Vell to the present day. Unfortunately, he knew that he would eventually have to return to his own time and would not be able to escape his ultimate fate. This version of Mar-Vell was later revealed to be a Skrull imposter in the *Secret Invasion* mega-crossover (2008).

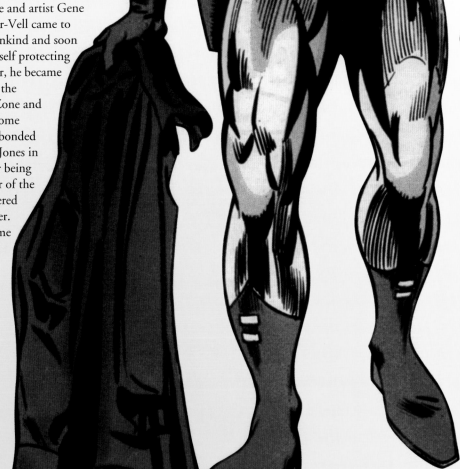

Fawcett Publications had published the adventures of a Captain Marvel in the 1940s and 1950s, but the title then fell into the public domain. Since Stan Lee didn't want anyone else to use the word Marvel, he created the comic Captain Marvel*—even though the character's real name was Mar-Vell.*

M *Fantasy Masterpieces* became *Marvel Super Heroes* with issue #12.

MEANWHILE IN 1967...

SIX-DAY WAR IN THE MIDDLE EAST

Israel triumphs over its Arab neighbors, seizing the Gaza Strip, the Sinai Peninsula, the West Bank of Jordan, and the Golan Heights.

"SUMMER OF LOVE"

The hippie counterculture movement hits the public consciousness when 100,000 young people gather in San Francisco for a festival in the spirit of cultural and political rebellion.

TWIGGY TAKES NEW YORK BY STORM

The first teenage female supermodel becomes an instant icon. She is known for her Mary Quant-influenced high-fashion mod look, large eyes, and skinny figure.

A NEW ERA OF MAGAZINES

Rolling Stone *and* New York Magazine *launch a new trend for special-interest and regional magazines.*

DONALD CAMPBELL KILLED IN WORLD RECORD ATTEMPT

The world-record holder was trying to beat his own water-speed record when his jet-powered Bluebird flew off course on Coniston Water in the UK.

FIRST HEART TRANSPLANT

The first heart transplant is conducted in South Africa by Professor C.N. Barnard on fifty-three-year-old Lewis Washkansky.

RECORD PRICE FOR A PICASSO PAINTING

Picasso's Mother and Child by the Sea *sells at auction for $532,000, a record price for a painting by a living artist.*

A NEW WAY TO COOK

Amana launches the first microwave for home use and revolutionizes the way people cook.

"MOUSE" ENTERS COMPUTER SPEAK

Douglas Engelbart files a patent for his prototype of a computer mouse. The wooden frame on two metal wheels was so named because "the tail came out the end."

AND AT THE MOVIES...

The Graduate, *a daring comedy about a student seduced by an older woman before falling for her daughter, which evokes the promiscuous 1960s;* Bonnie and Clyde, *Arthur Penn's stylized and amoral retelling of the outlaw couple's violent life and death;* The Jungle Book, *Disney's musical adaptation of the Kipling stories about the boy-cub Mowgli features some of its best characters and songs;* Thoroughly Modern Millie, *a musical comedy starring Julie Andrews;* You Only Live Twice, *the fifth James Bond film.*

The Mighty Thor #137 (Feb., 1967) written by Stan Lee, art by Jack Kirby, inked by Vince Colletta.
No one could draw a fight scene as well as Jack Kirby. A master when it came to exciting visual story-telling, Jack's characters rippled with raw power and thrilled readers with each bone-breaking blow. Stan Lee had a flair for dramatic dialogue—whether it was Peter Parker's contemporary quips or Thor's almost Shakespearian speeches. Together, the two creators produced pure Marvel magic!

CONTINUED AFTER NEXT PAGE

THERE IS NO *RIGHT*--THERE IS NO *WRONG*--
ONLY *MY COMMAND!*

1968

THE SECOND AGE OF MARVEL COMICS

As 1968 commenced, Marvel's Martin Goodman put extra pressure on his distributor Independent News. Their contract was coming to an end and his comics were now drastically outselling the competition. *T.V. Guide* reported that Marvel was selling nearly fifty million comics a year. In 1967, Marvel had been restricted to fourteen to eighteen titles a month, but for 1968 Goodman drove the limit up to twenty-four.

Hailing 1968 as the beginning of the "Second Age of Marvel Comics," and with more titles to play with, editor Stan Lee discarded his split books and gave more characters their own titles: *Tales Of Suspense* #99 was followed by *Captain America* #100, *Tales To Astonish* #101 by *The Incredible Hulk* #102, and *Strange Tales* #168 by *Dr. Strange* #169. The Sub-Mariner, Iron Man, Nick Fury, and even Captain Mar-Vell were all given their own titles. Lee used *Marvel Super Heroes* to showcase new features and existing characters like Medusa and Ka-Zar in their own stories. Marvel also created two new magazines, *Groovy* and *The Adventures Of Pussycat*, which was aimed at older readers. Lee said he would no longer refer to the competition as "Brand Echh"—while it had been okay to poke fun at other companies when they were bigger than Marvel, it no longer seemed appropriate now that his comics dominated the market.

JANUARY

THE BLACK KNIGHT LIVES AGAIN

"I—I know I was wrong, boy! But it's too late for me now! But it's not too late for you! You must swear to use my researches for good... as I used them for evil!"

• *The Avengers* #48

Writer Roy Thomas was an early believer in creator's rights. He hesitated when it came to creating new Super Heroes that Marvel would own because he knew that he would resent the company if any of his characters made it big. So, instead of coming up with new heroes, he often employed a name that Marvel already owned and built a new character around it. Such was the case with the Black Knight. The first Black Knight, Sir Percy of Scandia, had appeared in an Atlas comic in the 1950s. The second was a Super Villain who fought Iron Man and later became a member of the first Baron Zemo's Masters of Evil team. Thomas' version was the third incarnation of the Black Knight.

Dane Whitman became the third Black Knight in *The Avengers* #48, although his civilian identity had already been introduced in the previous issue. Whitman was the nephew of the evil second Knight, Nathan Garrett. After Garrett died, Whitman decided to atone for his uncle's misdeeds by using the Black Knight identity in the cause of justice. Unfortunately, the Avengers mistook Dane for his uncle and attacked him. However, he eventually proved his good intentions and later became a member of the team.

In *Marvel Super Heroes* #17 (Nov., 1968), by Roy Thomas and artist Howard Purcell, Dane met Sir Percy, the original Black Knight, and obtained his invincible ebony sword. Able to cut through any object, the sword dramatically increased the Knight's power, but it also came with a curse: it sought to control its master whenever it tasted blood.

THEN, AS THE YOUNG SCIENTIST *CONCLUDES* HIS REVERIE...
SO, THE TIME HAS *COME!*
I MUST DON THE *IMPROVED ARMOR* I'VE DEVELOPED, AND REDEEM THE NAME OF-- *THE BLACK KNIGHT!*

Using his uncle's scientific notes, Dane Whitman mutated a winged steed that he named Aragorn.

MADAME MASQUE APPEARS

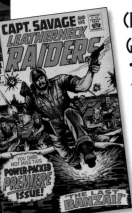

• *Tales Of Suspense* #97

Because Tony Stark was the ultimate ladies' man, Stan Lee and artist Gene Colan decided to pit him against a powerful female criminal.

The biological daughter of Count Nefaria, Whitney Frost took her name from her adoptive father Byron Frost, but she assumed control of the Count's criminal organization called the Maggia after he was imprisoned. Her face was later disfigured during a raid on Stark Industries and she took to wearing a golden mask and calling herself Madame Masque. Tony Stark's charms eventually won her over and she fell in love with him.

Tales Of Suspense #97 also introduced Whiplash (who later changed his name to Blacklash), who employed two cybernetically controlled whips.

MEET GWEN STACY'S FATHER

• *The Amazing Spider-Man* #56

Co-created by Stan Lee and artist John Romita, George Stacy was the father of Spider-Man's girlfriend Gwen Stacy. He was a retired police captain and close friend of the *Daily Bugle*'s Joe Robertson. The two men often met to discuss Spider-Man and Stacy eventually began to suspect that Peter Parker was the wall-crawler. Stacy died while saving a child from a falling chimney in *The Amazing Spider-Man* #90 (Nov., 1970).

CAPTAIN SAVAGE GETS HIS OWN TITLE

• *Capt. Savage And His Leatherneck Raiders* #1

Super Heroes may have been dominating Marvel's sales, but the war comic *Sgt. Fury And His Howling Commandos* was also doing well. Captain Savage had been introduced as a submarine commander simply called "the Skipper" in *Sgt. Fury* #10 (Sep., 1964). He went on to appear in five more issues before he was given a name and awarded his own title. In *Capt. Savage And His Leatherneck Raiders* #1, Captain Simon Savage was transferred from the Navy to the Marines to lead an elite attack force. The comic was created by writer Gary Friedrich and artist Dick Ayers and its title changed to *Capt. Savage And His Battlefield Raiders* with issue #9. The series lasted nineteen issues until March 1970.

Capt. Simon Savage modeled his squad after Sgt. Fury's Howling Commandos. Based in the Pacific, they usually fought the Japanese. Private Lee Baker was killed in action in Capt. Savage And His Battlefield Raiders *#11 (Feb., 1969).*

FEBRUARY

THE POUNDING POWER OF THE WRECKER

• *The Mighty Thor* #148

Dirk Gatherwaite smashed and destroyed for the sheer pleasure of it. He wielded a crowbar to remind him of his abusive father, a former construction worker. A case of mistaken identity in this issue caused him to be transformed into the Wrecker, a living engine of destruction, who left shattered buildings in his wake. In *The Defenders* #17 (Nov., 1974), he befriended three other convicts—Bulldozer, Piledriver, and Thunderball—and shared his power with them. Along with this destructive Wrecking Crew, Gatherwaite was drawn into crossovers like *Marvel Super Heroes Secret Wars* (1984) and *Civil War* (2007).

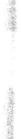

Karnilla, the Norn Queen, actually intended to super-charge Loki, the Asgardian God of Mischief, but she accidentally gave her powers to the Wrecker instead.

The Hulk and the Sub-Mariner features were combined into a single twenty-two-page battle to celebrate the one-hundreth issue of *Tales To Astonish*.

MARCH

DESTINY DEBUTS

• *Tales To Astonish* #101

This issue introduced Destiny, the man responsible for stripping the Sub-Mariner of his memory and causing the events that led to Johnny Storm finding him in *Fantastic Four* #4 (May, 1962).

THE DEATH OF PROFESSOR X

• *The X-Men* #42

"Not a hoax! Not a dream! Not an imaginary tale!" boasted the cover of *The X-Men* #42. Inside, Professor Charles Xavier, the leader of the X-Men, died during a battle with the sub-human Grotesk. Of course, the comic did not let on to readers that this particular Professor X was an imposter, who was eventually revealed to be the mutant metamorph the Changeling.

APRIL

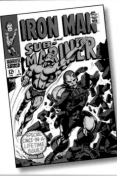

IRON MAN AND THE SUB MARINER

• *Iron Man And Sub-Mariner* #1

Marvel ended its split books with a special one-off edition called *Iron Man And Sub-Mariner*. Billed as a "special once-in-a-lifetime issue," it contained the last two eleven-page stories originally slotted for *Tales Of Suspense* and *Tales To Astonish*, and a letters page called "Astonishing Mails of Suspense."

MAY

THE GRIM REAPER APPEARS

"I am the embodiment of death... and I strike in the name of just vengeance!"

• *The Avengers* #52

The Grim Reaper slashed his way into the Marvel Universe in *The Avengers* #52, an issue written by Roy Thomas and drawn by John Buscema. Having read every issue of *The Avengers*, Thomas decided to do a follow-up to issue #9, which had introduced Wonder Man, aka Simon Williams. For issue #52, Thomas introduced Simon's brother Eric, who became the Grim Reaper. Armed with a scythe that fired bursts of electrical energy, he shocked his victims into coma-like states. Believing the Avengers responsible for his brother's death, Eric accused them of murder and sentenced them all to death.

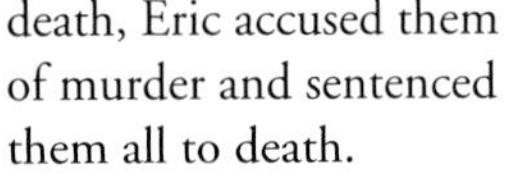

The Grim Reaper's scythe could rotate fast enough to deflect bullets. It also projected various types of gas and could be used like a buzz saw.

The scythe's handle fitted over the Grim Reaper's right hand. Aside from its ability to induce comas, it could also project devastating blasts of concussive force.

MAY

RED RAVEN RETURNS

• *The X-Men* #44

The Red Raven had originally been create by Joe Simon and Jack Kirby for his own title in August 1940, but he reappeared courtesy of Roy Thomas (plot), Gary Friedrich (dialogue), and Werner Roth (pencils). A fan of the Golden Age of Comics, Thomas brought Red Raven bac because he liked the name and the idea that the character was the last of his race.

SPIDER-MAN HEADLINES ANOTHER COMIC

• *Marvel Super Heroes* #14

Although Spider-Man was appearing in his own monthly title, *Marvel Super Heroes* #14 was the first time he headlined another comic book. Sadly, no one remembers the reasons for Spider-Man's appearance in a title that was used to showcase new features. It migh have come about because Stan Lee was trying to see whether Spider-Man could carry more than one title per month, or he might have been auditioning artist Ross Andru as a possible replacement for Spider-Man's artist at the time, John Romita.

JUNE

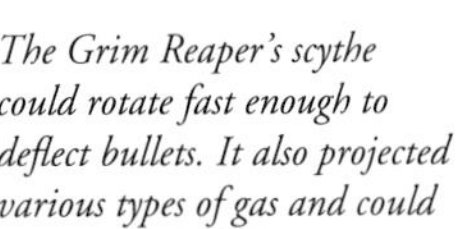

SCORPIO IS INTRODUCED

• *Nick Fury, Agent Of SHIELD* #1

Writer/artist Jim Steranko had begun to draw the "Nick Fury, Agent Of SHIELD" story in *Strange Tales* #151 and started writing it four issues later. When the feature got its own title, Steranko introduced Scorpio in issue #1. Scorpio was secretly Jack Fury, Nick's younger brother. Possessing a sentient weapon called the Zodiac Key that manipulated matter and energy, Scorpio routinely tried to spread terror across the United States and kill his own brother.

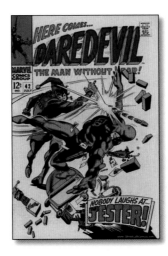

Jack Fury was actually the pawn of the sentient Zodiac Key, which kept creating new android bodies for him whenever he died.

JULY

THE JESTER'S FIRST APPEARANC

• *Daredevil* #42

Like most writers, Stan Lee had little use for critics. Thus, it came as no surprise when he and artist Gene Colan introduced Jonathan Powers, aka the Jester. An actor who had been savaged by critics, Powers turned to crime when his stage care faltered and he was forced to work a a clown on a children's television show. He dressed in a harlequin-lik costume and disguised his weapons so that they looked like toys.

THE MANY FORMS OF ULTRON

"You may have eluded me this time, Avengers... but there are other ways of striking at you... more deadly ways! You shall all die... by the hand of Ultron-5!"

• *The Avengers* #54

A precursor of the unstoppable robot in the *Terminator* films, Ultron sprang from the creative minds of writer Roy Thomas and artist John Buscema, although his name Ultron wasn't revealed until the following issue. Calling himself the Crimson Cowl at first, Ultron brought together a new Masters of Evil group that consisted of the Klaw, Whirlwind, the Melter, the third Black Knight (who only pretended to be evil), and Radioactive Man. He also brainwashed Edwin Jarvis, the Avengers' butler, and forced him to betray them. Ultron had been built by Hank Pym and was programmed with his master's brain patterns, but, like Frankenstein's monster, he rebelled against his creator and later tried to destroy him.

Ultron had two main desires: to survive and to bring peace and order to the universe. Unfortunately, he could only accomplish his second goal by eliminating all intelligent life. Ultron constantly upgraded himself and built more powerful models. He began with Ultron-5 and, by *Mighty Avengers* #1 (May, 2008), reached Ultron-18. He even incorporated the indestructible metal called adamantium into his body. Ultron also created two mates for himself: Jocasta, programmed with the Wasp's brain patterns, and Alkhema, who had the personality and intelligence of the New Avengers founder, Mockingbird. Ultron-12 became a member of the Lethal Legion and Ultron-15 built thousands of duplicates and conquered the small fictional European country of Slorenia.

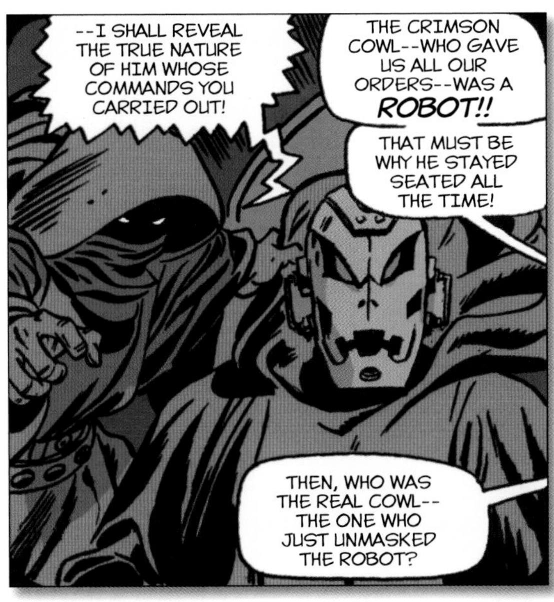

--I SHALL REVEAL THE TRUE NATURE OF HIM WHOSE COMMANDS YOU CARRIED OUT!
THE CRIMSON COWL--WHO GAVE US ALL OUR ORDERS--WAS A ROBOT!!
THAT MUST BE WHY HE STAYED SEATED ALL THE TIME!
THEN, WHO WAS THE REAL COWL--THE ONE WHO JUST UNMASKED THE ROBOT?

Ultron tricked the readers of Avengers *#54. He revealed his face, but pretended that Edwin Jarvis was the real criminal mastermind. It wasn't until the following issue that readers discovered that Jarvis was actually Ultron's pawn.*

MANGOG APPEARS

• *The Mighty Thor* #154

A creature born of hatred, Mangog lived only for vengeance. He was a demonic entity who hated the Asgardians and was created by Stan Lee and Jack Kirby. Mangog devoted his life to punishing Odin for defeating the evil alien race that spawned him. Virtually indestructible and unstoppable, Mangog has often tried to pull the Odin-sword from its scabbard. This action would set in motion a series of events that would climax with the destruction of Asgard.

JULY

A MAGAZINE FOR SPIDER-MAN

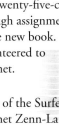

• *The Spectacular Spider-Man Magazine* #1

Since publisher/owner Martin Goodman also published a line of magazines, Stan Lee saw the opportunity to expand his readership. He convinced Goodman that Marvel should publish a black-and-white comic magazine specifically targeted toward older, more sophisticated readers. *The Spectacular Spider-Man Magazine* #1 was the result, featuring a lead story by Lee and John Romita and a retelling of Spider-Man's origin, pencilled by Larry Lieber. The second issue of the magazine went to full color, but unfortunately, the world wasn't ready for such an ambitious project and the material prepared for a third issue eventually saw print in a regular comic book.

AUGUST

THE SILVER SURFER GETS HIS OWN TITLE

• *The Silver Surfer* #1

Readers had been demanding to see more of the Silver Surfer ever since he had appeared in *Fantastic Four* #48 (March, 1966). So, when Stan Lee was told to expand the Marvel line, he immediately gave the Surfer his own title. However, such a special character deserved a special format, so instead of a traditional thirty-two-paged, twelve-cent comic, Lee bestowed a forty-eight-page, twenty-five-cent format on him. Since Jack Kirby had more than enough assignments, Lee assigned John Buscema the task of illustrating the new book. At long last, readers learned how the Surfer had volunteered to become Galactus' herald in order to save his own planet.

M *The Silver Surfer* #1 also introduced the great love of the Surfer's life—the beautiful Shalla-Bal, Empress of the planet Zenn-La.

SEPTEMBER

PHANTOM EAGLE APPEARS

• *Marvel Super Heroes* #16

Aviation buff Herb Trimpe, who flew his own biplane for many years, teamed up with writer Gary Friedrich to create flying ace the Phantom Eagle. Karl Kaufman was a second-generation American of German origin, who wanted to join the Allies against the Central Powers during World War I. Because his parents had moved back to Germany, he disguised himself as the Phantom Eagle so that they would not be harmed.

TIGER SHARK IS CREATED

• *Sub-Mariner* #5

The making of the super-criminal Tiger Shark began when Todd Arliss, a former Olympic swimmer, damaged his spinal chord while rescuing a drowning man. To regain his swimming abilities, he agreed to undergo a dangerous experiment, which resulted in him being transformed into a relentless monster. Created by writer Roy Thomas and artist John Buscema, Tiger Shark was super-strong and had razor-sharp teeth.

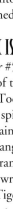

OCTOBER

VISION DEBUTS

"What cannot be touched... cannot be harmed!"

• *The Avengers* #57

"He moves silently, effortlessly—floating through the night like some great, vengeful bird of prey!" The updated Vision was created by writer Roy Thomas, who continued his trick of taking a name that Marvel already owned and creating a new Super Hero around it. Originally created by the writer-artist team of Joe Simon and Jack Kirby for *Marvel Mystery Comics* #13 (Nov., 1940), the Timely Comics version of the Vision had been an alien police officer from a dimension called Smokeworld, who had the ability to transport himself through mist or smoke.

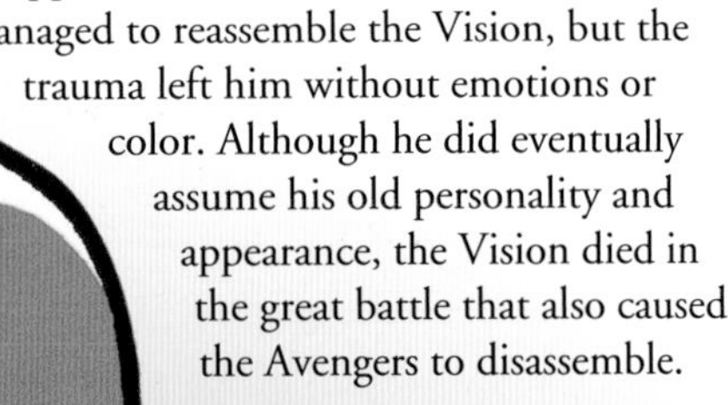

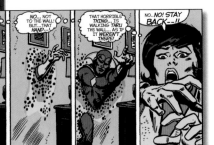

The Vision could lower his density to the point that he could pass through solid objects.

The new Vision, drawn by John Buscema, was a synthozoid—an android with synthetic human organs—who could control his density and discharge blasts of solar energy.

Built by Ultron, the new Vision was programmed to destroy the Avengers. The Vision was built from a duplicate of the android body of the original Human Torch and was programmed with the brain patterns of Simon (Wonder Man) Williams. However, the Vision eventually revolted and turned against his creator, just as Ultron did against Hank Pym. Later, after becoming an Avenger, the Vision married the Scarlet Witch, but his marriage was put in severe jeopardy when rogue government agents kidnapped and dismantled him. Hank Pym managed to reassemble the Vision, but the trauma left him without emotions or color. Although he did eventually assume his old personality and appearance, the Vision died in the great battle that also caused the Avengers to disassemble.

The small solar jewel on the Vision's forehead supplied him with power by drawing energy directly from the sun.

OCTOBER

THE FIRST APPEARANCE OF LORNA DANE

• *The X-Men* #49

Lorna Dane's green hair marked her as a mutant. Her magnetic powers told the world that she was the daughter of Magneto. Lorna learned she was a mutant when she responded to a psychic summons in *The X-Men* #49, an issue written by Arnold Drake and illustrated by Don Heck and Werner Roth. She soon found herself caught between the X-Men and the followers of Magneto.

Although she often tried to avoid using her powers, she did at times join the fight against evil mutants as a member of both X-Factor and the X-Men.

MESMERO DEBUTS

• *The X-Men* #49

Mesmero was a mutant super-hypnotist. He originally used his hypnotic powers for petty crime, but later led a group called the Demi-Men in the service of Magneto. Mesmero has clashed with Spider-Man as well as the X-Men. In 2007, at the end of the mega-crossover called *House Of M*, he lost his mutant powers which led him to try and live as a normal human.

THE BROTHERHOOD OF BADOON

• *The Silver Surfer* #2

This issue by editor Stan Lee and artist John Buscema introduced the reptilian Brotherhood of the Badoon, an alien race that was attempting to conquer the galaxy. They achieved their goal in the thirty-first century, having enslaved the Milky Way in the "Guardians Of The Galaxy" series, which debuted in *Marvel Super Heroes* #18 (Jan., 1969).

- Ben Grimm—who became the Thing after World War II—guest-starred in *Captain Savage And His Leatherneck Raiders* #7.
- As westerns were still selling, *Mighty Marvel Western* was launched. The first issue reprinted the adventures of Kid Colt, the Rawhide Kid, and the Two-Gun Kid.

DR. FAUSTUS

• *Captain America* #107

Before destroying his victims, Dr. Faustus would first send them mad. Created by Stan Lee and Jack Kirby, Faustus was a super-psychiatrist and master manipulator. His approach was to use a person's own mind against them by attacking their psychological weaknesses. Under the direction of the Red Skull, he later brainwashed Sharon Carter and programmed her to assassinate Captain America.

- In *The Amazing Spider-Man Annual* #5 by Stan Lee and Larry Lieber, Peter Parker learned that his parents were actually secret agents who died while on a mission to Algeria.

MEET ANNIHILUS!

• *Fantastic Four Annual* #6

Once a helpless insect-like alien, Annihilus built an armored exoskeleton for himself and created the Cosmic Control Rod—a weapon to control a vast area of the dimension known as the Negative Zone. He was obsessed with survival and believed he could only guarantee his safety if he destroyed every sentient creature that could pose a threat to him. Annihilus first encountered humanity when Mr. Fantastic, the Human Torch, and the Thing entered the Negative Zone in search of anti-matter particles, which they needed to save the life of the Invisible Woman. Once aware of Earth, he became obsessed with eliminating mankind.

FRANKLIN RICHARDS IS BORN

• *Fantastic Four Annual* #6

November saw the birth of Franklin Richards, the son of Reed and Sue. A mutant as a result of his parents' exposure to cosmic rays, Franklin exhibited psionic powers. Employing his ability to foresee possible futures, he briefly joined the Power Pack under the code name Tattletale. In one possible future, he fled to an alternate reality with his grandfather as the Super Hero called Psi-Lord. He later appeared in mini-series, collected editions, and one-shots aimed at all ages like *Franklin Richards, Son Of A Genius, Franklin Richards: Lab Brat,* and *Franklin Richards: Not-So-Secret Invasion.*

CRYSTAL REPLACES SUE

• *Fantastic Four* #81

While Sue Richards took some time off to care for her new baby, Johnny Storm's girlfriend—the Inhuman elemental Crystal—filled in for her on the Fantastic Four, from issue #81 until *Fantastic Four* #105 (Dec., 1970).

YELLOWJACKET APPEARS

• *The Avengers* #59

In this issue, by writer Roy Thomas and artist John Buscema, a creature called Yellowjacket appeared. Claiming to have "polished off" Hank Pym, he took the Wasp hostage when she attacked him. She stared into his eyes and immediately decided to marry him because she could see what the others didn't: Yellowjacket was actually Hank Pym! Hank had suffered a mental breakdown and created this new identity. In *The Avengers* #264 (Feb., 1986), Rita DeMara, a petty crook, stole Pym's costume and became the new Yellowjacket.

DECEMBER

MEPHISTO DEBUTS

"Since the dawn of time—seldom have I sensed such goodness of soul—such purity of spirit—as I sense with the Silver Surfer! All that you are—all that you stand for—is abhorrent to the Lord of the Lower Depths!"

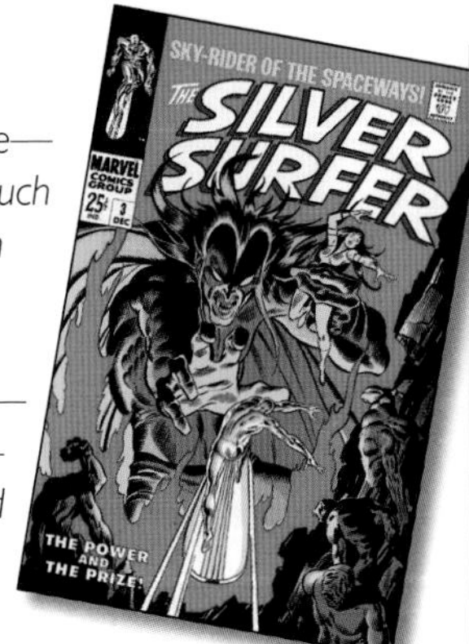

• *The Silver Surfer* #3

Although he was actually an extradimensional demon of immense power, Mephisto often pretended to be Satan in order to strike terror into the hearts of the superstitious and the religious. Created by editor Stan Lee and artist John Buscema, Mephisto hated the Surfer the moment he became aware of him because of his innate purity and goodness. Determined to bring him down, Mephisto lured the Surfer's girlfriend Shalla-Bal to Earth to use her as a bargaining chip, but he ended up sending her back to her home planet of Zenn-La when the Surfer refused to swear allegiance to him.

As well as challenging the Surfer, Mephisto also matched his wits against Thor, Dr. Strange, Spider-Man, and the Fantastic Four. He was the one who bound the demon Zarathos to Johnny Blaze to form the Ghost Rider. It was also Mephisto who made a deal with Peter and Mary Jane Parker: in exchange for Aunt May's life, he changed history, dissolving their marriage so it was as though it had never occurred. Mephisto's son, Blackheart, often plagued Daredevil and was prominently featured in the 2007 movie *Ghost Rider*.

Mephisto collected souls, which he tortured and forced to serve him for eternity.

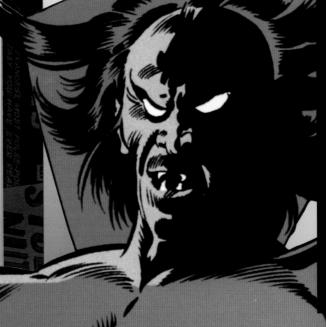

MEANWHILE IN 1968...

MARTIN LUTHER KING ASSASSINATED

The civil rights leader is shot dead in Memphis, Tennessee. Racial tensions boil over and within hours of his death there are riots across America.

STUDENT RIOTS SHAKE SOCIETY

Seeds of student rebellion spread around the world. Student protests and the "Month of the Barricades" in Paris mark a shift from conservative morality to more liberal values of equality, sexual liberation, and human rights.

BOBBY KENNEDY FATALLY SHOT

Senator Robert Kennedy, brother of the assassinated President, is shot dead after making a speech at a hotel in Los Angeles, where he had just won the California primary.

RUSSIAN TROOPS SUPPRESS THE PRAGUE SPRING

Following a thawing of Soviet rule in Czechoslovakia, Russian and other Warsaw Pact forces enter the country to restore the iron fist of "socialist solidarity."

FIRST MEN IN ORBIT AROUND THE MOON

The crew of Apollo 8 *becomes the first to enter the moon's orbit. From their spacecraft the astronauts make a Christmas Eve television broadcast, which is the most watched TV program in history to date.*

USS PUEBLO CAPTURED

An American intelligence-gathering vessel is captured by North Korea, who claim it was spying in their territorial waters. The crew is released, but not the ship.

A STEP FORWARD FOR THE WOMEN'S MOVEMENT

The Equal Employment Opportunity Commission (EEOC) rules that it is illegal for job adverts to specify which gender can apply.

YELLOW SUBMARINE

The Beatles release a feature-length film based on their songs. It is animated in a distinctive new style that pioneers psychedelia.

AND AT THE MOVIES...

Planet of the Apes, *a science fiction film set on a planet where apes rule and humans are slaves;* Night of the Living Dead, *a low-budget, cult horror film about a group of people defending themselves against a mob of zombies;* 2001: A Space Odyssey, *Stanley Kubrick's ambitious story traces humankind's evolution from ape to star child via a mysterious monolith;* Once Upon a Time in the West, *Sergio Leone's epic tribute to the men and women who developed America's frontiers as the railroad expanded westwards;* Chitty Chitty Bang Bang, *a children's musical featuring a flying car.*

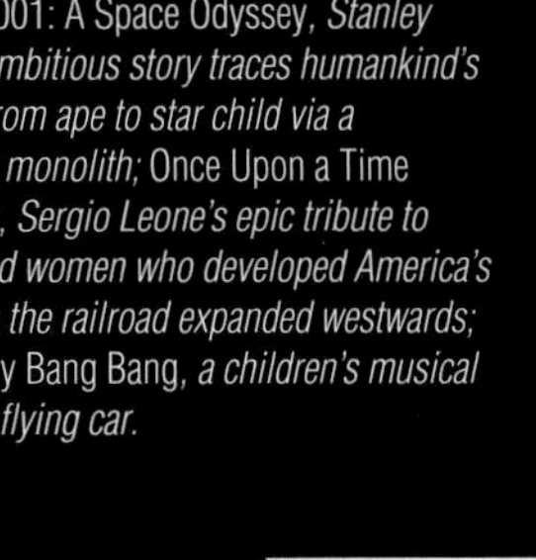

1969

A WHOLE NEW WORLD

The times they were a-changin' at Marvel as the swinging sixties drew to a close. The January *Bullpen Bulletins* announced the wedding of Roy Thomas and the June edition congratulated Jack Kirby on his move to sunny California. Stan Lee returned to writing *The Incredible Hulk*, which was being drawn by Herb Trimpe, one of Lee's favorite visual-storytellers. The artists Barry Windsor-Smith, Gil Kane, Neal Adams, and Sal Buscema joined the expanding Bullpen.

Marvel madness was spreading: Dr. Strange appeared on a Pink Floyd record cover, the song *Marvel Group* featured on Mother Earth's *Living With The Animals* album, and magazines like *Esquire* and *Eye* treated readers to a Marvel mini-comic insert. Stan Lee was in demand on the lecture circuit.

Marvel switched printers in May and raised its cover price from twelve to fifteen cents. But the biggest change came when the company's distribution deal with Independent News finally expired and Martin Goodman signed with Curtis Circulation. No longer would he be limited to a set number of titles. He could now publish all the titles he wanted. The Second Age of Marvel Comics had truly begun!

JANUARY

WEDDING BELLS FOR THE WASP AND ANT-MAN

• *The Avengers* #60

Although their marriage was destined to end in divorce, Janet Van Dyne (the Wasp) and Hank Pym (Ant-Man) finally tied the knot in *The Avengers* #60.

THE GUARDIANS OF THE GALAXY DEBUT

• *Marvel Super Heroes* #18

The Guardians of the Galaxy were a science-fiction version of the group from the movie *Dirty Dozen* (1967) and were created by writer Arnold Drake and artist Gene Colan. Three aliens—each the last of their respective races—teamed up with a human space explorer who had been in suspended animation for a thousand year Together they led a rebellion in the thirty-first century to free the solar system from the reptilian Brotherhood of the Badoon. They didn't return again until a ten-issue run in *Marvel Presents* #3 (Feb. 1976). After guest-starring in other publications, they were awardec their own title in June 1990, which was produced by writer/artist Jim Valentino.

The original Guardians were American astronaut Major Vance Astro, Jupiter solider Charlie-27, Martinex of Pluto, and Yondu, a primitive warrior from Beta Centauri IV.

M *Sgt. Fury And His Howling Commandos* #62 featured the story "The Basic Training Of Nick Fury," which showed how Sergea Bass taught Fury to be a great leader.

FEBRUARY

The right side of Madame Hydra/Viper's face had been horribly disfigured and she tinted her hair green.

MADAME HYDRA DEBUTS

• *Captain America* #110

"Destroy him!" Madame Hydra shouted about Cap, when she first appeared in *Captain America* #110, an issue by writer/artist Jim Steranko. She proved that the female is the deadlier of the species one issue later when her underlings blasted Cap as he leaped off a dock and was apparently killed. She later changed her name to the Viper, shared a brief marriage of convenience with Wolverine, and joined the early 2000s' incarnation of the Hellfire Club.

RICK JONES JOINS CAP

• *Captain America* #110

After tagging alongside both the Hulk and the Avengers, Rick Jones, the leader of the Teen Brigade, became Cap's official partner in *Captain America* #110, but they parted company after only three issues, when Captain America adopted a new secret identity and the artist Jim Steranko left the book.

Rick Jones first donned Bucky's costume in The Avengers *#7 (Aug., 1964), but at that point Cap was not yet ready for another partner.*

DOC'S NEW DUDS

• *Doctor Strange* #177

In an attempt to update Dr. Strange and make him more appealing to Super Hero fans, writer Roy Thomas had artist Gene Colan redesign Strange's costume and provide the master of the mystic arts with a mask.

MARCH

M'BAKU BECOMES MAN-APE

• *The Avengers* #62

A fierce warrior and a skilled hunter, M'Baku desired the Black Panther's throne of Wakanda, a country which he wanted to return to a primitive state. After joining the outlawed White Gorilla cult, he participated in a forbidden ceremony to become the Man-Ape in *The Avengers* #62, a comic by writer Roy Thomas and artist John Buscema. This gave him the powers of super-strength, agility, and resistance to injury. Man-Ape tracked the Black Panther to America, where he battled the Avengers. During his career, he also joined the original Lethal Legion of Super Villains and later the Masters of Evil.

MARCH

ALEX SUMMERS DISCOVERS HIS IDENTITY

"What's the matter? You afraid I'm going to be ashamed of being the kid brother of the leader of the X-Men?"

• *The X-Men* #54

Alex was the younger brother of the X-Man Scott "Cyclops" Summers. He appeared in *The X-Men* #54, by writer Arnold Drake and artist Don Heck. The two Summers boys had been put into an orphanage after the apparent death of their parents and were separated when Alex was adopted. Alex went on to study geophysics in college, where he met the X-Men and Lorna Dane, whom he later fell in love with. Alex first learned of his mutant powers when Ahmet Abdol, the Living Pharaoh, kidnapped him. Alex then took on the name Havok and wore a costume designed by artist Neal Adams.

At first, Alex was unable to control his power to absorb and discharge cosmic energy, so he only employed it when absolutely necessary. He and Lorna would help the X-Men on occasion, but neither wanted to actually join the team.

He later became the leader of the government-sponsored mutant team called X-Factor until an accident cast him into a parallel world and a series called *Mutant X* that began in 1998. In this plane of reality, Havok had been a member of the original X-Men and was now the leader of Six, a team of mutant heroes who were the X-Men of their world.

Alex eventually rejoined the real X-Men and resumed his relationship with Lorna Dane. When Lorna lost her mutant powers in the *House Of M* mega-crossover (2005), Havok temporarily left the X-Men with her, but later returned to help prevent Apocalypse from decimating the human population. Havok has appeared in the animated television series *X-Men* (1992–1997) and *X-Men: Evolution* (2000–2003) and in numerous video games.

THE LIVING PHARAOH STRIKES

• *The X-Men* #54

At first, the mutant terrorist Ahmet Abdol referred to himself as the Living Pharaoh, though he soon became known as the Living Monolith. He longed to conquer the world using his ability to absorb cosmic energy. When Abdol learned that Alex Summers possessed the same power, he kidnapped him. With Summers out of the way, Abdol was able to absorb more power than ever before and he grew to tremendous size.

MARCH

VANESSA FISK IS THE "MISSUS"

• *The Amazing Spider-Man* #70

Stan Lee believed there was a little good in even the worst of people, so, in an attempt to humanize the Kingpin of Crime, he and artist John Romita gave him a wife and made him a loving and devoted husband. First mentioned in the previous issue as the "missus," Vanessa Fisk's face was hidden when she appeared in this issue. Romita modeled her after an older Dragon Lady from Milton Caniff's comic strip *Terry And The Pirates*, when he finally showed her face in *The Amazing Spider-Man* #83 (April, 1970).

Although she usually stayed out of the Kingpin's affairs, Vanessa once helped him escape the police.

YOU ARRIVED JUST IN TIME, MY DEAR!
NOW DRIVE ON!

THE ORIGIN OF GALACTUS IS REVEALED

• *The Mighty Thor* #162

The Asgardian leader Odin sent Thor to learn the secret of Galactus' past in this story by Stan Lee and Jack Kirby. He discovered that the planet-eater had once been an alien called Galen, who had lived on the planet Taa in an earlier Universe. Because his universe was drawing to an end and this one was just beginning, Galen piloted a space vessel into the heart of the Big Bang. He somehow survived the explosion and slept for billions of years before awaking with his insatiable hunger for planets.

APRIL

EVERYONE'S MAD ABOUT MILLIE

• *Mad About Millie* #1

Despite the craze for Super Heroes, *Millie The Model* was still selling well, so Stan Lee launched the spin-off title, *Mad About Millie*. Lasting seventeen issues with one "Queen-Sized" special, it was drawn by Stan Goldberg, who later moved on to Archie Comics.

A SECOND GOLIATH

• *The Avengers* #63

Since Hank Pym had become Yellowjacket, the Super Hero Hawkeye decided to increase his powers by commandeering the growth formula that Pym had used to become Giant-Man and Goliath. Hawkeye also adopted Pym's most recent name, and called himself Goliath.

APRIL

THE COMING OF THE CONTROLLER

• *The Invincible Iron Man* #12

After scientist Basil Sandhurst was crippled in a lab accident, he donned an exoskeleton that was powered by mental energy. This act, written by Archie Goodwin and drawn by George Tuska, turned him into the Controller. Like the aliens in Robert A. Heinlein's science-fiction novel *The Puppet Masters*, the Controller soon learned that he could place "slave discs" on people, which allowed him to control their actions and siphon their mental energy.

MAY

A TITLE FOR MILLIE'S RIVAL

• *Chili* #1

Millie the Model's rival, the red-haired Chili Storm, was awarded her own title in May. Like Millie's titles, *Chili* was drawn by Stan Goldberg. It was the final *Millie* spin-off and ran for twenty-six issues until December 1973.

JUNE

SILVERMANE

• *The Amazing Spider-Man* #73

As he grew older, Silvermane began to seek artificial ways to extend his life.

In the same year that Mario Puzo's *The Godfather* published, Stan Lee and John Romita introduced Silvermane, the head of the New York branch of the Maggia crime syndicate.

Tall, distinguished, and genteel, Silvio "Silvermane" Manfredi evoked the perfect image of the sophisticated crimelord. Nearly killed a few years later, his brain was transplanted into a cyborg body so that he could continue to rule his criminal kingdom.

JULY

ADAMANTIUM

• *The Avengers* #66

Practically indestructible, adamantium is a fictional metal alloy that first appeared in this issue by writer Roy Thomas and artist Barry Windsor-Smith. Created by Dr. Myron McClain—the man who had formed Captain America's shield in the early 1940s—this material was later fused to Wolverine's skeleton and his natural bone claws. His claws could now cut through any material and there was no danger of shattering them. The additions to his skeleton drastically increased his physical strength and resiliency.

Desperate to escape the tormen[ts] of Mephisto's realm, the Gho[st Rider] agreed to deliver the Silver Surfer['s] soul in exchange for his ow[n].

SEPTEMBER

GETTING AROUND THE RULES

• *The X-Men* #60

The Comics Code Authority, which governed all mass-market comic books, had a strict rule against using werewolves. Writer Roy Thomas and artist Neal Adams got around this restriction by creating a were-pterodactyl instead. In *The X-Men* #60 they introduced Dr. Karl Lykos, a geneticist who was bitten by a pterodactyl while on an expedition to the Savage Land and became Sauron, an enemy of the X-Men. Unlike a werewolf, Sauron was not controlled by the moon, and so had control over when he changed form.

INTRODUCING THE GHOST

• *The Silver Surfer* #8

Roughly based on the Flying Dutchman legend of a ghost ship that can never go home, Stan Lee and artist John Buscema introduced a character they simply called the Ghost. The Ghost had once been Captain Joost van Straaten, who had deliberately led his ship into a storm that cost the lives of his crew. He was cursed to spend eternity as the slave of Mephisto and has often battled the Silver Surfer.

SEPTEMBER

MYSTERY/SUSPENSE TITLES RETURN

• *Tower Of Shadows* #1

With the public thirst for mystery/suspense titles, Marvel moved back into the field. Its first title was *Tower Of Shadows*, which contained the artwork of Jim Steranko, Johnny Craig, John Buscema, and Don Heck. Despite using top talent, the title failed to find an audience. With its tenth issue, it became *Creatures On The Loose* and eventually printed stories starring King Kull, Thongor the Barbarian, and Man-Wolf.

The stories in Tower Of Shadows *were usually hosted by Digger, a macabre grave digger.*

REVIVING ROMANCE

• *My Love* #1

Having recently added two new teenage/ humor titles, *Chili* and *Mad About Millie*, Stan Lee—remembering the days when romance titles were among his best sellers—attempted to revive the genre with *My Love*.

Lee utilized artists like John Buscema, John Romita, Gene Colan, Neal Adams, and Jim Steranko for this title, which ran for thirty-nine issues.

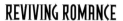

A BLACK AMERICAN SUPER HERO

• *Captain America* #117

The Black Panther may have broken the mold as Marvel's first black Super Hero, but he was from Africa. The Falcon, however, was the first black American Super Hero. Introduced by Stan Lee and artist Gene Colan, Sam "Snap" Wilson was a former community volunteer who turned to crime after his parents were brutally murdered. He encountered Captain America on Exile Island and eventually became his partner. A skilled fighter, Sam possessed artificial wings that enabled him to fly and a telepathic link with his trained falcon, Redwing. He briefly served as an Avenger and was dedicated to protecting the people of Harlem.

The Falcon was a natural athlete, tutored in acrobatics and hand-to-hand combat by Cap.

ENTER THE SQUADRON SINISTER

• *The Avengers* #69

Writer Roy Thomas was poking fun at his distinguished competition when he and artist Sal Buscema presented the Squadron Sinister on the last page of *The Avengers* #69. They designed the four members of the Squadron—Dr. Spectrum, Hyperion, Nighthawk, and Whizzer—to evoke DC Comics' Justice League of America team featuring Green Lantern, Batman, Superman, and Flash. This unofficial crossover between the two companies allowed the Avengers to battle a smaller version of the JLA, the comic which had inadvertently led to the creation of the Fantastic Four. The Squadron Sinister proved so popular that Thomas eventually introduced the Squadron Supreme in *The Avengers* #85 (Feb., 1971), a team of Super Heroes from an alternate Earth. A version of the Squadron Supreme was later published under the overall title of *The Supreme Power*, which began in 2003.

THE GRANDMASTER DEBUTS

• *The Avengers* #69

Five years before *Dungeons And Dragons* made fantasy role-playing games popular, Roy Thomas and Sal Buscema introduced a cosmic gamesman. The Grandmaster was an elder of the Universe, a virtually immortal being who dated back to the Big Bang. With his god-like powers, he specialized in games of skill and strategy. Playing against Kang, the Grandmaster orchestrated the fight between the Avengers and the Squadron Sinister. He later challenged Death for the life of his brother in a game, which resulted in the *Contest Of Champions* series in 1982.

DAREDEVIL REVEALS HIS IDENTITY

• *Daredevil* #57

Matt Murdock revealed that he was Daredevil to his girlfriend Karen Page. However, this decision would come back to haunt him when Karen passed his secret on to the Kingpin of Crime in the story line that became known as "Daredevil: Born Again" in *Daredevil* #227 (Feb., 1986).

CAPTAIN MAR-VELL AND RICK JONES

• *Captain Marvel* #17

Rick Jones, the perennial sidekick and former Avengers mascot, became bonded to Captain Mar-Vell thanks to Roy Thomas and artist Gil Kane. Inspired by Fawcett Comics' *Captain Marvel* series from the 1940s—in which a boy switched places with an older Super Hero—the relationship between Rick and Mar-Vell became a pivotal moment in the plot of the Kree-Skrull War that ran through *The Avengers* #93-97 in the early 1970s.

TORGO APPEARS

• *Fantastic Four* #91

The Thing met the mechanical life-form Torgo when he was captured by the Skrulls and sent to a distant planet to become a super-powered gladiator. Although the two were supposed to battle to the death, they ultimately became friends and defied their masters during their fight by refusing to harm each other.

- M A companion title to *Tower Of Shadows* in the mystery/suspense genre, *Chamber Of Darkness* #1 published. The title lasted for eight issues before it was renamed *Monsters On The Prowl*.
- M *Our Love Story* #1 was Marvel's second entry into the romance field. The series lasted thirty-eight issues.

NOVEMBER

THE NIGHT OF THE PROWLER

• *The Amazing Spider-Man* #78

Future Marvel artist John Romita Jr.—who was thirteen years old at the time—came up with a character called the Prowler and sent a drawing to Stan Lee. Lee liked the name, but wanted a different costume, so John Romita Sr. suggested using the costume that had been intended for the villain in the now-cancelled *The Spectacular Spider-Man Magazine* #3. The result appeared in *The Amazing Spider-Man* #78, by Lee and artist John Buscema. Hobie Brown was a would-be inventor who was stuck in a dead-end job as a window washer until he decided to use his inventions to create a costumed identity and become the Prowler. Although he was first introduced as a Super Villain, the Prowler ultimately became one of Spider-Man's best friends.

The Prowler's wrist cartridges fired compressed air and he used his steel-tip gloves to scale buildings.

THE STUNT-MASTER ROARS INTO MURDOCK'S LIFE

• *Daredevil* #58

Created by Stan Lee and artist Gene Colan, the Stunt-Master was an ex-Hollywood stunt man who sought fame as the man who killed Daredevil. He followed in the tradition of the real-life famed motorcycle stunt man, "Evel" Knievel.

THE GLOB APPEARS

• *The Incredible Hulk* #121

The Glob was modeled after the swamp monster from Theodore Sturgeon's science fiction short story *It*. He was created when petty criminal Joe Timms was exposed to radioactive waste after falling into the Florida Everglades. The Glob's origin may have later inspired the creation of Marvel's *Man-Thing* and DC Comics' *Swamp Thing*.

NOVEMBER

STINGRAY IS HERE!

• *Sub-Mariner* #19

Oceanographer Dr. Walter Newell became Stingray when he donned his underwater battle-suit, the design of which was roughly based on a manta ray. The character was created by writer Roy Thomas and artist Bill Everett. Stingray later aided the Thing in the "Serpent Crown Affair" story line in the 1980s, and he allowed the Avengers to use his Hydro-Base for their temporary headquarters. Stingray was a member of Captain America's outlaw band of Secret Avengers during the mega-crossover *Civil War* (2007) and later accepted Tony Stark's offer of a full pardon.

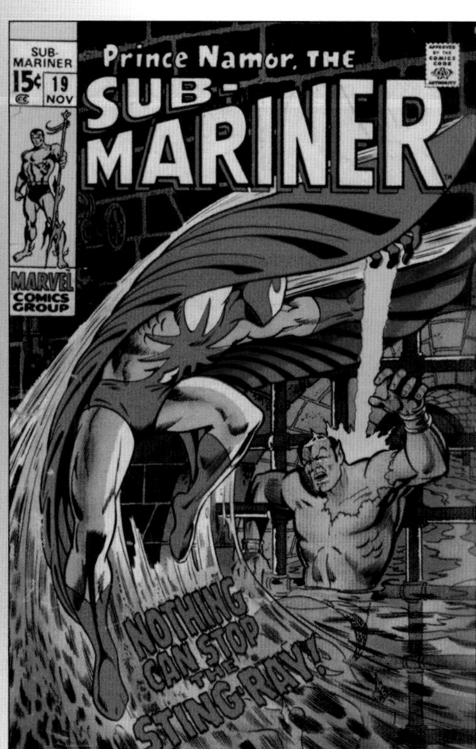

M *Kid Colt, Outlaw,* the longest running western comic, returned with issue #140. It continued until issue #229 (April, 1979).

DECEMBER

TORPEDO DEBUTS

• *Daredevil* #59

The first Torpedo—a costumed Los Angeles hit man—attempted to assassinate Daredevil in *Daredevil* #59, a issue by Stan Lee and artist Gene Colan. Later, the scientist Michael Stivak assumed the name when he designed a flying battle-suit in *Daredevil* #129 (Jan., 1976). His suit was then passed down to Brock Jones, the third Torpedo, and was eventually used by Turbo in the *New Warriors* in the 1990s.

MEANWHILE IN 1969...

MEN ON THE MOON

Americans Neil Armstrong and Edwin "Buzz" Aldrin take the first steps on the moon in "one small step for man, one giant leap for mankind."

NIXON IS PRESIDENT

Richard Nixon is sworn in as the thirty-seventh President of the United States.

A "BED-IN" FOR PEACE

On their honeymoon, Beatles musician John Lennon and Yoko Ono begin a week-long "bed-in for peace" in the presidential suite of the Hilton Hotel in Amsterdam.

THE "DAYS OF RAGE" IN CHICAGO

The National Guard steps in to control the Days of Rage rally in Chicago, arranged by the radical left-wing group the Weathermen. The event coincides with the trial of the Chicago Eight, charged with offenses relating to previous riots.

MAIDEN VOYAGE OF THE QE2

The luxury Cunard Line ocean liner arrives in New York after making her maiden voyage across the Atlantic from Southampton.

"NO FAULT" DIVORCE LAWS

In a step forward for the women's movement, California is the first state to introduce a "no fault" divorce law, whereby couples can divorce merely by mutual consent.

SUPERSONIC PASSENGER SERVICE

The Soviet-designed plane Tupolev Tu-144 is the first transport aircraft to reach supersonic speed.

SEX, DRUGS, AND ROCK 'N' ROLL AT WOODSTOCK

Five hundred thousand hippies gather for four days of peace and music at the Woodstock festival, a celebration of youthful hedonism and 1960s excess. Performers include Janis Joplin, Jimi Hendrix, and The Who.

JACKSON 5 ON THE ED SULLIVAN SHOW

The Jackson brothers from the popular music quintet make their first television appearance on The Ed Sullivan Show. *Michael Jackson is eleven years old.*

AND AT THE MOVIES...

The Wild Bunch, *Sam Peckinpah's lyrical, violent western about a gang of outlaws who go out in a blaze of gory glory;* Butch Cassidy and the Sundance Kid, *a Western about a bank robber and his partner;* Goodbye, Mr. Chips, *a musical in which an English school teacher falls in love with a showgirl;* A Boy Named Charlie Brown, *the first animation film based on the Peanuts comic strip;* On Her Majesty's Secret Service, *the sixth James Bond film.*

Nick Fury, Agent Of SHIELD *#1 (June, 1968) editor Stan Lee, writer/illustrator Jim Steranko, inker Joe Sinnott.*

Writer/artist Jim Steranko started drawing comics for Joe Simon at Harvey Comics in 1965 and quickly moved to Marvel where he worked on the "Nick Fury, Agent of SHIELD" feature in Strange Tales. *Initially, he finished the artwork on stories that had been broken down panel by panel by Jack Kirby, but he soon moved up to writing and drawing Fury, using innovative layouts, intriguing page designs, and high-voltage action-driven stories. His graphic influences included Peter Max, Andy Warhol, and Salvador Dali.*

STERANKO
WHO IS SCORPIO

1970s

The great Marvel comics of the 1960s had fired the imaginations of their readers. In the 1970s, a new generation of writers and artists emerged, who were inspired by the work of Stan Lee and his collaborators and were ambitious to push the artistic envelope of comics even further. Writers such as Roy Thomas, Marv Wolfman, Steve Englehart, Steve Gerber, Don McGregor, Doug Moench, Jim Starlin, and Chris Claremont were creative revolutionaries, who took Marvel Comics in imaginative new directions and put the stamp of their own personalities on their work. Jack Kirby left Marvel only to return half a decade later and produce a final series of creations as his legacy. Not only did the new generation continue to develop the Super Heroes, but they diversified the Marvel line into other genres, including horror, science fiction, and martial arts. Through licensing deals, Marvel explored other fictional mythologies, such as the sword and sorcery of author Robert E. Howard's *Conan The Barbarian* and the space opera of director George Lucas's *Star Wars*. By the end of the decade, Stan Lee and Jack Kirby had stopped making comic books together, but a brand new wave of talent was continuing the Marvel revolution.

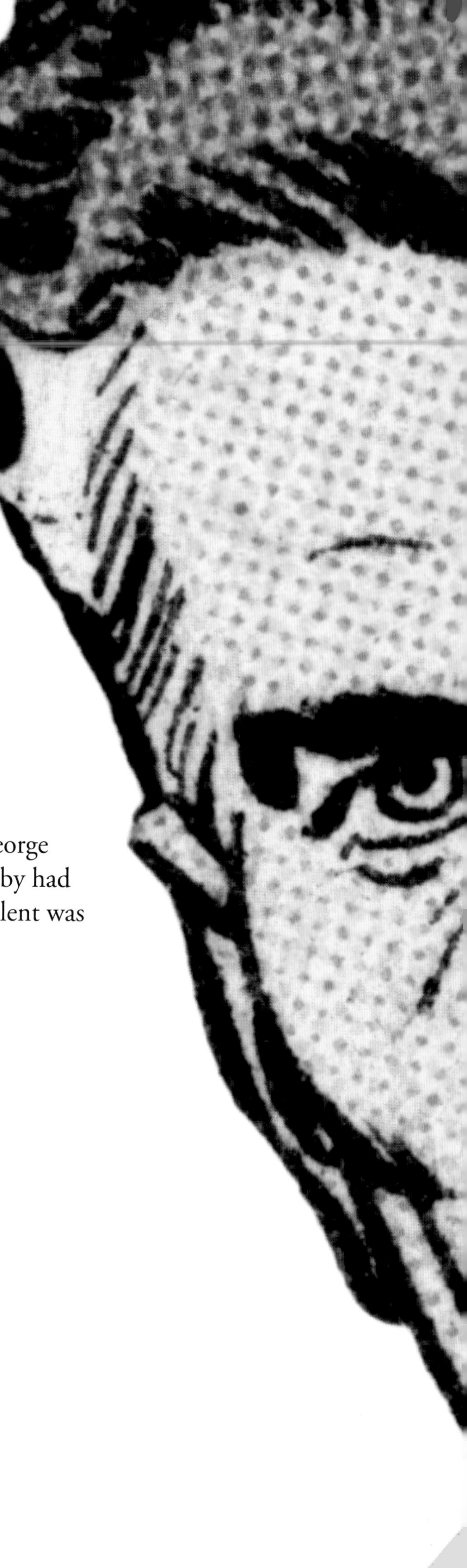

SHE IS DEAD! WEAK FROM HUNGER, SHE WAS NO MATCH FOR MY TOMAHAWK!

1970

THE END OF AN ERA

Comics scholars generally refer to the late 1950s through the 1960s—the era of the birth of the Super Hero genre—as the "Silver Age of Comics." In 1970, this age began its end with the departure of artist Jack Kirby. Kirby had revolutionized comic book art throughout the 1960s and, together with editor Stan Lee, had created scores of characters. In 1970, Kirby left Marvel for DC Comics, marking the end of the most creative period in Marvel history.

The year also saw the cancellation of *X-Men* due to poor sales. Written by Roy Thomas with art by Neal Adams, the series was revived as a reprint, but there would be no new stories for half a decade.

Despite these dramatic developments, Marvel began to move in new directions with *Conan The Barbarian*, having licensed the comics rights for author Robert E. Howard's hero. Indeed, *Conan* would become one of Marvel's greatest successes over the next two decades.

JANUARY

INTRODUCING AGATHA HARKNESS

• *Fantastic Four* #94

Although Fantastic Four leader Reed Richards was a man of science, he chose a sorceress to be governess to his infant son, Franklin. Issue #94 of *Fantastic Four* introduced Agatha Harkness, the kindly witch who dwelt in a Gothic mansion atop Whisper Hill. She lived with her black cat, Ebony, who could transform into a ferocious beast. In this story, Agatha demonstrated that she could protect Franklin by turning her spells against the Frightful Four, the FF's opposite number

A SUBSTITUTE IRON MAN

• *The Invincible Iron Man* #21

Boxer Eddie March was the first African-American to wear Iron Man's armor. Inventor Tony Stark was concerned that going into combat as Iron Man could endanger his surgically repaired heart, so he began training March to take his place. March went into battle against a new armor-wearing Crimson Dynamo, but was felled by a blood clot in his brain. His injury was not fatal, but Stark returned to his role as Iron Man.

SUNFIRE DEBUTS

• *X-Men* #64

Created by writer Roy Thomas and artist Don Heck, Sunfire was one of the first Marvel mutants to be born outside the United States. Exposed to lethal radiation during the bombing of Hiroshima at the end of World War II, Shiro Yoshida's mother died giving birth to him. The radiation endowed Shiro, alias Sunfire, with mutant powers that enabled him to fly and generate heat and radiation. Under the influence of his fanatical Uncle Tomo, Sunfire attacked the US Capitol building and fought the X-Men. But when Tomo murdered Shiro's father, Sunfire slew him and surrendered to the authorities. Later, Sunfire briefly joined the X-Men.

JANUARY

RETURN OF NICK FURY

• *The Avengers* #72

Following his seeming demise, super-spy Nick Fury returned, impersonating his enigmatic nemesis Scorpio. The real Scorpio was Nick's brother Jake and also one of the twelve members of Zodiac, a criminal organization with an astrological theme.

FEBRUARY

WEDDING PLANS GONE WRONG

• *The Incredible Hulk* #124

Bruce Banner had reached the point where he was able to retain his normal personality as the Hulk, thanks to help from scientist Reed Richards, so Bruce and Betty Ross decided to get married. But on their wedding day, Banner's archenemy, the Leader, hit Bruce with radiation that turned him once more into a savage, uncontrollable Hulk. Bruce finally succeeded in marrying Betty in issue #319 of *The Incredible Hulk* (May, 1986).

XAVIER IS RESURRECTED

"Greetings, X-Men! I'm delighted to be with you again!

• *X-Men* #65

In a story in *X-Men* #42 (March, 1968), Professor Charles Xavier, the founder of the X-Men, had seemingly sacrificed his life to prevent a device called the oscillotron from destroying the Earth. Soon afterward, the X-Men split up. In *X-Men* #65, the reunited X-Men returned to Xavier's mansion after their long travels and got the shock of their young lives: Professor Xavier was alive! But how?

In fact, *X-Men*'s sales were low, and Marvel had split the Super Hero team up in an attempt to revitalize the series. It hadn't worked, so now Marvel faced the dilemma of how to resurrect the Professor. In this issue, writer Denny O'Neil revealed that it was not Xavier who had perished, but a shape-shifter called the Changeling, who had once worked for the X-Men's enemies, Factor Three. Prior to his apparent death, Xavier had learned that an alien race, the Z'nox, was plotting to invade Earth. In order to prepare a defense, Xavier went into seclusion, while allowing the reformed Changeling to impersonate him.

On his return, Xavier exerted his telepathic powers to the utmost. In an amazing sequence, he psychically linked the minds of every person on Earth and, along with the X-Men, succeeded in turning this combined psychic energy against the Z'nox. The alien invaders were driven off and the Earth was saved.

This epic tale provided an appropriately grand finale for the work of legendary artist Neal Adams. But not even Adams' extraordinary work could save *X-Men*: the series only lasted for one more issue.

THE BLACK PANTHER IS FRAMED

• *The Avengers* #73

The Sons of the Serpent, a cabal of costumed racists, schemed to foment racial hatred by framing the Black Panther as a criminal in this story written by Roy Thomas. However, the Black Panther thwarted their plot and continued his success as Marvel's first black Super Hero.

X-MEN IS CANCELED

• *X-Men* #66

After the tremendous strain of using his telepathic powers to save the Earth in *X-Men* #65, Professor Charles Xavier fell into a life-threatening coma in what would be the series' last issue, by Roy Thomas and artist Sal Buscema. Having discovered that Bruce Banner held the key to saving the Professor's life, the X-Men flew to Las Vegas, where they battled Banner's other self, the savage Hulk. Reverting to human form, Banner gave the X-Men a device that he and Xavier had invented, which was then used to save Xavier and bring him out of his coma. However, the X-Men could not save their own series, which was cancelled due to poor sales.

Orka, the Human Killer Whale, an Atlantean villain with the powers of the fierce sea creature, debuted in *Sub-Mariner* #23.

APRIL

THE KINGPIN'S SON AND RIVAL

• *The Amazing Spider-Man* #83

This issue introduced a new criminal mastermind called the Schemer, who became a rival to the Kingpin of Crime. Beneath his face mask, the Schemer turned out to be the Kingpin's own son, Richard Fisk, who went on to adopt many criminal guises.

ENTER ARKON

• *The Avengers* #75

What would happen if a hero of the sword-and-sorcery genre met a Super Hero? Roy Thomas and artist John Buscema—the future *Conan* team—found out when warlord Arkon the Imperion tried to destroy Earth in order to provide enough energy to save his homeworld, Polemachus. Arkon battled the Avengers, but they made peace when Iron Man found an alternate way to save Polemachus.

With his own series canceled, Dr. Strange retired—temporarily—as Master of the Mystic Arts in *The Incredible Hulk* #126.

JUNE

CAPTAIN MARVEL RETURNS—AND LEAVES

• *Captain Marvel* #20

After a gap of six months, *Captain Marvel* returned to publication, again written by Roy Thomas and drawn by Gil Kane. But after this two-issue story line that pitted Mar-Vell against the Hulk, the series was cancelled and only returned in September, 1972.

JULY

THE *FANTASTIC FOUR*'S CENTENNIAL

• *Fantastic Four* #100

In July, *Fantastic Four*, the first series from the Marvel Age of Comics, reached its hundredth issue. Creators Stan Lee and Jack Kirby marked the important occasion with a story in which criminal mastermind the Mad Thinker and mind-controller the Puppet Master attacked the Fantastic Four with android doubles of their past foes.

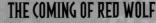

The Inhumans and the Black Widow shared the split cover of the first issue of Amazing Adventures. *As it said on the cover, "Double dynamite from Mighty Marvel!"*

AUGUST

THE INHUMANS AND THE BLACK WIDOW SHARE A COMIC

• *Amazing Adventures* #1

As Marvel was expanding its line of comics, the company decided to introduce two new "split" books in the tradition of *Tales Of Suspense* and *Tales To Astonish—Amazing Adventures* and *Astonishing Tales*. *Amazing Adventures* contained a series about the genetically enhanced Inhumans and a series about intelligence agent the Black Widow. The adventures of the Inhuman Royal Family—Black Bolt, Medusa, Gorgon, Karnak, and Triton—were plotted and drawn by their co-creator, Jack Kirby. New Marvel writer Gary Friedrich and artist John Buscema teamed up for the adventures of the Black Widow, the former Russian spy turned American Super Hero. As well as the comic being split, its first cover was also divided between two pencillers: Jack Kirby drew Black Bolt and his fellow Inhumans, while Marie Severin portrayed the Black Widow in acrobatic action.

KA-ZAR AND DR. DOOM TOGETHER

• *Astonishing Tales* #1

Marvel's second split book of 1970 gave two longtime Marvel stars their own series. Stan Lee and Jack Kirby collaborated on the first installment of the new series starring Ka-Zar, the lord of the prehistoric Savage Land, who had guest-starred in *X-Men*, *Daredevil*, and *The Amazing Spider-Man*. Marvel's greatest villain, Dr. Doom, also received his own series, scripted by Roy Thomas and drawn and inked by the legendary cartoonist Wally Wood.

- Jack Kirby's final complete issue of *Fantastic Four* (issue #101) saw Magneto team up with the Sub-Mariner.
- In Jack Kirby's final issue of *The Mighty Thor* (#179), the evil Loki temporarily switched bodies with the God of Thunder.

SEPTEMBER

THE COMING OF RED WOLF

• *The Avengers* #80

Red Wolf was Marvel's first Native American Super Hero. Will Talltrees' father, leader of the Cheyenne tribe, was killed on the orders of business mogul Cornelius Van Lunt. Talltrees went to New York as Red Wolf, where the Avengers helped him take vengeance on Van Lunt. He was later revealed as the successor of Johnny Wakely, the nineteenth-century Red Wolf.

ENTER JIM WILSON

• *The Incredible Hulk* #131

This issue saw the introduction of Jim Wilson, a character created by writer Roy Thomas and artist Herb Trimpe. An African-American boy from Watts, a Los Angeles ghetto, Wilson became a friend and confidante of both Bruce Banner and the Hulk, who at the time had been split into two different beings.

OCTOBER

THE PETRIFIED MAN APPEARS

• *Astonishing Tales* #2

When he quit Marvel, Jack Kirby left the Ka-Zar series in *Astonishing Tales*. But in a single panel in this issue, he introduced Garokk, a British sailor who gained immortality at the price of becoming a "petrified man" who would go on to menace both Ka-Zar and the X-Men.

SWORD AND SORCERY

Writer Roy Thomas and British artist Barry Smith (later known as Barry Windsor-Smith) launched Marvel's sword-and-sorcery comics with *Conan The Barbarian*, in a series that ran for 275 issues. Conan was a warrior who lived in the fictional Hyborian Age between the sinking of Atlantis and the start of recorded history. The success of Conan prompted Marvel comics to feature other warrior characters, including King Kull, an Atlantean warrior who became ruler of the civilized nation of Valusia long before the sinking of Atlantis, and Red Sonja—the She-Devil with a Sword—who gained her own comic book series in 1977.

NOVEMBER

DEATH STRIKES ONCE MORE

"Why must it happen? Why? Why? First, I lost Uncle Ben, those long years ago! And now, the second best friend I've ever had!"

• *The Amazing Spider-Man* #90

Disaster struck Peter Parker's world with the death of Captain George Stacy, in this landmark story by scripter Stan Lee and artist John Romita Sr. Not only was retired police officer Stacy the father of Peter Parker's first true love, Gwen, but he had also become a valuable friend and mentor to Peter himself. Moreover, whereas so much of the public regarded Spider-Man as a menace on society, Captain Stacy believed him to be a hero.

As a battle raged between Spider-Man and Dr. Octopus atop a Manhattan building, pieces of concrete came loose and began to fall to the street below. Witnessing the combat, Captain Stacy saw debris plunging down toward a small child on the street. Without a second

NOVEMBER

thought, he courageously plunged forward, pushing the child out of the way, only to be crushed by the concrete himself. Horrified, Spider-Man broke off his fight with Dr. Octopus and swung down to the street to be with his friend.

To his astonishment, the dying Captain addressed Spider-Man as "Peter." Referring to Gwen, he bid Peter, "Be good to her, son! Be good to her. She loves you so very much." And then he passed away.

Peter Parker had already lost one father figure, his Uncle Ben, when he failed to stop the burglar who murdered him. Now Spider-Man had lost another father figure, and, again, he blamed himself. Gwen herself believed that Spider-Man had killed her father, and Peter realized that now he could never reveal his other identity to the woman he loved.

Spider-Man raced to help Captain George Stacy, fatally wounded beneath fallen masonry in The Amazing Spider-Man *#90.*

DECEMBER

LLYRA, A FEMME FATALE

• *Sub-Mariner* #32

Llyra, the greatest Super Villain in the history of the *Sub-Mariner* series, was introduced by writer Roy Thomas and artist Sal Buscema. Like Namor, Llyra was a hybrid of *Homo sapiens* and the water-breathing *Homo mermanus*. Her mother, Rhonda Morris, was a woman from the surface world, but her father was from the undersea kingdom of Lemuria. The Lemurians were of the same species as the Atlanteans, but dwelt in the Pacific rather than the Atlantic Ocean. The insane Llyra overthrew the King of Lemuria, Namor's friend Karthon, and battled the Sub-Mariner. Seemingly killed at this issue's end, Llyra later returned to take a dreadful vengeance on Namor.

- The Valkyrie first appeared in *The Avengers* #83 as a guise of the evil Enchantress. A heroic Valkyrie was introduced later.
- Barry Smith, the first artist on *Conan The Barbarian*, took over drawing *Astonishing Tales* with issue #3, which introduced the Savage Land sorceress, Zaladane.

The panel showing Spider-Man lifting his friend Captain Stacy from the rubble was redrawn for the issue's cover, with the crowds below blaming Spidey for Stacy's death.

MEANWHILE IN 1970...

US FORCES IN CAMBODIA
The US sends troops into Cambodia to attack supply bases as part of the ongoing campaign in Vietnam against the Viet Cong. This action is met with a tidal wave of public objection in America.

KENT STATE SHOOTINGS LEAVE AMERICA IN SHOCK
The anti-Vietnam War movement reaches crisis point when National Guardsmen shoot dead four students during protests at Kent State University in Ohio. Ten days later two more students are shot during protests at Jackson State University, Mississippi.

NUCLEAR NON-PROLIFERATION TREATY
A treaty aimed at limiting the spread of nuclear weapons comes into effect after ratification from forty-three countries.

ELVIS VISITS THE WHITE HOUSE
Elvis Presley is granted an audience with President Nixon in the Oval Office to discuss his concerns about the drug culture in American society.

CHINA JOINS THE SPACE RACE
The People's Republic of China officially enters the space age when it launches its first satellite into orbit.

EARTH DAY
Tens of thousands of American schools and colleges celebrate the first Earth Day, which marks an increased awareness of environmental issues.

SKYJACK SUNDAY
Palestinian militants hijack four New York bound airplanes over Europe. Hundreds of passengers are held hostage when the planes land in the Middle East.

JIMI HENDRIX DIES
The musician who changed the sound of rock music forever dies from a drug-related incident aged just twenty seven.

WORLD TRADE CENTER TOWER ONE COMPLETED
Building work on One World Trade Center in New York finishes.

BAR CODES INTRODUCED IN UK
England starts using bar codes for retail and industrial use.

AND AT THE MOVIES...
M*A*S*H, *Robert Altman's subversive black comedy set in a Korean War mobile hospital about insolent, women-chasing surgeons;* The Aristocats, *a Walt Disney Production animation about a family of aristocratic cats;* Woodstock, *four-hour documentary uses twenty cameras to capture all the peace and love of the legendary outdoor music festival.*

YOU COSTUMED CRETINS WON'T STOP BRAINCHILD FROM BLOWING UP THE WORLD!

1971

EXPANDING UNIVERSE

For Marvel, 1971 was a period of progression and breaking down boundaries.

In the late 1960s, Roy Thomas had rapidly risen to become Marvel's most important writer next to Stan Lee. Not only a comics writer but also a pioneering comics historian, Thomas recognized that Stan Lee, Jack Kirby, and Lee's other collaborators had created a fictional universe replete with creative potential. Thomas sought to build upon the characters and concepts that Marvel had established in the 1960s and to closely connect together the disparate elements of the expanding Marvel Universe. Thomas's most spectacular early achievement was the Kree-Skrull War in *The Avengers* in 1971. This nine-part story line brought together past and present members of the Avengers, Captain Mar-Vell, the Inhumans, and SHIELD as two extraterrestrial empires, the Kree and the Skrulls, clashed in intergalactic combat. This story line would also influence later "event" comics like *Secret Wars* and *Civil War*.

Also in 1971, Marvel took steps to move beyond the restrictions imposed by the Comics Code Authority on the kind of stories that could be shown in comics. In defiance of the 1957 Code, Marvel published an anti-drug story line in *The Amazing Spider-Man* and experimented with non-Code magazines for adult readers.

JANUARY

ENTER THE SPYMASTER

• *The Invincible Iron Man* #33

The sinister Spymaster and his team of assistants, the Espionage Elite, first fought Iron Man in this issue of the armored avenger's comic.

MODERN AGE NAMORA

• *Sub-Mariner* #33

Namor's cousin Namora made her first modern day appearance in *Sub-Mariner* #33.

FEBRUARY

INTRODUCING THE SQUADRON SUPREME

• *The Avengers* #85

Traversing dimensions, Vision, Quicksilver, Scarlet Witch, and Goliath from the Avengers found themselves on a parallel Earth with its own team of Super Heroes created by writer Roy Thomas and artist John Buscema—the Squadron Supreme. Some of the team—Hyperion, Nighthawk, the Whizzer, and Doctor Spectrum—were heroic counterparts of members of the villainous Squadron Sinister, whom the Avengers had encountered in *The Avengers* #69 (Oct., 1969). Other Squadron Supreme members included American Eagle, Lady Lark, Tom Thumb, and even their own archer named Hawkeye. Each Squadron member was an affectionate parody of another Super Hero. The Avengers and Squadron Supreme ultimately joined forces against a highly intelligent menace called Brainchild and parted as allies.

NOT UNTIL SOME POINTED QUESTIONS ARE ANSWERED, MY IMPETUOUS FRIEND!
IT'S LIKE--HITTING A ROCK--OR A SOLID STEEL STATUE!

The Avengers tried to avert the destruction of the Squadron Supreme's Earth.

CAPTAIN AMERICA'S NEW CO-STAR

• *Captain America And The Falcon* #134

Marvel's first African-American Super Hero, the Falcon, won star billing when *Captain America* was retitled *Captain America And The Falcon* with issue #134. Captain America would share his comic book series and title with his partner through issue #222 in June, 1978.

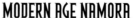

M Two of Marvel's greatest villains clashed when Dr. Doom met the Red Skull in *Astonishing Tales* #4, and also in #5 in April.

MARCH

KIRBY'S FAREWELL

• *Fantastic Four* #108

One of the last stories that Jack Kirby drew for *Fantastic Four* would not be published in complete form for over thirty years. Beginning with issue #107 in February, writer/editor Stan Lee and artist John Buscema constructed a new story line around the villain Janus, incorporating portions of Kirby's original artwork into issue #108. However, not until 2008 did Marvel finally publish Kirby's complete version of the Janus story in *Fantastic Four: The Lost Adventure*.

MAY

THE HULK IS SPACEBOUND

• *The Hulk* #137

Writers Gerry Conway and Roy Thomas and artist Herb Trimpe placed the Hulk in a sci-fi version of Herman Melville's classic whaling novel, *Moby-Dick*, that finished in March. The Hulk was shanghaied aboard the spaceship *Andromeda* by Xeron the Star-Slayer, an alien wielding "energy harpoons," and became entangled in the deadly obsession of Captain Cybor, the ship's commander, to destroy an immense space monster named Klaatu.

DEATH OF DORMA

• *Sub-Mariner* #36

After many years, Namor, Prince of Atlantis, married his true love, the royal Lady Dorma in this two-issue story line, beginning in April. But once the pair were pronounced man and wife, the bride's facial features began to change. This Dorma was really Namor's implacable enemy Llyra, who had abducted Dorma and disguised herself as Namor's love. Much to Llyra's disgust, Atlantean law decreed that Dorma was still Namor's wife and so Llyra murdered the water-breathing Dorma by forcing her to suffocate in open air.

HARLAN ELLISON AT MARVEL

• *The Avengers* #88

Harlan Ellison, legendary television, movie, and science-fiction writer, was an early and enthusiastic fan of Marvel Comics. In the 1970s, Ellison devised a plot for a two-part story, scripted by Roy Thomas, that began in *The Avengers* #88 and led into *The Incredible Hulk* #140. In this issue, drawn by Sal Buscema, an insect-like being called Psyklop fought against the Avengers and shrank the Hulk into seeming nothingness.

MARVEL'S ADULT LINE

• *Savage Tales* #1

The Comics Code, adopted in 1955, greatly restricted the kind of content that could be depicted in comic books. Sex and nudity, graphic violence, and even classic horror monsters like vampires were all forbidden. At the start of the 1970s, Marvel found a way to avoid the Code's restrictions by publishing comics stories in magazine formats, squarely aimed at adult audiences. One such magazine was *Savage Tales*, the first issue of which starred Conan the Barbarian. But this issue was more notable for the debut of Marvel's mindless swamp monster, the Man-Thing, in an origin story written by Gerry Conway and illustrated by Gray Morrow.

MARVEL SAYS NO TO DRUGS

"Any drug strong enough to give you that kind of trip can damage your brain—but bad!"

• *The Amazing Spider-Man* #96

In 1971, the US government's Department of Health, Education, and Welfare sent a letter to Marvel editor Stan Lee asking him to use his comics to warn his young audience about the rising use of dangerous, addictive drugs among their generation. Stan Lee agreed to do so, but there was a problem. In the 1950s, the comics industry had instituted the Comics Code Authority as a means of self-censorship and the Comics Code forbade any mention of drugs for any purpose.

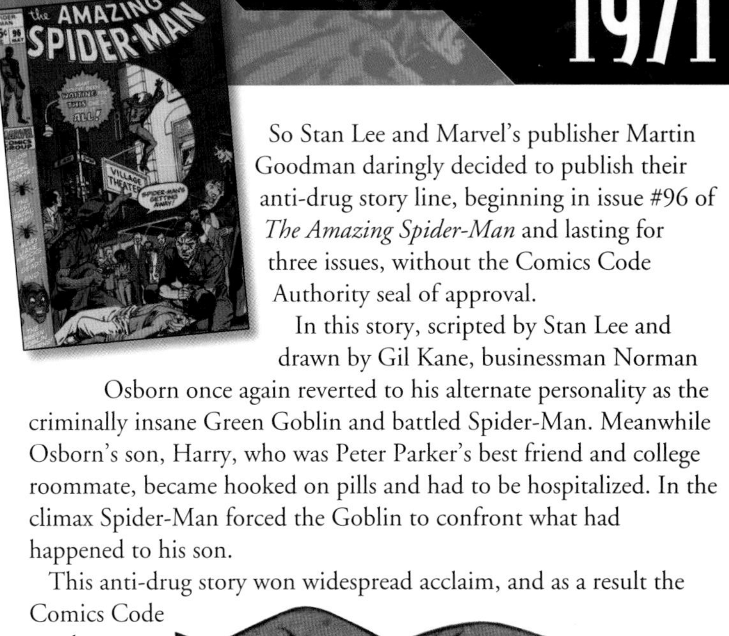

So Stan Lee and Marvel's publisher Martin Goodman daringly decided to publish their anti-drug story line, beginning in issue #96 of *The Amazing Spider-Man* and lasting for three issues, without the Comics Code Authority seal of approval.

In this story, scripted by Stan Lee and drawn by Gil Kane, businessman Norman Osborn once again reverted to his alternate personality as the criminally insane Green Goblin and battled Spider-Man. Meanwhile Osborn's son, Harry, who was Peter Parker's best friend and college roommate, became hooked on pills and had to be hospitalized. In the climax Spider-Man forced the Goblin to confront what had happened to his son.

This anti-drug story won widespread acclaim, and as a result the Comics Code was later revised, with restrictions on drugs and "vampires, ghouls, and werewolves" partially lifted. This gave American comics, including Marvel, greater creative freedom.

Once again Spider-Man battled one of his greatest enemies, the Green Goblin, but this time the fate of the Goblin's own son was in the balance.

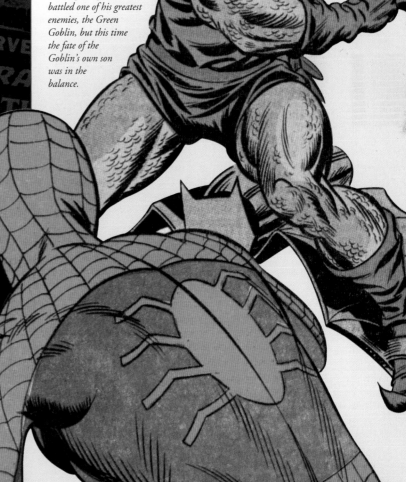

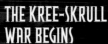

JUNE

THE KREE-SKRULL WAR BEGINS

• *The Avengers* #89

Editor Stan Lee and artist Jack Kirby had introduced two immense galactic empires in *Fantastic Four* : the Skrulls and the Kree. Now, writer Roy Thomas pitted the two empires against each other, with Earth caught in the middle, in the great Kree-Skrull War. Unprecedented in Marvel history, this epic spanned nine issues of *The Avengers*. The saga began in issue #89, as Ronan the Accuser seized control of the Kree Empire and ordered the assassination of the Kree's Captain Mar-Vell on Earth.

PRESENTING JARELLA

• *The Incredible Hulk* #140

Continuing the story line he began in *The Avengers* #88 in May, science fiction great Harlan Ellison showed how the Hulk was transported to a "microverse," a universe smaller than an atom. In the microverse, the Hulk rescued the beautiful green-skinned Princess Jarella from gigantic monsters. The grateful Jarella's sorcerers cast a spell on the Hulk that gave him Bruce Banner's rational personality. It seemed as if the Hulk had found paradise: He and Jarella were in love, and Jarella's people acclaimed the Hulk as a hero. But Ellison's saga ended in tragedy, when the evil Psyklop parted the lovers, returning the Hulk to Earth and to savagery.

- Kull the Conqueror launched in his own comic, *Kull The Conqueror* #1, initially written by Roy Thomas, drawn by Ross Andru, and inked by Wally Wood. Soon the art chores were taken over by brother and sister John and Marie Severin.

JULY

DOC SAMSON'S DEBUT

• *The Incredible Hulk* #141

Created by Roy Thomas and artist Herb Trimpe, Dr. Leonard Samson was a psychiatrist whose patient, Bruce Banner, had recently been cured of transforming into the Hulk. But Samson irradiated himself with gamma rays and transformed into a super-strong being with long, green hair, reminiscent of his biblical namesake. Jealous of Doc Samson's subsequent flirting with Betty Ross, Banner exposed himself to gamma radiation, became the Hulk once more, and battled Samson. At the end of this issue's story, Samson lost his powers but would later regain them. Doc Samson eventually became an ally of Banner and a frequent member of the Hulk's supporting cast.

- Steve Rogers, alias Captain America, joined the New York City police force in *Captain America And The Falcon* #139.

SEPTEMBER

FOREWARNED IS FOREARMED

• *The Amazing Spider-Man* #100

Peter Parker was no longer sure that his powers made him happy, so he concocted a serum to take away his spider-powers in his comic's 100th issue. In a vision, Uncle Ben's spirit reminded Peter that with great power must come great responsibility so Peter resumed his Spider-Man career, only to discover the serum had given him four extra arms!

OCTOBER

MEET MORBIUS

• *The Amazing Spider-Man* #101

To get around the fact that the Comic Code forbade the depiction of supernatural vampires, Roy Thomas and artist Gil Kane created Morbius, a sci-fi vampire. Seeking to cure himself of a blood disease, biochemist Michael inadvertently transformed himself into Morbius the Living Vampire. In this two-part story, Spider-Man, who had grown four extra arms in issue #100, battled Morbius and his old foe, the Lizard. Later, with the aid of the Lizard's human self, Spider-Man used a serum to rid himself of his extra arms. Morbius would go on to star in his own Marvel series in 1975.

NOVEMBER

ADAMS'S AVENGERS

• *The Avengers* #93

Following their collaboration on *X-Men*, Roy Thomas and artist Neal Adams teamed up again for the fifth installment of the Kree-Skrull War story line. Politician H. Warren Craddock was rallying public opinion against the Avengers, and members Thor, Iron Man, and Captain America disbanded the team. But these versions of the characters turned out to be shape-shifting Skrulls in disguise! Now the real Cap, Iron Man, and Thor returned to the Avengers in time to battle a group of Skrulls masquerading as the aliens' old nemeses, the Fantastic Four.

ANOTHER RED WOLF

• *Marvel Spotlight* #1

Marvel had already introduced the modern Red Wolf in *The Avengers* #80 (Sept., 1970). Now, writer Gardner Fox and artist Syd Shores created the Red Wolf of the nineteenth-century American West in this new Marvel series. Johnny Wakely was a Cheyenne whose tribe was slaughtered by soldiers and whose white foster parents were murdered by Native Americans. The God Owayodata chose Wakely to bring justice to the West as Red Wolf.

- The Black Widow began her long run as the Man Without Fear's co-star in *Daredevil* #81.
- Stan Lee scripted his final issue of the God of Thunder's adventures in *The Mighty Thor* #193.

TRIBUTE TO KONG

• *The Amazing Spider-Man* #103

Roy Thomas and artist Gil Kane created an entertaining homage to King Kong in this issue of *The Amazing Spider-Man.* As a publicity stunt, *Daily Bugle* publisher J. Jonah Jameson organized an expedition to the prehistoric Savage Land, taking along Peter Parker to shoot photographs and Peter's girlfriend, Gwen Stacy, to pose for the pictures. While there, they encountered a gigantic alien creature called Gog and Peter was forced to swing into action as Spider-Man to rescue Gwen from the alien's clutches.

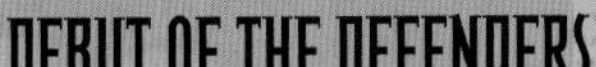

DEBUT OF THE DEFENDERS

"Defenders! A fitting name for such a grouping as we—if ever we've need to meet again."

• *Marvel Feature* #1

Roy Thomas was familiar with Marvel teams. He had already teamed Doctor Strange up, first with the Sub-Mariner and then with the Hulk, in Strange's war against the otherdimensional invaders called the Nameless Ones in 1970. Then in *Sub-Mariner* #34 and 35 (Feb. and March, 1971), Thomas banded the Hulk, the Sub-Mariner, and the Silver Surfer together in a short-lived alliance called the Titans Three. Now, for the first issue of a new series, *Marvel Feature,* Thomas and artist Ross Andru reunited Strange, the Hulk, and Namor as a brand new Marvel Super Hero team—the Defenders. In this initial story, Strange emerged from retirement and enlisted the help of Namor and the Hulk in his attempt to prevent his old enemy Yandroth's Omegatron computer from destroying the Earth. Following their success, Strange, Namor, and the Hulk pledged to reunite whenever it was necessary to defend the Earth. The new team would move to their own *Defenders* comic book in August, 1972, and would be joined by additional, unusual recruits including the Silver Surfer, the demigoddess Valkyrie, and a reformed Nighthawk, formerly of the Squadron Sinister.

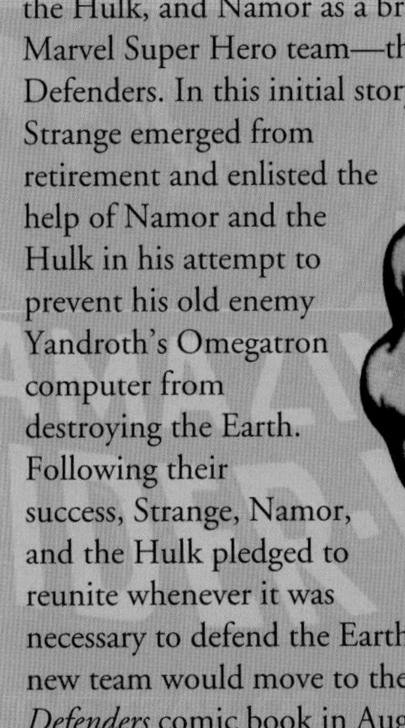

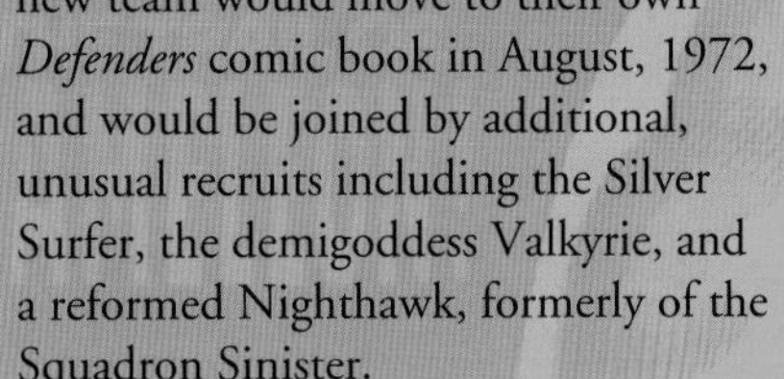

Though regarded by the public to be dangerous menaces, the Hulk and Namor joined forces with Doctor Strange to protect Earth as its Defenders.

MEANWHILE IN 1971...

VOTING AGE LOWERED TO EIGHTEEN

President Nixon certifies the 26th Amendment to the US Constitution, which lowers the voting age from twenty-one to eighteen. Many young people were being drafted to fight in Vietnam despite not having suffrage.

PENTAGON PAPERS LEAKED

A 7,000-page secret report on the US government's policy and planning of the Vietnam War is leaked to the press and further widens the credibility gap between the Nixon administration and the American people.

CULT LEADER AND FOLLOWERS GUILTY OF MURDERS

Charles Manson, the leader of a hippy cult community, and his accomplices are found guilty of a string of violent murders, including the Tate-LaBianca "ritualistic" murders.

THE 4004 MICROPROCESSOR

Intel creates its first microprocessor—"computer on a chip"—which opens the door to embedding intelligence in inanimate objects.

PAPARAZZI ROW OVER WEDDING

Rolling Stone Mick Jagger and Bianca Perez Morena de Macias' wedding in St. Tropez is delayed due to rows over the 100 or so cameramen and journalists at the venue.

NEW COUNTRY OF BANGLADESH

East Pakistan is granted independence from Pakistan and is named Bangladesh.

AND AT THE MOVIES...

The French Connection, *William Friedkin's raw account of a drugs squad trailing a drugs consignment features an amazing car chase;* Dirty Harry, *Clint Eastwood's vigilante cop tackles the Scorpio Killer on San Francisco's bumpy streets;* A Clockwork Orange, *Stanley Kubrick's controversial and arresting adaptation of Anthony Burgess's dystopic novel.*

The Amazing Spider-Man *#83 (April, 1970)*

Throughout Stan Lee's run as writer of The Amazing Spider-Man, *he presented a series of criminal masterminds who sought to control the New York City underworld. The Kingpin of Crime wore no mask, but others, like the Big Man, the Crime-Master, and, above all, the Green Goblin, all concealed their true identities. This characteristically powerful cover drawn by John Romita Sr. for* The Amazing Spider-Man *#83 showed Spider-Man encountering the latest of these mystery villains—the Schemer. The criminal's face was actually an astonishingly realistic mask, behind which hid the youthful features of Richard Fisk, the son of the Kingpin.*

SPIDEY TANGLES WITH A STRANGE
NEW SUPER-VILLAIN...
AND A DEADLY OLD-TIME ENEMY!

THE COMING OF...
THE SCHEMER!

I'M THE BEAST--AND I'M GOING PAST YOU--
OVER YOU--OR THROUGH YOU!

1972

HORROR UNLEASHED!

In the 1950s, much of the public, as well as members of Congress, had been outraged by the alleged excesses of the horror comics of that decade. The comics industry's Comics Code of 1957 had put an end to the horror genre in comics. Two decades later, and the hysteria directed against comics in the 1950s was long dead. Thanks in large part to Marvel, comic books were increasingly winning an older, more mature audience. Moreover, through his courageous anti-drug story line in *The Amazing Spider-Man* in 1971, Stan Lee had proved that the Comics Code was overdue for revision.

So the Comics Code was altered, and comics could now venture once more into the classic horror genre. Marvel quickly responded, launching *The Tomb Of Dracula*, *Werewolf By Night*, the new *Ghost Rider*, and a *Man-Thing* color comics series, all within a single year.

This was also the year that Stan Lee, the man who had revolutionized Super Hero comics, was promoted to the position of publisher. Lee's brilliant protégé, Roy Thomas, became Marvel's new Editor-in-Chief, guiding the comics line into horror and other new genres. Under Thomas's control, a new generation of comics creators, inspired by Stan Lee, was taking center stage.

JANUARY

THE KREE-SKRULL WAR CONTINUES

• *The Avengers* #95

In the seventh part of the Kree-Skrull War saga, the Avengers journeyed to the Inhumans' Great Refuge. There they clashed with Maximus, the brother of the Inhumans' rightful ruler, Black Bolt, as portrayed by writer Roy Thomas, penciller Neal Adams, and inker Tom Palmer.

FEBRUARY

FULL MOON OVER MARVEL

• *Marvel Spotlight* #2

With the changes to the Comics Code in place, Roy Thomas came up with the idea fo a series called "I, Werewolf," narrated in the first person by a teenager who transformed into a werewolf. Stan Lee liked the concept, but decided to rename it "Werewolf By Night." The initial creative team on the serie was scripter Gerry Conway and artist Mike Ploog, though they would eventually be succeeded by writer Doug Moench and penciller Don Perlin.

Teenager Jack Russell was born as Jacob Russoff in Transylvania. On his eighteenth birthday, he inherited the family curse and turned into a werewolf under the full moon. Initially, Jack had no control over his actions as this beast.

In *The Avengers* #96, the Avengers traveled into outer space in Neal Adams's final issue drawing the Kree-Skrull War.

MARCH

HAIR-RAISING CHANGES

• *Amazing Adventures* #11

Marvel had a problem: What was to be done with the X-Men now that their comic had turned into a reprint series? It experimented with various solutions, one of which was to spin off the Beast into his own series, in March, and to radically revamp the character's look. In *Amazing Adventures* #11, by writer Gerry Conway and artist Tom Sutton, Hank McCoy, the Beast's alter ego, completed his doctoral studies at Professor Xavier's school and took a job as a scientist. Drinking a serum he concocted, McCoy mutated, growing gray fur all over his body. The fur later turned blue, and, except for a brief period in *X-Factor* #11 (Dec., 2007), the Beast retained an animalistic appearance.

Marvel Team-Up #1 inaugurated a new series in which Spider-Man teamed with a different hero in each issue. In this issue, Spidey and the Human Torch fought the Sandman.

THE KREE-SKRULL WAR ENDS

"For untold eons, Skrull and Kree have stalked the cosmic corridors like twin races of malevolent gods... never knowing that each of their star-spanning clans has reached... a dead end."

• *The Avengers* #97

Over the course of eight issues of *The Avengers*, Roy Thomas had crafted an adventure saga longer than any before in Marvel history, ranging over three galaxies. Ronan the Accuser had seized control of the galactic Kree Empire away from its ruler, the Supreme Intelligence. Now the Kree were once again at war with their eternal rivals, the shape-shifting Skrulls. Their conflict had enveloped Earth, and the Avengers had traveled into outer space to defend their planet.

This dramatic concluding issue was drawn by John Buscema and inked by Tom Palmer, with a cover by Gil Kane and Bill Everett, and it saw the return of several Golden Age heroes. Rick Jones, friend of the Hulk and Avengers, was separated from his ally, Captain Mar-Vell, and found himself in the capital of the Kree Empire. The Supreme Intelligence knew that the Kree and the Skrulls had both reached evolutionary dead ends. But humanity still had great untapped potential, and the Supreme Intelligence temporarily unleashed latent powers within Rick Jones's mind. To combat Ronan's forces, Rick created simulacrums of Timely Super Heroes: Captain America, the original Human Torch, the Sub-Mariner, the Golden Age Angel, the Blazing Skull, the Fin, the Patriot, and the Golden Age Vision. Then, Rick used his powers to immobilize the entire space fleets of the Kree and the Skrulls, causing the end of the Kree-Skrull War. Exercising such vast power was too much for Rick, however, and Captain Mar-Vell once again merged with the youth to save his life. This unforgettable epic ended with the Supreme Intelligence returning the Avengers to the safety of their mansion.

Rick Jones conjured up the Super Heroes of Marvel's Golden Age.

APRIL

REMAKING "HIM"

• *Marvel Premiere* #1

In *Fantastic Four* #67 (Oct., 1967), Stan Lee and Jack Kirby had created a golden humanoid with superhuman powers known only as "Him." Five years later, Roy Thomas and artist Gil Kane allowed "Him" to meet another Lee-Kirby character, the godlike High Evolutionary, who created Counter-Earth, another world on the opposite side of the sun. After the satanic Man-Beast corrupted this human race, the High Evolutionary sent "Him" to be their savior.

DRACULA RISES

• *The Tomb Of Dracula* #1

Following the revision of the Comics Code, Stan Lee was eager to do a comics series about the archetypal vampire, novelist Bram Stoker's Dracula. Based on a few ideas from Lee, Roy Thomas plotted the first issue of *The Tomb Of Dracula*, which Gerry Conway then scripted. The interior art was pencilled by Gene Colan, a master of mood and characterization.

In this first issue, Dracula's American descendant, Frank Drake, journeyed to a Transylvanian castle he inherited, where his friend Clifton Graves resurrected Dracula.

The team of writer Marv Wolfman, penciller Colan, and inker Tom Palmer took over the series with issue #7.

MAY

GO WEST, YOUNG DAREDEVIL

• *Daredevil* #87

In May, writer Gerry Conway transported Daredevil and his crime-fighting partner, the Black Widow, into a mansion in San Francisco. However, Marvel's experiments in moving its heroes out of New York rarely worked for long, and Daredevil went back to Manhattan.

JUNE

LUKE CAGE DEBUTS

• *Luke Cage, Hero For Hire* #1

In the early 1970s there was a wave of movies about African-American adventure heroes. Marvel responded to this with *Luke Cage, Hero For Hire*, by writer Archie Goodwin and artist John Romita Sr. Sent to Seagate Prison for a crime he did not commit, Carl Lucas participated in an experiment that gave him super-strength and bulletproof skin. Fleeing Seagate, Lucas renamed himself "Luke Cage," set up an office, and offered his services as a "Hero for Hire."

NAMOR'S LITTLE COUSIN

• *Sub-Mariner* #50

Writer-artist Bill Everett, who had conceived Namor, the Sub-Mariner in 1939, returned to his most famous creation with the fiftieth issue of the current *Sub-Mariner* comic. In this story, which he wrote, drew, and inked, Everett introduced the Sub-Mariner's high-spirited adolescent cousin, Namorita, the daughter of the Golden Age character Namora. Later, Namor and Namorita fought against the Sub-Mariner's 1940s rival, Byrrah.

JULY

PATSY WALKER REAPPEARS

• *Amazing Adventures* #13

New Marvel writer Steve Englehart reintroduced Timely teen Patsy Walker into the Marvel Universe as a supporting character in the Beast's new series. Patsy and her love, Buzz Baxter, were married, but while Patsy became the Beast's ally, the Beast became the pair's nemesis.

DOCTOR STRANGE RETURNS

• *Marvel Premiere* #3

Having emerged from retirement to form the Defenders, Dr. Strange began a new series of solo adventures. He got off to an impressive start with this story scripted by Stan Lee and illustrated by Barry Windsor-Smith that pit him against his old foe Nightmare.

- Stan Lee retired from writing monthly comic books with *The Amazing Spider-Man* #110. Newcomer Gerry Conway succeeded him with the following issue.
- Created by writer Archie Goodwin and artist Gene Colan, the blonde vampire slayer Rachel Van Helsing debuted in *The Tomb Of Dracula* #3.

AUGUST

STARRING ADAM WARLOCK

• *The Power Of... Warlock* #1

Adam Warlock received his own bimonthly comic book in August, written by Roy Thomas and pencilled by Gil Kane. Having come to Counter-Earth, Warlock strove to save its population from the Man-Beast, who was masquerading as a false prophet.

- Roy Thomas revealed that the ionic-bodied Wonder Man was still alive, but comatose, in the beginning of the Sentinels story line in *The Avengers* #102.
- The Defenders moved into their own bimonthly comic book with *The Defenders* #1, written by Steve Englehart and pencilled by Sal Buscema.

AUGUST

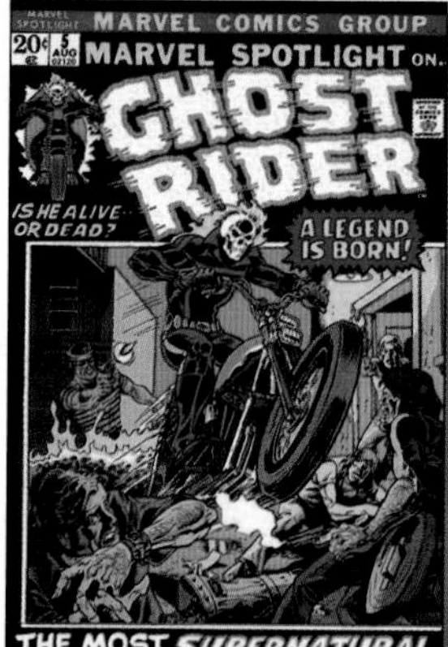

GHOST RIDER BLAZES FORTH

"Will I ever be... free? Or am I doomed to a dual life... man by day... and monster by night?!"

• *Marvel Spotlight* #5

Marvel's first Ghost Rider, who debuted in February, 1967, was a Western hero, living in the nineteenth century, who used a phosphorescent costume to appear to be a vengeful spirit. That character was subsequently renamed the Phantom Rider, because, in August, 1972, Marvel recycled the name "Ghost Rider" for a new hero, set in the present, who had actual supernatural powers.

Co-created by editor Roy Thomas, writer Gary Friedrich, and artist Mike Ploog, the new Ghost Rider was Johnny Blaze, a motorcycle stunt performer.

The orphaned Blaze was adopted and raised by Crash Simpson, the owner of a motorcycle stunt show, and, ultimately, fell in love with Crash's daughter, Roxanne. Discovering that Crash had a lethal illness, Blaze made a deal with the devil—actually the demon Mephisto—to save Crash from the disease. Mephisto kept the bargain, but then allowed Crash to die instead in a motorcycle stunt. However, Blaze still had to pay his price: Mephisto bonded his soul to the demon Zarathos, causing Blaze to transform into a demonic cyclist whose body appeared as a flaming skeleton. As the Ghost Rider, he could shoot "hellfire" from his hands, and even create a motorcycle from this blazing fire.

In these early adventures, Blaze could control his demonic form, and even used his Ghost Rider identity to fight evildoers. In later stories, however, Zarathos' personality became dominant in Blaze's Ghost Rider form.

This new Ghost Rider became a long-running success in the 1970s, and, in 2007, actor Nicolas Cage would star as Johnny Blaze in the *Ghost Rider* movie.

SEPTEMBER

CAP VERSUS CAP

• *Captain America And The Falcon* #153

If Captain America went into suspended animation after his sidekick, Bucky, died in 1945, then who were the Captain America and Bucky who appeared in *Young Men* #24 in December, 1953? In his first story line as *Captain America And The Falcon* writer, Steve Englehart revealed that an unnamed teacher had rediscovered the "Super-Soldier serum" in the 1950s and he and a student used it to turn themselves into new versions of Captain America and Bucky. However, their fanatical anti-communism devolved into madness, and both were involved in a battle with the original Captain America in this saga.

SEPTEMBER

THE CHANGING OF THE GUARD

• *Fantastic Four* #126

September witnessed a new generation taking command at Marvel Comics. Roy Thomas not only became writer of "The World's Greatest Comic Magazine" with *Fantastic Four* #126, but also simultaneously became Marvel's Editor-in-Chief, while Stan Lee ascended to the position of publisher.

- The cursed Jack Russell graduated into his own ongoing comic book with *Werewolf By Night* #1.

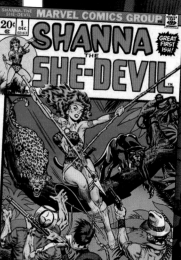

OCTOBER

- Beginning with issue #92, *Daredevil* was retitled *Daredevil And The Black Widow*, after the Man Without Fear's new partner.
- A pulp magazine favorite got his own comic with *Doc Savage* #1, plotted by Roy Thomas and penciled by Ross Andru.

MAN-THING

• *Adventure Into Fear* #10

The macabre Man-Thing made his way into color comic books in October. Having debuted in May, 1971, in Savage Tales #1, Man-Thing received a ten-page feature in the tenth issue of *Adventure Into Fear*. By issue #15, the feature had extended to nineteen pages, which was the standard length for a Marvel Super Hero comic. After issue #19 Man-Thing received his own series. Ted Sallis had transformed into the swamp creature Man-Thing when he fell into a swamp, which turned out to be the Nexus of All Realities.

NOVEMBER

FELINE FEMALE

• *The Claws Of The Cat* #1

Greer Grant Nelson, the widow of a policeman, was endowed with superhuman abilities through a series of experiments and became the crime-fighter the Cat. Written by Linda Fite and originally drawn by Marie Severin, the series lasted merely four issues, but the Cat later became Tigra.

- Steve Englehart took command of "Earth's Mightiest Heroes" with *The Avengers* #105, inaugurating his run as one of the series' most imaginative writers.

DECEMBER

JUNGLE HEROINE

• *Shanna The She-Devil* #1

Raised in Africa in the jungles of Zaire, Shanna O'Hara Plunder became a veterinarian and went to work at a Central Park Municipal Zoo in New York City. With her strong love of animals, she was horrified when the zoo's big cats were slaughtered, including her beloved leopard. Shanna returned to Africa where, wearing a costume made from the leopard's pelt, she personally fought poachers and other menaces as Shanna the She-Devil. Writers Carole Seuling and Steve Gerber crafted Shanna's origin story with artist George Tuska.

- Bruce Banner's former fiancée, Betty Ross, married Banner's rival and nemesis Glenn Talbot in *The Incredible Hulk* #158.

MEANWHILE IN 1972...

MEN ARRESTED AT WATERGATE

Five men are arrested while breaking into the Democratic Party's headquarters in the Watergate complex in Washington. The police claim they were attempting to bug the offices. One of the men is a member of the Republican committee to re-elect President Nixon.

OUT OF VIETNAM

After a cease-fire agreement in Paris, the last of the US's ground troops withdraw from Vietnam, bringing an end to America's role in the ground war. However, US forces continue to battle it out in the air.

US AND USSR SIGN MOSCOW PACT

During the first visit of an American President to Moscow, President Nixon and Leonid Brezhnev sign a pact aimed at reducing the danger of nuclear war.

TERROR RAID ON OLYMPIC VILLAGE

Palestinian gunmen storm the Israeli building in the Olympic village near Munich, shoot athletes dead, and take nine hostages. Fourteen people are killed in the ensuing gun battle with German police.

BRITAIN JOINS THE EEC

The Treaty of Brussels is signed, bringing the number of members of the Economic European Community to ten. The new member states are Britain, Ireland, Denmark, and Norway.

BLOODY SUNDAY IN NORTHERN IRELAND

A resolution to the ongoing Troubles in Northern Ireland seems further away than ever after the British Army open fire on civil rights protesters marching in Londonderry and kill fourteen.

"MEDIA VIOLENCE AFFECTS CHILDREN"

The National Institute of Mental Health and the Surgeon General issues a report that states that exposure of violence on television can foster aggression in children.

FIRST POCKET-SIZED SCIENTIFIC CALCULATOR

Hewlett-Packard releases the HP-35, the first hand-held calculator capable of scientific calculations. It goes on sale for $395.

AND AT THE MOVIES...

The Godfather, *Francis Ford Coppola's mythic Mafia saga, adapted from Mario Puzo's novel, charts the Corleone family's vicious struggle for Mafia supremacy;* Deliverance, *a film about man's inhumanity disguised as a wild, water adventure about four city friends in search of paradise lost;* Cabaret, *Bob Fosse's iconically choreographed vision of the sleazy Kit Kat Club in 1930s Berlin set against the rising Nazi threat.*

YOU'VE SHOUTED YOUR LAST THREATS, KILLRAVEN. BY DAY'S END YOUR ARROGANT MOUTH WILL BE STILLED!

1973

MARVEL'S TURNING POINT

When did the Silver Age of Marvel truly end? Was it when Jack Kirby left the company in 1970? Or was it when Stan Lee stopped writing comic books on a regular basis in 1972? It was difficult for comic book scholars and fans to pinpoint the answer. But there was one monumental event in 1973 that made it clear that if the Silver Age had not already ended, then it was really over now. It was not about a real person leaving Marvel; it was the departure of a fictional character. In June, 1973, in the pages of *The Amazing Spider-Man* #121, Peter Parker's love, Gwen Stacy, died.

From the beginning of Marvel's Super Hero renaissance of the 1960s, Stan Lee had made it clear that, in the Marvel Universe, life was not always fair, and the innocent sometimes suffered. In Spider-Man's origin story, his Uncle Ben was murdered. Since then Betty Brant's brother Bennett, *Daily Bugle* reporter Fred Foswell, and Captain George Stacy had all died in Stan Lee's Spider-Man stories.

Nevertheless readers were shocked when Spidey's own leading lady, Gwen Stacy, met her tragic end. In 1994, in their series *Marvels*, writer Kurt Busiek and painter Alex Ross claimed Gwen's death was a turning point in Marvel history. Happy endings were no longer guaranteed. Super Hero comics had lost their innocence.

JANUARY

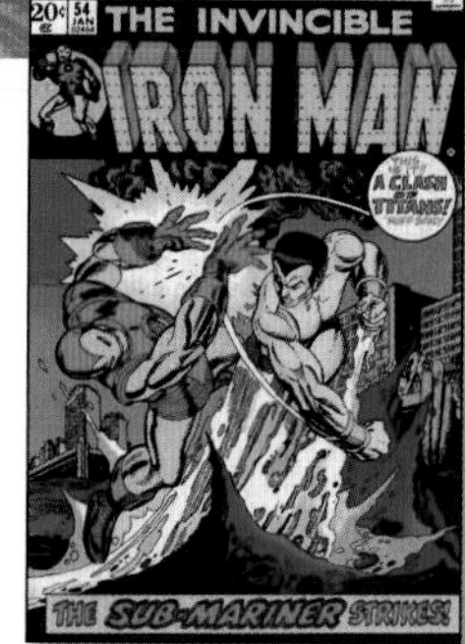

MOONDRAGON IN DISGUISE

• *The Invincible Iron Man* #54

In January, a mysterious, shaven-headed woman calling herself Madame MacEvil manipulated Iron Man into battling the Sub-Mariner. She later became known as Moondragon, an Earthwoman raised on Titan who had developed psionic powers.

THE MONSTER AWAKES

• *The Monster Of Frankenstein* #1

Marvel's new series about Frankenstein's monster ran until 1975. It began with a faithful comics adaptation of Mary Shelley's original novel, by writer Gary Friedrich and artist Mike Ploog. In Marvel's series, the Monster was in a state of suspended animation brought on after he fled from Frankenstein and found himself in the Arctic. He briefly awoke from this state in the nineteenth century and later appeared in the modern world.

Ⓜ Artist Bill Everett revived his 1950s character, the goddess Venu in *Sub-Mariner* #57.

FEBRUARY

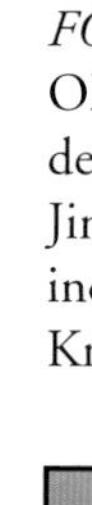

FRIENDS OF OL' MARVEL

• *FOOM* #1

Marvel launched its first official fan magazine to be produced in-house. *FOOM*, standing for "Friends of Ol' Marvel," was edited and designed by SHIELD writer/artist Jim Steranko. Later *FOOM* editors included Chris Claremont, Dave Kraft, and Jim Salicrup.

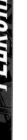

RIDE OF THE VALKYRIE

• *The Defenders* #4

Amora, Enchantress of Asgard, endowed Barbara Norriss with the consciousness, physical appearance, and superhuman powers of Brunnhilde, leader of the Valkyries. Known as the Valkyrie, she joined the Defenders, and later regained her original, immortal body.

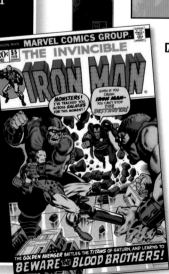

Ⓜ Conan first met Red Sonja, the woman with fiery red hair who was his equal as a warrior, in *Conan The Barbarian* #23.

THE GODS OF TITAN

• *The Invincible Iron Man* #55

In this issue, scripted by Mike Friedrich, plotter and penciller Jim Starlin introduced a miniature mythos of his creations. There was Mentor, the immortal ruler of Titan; his son Eros, later known as Starfox; and, most importantly, Mentor's other son, Thanos, who would later seek godlike power and serve the personification of Death.

THANOS STRIKES

• *Captain Marvel* #25

In March, the first of artist Jim Starlin's many sagas of the Marvel heroes' wars against Thanos began. Scripted by Mike Friedrich, this tale saw Captain Mar-Vell first meet the villainous "Masterlord," who later proved to be the Mad Titan, Thanos.

M In *Fantastic Four* #132, Medusa of the Inhumans replaced Susan Richards briefly on the FF, as Medusa's younger sister, Crystal, had once done.

DRACULA DEBUTS

• *Dracula Lives!* #1

Marvel added to its black-and-white magazine line with this anthology of stories about the vampire lord Dracula. In this first issue, Roy Thomas and artist Dick Giordano began a comics adaptation of Bram Stoker's original novel that would not be completed for three decades.

THE COMING OF KILLRAVEN

• *Amazing Adventures* #18

Roy Thomas conceived the initial idea of an alternate-future Earth sequel to H.G. Wells' classic science fiction novel, *The War Of The Worlds*, which began with this issue. After their failed attempt to conquer the Earth, the Martians returned a hundred years later—in 2001—and, this time, succeeded. Jonathan Raven was raised to fight in their gladiatorial arena, where he was given the name "Killraven." Managing to escape, he became the leader of a band of rebels, the Freemen, who were determined to free humanity from their Martian masters. Neal Adams created Killraven and plotted the first story with a script by Gerry Conway and art by Adams and Howard Chaykin.

JUNE

THE DEATH OF GWEN STACY

"How can Spider-Man go on, after being faced with this almost unbelievable death?"

• *The Amazing Spider-Man* #121

In June, Marvel embarked on a story that would have far-reaching effects. *The Amazing Spider-Man* artist John Romita Sr. suggested killing off Peter Parker's beloved Gwen Stacy in order to shake up the book's status quo.

In this story, written by Gerry Conway and drawn by Gil Kane, Norman Osborn regained his memory that he was the Green Goblin—and that Peter Parker was his foremost enemy, Spider-Man. He abducted Gwen Stacy and took her to the top of a towering New York City bridge. (Oddly, Conway's script referred to it as the George Washington Bridge, but Kane clearly drew the Brooklyn Bridge.) Before Spider-Man's horrified eyes, the Goblin pushed Gwen off the bridge toward the waters below. Spider-Man managed to swoop down on his webbing and catch Gwen, but when he finally got her to safety, he discovered she was dead.

Spider-Man attributed Gwen's death to the shock of her fall. But was the truth even worse? Conway inserted a snapping sound effect when Spider-Man caught Gwen, implying that the shock of being caught while falling at great speed had broken her neck. Whatever the case, Peter Parker would once again blame himself: the woman he loved had died because he was Spider-Man.

Probably no one at Marvel anticipated how much the death of Gwen would shock their readers. Yet even though Conway later introduced the Jackal's clone of Gwen Stacy, the real Gwen's demise was never undone. It served as evidence that Spider-Man lived in a world in which the good guys did not always win, and in which tragedy was real.

MEET MANTIS

• *The Avengers* #112

In this issue, writer Steve Englehart and artist Don Heck introduced Mantis, a mistress of the martial arts. In Vietnam, she became the companion of the skilled Swordsman, and accompanied him to New York where he rejoined the Avengers.

JULY

UNSHEATHING BLADE

• *The Tomb Of Dracula* #10

Early in their collaboration on *The Tomb Of Dracula*, writer Marv Wolfman and artist Gene Colan co-created Blade, a black man who stalked and killed vampires with the wooden blades after which he named himself.

When Eric Brooks's mother was in labor, she was visited by a supposed doctor, who was actually the vampire Deacon Frost. Frost attacked and killed her as she was giving birth, and, as a result her son, the future Blade, was born with an immunity to a vampire's bite. Moreover, he grew up determined to avenge his mother's death by hunting all vampires—and finding his mother's killer.

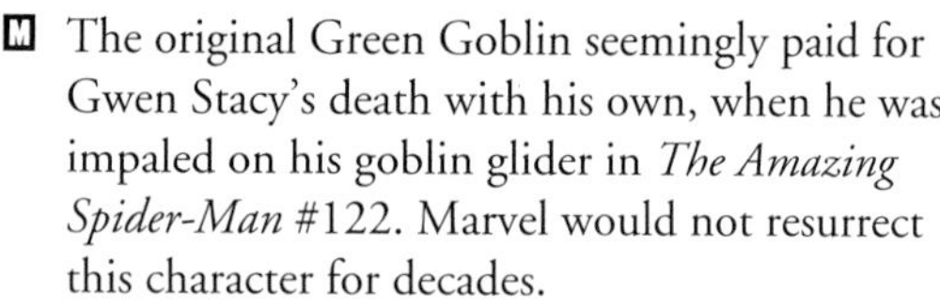

- The original Green Goblin seemingly paid for Gwen Stacy's death with his own, when he was impaled on his goblin glider in *The Amazing Spider-Man* #122. Marvel would not resurrect this character for decades.
- Marvel published a new black-and-white magazine, *Monsters Unleashed*. The first issue featured author Robert E. Howard's Puritan adventurer Solomon Kane.
- Writer Steve Englehart and artist Frank Brunner first joined forces on the "Dr. Strange" story in *Marvel Premiere* #9.

AUGUST

DEAD MEN'S TALES

• *Tales Of The Zombie* #1

In July, 1953, writer Stan Lee and artist Bill Everett created a story called "Zombie" in *Menace* #5. Now, Marvel built a new magazine series around that mystical Zombie. Writers Roy Thomas and Steve Gerber collaborated on the first new Zombie story.

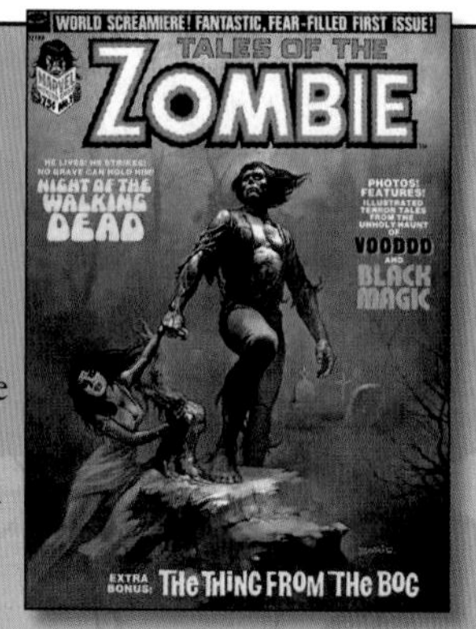

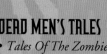

- The original Yellow Claw—not Jim Steranko's robot double from SHIELD—made his first modern appearance in *Captain America And The Falcon* #164.
- Marvel debuted black-and-white horror magazine *Vampire Tales*, whose first issue featured a story by Steve Gerber about the Living Vampire Morbius.

SEPTEMBER

STARRING THE BLACK PANTHER

"Tomorrow's sun will rise on a new king of the Wakandas!"

• *Jungle Action* #6

Stan Lee and Jack Kirby had made comics history by creating the first significant black Super Hero, the Black Panther, in July, 1966. Falcon, Marvel's first African-American Super Hero, who had debuted in September, 1969, was currently sharing billing with Captain America in the latter's comic book. But now Marvel took another major step forward, by making the Black Panther its first black character to star in his own comic book series.

Marvel assigned Don McGregor, a uniquely talented writer, to write this series. McGregor's initial idea for this Black Panther series was an ambitious thirteen-part story line, Panther's Rage, which continued for two years. Rich Buckler, Gil Kane, and Billy Graham all contributed art to the saga. Due not only to its length but to McGregor's skill with exploring characterization, this story line was declared to be Marvel's first graphic novel, despite its serialized form.

The principal antagonist was Erik Killmonger, who was bent on overthrowing the Panther's rule of the African kingdom of Wakand McGregor co-created a long line of additional villains, including human mutates Baron Macabre and King Cadaver. But McGregor' greater talent lay in delineating vivid multidimensional personalities for each member of his cast, from leading lady Monica Lynne to minor members of the Wakandan court. As for the Panther himself McGregor portrayed T'Challa as a complex and credible hero, nobl yet vulnerable, capable of enduring great suffering yet still determined struggling toward victory. This series along with *Killraven* deservedly won McGregor a cult following among comics fans of the 1970s.

- The new Ghost Rider became the title character of his comic book and *Ghost Rider* #1 gave readers their first glimpse of demonologist Daimon Hellstrom.

OCTOBER

SON OF SATAN

• *Marvel Spotlight* #12

Stan Lee suggested doing a series called *Mark Of Satan*, and Roy Thomas amended the idea to "The Son Of Satan" in this issue of *Marvel Spotlight*. The son of a demon called Satan and a mortal woman, Daimon Hellstrom battled supernatural evil.

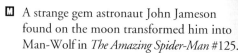

- A strange gem astronaut John Jameson found on the moon transformed him into Man-Wolf in *The Amazing Spider-Man* #125.
- Magical Loki and Dormammu manipulated two super-teams into the Avengers-Defenders war, starting in *The Avengers* #116 and *The Defenders* #9 in October.
- Marvel launched its humor magazine *Crazy*, which would run until October, 1983, and featured such recurring characters as Obnoxio the Clown and Teen Hulk.

NOVEMBER

McGREGOR AND MARTIANS

• *Amazing Adventures* #21

Marvel's "War Of The Worlds" series in *Amazing Adventures* became a true classic when Don McGregor took over as writer. McGregor began his memorable collaboration with artist P. Craig Russell in issue #21, and the series was renamed *Killraven* with issue #29.

M The telepathic Madame MacEvil got the far more poetic name of Moondragon in *Daredevil* #105.

DECEMBER

A STAR IS HATCHED

• *Adventure Into Fear* #19

December saw the debut of the cigar-smoking Howard the Duck. In this story by writer Steve Gerber and artist Val Mayerik, various beings from different realities had begun turning up in the Man-Thing's Florida swamp, including this bad-tempered talking duck. It transpired that the swamp was actually the "nexus of all realities," where many dimensions met.

DECEMBER

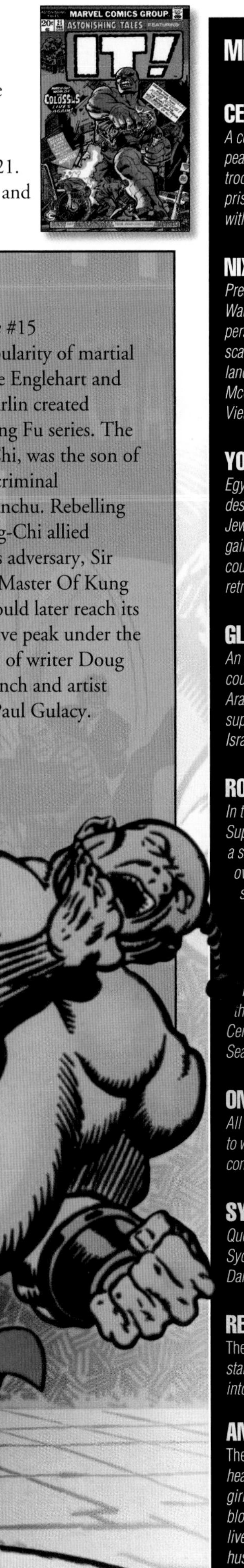

IT, THE LIVING COLOSSUS

• *Astonishing Tales* #21

It, the immense stone statue from *Tales Of Suspense* #14 (Feb., 1961), won his own series in *Astonishing Tales* #21. However, it was short-lived and finished in June, 1974.

ENTER SHANG-CHI

• *Special Marvel Edition* #15

Capitalizing on the popularity of martial arts movies, writer Steve Englehart and artist/co-plotter Jim Starlin created Marvel's Master Of Kung Fu series. The title character, Shang-Chi, was the son of novelist Sax Rohmer's criminal mastermind Dr. Fu Manchu. Rebelling against his father, Shang-Chi allied himself with his father's adversary, Sir Denis Nayland Smith. Master Of Kung Fu would later reach its creative peak under the team of writer Doug Moench and artist Paul Gulacy.

MEANWHILE IN 1973...

CEASE-FIRE IN VIETNAM

A cease-fire agreement is reached at the Paris peace talks. The treaty states that all American troops will be withdrawn and all military prisoners on both sides will be exchanged within sixty days.

NIXON LINKED WITH WATERGATE

President Nixon takes responsibility for the Watergate scandal, though he denies any personal involvement. Despite the Watergate scandal, he was re-elected in 1972 in a landslide victory against Democrat George McGovern, who was an outspoken critic of the Vietnam War.

YOM KIPPUR OFFENSIVE

Egypt and Syria attack Israeli troops in the Sinai desert and the Golan Heights on the day of the Jewish festival Yom Kippur. Despite initial Arab gains, the Israelis are successful in their counter-offensive and the attacking forces retreat.

GLOBAL OIL CRISIS

An energy crisis hits oil-dependent Western countries when members of the Organization of Arab Petroleum Exporting Countries stop supplying oil to countries that are supporting Israel in the Yom Kippur war.

ROE V. WADE

In the landmark case of Roe v. Wade, the US Supreme Court establishes a woman's right to a safe abortion. This controversial judgment overrides the anti-abortion laws of many states.

WORLD TRADE CENTER OPENS

New York celebrates the official opening of the 110-storey twin towers. The World Trade Center is the world's tallest building until the Sears Tower opens in Chicago in May.

ONE BILLION WATCH ELVIS

All around the world one billion people tune in to watch Elvis Presley's Aloha from Hawaii *concert.*

SYDNEY OPERA HOUSE OPENS

Queen Elizabeth II officially opens the iconic Sydney Opera House, which was designed by Dane Jorn Utzon.

REGGAE MUSIC TAKES OFF

The Harder They Come, *a Jamaican film starring Jimmy Cliff, launches Reggae music into the American mainstream.*

AND AT THE MOVIES...

The Exorcist, *William Friedkin's spitting, head-spinning account of a demonic teenage girl's exorcism is the first true horror blockbuster;* Mean Streets, *Martin Scorsese's lively, sharp-suited account of Little Italy hustlers, set to a snappy soundtrack and starring Robert de Niro;* Don't Look Now, *Nicolas Roeg's haunting adaptation of*

The Avengers *#113 (July, 1973)*

As the Avengers attempted to put the Statue of Liberty back together again after the monster Gog had torn it up, the Vision was attacked by the Living Bombs. This extremist group were horrified by the idea of an Avengers romance between the Vision, an android, and the Scarlet Witch, a mutant. In this story scripted by Steve Englehart with art by Bob Brown, it seemed that the Vision would die, but his fellow Avenger team mates managed to save his life, to the relief of the Scarlet Witch.

--AND I'M GOING TO MAKE YOU PAY!!
YOUR YOUNG MEN SHALL SLAY VISIONS!
BUCKLER/SINNOTT

PLEASE... SURRENDER YOURSELVES..! I HAVE NO WISH TO DO YOU ANY HARM...!

1974

THE GRIM AND THE GRITTY

In 1974, two of Marvel's most famous characters made their debuts. These heroes were very different from those Stan Lee and his collaborators had created back in the idealistic 1960s. The Super Heroes of the Silver Age never used guns or knives and were morally opposed to killing under any circumstances. But by the 1970s, disillusionment had set in and the success of the savage *Conan The Barbarian* in 1970 showed that Marvel's audience was ready to accept a more ruthless sort of hero for less innocent times. The comic book world was ready for the arrival of Wolverine and the Punisher.

Previous Marvel Super Heroes had fought with their fists, and, to a certain extent, Wolverine was no different. However, his fists contained razor-sharp, unbreakable claws, and the short-tempered mutant would not hesitate to use them on anyone who crossed his path.

The Punisher was a vigilante who acted outside the law. He carried guns, wore a death's-head symbol on his costume, and saw himself as a soldier conducting a one-man war on crime.

Although Marvel introduced the Punisher and Wolverine as supporting characters, they would soon become stars. These two antiheroes were the first major figures in a new, darker style of Super Hero comics that would become prominent in the 1980s: "grim and gritty" comics.

JANUARY

CONSPIRACY AGAINST CAP

• *Captain America And The Falcon* #169

Inspired by the real life Watergate scandals, writer Steve Englehart devised a story line about a conspiracy within the US government. In this issue, the Committee to Regain America's Principles framed Captain America for murdering a costumed criminal, named the Tumbler.

JUNGLE LORD

• *Ka-Zar* #1

Ka-Zar, lord of the prehistoric Savage Land, had received his own three-issue series in 1970. Following his stint in *Astonishing Tales*, Ka-Zar now won a brand new comic book series, whose first issue guest starred his future wife—Shanna the She-Devil.

SWAMP STAR

• *Man-Thing* #1

After his success in *Fear*, the Man-Thing won his own comic. In the first issue, writer Steve Gerber wound up the story of the "Congress of Realities" and Howard the Duck seemingly fell to his doom.

- The Thing got his own comic book with the first issue of *Marvel Two-In-One*, a series that teamed him up with other Super Heroes.
- Doctor Strange encountered Sise-Neg, a sorcerer who traveled back in time to become God, in *Marvel Premiere* #13 by writer Steve Englehart and artist Frank Brunner.

MARCH

PRESENTING THE PUNISHER

"He's different! He's deadly! He's... the Punisher!"

• *The Amazing Spider-Man* #130

Inspired by crime fiction, new *Spider-Man* writer Gerry Conway co-created the Punisher, a vigilante who believed that the police and the courts were ineffective in stopping criminals. The Punisher acted as judge, jury, and executioner—seeking out and destroying those he considered evildoers that were beyond the reach of the law. Artist John Romita Sr. developed the Punisher's visual appearance, while Ross Andru drew his initial story in this issue of *The Amazing Spider-Man*.

In his first appearance, the Punisher was deceived by his costumed ally, the Jackal, into believing that Spider-Man himself was a criminal who must be stopped—permanently. By the end of the issue, Spider-Man had proved to the Punisher that the Jackal was their real enemy.

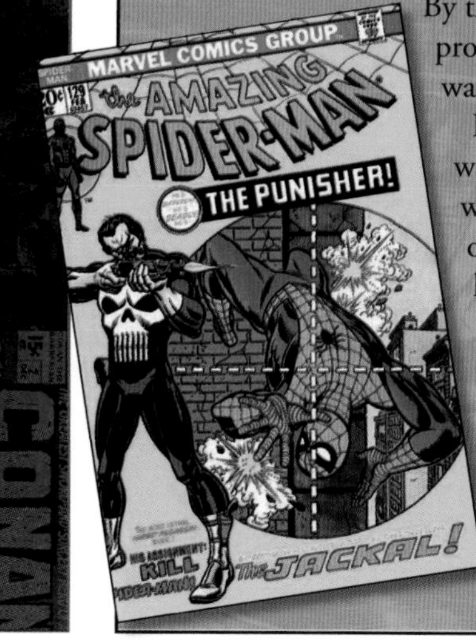

Later stories revealed that the Punisher was Frank Castle, a former US Marine who sought vengeance for the murder of his family by criminals. At the height of his popularity, the Punisher simultaneously starred in four monthly comics and so far there have been three Punisher movies, in 1989, 2004, and 2008, with the eponymous vigilante played by Dolph Lundgren, Thomas Jane, and Ray Stevenson, respectively.

MARCH

MOTOR MANIA

• *The Amazing Spider-Man* #130

As the result of a merchandising deal with Corona Motors, Spider-Man also ended up driving his own car, the Spidermobile, in *The Amazing Spider-Man* #130. But neither the writers nor the fans liked it, and Spider-Man finally got rid of the Spidermobile in issue #160.

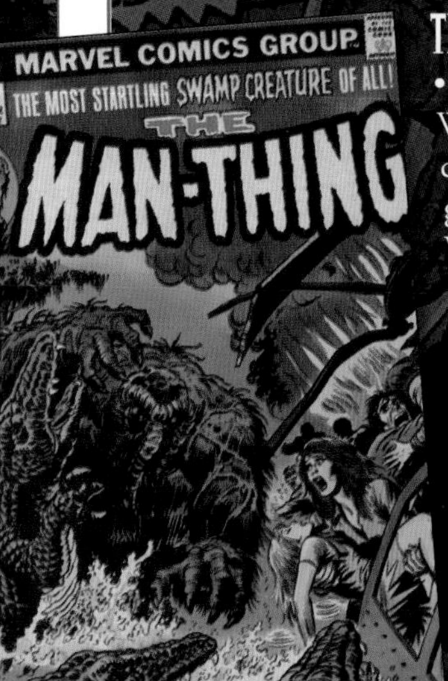

THE FIRST FOOLKILLER

• *The Man-Thing* #3

Writer Steve Gerber made his own comment on the rise of "grim and gritty" vigilantes when he and artist Val Mayerik created the Foolkiller in *The Man-Thing* #3. The Foolkiller believed that he had been chosen by God to destroy criminals, sinners, and political dissidents, all of whom he considered to be "fools." He would send them his victims a card, warning that they had twenty-four hours to live. If they did not repent, he would use his "purification gun" to disintegrate them. Clearly insane, the Foolkiller perished in combat with the Man-Thing, but other men would subsequently adopt the Foolkiller's costumed identity.

- Injecting himself with dinosaur DNA from the Savage Land, Dr. Vincent Stegron became a reptilian menace known as Stegron the Dinosaur Man, in *Marvel Team-Up* #19.

APRIL

ALMOST AN UNCLE

• *The Amazing Spider-Man* #131

In the first *Amazing Spider-Man* annual in 1964, Peter Parker's trusting Aunt May first met Doctor Octopus, whom she believed to be a chivalrous gentleman. In issue #131 of *The Amazing Spider-Man*, Spidey narrowly stopped Doc Ock from marrying May to gain control of an atomic processing plant that she had unexpectedly inherited!

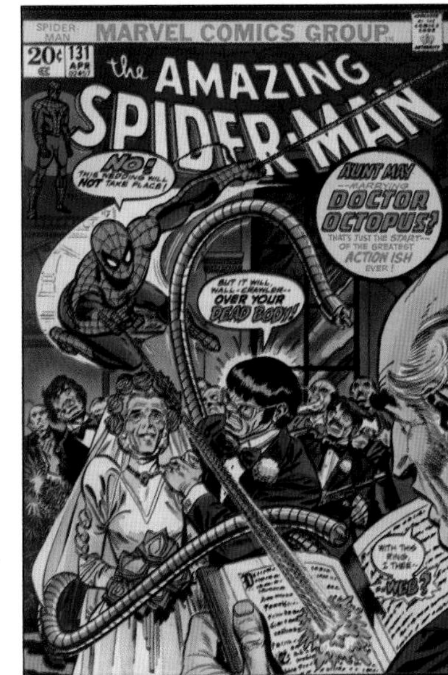

SONS OF THE TIGER

• *The Deadly Hands Of Kung Fu* #1

Marvel's magazine line moved into martial arts with the first issue of *The Deadly Hands Of Kung Fu*, starring Shang-Chi, the Master of Kung Fu. The first issue also introduced the Sons of the Tiger, a martial arts team.

- *Special Marvel Edition* was renamed *Master Of Kung Fu* with issue #17.

MAY

TURNING INTO TIGRA

• *Giant-Size Creatures* #1

Like other popular Marvel stars, the Werewolf by Night began starring in his own double-sized quarterly comic book. Originally titled *Giant-Size Creatures*, it was later renamed *Giant-Size Werewolf* with issue #2. In the first issue, Greer Nelson, the Super Hero known as the Cat, was exposed to lethal radiation. To save her life, members of an ancient race called the Cat People transformed her into Tigra the Were-Woman, a catlike being.

INTRODUCING IRON FIST

• *Marvel Premiere* #15

Marvel combined the Super Hero and martial arts genres when writer Roy Thomas and artist Gil Kane created Iron Fist in *Marvel Premiere* #15. When Danny Rand was a boy, his parents Wendell and Heather took him on an expedition to Asia to find the mystical realm of K'un-L'un. Wendell and Heather both perished, but Daniel was rescued and raised in K'un-L'un. There, Daniel became a supreme martial artist, and, by plunging his hands into the heart of a dragon, gained the power of the "iron fist," which enhanced his natural abilities. Later, Daniel returned to New York City, where he eventually became a crimefighting Super Hero—Iron Fist.

- The Fantastic Four began starring in a double-size quarterly comic book, *Giant-Size Super-Stars*, which became *Giant-Size Fantastic Four* with issue #2 in August.
- Marvel launched *Haunt Of Horror*, a new black and white horror comics anthology magazine.

JUNE

ENTER LILITH

• *Giant-Size Chillers* #1

Dracula won his own double-sized quarterly comic, *Giant-Size Chillers*, which became *Giant-Size Dracula* with its second issue in September. Issue #1 introduced Lilith, Dracula's daughter and enemy. Created by Marv Wolfman and Gene Colan, Lilith took possession of host bodies of women who, like her, despised their fathers.

- Silver Dagger was introduced in the new *Dr. Strange* comic.

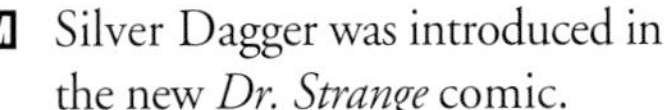

JULY

WHITE HOUSE WAR

• *Captain America And The Falcon* #175

In the conclusion of writer Steve Englehart's Watergate-inspired story line, Captain America battled the Secret Empire on the White House lawn. It was implied that, when unmasked, the Secret Empire's leader was revealed to be the President!

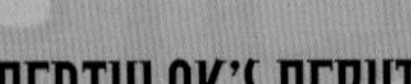

SILVER SAMURAI

• *Daredevil* #111

In one of the first signs of Japanese influence on American Super Hero comics, Daredevil came up against a new Super Villain, the Silver Samurai.

- Formerly a member of the villainous Squadron Sinister, millionaire Kyle Richmond, alias Nighthawk, turned hero and joined the Defenders in *The Defenders* #14.
- In the first crossover between Marvel's Super Hero books and its horror line, Spider-Man and Dracula both appeared in *Giant-Size Spider-Man* #1.

AUGUST

DEATHLOK'S DEBUT

• *Astonishing Tales* #25

Before there were Robocop and the Terminator, there was Deathlok the Demolisher. Created by artist Rich Buckler and writer Doug Moench, the original Deathlok was Colonel Luther Manning, a soldier in an alternate, post-apocalyptic future, which was set in the 1980s. Severely injured in war games, Manning was converted into a cyborg warrior, part man and part machine. Several other Deathloks would appear in later years.

WHIZZER AND SON

• *Giant-Size Avengers* #1

The original Whizzer made his first modern appearance in a story by Roy Thomas in *Giant-Size Avengers* #1. The first issue of this new quarterly series also featured the debut of Nuklo, the nuclear-powered son of the Whizzer and Miss America.

- Adam Warlock rose from the dead to defeat Man-Beast and his New Men on Counter-Earth in issue #178 of *Incredible Hulk*.
- Marvel launched a new black-and-white magazine based on Twentieth Century Fox's *Planet Of The Apes* movies in August. Doug Moench was the principal writer, and artists included Mike Ploog, Tom Sutton, Alfredo Alcala, and George Tuska.

SEPTEMBER

BEGINNING OF THE END

• *Captain Marvel* #34

Jim Starlin and Steve Englehart introduced Nitro, a Super Villain who could explode and then re-form his body, in *Captain Marvel* #34. In this story, Nitro exposed Kree Super Hero Mar-Vell to the nerve gas that caused the cancer that would eventually kill him.

- The Man Without Fear's former foe, the Exterminator, first appeared in his new guise as the Death-Stalker in *Daredevil* #113.
- Crystal of the Royal Family of the Inhumans married Quicksilver of the Avengers in *Fantastic Four* #150.

OCTOBER

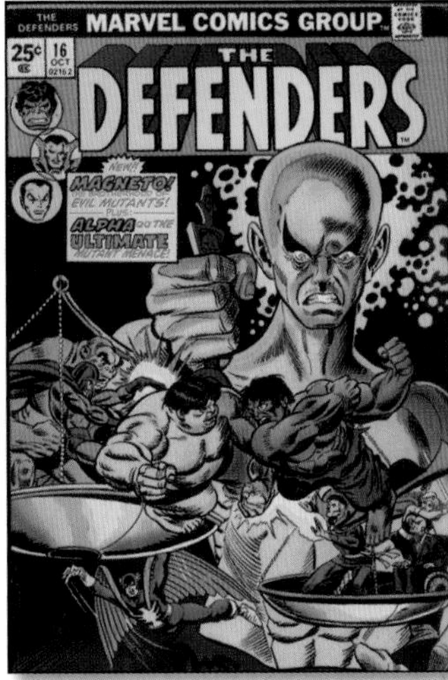

ALPHA THE ULTIMATE MUTANT

• *The Defenders* #16

While *X-Men* remained in reprints Professor Charles Xavier teamed up with the Defenders to oppose Magneto, the Brotherhood of Evil Mutants, and Magneto's creation, Alpha the Ultimate Mutant. In the following issue, Alpha rebelled and devolved Magneto into an infant.

Genetically engineered by Magneto, the all-powerful Alpha the Ultimate Mutant determined the outcome of the conflict between the Defenders and Magneto's Brotherhood.

WENDIGO AND WOLVERINE

• *The Incredible Hulk* #180

Returning to Canada, the Hulk again did battle with a flesh-eating monster called the Wendigo. Written by Len Wein and drawn by Herb Trimpe, this issue also gave readers their first glimpse of the Canadian government's special agent, Weapon X, alias Wolverine.

DEATH AND THE DOCTOR

• *Doctor Strange* #4

Within the surreal world inside the mystic Orb of Agamotto, Doctor Strange surrendered to Death incarnate. But after his spirit encountered the sorcerer supreme, the Ancient One, Strange returned to life in the next chapter of this classic saga by writer Steve Englehart and artist Frank Brunner.

- Harry Osborn first appeared as his father's successor, the second Green Goblin, in *The Amazing Spider-Man* #136.

NOVEMBER

CELESTIAL MADONNA

• *The Avengers* #129

Writer Steve Englehart started an epic story line in which Kang the Conqueror tried to locate the Celestial Madonna, who was destined to become the mother of the Celestial Messiah, the most "important being in the universe." The Madonna proved to be Super Hero, Mantis.

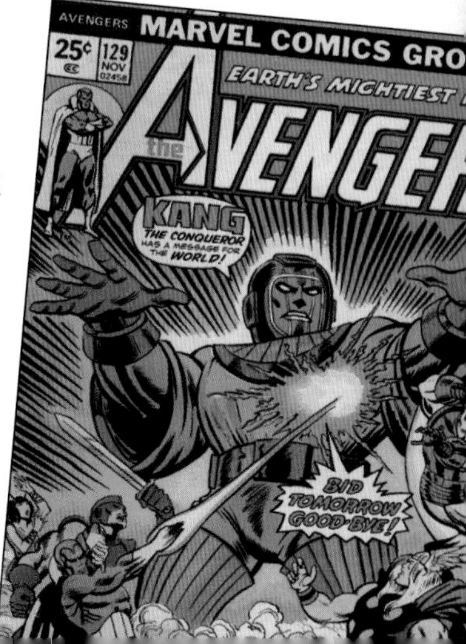

NOVEMBER

AND NOW, THE WOLVERINE

"This gaudily-garbed gentleman intrudes upon the scene, claws bared, teeth clenched, his face awash with almost feral fury!"

• *The Incredible Hulk* #181

Marvel's Wolverine had many "fathers." Editor-in-Chief Roy Thomas and writer Len Wein each appear to have separately come up with the idea of naming a mutant after the short, ferocious beast with sharp claws that dwells in Canada—the wolverine. John Romita Sr. designed the character, while Len Wein wrote and Herb Trimpe drew Wolverine's cameo appearance in *The Incredible Hulk* #180 and his premiere in issue #181.

Roy Thomas had introduced adamantium, an unbreakable steel alloy, back in *The Avengers* #66 (July, 1969) as part of android Ultron's outer shell. From the start, Wolverine's retractable claws were composed of adamantium. But Len Wein's original concept of the character was very different from the Wolverine we know today. Wein meant for the claws to be part of Wolverine's costume, not his body. Moreover, Wein intended the mutant Wolverine to be a teenager, like the original members of the X-Men in the 1960s, but with a hot temper.

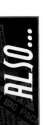

All of this would change after Wolverine joined the "new" X-Men in 1975 and new writer Chris Claremont and artist Dave Cockrum began reworking the character. Claremont established that the claws were part of Wolverine's skeleton, which had been laced with molecules of adamantium to make it unbreakable. Not only was Claremont's Wolverine an adult, but he was far older than he looked, thanks to a mutant "rapid healing" ability that greatly slowed his aging. Claremont and Cockrum also made it clear that Wolverine's temper could easily lead to terrifying rages without any warning.

M The Wrecker joined with fellow super-powered convicts to become the criminal Wrecking Crew in *The Defenders* #17.

DECEMBER

CAPTAIN AMERICA NO MORE

• *Captain America And The Falcon* #180

Shocked by learning the identity of Number One of the Secret Empire, Steve Rogers abandoned his Captain America role and adopted a new costumed identity, Nomad. His enemy Madame Hydra also took a new identity, becoming the new Viper.

M Female samurai Colleen Wing made her debut as Iron Fist's friend and ally in *Marvel Premiere* #19.

ALSO...

MARVEL GOES UNDERGROUND

• *Comix Book* #1

In an unusual move, Marvel hired underground comic artist Denis Kitchen to edit *Comix Book*, an anthology of underground comics. Among the artists featured in its run were Howard Cruse, Kim Deitch, Justin Green, Trina Robbins, Art Spiegelman, Skip Williamson, and Basil Wolverton.

MEANWHILE IN 1974...

PRESIDENT NIXON RESIGNS

Richard Nixon becomes the first US President to resign. He does so to avoid impeachment over claims he misused government agencies during the course of the Watergate cover-up.

FORD IS PRESIDENT

Gerald R. Ford is sworn in as the 38th President of the US in mid-term after Nixon resigns. He is the first ever unelected US President.

BRITISH PARLIAMENT BOMBED

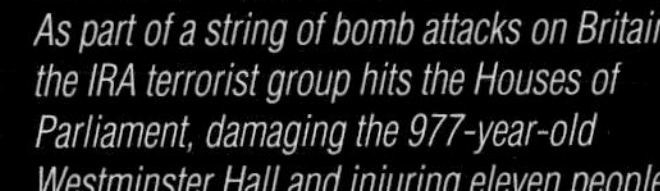

As part of a string of bomb attacks on Britain, the IRA terrorist group hits the Houses of Parliament, damaging the 977-year-old Westminster Hall and injuring eleven people.

AND AT THE MOVIES...

Chinatown, *Roman Polanski and Robert Towne's intricately scripted noir film is a conspiracy about corruption, irrigation, and intrigue in 1930s LA;* The Godfather Part II, *a compelling companion piece to the original Godfather movie, marked by its complex, historical interweaving of the lives of two Corleone Dons.*

LOOK OUT, WORLD-BEATERS! HERE COMES THE NOMAD!

Disillusioned with the US government, Captain America assumed the new heroic identity of Nomad, the man without a country, in December.

I'LL NOT REST UNTIL I'VE LAID LOW THE FORCES OF GREED AND INJUSTICE!

1975

THE X-MEN ARE REBORN

Though it was beloved of true Marvel aficionados, the original *X-Men* comic had never been a Marvel series of the first rank. It was also a commercial failure and was cancelled in March, 1970. In 1975, Editor-in-Chief Roy Thomas, writer Len Wein, and artist Dave Cockrum reconceived and reintroduced the mutant team in *Giant-Size X-Men* #1 with a new international cast. Though Marvel couldn't have known it at the time, this series would change Super Hero comics forever. Wein and Cockrum also introduced strange new characters like Wolverine, Nightcrawler, and the ethereal Storm.

The gamble succeeded far more than anyone could have imagined. Within a decade the "new" *X-Men* would become Marvel's biggest hit, outshining even *The Amazing Spider-Man*. The series would go on to spawn a whole family of comics featuring mutant heroes.

JANUARY

MARVEL GOES SCI-FI

• *Unknown Worlds Of Science Fiction* #1

In an aim to broaden its horizons, Marvel launched a new magazine, *Unknown Worlds Of Science Fiction*, which was an anthology of science fiction tales, both old and new, in comics form. This was a successor to Marvel's color comics science fiction anthology, *Worlds Unknown*, which ran from May, 1973, to August, 1974. During its six-issue run, *Worlds Unknown* adapted classic stories by authors Alfred Bester, Harlan Ellison, Frank Herbert, Michael Moorcock, Larry Niven, Robert Silverburg, A.E. Van Vogt, and John Wyndham. Artists included Neal Adams, Frank Brunner, and Howard Chaykin.

FEBRUARY

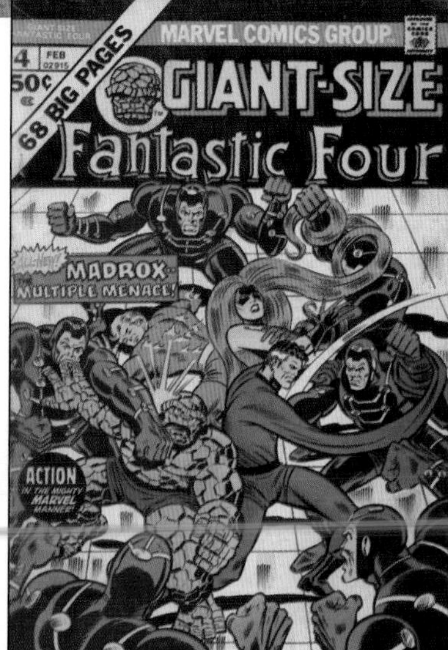

A malfunction in his containment suit caused Madrox to go on the rampage and attack the Fantastic Four.

THE MULTIPLE MAN

• *Giant-Size Fantastic Four* #4

In this issue, new Marvel writer Chris Claremont and artist John Buscema introduced Madrox the Multiple Man, a mutant who could duplicate his own body over and over. Madrox would eventually become a member of the cast of *X-Men*, and Claremont would soon become its writer.

COSMIC TRAVELS

• *Strange Tales* #178

Recently resurrected in *The Incredible Hulk*, artificial human Adam Warlock returned in a new series, taking over *Strange Tales* for four issues, the content of which was previously dedicated to purple monster the Golem. Jim Starlin both wrote and drew Warlock's new adventures through time and space. The original *Warlock* comic book would return with issue #9 in October.

M In *Doctor Strange* #6, writer Steve Englehart and artist Gene Colan introduced Mother Earth, also known as the goddess Gaea, who would eventually be revealed to be the Mighty Thor's mother.

MARCH

THE ENDLESS WAR

• *The Avengers* #133

In this issue, writer Steve Englehart revealed how the ongoing intergalactic Kree-Skrull war started. It began when the Skrull race held a competition between the primitive Kree and aliens called the Cotati to see who was worthy to join them.

RECLAIMING THE SHIELD

• *Captain America And The Falcon* #183

While Steve Rogers continued in his new heroic identity as Nomad, a young boy named Roscoe adopted Rogers' role as Captain America. But in this tale by writer Steve Englehart and artist Frank Robbins, Captain America's greatest enemy, the Red Skull, resurfaced and killed the Super Hero. Shocked by the sight of the murdered Roscoe, in Cap's uniform, Steve Rogers at last reclaimed his identity of Captain America.

DOOM AND NAMOR

• *Giant-Size Super-Villain Team-Up* #1

Namor, the Sub-Mariner sought a new alliance with Dr. Doom in this giant-size comic. After two giant-size issues, *Super-Villain Team-Up* switched to a thirty-two-page format in August of this year.

MARCH

ENTER THE HEADMEN

• *The Defenders* #21

Writer Steve Gerber teamed up three villains from old Marvel science fiction stories—Dr. Arthur Nagan (alias Gorilla-Man), Dr. Jerry Morgan, and Chondu the Mystic—as the Headmen, a group of would-be criminal masterminds.

MAY

HOWARD THE DUCK RETURNS

• *Giant-Size Man-Thing* #4

After plunging to his apparent doom in *Man-Thing* #1, Howard the Duck returned in a new series of stories by writer/creator Steve Gerber and artist Frank Brunner in the back of *Giant-Size Man-Thing*. In this issue, Howard's plunge through the interdimensional void landed him in Cleveland, Ohio. There Howard contended against the first of his many ludicrous adversaries: Garko the Man-Frog!

MAY

SECOND GENESIS

"From the ashes of the past there grow the fires of the future! The grandeur and the glory begin anew with Second Genesis."

• *Giant-Size X-Men* #1

Ever since their series was cancelled in March, 1970, the X-Men had continued to appear as guest stars in series such as *The Avengers*, *Captain America And The Falcon*, and *Marvel Team-Up*. Marvel even started publishing the *X-Men* comic again, this time as a reprint series. But it was former *X-Men* writer Roy Thomas, who had succeeded Stan Lee as Editor-in-Chief, who realized that if *X-Men* was to be successfully revived, it needed an exciting new concept. Thomas came up with just such an idea: the X-Men would become an international team, with members from other countries as well as the United States.

Writer Len Wein and artist Dave Cockrum were assigned to the new project, and the result was *Giant-Size X-Men* #1. In this landmark issue, the original X-Men were trapped on a mysterious island called Krakoa. Only Cyclops narrowly managed to escape and return to Professor Charles Xavier's mansion. Xavier set about organizing a new team of mutant X-Men from around the globe to rescue his imprisoned students. Among his new recruits were two of the X-Men's former adversaries: Sean Cassidy, alias the Banshee, from Ireland, and Shiro Yoshida, alias Sunfire, from Japan. Wolverine, whom Wein had introduced in *The Incredible Hulk* #180 (Oct., 1974), quit his work for the Canadian government when Xavier issued his invitation.

There were new characters who joined the new X-Men team to save the original X-Men: Thunderbird was a Native American with superhuman strength; Colossus could change into a powerful being of organic metal; Nightcrawler was a teleporting mutant who Xavier rescued from an angry mob in Germany; and Storm was a beautiful mutant who could control the weather.

Among the members of the "new" international X-Men were three stars in the making: Wolverine, Storm, and Colossus.

JUNE

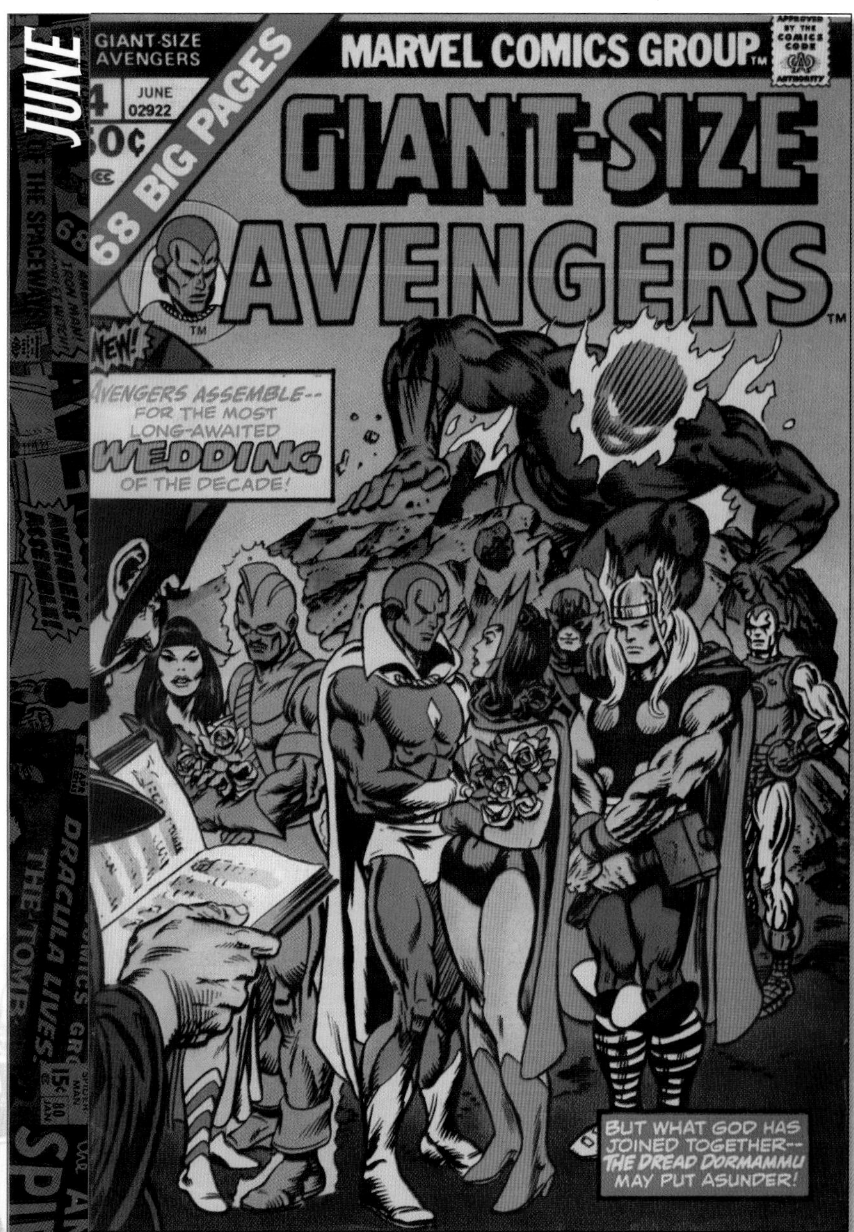

DOUBLE WEDDING

• *Giant-Size Avengers* #4

Writer Steve Englehart and veteran *Avengers* artist Don Heck presented the grand finale of the long-running "Celestial Madonna" saga. The Madonna, destined to become mother of the "most important" being in the cosmos, was the Avengers' ally Mantis. Her lover, the Swordsman, was slain by Kang the Conqueror, but his body was reanimated by a member of the alien Cotati. Kang's alternate future self, Immortus, presided over the double wedding of Mantis to the resurrected Swordsman, and the android Vision to the Scarlet Witch. Then Mantis, newly made an Avenger, and her husband departed for outer space, while the Vision and Scarlet Witch left for their earthly honeymoon.

JUNE

OKAY, AXIS, HERE WE COME!

"Captain America! Human Torch! Sub-Mariner! In a fury-filled first issue!"

• *Giant-Size Invaders* #1

In 1946, Timely Comics had teamed up its leading heroes—Captain America, Bucky, the Human Torch, Toro, the Sub-Mariner, the Whizzer, and Miss America—as the All Winners Squad. Marvel writer and editor Roy Thomas had long been a fervent fan of the comics of the Golden Age of the 1940s and wanted to create a Super Hero team similar to the All Winners Squad. The seeds of this idea were sown in *The Avengers* #71 (Dec., 1969), when Thomas dispatched several members of the Avengers back through time to World War II Paris, where they battled a team of Captain America, the original Human Torch, and the Sub-Mariner.

In 1975, Thomas and adventure comic strip artist Frank Robbins created the Invaders, who were the core of the All Winners Squad as it would have been if active during World War II. As well as illustrating comic books, Frank Robbins had been drawing the adventure comic strip *Johnny Hazard* since 1944, and his work bore the influence of the master of the wartime adventure strip, Milton Caniff.

In this first story, set shortly after the Japanese attack on Pearl Harbor in December 1941, Captain America and Bucky, the original Human Torch and Toro, and the Sub-Mariner worked together to save British Prime Minister Winston Churchill from assassination by the super-strong Nazi warrior Master Man. The grateful Churchill proposed that these Super Heroes band together as a team to combat the Axis powers of Germany, Italy, and Japan. Together these heroes could fight the Nazis in Europe before the Allies' armed forces could invade. This new Super Hero team became known as the Invaders, whose battle cry was "Okay, Axis, here we come!"

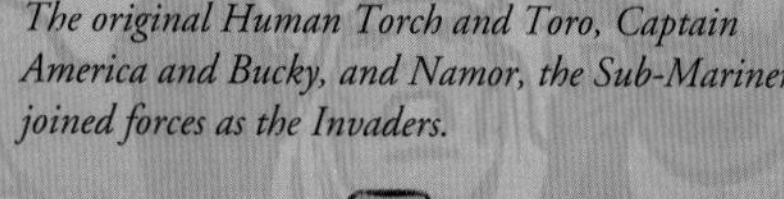

The original Human Torch and Toro, Captain America and Bucky, and Namor, the Sub-Mariner joined forces as the Invaders.

JULY

BEAST JOINS AVENGERS

• *The Avengers* #137

Following the end of his series in *Amazing Adventures* #17 (March, 1983) the newly furry Beast joined the Avengers on a provisional basis. He was the first member of the X-Men to join another Super Hero team.

AUGUST

MOON KNIGHT RISING

• *Werewolf By Night* #32

In August, Jack Russell, the Werewolf by Night, encountered a new mysterious enemy called Moon Knight, created by writer Doug Moench and artist Don Perlin. Moon Knight was hired by an organization called the Committee to capture Russell. But after doir so, Moon Knight set the Werewolf free to attack the Committee, ar then escaped. Moench would later establish that Moon Knight, whose real name was Marc Spector, pretended to work for the Committee in order to bring it to justice. Moon Knight would later star in his own series as a Super Hero, first in *The Hulk* and then in his own comic book.

CLAREMONT JOINS THE X-MEN

• *X-Men* #94

The "new" X-Men team, created for *Giant-Size X-Men* #1 in May, moved into this thirty-two-page bimonthly comic, continuing the numbering of the original *X-Men* series. In this issue, the original X-Men quit the team, except for Cyclops and Professor X, and writ Chris Claremont took over the scripting.

SEPTEMBER

STARRING STARHAWK

• *The Defenders* #27

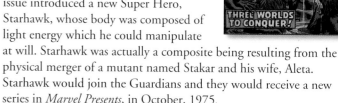

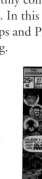

In this story line by writer Steve Gerber and artist Sal Buscema, the Defenders had traveled to an alternate future, in which they aided the Guardians of the Galaxy against Earth's conquerors, the alien Brotherhood of the Badoon. This issue introduced a new Super Hero, Starhawk, whose body was composed of light energy which he could manipulate at will. Starhawk was actually a composite being resulting from the physical merger of a mutant named Stakar and his wife, Aleta. Starhawk would join the Guardians and they would receive a new series in *Marvel Presents*, in October, 1975.

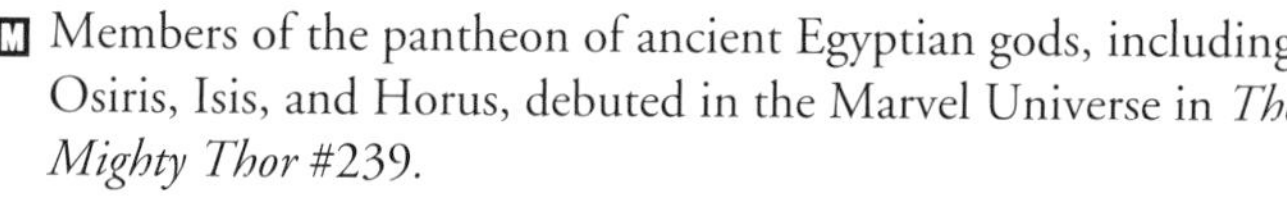

Members of the pantheon of ancient Egyptian gods, including Osiris, Isis, and Horus, debuted in the Marvel Universe in *The Mighty Thor* #239.

OCTOBER

SEND IN THE CLONE

• *The Amazing Spider-Man* #149

The criminal mastermind known as the Jackal was actually biologist Miles Warren, who had succeeded in creating a clone of Peter Parker's girlfriend, the late Gwen Stacy. Now the Jackal pitted Spider-Man against a Spidey clone, and neither Spider-Man could be certain who was the original. One of the Spider-Men seemingly died in an explosion, but twenty years later, the clone would return.

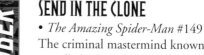

OCTOBER

WE ARE THE CHAMPIONS

• *The Champions* #1

After the Angel and Iceman quit the X-Men in *X-Men* #94 (Aug.), it was not long before they helped to start a new Super Hero team. Created by writer Tony Isabella and artist Don Heck, the Champions consisted of Angel, Iceman, Hercules, the Black Widow, and Ghost Rider. Unlike most other Marvel heroes, who were based in New York, the Champions were based in Los Angeles. The series lasted seventeen issues.

SUDDEN DEATH

• *X-Men* #95

With this issue the X-Men received an unexpected shock. In only his third appearance, Thunderbird, the Native American member of the new X-Men, leapt aboard the aircraft of the evil Count Nefaria to try to stop his escape. The aircraft exploded, causing Thunderbird to die. Meanwhile, Count Nefaria survived.

BLOODSTONE STRIKES

• *Marvel Presents* #1

The first issue of *Marvel Presents* introduced the monster hunter Ulysses Bloodstone. Originally a prehistoric warrior, Bloodstone was endowed with superhuman abilities, including immortality, from a mystical bloodstone imbedded in his chest.

- Sub-Mariner's Golden Age leading lady, Betty Dean Prentiss, died saving Namor's life in *Super-Villain Team-Up* #2.

NOVEMBER

MARVEL BOY RETURNS

• *Fantastic Four* #164

The 1950s Super Hero Marvel Boy made a dramatic return as the insane adult Crusader in *Fantastic Four* #164, in this story by writer Roy Thomas and artist George Pérez. After battling the Fantastic Four, the Crusader perished in the following issue in December.

- With *Iron Fist* #1 the eponymous hero received his own comic book, written and drawn by Chris Claremont and John Byrne.

DECEMBER

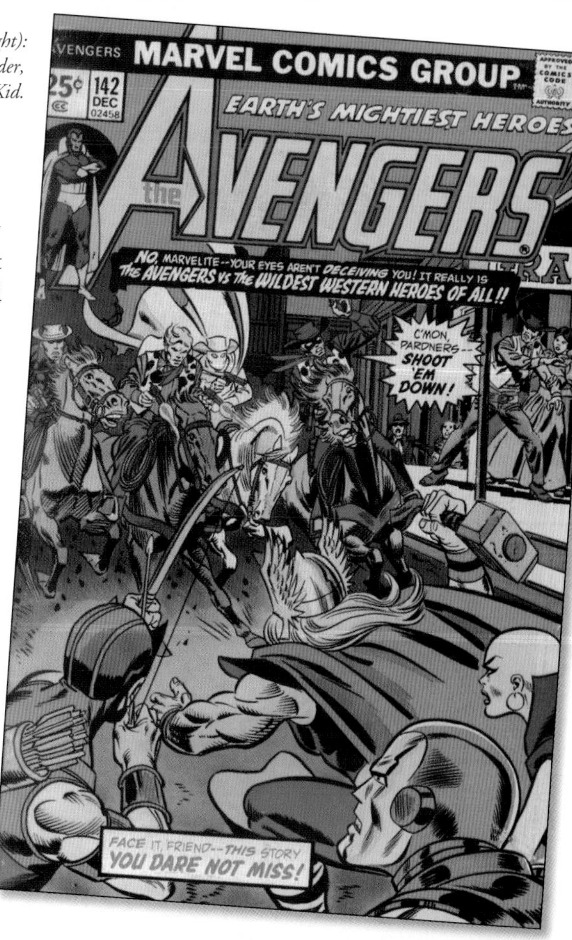

Western heroes (back row from left to right): Rawhide Kid, Kid Colt, Phantom Rider, and Two-Gun Kid.

INTO THE WILD WEST

• *The Avengers* #142

In the Go West, Young Gods story by writer Steve Englehart and artist George Pérez, Thor, Hawkeye, and Moondragon traveled back in time to 1873, where Kang the Conqueror had invaded the American West. There, Thor and company encountered Kid Colt, Rawhide Kid, the Two-Gun Kid, and the nineteenth-century Ghost Rider (now known as the Phantom Rider).

MOIRA MACTAGGERT DEBUTS

• *X-Men* #96

In this issue, the first to be plotted as well as scripted by Chris Claremont, Claremont and artist Dave Cockrum introduced geneticist Dr. Moira MacTaggert, Charles Xavier's colleague and former fiancée. Moira made a memorable first impression when she unexpectedly fired a machine gun at Kierrok the Damned, one of the N'garai demons.

ALSO PUBLISHED

MARVEL AND DC TOGETHER

• *MGM's Marvelous Wizard Of Oz* #1

Marvel and DC Comics collaborated together on the comics adaptation of the classic 1939 MGM movie *The Wizard Of Oz*. The film was itself based on the novel *The Wonderful Wizard Of Oz* by L. Frank Baum, written in 1900.

- The Punisher's origin was first revealed in *Marvel Preview* #2.
- Also in *Marvel Preview* #2, 1930s adventurer Dominic Fortune, created by Howard Chaykin, made his debut.

MEANWHILE IN 1975...

SAIGON FALLS

The city of Saigon surrenders to North Vietnamese forces, marking a final end to the war in Vietnam. Remaining Americans are evacuated from the US Embassy.

OIL CRISIS AFFECTS THE CLOCKS

In response to the oil crisis caused by events in the Middle East, the US introduces daylight saving time two months early in the hope of saving electricity.

AMERICANS & RUSSIANS HOOK UP IN SPACE

In a space-race and cold-war first, the crews of the American Apollo *and the Russian* Soyuz *spacecrafts dock in space and share meals, undertake joint experiments, and make live television broadcasts together.*

MICROSOFT FOUNDED

In Albuquerque, New Mexico, technology enthusiast Bill Gates founds a computer software company called Microsoft.

AND AT THE MOVIES...

One Flew Over the Cuckoo's Nest, *Jack Nicholson's virtuoso performance as the faux-crazy McMurphy elevates Milos Forman's superb adaptation of Ken Kesey's novel about mental illness to another level;* Jaws, *Steven Spielberg's perfectly cast and scored box-office hit slowly builds the tension around a killer shark terrorizing an island resort.*

Fantastic Four ***#164 (Nov., 1975)***

Over the seven-decade span of Marvel's history, continuity was subject to reinterpretation. When writer Roy Thomas and artist George Pérez introduced the Crusader in Fantastic Four *#164, they intended him to be Robert Grayson, the 1950s Super Hero Marvel Boy, grown into an insane adult. When the Crusader perished in an explosion, his energy-manipulating "quantum bands" came into the possession of a new Super Hero, Wendell Vaughn, alias Quasar. However, more recently it was revealed that the Crusader was really a flawed duplicate of Grayson, and that the real Marvel Boy had joined the contemporary team of 1950s heroes, the Agents of Atlas.*

C'MON, YOU GUYS!
WE'VE GOTTA FIGHT--THE INVADERS!

1976

HISTORY IN THE MAKING

The year 1976 was the 200th anniversary of the United States' Declaration of Independence. So it was appropriate that several of the major events in Marvel history that year dealt with political themes.

Jack Kirby returned to Marvel after an absence of over five years. Under his new deal, Kirby edited and scripted his stories as well as plotting and drawing them. In July, he created his last great series, *The Eternals*. But he also returned to his early co-creation, Captain America, devising story lines appropriate to the nation's anniversary both in the Captain's monthly comic and in the special *Captain America's Bicentennial Battles.*

In September, just before departing from Marvel for DC Comics, writer Steve Englehart sent Dr. Strange back through time to meet one of the men responsible for the Declaration of Independence, Benjamin Franklin, while in December, writer Steve Gerber's Howard the Duck ran for President.

JANUARY

HOWARD THE DUCK GETS HIS OWN COMIC

"Sure, I'll go with a flourish, the big splash, the last hurrah, why not? I mean it's not like anyone'll notice."

• *Howard The Duck* #1

From the moment he first waddled into a Man-Thing story in *Adventure Into Fear* #19 (Dec., 1973), Howard the Duck had captured the imaginations of Marvel readers. Conceived by writer Steve Gerber and first drawn by artist Val Mayerik, this talking duck with his omnipresent cigar was like characters from "funny animal" cartoons readers had watched as children, transplanted into the more adult world of the Marvel Universe. Gerber and artist Frank Brunner quickly brought Howard back in *Giant-Size Man-Thing* #4 (April, 1975) and then in his own comic book.

Though he was born—or hatched—on a world of talking ducks, Howard found himself marooned on Earth among what he called "hairless apes," meaning human beings. According to the series' catchphrase, Howard was "trapped in a world he never made." Through Howard, Gerber found a new metaphor for the alienation of the typical Marvel hero.

Gerber used Howard to parody different comic book genres. In this first issue, his target was the sword-and-sorcery genre, as Howard, dressed like Conan, contended against Pro-Rata, an accountant turned evil wizard. Howard also met Pro-Rata's captive, a model named Beverly Switzler. Howard and Beverly quickly formed a bond that later evolved into an unlikely romance.

Howard the Duck was Steve Gerber's most celebrated creation. Through Howard, Gerber employed his great talents to satirize not only comics, but popular culture, American society, politics, and more. Howard was also a brilliant character, mixing his exasperation at the world's idiocies with a steadfast commitment to his principles and an ironic sense of humor.

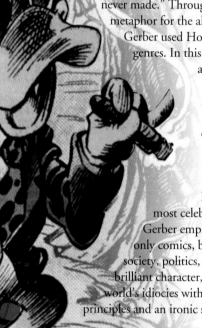

Drawn here by Frank Brunner, Howard the Duck was known to quack "Waaaugh!" at each new example of human foolishness.

WELCOME TO WEIRDWORLD

• *Marvel Super Action* #1

In the tradition of J.R.R. Tolkien's *The Lord of the Rings*, the prolific writer Doug Moench and artist Mike Ploog created "Weirdworld." This fantasy series began in the pages of *Marvel Super Action* and starred two elves from the floating island of Klarn. The series continued in various Marvel publications throughout the 1970s and 1980s.

FEBRUARY

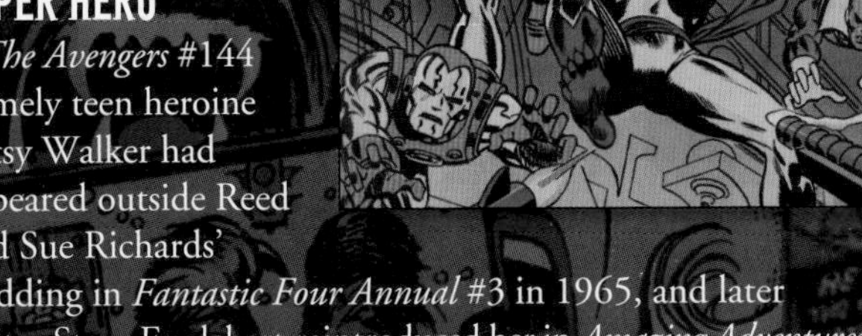

PATSY WALKER, SUPER HERO

• *The Avengers* #144

Timely teen heroine Patsy Walker had appeared outside Reed and Sue Richards' wedding in *Fantastic Four Annual* #3 in 1965, and later writer Steve Englehart reintroduced her in *Amazing Adventures* #13 (July, 1972). Disillusioned with her marriage to Buzz Baxter, Patsy was determined to become a Super Hero. In this issue she did, and became the yellow-costumed Hellcat.

JACK KIRBY RETURNS

• *Captain America And The Falcon* #194

After an absence of half a decade, Jack Kirby returned to Marvel Comics as writer, penciller, and editor of the series he and Joe Simon created back in 1941. In this issue, Kirby introduced Captain America's ancestor, the Steven Rogers of the 1770s, who was a masked hero in the American Revolution. Kirby also introduced the Royalists, who dressed in eighteenth-century wigs and costumes and sought to restore monarchy to America.

GUARDIANS OF THE GALAXY

• *Marvel Presents* #3

A team of super-powered freedom fighters from different planets in an alternate thirty-first century future, the Guardians of the Galaxy finally received their own ongoing series in *Marvel Presents* #3, written by Steve Gerber and pencilled by Al Milgrom.

- Endowed with Henry Pym's ability to grow to giant size, African-American Super Hero Bill Foster won his own comic book with *Black Goliath* #1.
- Lorna Dane, the green-haired mutant with magnetic powers, first appeared as Polaris in *X-Men* #97.
- Writer Chris Claremont and artist Dave Cockrum also introduced the alien Shi'ar race, the Shi'ar's Princess Lilandra, and covert agent Erik the Red in *X-Men* #97.

MARCH

HITTING THE BULLSEYE

• *Daredevil* #131

In March, writer Marv Wolfman and artist Bob Brown co-created one of the Man Without Fear's greatest nemeses, Bullseye. With his extraordinary aim, Bullseye could turn any ordinary object into a lethal weapon by hurling it at an opponent. Writer/artist Frank Miller would further develop the character in his run on *Daredevil*, beginning with issue #158 in May, 1979.

THE MYSTERY OF OMEGA

• *Omega The Unknown* #1

In March, a new Super Hero series began called *Omega The Unknown*, created by writers Steve Gerber and Mary Skrenes and artist Jim Mooney. The title character was an alien humanoid, who rarely spoke and served as protector to an eerily precocious young boy, James-Michael Starling. The original *Omega The Unknown* was not a commercial success but would become a cult classic.

APRIL

THE LIBERTY LEGION

• *Marvel Premiere* #29

Golden Age Super Hero team the Invaders had battled the Nazi menace abroad during World War II. *Invaders* writer/editor Roy Thomas decided to create another team of Golden Age Super Heroes who would, this time, fight saboteurs, spies, and fifth columnists on the homefront. The result was the Liberty Legion, which included the Blue Diamond, the original Jack Frost, Miss America, the Patriot, the Red Raven, the Thin Man, and the original Whizzer.

- Writer Steve Englehart and artist Herb Trimpe created the Shroud, a blind vigilante with mystical abilities, in *Super-Villain Team-Up* #5.

MAY

DOCTOR VERSUS DRACULA

• *The Tomb Of Dracula* #44

The great Marvel artist Gene Colan was doing superb work illustrating both *Doctor Strange* and *The Tomb Of Dracula*. So it made sense for *Strange* writer Steve Englehart and *Tomb* author Marv Wolfman to devise a crossover story pitting Marvel's sorcerer supreme against the vampire lord that appeared in issue #14 of *Doctor Strange* and issue #44 of *The Tomb Of Dracula*.

JULY

UNION JACK AND BARON BLOOD

• *The Invaders* #7

In the Marvel Universe there were costumed Super Heroes who served in both World Wars. In July, Roy Thomas and artist Frank Robbins introduced the British World War I hero Union Jack, and his enemy, the vampire Baron Blood, who had served the Nazis during World War II.

RETURN OF THE SPACE GODS

• *The Eternals* #1

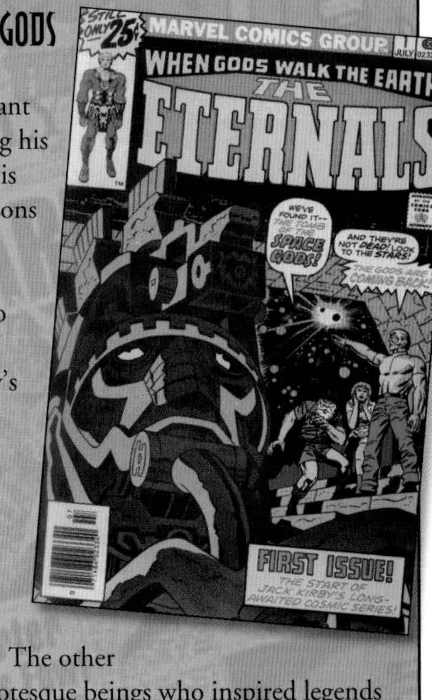

Jack Kirby's most important creation for Marvel during his return in the 1970s was his epic series *The Eternals*. Eons ago, gigantic, enigmatic space gods (called the Celestials) visited Earth to conduct genetic experiments on humanity's ancestors. The Celestials created two genetic offshoots of humankind. One was the Eternals, a race of immortal, superhuman beings, whom mankind mistook for gods in ancient times. The other race was the Deviants, grotesque beings who inspired legends of demons and devils. Now the Celestials had returned to stand in judgment on their creations.

August

The new X-Men battled robot versions of the original team in X-Men's hundredth issue.

JEAN GREY'S SACRIFICE

• *X-Men* #100

Aboard a space station orbiting Earth, the X-Men, including original member Jean Grey, battled against the robot Sentinels in the 100th issue of *X-Men*. Jean voluntarily exposed herself to a radiation storm while piloting the X-Men's escape craft back to Earth, with results that would shock them.

September

THE HUMAN ROCKET

• *The Man Called Nova* #1

Seeking to create a new teenage Marvel Super Hero in the tradition of Spider-Man, writer Marv Wolfman and artist John Buscema presented Richard Rider, alias Nova, the Human Rocket. A high school student living on New York's Long Island, Richard was endowed with super-powers by the mortally wounded alien Rhomann Dey, a member of the Nova Corps of the planet Xandar. As Nova, Richard could fly and would later become a founding member of the New Warriors.

- Once thought dead, and then found in a comatose state, Wonder Man was at last resurrected in *Avengers Assemble!* #151.
- In his final issue as writer, Steve Englehart had the time-traveling Stephen Strange explore the "occult history of America" and meet Benjamin Franklin in *Doctor Strange* issue #18.

October

MARVEL IN THE UK

• *Captain Britain* #1

Since 1972, Marvel's UK line had created comics for the British market reprinting stories from its American comics. Now, British-born writer Chris Claremont and artist Herb Trimpe created a new Super Hero specifically for Marvel's readers in the United Kingdom. Student Brian Braddock was severely injured in a motorcycle accident, but was transformed into his homeland's own superheroic guardian, Captain Britain.

- Jigsaw, one of the Punisher's few recurring foes, made his debut appearance in *The Amazing Spider-Man* #161.

October

PHOENIX RISING

"Hear me X-Men! No longer am I the woman you knew! I am Fire! And life incarnate! Now and forever—I am Phoenix!"

• *X-Men* #101

The transformation of Jean Grey into Phoenix was a dramatic affair. Piloting the X-Men's escape craft to Earth after their battle in space with the Sentinels, Jean had courageously volunteered to sit in a cabin that lacked sufficient radiation shielding. At the end of *X-Men* #100, she was bathed in lethal solar radiation. In the following issue, the X-Men's spacecraft crash-landed into a bay off the New York City coast. As the X-Men watched in astonishment, Jean rose out of the water into the air, proclaiming herself to be Phoenix.

Writer Chris Claremont and artist Dave Cockrum's intent in transforming Jean Grey into Phoenix was to boost Jean's powers to a higher level. She now possessed seemingly limitless powers over matter and energy. She could manifest her power as cosmic energy in the form of a large bird of prey. As Phoenix, Jean soon rejoined the X-Men.

However, a question arose: Was this really Jean? Later stories indicated that the sentient Phoenix Force had created a duplicate of Jean's body for itself, and that the real Jean lay in suspended animation at the bottom of the bay. But Claremont would establish that the Phoenix had also borrowed a portion of Jean's own consciousness.

Claremont became renowned for his formidable female characters, who were the equals of the men in his comics. The creation of Phoenix led eventually to one of the greatest epics in Marvel history, Claremont and artist John Byrne's Dark Phoenix Saga story line.

November

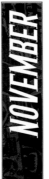

MEET MARLA MADISON

• *The Amazing Spider-Man* #162

The *Daily Bugle*'s hot-tempered publisher, J. Jonah Jameson, was a widower and might seem an unlikely candidate for romance. But in this issue Jameson met his future second wife, scientist Dr. Marla Madison, who designed a new Spider-Slayer robot for him.

MISSION IMPOSSIBLE

• *Fantastic Four* #176

In a venture into metafictional comedy, the mischievous Impossible Man visited the Marvel offices, where he met his creators, Stan Lee and Jack Kirby, as well as the collaborators on his current story, writer Roy Thomas and artist George Pérez!

DEATH OF JARELLA

• *The Incredible Hulk* #205

Jarella, the green-skinned princess from the microverse, was reunited with the Hulk back on Earth. During a battle between the Hulk and the Crypto-Man, Jarella saved a child from a collapsing wall, which crushed her to death instead.

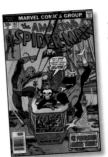

HOWARD FOR PRESIDENT!

• *Howard The Duck* #7

Working as a security guard at the All-Night Party's political convention in New York City, Howard the Duck ended up being nominated as their presidential candidate! With the campaign slogan "Get down, America!," writer Steve Gerber thus ran Howard against Jimmy Carter and Gerald Ford in the 1976 election.

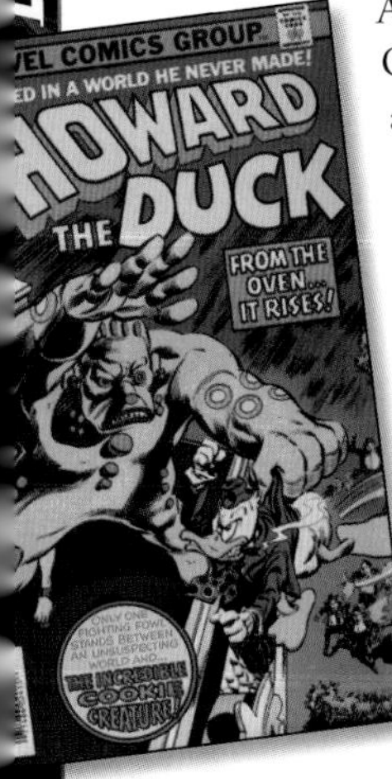

Howard also contended against an edible version of Frankenstein's Monster, the Gingerbread Man.

ALSO PUBLISHED

WHEN TITANS CLASH

• *Superman Vs. The Amazing Spider-Man*

Comics fans might have fantasized that someday DC Comics' Superman might meet Marvel's Spider-Man. But it was still a monumental surprise when America's "Big Two" Super Hero comics companies joined forces to produce their first crossover book. Written by Gerry Conway and drawn by Ross Andru, this landmark tale also featured the title heroes' leading ladies, Lois Lane and Mary Jane Watson, and their archvillains, Lex Luthor and Doctor Octopus.

M Marking the anniversary of American independence, Jack Kirby wrote and drew *Captain America's Bicentennial Battles.*

MEANWHILE IN 1976...

THE APPLE COMPUTER COMPANY BEGINS TO GROW

In Los Altos, California, Steve Jobs and Steve Wozniak start producing a personal computer kit, the Apple I.

"FACE ON MARS" PICTURE

The Viking spacecraft transmits images of Mars back to Earth, including one of a rock formation that looks like a human face. Some argue that the face is artificial and is evidence of Martian civilization.

MAFIA "BOSS OF BOSSES" DIES

Carlo Gambino dies in his sleep. Head of five New York families, he was in charge of an empire of gambling, narcotics, and loan sharking.

AND AT THE MOVIES...

Rocky, *Sylvester Stallone's boxing tale about an underdog who takes on the heavyweight champ —and loses;* Taxi Driver, *a claustrophobic vision of anti-hero Travis Bickle's obsession with cleaning up New York's mean streets;* All the President's Men, *a gripping story of the* Washington Post *reporters who exposed the Watergate affair.*

In the first issue of Peter Parker, The Spectacular Spider-Man, *the web-slinger again battled the spider-themed criminal from Latin America, the Tarantula, whose boots carried retractable spikes tipped with poison.*

SPIDER-MAN'S THIRD SERIES

• *Peter Parker, The Spectacular Spider-Man* #1

Spider-Man already starred in two monthly series: *The Amazing Spider-Man* and *Marvel Team-Up*. Now Marvel added a third, *Peter Parker, The Spectacular Spider-Man,* initially written by Gerry Conway with art by Sal Buscema and Mike Esposito.

BRITAIN'S SISTER

• *Captain Britain* #8

Writer Chris Claremont and artist Herb Trimpe introduced Captain Britain's sister, Elisabeth "Betsy" Braddock, the future Psylocke, in Marvel UK's *Captain Britain* #8.

I AM GRAVITON! AND SOON THE WORLD WILL FEAR THAT NAME!

1977

MARVEL AND THE MEDIA

Stan Lee had given up writing Spider-Man in monthly comic books, but he hadn't given up writing Spidey completely. On January 3, 1977, *The Amazing Spider-Man* newspaper comic strip premiered, written by Stan Lee and drawn by John Romita Sr. *The Amazing Spider-Man* was to become the most successful American adventure comic strip to be launched in the last thirty years. Its success led to other Marvel newspaper strips, including *The Incredible Hulk*, *Conan The Barbarian*, and *Howard The Duck*, but these did not last long. However, *The Amazing Spider-Man* comic strip continues today, still scripted by Stan Lee, whose brother Larry Lieber draws the weekday installments.

In 1977, the CBS television network broadcast two live-action *Incredible Hulk* movies developed for television. Bill Bixby starred as David Banner (his name changed from Bruce) and bodybuilder Lou Ferrigno portrayed the Hulk. The movies' success led to the classic weekly television series *The Incredible Hulk*.

Also in 1977, thanks to the persuasive efforts of Roy Thomas, Marvel took a gamble by starting to publish an adaptation of a new science fiction adventure movie into comics form before it premiered in theaters. No one, not even Thomas, anticipated that *Star Wars* would be the blockbuster it soon became.

JANUARY

BLACK-AND-WHITE HULK

• *The Rampaging Hulk* #1

This black-and-white magazine starred the Hulk in adventures set i Europe shortly after his original six-issue series. In these stories, written by Doug Moench and drawn by Walter Simonson, the Hu contended against an invading race of aliens called the Krylorians, who have established a base at the bottom of the sea off the coast o Italy and planned to infiltrate Earth by taking on human forms.

SPITFIRE'S DEBUT

• *The Invaders* #12

Jacqueline Falsworth was the daughter of British Super Hero, Union Jack. She was bitten by the vampire Baron Blood, and given a transfusion of the original Human Torch's blood, thus gaining the power of superspeed and becoming Spitfire.

BECOMING MS. MARVEL

• *Ms. Marvel* #1

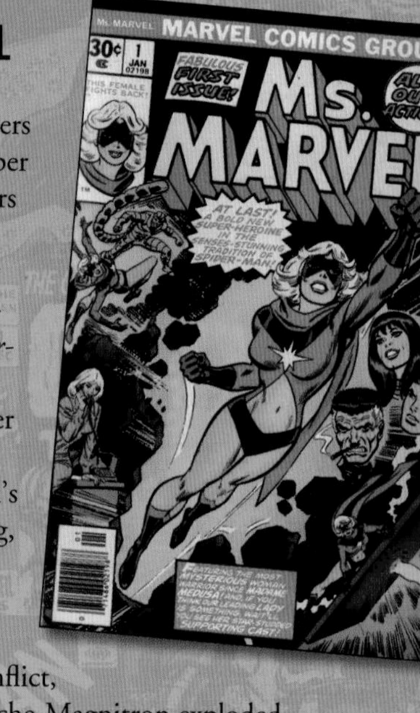

In this series, Carol Danvers became the costumed Super Hero Ms. Marvel. Danvers first appeared in March, 1968, as a NASA security chief in the Captain Mar-Vell story in *Marvel Super-Heroes* #13, and was originally created by writer Roy Thomas and artist Gene Colan. The Captain's enemy, Colonel Yon-Rogg, a member of the Kree race, abducted Danvers and Mar-Vell went to her rescue. In the ensuing conflict, a Kree device called a Psyche-Magnitron exploded, irradiating Danvers. As a result, Danvers became Ms. Marvel—half-Earthwoman, half-Kree—and she developed super-powers including super-strength and the ability to fly.

DUCK'S DOWNFALL

• *Howard The Duck* #8

Daring to tell the truth to the American public, Howard the Duck became a sensation in his campaign for president. He also made powerful enemies in the corporate world and became the target of assassination attempts. But in this story by writer Steve Gerber and artist Gene Colan, Howard's candidacy finally ended in scandal when a faked photo showed him taking a bath with campaign aide Beverly Switzler!

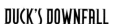

M Red Sonja, the female warrior from the age of Conan the Barbarian, garnered such great popularity that Marvel gave her her own comic book series. By now Red Sonja had acquired her most familiar costume, the chain mail bikini, designed by Spani artist Esteban Maroto.

FIRST OF THE SPIDER-WOMEN

"But I no longer belong to anyone, I'm free now. I'm by myself at last. But, heaven help me, it still makes no difference!"

• *Marvel Spotlight* #32

It was inevitable that Marvel would someday come up with a female counterpart to Spider-Man. But Marvel didn't get it right initially. According to this first story by writer Archie Goodwin and artists Sal Buscema and Jim Mooney, Jessica Drew, alias Spider-Woman, was an actual spider who had been evolved into human form by the geneticist, the High Evolutionary.

Stan Lee disliked this origin, so it was later revealed that it was a hoax. Instead, Jessica had always been human, but her scientist father had injected her with a serum including irradiated spider's blood when she was a small child. In 2006, in *Spider-Woman: Origin*, this account would be revised, so that Jessica's mother was struck by a laser beam that implanted the DNA patterns from different spiders upon her unborn daughter. Whatever the origin of her super-powers, Spider-Woman possessed superhuman strength. Like her male counterpart, she could adhere to walls with her hands and feet, and was able to project blasts of bioelectricity from her hands.

At first, Jessica was recruited into the subversive organization HYDRA. But she eventually rebelled against them and found a new mentor, the sorcerer named Magnus. She moved to Los Angeles, where she became a crime-fighting Super Hero. Jessica once gave up her costumed career and even lost her super-powers for a time. Later, two others adopted the name of Spider-Woman. However, in recent years, Jessica regained her super-powers and returned to her superheroic identity as Spider-Woman.

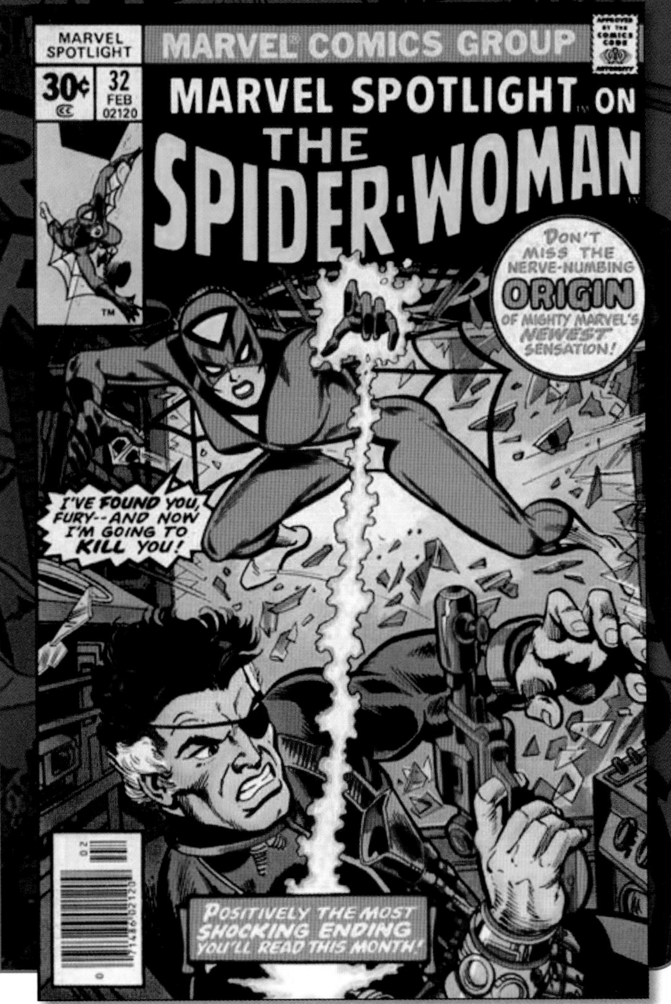

APRIL

GRAVITON RISES

• *The Avengers* #158

In this story by writer Jim Shooter and artist Sal Buscema, physicist Franklin Hall became the Avengers' latest costumed enemy, Graviton. An accident during a scientific experiment endowed Hall with the superhuman ability to control the force of gravity.

3-D SUPER HERO

• *Marvel Premiere* #35

In Roy Thomas' story set in the 1950s, test pilot Chuck Chandler literally vanished after being captured by the alien Skrulls, but his image was somehow imprinted on his brother Hal's glasses. By concentrating, Hal could cause Chuck to materialize as the 3-D Man.

MAY

ARNIM ZOLA DEBUTS

• *Captain America And The Falcon* #209

In many ways, Jack Kirby was way ahead of his time. In this issue, he depicted the effects of genetic engineering. Kirby introduced the Red Skull's ally, the Nazi genetic engineer Arnim Zola, who had created a new body for himself. Zola's brain was now located within his chest cavity for protection, and he substituted an ESP Box for his head, which enabled him to see and hear by psychic means. Ever busy, Kirby was simultaneously writing and drawing a new *Black Panther* series, whilst working on this comic.

In his new body, Arnim Zola had no head. A hologram image of his original face appeared in a viewscreen on his chest.

JUNE

- The *Conan The Barbarian* team of writer Roy Thomas and artist John Buscema created Marvel's new *Tarzan* series, based on author Edgar Rice Burroughs's character.
- Writer Marv Wolfman and artists Gil Kane and Dave Cockrum produced *John Carter, Warlord Of Mars*, based on another Edgar Rice Burroughs's character.

JULY

THE NEW DESTROYER

• *The Invaders* #18

Stan Lee's Golden Age co-creation, the Destroyer, was American reporter Kevin "Keen" Marlow, who, in his costumed identity, battled the Nazis behind enemy lines. In this July issue, writer Roy Thomas and artist Frank Robbins cast Union Jack's son Brian Falsworth as the Mighty Destroyer. Falsworth would eventually succeed his father as Union Jack.

LICENSING AT MARVEL

The late 1970s saw a diversification of Marvel's licensed property comics, with collaborations based on sci-fi movies, toy lines, musical artists, and TV series.

It had begun in December, 1976, when Marvel published its adaptation of director Stanley Kubrick and writer Arthur C. Clarke's classic science fiction film *2001: A Space Odyssey* as an oversize *Marvel Treasury Special*. The series lasted for ten issues.

In July, 1977, Marvel's comics adaptation of George Lucas's *Star Wars* movie was released, created by writer Roy Thomas and artist Howard Chaykin, although after issue #1 Chaykin could only do layouts. Other artists, including Steve Leialoha, Rick Hoberg, and inkers Bill Wray and Dave Stevens completed the artwork. The six-part adaptation began coming out weeks before the movie appeared in theaters and surely persuaded Marvel readers to go see the new film. Marvel continued publishing the *Star Wars* comic until July, 1986, by such talents as writers Archie Goodwin and Jo Duffy and artists Carmine Infantino, Cynthia Martin, and Al Williamson.

In August, 1977, Marvel produced comics featuring the most famous monster in Japanese cinema, Godzilla, in a series by writer Doug Moench and penciller Herb Trimpe. Godzilla came ashore in Alaska, and then crossed the United States from west to east, battling other monsters, SHIELD, the villainous Doctor Demonicus, Devil Dinosaur, and Marvel Super Heroes along the way.

In September, 1977, *Marvel Super Special* #1 featured the rock band KISS as Super Heroes battling Mephisto and Doctor Doom, aided by The Avengers, The Defenders, Spider-Man, and The Fantastic Four.

In October, 1978, *Marvel Team-Up* #74 featured the cast of NBC's long-running comedy variety series *Saturday Night Live* alongside Spider-Man, a Super Villain called the Silver Samurai, and even Stan Lee himself (as guest host).

The *Micronauts* comics series, dating from January, 1979, was based on toys made by Japanese company Takara and distributed in the United States by the Mego Corporation. In the comics, Commander Arcturus Rann organized a band of freedom fighters to oppose the tyranny of dictator Baron Karza.

In February, 1979, Marvel published *Shogun Warriors*, based on a line of Japanese toys imported by Mattel. These colossal robots were piloted by humans to combat the dangerous extraterrestrial Myndai.

In December, 1979, Marvel's *ROM Spaceknight* series emerged, based on a Parker Brothers toy. ROM was a humanoid native of the planet Galador who was converted into a cyborg warrior to combat a deadly race of shape-shifting aliens known as the Dire Wraiths.

AUGUST

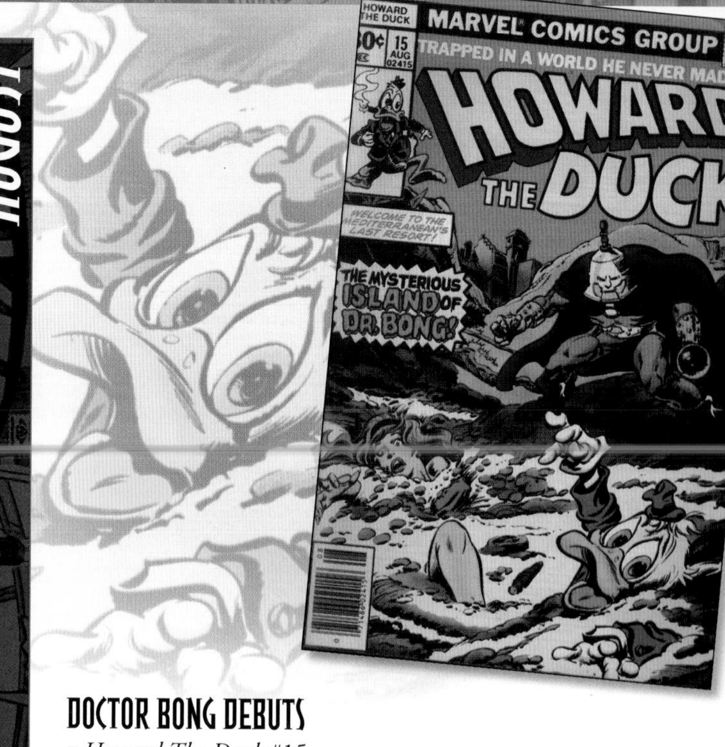

DOCTOR BONG DEBUTS

• *Howard The Duck* #15

As Howard the Duck continued his adventures, Marvel realized he was lacking a mad scientist for an archenemy! So, in this parody of H.G. Wells' *The Island of Dr. Moreau*, writer Steve Gerber and artist Gene Colan created Doctor Bong, a former music critic who was obsessed with Howard's companion, Beverly Switzler. A master of genetic engineering, Doctor Bong even temporarily turned Howard into a human being.

To announce his arrival, Doctor Bong strikes his bell-like helmet, creating various sonic effects.

AUGUST

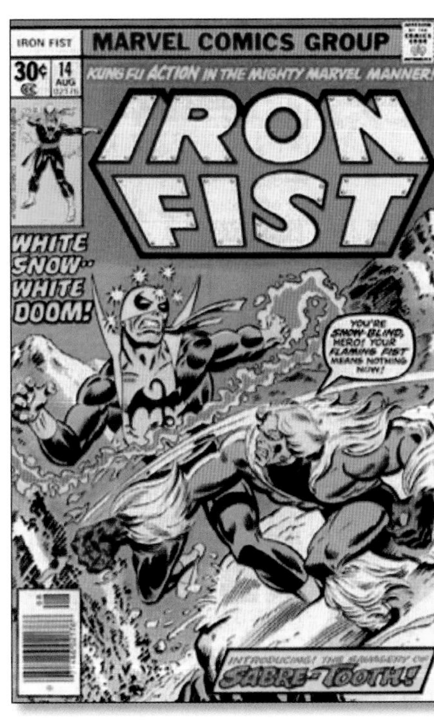

SABRETOOTH STRIKES

• *Iron Fist* #14

In August, writer Chris Claremont and artist John Byrne presented martial arts expert Iron Fist with a formidable new adversary, Sabretooth, whose animal-like fangs and claws were matched by his bestial savagery. Readers might well have noticed that Sabretooth seemed like a bigger, stronger version of Wolverine. That was intentional. Sabretooth was also a mutant, and it was suggested that he had some mysterious connection to Wolverine. Later, Claremont would pit Sabretooth against Wolverine time and again. While Wolverine struggled to control his capacity for berserker madness, Sabretooth not only gave in to his murderous insanity but reveled in it.

As the cover stated, "Kung Fu Action in the Mighty Marvel Manner" was seen as Iron Fist battled new adversary Sabretooth in a moment from the story "Snowfire" contained within.

OCTOBER

DAVE COCKRUM'S CREW

• *X-Men* #107

Dave Cockrum, the artist who co-created the "new" X-Men in *Giant-Size X-Men* #1 in May, 1975, was renowned in the comics profession for his inexhaustible visual imagination. This final issue of his first stint as penciller of *X-Men* showcased just what Cockrum could do given free rein.

Transported to a world in the Shi'ar galactic empire, the X-Men confronted a sort of superhuman legion, the Imperial Guard. Each member of the Guard came from a different alien race and had a different look, costume, and set of super-powers.

Also in this issue, Cockrum and writer Chris Claremont introduced the Starjammers, a band of space pirates led by Corsair, who turned out to be Cyclops's long-missing father!

DECEMBER

JOHN BYRNE JOINS *X-MEN*

• *X-Men* #108

When "new" *X-Men* co-creator Dave Cockrum left the series, John Byrne took over as penciller and co-plotter. In his first issue, Byrne and writer Chris Claremont wound up the Shi'ar story arc, as Phoenix first used the full extent of her powers to save the cosmos from annihilation by the powerful M'Kraan Crystal.

MEANWHILE IN 1977...

CARTER IS PRESIDENT
Jimmy Carter succeeds Gerald Ford and becomes the thirty-ninth President of the United States.

OPTICAL FIBER TELEPHONE CALL
The first live telephone traffic is sent down cables containing fiber optics, transforming communications technology.

BLACKOUT IN NEW YORK CITY
Lightning strikes and equipment failures cause a twenty-five-hour blackout in New York, which results in looting and disorder.

LIGHTNING STRIKES THE SAME PLACE SEVEN TIMES
Virginia Park ranger Roy Sullivan is hit by lightning for the seventh time since 1942. Despite suffering various injuries in the strikes, he has survived them all.

ALASKA PIPELINE CONNECTED
After years of construction, the Alaska Pipeline opens. It runs nearly 800 miles (1,300 kilometers) across Alaska from oil fields in the north to a port where it can be shipped south to the Continental States.

LONG LIVE THE KING!
Elvis Presley, the King of Rock 'n' Roll, who revolutionized music in the 1950s, dies of a heart attack at his home in Memphis, Tennessee.

SMALLPOX OBLITERATED
In a triumph of modern science and vaccination, the World Health Organization eradicates the smallpox disease after the last case is discovered in Somalia. Just ten years earlier, it was claiming two million lives a year.

THE RISE OF COUNTRY MUSIC
Country singer Kenny Rogers brings country into the mainstream. He has many hits, such as Lucille, *which are popular in both the country and the pop charts.*

SILVER JUBILEE
England's Queen Elizabeth II celebrates twenty-five years on the throne.

IN A GALAXY FAR, FAR AWAY...
Science fiction movie Star Wars *releases and becomes the highest grossing film ever. Its ground-breaking special effects and new marketing strategy marks the start of big-budget blockbusters aimed at younger audiences.*

AND AT THE MOVIES...
Annie Hall, *Woody Allen's witty, neurotic, romantic take on screwball comedies of the 1930s marks a turning point in his career;* Close Encounters of the Third Kind, *Steven Spielberg's haunting sci-fi mystery about a first contact with extraterrestrials.*

The Rampaging Hulk *#1 (Jan., 1977)*

Writer Doug Moench and artist Walter Simonson set the lead stories in The Rampaging Hulk *in the time period between the end of the Hulk's original six-issue series (March, 1963) and his return in* Tales To Astonish *(Sept., 1964). In those initial six issues, writer Stan Lee and artists Jack Kirby and Steve Ditko had presented a Hulk who was more intelligent, more articulate, and perhaps more consciously brutal than the Hulk of the later 1960s and 1970s. He was a Hulk who had the mind and personality of a bad-tempered child in a super-powerful adult body. In this sequence, Moench and Simonson recreated the Hulk as he had been in his origin story.*

YES--I CHANGED, YOU FOOL!!

NOW GET OUT OF MY WAY--I WANT OUT!!

EVERYTHING, OUT OF MY WAY--!!

ROOM
WALLS...!!
EVEN SOLDIERS--!!
WEAKLING SCIENTIST GONE...
NOW ONLY ME... ME!!
HOLY HANNAH--! WH-WHAT IN THE WORLD WAS THAT... THAT...THAT WALKING --

NICE TRY FRIEND BUT YOU COULDN'T MAKE THE METS' *SECOND STRING* WITH A PITCH LIKE THAT!

1978

EXIT KIRBY, ENTER SHOOTER

The year 1978 was a time of change among the Marvel personnel. Jack Kirby had proved to be as prolific as ever since returning to Marvel in 1976. He wrote and drew *Captain America And The Falcon* and a new *Black Panther* series, created *The Eternals* and *Devil Dinosaur*, and turned his *2001: A Space Odyssey* comic into a series about his new creation Machine Man. Kirby also drew covers for series he had co-created, and he and Stan Lee even reunited to create one of the first modern graphic novels, *The Silver Surfer*.

Ironically, Kirby's 1970s work at Marvel would go on to be regarded as classic, although it was not thought commercially successful at the time. In 1978, Kirby ended up leaving Marvel Comics for the last time to work in animation. One of his first projects was the *Fantastic Four* animated series.

Stan Lee had served as Marvel's Editor-in-Chief from late 1941, succeeding Joe Simon, until he became Marvel's publisher in 1972. Roy Thomas then became the new Editor-in-Chief, but stepped down in 1974 to edit only the comics he wrote himself. A rapid succession of new Editors-in-Chief followed, including Len Wein, Marv Wolfman, Gerry Conway, and Archie Goodwin. Finally, Associate Editor Jim Shooter, who had been writing comics professionally since he was fourteen, was promoted to Editor-in-Chief in 1978.

JANUARY

THE COMING OF QUASAR

• *Captain America And The Falcon* #217

This story, plotted by Roy Thomas, scripted by Don Glut, and pencilled by John Buscema, introduced Marvel Man, one of the SHIELD Super Agents. Marvel Man wore the wristbands that formerly belonged to the 1950s Super Hero Marvel Boy and they enabled him to mentally manipulate energy. Readers would later learn that Marvel Man's real name was Wendell Vaughn, who then became the Super Hero Quasa

CAPTAIN BRITAIN AND ARCADE

• *Marvel Team-Up* #65

Captain Britain made his first appearance in American comics when he teamed up with Spider-Man against Arcade, a villain making hi comics debut. A flamboyantly dressed assassin, Arcade entrapped his targets in Murderworld, a lethal sort of amusement park filled with death traps disguised as toys or carnival rides. Arcade was the creation of writer Chris Claremont, wh also co-created Captain Britain, and his regular 1970s collaborator, artist John Byrne.

- Writer Jim Shooter and artist George Pérez began their saga pitting their seemingly omnipotent villain, Michael Korvac, against Earth's Mightiest Heroes in *The Avengers* #167.
- *Daredevil* #150 introduced the costumed mercenary Paladin, created by Jim Shooter and artist Carmine Infantino.

FEBRUARY

WEAPON ALPHA

• *X-Men* #109

The Canadian government was not happy that Wolverine had resigned as their special agent to join the X-Men. This issue, written by Chris Claremont, introduced the costumed Weapon Alpha who attempted to bring Wolverine back to Canada by force. Created by Canadian artist John Byrne, Weapon Alpha was, in reality, Wolverine's former friend James MacDonald Hudson, the scientist hero who later became known as Vindicator and Guardian.

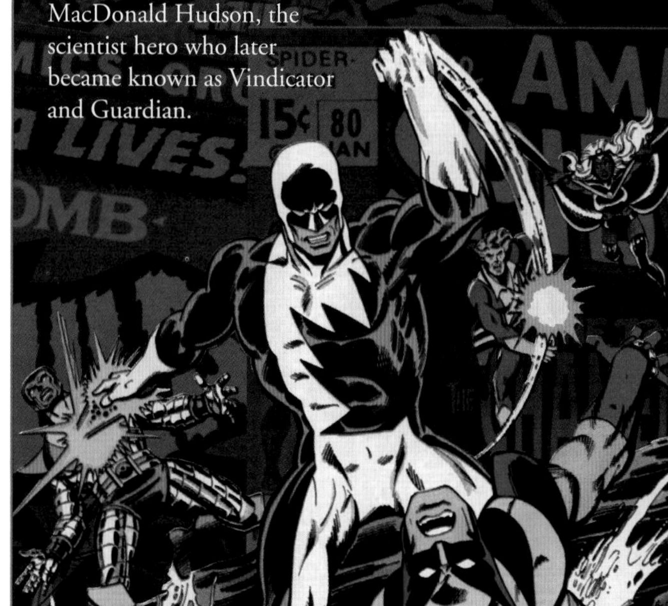

BOY MEETS DINOSAUR

• *Devil Dinosaur* #1

Jack Kirby's final major creation for Marvel Comics was perhaps his most unusual hero: an intelligent dinosaur resembling a *Tyrannosaurus rex*. Devil Dinosaur was captured by the "Killer-Folk," a tribe of hostile beings who nearly burned him to death. A young, fur-covered proto-human named Moon-Boy rescued the dinosaur, whose hide the flames had turned bright red. Ever after, Moon-Boy and Devil Dinosaur were inseparable friends. Kirby intended the *Devil Dinosaur* series to be set on prehistoric Earth, but later stories established that the dinosaur and Moon-Boy originated on another planet. The nine-issue comic would become a cult classic among Kirby fans.

CAUGHT IN HER WEB

• *Spider-Woman* #1

In April, Jessica Drew, alias Spider-Woman, received her own comic book, written by Marv Wolfman and drawn by Carmine Infantino. The first issue revealed her newly revised origin, in which Jessica was a human who was endowed with spider-like super-powers, rather than a spider who became a super-powered human. Later writers in the fifty-issue run of this series included Chris Claremont, a specialist in portraying self-reliant heroines, and Mark Gruenwald.

MACHINE OR MAN?

"He looks like a man... he thinks like a man... but nowhere in this world is there anyone as exciting and different as... Machine Man."

• *Machine Man* #1

When he returned to Marvel in the mid-1970s, one of Jack Kirby's projects was writing and drawing a comic book series based on Stanley Kubrick's MGM science fiction film *2001: A Space Odyssey*. In issue #8, cover-dated July, 1977, Kirby introduced a robot whom he originally dubbed "Mister Machine." Marvel's *2001* series eventually came to an end, but Kirby's robot protagonist went on to star in his own comic book series as Machine Man.

Machine Man's original name was X-51, because he was the fifty-first of a series of experimental robots that were created for a top secret United States military project. One of the project scientists, Dr. Abel Stack, took X-51 home with him and treated him as if he were his own son. Dr. Stack even designed an artificial facade for X-51. The project's other robots developed psychotic personalities, so the project destroyed them by remote control. Dr. Stack removed the self-destruct mechanism from X-51, but the device killed him instead. Having thus lost his "father," X-51 tried to find a place for himself in the world of humans. He even adopted a human identity, Aaron Stack, but as Machine Man he was hunted as a potential menace by the US military.

Jack Kirby wrote and drew the initial nine issues of *Machine Man*. In August, 1979, the series was revived by writer Marv Wolfman and artist Steve Ditko. Though the series was cancelled in February, 1981, Machine Man continued to appear in Marvel stories.

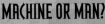

- *The Invincible Iron Man* #109 introduced the Soviet Super-Soldiers, including the new Crimson Dynamo and the superhuman twin siblings Darkstar and Vanguard.
- In *Marvel Team-Up* #68, Spider-Man teamed with Man-Thing against the demon D'Spayre.
- Now that Iron Fist had become Luke Cage's crime-fighting partner, Cage's series was retitled *Power Man And Iron Fist* with issue #50.

1978

MAY

THE KID COMMANDOS DEBUT

• *The Invaders* #28

In May, the *Invaders* team of writer Roy Thomas and artist Frank Robbins introduced the Kid Commandos, a World War II team of costumed teen Super Heroes. Members included Captain America's sidekick Bucky, the original Human Torch's protégé Toro, the Human Top, and Golden Girl. The Human Top and Golden Girl were both named after Timely characters of the 1940s.

JUNE

MYSTIQUE'S APPEARANCE

• *Ms. Marvel* #18

In *Ms. Marvel* #16 the *X-Men* team of writer Chris Claremont and artist Dave Cockrum had introduced a mysterious and sinister woman named Raven Darkholme, who could alter her appearance into that of any other person, male or female. In issue #18, Cockrum revealed Darkholme's true appearance of dark, indigo blue skin, red hair, and strange, yellow eyes. Later, readers learned that Darkholme was a mutant terrorist who called herself Mystique.

AUGUST

TV TIE-IN

• *The Hulk!* #10

To appeal to the audience of the popular new *Incredible Hulk* TV series, Marvel revamped *The Rampaging Hulk* magazine, calling it *The Hulk!* Backup stories in later issues of this comic featured Moon Knight, created by writer Doug Moench and artist Bill Sienkiewicz.

OCTOBER

THE NEW MOONSTONE

• *The Incredible Hulk* #228

In this issue, co-written by Roger Stern and Peter Gillis, the sinister psychologist Dr. Karla Sofen adopted a costumed identity. Originally created by writer Marv Wolfman and artist Frank Robbins in *Captain America And The Falcon* #192, Dr. Sofen induced the original Moonstone into revealing that he derived his super-powers from an extraterrestrial gem. She absorbed the gem's powers herself, becoming the new Moonstone. Later, the female Moonstone became a founding member of the Thunderbolts.

MS. MARVEL'S MAKEOVER

• *Ms. Marvel* #20

Ms. Marvel's original costume, with its bare midriff, was often voted Worst Female Super Hero Costume amongst comic book fans. But by now her series was in the hands of Chris Claremont, a specialist in writing smart and capable women characters, and Dave Cockrum, a master of imaginative costume design. In this issue, Claremont and Cockrum unveiled the latter's new, stylish black costume for Ms. Marvel. The costume also featured a yellow thunderbolt design and red sash around the waist.

M *X-Men* changed its title to *The Uncanny X-Men* with issue #114.

NOVEMBER

KORVAC'S CONCLUSION

• *The Avengers* #177

The long saga of the near-omnipotent Michael Korvac came to a cataclysmic climax, courtesy of writer Jim Shooter and artist George Pérez. Korvac was confronted in his home by his various opponents. He succeeded in slaying virtually all of them. But, sensing the reactions of Carina, the woman he loved, as she witnessed the slaughter, Korvac committed suicide, restoring his adversaries to life as his final act.

M Writer David Michelinie and inker Bob Layton began their classic run co-plotting *The Invincible Iron Man* with issue #116.

DECEMBER

INTRODUCING BETHANY CABE

• *The Invincible Iron Man* #117

In December, co-plotters David Michelinie and Bob Layton, and penciller John Romita Jr. (the son of the 1960s' *Spider-Man* artist) came up with Bethany Cabe, a highly capable professional bodyguard and a different sort of leading lady. She reflected the rise of feminism and the more independent women who started appearing in comics in the 1970s. In this issue, Tony Stark met Bethany and the pair soon became romantically involved.

MARVEL'S FIRST GRAPHIC NOVEL

In 1978, Will Eisner, one of the founding fathers of comic books, best known as creator of *The Spirit*, pioneered a new format for comics. *A Contract With God*, a collection of Eisner's short stories in comics form, is generally regarded as the first contemporary graphic novel. In that same year, Simon & Schuster's Fireside Books published a paperback book titled *The Silver Surfer* by Stan Lee and Jack Kirby. The final significant collaboration by Lee and Kirby, this was an original work which was, in effect, a reworking of their original Galactus Trilogy story line about the Surfer and his master Galactus, minus the Fantastic Four. This book was later recognized as Marvel's first true graphic novel.

MEANWHILE IN 1978...

CAMP DAVID ACCORDS

The Middle East peace process is rejuvenated when President Carter hosts the Camp David Accords which lead to the 1979 Israel-Egypt Peace Treaty.

"SON OF SAM" MURDERER PLEADS GUILTY

David Berkowitz pleads guilty to killing six people in a shooting spree that terrorized New York for over a year. He gave himself the nickname "Son of Sam" in taunting letters he wrote to the police, which were published in newspapers.

CHARLIE CHAPLIN'S STOLEN BODY FOUND

The coffin containing the body of legendary comic actor Charlie Chaplin is recovered from a field not far from his family home eleven weeks after kidnappers stole it from his grave in Switzerland.

MASS SUICIDE IN GUYANA

More than 900 members of an American religious cult, the People's Temple, led by the Rev. Jim Jones, are found dead in the jungles of Guyana. Survivors claim that Jones forced them all to drink a mixture of soft drink Kool-Aid laced with cyanide.

FIRST "TEST-TUBE BABY" BORN

Louise Brown is the first baby to be born through in vitro fertility (IVF) treatment, where the embryo is implanted after fertilization has taken place in a laboratory.

POPE JOHN PAUL II HEADS CATHOLIC CHURCH

Cardinal Karol Wojtyla of Poland becomes Pope, taking the name of John Paul II in honor of his short-lived predecessor who died after only 33 days in office.

SONY RELEASE THE WALKMAN

Sony introduces the Walkman, a portable cassette tape player, which changes the way people interact with music. It becomes a symbol of youth culture, through which people can listen to their own music on their own terms.

NEW GAME INVADES VIDEO ARCADES

A new Japanese computer game called Space Invaders *appears and launches a craze for computer video games, which brings arcade gaming out of seedy arcade halls and into the mainstream.*

AND AT THE MOVIES...

Grease, *a hit musical starring John Travolta and Olivia Newton-John;* The Deer Hunter, *Michael Cimino's epic elegy to America's loss of innocence during the Vietnam War,* Invasion of the Body Snatchers, *a remake of 1956 sci-fi film, starring Donald Sutherland;* Halloween, *John Carpenter's slasher horror about a prowling, masked psychopath foiled by a virgin's purity.*

HOW COULD LITTLE ME EVER ESCAPE YOU? YOU'RE SO STRONG, SO POWERFUL.

1979

THE NEW MASTERS

In the 1960s, Marvel's greatest creative team was unquestionably Stan Lee and Jack Kirby. By the end of the 1970s, that title belonged to writer Chris Claremont and writer/artist John Byrne. They both began working for Marvel in the 1970s and became a team on *Iron Fist*, *Marvel Team-Up*, and the science fiction adventure *Star-Lord*. But their collaboration reached its peak when Byrne joined Claremont on *X-Men* for issue #1 in December, 1977, after artist Dave Cockrum left the series.

Claremont and Byrne co-plotted their stories, though they often had disagreements since each man had a strong creative vision of his own. But during their collaboration on *X-Men*, Claremont and Byrne's creative synergy resulted in an astonishing series of new characters and thrilling adventures that made *X-Men* the cutting edge Super Hero series of that time.

Claremont and Byrne also began laying the groundwork for what would become their greatest story line, The Dark Phoenix Saga. Jean Grey fell under the mental influence of a handsome stranger named Jason Wyngarde, who was actually the X-Men's enemy Mastermind. Ultimately, this epic story line would end in tragedy for Jean and would become one of the most well-known among Marvel fans.

JANUARY

THE SHADOW KING DEBUTS

• *The Uncanny X-Men* #117

In this issue, a flashback showed the young Charles Xavier, before he lost the use of his legs, visiting Egypt. There he met a child pickpocket, who would grow up to become Storm. More ominously, Xavier met and waged psychic battle with the first evil mutant he ever met: a telepath named Amahl Farouk. Created by Chris Claremont and John Byrne, Farouk would later be known as the Shadow King.

Writer David Michelinie and artists John Byrne and Bob Layton introduced James Rhodes, Tony Stark's best friend and future Super Hero War Machine, in *The Invincible Iron Man* #118.

Writer Bill Mantlo and artist Michael Golden created a Marvel comic series around the Micronauts toys set in the Microverse.

FEBRUARY

PRESENTING MARIKO

• *The Uncanny X-Men* #118

In this issue, by Chris Claremont and John Byrne, the X-Men arrived in Japan, where Wolverine met and fell in love with a shy, quiet Japanese woman named Mariko Yashida. The unlikely romance would end tragically with Mariko's death.

Writer Doug Moench and artist Herb Trimpe created *Shogun Warriors*, a Marvel comics series based on a line of Japanese toys imported by Mattel that were inspired by animé about giant robots.

JUSTIN HAMMER

• *The Invincible Iron Man* #120

Tony Stark's billionaire nemesis Justin Hammer made his first appearance in *The Invincible Iron Man* #120 by writer David Michelinie and artists John Romita Jr. and Bob Layton. Hammer was a brilliant criminal financier and arms manufacturer who supported, outfitted, and financed operations for many costumed criminals, including Blizzard, Boomerang, and Water Wizard.

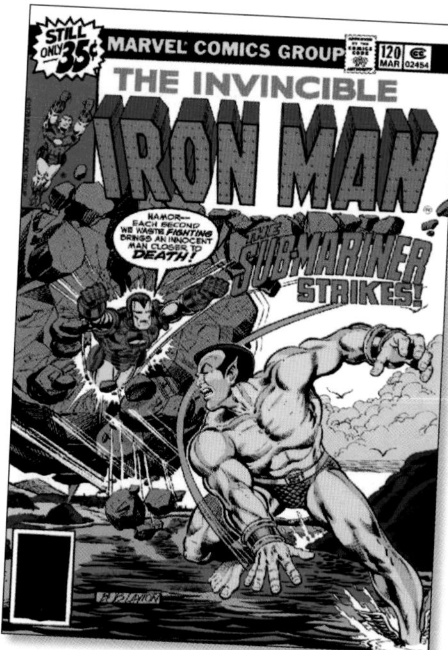

In Claremont and Byrne's classic *Marvel Team-Up* #79, Spider-Man and Red Sonja, whose spirit had taken possession of Mary Jane Watson, defeated sinister sorceror Kulan Garth.

MAY

MILLER TIME

• *Daredevil* #158

In May, the Man Without Fear had his final showdown with the Death-Stalker. More importantly, in this issue the great longtime *Daredevil* artist Gene Colan was succeeded by a new penciller who would become a star himself: Frank Miller. Initially, Miller collaborated on *Daredevil* with writer Roger McKenzie, but he would take over the writing with issue #168 (Jan., 1981).

JUNE

WHEN IMMORTALS MEET

• *The Mighty Thor* #284

Stan Lee and Jack Kirby's version of the Norse god Thor encountered Kirby's creations the Eternals, as writer/editor Roy Thomas began clearly integrating Kirby's Eternals mythos into the Marvel Universe.

CHAOS IN CANADA!

ALPHA FLIGHT ASCENDANT

"I was operational when Hudson gathered the rest of Alpha Flight. Outside of him, I don't know who we're up against or how many."

• *The Uncanny X-Men* #120

Although he was born in England, John Byrne moved to Canada with his family as a boy, and lived there until he moved to the United States in the 1980s. On becoming the new artist on *X-Men*, Byrne took particular interest in his fellow Canadian, Wolverine. In issue #109 of *X-Men* (Feb., 1978), which was only Byrne's second issue, he introduced another Canadian Super Hero, James MacDonald Hudson alias Weapon Alpha.

Beginning with *The Uncanny X-Men* #120, which was written by Chris Claremont and pencilled by Byrne, the X-Men found themselves in Calgary, Canada. Hudson had intended Wolverine to join the team of superhuman agents he organized for the Canadian government, Alpha Flight. Now calling himself Vindicator, Hudson led Alpha Flight in a new attempt to capture Wolverine. Byrne created Alpha Flight, and this story, which lasted for two issues, introduced its original members. Among them were Jean-Paul and Jeanne-Marie Beaubier, the French Canadian twins gifted with superhuman speed, known as Northstar and Aurora. Alpha Flight battled the X-Men until Wolverine decided to surrender; of course, Wolverine immediately escaped custody and returned to the X-Men. He eventually made peace with Hudson in *The Uncanny X-Men* #139 and #140 (Nov. and Dec., 1980). In 1983, Alpha Flight won their own monthly comic book, which Byrne originally wrote and drew.

JULY

BEWARE THE BLACK CAT

• *The Amazing Spider-Man* #194

Inspired by Tex Avery's MGM animated cartoon *Bad Luck Blackie* about a black cat who brought bad luck, writer Marv Wolfman came up with the idea for the Super Hero the Black Cat. The daughter of a cat burglar, Felicia Hardy decided to follow in her father's footsteps. She soon crossed Spider-Man's path and found herself attracted to her web-slinging adversary. She eventually became Spider-Man's ally and even, for a time, his girlfriend. Later, Black Cat became a private investigator. Dave Cockrum designed the Black Cat's visual appearance and Keith Pollard drew her first story.

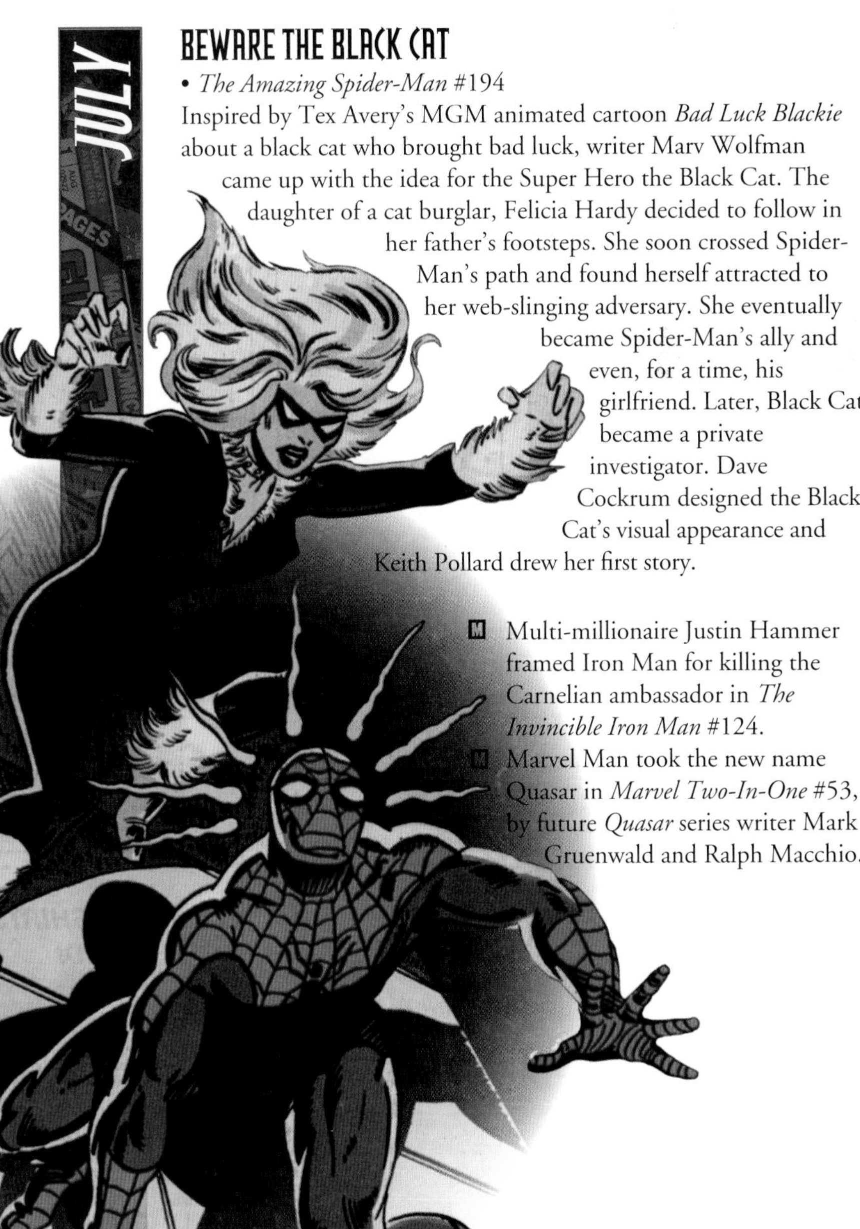

Multi-millionaire Justin Hammer framed Iron Man for killing the Carnelian ambassador in *The Invincible Iron Man* #124.

Marvel Man took the new name Quasar in *Marvel Two-In-One* #53, by future *Quasar* series writer Mark Gruenwald and Ralph Macchio.

AUGUST

"...AND THEN LIKE SOME MANIFESTING GOD, HE PLACED THEM IN THE CARE OF THE TRIBE'S SHAMAN , DJANGO MAXIMOFF, AND HIS WIFE, WITH INSTRUCTIONS TO RAISE THE TWINS AS THEIR OWN.
"THE MAXIMOFFS WHO HAD RECENTLY LOST THEIR OWN CHILDREN --ANA AND MATEO-- COMPLIED."

SECRET ORIGINS REVEALED

• *The Avengers* #186

The origins of mutant Avengers Quicksilver and the Scarlet Witch were finally revealed in August. Readers learned how a mysterious woman, Magda, gave birth to the mutant twins at Wundagore Mountain before disappearing into the wilderness. A page that Byrne originally drew for *The Uncanny X-Men* #125 (Sept., 1979) revealed that Magda was the wife of Magneto, making him the unknowing father of Quicksilver and the Scarlet Witch.

HELLO TO H.E.R.B.I.E.

• *Fantastic Four* #209

Oddly, the 1978 *Fantastic Four* animated series, produced by animation company DePatie-Freleng Enterprises, was unable to use the Human Torch, who had been optioned for a film project that never happened. As a substitute, Stan Lee and Jack Kirby created the robot H.E.R.B.I.E., who made his comics debut in this issue. His name was an acronym for Humanoid Experimental Robot, B-type, Integrated Electronics.

SEPTEMBER

THE DRAMATIC RETURN OF PHOENIX

MUTANT X DEBUTS

• *The Uncanny X-Men* #125

The mysterious Mutant X made his first appearance in this story by Chris Claremont and John Byrne. He was Dr. Moira MacTaggert's mad son, known as Proteus, who took possession of host bodies and had the power to distort reality.

OCTOBER

THE TERROR OF TERRAX BEGINS

• *Fantastic Four* #211

The world-devouring Galactus chose the ruthless alien tyrant Tyros to be his next herald, as he wanted one that would possess no sympathy for other living beings. Galactus transformed him into the cosmic-powered Terrax the Tamer and, in doing so, magnified Terrax's mental ability to control earth and rock. Created by writer Marv Wolfman and artist John Byrne, Terrax would not only become a threat to the Fantastic Four but also Galactus himself.

"BEHOLD HIM NOW! WITH HIS COSMIC AXE IN HIS HAND, TERRAX IS INVINCIBLE!
"FOR, WITH THIS AXE, HE CAN CLEAVE THE COSMIC STRATUM ITSELF!

M Writers Jim Salicrup, Roger Stern, and Ed Hannigan and artists Tom Sutton and Terry Austin collaborated with musician Alice Cooper on *Marvel Premiere* #50, a one-shot comic.

NOVEMBER

WAITING FOR THE END OF THE WORLD!

THE MYSTERY SOLVED?

• *The Defenders* #77

When *Omega The Unknown* was cancelled in October, 1977, the title character had apparently been shot dead. Omega's co-creator Steve Gerber subsequently left Marvel, and writer Steven Grant devised this wrap-up of the Omega story line, killing off the other protagonist, James-Michael Starling. The mysterious connection between Omega and Starling was never elaborated upon.

MAN-THING RESURFACES

• *The Man-Thing* #1

The Man-Thing returned in a new short-lived series, originally written by Michael Fleisher with pencil art by Jim Mooney. Fleisher was soon succeeded as writer by Chris Claremont, who brought back Steve Gerber characters such as sorceress Jennifer Kale.

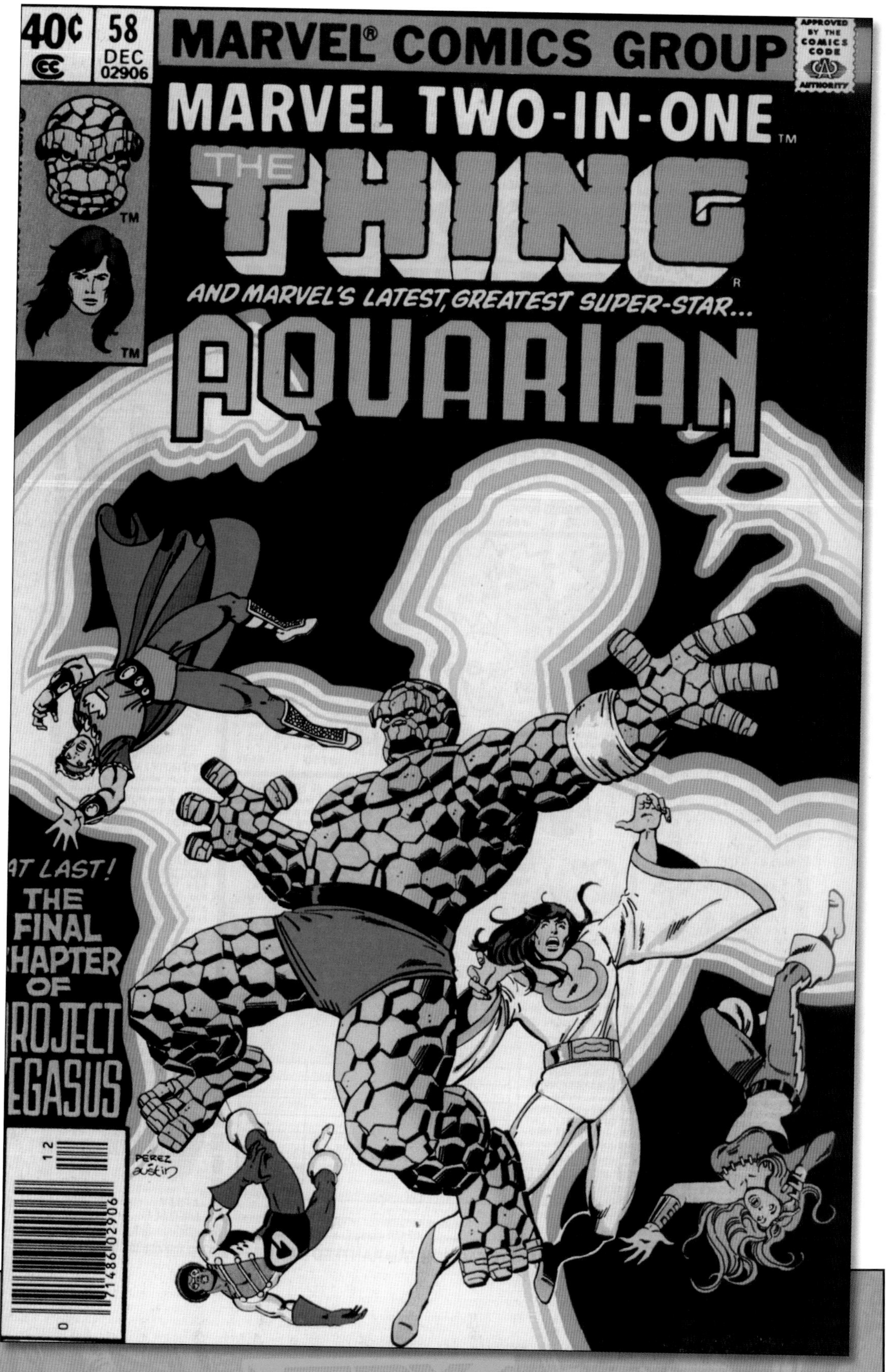

MEANWHILE IN 1979...

ATOMIC LEAK CAUSES CONCERN IN AMERICA

Nuclear disaster is narrowly averted at the Three Mile Island power station in Pennsylvania when partial core meltdown occurs and radiation leaks into the environment. No casualties are reported, but the event is a public relations crisis for the American nuclear industry.

WOMAN PRIME MINISTER FOR BRITAIN

Conservative Party leader Margaret Thatcher wins the general election and becomes the first female Prime Minister of Great Britain.

REVOLUTION IN IRAN

The Iranian revolution transforms the autocratic, pro-western monarchy into an Islamic, theocratic government, ruled by Ayatollah Khomeini.

PANIC FUELS ENERGY CRISIS

The second oil crisis is sparked by the Iranian Revolution. Decreased production, higher prices, and panic disrupt the supply to oil-dependent Western countries.

US HOSTAGE CRISIS IN IRAN

Distrust between the new revolutionary leadership in Iran and the West is fueled by the 444-day hostage crisis that begins when radical students storm the US embassy in Tehran.

SECRET DIRECTIVE TO HELP ANTI-SOVIETS IN AFGHANISTAN

After the USSR invades Afghanistan, President Carter signs a directive to supply secret aid to the opponents of the new regime.

CAMBODIAN HORROR REVEALED

Vietnamese troops invading Cambodia overthrow Pol Pot. He is sentenced to death for genocide for his lethal regime in which over a million people died through execution, starvation, and forced labor after his Khmer Rouge took over the country in 1975.

"PRESIDENT ATTACKED BY RABBIT"

President Carter is lambasted as hapless and enfeebled by the media when a story breaks that he was persecuted while fishing by an aggressive swamp rabbit, which tried to get onto his small fishing boat.

SNOW IN THE SAHARA

The Sahara Desert experiences snow for thirty minutes.

AND AT THE MOVIES...

Apocolypse Now, *Francis Ford Coppola's powerful adaptation of Joseph Conrad's novella, transposed to Vietnam, provides a gripping allegory of war's insanity;* Alien, *Ridley Scott's mastery of high-budget visuals and dramatic tension creates a very scary space-monster movie;* Manhattan, *Woody Allen's love-story to New York follows a TV comedy writer and sums up all his neuroses and confessional comic obsessions.*

BORN AGAIN WUNDARR

• *Marvel Two-In-One* #58

Created by writer Steve Gerber and artist Val Mayerik in *Fear* #17, Wundarr was a super-powered adult alien with the mind of a child. In this finale of the Project: PEGASUS saga, Wundarr became the Aquarian, a prophet of peace and spiritual enlightenment.

M Prolific writer Bill Mantlo and artist Sal Buscema created a Marvel comics series and a whole mythology around Parker Brothers's toy "ROM." *ROM Spaceknight* comic ran for seventy-five issues.

The Hulk! #10 ***(Aug., 1978)***
After starring in two made-for-television movies, the Hulk graduated to his own weekly television series, The Incredible Hulk. *Like another classic show,* The Fugitive, *the show turned its protagonist David (changed from Bruce) Banner into a homeless wanderer, staying one step ahead of a pursuing reporter. Without any Super Villains to fight, it was more like a show about a monster than a true Super Hero series. The huge success of the television series gave rise to Hulk games, toys, coloring books, action figures, and savings banks. "Hulkmania has made our jade giant a modern day myth, a creative mainstay of our culture," proclaimed the introduction to issue #10 of* The Hulk!.

1980s

Since the beginning of the comic book industry, comics had usually been sold through newsagents and spinner racks located in small "Mom and Pop" stores around the country, and retailers could return unsold copies to the publisher. Comic-book stores had begun to appear in the 1970s and Phil Sueling, the Brooklyn high-school teacher who had founded the Comic Art Convention in New York City, convinced Marvel to start selling its product on a firm sale, non-refundable basis to these new stores. At the beginning of the 1980s there were only a few hundred comic-book stores, but Marvel began actively to support them and even published their names and addresses. Marvel also noticed that some smaller publishing companies were producing comics that were sold exclusively through these stores, so the company decided to publish its first "direct only" title—so named because it was sold directly to the independent distributors who only supplied comic-book stores. The chosen title was *Dazzler* #1, which sold over 400,000 copies. Within months, Marvel made three of its monthly titles—*Moon Knight*, *Micronauts*, and *Ka-Zar*—"direct only" and the company was soon creating new titles (for example, *Marvel Fanfare*), new formats (like Marvel Graphic Novels), and entire lines (such as the Epic Comics Group imprint) that were reserved exclusively for comic-book stores. With Marvel's support, the number of stores grew at a phenomenal rate... and so did the industry's dependence upon them.

NICE TEAM WORK, PEOPLE.
SO WHAT'S OUR NEXT MOVE?

1980

ONE COMPANY, TWO COASTS

Editor-in-Chief Jim Shooter prepared Marvel to face a new decade. The company was producing between thirty-one and thirty-five comics a month as well as magazines aimed at older readers like *The Savage Sword Of Conan*, *Tomb Of Dracula*, and *Crazy*. Aside from Roy Thomas and Marv Wolfman, Shooter's editorial staff included Denny O'Neil, Allen Milgrom, Louise Simonson, Jim Salicrup, and Larry Hama.

The *Bullpen Bulletins* announced that Stan Lee had moved to Los Angeles to help supervise a number of soon-to-be-produced Marvel television shows and movies. *The Incredible Hulk*, starring Bill Bixby and Lou Ferrigno, was still being aired on American television, as were a new animated series starring Spider-Woman and one roughly based on the Thing. A second Captain America live-action television movie had been scheduled and Lee proudly proclaimed that work had begun on a major Silver Surfer movie, scheduled to be released in the summer of 1982, although it ultimately failed to materialize.

Regular Marvel comics were priced at forty cents at the beginning of 1980, but went up to fifty cents with the September-dated books. Jim Shooter publicly apologized for the increase and announced "The Mighty Marvel Win-Yourself Some-Big-Bucks Contest" as a way to reward readers for their continued loyalty.

JANUARY

THE DARK PHOENIX SAGA BEGINS

"Hear me, X-Men! No longer am I the woman you knew! I am fire! And life incarnate! Now and forever—I am PHOENIX!"

• *The Uncanny X-Men* #129

In January a nine-part story began that changed the X-Men forever. Never one of Marvel's top sellers, *The Uncanny X-Men* had been slowly gaining momentum under the creative direction of writer Chris Claremont and artist Dave Cockrum (who was later followed by John Byrne). Claremont proposed a story that would show how Jean Grey—one of the original members of the X-Men—had become corrupted by her new Phoenix power. She would become a great threat, would destroy an inhabited world, and would have to be punished. In the original story line, Jean's punishment was a psychic lobotomy that removed all her mutant powers, but Editor-in-Chief Jim Shooter didn't think that was enough and decided that Phoenix had to die for her crimes. The final pages of the story line in *X-Men* #137 were redrawn to incorporate the new ending. When word of the changes leaked out, comic book fans became outraged. They couldn't believe that a beloved character from the 1960s would actually die. Sales of *The Uncanny X-Men* immediately began to grow and the title was soon challenging *The Amazing Spider-Man* and *Star Wars* for the top of Marvel's sales chart.

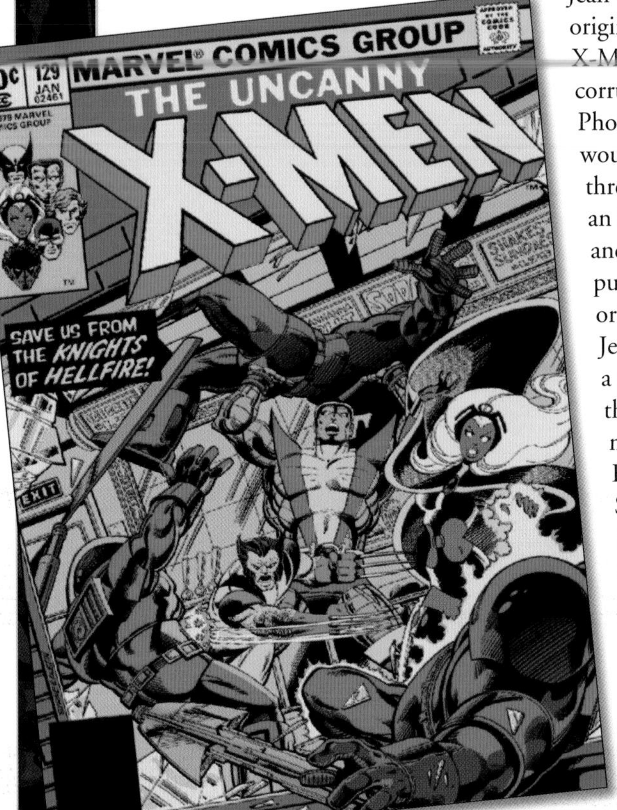

The Uncanny X-Men #129 introduced the Hellfire Club, an exclusive social club that secretly sought world domination. Also introduced in this issue were longtime X-Men foe Sebastian Shaw, the future Black King of the Hellfire Club, and Emma Frost, a mutant with telepathic powers, who later joined the X-Men.

SPIDEY'S TWO-HUNDREDTH ISSUE

• *Amazing Spider-Man* #200

Writer/editor Marv Wolfman wanted a very special story to celebrate this two-hundredth issue. He wrote a story in which Spidey confronted his feelings about the burglar who had murdered his uncle. This event was still quite recent to Peter, as, thanks to the magic of comics, only four or five years had passed since he had been bitten by the spider. Keith Pollard pencilled the story, Jim Mooney did the inking, and Stan Lee came back to write the final page.

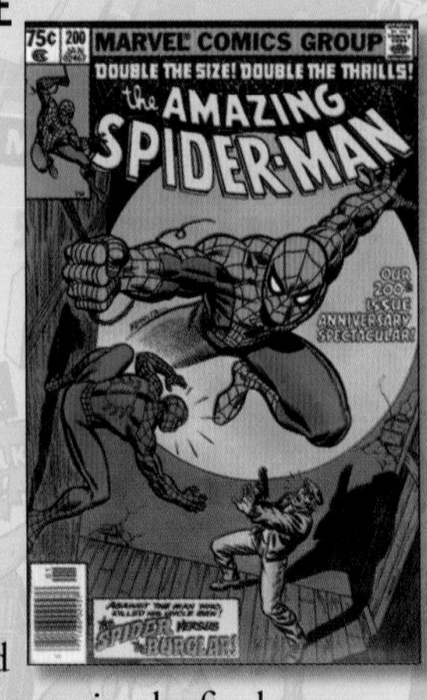

A DAZZLER FOR A DISCO ERA

• *The Uncanny X-Men* #130

Hoping to cash in on the disco craze, Casablanca Records approached Marvel and the movie company Filmworks about creating a new character who could appear across records, comics, and movies. The three companies settled on the name Dazzler and commissioned John Romita Jr. to design her. He was first told to model her after the singer Grace Jones, but that was changed to the actress Bo Derek when she agreed to star in the movie. Writer Tom DeFalco, who was hired to develop the character, decided that Dazzler would be a mutant with the ability to convert sound waves into a beam of concussive force. The movie deal ultimately fell apart, but the character was still a success for Marvel.

JENNIFER WALTERS BECOMES THE SHE-HULK

"I've never felt like this before! I can do anything! I'm throbbing with power!"

• *The Savage She-Hulk* #1

Stan Lee decided to introduce a female version of the Hulk amid fears that the producers of the television series *The Incredible Hulk* might introduce their own spinoff that they would own the rights to—like Universal had done when they spun *The Bionic Woman* off *The Six Million Dollar Man*, a property based on Martin Caidin's novel *Cyborg*. With the help of artist John Buscema, Lee created Jennifer Walters, the cousin of Bruce Banner. When she was seriously wounded, Banner used his blood to perform an emergency blood transfusion that turned her into a green-skinned She-Hulk.

Although Jennifer's strength was greatly increased, she could still think clearly and she rarely had uncontrollable rages like the Hulk. Her transformations were initially triggered by anger, but she soon became able to control them.

The She-Hulk was the last major Marvel character created by Lee. She went on to be a member of the Avengers, the Fantastic Four, Heroes for Hire, the Defenders, and SHIELD. While *The Savage She-Hulk* ended with issue #25, the character later appeared in *Marvel Graphic Novel* #18*: The Sensational She-Hulk* (1985). This was written and drawn by John Byrne, who went on to produce the monthly title *The Sensational She-Hulk*, which ran for sixty issues. She also appeared in the two-issue *She-Hulk: Ceremony* (1989) and *Thing And She-Hulk: The Long Night* (2002). A new monthly title, *She-Hulk*, was launched in December, 2005.

Although the She-Hulk's strength didn't increase in proportion to her anger, and she wasn't nearly as strong as her cousin the Hulk, she could still tear steel with her bare hands.

MARCH

AN EPIC JOURNEY BEGINS

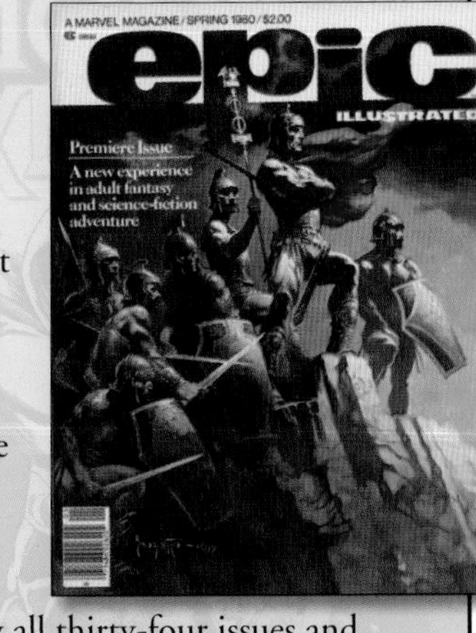

• *Epic Illustrated* #1

This title was Marvel's attempt to compete with the popular *Heavy Metal Magazine*, which printed more mature material for the adult market and work by European artists. *Epic* offered its creators ownership of the material and paid them royalties rather than the traditional page rates. Each issue featured both complete short stories and serials. Former Editor-in-Chief Archie Goodwin oversaw all thirty-four issues and published work by the likes of Barry Windsor-Smith, Jim Starlin, John Bolton, Wendy Pini, and Dave Sim.

- M Tako Shamara became the Dragon Lord in *Marvel Spotlight* #5, by writer/editor Marv Wolfman and artist Steve Ditko.
- M *King Conan* #1 was launched, a title that followed the adventures of an older Conan, as the King of Aquilonia. It changed its title to *Conan The King* with issue #20 and ran for fifty-five issues.

MAY

TASKMASTER DEBUTS

• *The Avengers* #195

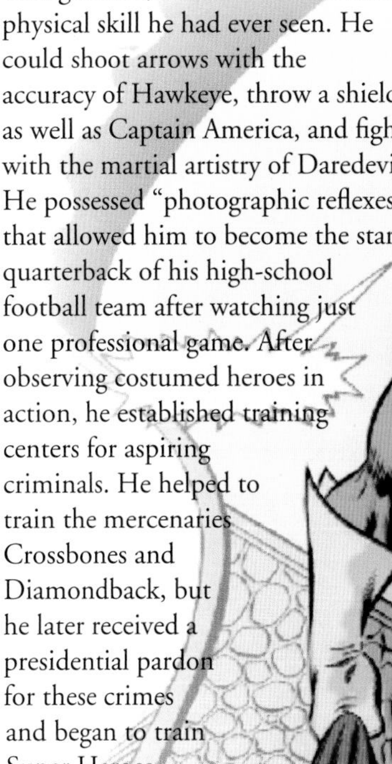

Created by writer David Michelinie and artist George Pérez, Taskmaster could mimic any physical skill he had ever seen. He could shoot arrows with the accuracy of Hawkeye, throw a shield as well as Captain America, and fight with the martial artistry of Daredevil. He possessed "photographic reflexes" that allowed him to become the star quarterback of his high-school football team after watching just one professional game. After observing costumed heroes in action, he established training centers for aspiring criminals. He helped to train the mercenaries Crossbones and Diamondback, but he later received a presidential pardon for these crimes and began to train Super Heroes.

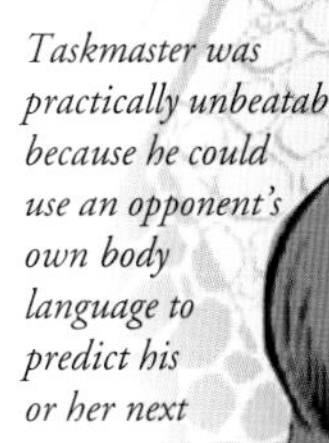

Taskmaster was practically unbeatable because he could use an opponent's own body language to predict his or her next move.

OCTOBER

In Spectacular Spider-Man *#47, Spidey battled a new and vicious Prowler, who was later revealed to be the Cat Burglar from* Amazing Spider-Man *#30.*

A BEAU FOR AUNT MAY

• *The Spectacular Spider-Man* #47

Nathan Lubensky met Spider-Man's Aunt May in a nursing home where she was recuperating from a heart attack in *Spectacular Spider-Man* #47, an issue by writer Roger Stern and artist Marie Severin. Nathan and May later became engaged and set up a boarding house together, but tragically, Nathan died from heart failure before they could wed.

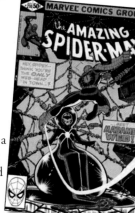

CAP FOR PRESIDENT!

• *Captain America* #250

The National Populist Party asked Captain America to run for President of the United States in this issue by writer Roger Stern and artist John Byrne. Cap refused the request because he believed that his dedication to the American Dream would hinder his ability to deal with the realities of public office.

AUGUST

LOVE IN THE AIR FOR CAP

• *Captain America* #248

Bernie Rosenthal was a professional glass-blower and former college activist, who was created by writer Roger Stern and penciller John Byrne. She met Steve Rogers when he was a freelance artist in Brooklyn Heights, but soon after they met, he had to change into Captain America to fight Dragon Man. Despite his frequent disappearances, they fell in love, but their relationship deteriorated when she moved to another state to attend law school.

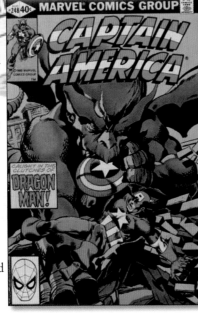

NOVEMBER

MADAME WEB DEBUTS

• *The Amazing Spider-Man* #210

Cassandra Webb was a mutant whose powers included telepathy and clairvoyance. Created by writer/editor Denny O'Neil and artist John Romita Jr., Webb was blind and suffered from a nerve disease which left her dependent on a life-support system that resembled a giant web. She psionically learned Spider-Man's secret identity and helped him find K.J. Clayton, the missing publisher of the *Daily Globe*. Spidey later returned the favor when he stopped the Juggernaut kidnapping her. Madame Webb briefly served as mentor to the Mattie Franklin version of Spider-Woman and later appeared to be cured of her nerve disease.

MOON KNIGHT GETS HIS OWN COMIC

• *Moon Knight* #1

Created by writer Doug Moench and artist Don Perlin, Moon Knight first appeared in *Werewolf By Night* #32 (Aug., 1975). When the mercenary Marc Spector was left for dead in the desert, he was laid before a statue of the Egyptian God Khonshu, who gave him a chance to redeem himself in issue #1. Using the identities of the millionaire Steven Grant and the cab driver Jake Lockley, Spector waged a war on crime as Moon Knight. He appeared in *Marvel Spotlight*, *Spectacular Spider-Man*, *Marvel Two-In-One*, *Defenders*, and *The Incredible Hulk* magazine before being awarded his own comic.

SEPTEMBER

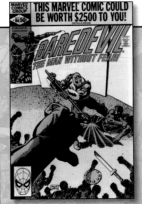

FOGGY NELSON'S WEDDING

• *Daredevil* #166

With Matt Murdock as his best man, Franklin "Foggy" Nelson married his high-school sweetheart, Deborah Harris, in this issue scripted by Roger McKenzie and pencilled by Frank Miller. Sadly, their marriage ended when Harris became attracted to the jungle crimelord, Micah Synn.

A FORAY INTO RELIGIOUS BIOGRAPHIES

• *Francis, Brother Of The Universe*

With the aid of Father Roy Gasnick, writer Mary Jo Duffy and artists John Buscema and Marie Severin produced this biography of St. Francis of Assisi. This was later followed by *The Life Of Pope John Paul II* (1982) and *Mother Teresa Of Calcutta* (1984).

THE U-FOES DEBUT

"We're murderers—but what does it matter? Like he said, we ain't human, anymore! There ain't no laws we have to obey—no prisons that could hold us!"

• *The Incredible Hulk* #254

Inspired by the 1979 Graham Parker song, *Waiting for the UFOs*, the creation of the U-Foes was truly a team effort. Writer Bill Mantlo and artist Sal Buscema produced the first U-Foes story, but editor Al Milgrom helped design the costumes and Editor-in-Chief Jim Shooter suggested some of the names.

Millionaire and former politician Simon Utrecht had a dream. Desiring power for its own sake, he funded a mission into space to gain super-powers as the Fantastic Four had done. He hired Ann Darnell as his life-support engineer, her brother Jimmy as the fuel-propulsion systems engineer, and Mike Steel to pilot the spacecraft. They blasted off and deliberately flew into the heart of a cosmic storm. Everything was going according to plan until Dr. Bruce Banner accidentally stumbled into their command center and recalled them to Earth. But the cosmic rays had already done their work! Simon had become Vector, with the power to attract or repel matter. Ann was able to transform herself into any known gas and called herself Vapor. Jimmy dubbed himself X-Ray after he was permanently converted into a living energy field with the power to fire deadly blasts of radiation. Mike gained super-strength, an armored covering, the ability to increase or decrease his own weight, and the name Ironclad. After numerous battles with the Hulk, the U-Foes were offered membership of the villainous group, the Thunderbolts.

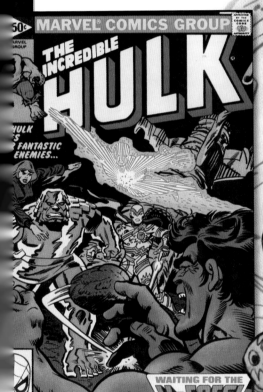

MEANWHILE IN 1980...

US SEVERS DIPLOMATIC RELATIONS WITH IRAN

Following the seizing of American hostages at the US Embassy in Tehran in November, 1979, the US cuts diplomatic ties and imposes economic sanctions on Iran.

JOHN LENNON SHOT DEAD

Beatles musician and peace campaigner John Lennon is shot dead outside his home in New York by a man who asked for his autograph only hours earlier.

VOLCANO ERUPTION IN WASHINGTON

Mount St. Helens blows its top in the deadliest eruption in the US, killing fifty-seven people.

AND AT THE MOVIES...

The Empire Strikes Back, *the darkest installment of the Star Wars trilogy features Luke Skywalker being Jedi-trained by the mystic Yoda;* The Shining, *Stanley Kubrick's memorable adaptation of Stephen King's haunted-house horror about a writer slowly going insane;* Raging Bull, *Martin Scorsese's brutal boxing biopic about Jake LaMotta.*

The cover of issue #254 featured the entire U-Foes team. From left to right, they are Vapor, Ironclad, Vector, and X-Ray.

Instead of thanking Bruce Banner for saving their lives, the U-Foes attacked him. They were enraged because they believed that, without his interference, they would have become even more powerful.

Marvel's branch in the UK published *Dr. Who Weekly*, a comic that contained black-and-white comic strips featuring the adventures of the popular BBC television character.

MUTANTS, YOU ARE ADVISED TO SURRENDER OR FACE IMMEDIATE TERMINATION. THIS IS YOUR ONLY WARNING.

1981

KICKING INTO HIGH GEAR

Marvel was on the move again. The company's main channel for selling its comics had been newsagents and small "Mom and Pop" stores. While it had been selling to comic-book stores since 1976, the company decided to take a big gamble: it launched the first issue of a new monthly title exclusively through comic-book stores. The gamble paid off. *Dazzler* #1 sold 428,000 copies and proved that comic-book stores were here to stay.

Editor-in-Chief, Jim Shooter revamped the *Bullpen Bulletins* page, devoting it more to news and gossip than sales hype. Going back to the early days of Marvel, Shooter wrote these pages himself to establish a greater personal rapport with the readers. He announced weddings, births, and other significant events in the lives of Marvel's creative community. On the creative front, Frank Miller was redefining *Daredevil* by focusing on urban crimes and John Byrne went back to basics with the *Fantastic Four* and evoked the title's early days of Stan Lee and Jack Kirby by focusing on character-driven stories. On the editorial front, Michael Z. Hobson, who had a background in children's books, was hired to oversee the company's publishing, and writer Tom DeFalco, who had begun his career as an editorial assistant at Archie Comics, became editor of the *Spider-Man* titles.

JANUARY

HYDRO-MAN SPLASHES ONTO THE SCENE

• *The Amazing Spider-Man* #212

Created by writer Denny O'Neil and artist John Romita Jr., Hydro-Man was a watery version of Sandman, who could change his body at will. Morris Bench was a crewman on a cargo ship who gained his Hydro-Man powers when he accidentally fell overboard and was exposed to a mystery form of radiation. Like Sandman, he originally wore a black T-shirt and jeans, but he switched to a distinctive jumpsuit when he joined the villainous Frightful Four. Hydro-Man has also been a member of the Sinister Syndicate, the Masters of Evil, and the Sinister Twelve. For a brief period, he even merged with Sandman to form a giant mud-creature.

Hydro-Man could change the shape of his watery form, fire concentrated streams of water and merge with large bodies of water.

THE DAYS OF FUTURE PAST STORY BEGINS

"Forgive us, my friends. We cannot avenge you—for what point is vengeance against an unfeeling machine? But at least we can try to ensure that this nightmare never happens, never even begins!"

• *The Uncanny X-Men* #141

The Sentinels ruled the earth in an alternate reality. These giant metal monsters hunted mutants and humans who possessed superhuman powers. An older Wolverine and Kate "Kitty" Pryde planned to strike back by taking a dangerous gamble. They decided to mentally project Kitty's mind back into the past, hoping that she could warn the X-Men in time to prevent this future from ever happening. Days Of Future Past proved so popular that it merited a number of sequels, including *Days Of Future Tense* and a three-part miniseries called *Wolverine: Days Of Future Past* (1997), which explained this alternate timeline.

The Uncanny X-Men #141 also introduced Rachel Summers, the daughter of Scott Summers and Jean Grey, who was born in the "Days Of Future Past" timeline. A powerful mutant with telepathic and telekinetic powers, Rachel had been a Hound—a mutant who hunted other mutants—until she joined the resistance movement. She later journeyed through time calling herself Phoenix in honor of her deceased mother. She briefly joined the X-Men and cofounded the British team, Excalibur.

JANUARY

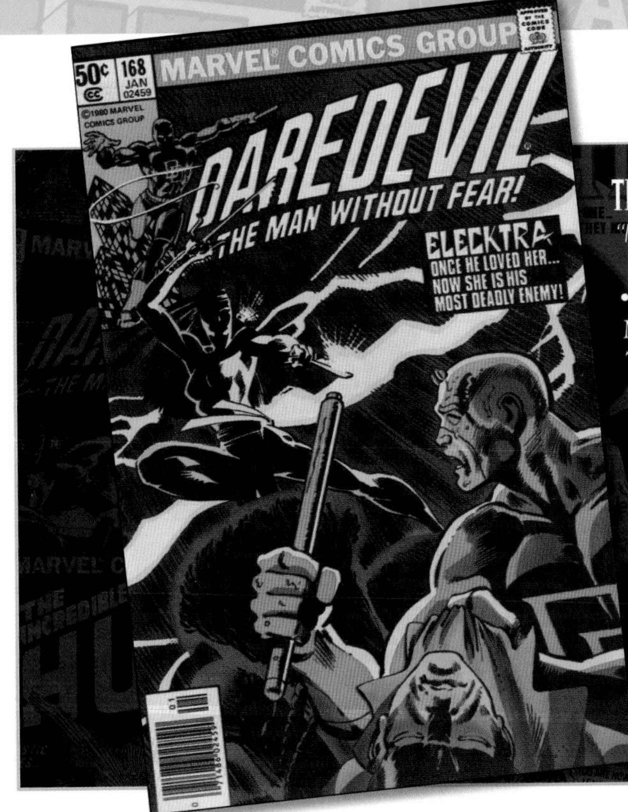

THE FIRST APPEARANCE OF ELEKTRA

"I serve no cause—no law—and no man."

• *Daredevil* #168

Matt Murdock's college sweetheart first appeared in this issue by writer/artist Frank Miller. The daughter of a Greek diplomat who had been murdered by terrorists, Elektra Natchios was a woman who sought vengeance, like the Electra of Greek myth. Trained in the martial arts so that she could protect herself, she met Murdock while attending Columbia University in New York. After her father was killed, she fell into a severe depression, dropped out of law school, and eventually joined the league of assassins known as the Hand. She became an independent mercenary and soon found herself battling Daredevil. She even briefly served as the Kingpin of Crime's chief assassin. When Wolverine regressed to a more bestial form, Elektra helped restore him so that he could think and act as a human again. In an alternate timeline, Elektra and Wolverine married and had a mutant daughter who took on the name of Wild Thing.

Elektra appeared in two major motion pictures: *Daredevil* (2003) and *Elektra* (2005) and was played by the actress Jennifer Garner. In the *Secret Invasion* mega-crossover (2008), it was revealed that Elektra had been replaced by a Skrull imposter.

In the dystopian future of "Days Of Future Past," the Sentinels had already slain Cyclops, Beast, Nightcrawler, Angel, and Iceman. Wolverine became a member of the Canadian Resistance Army and Kitty Pryde lived in a concentration camp reserved for mutants and wore an inhibitor collar to negate her mutant abilities.

APRIL

ENTER THE SOVIET SUPER-SOLDIERS

• *The Incredible Hulk* #258

The Soviet Super-Soldiers, the Russian equivalent of the Avengers, were a team of super-powered individuals assembled by the Soviet government in this issue by writer Bill Mantlo and artist Sal Buscema. The team consisted of Mikhail Ursus/Ursa Major, who had the ability to transform himself into a super-strong bear-like creature, Laynia Petrovna/Darkstar, a mutant who could psionically access and employ energy from another dimension to form solid objects and fire blasts, Nikolai Krylenko/Vanguard, who could repel any force, and Dmitri Bukharin, the fifth man to don the Crimson Dynamo's armor. After the team refused to obey their government, they were replaced by the Supreme Soviet.

SEPTEMBER

THE HAND STRIKES!

• *Daredevil* #174

Like the five islands of Japan, a hand has five separate fingers, none of which is very powerful. But when they form a fist, the hand can become an object of incredible power! The Hand was a league of ninja assassins who employed dark magic, which originated about 800 years ago in feudal Japan. Introduced in *Daredevil* #174 by writer/artist Frank Miller, this group of deadly warriors had been hired by the Kingpin of Crime to exterminate Matt Murdock. The plot was uncovered by Elektra, who was a former member of the league. As punishment for warning Murdock, she was also sentenced to death by Kirigi, the Hand's deadliest ninja. Although Elektra managed to kill Kirigi, the Hand employed its magic to resurrect him. The Hand was eventually driven away from Murdock by their longtime foes, a band of rival ninja enemies called the Chase.

Like all ninja, the members of the Hand were skilled fighters and masters of various forms of weaponry, subterfuge, and the martial arts. The Hand could also murder a person and then resurrect him or her as a mindless servant. Only Elektra, Psylocke, and Wolverine managed to free themselves from the Hand's control.

MARVEL PRODUCTIONS

In the early 1980s, Marvel Productions, the newly formed west-coast branch of the company, produced two key animated series for television: *Spider-Man And His Amazing Friends* (first aired in September, 1981) and *The Incredible Hulk* (first aired in September, 1982). *Spider-Man And His Amazing Friends* was the first animated series produced by Marvel Productions, and, with Stan Lee as its creative director, the show ran for twenty-four episodes. It featured the adventures of Peter Parker, aka Spider-Man, Bobby Drake, aka Iceman, and a new character named Angelica Jones, who called herself Firestar. *The Incredible Hulk* was shown together with the Spider-Man animated series. Narrated by Stan Lee, it included characters like the Leader, side-kick Rick Jones, and Banner's girlfriend Betty Ross.

NOVEMBER

Stick led a group of mystical ninjas who called themselves the Chase. They sought spiritual purity and enlightenment through perfection of the martial arts.

THE FIRST APPEARANCE OF THE STICK

• *Daredevil* #176

Stick was the ninja master who helped train Elektra and taught Matt Murdock to control his hyper-senses and hone his acrobatic skills. Possibly modeled after Nantembo, a Zen master who reputedly disciplined his students by striking them with his nantin staff, Stick first appeared in this issue by Frank Miller. He later died in battle with the Hand, but his soul was reincarnated into a newborn child.

- M James Sanders had debuted in *The Avengers* #70 as Whizzer, but he renamed himself Speed Demon in *Amazing Spider-Man* #222.
- M Anticipating the Star Comics imprint, Marvel secured rights to Hank Ketchum's famous comic-strip character and published *Dennis The Menace* #1, but the title only ran for thirteen issues.

DECEMBER

GREENBERG, AN UNUSUAL VAMPIRE

• *Bizarre Adventures* #29

Writer J.M. DeMatteis and artist Steve Leiloha explored a new take on the vampire myth with Greenberg. The grandson of a rabbi, Oscar Greenberg wrote horror stories for a living and was accidentally turned into a vampire during a romantic escapade. Too squeamish to ever attack anyone, Greenberg drank animal blood while trying to maintain his normal life.

A DEAL WITH DC COMICS

Marvel had worked with their rival DC Comics on *MGM's Marvelous Wizard Of Oz* (1975) and *Superman Vs. Spider-Man* (1976). In 1981 they signed a deal to produce more crossovers: a Superman/Spider-Man and Batman/Hulk title in 1981 and an X-Men/Teen Titans one in 1982. But negotiations caused delay and the JLA/Avengers four-part series did not publish until 2003.

- M In *The Invincible Iron Man* #153, Iron Man unveiled his all-black stealth armor, which used technology similar to that of spy planes.
- M Marvel said goodbye to war comics with *Sgt. Fury And His Howling Commandos* #167, which reprinted the team's first issue.

ALSO PUBLISHED...

INTRODUCING ROGUE

"Poor L'il Cap. You never had a chance, Dahlin'. Ah possess all Ms. Marvel's mem'ries. Ah know how you fight, how you think. That made it easy to catch you off guard. Most importantly, Ah possess her power!"

• *The Avengers Annual* #10

Rogue had originally been scheduled to appear in *Ms. Marvel* #25, but was left homeless when that title was cancelled with issue #23 in 1979. Her first published appearance occurred in *The Avengers Annual* #10 by Chris Claremont and Michael Golden. The mutant Rogue had the ability to absorb the psyches, memories, characteristics, skills, and powers of anyone she physically touched. She left her victims weakened or unconscious. This transfer of power was usually temporary, but could become permanent if she maintained contact for too long.

When she first appeared, Rogue was a member of Mystique's Brotherhood of Evil Mutants, which also included the Super Villains Destiny, the Blob, Pyro, and Avalanche. Rogue had already confronted the Super Hero Ms. Marvel, aka Carol Danvers, and permanently absorbed her psyche, superhuman strength, and ability to fly. But, as Rogue continued to use her powers, her mind became clouded with the psyches and memories of her victims, so she turned to Professor Charles Xavier for help. The X-Men, however, initially viewed her as a potential threat. In contrast to the way their relationship is portrayed in the *X-Men* films, Wolverine was especially suspicious, but Rogue eventually gained the team's trust and respect.

Despite her inability to touch or kiss, she later began a longtime romantic relationship with the mutant Gambit. Rogue briefly joined Storm's X-Treme X-Men team, but later returned to the original X-Men. She has starred in two limited series as well as her own monthly title and she was played by actress Anna Paquin in all three *X-Men* films.

Rogue, who debuted in The Avengers Annual *#10, first learned she was a mutant when she kissed her first boyfriend. She was traumatized, thinking she had killed him when he fell unconscious and she absorbed all his memories.*

Rogue launched a sneak attack on the Earth's Mightiest Heroes in The Avengers Annual *#10. Her goal was to absorb their powers so that she would have the strength to free the Blob, Avalanche, Pyro, and Destiny, who were being held in police custody in Ryker's Island Prison.*

AN' WHEN AH TOUCH YOU, AS AH DID HER, AH'LL ABSORB YOUR POWER AN' MEM'RIES AS WELL. ANY FLESH-TO-FLESH CONTACT--NO MATTER HOW SLIGHT--WILL SUFFICE FOR THE TRANSFER...

MEANWHILE IN 1981...

REAGAN IS PRESIDENT
Ronald Reagan becomes the fortieth President of the United States.

IRAN FREES US HOSTAGES
After 444 days, fifty-two American hostages are freed from the US Embassy in Tehran.

PRESIDENT SHOT
President Reagan has life-saving surgery after an assassination attempt.

WOMAN ON US SUPREME COURT
Sandra Day O'Connor is the first woman to serve on the US Supreme Court.

CHARLES AND DI WED
In the new era of mass telecommunications, 750 million people around the world watch the royal ceremony on TV.

AND AT THE MOVIES...
Raiders of the Lost Ark, *a spirited action adventure about nomadic archaeologist Indiana Jones;* Das Boot, *an underwater drama that captures the claustrophobia of a U-boat;* An American Werewolf in London, *imaginative horror about an American backpacker who wakes up with a taste for human flesh;* Southern Comfort, *a life-or-death battle in swamplands is a metaphor for America's struggle in Vietnam.*

NOW LET'S SEE HOW TOUGH YOU ARE--AGAINST ME!

IT'S A GIRL! BUT-- LOOK AT THE SIZE OF HER!
HER SKIN! IT-IT'S GREEN!
IT'S LIKE-- SHE'S SOME KIND'A SHE-HULK!

THE ARTIST JOHN BUSCEMA

The Savage She-Hulk #1 (Feb., 1980) Written by Stan Lee, pencilled by John Buscema, and inked by Chic Stone.

John Buscema was born in Brooklyn, New York on December 11, 1927. He was a graduate of Manhattan's High School of Music and Art and he also took classes in life drawing and design at Pratt Institute and the Brooklyn Museum. His earliest comic strip influences were Hal Foster's *Prince Valiant* and Alex Raymond's *Flash Gordon*. He began at Timely Comics in 1948 and then worked for a variety of comic book publishers in the 1950s and spent eight years in the commercial art field before returning to Marvel Comics in 1966. Buscema's credits are much too numerous to list, but he had notable runs on *The Avengers*, *The Silver Surfer*, and *Conan The Barbarian*. He founded his own art school and also wrote the book *How To Draw Comics The Marvel Way* with Stan Lee.

BUB, YOU'VE JUST SIGNED YOUR *DEATH WARRANT!*

1982

NEW FACES AND RELATIONSHIPS

Editor-in-Chief Jim Shooter thought that it was about time Marvel presented a new face to its fans. He started with his own, publishing a picture of himself in a cowboy hat and calling himself "J.S."—a reference to Larry Hagman's character "J.R." on the popular television show *Dallas*. He followed it with pictures of his editors and the names of everyone in his editorial and production departments.

In 1982, Marvel also began a pivotal relationship that lasted well into the 1990s with Hasbro Industries, a toy company primarily known for its toys Mr. Potato Head and G.I. Joe—a military-themed line of twelve-inch figures that had been popular from 1964 to 1978. In 1982, Hasbro re-launched the line as smaller, three-and-three-quarter-inch action figures. Since there were numerous restrictions on the way toys could be advertised on television, Hasbro's advertising agency—Griffin Bacal—proposed a bold idea: Hasbro should promote a comic book, which would have no advertising restrictions. Hasbro went to Marvel. A creative team that included Jim Shooter, Archie Goodwin, Larry Hama, and Tom DeFalco was immediately assigned to develop G.I. Joe as a comic book and, possibly, an animated television series. The comic book, the toy line, and, eventually, the animated series all proved highly successful.

MARCH

The first Marvel Fanfare *story starred Spider-Man, the X-Men, and Ka-Zar. It was produced by writer Chris Claremont and artist Michael Golden.*

A TITLE EXCLUSIVELY FOR COMIC-BOOK STORES

• *Marvel Fanfare* #1

March, 1982 saw the first Marvel comic book designed to be sold only in comic-book stores. Initially priced at $1.25—at a time whe most of Marvel's line was still sixty cents—*Marvel Fanfare* containe thirty-six pages of editorial material (including the covers) and was printed on high-quality, glossy paper with vivid colors. It was an anthology that featured work by talented newcomers as well as wor by the company's most popular creators and its first volume ran for sixty bimonthly issues. The only regular feature was *Editori-Al*, a humorous strip that discussed the issue's contents, written and drawn by *Marvel Fanfare*'s editor, Al Milgrom.

THE BROOD DEBUT

• *The Uncanny X-Men* #155

The Brood was an evil alien race introduced by writer Chris Claremont and artist Dave Cockrum, and was modeled after the creatures in the movie *Alien*. The Brood stole the bodies of others and placed their eggs within these unwilling hosts. As soon as the egg hatched, the host was physically transformed into a member of the Brood. Allied with rebels to overthrow the rightful ruler of the Shi'ar Empire, the Brood attempted to recruit the bodies of the Shi'ar Empress, Lilandra, and her friends, the X-Men. Wolverine's healing power saved him from transformation and he later rescued the rest of the team. The Brood often returned, but *Annihilation: Prologue* (2006) reported that most of them had been exterminated.

The character Cloak could become intangible and instantly teleport himself and others to the Dark Dimension. His companion, Dagger, gained the ability to create psionic "light daggers" that obeyed her will.

APRIL

THE DEATH OF ELEKTRA

• *Daredevil* #181

Writer/artist Frank Miller did the unthinkable when he killed off the popular Elektra in *Daredevil* #181. She was targeted by the professional killer Bullseye because she was his only competition for the job of the Kingpin of Crime's chief assassin. He hunted her down and they faced off in a brutal five-page battle that climaxed when he used her own sai—a three-pronged dagger—against her. Elektra somehow found the strength to survive long enough to die in the arms of Matt Murdock, who later avenged her death as Daredevil. The evil league of assassins known as the Hand attempted to resurrect her. Although they failed, their enemies—the Chaste—succeeded in *Daredevil* #190 (Jan., 1983).

Daredevil *#181 immediately sold out in comic-book stores and sent fans and retailers to raid mass-market newsstands for all the remaining copies.*

INTRODUCING CLOAK AND DAGGER

"It is not justice we want, Spider-Man. It is vengeance!"

• *The Spectacular Spider-Man* #64

In a world where teenage runaways were kidnapped and used as guinea pigs to test an experimental new street drug, two such subjects—Tyrone "Ty" Johnson and Tandy Bowen—survived. Destined to be known as Cloak and Dagger, these two became costumed vigilantes who targeted drug dealers and street predators. Ty suffered from a speech impediment and had fled his home when his nervous stammer prevented him from getting the words out that might have saved his friend's life. Tandy had run away from home because her super-model mother was too busy to pay her any attention.

Cloak and Dagger's first appearance was written by Bill Mantlo and illustrated by Ed Hannigan. A socially conscious writer, Mantlo used the characters to address the problems of teenage runaways and the dangers of illegal drugs. He also came out against racism by pairing Tandy, a teenage white girl, with Ty, an African-American.

The characters Cloak and Dagger were immediate hits and appeared in subsequent issues of *The Spectacular Spider-Man*. They also met the New Mutants in *Marvel Team-Up Annual* #6 (1983), were awarded a four-issue limited series (Oct., 1983–Jan., 1984), and were given their first monthly title in July, 1985. Although their comic only lasted eleven issues, they returned in 1988 in the graphic novel *Cloak And Dagger: Predator And Prey* and in October, 1988, they began a second monthly title, *The Mutant Misadventures Of Cloak And Dagger*. The pair appeared prominently in *Spider-Man: Maximum Carnage* (1993), *Civil Wars* (2007), and *Secret Invasion* (2008).

In the story called "Last Hand," Elektra's death merited a special forty-eight-paged issue that was priced at $1.00 rather than the usual sixty cents.

A MARVEL GRAPHIC NOVEL

• *The Death Of Captain Marvel*

This title by Jim Starlin was the first of a new series of Marvel Graphic Novels. Running between forty-eight and ninety-six pages, these paperback books were an attempt to compete with the European-style graphic albums. They featured complete stories by top creators and measured eight-and-a-half by eleven inches. The format was used between 1982 and 1994, but eventually gave way to the more popular "bookshelf" format that was roughly the same dimensions as regular comic books.

- Marvel published *Dennis The Menace Digest* #1, reprinting Hank Ketchum's famous comic-strip in ninety-six-paged paperback books.
- Although the first issue of *G.I. Joe,* by editor Larry Hama and artist Herb Trimpe, was cover-dated July, April saw the first ever television adverts for a comic when it was featured on television.

JUNE

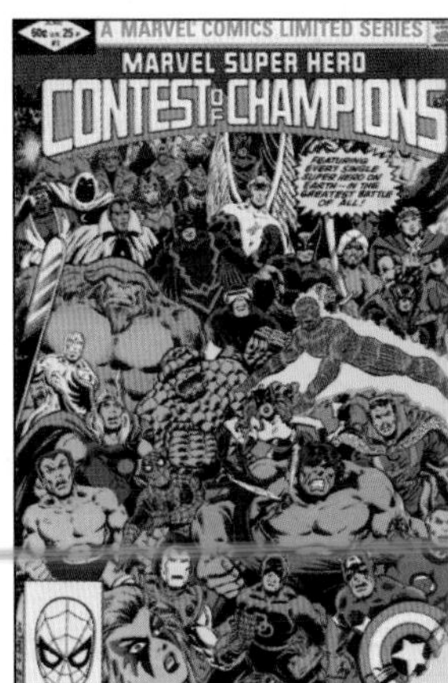

INSPIRED BY SPORT

• *Contest Of Champions* #1

In celebration of the 1980 Moscow Olympics, Marvel began work on a special sixty-four-paged comic that pitted its heroes in various competitions. Unfortunately, the United States decided to boycott the event after the Soviet Union invaded Afghanistan. Since most of the comic had already been pencilled and scripted, Marvel decided to publish it after sufficient time had passed. Plotted by Mark Gruenwald, Steven Grant, and Bill Mantlo, and pencilled by John Romita Jr., *Contest Of Champions* #1 eventually saw print in June, 1982. The re-worked story centered on a cosmic game between the Grandmaster and Death for the life of the Grandmaster's brother, the Collector.

M In a deal similar to the one with Hasbro, the Ideal Toy Company commissioned Marvel to develop *Team America*, which was roughly based on their line of Evel Knievel stunt racing toys.

SEPTEMBER

HERCULES TRAVELS THE UNIVERSE

• *Hercules, Prince of Power* #1

Written and drawn by Bob Layton, *Hercules, Prince of Power* was a four-issue limited series set in the twenty-fourth century. Temporarily exiled from Olympus, Hercules explored the universe with a robotic Rigellian scout called the Recorder. He confronted Galactus and provided the planet-eater—who found him to be an amusing buffoon—with his first laugh in millennia.

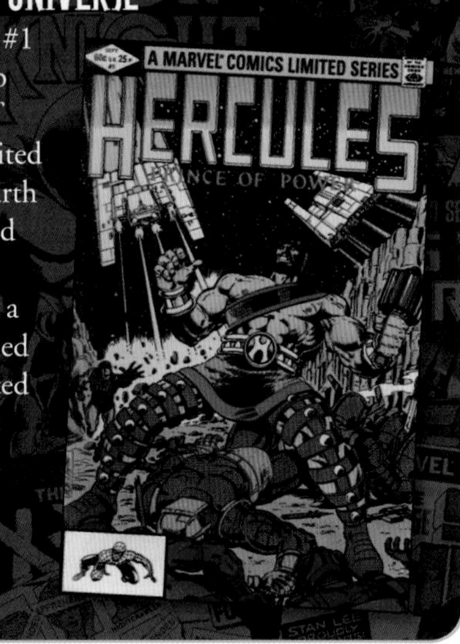

WOLVERINE GETS HIS OWN TITLE

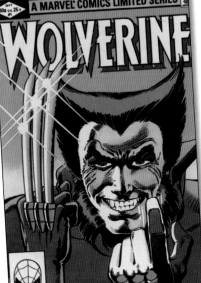

• *Wolverine* #1

The most popular member of the X-Men was finally featured in his first solo title, a four-issue limited series by writer Chris Claremont and writer/artist Frank Miller. *Wolverine* introduced the character's most famous catch phrase, "I am the best at what I do." The story began in the Canadian wilderness and ended in Tokyo where Wolverine learned that the woman he loved, Mariko Yashida, had been forced to marry another out of a sense of obligation to her father. He battled legions of Ninja assassins and eventually managed to set her free. The story ended with an invitation for the X-Men to the wedding of Wolverine and Mariko.

NOVEMBER

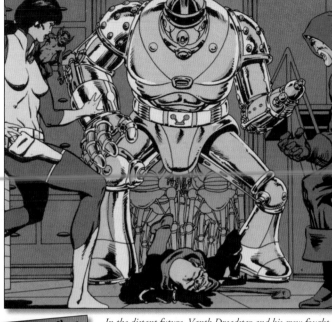

In the distant future, Vanth Dreadstar and his crew fought against the Church of the Instrumentality, which was led by th evil Lord High Papal.

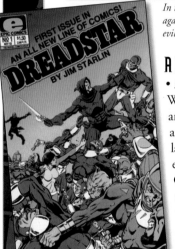

A NEW LINE JUST FOR COMIC STORES

• *Dreadstar* #1

With the growing number of comic-book stor and the success of *Epic Illustrated* and the first Marvel Graphic Novels, Marvel launched an entire new line that was targeted exclusively at comic-book stores. Marvel's Ep Comics Group imprint allowed creators to retain ownership of their work and guarante them a share in the profits. The first title produced for this line was *Dreadstar*, a space opera by writer/artist Jim Starlin.

BERNIE DISCOVERS CAP'S IDENTITY

• *Captain America* #275

When a neo-Nazi group arranged a demonstration in New York, Steve Rogers' girlfriend Bernie Rosenthal convinced him to attend a counter-demonstration. When violence erupted, Steve sneaked off to change into Cap to stop the fight. Bernie recognized his voice and realized that her boyfriend was secretly Captain America. At first she was shocked, but she later asked him to marry her.

M *Vision And The Scarlet Witch* #1 starred these two eponymous Avengers in a four-issue series by Bill Mantlo and Rick Leonardi

DECEMBER

KING KULL IN A SOLO TITLE

• *Kull The Conqueror* #1

This title by writer Alan Zelenetz and artist John Buscema was Marvel's third attempt to launch a successful monthly title based or Robert E. Howard's Barbarian king. The story "The Phoenix On T Sword" was a rewrite of an early Kull story, "By This Axe, I Rule."

M Marvel published *Smurfs* #1, the first of three issues based on th internationally popular characters, created by the cartoonist Pey

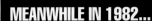

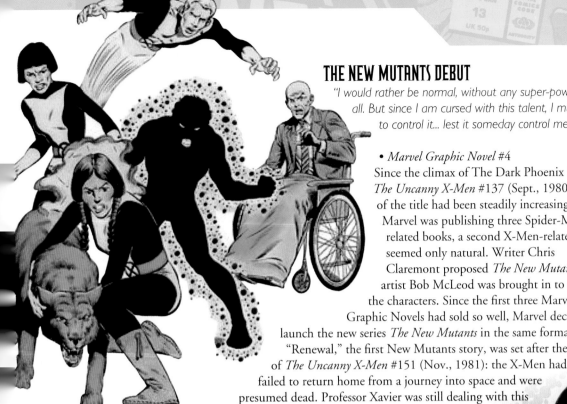

THE NEW MUTANTS DEBUT

"I would rather be normal, without any super-powers at all. But since I am cursed with this talent, I must learn to control it... lest it someday control me."

• *Marvel Graphic Novel* #4

Since the climax of The Dark Phoenix Saga in *The Uncanny X-Men* #137 (Sept., 1980), sales of the title had been steadily increasing. Since Marvel was publishing three Spider-Man-related books, a second X-Men-related title seemed only natural. Writer Chris Claremont proposed *The New Mutants* and artist Bob McLeod was brought in to design the characters. Since the first three Marvel Graphic Novels had sold so well, Marvel decided to launch the new series *The New Mutants* in the same format.

"Renewal," the first New Mutants story, was set after the events of *The Uncanny X-Men* #151 (Nov., 1981): the X-Men had failed to return home from a journey into space and were presumed dead. Professor Xavier was still dealing with this terrible loss when his associate Moria MacTaggert asked him to help train fourteen-year-old Rahne Sinclair, a shape-shifting mutant called Wolfsbane. Xavier was already attempting to teach Xi'an Coy Manh/Karma, another young mutant, how to hone her ability to mentally possess other people's bodies. Tired of training mutants only to send them to their deaths, Xavier was hesitant to take on new students, but he changed his mind when Danielle Moonstar/Mirage, the mutant granddaughter of an old friend, also needed his help in using her ability to create illusions.

Xavier soon found himself leading a new team of young mutants after he also agreed to tutor Samuel Guthrie/Cannonball, who could propel himself through the air like a human cannonball, and Roberto da Costa/Sunspot, a Brazilian able to transform into a mass of super-strong dark energy that could expel heat.

MEANWHILE IN 1982...

CONFLICT IN THE FALKLANDS
Argentina surrenders to Britain after three months of battle for sovereignty of the Falklands.

HRH PRINCE WILLIAM IS BORN
Princess Diana gives birth to Prince William Arthur Philip Louis, who is second in line to the British throne.

PRINCESS GRACE DIES
Princess Grace of Monaco, formerly Grace Kelly, dies in a car crash in Monaco.

THE "VALLEY GIRL" LOOK
Teen fashions draw inspiration from professional dancers as girls adopt leg-warmers, headbands, and the rediscovered 1960s mini skirt.

THE RUBIK'S CUBE
Erno Rubik's colorful cube puzzle sweeps across America.

AND AT THE MOVIES...
ET, *an alien is befriended by a young boy in Steven Spielberg's extraterrestrial fairytale;* Gandhi, *Richard Attenborough's stunning biography of the Indian peace activist;* Blade Runner, *a futuristic thriller that follows a detective hunting down human-looking androids.*

THE NEW CAPTAIN MARVEL

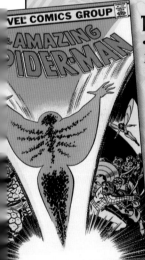

• *The Amazing Spider-Man Annual* #16

Monica Rambeau was a lieutenant in the New Orleans harbor patrol. When an old family friend asked her for help, she was accidentally bombarded by unknown forces from another dimension and gained the ability to convert her body into any form of energy. She used these new powers to fight crime and the media started to call her Captain Marvel. Created by writer Roger Stern and artist John Romita Jr., this new Captain Marvel soon went to New York to ask the Avengers to teach her how to control her new abilities. She became a full member of the team in *The Avengers* #231 (May, 1983) and replaced the Wasp as team leader in *The Avengers* #279 (May, 1987).

THE ORIGIN OF WILL O'THE WISP

• *The Amazing Spider-Man* #235

Will O'the Wisp was created for *The Amazing Spider-Man* #167 (April, 1977), but little was known about him until writer Roger Stern and artist John Romita Jr. told his origin story in this issue. Jackson Arvad was an overworked scientist. Pushed to exhaustion by a demanding boss, he was exposed to a high-frequency electromagnetic field that caused the molecules in his body to separate from one another. He soon learned he could control his density and hypnotize others.

Monica Rambeau, the new Captain Marvel, could project various types of energy while in human form. She also possessed enhanced physical strength and the ability to fly.

MY FAMILY ARE PEOPLE OF *HONOR* AND COURAGE, PROFESSOR. YOU'LL FIND *I'M* CAST FROM THE SAME *MOLD*!

1983

AN EVER-EVOLVING UNIVERSE

Never content to rest on his laurels, Editor-in-Chief Jim Shooter briefly flirted with the idea of shaking up the entire Marvel Universe and re-launching all the titles from scratch. Brand new characters, using the same familiar names, would be given updated origins and costumes, in a similar way to what DC Comics had done with the new Flash and Green Lantern in the 1950s. After a few discussions with his top creative people, Shooter was convinced to abandon the idea. However, word of it leaked out and outraged fans sent in letters of protest. Shooter addressed these concerns in the February *Bullpen Bulletins*, assuring fans that their beloved characters were safe, but he also warned that change was the "essence" of the Marvel Universe. Ironically, Marvel eventually did introduce new versions of their characters when the company began publishing *Ultimate Spider-Man* #1 in 2000 to great acclaim. Shooter was, it seems, years ahead of his time.

The editorial staff also changed in 1983. Mark Gruenwald, Ralph Macchio, and Carl Potts all became editors, and Tom DeFalco was promoted to executive editor, which involved developing new titles and overseeing special projects like Marvel's adaptations of *Indiana Jones And The Temple Of Doom*.

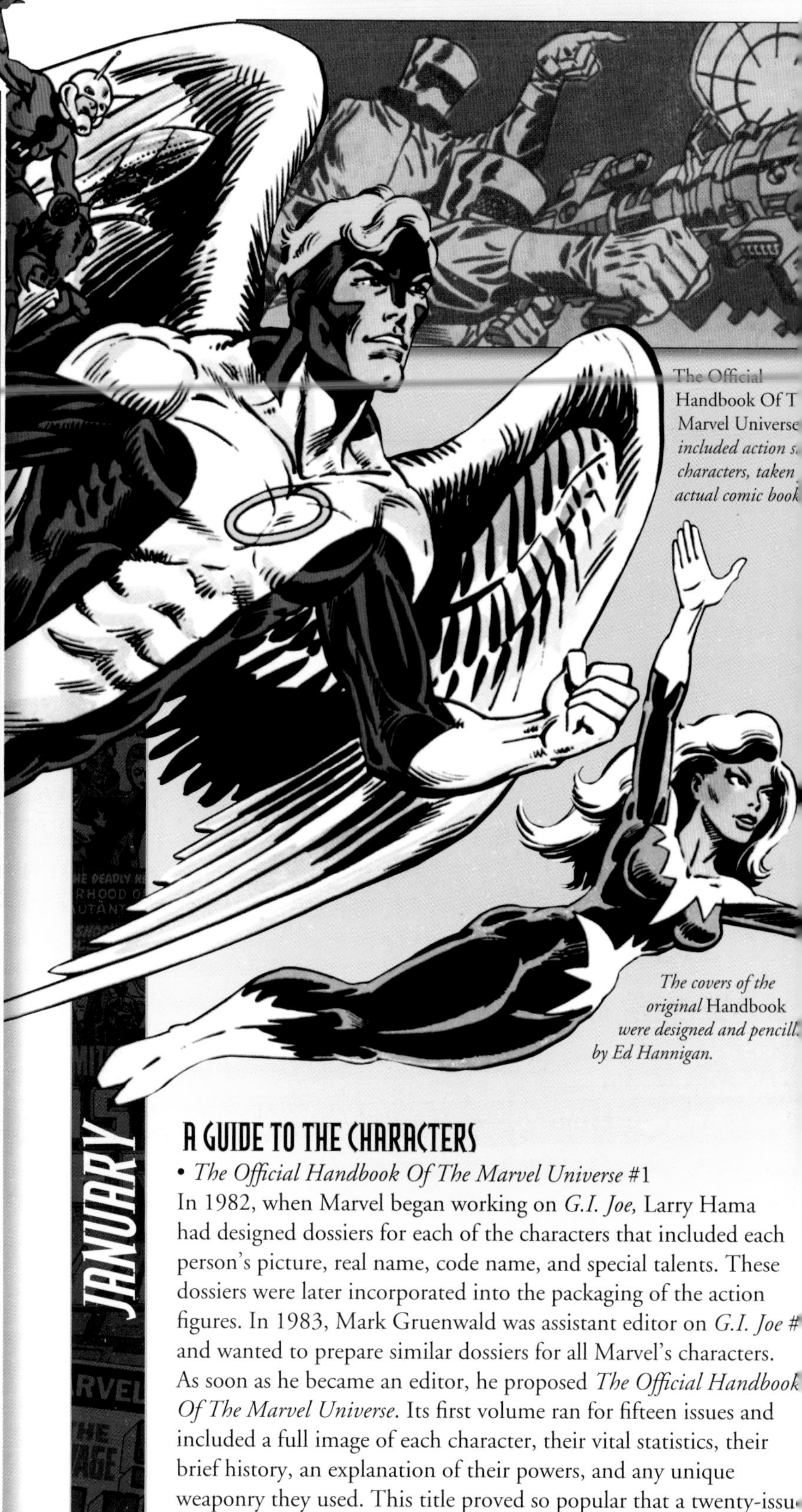

The Official Handbook Of T Marvel Universe *included action s characters, taken actual comic book*

The covers of the original Handbook *were designed and pencill by Ed Hannigan.*

JANUARY

A GUIDE TO THE CHARACTERS

• *The Official Handbook Of The Marvel Universe* #1

In 1982, when Marvel began working on *G.I. Joe,* Larry Hama had designed dossiers for each of the characters that included each person's picture, real name, code name, and special talents. These dossiers were later incorporated into the packaging of the action figures. In 1983, Mark Gruenwald was assistant editor on *G.I. Joe* # and wanted to prepare similar dossiers for all Marvel's characters. As soon as he became an editor, he proposed *The Official Handbook Of The Marvel Universe*. Its first volume ran for fifteen issues and included a full image of each character, their vital statistics, their brief history, an explanation of their powers, and any unique weaponry they used. This title proved so popular that a twenty-issu second edition was released in 1985, along with an eight-issue update in 1989, and a thirty-six-issue Master Edition in 1990. In 2008, Marvel began publishing the *Handbook* as a twelve-volume set of 240-paged hardcover books.

THE MARVEL NO-PRIZE BOOK

• *The Official Marvel No-Prize Book* #1

Stan Lee had started awarding the coveted "Marvel No-Prize" in the early 1960s to readers who spotte mistakes. *The Official Marvel No-Prize Book* published some of the famous blunders, like the time Cap shouted, "Only one of us is going to wa out of here under his own steam… and it won't be me!" in *Tales Of Suspense* #92 (Aug., 1967).

INTRODUCING THE HOBGOBLIN

"Norman Osborn may have died, but his legacy—his power—will live on! And this time it shall be shaped by a man who knows how to use power!"

• *The Amazing Spider-Man* #238
Norman Osborn, the original Green Goblin, had died in *The Amazing Spider-Man* #122 (July, 1973). Since fans were always clamoring for the return of old Super Villains, writer Roger Stern decided to meet them halfway. He introduced a new character who would steal the Goblin's old equipment and update it. While seeking safety in the sewers, an escaping bank robber stumbled upon one of Osborn's old hideouts. He contacted someone he knew would be interested. This someone murdered the bank robber, took the equipment, and designed a new costume for himself as the Hobgoblin. Using Osborn's old journals to guide him, he became one of Spider-Man's deadliest enemies.

Following Stan Lee's lead with the original Goblin, Stern had planned to keep the character's real identity secret for twenty-nine issues—one more than the original story line—and reveal it in issue #267 (Aug., 1985). But, Stern left the title earlier than that and the creative teams who followed him had their own ideas. Ned Leeds, who had married Peter Parker's former girlfriend Betty Brant, was accused in issue #289 (June, 1987), but Stern corrected that mistake when he returned to write the three-issue series *Spider-Man: Hobgoblin Lives* (1997), which revealed that the real culprit was Roderick Kingsley.

APRIL

THE GOBLIN QUEEN DEBUTS

• *The Uncanny X-Men* #168
Created by the X-Men's enemy Mister Sinister, Madelyne Pryor was a clone of Jean Grey, although this wasn't known at first. Since she bore a striking resemblance to Jean, Scott Summers became attracted to her. They married and had a son, but Scott abandoned them when the real Jean seemingly returned from the dead. Madelyne later became the Goblin Queen in issue #240 (Jan., 1989), and was determined to punish Scott.

JIM RHODES TAKES OVER AS IRON MAN

• *The Invincible Iron Man* #169
Jim Rhodes had first appeared in *The Invincible Iron Man* #118, but he had previously met Tony Stark in Vietnam. Through flashbacks, readers learned that Rhodes had been repairing his damaged helicopter when Stark arrived, still dressed in the bulky prototype armor from his origin story in *Tales Of Suspense* #39 (March, 1963). When Stark became Iron Man, he hired Rhodes to be his pilot.

As one of the few people who knew Tony's secret identity, Jim was the natural choice to replace him as Iron Man when Tony's problems with alcohol prevented him from doing the job. Jim continued in his role until *The Invincible Iron Man* #199 (Oct., 1985).

THE NEW MUTANTS IN THEIR OWN TITLE

• *The New Mutants* #1
After their initial appearance in *Marvel Graphic Novel* #4 (Dec., 1982), Professor Xavier's young students were given their own monthly title. It was written by Chris Claremont and drawn by Bob McLeod. Sal Buscema took over the pencilling chores with issue #4, followed by Bill Sienkiewicz, who illustrated #18 to #31. The New Mutants often battled the Hellions—mutant students under the instruction of Emma Frost. The title lasted one hundred issues and was replaced by *X-Force* in 1991, which featured many of the former New Mutants.

A MARVEL FAN MAGAZINE

• *Marvel Age* #1
As the number of comic-book stores grew, fans became more organized. Conventions and fan magazines devoted to comics also began to proliferate, but their coverage was not always favorable to Marvel. Jim Shooter decided it was time for Marvel to publish its own fan magazine. Very similar to the *Merry Marvel Messenger* of the late 1960s, *Marvel Age* featured news of future story lines, previews of artwork, articles about the characters, and interviews with Marvel creators. It also contained regular columns like Mark Gruenwald's *Mark's Remarks*. Initially priced at a mere twenty-five cents, *Marvel Age* ran for 140 issues.

Hobgoblin, who debuted in March in The Amazing Spider-Man *#238 used a flying bat-glider.*

MAY

INTRODUCING CALLISTO AND THE MORLOCKS

"As for why Angel's here—every princess must have a prince and, for me, who more fitting than the most beautiful man in all the world?"

• *The Uncanny X-Men* #169
When Angel's girlfriend found a trail of feathers and blood, she immediately called the X-Men for help. Employing a mutant-tracking device to find Angel, the team entered the subway system and kept descending until they reached the Alley, a huge tunnel under Manhattan that was built by the military in case of a nuclear war. It was here that the X-Men first encountered Callisto and the Morlocks, in this issue by writer Chris Claremont and artist Paul Smith.

Once beautiful, Callisto was now permanently scarred and missing her right eye. She was a mutant with enhanced senses and exceptional night vision and was the leader of the Morlocks. Named after the underground creatures in H.G. Wells' science-fiction novel *The Time Machine*, the Morlocks were unable to pass for normal humans because of the physical effects their mutations had had on their outward appearances, so they gathered underground in a large community of social outcasts.

Callisto had kidnapped Angel with the intention of forcing him to become her mate, but Storm defeated her in a duel for Angel's freedom and became the Morlocks' leader. However, Storm allowed Callisto to rule in her absence when she returned to the surface with the X-Men.

The evil geneticist Mister Sinister later sent his band of Marauders down into the Alley to murder the Morlocks in *The Mutant Massacre* (1988). This title was a company-wide crossover—a comic that combined characters from many different comics. Callisto, however, survived and her wounds were treated by Professor Xavier's associate Moira MacTaggart at her base on Muir Island.

In 2005, Callisto lost her mutant abilities at the conclusion of the mega-crossover, *The House Of M*, and then attempted to live a normal life.

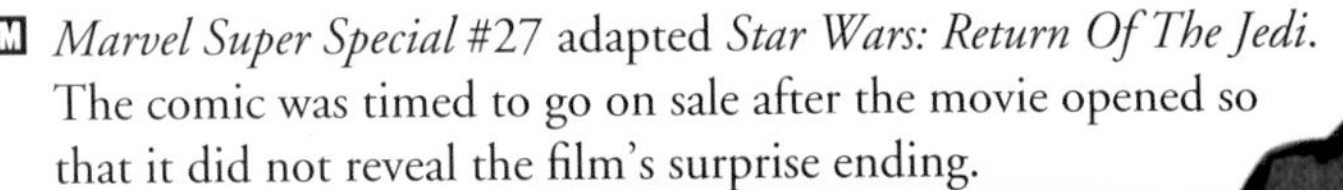

M *Marvel Super Special* #27 adapted *Star Wars: Return Of The Jedi*. The comic was timed to go on sale after the movie opened so that it did not reveal the film's surprise ending.

JUNE

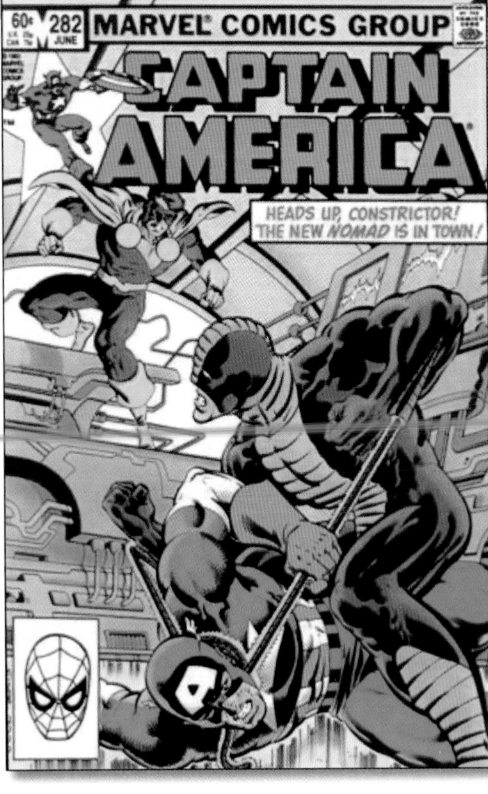

JACK MONROE BECOMES NOMAD

"C'mon, Jack—you volunteered for this job because you wanted to prove to yourself—and to Cap—that you could hold your own! That you're something more than an over-the-hill boy sidekick!"

• *Captain America* #282
In the 1950s, Jack Monroe had been a teenager. He joined a top-secret government program to become "Bucky" in *Young Men* #24 (Dec., 1953) and, with an unnamed partner who assumed Cap's role, went on to feature in all the Atlas Captain America stories of 1953 and 1954. Having been in suspended animation since the 1950s, Monroe was reawakened in *Captain America* #155 (Nov., 1972) by writer Steve Englehart and artist Sal Buscema. He and his partner battled the real Captain America, who they believed to be an imposter, and Jack was turned over to SHIELD. In this issue, Monroe was sent to rescue Cap, who had been captured by the criminal Viper. Nick Fury, the leader of SHIELD, suggested that, rather than go as Bucky, Jack should become Nomad—an identity that Cap had briefly assumed for issues #180–184 (Dec., 1974–April, 1975). After helping Cap escape, Nomad became his partner until issue #309 (Sep., 1985) and he reappeared intermittently after they no longer worked together. In 1990, Nomad was given his own four-issue limited series, written by Fabian Nicieza and illustrated by James Fry. Nomad assumed custody of a baby girl, whom he named Bucky. The miniseries proved popular enough for Nomad to be awarded his own monthly title in 1992, in which he and Bucky moved from town to town as urban vigilantes, dispensing frontier-style justice. Jack Monroe was ultimately assassinated i *Captain America* #7 (July, 200 by the Winter Soldier, who was revealed to b the original Bucky fro Timely's Captain Ameri stories of the 1940s.

Nomad had the strength, speed, endurance, and agility of an Olympic athl His first costume had a pair of stun discs on ea shoulder that could be used as throwing weap

A PARODY OF MARVEL

• *Marvel Tails Starring Peter Porker, The Spectacular Spider-Ham* #1
Put two Marvel editors together and anything could happen. Larry Hama and Tom DeFalco were discussing genres that Marvel no longer published. Both had an interest in funny animal comics, but neither thought they would sell to Super Hero fans. Not unless they could put a funny animal in a Spider-Man costume. Intrigued, they wrote a proposal and convinced Jim Shooter to approve the one-off comic *Marvel Tails Starring Peter Porker, The Spectacular Spider-Ham.*

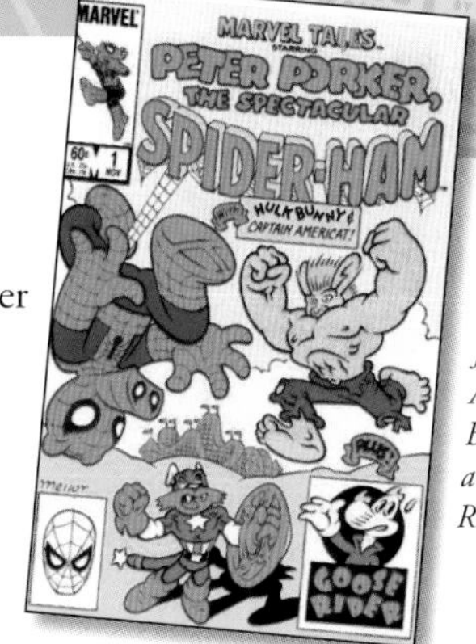

Along with Spider-Ham, Marvel Tails *#1 introduced J. Jonah Jackal, Captain Americat, and Hulk-Bunny, and featured a five-page "Goose Rider" story.*

ENTER BETA RAY BILL

"I... I can feel the power of the demon himself added to my own! Power enough to shake this planet to its foundations!"

• *The Mighty Thor* #337
This issue began a highly acclaimed run by writer/artist Walter Simonson that would last for nearly four years and end with issue #382 (Aug., 1987), which was also the 300th appearance of Thor since his introduction in *Journey Into Mystery* #83 (Aug., 1962).

Dr. Don Blake, aka Thor, was casually strolling through Chicago's Grant Park when he was taken into custody by two SHIELD agents. Their leader, Nick Fury, informed Blake that an alien ship was headed for their solar system—a ship that gathered fuel by sucking suns dry of energy! Thor was sent to investigate. He encountered a sentient spacecraft called Skuttlebutt and its guardian Beta Ray Bill. Bill belonged to an extraterrestrial race called the Korbinites, whose homeworld had been destroyed when their galaxy exploded. The surviving Korbinites fled in a fleet of spaceships in search of a new world. Beta Ray Bill, who had volunteered for an experiment that transferred his consciousness into the body of a mutated, beast-like cyborg, guarded the ship while the rest of the Korbinites were held in suspended animation for the duration of the flight.

Thor and Bill battled until the Thunder God became temporarily separated from his enchanted hammer and reverted to Don Blake. Picking up Blake's cane, Bill struck the ground and was transformed into a Thor-like version of himself. According to the hammer's enchantment, "Whosoever holds this hammer, if he be worthy, shall possess the power of Thor!" Bill, who had sacrificed himself to protect his race, was clearly worthy.

Odin later learnt of what was happening and in issue #339 (Jan., 1984) granted Bill his own enchanted hammer, called Stormbreaker. Beta Ray Bill continued to appear over the years and was even given his own six-issue limited series called *Stormbreaker: The Saga of Beta Ray Bill* (2005), during which his consciousness was transferred into the body of a man named Simon Walters.

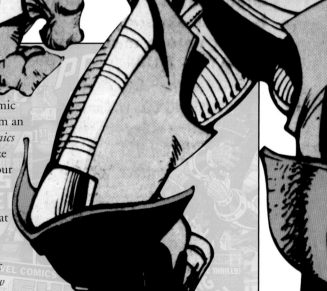

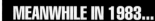

MEANWHILE IN 1983...

"STAR WARS" PROTECTION
The President announces an anti-Soviet-missile shield across America, dubbed "Star Wars."

FIRST US WOMAN IN SPACE
Sally K. Ride makes history as the first American woman to be launched into space.

A FINAL GOODBYE TO *M*A*S*H*
The final episode of M*A*S*H *airs and is the most-watched television episode in US history.*

KIDS' MASS MERCHANDISING
He-Man *launches the era of crossovers between television characters and mass merchandising.*

SUPER HERO-STYLE FEAT
Six men walk underwater across Sydney Harbor; 51.5 miles (82.9 km) in forty-eight hours.

AND AT THE MOVIES...
Scarface, *a ruthless Cuban rises to the top;* Trading Places, *a snooty investor and street panhandler find their positions reversed after a $1 bet.*

SHARING THE SECRETS OF COMICS

• *The Official Marvel Comics Try-Out Book*
Realizing that many comic book fans dreamt of becoming comic book professionals some day, Jim Shooter decided to give them an opportunity to prove their skills with *The Official Marvel Comics Try-Out Book.* Measuring eleven-by-seventeen inches—the size professionals used for their original artwork—the book had four fully written, drawn, colored, and lettered pages of a story. These were followed by an explanation of coloring, and four uncolored pages. The book allowed readers to test their skills at plotting, pencilling, inking, scripting, and lettering. Shooter also announced a contest that promised a trip to the Marvel offices. Mark Bagley won the pencilling competition and later went on to become the regular penciller on titles like *The New Warriors, The Amazing Spider-Man,* and *Ultimate Spider-Man.*

A MOMENT AGO, THEY HAD BEEN ON EARTH.
WHAT HAPPENED?!
WHERE THE DEVIL ARE WE?!
LET ME PUT IT THIS WAY CYKE--
--I DON'T THINK WE'RE IN KANSAS ANYMORE.
CUTE, BEAST, REAL CUTE. BUT WHO ARE THESE... PEOPLE?! WHAT DO THEY WANT WITH US?!
WE'RE SURROUNDED BY ARMED AND ARMORED WARRIORS, ANGEL, SO I DOUBT IT IS ANYTHING GOOD.

Phoenix: The Untold Story ***(April, 1984) Written by Chris Claremont, pencilled by John Byrne, and inked by Terry Austin.***
Chris Claremont was born in England in 1950 and settled in America in 1958. As a child he read English comics—mostly Eagle*—and was a big fan of* Dan Dare. *His first Marvel comic was* Fantastic Four *#49. During his first year of college in 1969, he got a job as a go-fer at Marvel, where he soon began selling plots to editor Roy Thomas and was assigned his own titles. Claremont probably created more original characters that anyone, except possibly Stan Lee. He was easily the most popular and influential comic book writer of the 1970s and 1980s and his work continues to entertain hundreds of thousands of readers every month.*

GO, LITTLE BROTHER! GUARD WELL THE ETERNAL FLAME AND RULE WISELY THE REALM OF OUR FATHERS!

1984

ASSISTANT EDITORS AND STRATEGIC ALLIANCES

The January-dated books in 1984 featured a company-wide event that became known as "Assistant Editors' Month." Editor-in-Chief Jim Shooter took all his editors on a two-week trip to attend major comic book conventions in Chicago and San Diego. He claimed that, in their absence, the assistant editors had assumed control of the office and were now in charge of all editorial content. Assistant Editors' Month was never intended to be real, but the assistants—led by Mike Carlin, who later became the editor of *Superman* at DC Comics—decided to take it seriously. The results ranged from a humorous story in *Marvel Team-Up* #137 that featured Aunt May as the new herald of Galactus, to the highly acclaimed "Kid Who Collects Spider-Man" story in *The Amazing Spider-Man* #248 (Jan., 1984).

In 1984, Marvel also cemented its relationship with Hasbro Toys by developing *Transformers*, just like it had done for G.I. Joe. Based on Marvel's success with Hasbro, Tomy Toys asked the company to develop another robotic line of toys called The Starriors. Marvel also entered into an agreement with the computer gaming company Adventure International and produced a Marvel-themed game series called *Questprobe* that starred the Hulk and Dr. Strange. And then, Marvel teamed up with Mattel to produce *Marvel Super Heroes Secret Wars.*

FEBRUARY

MOTHER SUPERIOR

• *Captain America* #290

The depraved Red Skull wanted an heir—someone to carry on his work in the unlikely event of his death. He fathered a child with a washerwoman, but almost killed it when he learned it was a girl. One of the Skull's assistants—Susan Scarbo/Mother Night—convinced him to let the child live. Scarbo volunteered to tutor Synthia Shmidt and hone her into a suitable heir. Synthia became the leader of the Sisters of Sin group and assumed the name of Mother Superior when she first appeared in this issue by writer J.M. DeMatteis and artist/writer Paul Neary. She later shortened her name to Sin.

An expert in explosives and a highly skilled marksman, Mother Superior was also a master of bladed weapons, interrogation, torture, and several martial arts.

Elektra's history with Daredevil began in a four-part series with *Elektra Saga* #1.

MARCH

A RETURN TO POWER

• *Hercules, Prince of Power #1*

The first *Hercules, Prince of Power* limited series (1982) sold so well that writer/artist Bob Layton was commissioned to do another. When Zeus had apparently gone mad and slain all the Gods of Olympus, Hercules returned home and attempted to subdue him. Hercules soon learned that this was all a charade and that the other Gods were not really dead—Zeus had just wanted to test whether Hercules would be worthy of siring a new race of Gods for a new world.

Marvel licensed the rights to publish a three-issue limited series based on the popular television show *The A-Team*.

THE FACES BEHIND THE COMICS

• *The Marvel Fumetti Book* #1

This fumetti title—"a story illustrated with photographs"—showed members of staff, along with popular freelancers like writer Chris Claremont, writer/artist John Byrne, and artist Walter Simonson, in humorous situations, and featured a centerfold of Stan Lee with his head on the Hulk's body.

A DIFFERENT ENDING FOR PHOENIX

• *Phoenix: The Untold Story* #1

Three years had passed since the death of Phoenix at the end of *X-Men* #137 (April, 1982) and fans were still angry over it. Jim Shooter decided to let them see what could have been. Not only were the faithful treated to the original ending of *X-Men* #137, in which Phoenix did not die, but they were also given an extended interview with the creators that explained all the behind-the-scenes events that had led to the controversial story.

MAY

THE ALIEN COSTUME SAGA

• *The Amazing Spider-Man* #252

A comic fan named Randy Schueller sent in an idea for a story in which Spider-Man got a black costume with a red spider emblem that enhanced his ability to stick to walls because it was made of unstable molecules—the material invented by Reed Richards. Jim Shooter bought the idea, but Schueller failed to write a publishable story based on it.

Later, Shooter remembered Schueller's idea and gave Spider-Man a new costume. Designed by Mike Zeck, it became a black-and-white alien symbiote that could produce unlimited webbing and respond to Spider-Man's thoughts. It first appeared in *The Amazing Spider-Man* #252, written by Roger Stern and Tom DeFalco and pencilled by Ron Frenz.

M *Marvel Comics Super Special* #30 adapted *Indiana Jones And The Temple Of Doom* to coincide with the movie's release.

THE FIRST COMPANY-WIDE CROSSOVER

"I am from beyond! Slay your enemies and all you desire shall be yours! Nothing you dream of is impossible for me to accomplish!"

• *Marvel Super Heroes Secret Wars* #1

Action figure toys had become big sellers in the early 1980s. The toy company Mattel produced action figures of Marvel's most popular characters and sold them with a lenticular lens that contained a secret code. Mattel just needed Marvel to come up with an editorial concept that would explain why all these characters had gathered together.

The response of Editor-in-Chief Jim Shooter was to publish the first company-wide crossover in the history of comics. Anchored by a twelve-issue limited series, other titles were tied into the main story.

For a couple of months, characters like Spider-Man and Professor Xavier sensed a mysterious danger. In the April-dated books, they journeyed to New York's Central Park where they found an alien structure, entered it, and vanished. *Marvel Super Heroes Secret Wars* #1 published in May, as all the heroes materialized in a different universe. They had been brought together by an all-powerful alien creature called the Beyonder, who had decided to pit them against their deadliest super-foes in a secret war. Meanwhile, in their own titles, the heroes returned, but some had experienced startling changes: the Hulk now had a broken leg and the Fantastic Four had replaced the Thing with the She-Hulk.

Spider-Man, the Hulk, the X-Men, the Avengers, and the Fantastic Four all appeared in Marvel Super Heroes Secret Wars.

JUNE

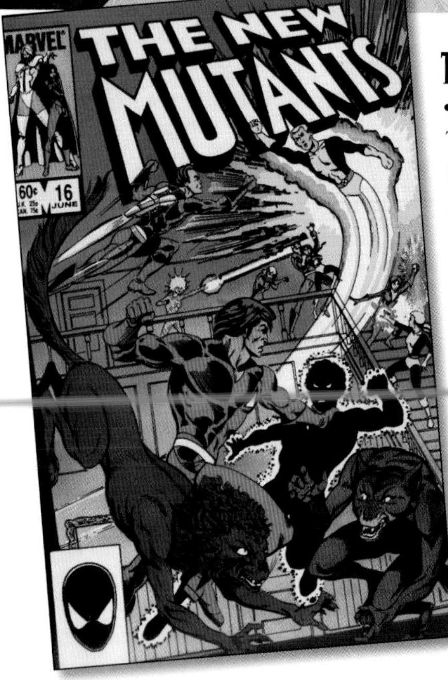

THE HELLIONS DEBUT

• *The New Mutants* #16

The students of Emma Frost's Massachusetts Academy—enemies of the New Mutants—were introduced in this issue. Dubbed the Hellions, they were Sharon Smith/Catseye, Manuel de la Roche/Empath, Haroun ibn Sallah al-Rashid/Jetstream, Jennifer Stavros/Roulette, Marie-Ange Colbert/Tarot, and James Proudstar/Thunderbird.

THE ROSE APPEARS

• *The Amazing Spider-Man* #253

If the Kingpin of Crime ran the underworld like a business, the Rose was middle management. Created by writer Tom DeFalco and artist Rick Leonardi, the villain tended his rose garden as he casually ran his various criminal enterprises. He wore a leather mask and tried to avoid direct conflict with Super Heroes like Spider-Man.

The Rose was eventually revealed to be Richard Fisk, the Kingpin of Crime's son.

AUGUST

FORGE DEBUTS

• *The Uncanny X-Men* #184

A brilliant weapons inventor, Forge was the man the government hired when Tony Stark stopped building munitions. Trained as a medicine man, Forge was a Native American mutant with a superhuman ability to invent and instantly understand mechanical devices. After losing his right leg and right hand in combat, he built cybernetic replacements that contained concealed weapons. In this issue by writer Chris Claremont and artist John Romita Jr., Forge was hired by the government to design a weapon capable of removing a mutant's powers. He accidentally shot Storm, causing her to temporarily lose her powers. The pair later went on to have a rocky romantic relationship.

AUGUST

TERMINUS APPEARS

• *Fantastic Four* #269

Writer/artist John Byrne had reinvigorated Marvel's first family when he began his critically acclaimed run with *Fantastic Four* #232 (July, 1981). Byrne wanted to introduce a huge cosmic thug into the Marvel Universe so, for issue #269, he created Terminus. Employing a 240-foot power lance, this armored giant announced his presence by burning a message across America in letters a half-mile wide, "I claim this world—Terminus."

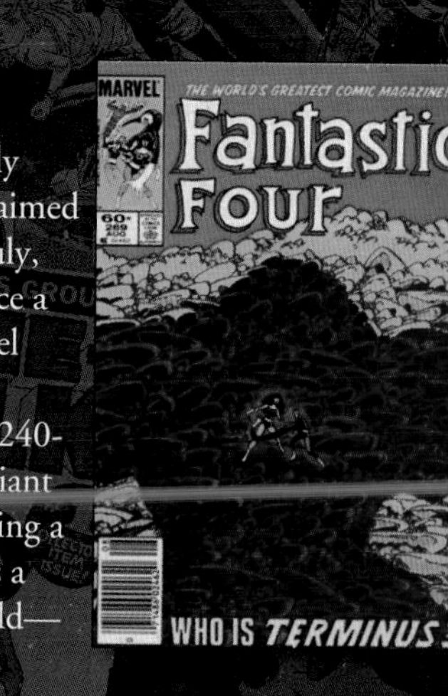

INTRODUCING THE POWER PACK

"I can split up my powers among you. And you will not have to ask permission to save your own world!"

• *Power Pack* #1

Louise Jones had begun her comic book career at Warren Publishing working on titles like *Creepy* and *Eerie*. She became an editor at Marvel in 1980 and later married writer/artist Walter Simonson. After leaving her editing job in 1983, she became a freelance writer under her married name, Louise Simonson. Working with artist June Brigman, who went on to draw the newspaper comic strip *Brenda Starr*, Louise created the preteen Super-Hero team called Power Pack.

Dr. James Power was a physicist who invented a device that could generate energy from anti-matter. Unfortunately, his device was faulty and was liable to start a chain action and destroy the Earth. Aelfyre Whitemane, an extraterrestrial who resembled a horse, learned of the problem, but before he could fix it, he was mortally wounded by rival aliens, who kidnapped James and his wife, Margaret, because they wanted his invention.

The dying Aelfyre bestowed his alien powers and his "smartship"—a sentient starship called Friday—on the Power children, who became the Power Pack. Twelve-year-old Alex became able to control gravity; ten-year-old Julie could fly, leaving a trail of colored lights behind her; eight-year-old Jack could compress his mass to shrink his size or expand into a giant cloud; and five-year-old Katie could absorb energy and discharge it in concussive blasts. However, on at least two occasions, the children switched powers with each other and had to learn to master their new abilities all over again.

Power Pack *#1 also introduced the reptilian race, the Zn'rx, whom Whitemane nicknamed the "Snarks," after the monster in Lewis Carroll's poem* The Hunting of the Snark.

FIRST APPEARANCE OF PUMA

• *The Amazing Spider-Man* #256

Tom DeFalco and Ron Frenz created Puma, an updated version of Kraven the Hunter, in *The Amazing Spider-Man* #256. The Native American Thomas Fireheart was the result of centuries of selective breeding and mystical ceremonies. As well as transforming into the mountain lion-like Puma, he was also the CEO of a global corporation. Charged with being the guardian of his people, the Puma frequently freelanced as a mercenary to keep his skills sharp.

Possessing superhuman strength and enhanced senses, the Puma could track anyone anywhere.

A NEW BRANCH OF THE AVENGERS

• *West Coast Avengers* #1

As the Earth's mightiest heroes, the Avengers considered it their responsibility to protect the entire world. Their base in New York City limited their ability to respond quickly to a crisis on the other side of the planet. Since many countries would balk at the idea of allowing the mostly American Avengers to establish a presence on their soil, the team decided to open a branch on the West Coast of the USA.

Hawkeye and his new wife, Mockingbird, were given the job of running the West Coast branch in this issue. The initial four-issue limited series proved so popular that it become a regular monthly book that ran for 102 issues.

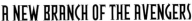

- *Prince Namor, The Sub-Mariner* #1 began a four-issue limited series by J.M. DeMatteis and Bob Budiansky that involved a confrontation with the United Nations about pollution.
- Initially conceived as a four-issue limited series, *Transformers* #1 published. The title went on to last eighty issues and spawn a handful of related limited series.

MACHINE MAN RETURNS

• *Machine Man* #1

Created by Jack Kirby in *2001: A Space Odyssey* #8 (July, 1977), X-51, aka Machine Man, was a living robot who was re-launched in 1984 by Tom DeFalco, Herb Trimpe, and Barry Windsor-Smith.

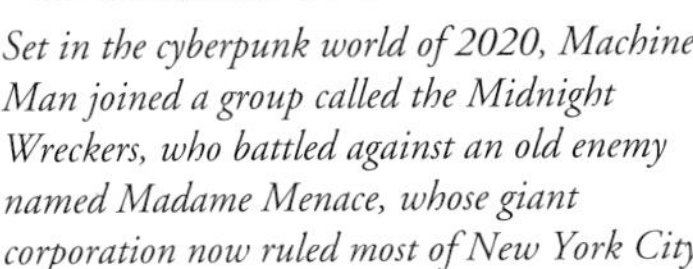

Set in the cyberpunk world of 2020, Machine Man joined a group called the Midnight Wreckers, who battled against an old enemy named Madame Menace, whose giant corporation now ruled most of New York City.

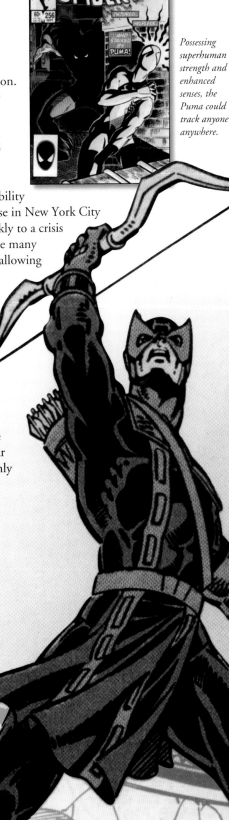

MEANWHILE IN 1984...

REAGAN IN LANDSLIDE VICTORY
President Ronald Reagan is elected for a second term—carrying forty-nine of the fifty States—over the Democratic candidate, former Vice President, Walter Mondale.

"GREENHOUSE EFFECT" WARNINGS
Concern is growing about the increasing burning of fossil fuels for energy and the resulting carbon dioxide, which some suggest is affecting the Earth's climate.

FIRST SOLO TRANSATLANTIC BALLOON FLIGHT
Joseph W. Kittinger flies into the history books when he travels for four days across the Atlantic suspended from a hydrogen balloon.

BAND AID FOUNDED
In reaction to famine in Ethiopia, Bob Geldof and Midge Ure found Band Aid and record the song Do They Know It's Christmas?

APPLE'S PERSONAL COMPUTER
Apple's Mackintosh 128k, *the first personal computer with a mouse and graphical user interface, goes on sale.*

RAP MUSIC AND BREAK-DANCING
Rap music reaches the mainstream and break-dancing hits the streets, in part thanks to the movies Beat Street *and* Breakin'.

MIAMI VICE
The first episode of the iconic cop show broadcasts and combines film-like production values with MTV-style music-video sequences.

AND AT THE MOVIES...
The Terminator, *James Cameron's stylish "tech noir" places Arnie center-stage as the robotic assassin sent back in time to terminate a future resistance leader;* A Nightmare On Elm Street, *Wes Craven's signature film, a creative combination of horror and humor, unleashes a new monster, Freddy Krueger, into the popular psyche;* Ghostbusters, *Dan Aykroyd's ghostbusting team sets up business in NYC to flush out all the spooks in this supernatural comedy;* This Is Spinal Tap, *Rob Reiner's cult mockumentary follows life on the road with a dim-witted heavy rock band.*

BUT... BUT HE ***IS THE REAL WORLD***, MS. WELSH. JOHNNY STORM IS THE GREATEST HERO EVER!

1985

SEQUELS, SERGIO, AND SADNESS

Mattel's Marvel Super Heroes Secret Wars action figures did not have much of a marketing campaign behind them, but that didn't matter as far as the comics were concerned—*Marvel Super Heroes Secret Wars* proved to be Marvel's best-selling title of the year. Jim Shooter immediately approved an eight-issue sequel that appeared across numerous titles and showed the Beyonder coming to Earth.

Marvel's Epic Comics imprint also launched their longest running and most successful title, *Groo The Wanderer*. It was drawn by Sergio Aragonés (whose cartoons regularly appeared in *MAD Magazine* and on television) and was written by Mark Evanier (the former fan who had suggested the ranks of the Merry Marvel Marching Society back in the 1960s and was now a successful television writer). The character Groo had first appeared in *Destroyer Duck* (1982), which had been published to raise money for a lawsuit against Marvel. *Groo The Wanderer* lasted for 120 issues, two graphic novels, and several trade paperback reprints before moving to the company Image Comics in 1994.

The Bullpen suffered two major losses in 1985. Longtime letterer and production man, Morrie Kuramoto, passed away of a heart attack aged 64 and beloved art/production supervisor and top letterer Danny Crespi died of leukemia at 59.

APRIL

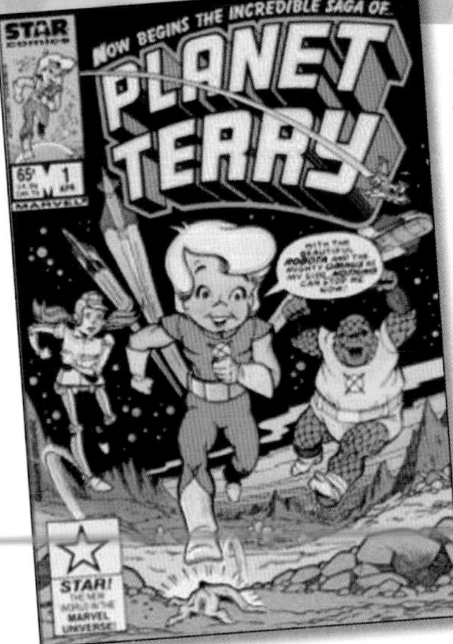

A NEW CHILDREN'S IMPRIN

• *Planet Terry* #1

Harvey Comics, one of Marvel's competitors who specialized in comics for young readers like *Casper Th Friendly Ghost* and *Hot Stuff* had ceased publication and was up for sale. A deal was struck for Marvel to buy it. The plan was that executive editor Tom DeFalco would serve as a quasi-Editor-in-Chief of the new titles, but longtime Harvey editor Sid Jacobson would continue to edit them. Jacobson was a former songwriter and had written novels like *Streets Of Gold*. In anticipation of the deal, he moved into the Marvel offices and set up shop. But the deal kept getting delayed and never actually happened. Undaunted, Marvel decided to go ahead with its own children's line under DeFalco and Jacobson. Marvel created new characters and licensed the rights to other popular properties under the name of Star Comics.

The new titles from Star Comics were *Wally The Wizard*, the adventures of a young wizard during feudal times; *Top Dog*, a brilliant talking dog and his pet boy; *Royal Roy*, a rich prince in the then-present day; *Planet Terry*, a young space explorer; *Meet Misty*, about Millie the Model's niece, who took up where she had left off and *Sweet XVI* (Sixteen), about teenagers in Roman times.

Some of the properties that Star Comics licensed from other companies were *Alf*, a then-popular television show; *Heathcliff*, a popular newspaper comic-strip cat; *Care Bears*, from greeting cards and television; and *Barbie*, Mattel's popular fashion doll.

Although the children's line continued well into 1995, it stopped calling itself Star Comics in March, 1988 and simply became part of the Marvel line in the hopes that the titles would get better newsstand distribution.

MAY

ENTER SCOURGE

• *The Invincible Iron Man* #194

The Scourge of the Underworld was a serial killer. His targets were all Super Villains, but that was the only pattern he followed—everything else changed, including his sex. The character first appeared in this issue by writer Denny O'Neil and artist Luke McDonnell, but was actually created by Mark Gruenwald, who convinced other Marvel writers to allow Scourge to appear in their titles and kill off their minor Super Villains. In the twenty-four years since *Fantastic Four* #1, many Super Villains had been created but some of them were rather lame, so writers devised story lines that eliminated the bad ones at the hands of the Scourge.

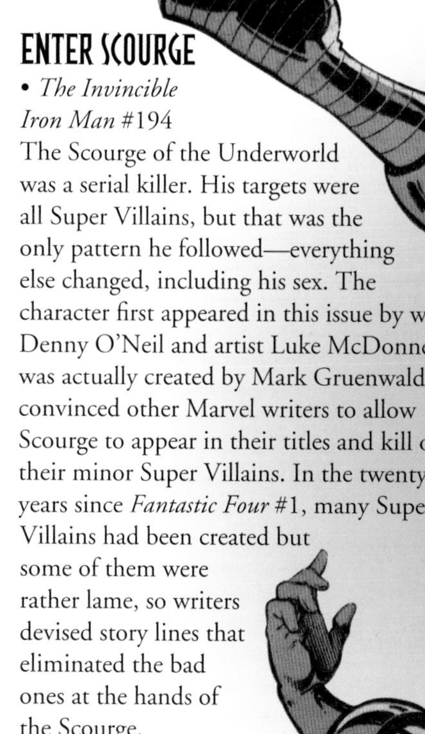

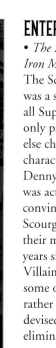

Scourge worked for the Angel, the former star of Timely Comic's Marvel Mystery Comics.

MAY

PETER PORKER GETS HIS OWN TITLE

• *Peter Porker, The Spectacular Spider-Ham* #1
Larry Hama and Tom DeFalco were called into the office of Jim Galton, the President of Marvel. The sales of *Marvel Tails* #1 (Nov., 1983) had been so good that Marvel's newsstand distributor wanted to know when he could expect the next issue. And so work was immediately begun on *Peter Porker, The Spectacular Spider-Ham* #1.

FIRESTAR PREVIEWS IN *X-MEN*

"I can't blame normal humans for fearing and distrusting mutants! We're freaks! Monsters! I hate the power which I can feel growing within me! I hate it!"

• *X-Men* #193
Marvel Productions had created the character Firestar for the animated television series *Spider-Man And His Amazing Friends*. Her name was Angelica Jones and she had heat powers similar to the Human Torch. Aside from the fact that she was a former X-Men member, Angelica's past was a blank slate. That was, at least, until Tom DeFalco and Mary Wilshire fleshed out her backstory in the four-issue *Firestar* limited series in 1986.

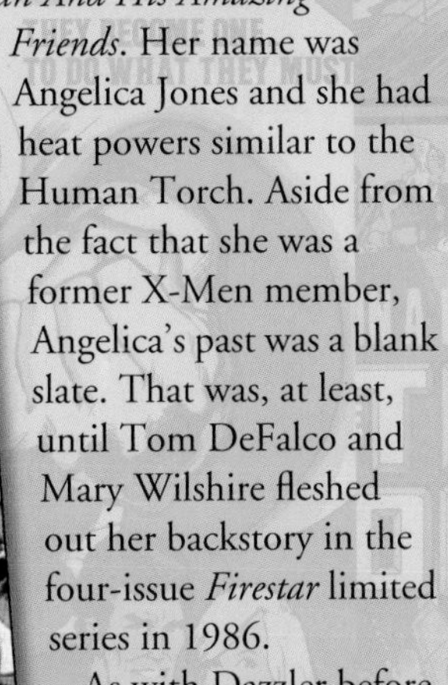

As with Dazzler before her, it was decided to whet the public's appetite for Firestar before her series premiered, so she first saw print in *X-Men* #193. Although published ten months later, the story line of the first two issues of her limited series occurred earlier than *X-Men* #193 and the last two happened after it. On the first page of her limited series, readers learned that Angelica bore the mark of a mutant—the letter "M" formed by the lines in the palm of her hand. Unknown to the anxious readers who were checking their own palms, most people have a vague "M." When Angelica began to exhibit her mutant powers, her befuddled widowed father didn't know what to do with her. Emma Frost solved the problem when she offered Angelica a full scholarship to the Massachusetts Academy. Under Emma's tutelage, Angelica became a member of the Hellions and learnt that her powers were based on microwaves. Realizing the advantages of these powers, Frost decided that Angelica would make a perfect assassin for the Hellfire Club. Firestar later became a founding member of the New Warriors and eventually joined the Avengers.

M Star Comics released *Ewoks* #1, a comic based on the furry characters from the *Star Wars* films and their popular animated television series.

JUNE

SILVER SABLE DEBUTS

• *The Amazing Spider-Man* #265
Based in the Balkan country of Symkaria—which bordered Dr. Doom's Latveria—Ernst Sablinova began hunting Nazi war criminals shortly after World War II. His daughter, Silver Sable, later took over the family business, but realizing that there were not many war criminals left, she and her Wild Pack began selling their services to major corporations, small countries, and wealthy individuals. Supplying bodyguards, mercenaries, and investigators, Silver Sable International became the major contributor to Symkaria's economy. Silver Sable first appeared in this issue by writer Tom DeFalco and artist Ron Frenz and in 1992 went on to star in her own monthly comic.

The Amazing Spider-Man #265 introduced the Black Fox, an aging international jewel thief who plagued Spider-Man on many occasions.

JULY

MALICE STRIKES SUSAN

• *Fantastic Four* #280
The Dark Phoenix Saga (Jan., 1980) had outraged fans by killing off one of their favorite characters. Wanting to do a story that evoked similar feelings, writer/artist John Byrne introduced Malice. Susan Richards was exposed to the Hate-Monger's Hate Ray. Secretly controlled by the Hate-Monger's master—the Psycho-Man—Susan adopted the new identity of Malice and viciously attacked the rest of the Fantastic Four, molding her invisible force-field into deadly spikes and razor-sharp knives. After freeing herself from the Psycho-Man's control, Susan changed her name from the Invisible Girl to the Invisible Woman. The Malice identity briefly resurfaced in the 1990s, but was expelled from Susan's mind by her son, Franklin.

LONGSHOT APPEARS FOR THE FIRST TIME

"Those troops want me bad! I wish I knew why! All their shots are missing me. But that's impossible! Either I'm already dead... or I've suddenly become wildly lucky!"

• *Longshot* #1

Editor Ann Nocenti wanted to introduce a character who was a clean slate. One with no history, no past, and no prejudices. A man without a memory. With Arthur Adams and Whilce Portacio providing the art, Nocenti wrote the six-issue limited series *Longshot*.

When readers first saw Longshot, soldiers were trying to kill him and he couldn't remember why. Nothing looked familiar, not even his own face. While fleeing, he chanced upon a warp in time and space that whisked him to upstate New York. Filled with innocence and exuberance, he studied his new surroundings. He did not recognize the sun and even mistook some storefront mannequins for real women. A gifted acrobat with superhuman agility, he was nicknamed "Longshot" because he had the ability to affect probability so that he had more than his share of good luck. In New York, Longshot stumbled upon a dog-like creature named Magog, who had actually been one of his pursuers and later turned against him. He also befriended Ricochet Rita, a professional stuntwoman.

Longshot eventually learned that he was an artificial man who had been created in a dimension known as the Mojoverse. Produced to be a slave, he had joined a rebellion against his masters, a race of aliens called the Spineless Ones. With the help of Dr. Strange, Longshot returned home to continue the revolution. He later returned to Earth in *The X-Men Annual* #10 (1986) and briefly joined the team. He became romantically involved with Dazzler and in *X-Factor* #33 (Sep., 2008) he joined the X-Factor team.

SHARON VENTURA

• *The Thing* #27

Sharon Ventura wanted to be a wrestler in the Unlimited Class Wrestling Federation, a league that featured super-powered wrestlers like the Thing. A promoter named Curtiss Jackson, who was also known as the Power Broker, had developed a process that created superhuman wrestlers and Sharon volunteered for it in this issue by writer Mike Carlin and artist Ron Wilson. However, she did not realize that Jackson addicted his test subjects to a drug and forced them to commit crimes to feed their habit. She managed to escape before Jackson exposed her to the drug and later began calling herself Ms. Marvel. At the Thing's urging, she briefly joined the Fantastic Four in the 1980s, and in *Fantastic Four* #310 (Jan., 1988), she was exposed to cosmic rays that mutated her into a female version of the Thing.

MARVEL
CAPTAIN AMERICA
IN THE ARMS OF ANACONDA!

A UNION FOR CRIMINALS

• *Captain America* #310

Seth Voelker missed his vocation as a labor organizer. Instead, he became the Super Villain called Sidewinder in *Marvel Two-In-One* #64 (June, 1980). He possessed a cloak that discharged stunning blasts of electricity and enabled him to teleport. Realizing that freelance criminals had no medical insurance or retirement plans, Voelker formed the Serpent Society in this issue written by Mark Gruenwald and pencilled by Paul Neary. It functioned like a union for super-criminals with serpent-themed powers or names like Sidewinder, Anaconda, Black Mamba, Death Adder, and Cobra. The Society provided its members with medical benefits, defense attorneys, hideouts, access to improved technology, and even helped them find criminal jobs in exchange for a fixed percentage of every crime they committed.

INTRODUCING MOJO

• *Longshot* #3

Mojo—who aged and corrupted everything he touched—was the ruler of an alien dimension called the Mojoverse. His people were the Spineless Ones who used motorized platforms because they were too obese to walk. Access to television transmissions had made the population so obsessed with entertainment that they created a slave race to provide it for them. Mojo frequently battled the New Mutants and X-Men.

- *Care Bears* #1 featured the stars of greeting cards and the hit animated television show.
- *Iron Man* #200 brought the long-awaited return of Tony Stark as Iron Man in a new armored costume.

DECEMBER

MARVEL: AN OFFICIAL HISTORY

• *The Marvel Saga* #1

Written by famed comic book historian Peter Sanderson, *Marvel Saga* was a twenty-five-issue limited series that told the official history of the Marvel Universe. Reprinting panels from the comics, Sanderson pieced together a coherent pictorial narration that put all the main characters and the biggest events into a historical time line. Readers finally learned when it was that Hank Pym had first shrunk to the size of an ant and what Wolverine was doing while Reed Richards built his spaceship. The four-issue *The Wolverine Saga* (Sep., 1989) and a *Spider-Man Saga* (Nov., 1991) soon followed.

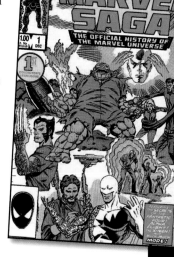

ALL PROCEEDS GO TO FAMINE RELIEF

• *Heroes For Hope Starring The X-Men* #1

Horrified by the plight of starving children in Africa, writer/artist Jim Starlin and illustrator Bernie Wrightson convinced Marvel to publish *Heroes For Hope*. It was a "jam" book—a comic created by many writers and artists who each contributed a page or more to the overall story—and all of Marvel's profits were donated to famine relief in Africa. Marvel's printer and distributor even waived their fees. The contributors included the best-selling authors Stephen King and Harlan Ellison.

- *The Official Marvel Index To The Fantastic Four* #1 summarized past FF stories.
- *Meet Misty* #1 asked readers to send in clothing suggestions for Misty to wear and brought paper dolls back to comics.
- Star Comics published *Thundercats* #1, based on the popular television animation.

MEANWHILE IN 1985...

NEW REFORMS FOR THE USSR

Mikhail Gorbachev becomes leader of the Soviet Union and initiates a new era of reform and liberalization, which leads to better relations with the West.

BOMB SINKS THE RAINBOW WARRIOR

French agents bomb Greenpeace's ship the Rainbow Warrior *in Auckland harbor. The ship was involved in campaigning against French nuclear testing in the Pacific.*

"NEW COKE" FLOPS

Coca-Cola changes the recipe of its best-selling drink, but it is a marketing disaster and original coke is back on the shelves within three months.

POLE-VAULTER JUMPS "THE IMPOSSIBLE"

Ukrainian Sergei Bubka is the first pole-vaulter to clear 19 feet and 8 inches (6 meters), a height long thought unattainable.

A HOLE IN THE OZONE LAYER

Scientists discover a hole above the Antarctic in the Ozone Layer. This finding launches one of the big environmental campaigns of the 1980s, to reduce CFCs.

LIVE AID CONCERT

Bob Geldof organizes a historic rock concert to raise money for famine relief in Ethiopia. The main concerts take place in London and Philadelphia and are watched on TV by 1.5 billion people across one hundred countries.

ROUTE 66 DECOMMISSIONED

Route 66—the road immortalized in literature, music, and television—is officially removed from the US Highway system.

VIDEO CASSETTES TAKE OFF

The first Blockbuster *video rental shop opens to meet the demand for video cassettes as the number of households that have video players rises dramatically.*

VEGETARIANISM HITS FAST FOOD

Wimpy is the first hamburger restaurant chain to add the vegetarian beanburger to its menu.

AND AT THE MOVIES...

Back To The Future, *a charming, time-traveling comedy in which Michael J. Fox meets his parents as teens;* The Breakfast Club, *five high-school kids—a jock, a princess, a misfit, a nerd, and a lout—meet in detention and discover common bonds;* The Goonies, *a fun rite-of-passage comedy in which a group of ordinary kids embark on an action adventure following a pirate's treasure map;* Brazil, *a young man dreams of escaping from a futuristic, bureaucratic dystopia in Terry Gilliam's stylish fantasy.*

Iron Man #200 ***(Nov., 1985) Written by Dennis O'Neil, pencilled by Mark Bright, and inked by Ian Akin and Brian Garvey.***

Dennis O'Neil was born in St. Louis, Missouri on May 3, 1939. When he graduated from Saint Louis University, he joined the Navy. After his discharge, he got a job on a newspaper, where his work caught the attention of Marvel editor Roy Thomas. When Marvel began to expand, Thomas hired O'Neil, who over the years, worked as an editor and writer for both Marvel and DC Comics. His work has won him high acclaim on titles like The Shadow, Green Lantern/Green Arrow, Batman, Daredevil *and, of course,* The Invincible Iron Man. *O'Neil also wrote for Charlton Comics under the pen name Sergius O'Shaugnessy.*

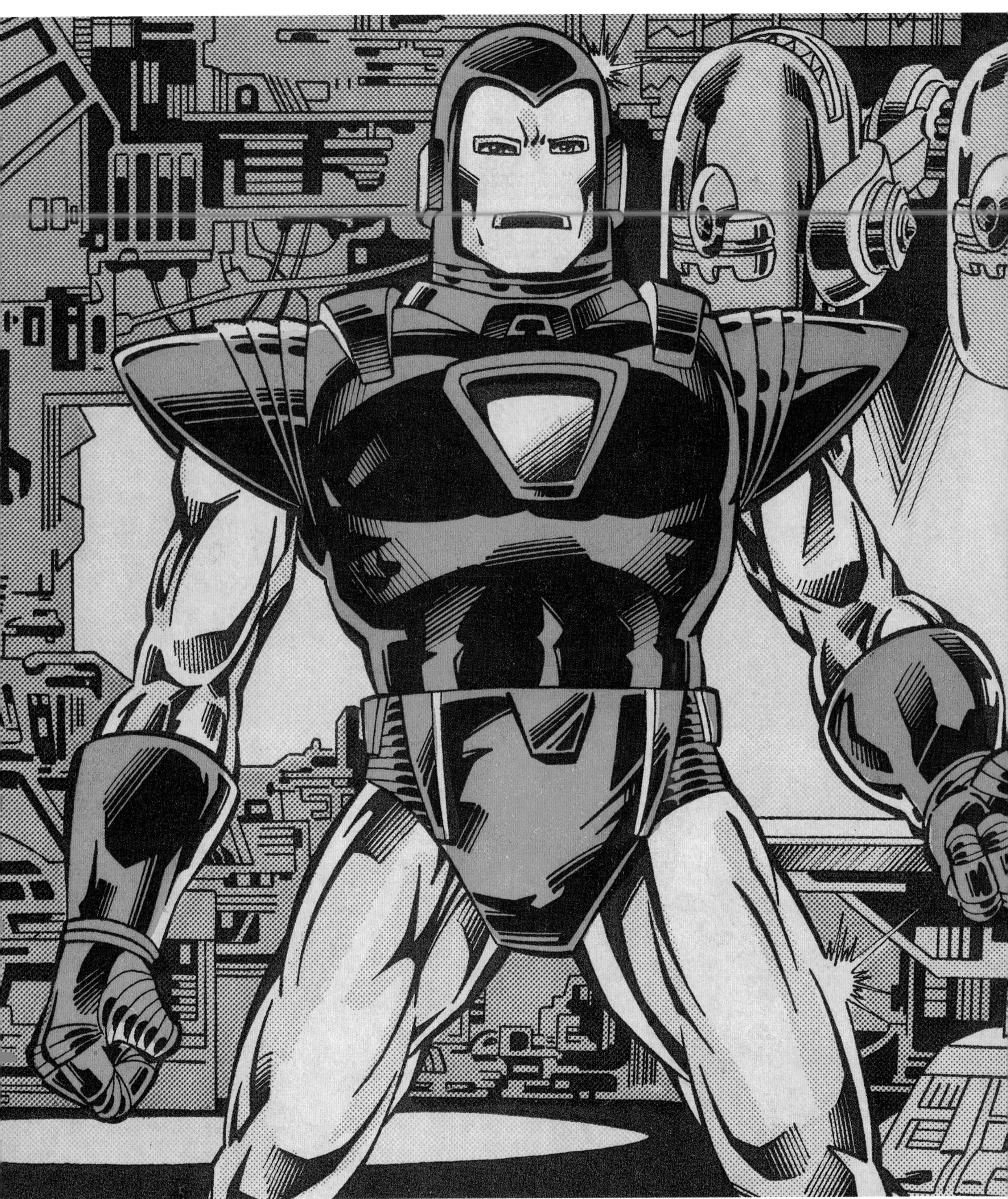

AFTER ALL THESE MONTHS OF TELLING US HE'LL NEVER WEAR ARMOR AGAIN, IT LOOKS LIKE HE'S CHANGED HIS MIND!
LOOK HONEY, SOMETHING TELLS ME WE'VE JUST SEEN THE REBIRTH OF IRON MAN!

1986

NEW WORLD AND A NEW UNIVERSE

The year 1986 was the twenty-fifth anniversary of the Marvel Universe, which had begun with *The Fantastic Four* #1 in November, 1961. Jim Shooter decided all November-dated books would mark the occasion with a portrait of the title's main character. He also embarked on his most ambitious project: he would celebrate the birth of one universe by creating a brand new one.

Appropriately dubbed the New Universe, the new comics were built around the idea of real people gaining superhuman powers. These new titles would inhabit a world that looked and behaved exactly like the one outside the reader's window. There would be no aliens, no magic, and no fictional technology. The titles would also operate in real time and characters would age with their readers.

In 1986, Marvel Comics was purchased by New World Pictures, a major film and television production company that had been established in 1970 by the legendary producer/director Roger Corman. New World Pictures planned to create a series of major films starring the Marvel characters. They produced *The Punisher* (1989) starring Dolph Lundgren, the direct-to-video *Captain America* (1990) with Matt Salinger, an unaired pilot of a television series based on the Power Pack, and three made-for-television Incredible Hulk movies.

JANUARY

A SON FOR CYCLOPS AND MADELYNE PRYOR

• *The Uncanny X-Men* #201

Nathan Christopher Summers was born to Scott "Cyclops" Summe[rs] and his wife, Madelyne Pryor, in this issue. He seemed to be a norm[al] baby boy at first. But little did he know that his mother was actua[lly] a clone of the deceased Jean Grey and that she had been created for the specific purpose of conceiving him. Mister Sinister carefully arranged Nathan's birth because he knew the child would have gre[at] powers—powers that Sinister planned to use to destroy Apocalyps[e]. Unfortunately, Apocalypse learned of Sinister's plan and infected Nathan with a techno-organic virus that would slowly kill him. Rachel Summers arrived from the future as an old woman and promised Cyclops that she could use technology from her era to save Nathan, so he sent him with her in *X-Factor* #68 (July, 1991).

HEY, KIDDO--
SAY HELLO TO
YOUR BIG
SISTER!
SHUSH!
CYCLOPS'L
HEAR! I
DON'T WAN
HIM TO
KNOW!
KITTY
WOULD
YOU LIKE
TO "HEAR
THE BABY'
THOUGHTS
I'LL
PSILINK
US.

Nathan Summers left the present as a baby to go into the future with Rachel Summers. In The New Mutants *#87 (March, 1990) he appeared as the adult called Cable.*

FEBRUARY

DAREDEVIL IS BORN AGAIN

• *Daredevil* #227

Born Again was a seven-issue story arc that appeared in *Daredevil*, from issue #227 to #233 (Feb.–Aug., 1986) by writer Frank Miller and artist David Mazzucchelli. Karen Page, Matt Murdock's former girlfriend, had become a drug addict and revealed Daredevil's secret identity to someone in the Kingpin of Crime's employ in exchange for drugs.

The Kingpin proceeded to wage a secret war against Murdock. He used his contacts to freeze the lawyer's bank accounts and foreclose on his house. Murdock was also disbarred when a crooked cop testified that he had paid a witness to perjure himself. Realizing that the Kingpin was destroying his life, Daredevil struck back and publicly exposed the Kingpin's underworld connections, ruining his image as an honest businessmen. No longer a high-priced attorney, Murdock was literary reborn as the protector of Hell's Kitchen.

THE ORIGINAL FIVE X-MEN ARE BACK

"Ironic isn't it, Iceman? Garbed as mutant hunters, we're welcomed with open arms! Garbed as mutants, we become Public Enemy #1!"

• *X-Factor* #1
Time had changed the X-Men. Professor X had gone into outer space to be with his girlfriend Lilandra, leaving his former enemy Magneto in charge of the New Mutants. Storm now led the main X-Men team, which consisted of Kitty Pryde, Nightcrawler, Rogue, Colossus, Wolverine, and Rachel Summers. Like many older fans, writer/artist Bob Layton longed for the good old days. He missed the original five X-Men and wanted to do a book that featured Cyclops, Angel, Beast, Iceman, and Marvel Girl. Unfortunately, Jean Grey, the original Marvel Girl, had died at the conclusion of the Dark Phoenix Saga in *X-Men* #137 (Sept., 1980). Marvel writer Kurt Busiek offered a solution: what if Jean Grey had never been Phoenix? What if Phoenix had been a different entity and Jean Grey was still alive in Jamaica Bay?

In *The Avengers* #263 (Jan., 1986), the team detected a cocoon at the bottom of Jamaica Bay. The same month, Reed Richards examined the cocoon in *Fantastic Four* #286 and was startled to discover Jean Grey inside. The original X-Men gathered in *X-Factor* #1 by Bob Layton and artist Jackson Guice and learned that Jean had been inside the cocoon since she had been exposed to cosmic rays in *X-Men* #100 (Aug., 1976)—the issue before Phoenix's first appearance. Even though it meant leaving his new wife and child, Cyclops joined with the others to set up their new team in New York City. Based on the concept used in the *Ghostbusters* movies, X-Factor posed as mutant hunters and publicly advertised their services. When called to deal with a mutant menace, they didn't harm the mutants they captured. Instead, unknown to their employers, they secretly trained the mutants in how to hone their skills so that they could fit into society.

During the course of Born Again, Daredevil realized that he had a responsibility to protect the innocent when he battled Nuke—a Rambo-like, drug-addicted member of America's Super-Solider program who did not hesitate before killing anyone in his way.

MAY

WEDDING BELLS

• *The Incredible Hulk* #319
Dr. Bruce Banner first met Betty Ross in *The Incredible Hulk* #1 (May, 1962) and finally married her in issue #319, by John Byrne. Temporarily separated from the Hulk, Banner raced to the wedding altar while Dr. Samson and the Hulkbusters battled his alter ego. Betty's father, a furious General "Thunderbolt" Ross, tried to stop the ceremony, but he only succeeded in shooting Banner's sidekick Rick Jones, who insisted the wedding continued.

JUNE

INTRODUCING APOCALYPSE AND HIS ALLIANCE OF EVIL

"You shall soon provide all mutantkind with a source of unlimited might—a race of super-mutants! And I shall lead them to war against the puny infection called—man!"

• *X-Factor* #5
Writer/artist Bob Layton intended to use Daredevil's foe, the Owl, as X-Factor's main villain. But Louise Simonson wanted X-Factor to battle someone new, so when Layton left the title with *X-Factor* #5, she had the final page redrawn, adding a shadowy figure named Apocalypse. Simonson liked the idea of introducing a Darwinian character who would initiate disasters to help stimulate humanity's evolution, by forcing people and mutants to keep evolving to higher and higher levels.

In *X-Factor* #6 (July, 1986), readers learned that Apocalypse had hired a mutant team called the Alliance of Evil, which consisted of Frenzy, a mutant with steel-hard skin and superhuman strength; Tower, who could increase his size; Stinger, who could project electrical blasts; and Timeshadow, who could teleport so fast that he appeared to be in several places at once. Apocalypse sent the Alliance to capture Michael Nowlan/Source, a mutant who could enhance other mutants' powers.

Apocalypse had been born nearly six thousand years ago and had been a slave of Rama-Tut, a previous identity of the time-traveling Kang. Virtually immortal, Apocalypse was one of the most powerful mutants ever born. He could alter his body's molecular structure at will and so could become as strong as he desired or assume any appearance he wanted. He was able to physically interface with technology and could generate force-fields and project concussive blasts of energy. Although he had apparently been killed on several occasions, Apocalypse always found a way to revive himself.

AUGUST

ELEKTRA'S OWN SERIES

• *Elektra: Assassin* #1

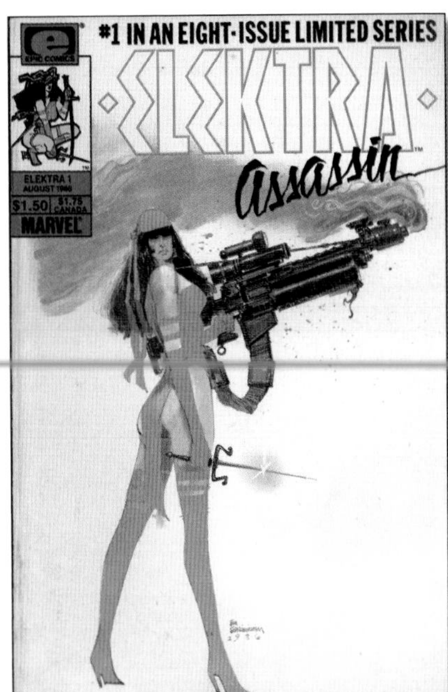

#1 IN AN EIGHT-ISSUE LIMITED SERIES
ELEKTRA
Assassin
MARVEL

Produced by Frank Miller and illustrated by Bill Sienkiewicz, *Elektra: Assassin* was an eight-issue limited series. Because its mature content was inappropriate for children, it was published by Marvel's Epic Comics imprint. The story was illustrated with a series of individual panels that were painted in watercolors rather than by the traditional method of pencilling and inking.

Elektra learned that a Presidential candidate intended to launch a nuclear war as soon as he was elected. Battling cyborgs, monsters, and SHIELD agents, she tried to prevent him from being elected. Although she failed, she did manage to stop the war by transferring the mind of a good man into the new President's body.

OCTOBER

INTRODUCING THE SUPER-PATRIOT

• *Captain America* #323

John Walker worshipped his older brother and was devastated when he was killed in Vietnam. To honor his brother's memory, John enlisted in the military. He later heard about Curtiss Jackson, the Power Broker, and signed up with him to gain superhuman strength. Walker was going to join the Unlimited Class Wrestling Federation until he met Ethan Thurm in *Captain America* #323, who suggested that Walker become a corporate-sponsored Super Hero. Thurm later organized a rally to criticize Captain America. Taking the name Super-Patriot, Walker believed that the American people should be able to decide who wore the uniform of Captain America and he began to campaign for the job. The Super-Patriot came to fame when he killed a terrorist to preve[nt] him from detonating a nuclear warhead in Washington D.C..

OCTOBER

THE MUTANT MASSACRE

• *The Uncanny X-Men* #210

THE UNCANNY
X-MEN
C'MON, MESS WITH US--MAKE OUR DAY!!
75¢
210
OCT

Although he had co-created the Morlocks in *The Uncanny X-Men* #169 (May, 1983), Chris Claremont did not like the idea of so many mutants living beneath New York City. He conceived a story line that would solve the problem and also introduce a new team of villains for the X-Men.

The Mutant Massacre was an eleven-issue story that ran from October, 1986, through *The Uncanny X-Men* #210–213, *The New Mutants* #46, *The Mighty Thor* #373–374, and *X-Factor* #9–11. Working for Mister Sinister, the Marauders—a team of mutant mercenaries—raided the Alley and callously slaughtered most of the Morlocks.

- *G.I. Joe* proved so popular that a second title, *G.I. Joe Special Missions* #1, was launched.
- Spider-Man guest-starred in *Top Dog* #10 in the first very crossover between characters from Marvel and Marvel's imprint Star Comics.

NOVEMBER

A MARVEL MOVIE

• *Marvel Super Special* #4[1]

Nº 41
MARVEL SUPER SPECIAL
$2.50
HOWARD THE DUCK
THE OFFICIAL COMIC BOOK ADAPTATION OF THE SPECTACULAR NEW MOVIE FROM LUCASFILM AND UNIVERSAL PICTURES!

This issue adapted the story line of *Howard Th[e] Duck*, the first major motion picture based o[n] a Marvel character. The comic showed Howard plucked from his home on Duckworld and take[n] to Cleveland, Ohio, where he met a young singer named Beverly. When Howard discover[ed] that an alien Dark Overlord was planning t[o] invade the Earth, he stopped the invasion by destroying the only device that could send him home. Produced by Lucasfilm and Universal Pictures, the film starred Lea Thompson and Tim Robbins.

A NEW UNIVERSE TITLE

• *D.P.7* #1

Created by editor Mark Gruenwald and artist Paul Ryan, *D.P.7* wa[s] published under the New Universe imprint. The title stood for the seven Displaced Paranormals—ordinary people with super powers —who met in a clinic where they had gone to learn how to deal with their new superhuman powers.

PROUDSTAR FORMS THE PSI-FORCE

• *Psi-Force* #1

This title was part of the New Universe imprint and lasted thirty-two issues. Created by editor Archie Goodwin and artist Mark Texeira, it focused on teenagers with psionic powers. Former CIA agent Emmett Proudstar had gained his powers from the mysterious "White Event" that had suddenly created paranormals—ordinary people with super powers—in the New Universe. His dreams led him to gather a group of teenagers who had various psionic powers. After Proudstar was murdered, the teens formed the powerful entity called the Psi-Hawk.

The Psi-Hawk possessed all the powers of the members of Psi-Force, but magnified to a much greater degree. The whole was far more powerful than the sum of its parts.

MEANWHILE IN 1986...

CHALLENGER EXPLODES
The American space shuttle Challenger *explodes just seventy-two seconds after lift-off, killing all seven astronauts on board.*

CHERNOBYL NUCLEAR DISASTER
Severe meltdown at the Ukrainian power plant causes the worst nuclear accident in history.

THE RISE OF THE "YUPPIE"
Young Urban Professionals—YUPPIES—put cash before compassion and make the most of the economic boom years.

OPRAH WINFREY SHOW LAUNCHES
A new type of daytime TV program hosted by Oprah Winfrey airs and popularizes the talk-show genre on television.

NINTENDO REACHES THE US
Super Mario Bros *and* The Legend of Zelda *games are instant hits on Nintendo.*

AND AT THE MOVIES...
Top Gun, *a gung-ho blockbuster about the macho exploits of students Iceman and Maverick at an elite naval flying school;* Stand By Me, *a group of adolescent kids discover a dead body in an adaptation of Stephen King's novella,* The Body; Blue Velvet, *David Lynch's stylish, off-kilter mystery reveals the horror that lurks behind America's suburban picket-fences.*

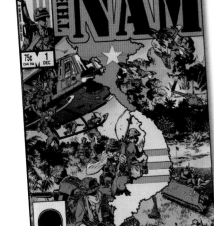

A NEW VIETNAM WAR COMIC

"Yeah, the perfect replacement. Green as grass and just stupid enough to fit in. Welcome to the jewel of Southeast Asia."

• *The 'Nam* #1

Oliver Stone's movie *Platoon* had already been released to critical acclaim when Editor-in-Chief Jim Shooter walked into editor Larry Hama's office one day. He carried a *G.I. Joe* cover with a new logo on it. The logo simply said "The 'Nam." Shooter asked Hama if he was interested in developing a new title that was set during the United States' war with Vietnam. Hama immediately called Doug Murray, a veteran who had served in Vietnam. Murray had written a feature about Vietnam called "The 5th Of The 1st" for Marvel's black-and-white magazine *Savage Tales* #1 (Oct., 1985) and *Savage Tales* #4 (April, 1986). Hama also called artist Michael Golden to draw the new title. Working together, Murray and Golden produced *The 'Nam* #1, the first of a twelve-year limited series It was their intention to produce one issue for every month the United States had been in Vietnam. They also planned for the book to occur in real time, so each issue detailed another month in the characters' lives. A glossary that explained military slang also appeared in most issues. The series was set from the average soldier's point of view. The first issue introduced Private First Class Ed Marks as he was saying goodbye to his family before flying to Vietnam. After being met with artillery fire as he landed in Saigon, Marks was handed a malaria pill, shipped off to join the 23rd Infantry, assigned to his squad, and sent on his first patrol.

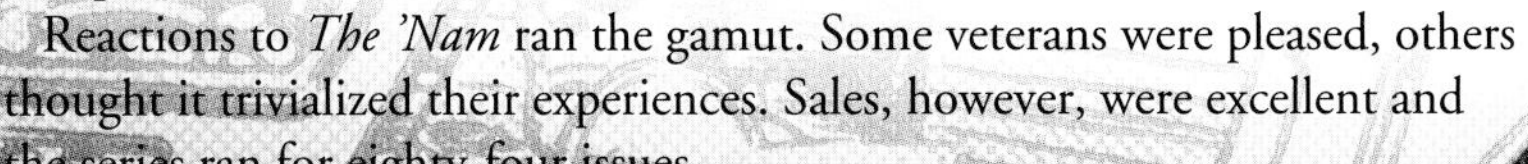

Reactions to *The 'Nam* ran the gamut. Some veterans were pleased, others thought it trivialized their experiences. Sales, however, were excellent and the series ran for eighty-four issues.

Although Ed Marks was rotated out of the title when he completed his twelve-month tour of duty with The 'Nam *#12, Doug Murray had intended to bring him back as a reporter who covered the war, although this never happened.*

1987

A NEW ORDER BEGINS

Jim Shooter used January's *Bullpen Bulletins* to apologize for a television interview with Stan Lee about Marvel's twenty-fifth anniversary. The interview had edited out any mention of Jack Kirby, Steve Ditko, Larry Lieber, and all the other creators who had helped launch the Marvel Universe in the 1960s. Shooter used the following month's *Bulletins* to describe the lesson he had learned about responsibility from reading *The Amazing Spider-Man*. It would be the last *Bullpen Bulletins* he ever wrote.

On April 15, 1987, a day when most Americans were thinking about their taxes, Tom DeFalco was informed that he had become Marvel's Editor-in-Chief. Where Shooter had deliberately put a spotlight on himself, DeFalco took a more low-key approach. He had always considered himself a freelancer who was only masquerading as a staff person and he never thought the job would last. DeFalco appointed Mark Gruenwald as executive editor. They initially wrote the *Bullpen Bulletins* together, but did not sign it. DeFalco could already foresee the day when his responsibilities would prevent him from working on it. He and Gruenwald immediately began formulating a publishing plan that would slowly increase the number of titles over the next five years. Marvel was on the move, again.

JANUARY

A NEW TYPE OF COMIC

• *Spider-Man Comics Magazine* #1

While working for Archie Comics in the 1970s, Tom DeFalco had spearheaded a line of highly successful digest-sized comics. Measuring about five by seven inches, they fitted into the racks for magazines like *Reader's Digest* and *T.V. Guide* that were displayed near cash registers in supermarkets across America. DeFalco introduced a similar line at Marvel that featured Spider-Man, G.I. Joe, the Transformers, Alf, and a general Star Comics anthology.

M *Defenders Of The Earth* #1 featured the famous comic strip her Flash Gordon, the Phantom, and Mandrake the Magician.

FEBRUARY

THE COMET MAN DEBUTS

• *The Comet Man* #1

Bill Mumy and Miguel Ferrer were writers, actors, and musicians who created this six-issue limited series. Astrophysicist Dr. Stephen Beckley was on a space mission when he was exposed to radiation. As a new Super Hero, he could rocket through the air, teleport himself, project his mind into others, and read peoples' thoughts.

THE LOST IN SPACE-TIME STORY BEGINS

• *The West Coast Avengers* #17

This issue began a seven-part story line called Lost In Space-Time that sent the Super Heroes Hawkeye, Iron Man, Tigra, Wonder Man, and Mockingbird into the past. Part of the team ended up i the old west and others were sent to ancient Egypt.

MARCH

DUNPHY BECOMES DEMOLITION MAN

• *Captain America* #328

Dennis Dunphy was a wrestler who gained superhuman strength thanks to the Power Broker. He worked for the Unlimited Class Wrestling Federation where he met Ben Grimm in *The Thing* #28 (Oct., 1985). He became Demolition Man—or D-Man—and teamed up with Cap to investigate the Power Broker's criminal activities. He stayed on as Cap's partner until he was frozen in a block of ice in issue #384 (April, 1991).

THE SUPER-PATRIOT TAKES OVER AS CAPTAIN AMERICA

"I cannot represent the American government: the President does that. I must represent the American people. I represent the American Dream, the freedom to strive, to become all that you dream of being. Being Captain America has been my dream."

• *Captain America* #332

This issue began a nineteen-part story arc called Captain America No More! The US President appointed a Commission on Superhuman Activities to supervise Americans with superhuman powers. When it ordered Captain America to work directly for the government, Steve Rogers turned in his shield and costume. The Commission appointed John Walker, the Super-Patriot, as the new Captain America.

Walker was trained in this new role by the Taskmaster and was partnered with a new Bucky—Lemar Hoskins—who later changed his name to Battlestar. Walker did his best to replace Rogers, but he was far more brutal than his predecessor and the job was not everything he had hoped. Walker's former friends became jealous of his success and turned on him. When a neo-Nazi group learned of his secret identity and murdered his parents, Walker flew into a rage and exacted a terrible revenge.

Meanwhile, a high-ranking member of the Commission was secretly working for the evil Red Skull, Cap's longtime enemy. The Skull had masterminded everything to destroy his old foe's reputation: he had deliberately forced Rogers into a corner, knowing he would quit. Mission accomplished, the Skull planned to kill Walker. When Steve Rogers learned that Walker had been captured by the Skull, he raced to his rescue. That was the moment John Walker finally realized that he was not ready to replace Cap. He soon resigned and allowed Rogers to resume his identity as the true Captain America.

- M *The Flintstone Kids* #1 showed the famous television characters—Fred, Wilma, Barney, and Betty—as young children.
- M Walter Simonson and Sal Buscema ended their popular run with *The Mighty Thor* in issue #382, which celebrated the 300th appearance of Thor. The Thunder God commemorated the occasion by breaking Loki's arm with his enchanted hammer.

SEPTEMBER

MISTER SINISTER APPEARS

• *The Uncanny X-Men* #221

Although he had been mentioned as early as issue #212 (Dec., 1986), Mister Sinister did not appear until this issue. Nathaniel Essex discovered Apocalypse lying in suspended animation. Apocalypse made him superhumanly strong and virtually immortal as Mister Sinister. A scientist interested in Darwin's Theory of Evolution, Essex had worked for the Nazis during World War II and was obsessed with studying mutant children. He tested the young Charles Xavier and, later, Scott Summers. He also hired the Marauders to massacre the Morlocks because he believed they would weaken mutantkind's ability to evolve.

OCTOBER

MARVEL PUBLISHES WORK BY MOEBIUS

• *Moebius* #1

The French comic book artist Jean Giraud, who signed his work Moebius, allowed Marvel's Epic Comics imprint to translate his work and publish it as a series of graphic novels. These included his *Blueberry* western series as well as many of his science-fiction fantasies.

SPIDER-MAN AND KRAVEN MEET IN FEARFUL SYMMETRY

• *Web Of Spider-Man* #31

J.M. DeMatteis had an intriguing idea. What if a villain put a hero in suspended animation and took over his costumed identity? He first tried this with the Grim Reaper and Wonder Man. When that didn't sell, he rewrote it to star Batman. When that failed, he substituted Spider-Man and a new villain. Finally, deciding the story would work better with a classic villain, he rewrote it a fourth time with Spider-Man and Kraven the Hunter.

The six-issue story arc, Fearful Symmetry, drawn by Mike Zeck and Bob McLeod began in this issue and ran through all the Spider-Man titles for two months, climaxing in *The Spectacular Spider-Man* #132 (Nov., 1987).

OCTOBER

SPIDER-MAN'S WEDDING

"I will take this man—this very special man—to be the most important thing in my life. Because that's exactly what I realize he already is."

• *The Amazing Spider-Man Annual* #21

In 1977, Stan Lee had begun writing a syndicated newspaper comic strip that starred Spider-Man. Realizing that adults were the primary market for newspapers, Lee tailored the strip accordingly, focusing on the soap-opera elements of Peter Parker's life and downplaying the superheroics. He wanted Parker to marry Mary Jane Watson in the comic strip and he mentioned the idea to Jim Shooter at a comic book convention. Shooter turned to the audience and asked their opinion. The shouts of approval convinced Shooter to approve the marriage.

Peter Parker had asked Mary Jane to marry him on at least two occasions, but, being a child of divorce, Mary Jane was afraid of committing to anyone for the rest of her life. She refused, but later realized that it was time to stop running away and accepted.

Neither Peter nor Mary Jane arrived on time for their wedding. Their friends feared neither would show up, but they did. Surrounded by their friends and family, Peter and Mary Jane were married on the front steps of City Hall.

The wedding occurred in *The Amazing Spider-Man Annual* #21, which sported two different covers: one with Peter Parker beside Mary Jane and one with Spider-Man in his place. The wedding was also recreated with actors in front of a live audience at New York's Shea Stadium on June 5, 1987 and was celebrated in the newspaper strip on June 21.

Mary Jane's wedding dress was created especially for her by the renowned fashion designer Willi Smith, who died unexpectedly before any of these ceremonies took place.

NOVEMBER

MARVEL MASTERWORKS

Tom DeFalco had barely moved into his new office as Editor-in-Chief when he was informed of a crisis. The New Universe comics had not sold as well as expected and the company needed to make up the budgetary difference. DeFalco had to create some new titles quickly or come up with another idea. His solution was *Marvel Masterworks*—a line of hardcover books that reprinted the earliest Marvel comics. He started with three titles: *The Amazing Spider-Man* #1–10, *The Fantastic Four* #1–10, and *The X-Men* #1–10. The sales department was thrilled with the idea and many different titles have been published as *Marvel Masterworks* ever since.

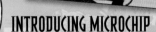

INTRODUCING MICROCHIP

• *The Punisher* #4

Linus "Microchip" Lieberman first appeared in this issue by writer Mike Baron and artist Klaus Janson. Inspired by Q from the James Bond films, Microchip had been secretly providing Frank Castle—the Punisher—with weaponry and technology for years and had even helped build the Punisher's battle van. Linus had a son named Louis who was also introduced in weapons technology. Nicknamed Microchip Jr., Louis was killed while aiding Castle in *The Punisher* #8 (May, 1988).

STEVE ROGERS CARRIES ON

• *Captain America* #335

Although he had resigned as Captain America in August, Steve Rogers resumed his superheroic duties as Cap in this issue, wearing a black version of hi famous costume. He continued to be a member o the Avengers and even set u an interim team when the Earth's Mightiest Heroes temporarily disbanded.

THE NORSE GODS MEET THE CELTIC GODS

• *The Mighty Thor* #386

While Thor was pursuing a dangerous beast, he crossed a dimensional rift that led him to Avalon, the home of the Celtic Gods, where he confronted Leir, the God of Lightning and the Spear. Leir later journeyed to Thor's homeland, Asgard, where he challenged Thor for the hand of Lady Sif. However, he was sent packing when Sif defeated him in a fair duel.

A TEAM OF BRITISH SUPER HEROES

• *Excalibur Special Edition*

Captain Britain had been created by Chris Claremont and Herb Trimpe for Marvel's London office and he first appeared in the weekly *Captain Britain* #1 (Oct. 13, 1976). Claremont always had a fondness for the character, as did Alan Davis, who had drawn many of his adventures. So it was only natural that they produced *Excalibur Special Edition*, a graphic novel about a team of Super Heroes based in England. It featured Captain Britain, Meggan (his shape-shifting girlfriend), the former X-Men members Nightcrawler and Phoenix (Rachel Summers), and Kitty Pryde and her pet dragon Lockheed. A regular *Excalibur* title was soon published that ran for 125 issues.

A SPLIT BOOK FOR THE 1980S

• *Solo Avengers* #1

Harkening back to the split books of the 1960s, *Solo Avengers* #1 was launched to fulfill two goals: it would give Hawkeye a regular eleven-page feature and it would also provide Marvel with a second eleven-page slot that could be used to try out new talent or to tell stories with the Avengers characters who did not have their own series. The backup story in issue #1 starred Mockingbird and was drawn by Jim Lee, who achieved fame drawing the X-Men. Backups in other issues featured Moondragon, the Swordsman, and Starfox. The title was changed to *Avengers Spotlight* with its twenty-first issue.

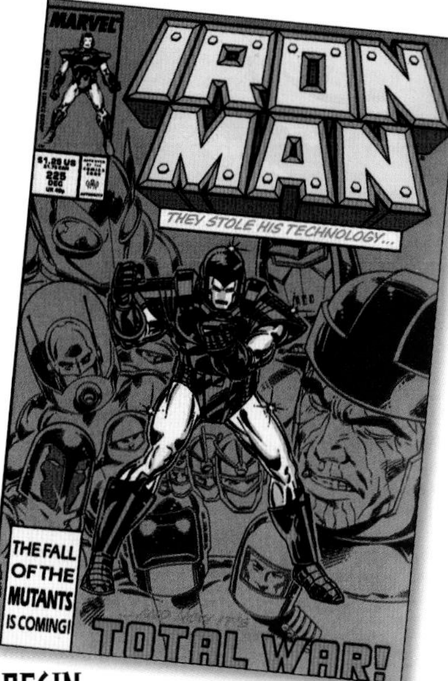

ARMOR WARS BEGIN

• *Iron Man* #225

Although actually called Stark Wars, the story arc that became known as Armor Wars began in this issue and ran until June, 1988. Written by David Michelinie and Bob Layton and drawn by Mark Bright, Tony Stark was horrified to learn that a mercenary called FORCE was using his own technology against him. Fearing other villains would do the same, Stark journeyed around the world to disable every armored suit that was using his stolen technology.

MEANWHILE IN 1987...

FIRST DNA CONVICTION

Robert Melias is the first person to be convicted of a crime in court using DNA evidence. He pleads guilty to rape when scientists work out that the chance of the sample not being from him is one in four million of the male population.

A THIRD TERM FOR THATCHER

Margaret Thatcher is elected for a third term as British Prime Minister.

BLACK MONDAY

The optimism and economic boom of the 1980s crashes to a halt with the biggest stock market collapse in history.

CFC REDUCTION TARGETS

Following the discovery of the hole in the ozone layer, an international treaty is signed in Montreal calling for a fifty per cent reduction in the use of CFCs by 2000.

SPYCATCHER IS BANNED

The autobiography by former intelligence officer Peter Wright, which reveals the workings of the British secret services, is banned from publication in Britain, despite being available in America and other countries.

MEET THE SIMPSONS

The animated satirical comedy The Simpsons *appears for the first time as a short on* The Tracey Ullman Show. *Matt Groening's yellow-skinned, dysfunctional family parodies the American middle-class way of life.*

A PROGRAM FOR THIRTYSOMETHINGS

Thirtysomething *debuts on ABC. The introspective drama and its self-absorbed characters address the angst felt by baby boomers and yuppies in the 1980s.*

SEEING CLEARLY

The first disposable soft contact lenses are introduced, forty-eight years after the first lenses were made from plastic.

AND AT THE MOVIES...

Robocop, *Paul Verhoeven's sci-fi action movie about a terminally wounded cop who returns to the force as a powerful cyborg haunted by his memories;* Full Metal Jacket, *Stanley Kubrick's epic Vietnam-set story exploring the dehumanizing effects of warfare on US Marine recruits;* Lethal Weapon, *an action thriller sees Danny Glover's veteran cop reluctantly partnered with Mel Gibson's homicidal cop to stop a gang of drug smugglers;* Dirty Dancing, *a dance-fueled, coming-of-age romance in which a young women falls in love with a bad-boy dance instructor on a family summer vacation;* Fatal Attraction, *Glenn Close becomes Michael Douglas's "bunny boiler" stalker after a one-night stand in this psychological thriller.*

CAPTAIN AMERICA®
NO MORE!

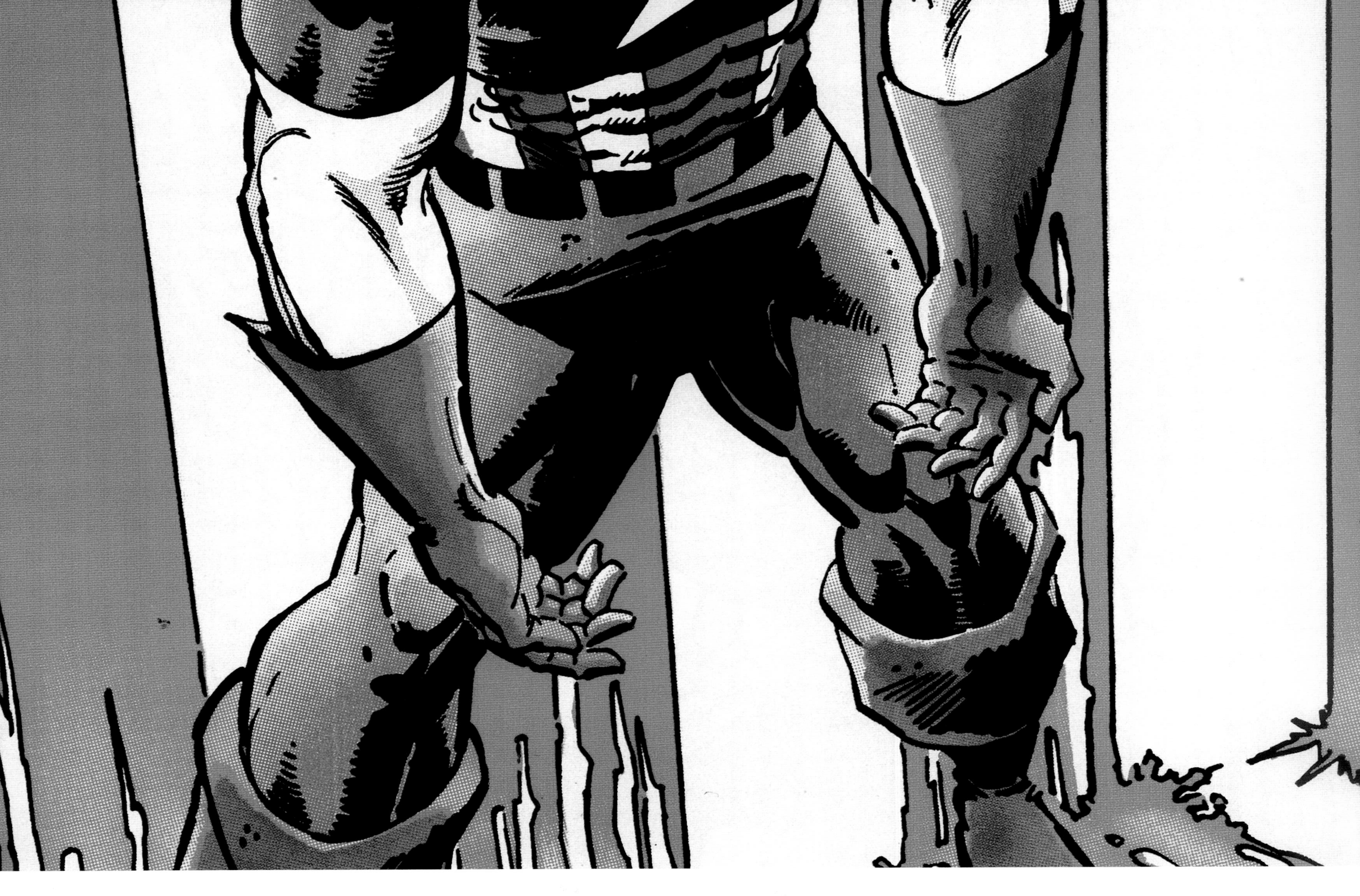

Captain America #332 (Aug., 1987) ***Written by Mark Gruenwald, cover pencilled by Mike Zeck and inked by Klaus Janson.***
*Mark Gruenwald was born in Oshkosh, Wisconsin on June 18, 1953 and bought his first comic book—*The Fantastic Four *#8—when he was nine years old. He became a serious fan and soon started drawing his own stories. He moved to New York City and got an editorial job at Marvel, where he wrote titles like* Marvel Two-In-One, The Spider-Woman, D.P.7, Quasar, *and, of course,* Captain America. *He is also famous for having spearheaded* The Official Handbook Of The Marvel Universe. *He died unexpectedly on August 12, 1996, and was named the patron saint of Marvel in 2006.*

FOR PEACE!
NO NUKES!!
MAKE LOVE NOT BOMBS!

1988

ONE UNIVERSE ENDS, OTHERS BEGIN

Marvel's editorial staff continued to evolve in 1988. Editors Larry Hama and Ann Nocenti left to pursue careers as full-time writers and were replaced by Bob Harras, Bobbie Chase, and Terry Kavanagh. Jim Novak resigned from his post as production department supervisor and was succeed by Virginia Romita (the wife of John Romita Sr.), whose skills as art traffic manager had assured that the comics all came out on time.

The *Bullpen Bulletins* congratulated Doug Murray, writer of *The 'Nam*, for winning the prestigious Veterans Achievement Award For Entertainment from BRAVO—the Brotherhood Rally of All Veterans Organization. And Marvel even used the pages to salute their distinguished competition—DC Comics—on Superman's fiftieth anniversary.

The New Universe came to an end with three graphic novels, *The Pitt*, *The Draft*, and *The War*. The city of Pittsburgh was destroyed, all the paranormals were drafted into the army, and nuclear war was barely averted by a Star Child, who took responsibility for protecting the world.

Marvel increased its number of monthly titles, adding a new one every month. In addition, the company expanded some of its already popular lines with two new X-Men-related titles (*Excalibur* and *Wolverine*), *The Punisher War Journal*, and *G.I. Joe European Missions*.

JANUARY

SHARON IS THE SHE-THING

• *Fantastic Four* #310

While returning from a space mission, Sharon Ventura/Ms. Marvel and the Thing were exposed to cosmic rays. The Thing's second exposure caused him to mutate even further and Sharon became a hideous She-Thing. Unable to cope with her appearance, she suffered a mental breakdown and was cared for by the adventurer Wyatt Wingfoot.

THE RETURN OF THE SIN-EATER

• *The Spectacular Spider-Man* #134

Obsessed with destroying anyone who sinned, the Sin-Eater had first appeared in issue #107 (Oct., 1985). Haunted by his crimes, he returned for a three-issue story that climaxed when he committed "suicide by cop" by threatening a child with an unloaded gun.

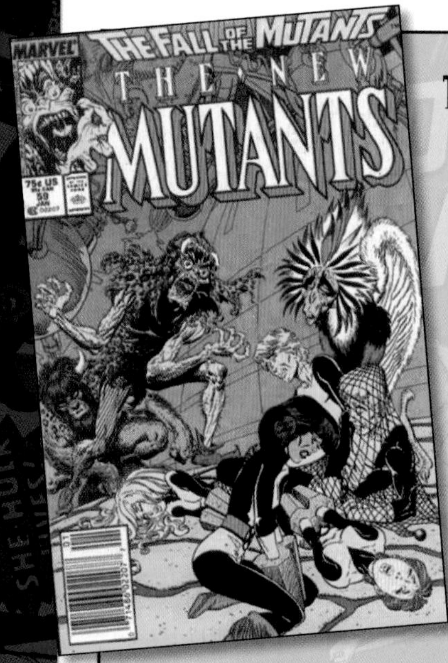

THE FALL OF THE MUTANTS

"Mutants are not inhuman monsters! They are people who are born with extraordinary abilities. That's all. Some are good. Others become criminals. But they, like you, deserve to be judged as individuals."

• *The New Mutants* #59

"Do you know what your child is?" Small cards with this question began appearing in comic-book stores as Marvel geared up its advertising campaign for The Fall Of The Mutants twelve-issue story arc that ran through *The New Mutants* #59–61, *The Uncanny X-Men* #225–227, and *X-Factor* #24–26. *Captain America* #339, *Daredevil* #252, *Fantastic Four* #312, *The Incredible Hulk* #340, and *Power Pack* #35 also tied into to the story. Against the backdrop of growing fear and suspicion of mutants, the government was considering a Mutant Registration Act, which would require all mutants to register themselves, as if they were dangerous weapons. (A similar law for those with superhuman powers was the basis for the 2007 company-wide crossover *Civil War*.)

The Fall of the Mutants was actually three separate stories—one in each of the X-Men titles. In *The Uncanny X-Men*, the team battled the government-sponsored Freedom Force and sacrificed themselves to banish a monster from their plane of existence. A goddess took pity on the team and restored them to life, but made them invisible to surveillance equipment so that the world would still think they were dead. In *X-Factor*, Apocalypse had turned the now-wingless Angel into a murderous cyborg and planned to unleash his Four Horsemen on New York City. X-Factor drove off the Horsemen and rescued their former teammate, now called Archangel. In *The New Mutants* the team tried to help semi-sentient creatures who were being abused. In the course of battle, Cypher was killed, and Magneto blamed his death on humanity.

THE DARKNESS THAT BLANKETS THIS CITY IS NOTHING. NOTHING! NOT COMPARED TO THE SHROUD THAT SPIDER-MAN PULLED OVER ME!
HE STOLE MY LIFE... SHATTERED IT...THEN CAST IT ASIDE LIKE YESTERDAY'S NEWS!
SO IT IS ONLY FITTING, ONLY FAIR, THAT I DO THE SAME TO HIM!
AND I WILL
SOON!
DOC OCK DOC TO TELL ALL
ELECTRO HUMILIATE WEB-SLING
HERO OR MENACE?
THE NEW SPIDER-MAN
MUTANT SPIDER
COSTUMED VIGILANTES
SPIDER-MAN SA CHILD FROM FIR

MARCH

THE FIRST APPEARANCE OF GATEWAY

• *The Uncanny X-Men* #227

The Australian Aborigine known as Gateway, who first appeared in this issue by writer Chris Claremont and artist Marc Silvestri, had the ability to open teleportation gateways. After being forced to aid the super-criminal cyborgs called the Reavers, he assisted the X-Men when they established a temporary base in the Australian outback.

- Written by Michael Gallagher and drawn by Dave Manak, *Alf* #1 was based on the popular television show and ran for fifty issues.
- *Captain Justice* #1 featured New World Pictures' television hero.

MAY

INTRODUCING ERIC MASTERSON

• *The Mighty Thor* #391

Eric Masterson was an architect working on a construction site in this issue by Tom DeFalco and Ron Frenz. He never wanted to be a hero. He just wanted to do his job, raise his son, and live a normal life. But fate decreed otherwise. When Thor and Spider-Man battled the Mongoose, Eric was injured as he pushed a coworker out of the way of falling debris. Eric and Thor became friends and when Eric was fatally injured, Thor merged himself with the human to save his life in issue #408 (Oct., 1989). Eric proved so worthy that Odin awarded him his own enchanted mace in issue #459 (Feb., 1993).

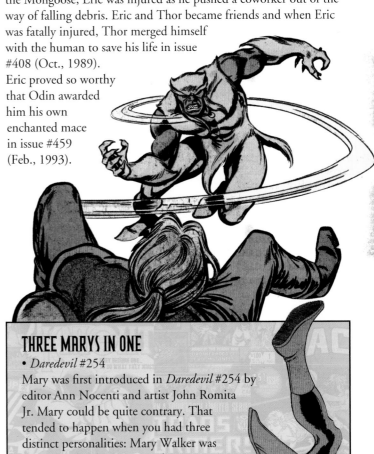

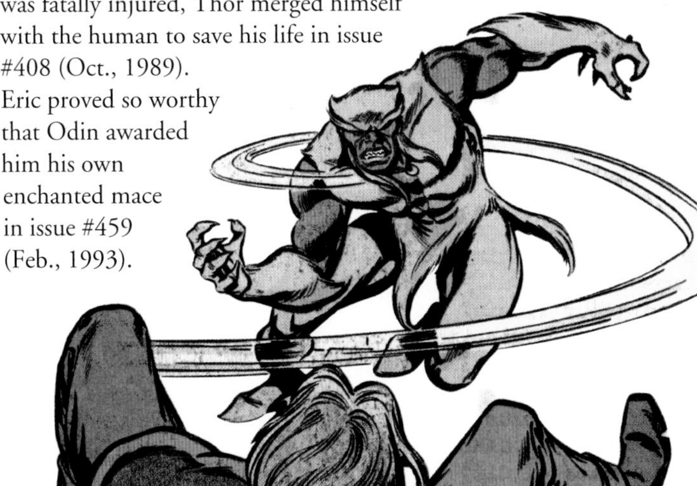

SPIDEY'S ALIEN COSTUME IS BACK!

"You may call me Venom—for that's what I'm paid to spew out these days! I'm your victim, Spider-Man—I'm the innocent you ruined!"

• *The Amazing Spider-Man* #298

The alien costume that Spider-Man had obtained in *Marvel Super Heroes Secret Wars* #8 (Dec., 1984) and that was later revealed to be a sentient symbiote was back. And it wanted revenge!

Daily Globe reporter Eddie Brock thought he was destined for a Pulitzer. The Sin-Eater had just begun his first murder spree when Brock received a call from someone claiming to be him. He revealed the Sin-Eater's identity and was the *Globe*'s star reporter... for about an hour. Then Spider-Man caught the real Sin-Eater and Brock's source was exposed as a fake. Brock was fired and began a downward spiral, his hatred of Spider-Man growing in proportion to how far he fell. Unable to go on, Brock went into a church to ask for guidance. As it turned out, this was the same church where the alien symbiote had allegedly perished during its final battle with Spider-Man in *Web Of Spider-Man* #1 (April, 1985). Sensing a kindred spirit, the symbiote bonded with Brock. The two became one. And that one was called Venom.

Since he could not be detected by Peter Parker's spider-sense, Venom's first act was to push Parker in front of a subway car in this issue by David Michelinie and Todd McFarlane, although all readers saw of him was his hand. In the next issue, he terrorized Mary Jane and issue #300 revealed his origin and showed his first battle with Spider-Man. Stronger and larger than the webhead, Venom honestly believed that Spider-Man was a monster and that it was his responsibility to protect other innocents from the wall-crawler.

THREE MARYS IN ONE

• *Daredevil* #254

Mary was first introduced in *Daredevil* #254 by editor Ann Nocenti and artist John Romita Jr. Mary could be quite contrary. That tended to happen when you had three distinct personalities: Mary Walker was timid; Typhoid Mary was adventurous; and Bloody Mary was sadistic.

All of them possessed telekinetic powers and the ability to mentally start fires.

As Mary Walker, she fell in love with Matt Murdock. But as Typhoid Mary, she worked as an assassin for the Kingpin and often tried to kill Daredevil, and as Bloody Mary, she would torture him.

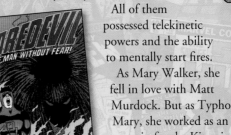

1988

JULY

INFECTIA'S KISS IS DEATH

• *X-Factor* #30

Introduced two issues earlier, the mutant Infectia set her sights on Iceman in *X-Factor* #30. She mutated a policeman into a monster so that Iceman would save her, but the Beast intercepted her lethal kiss and turned into a monster.

SEPTEMBER

A NEW SPLIT BOOK

• *Marvel Comics Presents* #1

This new comic came out twice a month and contained four stories that were eight pages each. Two of the stories featured popular characters and two were reserved for new talent or characters without their own titles. It ran for 175 issues.

- *Akira* #1 was based on a 2,000-paged manga by Katsuhiro Otomo. The original *Akira* had been printed in black and white and was designed to be read from right to left. Epic Comics colored their version and made the art read from left to right.

SEPTEMBER

SPEEDBALL GETS HIS OWN TITLE

• *Speedball* #1

Editor-in-Chief Tom DeFalco thought Marvel should publish more titles starring teenagers because they comprised the majority of Marvel's audience at that time. He wrote the basic scenario and character descriptions for a new series and hired Steve Ditko to design it. Accidentally exposed to energy from another dimension, Robbie Baldwin gained the ability to bounce like a living rubber ball. He first appeared in *The Amazing Spider-Man Annual* #22 in early 1988 and then in September in his own title. *Speedball* only lasted ten issues, but the character came back as a member of the New Warriors in 1989.

A MULTI-ANNUAL CROSSOVER

• *The Avengers Annual* #17

The Evolutionary War was a new kind of crossover. It was an eleven-part story that was told across the 1988 Annuals, including titles as diverse as *The Punisher Annual* #1 and *The Uncanny X-Men Annual* #12. It began with *X-Factor Annual* #3 and ended with *The Avengers Annual* #17 when the High Evolutionary attempted to jumpstart humanity's evolution by releasing a "Genetic Bomb."

OCTOBER

MUTANT APARTHEID

• *The Uncanny X-Men* #235

Intended to criticize South Africa's policy of apartheid, Genosha was a fictional island located off the east coast of Africa that first appeared in this issue by writer Chris Claremont and artist Rick Leonardi. Genosha had a high standard of living thanks to its mutant population which was considered the property of the state and was enslaved. David Moreau, the Genegineer, could modify mutants so that their powers could better serve the state. Seeing the potential of the X-Men, the Genegineer ordered their kidnap—a mistake that ultimately caused the collapse of his government.

THE LOBOS BECOME WEREWOLVES

• *The Spectacular Spider-Man* #143

Created by writer Gerry Conway and artist Sal Buscema, Carlos and Eduardo Lobo possessed the mutant ability to transform into werewolves. They used this ability to become major crimelords and started a gang war with the Kingpin.

- *Excalibur* #1 by Chris Claremont and Alan Davis was launched as a monthly series based on the group of British Super Heroes.
- *The Mutant Misadventures Of Cloak And Dagger* #1 was Marvel's second attempt to give the popular duo a regular title.

WOLVERINE HEADLINES HIS OWN TITLE

• *Wolverine* #1

When Tom DeFalco asked writer Chris Claremont and editor Bob Harras to produce a monthly Wolverine title, Claremont objected. He thought the character would be better served by a run of limited series, each marketed as a big event. Fearing that these series would never materialize, DeFalco scheduled *Wolverine* #1, which ran for 189 issues.

- Marvel published *Count Duckula* #1, based on the popular animated series.
- *Doctor Strange, Sorcerer Supreme* #1 propelled the master of mysticism on his longest running series.

A NEW WAR COMIC

• *Semper Fi* #1

Since the war comic *The 'Nam* was selling so well, Marvel created *Semper Fi* #1. The title—"always faithful" in Latin—was taken from the official motto of the United States Marine Corps. The comic focused on the Whittier family whose members had been Marines in various wars from 1777 to the present day. Each issue contained two stories written by Michael Palladino. John Severin, Andy Kubert, and Sam Glanzman provided the artwork.

Inspired by the comic strip Terry And The Pirates *and the film* Casablanca, *Chris Claremont set the new* Wolverine *series in the fictional country of Madripoor.*

MEANWHILE IN 1988...

PERESTROIKA: RESTRUCTURING BEGINS

Under President Gorbachev, the USSR begins a program of economic reforms that introduces private ownership, market economics, and foreign investment and brings a thaw in relations with the West.

TERRORIST EXPLOSION OVER LOCKERBIE

Pan Am flight 103 crashes over Scotland after Libyan intelligence agents place a bomb on board. All 259 passengers and eleven people in the Scottish town of Lockerbie are killed.

USSR FORCES LEAVE AFGHANISTAN

After eight years of conflict between Marxist and Mujahideen insurgents, the Red Army begins to withdraw from Afghanistan.

NASA RESUMES SPACE FLIGHTS

America's program of space travel begins again with the launch of Discovery, *the first voyage since all flights were grounded after the* Challenger *disaster in 1986.*

FIRST WOMAN PRIME MINISTER IN PAKISTAN

Benazir Bhutto wins the first democratic election in eleven years and becomes Prime Minister.

NEARLY ONE TV PER HOUSEHOLD

Ninety-eight per cent of American households now have at least one television set.

OPTICAL FIBERS UNDER OCEAN

TAT-8 is the eighth transatlantic telephone cable under the sea, but it represents a landmark in telecommunications because it is the first to use optical fibers.

CDS OUTSELL RECORDS

For the first time, music compact discs (CDs) are now outselling vinyl records.

FIRST "FAIRTRADE" LABEL

The first label promoting ethical standards in agriculture is brought to mainstream consumers thanks to an initiative with Mexican coffee producers. This move marks the beginning of increased consumer awareness of the impact of trade on the developing world.

AND AT THE MOVIES...

Die Hard, *Bruce Willis's one-man-army gets his shirt off in this taut thriller about a skyscraper taken over by terrorists;* Who Framed Roger Rabbit, *this comedy-noir whodunit plays the sexy Jessica Rabbit opposite Bob Hoskins' wisecracking PI in this flawless integration of animation and live-action;* Rain Man, *selfish yuppie (Tom Cruise) discovers he has a brother with Asperger's syndrome (Dustin Hoffman) and they set off on a road trip, which begins with financial motivations, but becomes a touching journey of discovery for both of them.*

EVIL IS A REAL FORCE AND IT'S GOING TO HAVE ITS WAY WITH SOME PEOPLE.

1989

A PRESIDENT READS AND A PERELMAN BUYS

As the decade drew to a close, Marvel received some rather unexpected publicity—President Ronald Reagan confessed that the first thing he read in the newspaper every morning was the syndicated *Spider-Man* comic strip.

Spider-Man was already an active spokesman for the National Committee to Prevent Child Abuse and in 1989 he was made an honorary chairperson for UNICEF's Halloween fundraising campaign.

Tom DeFalco and Mark Gruenwald began weekly "Assistant Editor Classes," in which they revealed the secrets of the comic book industry and taught the craft of visual storytelling to the next generation of editors.

In the June-dated comics, *Stan Lee's Soapbox* returned to the *Bullpen Bulletins* after an absence of nearly nine years. Along with its line of hardcover *Marvel Masterworks*, the company increased its production of trade paperbacks and actively distributed them to bookstores.

Having owned Marvel for three years, New World Entertainment sold it to a holding company owned by billionaire investor Ronald Perelman. Believing that Marvel had the potential to become as big as Disney, Perelman's people began to acquire other companies. For the first time in its history, Marvel was owned by someone who could afford to invest in its future, a future that suddenly seemed brighter…

MARCH

VISION QUEST COMMENCES

• *The West Coast Avengers* #42

Writer/artist John Byrne produced the story arc that came to be known as Vision Quest that ran through *The West Coast Avengers* #42–45. The Scarlet Witch awoke one morning to discover that her husband, the synthozoid Vision, was missing. He had been kidnapped by a consortium of intelligence agents from various governments, which viewed the Vision as a threat to world security because of his ability to infiltrate any computer network. The consortium dismantled him and erased his programming. Hank Pym managed to reassemble the Vision, but only in an all-white body that had lost all his emotions.

THE SUPER NOVA SAGA

• *The Avengers* #301

The solo survivor of a ravaged planet, Super Nova streaked toward Earth on a mission of vengeance in the story arc that ran through *The Avengers* #301–303 by editor/writer Ralph Macchio, writer/artist Bob Hall, and artist Rich Buckler. Mistakenly believing that the woman who had destroyed his world was an Avenger, he planned to incinerate the entire planet, but the Avengers stopped him.

DAMAGE CONTROL TO THE RESCUE!

• *Damage Control* #1

Has a spaceship crashed into your building? Are inhabitants from an underworld civilization ruining your lawn? Did the Hulk smash your house to smithereens? Call Damage Control! Created by writer Dwayne McDuffie and artist Ernie Colan, Damage Control was a construction company that specialized in the removal and repair of property damaged by anything out of the ordinary. It first appeared in the 1988 *Marvel Age Annual* and then in *Marvel Comics Presents* #19 (May, 1989). This four-issue limited series was followed by two others: *Damage Control: The Movie* (1991) and *World War Hulk Aftersmash: Damage Control* (2008).

MAY

INTRODUCING JUBILEE

"Rock'n'rude, that's Jubilee—especially with folks who torture my friends! So clear the road, Jack—before I cut loose my Fourth of July."

• *The Uncanny X-Men* #244

Jubilation Lee was a talented Chinese American gymnast. She appeared destined for the Olympics until her parents were murdered, when she ran away and lived in the Hollywood Mall. One day, while escaping mall security, she discovered that she had the mutant ability to generate explosive bursts of light like "fireworks" on the Fourth of July.

Frustrated by their inability to catch her, mall security hired a team of mutant hunters. In this issue, written by Chris Claremont and illustrated by Mark Silvestri, a group of X-Men happened to be shopping at the Mall and helped Jubilee to escape. She followed them into a portal that teleported her to their secret base in the Australian outback and, without their knowledge, hid in the tunnels that surrounded their base. The super-criminal cyborgs, the Reavers later attacked, capturing and torturing Wolverine. After Jubilee nursed him back to health, she became his unofficial sidekick, travelling the world with him and helping him on various missions. Professor Xavier later persuaded her to join a new team of young mutants called Generation X-Men, which was being instructed by Banshee and the recently reformed Emma Frost.

Jubilee lost her mutant powers in the mega-crossover *House Of M* (2005). After briefly running a halfway house for former mutants, she acquired a pair of gauntlets that gave her superhuman strength and, in 2008, she joined the regrouped New Warriors, using the name of Wondra.

M *The Sensational She-Hulk* #1 by writer/artist John Byrne took a tongue-in-cheek approach to superheroics.

JULY

A NEW TEAM OF CRIME-FIGHTERS

• *The West Coast Avengers* #46

When Craig Hollis discovered that he could not die, he decided to fight crime as Mr. Immortal. He advertised for other would-be crime-fighters and assembled the Great Lake Avengers: Dinah Soar, a winged creature who never spoke; Big Bertha, a model who gained superhuman strength by mentally becoming obese; Flatman, who could stretch his body thinner than paper; and Doorman, who could teleport. Squirrel Girl later joined the team, a mutant with squirrel-like powers—writer/artist John Byrne took a tongue-in-cheek approach to superheroics.

SEPTEMBER

BLACKHEART DEBUTS

• *Daredevil* #270

In 1658, a woman was brutally murdered on a hill. Her blood soaked the ground and attracted a flock of crows. Over time, other crimes occurred on the same hill and strange plants began to grow. Finally, in *Daredevil* #270 by editor Ann Nocenti and artist John Romita Jr., a grotesque creature emerged, a creature formed by the demon Mephisto to be his son. Mephisto sent Blackheart to explore the world of men and he soon found himself battling Daredevil and Spider-Man. He later fought Wonder Man and was ultimately destroyed by Ghost Rider. He appeared as the major villain in the film *Ghost Rider* (2007).

A HERD OF SUPER HERO ELEPHANTS

• *Power Pachyderms* #1

Originally entitled *Adult Thermonuclear Samurai Elephants, Power Pachyderms* #1 was a parody of Mirage's *Teenage Mutant Ninja Turtles* comic, which, itself, was a parody of Marvel's *The Uncanny X-Men* and Frank Miller's version of *Daredevil.*

M Based on the success of the *Nick Fury Vs. SHIELD* limited series, Marvel launched a second volume of *Nick Fury, Agent Of SHIELD.*

OCTOBER

M In October, Marvel published *Freddy Krueger's A Nightmare On Elm Street* #1, a black-and-white magazine for adults based on the 1984 horror film franchise that inspired six sequels.

INTRODUCING CROSSBONES

• *Captain America* #360

Captain America was in a race against Baron Zemo in this issue by editor Mark Gruenwald and artist Kieron Dwyer. Cap and the Baron were on an Indiana Jones-like hunt for fragments of the Bloodstone—a jewel that bestowed immortality. Determined to steal the Bloodstone for himself, the Red Skull sent his most trusted operative, the dangerous Crossbones, to steal it. The deadly Crossbones snuck aboard Captain America's ship, kidnapped his girlfriend Diamondback, and destroyed the jewel fragments to prevent them from falling in the hands of the Skull's enemies.

OCTOBER

QUASAR DEBUTS

"I'm still not sure what to make of these wristbands, whether they're safe or not. I'm going to some remote unpopulated area to work on controlling them. If I succeed in mastering them, I'll be back. If I don't, well, let me apologize in advance for ruining your project."

• *Quasar* #1

Wendell Vaughn did not seem destined to be a Super Hero. He joined SHIELD, but was not deemed good enough to be a field agent. Instead, he was assigned to protect a pair of alien wristbands that had once been worn by Atlas Comics' Marvel Boy.

Marvel Boy had returned to Earth in the 1970s and battled the Fantastic Four, but he lost control of his wristbands and was disintegrated. The wristbands were confiscated by SHIELD and when agent William Wesley was asked to test them, he, too, lost control and was disintegrated.

When AIM attempted to steal the wristbands in *Quasar* #1, an issue by Mark Gruenwald and Paul Ryan, Vaughn instinctively donned them and used their power to repel the attack. Fully expecting to suffer the same fate as Marvel Boy and Wesley, Vaughn flew into space. Nothing happened. He had somehow managed to keep control of the wristbands. He went on to call himself Quasar.

Although this issue finally revealed the origin of Quasar, the character had first appeared in *Captain America* #217 (Jan., 1978), using the name Marvel Boy. He occasionally guest-starred in *Captain America* and *Marvel Two-In-One* until he was awarded his own series, which ran for sixty issues. *Quasar* #1 predated all these appearances and *Quasar* #2 occurred after them. Later, Quasar joined the Avengers and in October, 2006, he was killed by Annihilus in *Annihilation: Nova* #4.

NOVEMBER

PUNISHER COMES TO LIFE

• *The Punisher Magazine* #1

This three-issue limited series adapted the *Punisher* film, starring Dolph Lundgren and Louis Gossett Jr. In this version of the story, Frank Castle was an ex-cop who, since the murder of his wife and children, lived in the sewers and served as judge, jury, and execution to the city's criminals. Directed by Mark Goldblatt (*X-Men: The L. Stand*, 2006) and written by Boaz Yakin (*Conan The Barbarian*, 2008), the movie was, unfortunately, a box-office failure.

M *Police Academy* #1 adapted the animated series that was based o the popular film franchise.

M *Marvel Comics Presents* #31 printed the first of an eight-part *Excalibur* serial by Michael Higgins and newcomer Erik Larsen.

SPIDEY'S COSMIC ADVENTURES

• *The Spectacular Spider-Man* #158

Spider-Man was a friendly neighborhood Super Hero. What if that changed? What if he was now powerful enough to take on Magneto or flatten the Hulk with a single blow? These were the questions that led to a scientific accident that temporarily super-charged Spidey. Spider-Man: The Cosmic Adventures story line began in *The Spectacular Spider-Man* #158. It ran through all three Spider-Man titles for two months and climaxed in *The Spectacular Spider-Man* #160.

YUPPIES FROM HELL

• *Sex, Lies, And Mutual Funds Of The Yuppies From Hell*

Written and illustrated by cartoonist Barbara Slate, this was a graphic album for older readers that contained short stories about finding true love in New York City, a theme that foreshadowed television shows like *Sex And The City*.

THE ACTS OF VENGEANCE CROSSOVER

• *Avengers Spotlight* #26

Acts Of Vengeance was a company-wide crossover that appeared in most of Marvel's Super Hero titles between December, 1989, and February, 1990. Loki, the Norse God of Mischief, gathered together the villains Dr. Doom, the Kingpin of Crime, Magneto, the Mandarin, the Red Skull, and the Wizard. He had a simple plan—instead of fighting their regular foes, everyone would fight a hero who was unfamiliar with their powers and abilities, for example Spider-Man fought Magneto from the X-Men titles. Unlike previous crossovers, it was not necessary to read other titles to get the gist of the story.

THE NEW WARRIORS DEBUT

• *The Mighty Thor* #411

As part of his five-year publishing plan, Tom DeFalco had intended to launch a team of teenage Super Heroes in 1990, but an opportunity came along in 1989. All he had to do was come up with a team. He made a list of every teenage Super Hero in the Marvel Universe and he learned from Marvel's newsstand distributor that the best-selling magazines among teenagers were those about skateboarding. Armed with this information, he assembled his team. The New Warriors consisted of the cosmic adventurer Nova; Angelica Jones, the mutant called Firestar; crime-fighter Speedball; Vance Astrovik as Marvel Boy; and a new character—Night Thrasher, who rode a motorized skateboard.

MEANWHILE IN 1989...

GEORGE BUSH IS PRESIDENT

George Herbert Walker Bush becomes the forty-first President of the United States.

THE QUAKE OF '89

A state of emergency is declared after the Loma Prieta Earthquake—7.1 on the Richter scale—hits San Francisco. More than sixty people are killed, over 3,000 injured, and 12,000 homeless.

BERLIN WALL TORN DOWN

After twenty-eight years of division, East and West Berlin are united as people begin to dismantle the Berlin Wall, paving the way for the reunification of Germany.

WAVE OF LIBERATION ACROSS EASTERN EUROPE

The iron curtain opens a little wider with moves toward democratic reform across Bulgaria, Romania, Czechoslovakia, Hungary, Poland, and East Germany. In Romania, Communist President Ceausescu and his wife are executed.

US TROOPS INVADE PANAMA

Operation Just Cause begins a six-week campaign to overthrow the Panama dictator, General Manuel Noriega.

MOVIE: THE SEQUEL

The 1980s sees the commercial high-budget "blockbuster" film aimed at mass audiences, a feature of which is the sequel. Sequels in 1989 include Ghostbusters II, Indiana Jones And The Last Crusade, Back To The Future Part II, *and* Lethal Weapon 2.

FIRST GAMEBOY IS RELEASED

The first compact video system—with a screen in shades of gray—is launched and marks the beginning of portable gaming.

THE WORLD WIDE WEB

The first World Wide Web server and browser are created by Tim Berners-Lee, paving the way for the future explosion of Internet usage.

MICROSOFT OFFICE ON SALE

Microsoft releases the first version of its bundle of software applications, which includes Microsoft Word for word processing and Mircrosoft Excel for using spreadsheets.

AND AT THE MOVIES...

Batman, *Tim Burton's dark vision of Gotham City features Jack Nicholson's electric Joker;* Do The Right Thing, *Spike Lee's lively polemic presents a provocative distillation of racial tensions in Brooklyn on a hot summer's day;* Born on the Fourth of July, *a biopic of Vietnam vet-turned-anti-war, pro-human rights political activist Ron Kovic;* When Harry Met Sally, *classic romcom that asks whether men and women can ever "just be friends" and introduces terms like "high-maintenance."*

The West Coast Avengers ***#46 (July, 1989) Written and pencilled by John Byrne and inked by Mike Machlan.***
John Byrne was born in West Bromwich, England on July 6, 1950 and settled in Canada when he was eight. His first exposure to Super Heroes was George Reeves in The Adventures Of Superman *television show. He broke into comics in 1974 when he started freelancing for Charlton Comics. He later moved to Marvel, where he worked on titles like* Iron Fist, The Champions *and* Marvel Team-Up *and, later on,* The X-Men *and* Fantastic Four. *Having established himself as both a writer and a penciller, Byrne would go on to revamp* Superman *for DC Comics with the best-selling* Man Of Steel *limited series and create new series like* John Byrne's Next Men *and* Danger Unlimited. *Byrne has also written three novels:* Fear Book, Whipping Boy, *and* Wonder Woman: Gods And Goddesses.

1990s

Comics were selling in the millions. The 1990s saw the peak of the direct market, as fans bought dozens of their favorite issues, hoping to see a return on their investment years later. Crossovers began to be commonplace, taking characters from their usual world and comic book title and placing them into the lives and titles of other heroes in order to birth massive team-up stories or unexpected battles. It was a time of superstar artists, flashy splash panels, and multi-issue epics where character development was often shelved in favor of violence and action. But that is not to say there weren't diamonds hidden in the heaps of cubic zirconium. As in any era of comics, groundbreaking works appeared, stunning a complacent audience, or at times even coming in beneath their radar. It was a decade that birthed criticism, records, and legends. And as always, Marvel was at the forefront of it all.

BUT I'VE GOT TO TELL YOU, WHEN IT COMES RIGHT DOWN TO IT, I CAN BE PRETTY AWESOME IF I WANT.

1990

BIRTH OF THE IMAGE AGE

By 1990, the era of the comic book superstar artist had begun. Todd McFarlane, Jim Lee, and Rob Liefeld had been amassing hoards of fans with their dramatic drawing styles in the pages of their respective titles *Amazing Spider-Man*, *The Uncanny X-Men*, and *The New Mutants*. Indeed, the artists had begun to enjoy such creative freedom that the writers at each title seemed to be taking a back seat. However, this new approach to comics was clearly working, and sales were hitting record highs. This culminated with Todd McFarlane's new monthly series, titled simply *Spider-Man*, which sold over 2.5 million copies, thanks in part to variant cover editions.

In 1990, Marvel enjoyed unparalleled success with the comics that McFarlane, Lee, and Liefeld created, with fans purchasing several copies of their favorite comics as a future investment of sorts. This resulted in mammoth sales figures that would only be exceeded in the year to follow. In recent years, Marvel had bred its own superstar artists, but by 1992, the comic company would lose them as McFarlane, Lee, and Liefeld went on to cofound Image Comics, along with four other Marvel luminaries: Erik Larsen, Whilce Portacio, Jim Valentino, and Marc Silvestri. But as of 1990, the stars were shining brighter than ever before, and the future looked just as brilliant.

FEBRUARY

HULK QUELLS THE RIOT SQUAD

• *The Incredible Hulk* #366

Continuing his legendary Hulk run, writer Peter David, along with artist Jeff Purves, created the Riot Squad, a team of super-powered villains intent on bringing down the Hulk. The team was under the employ of the Hulk's arch-foe the Leader, and included the aptly-named Rock, the heavily armed Redeemer, the telekinetic Jailbait, the fire-projecting Hotshot, and the bestial Ogress.

The fierce Ogress could nearly match the Hulk's physical strength and savagery.

M The Mutant Liberation Front, a team of terrorist mutants, debuted in the pages of *The New Mutants* #86 by writer Louise Simonson and penciller Rob Liefeld.

MARCH

CABLE VS. STRYFE

• *The New Mutants* #87

When the newly formed Mutant Liberation Front (MLF) staged an attack on a secret energy research station, writer Louise Simonson and penciller Rob Liefeld introduced one of the hottest stars of the 1990s, the mysterious mutant known only as Cable. Displaying an impressive array of telekinetic abilities, and toting a gun nearly as large as he was, Cable hunted the mutant terrorists for reasons solely his own. Also introduced in this issue was the evil leader of the MLF, Stryfe, whose past was as enigmatic as the man stalking him, and who seemed to share a common bond with his pursuer.

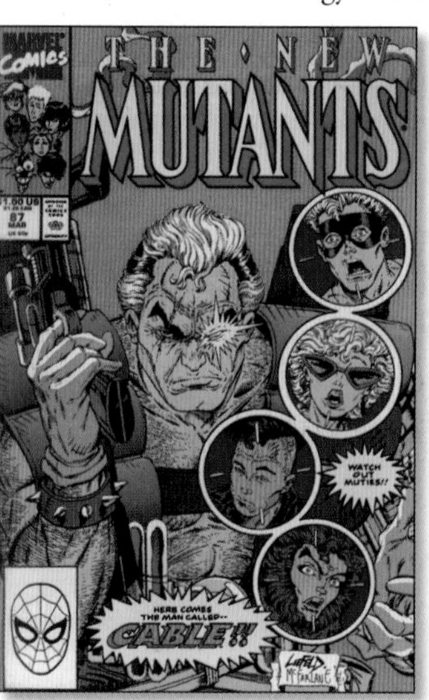

APRIL

NAMOR'S NEW LEASE

• *Namor The Sub-Mariner* #1

Comics superstar John Byrne revamped the classic Marvel character Namor in this new series that he both wrote and drew. The comic saw the avenging son of Atlantis meet Dr. Caleb Alexander, who had deduced that Namor had a blood imbalance that created fluctuations in his personality, explaining some of Namor's past fits of rage. With Dr. Alexander's help, Namor founded Oracle, Inc., a large corporation intent on saving the planet.

M Hulk's future teammates, the Pantheon, made their debut in a few panels of *The Incredible Hulk* #368.

GHOST RIDER RIDES AGAIN

• *Ghost Rider* #1

Popular writer Howard Mackie and penciller Javier Saltares had a sensation on their hands when they created Daniel Ketch, the second man to wear the mantle of the supernatural Ghost Rider. Accidentally wandering onto the scene of an underworld deal gone bad in a junkyard one night, Danny and his sister Barb hid underneath a mountain of junked cars, Barb bleeding badly from having been shot with an arrow by one of the criminals. With his hands covered in the blood of his innocent sister, Danny touched a glowing gas cap of a mysterious motorcycle and was transformed into the avenging Ghost Rider.

THE GUARDIANS RETURN

• *Guardians Of The Galaxy* #1

Marvel's 31st-century heroes finally received an ongoing series thanks to writer/artist Jim Valentino. The series featured the adventures of super-powered teammates Starhawk, Major Vance Astro, Charlie-27, Yondu, Nikki, and Martinex.

AUGUST

GAMBIT GUEST-STARS

• *The Uncanny X-Men* #266

When the X-Men's Storm attempted to break free from the home of the Shadow King, she encountered one of the most popular X-Men of the 1990s, the enigmatic thief called Gambit. Created by legendary X-scribe Chris Claremont and artist Michael Collins, Gambit's Southern charm, thick Cajun accent, and ability to supercharge objects with kinetic energy for explosive results won over the readers. He soon became a full-fledged member of the X-Men, forming an on-again/off-again romance with Southern belle member, Rogue.

NEW WARRIORS AND OLD FAVORITES

"Is it just me… or is this an incredibly dramatic and emotional turning point in our lives?"

• *The New Warriors* #1

Billed as "Heroes for the 90's--!", *The New Warriors* was the brainchild of writer/editor Tom DeFalco, who first debuted the team in the pages of *The Mighty Thor* #411 in December of the previous year. In this ongoing series, writer Fabian Nicieza with former Marvel Tryout art contest winner and future *Spider-Man* superstar Mark Bagley chronicled the tales of a team that not only thrived in this brave new decade, but continued to make an impact in the Marvel Universe over the years. *The New Warriors* lasted a solid seventy-five issues, perhaps enticing a generation of readers that wanted a young team they could get on board with from the beginning. The series also inspired two later follow-up series and a miniseries of the same title.

An eclectic bunch, the New Warriors consisted of Firestar, a character created for the popular *Spider-Man And His Amazing Friends* animated TV series; street-tough newcomer Night Thrasher; the young powerhouses Marvel Boy (later Justice) and Kid Nova (later Nova); Atlantian cousin of the Sub-Mariner, Namorita; and Steve Ditko's classic comic relief character, Speedball. Funded and organized by Night Thrasher's guardians' fortune, the New Warriors set up shop in a midtown Manhattan high-rise after Night Thrasher sought out Nova, Firestar, and Marvel Boy individually, deducing their secret identities one by one. Namorita and Speedball were not recruited, but joined as the team banded together for an impromptu fight against the earth-moving villain Terrax at the site of an outdoor genetic research study in Queens, solidifying the New Warriors' roster.

The New Warriors featured such talents as Speedball, Firestar, Namorita, Marvel Boy, Kid Nova, and Night Thrasher.

TODD MCFARLANE'S SPIDER-MAN

"The witch bleeds. Life drains from her—but she is blinded to it all. Consumed with an image that must be obliterated, cleansed from her mind. An image of—the spider."

• *Spider-Man* #1

Fan sensation Todd McFarlane was previously established only as an artist but finally got his chance at more creative freedom when he wrote, pencilled, and inked the new series created just for him—the adjective-free *Spider-Man*. Feeling restless in his role of penciller on *The Amazing Spider-Man* and wanting a new challenge, McFarlane spoke to his editor Jim Salicrup about the possibility of working on a title that he could both write and draw. Not wanting to lose the popular creator, Salicrup instead offered him his own new Spidey title, and McFarlane jumped at the chance. The result was Torment, McFarlane's first story arc that ran through the pages of the first five issues of *Spider-Man*, beginning in August.

Torment told the story of a mind-controlled Lizard lurking in Manhattan's sewers and on a mad killing rampage. Following a set of clues that revealed that Dr. Curt Connors was behind the recent string of murders, Spider-Man finally defeated the Lizard. He also managed to defeat the voodoo-wielding witch that was manipulating him, a woman who had been a former lover of Spider-Man's old foe, Kraven.

Famous for his depiction of Spidey's webs, McFarlane's art was given the foil treatment with three variant cover editions: silver, gold, and card-stock platinum.

Featuring a dark and moody tale, *Spider-Man* was printed on a hi grade of paper stock, previously unavailable to McFarlane on *The Amazing Spider-Man*, and one that allowed the details of his artwor to really be displayed for the first time. The series proved to be such hit that McFarlane left the book after fifteen issues to found his own comic company, Image Comics, with other well-known creators.

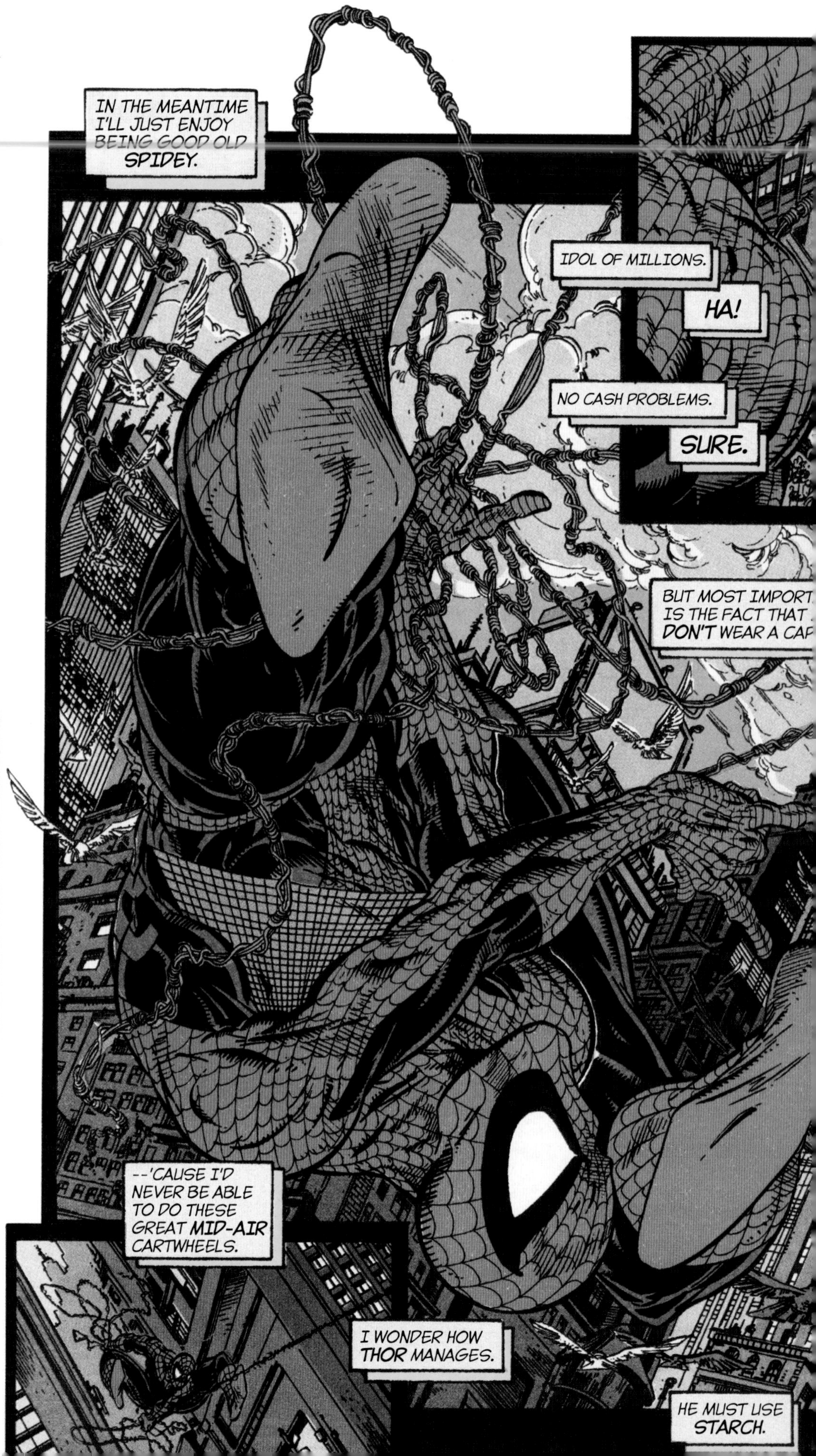

This sequence shows Peter Parker's optimism and upbeat attitude, traits that kept him going as his surroundings grew ever darker.

THE X-TINCTION AGENDA

"Goodbye, Selfriend. We're going to miss you."

• *The Uncanny X-Men* #270

With a marketplace primed for flashy event-oriented stories, the X-Men titles took full advantage with their epic crossover, "X-Tinction Agenda". The story line originated in November in issue 270 of *The Uncanny X-Men* and continued into *The New Mutants* and *X-Factor*. The powers that be at Marvel saw not only the selling potential of uniting their vast multitude of X-Men characters, but also the power of linking many of their popular creators on one narrative. Among those industry giants that helped craft this larger-than-life crossover story were writers Chris Claremont and Louise Simonson, and artists Jim Lee, Rob Liefeld, and Jon Bogdanove. The story featured the team-up of all three X-Men teams, allowing the fan favorite X-Men founders to mingle with the new class of super-popular heroes, a formula Marvel revisited a year later, when the titles were revamped.

The X-Tinction Agenda story line began when X-Factor's foe Cameron Hodge successfully survived decapitation at the hands of winged Archangel. He then kidnapped several members of the New Mutants and held them on Genosha, a small island nation off the coast of Africa, preparing to execute them for past crimes. In an attempt to free their friends, the remaining New Mutants and X-Factor members journeyed to the island, encountering the slave-like mutates that served as the bottom rung of society in this segregated nation. With the help of the X-Men, the teams rescued their captured friends and defeated Hodge, but at the cost of the life of New Mutant member Warlock.

The X-Tinction Agenda *also saw the brainwashed former X-Men member Havok lead an attack on Storm and the New Mutants.*

MEANWHILE IN 1990...

NELSON MANDELA FREED

After twenty-seven years of imprisonment in South Africa, Nelson Mandela is released from prison.

MILITARY DICTATOR OF PANAMA SURRENDERS TO US

Having fled after the American invasion of Panama in December, Manuel Noriega surrenders to US troops.

REUNIFICATION OF GERMANY

East Germany and West Germany officially reunify into a single country after fifty-five years of separation.

LEANING TOWER OF PISA CLOSES

Following safety concerns about its structural condition, the Leaning Tower of Pisa, which leans at an angle of 3.97 degrees, is closed to the public.

FIRST MCDONALD'S IN RUSSIA

The first McDonald's restaurant opens in Moscow in Pushkin Square.

AMERICANS WITH DISABILITIES ACT SIGNED

President George H.W. Bush signs legislation intended to protect disabled Americans from discrimination.

HUBBLE TELESCOPE LAUNCHES

The Hubble Telescope is the first space telescope to be launched into the Earth's orbit.

CHANNEL TUNNELERS MEET

The two halves of the Channel Tunnel being constructed between Britain and France are connected, linking the UK with mainland Europe for the first time since the Ice Age.

"NC-17" INTRODUCED

The Motion Picture Association of America (MPAA) introduces the NC-17 (No children under 17 admitted) rating for films.

CARTOONS FOR ADULTS

Following the success of The Simpsons, *animated cartoons aimed at adult audiences become popular. Later programs include* South Park, King of the Hill, Family Guy, *and* Futurama. *Highly satirical, the shows parody American life and society.*

AND AT THE MOVIES...

Edward Scissorhands, *social outcast Edward Scissorhands is adopted into society through his hedging and hairdressing skills in Tim Burton's updated Frankenstein fairytale;* Goodfellas, *Martin Scorsese's frantic account of the rise and fall of a real-life mobster;* Pretty Woman, *high-grossing 1940s-style romantic comedy starring Julia Roberts and Richard Gere, given the modern Cinderella treatment.*

THE LOOSE-LEAF MARVEL HANDBOOK

• *The Official Handbook of the Marvel Universe* #1

Having released two series of guides to their characters' powers and histories in a standard comic book format, Marvel debuted this thirty-six-issue series. The handbook was in a loose-leaf format and could be stored in three ring binders, providing its readers with easy updating potential.

DAYS OF FUTURE PRESENT

• *Fantastic Four Annual* #23

With the success of the now-classic X-Men story Days of Future Past, where mutants were held in concentration camps in an alternate future, the similarly titled Days of Future Present story line crossed over into four of the annuals of the 1990s and continued into *X-Factor*, *The New Mutants*, and *The Uncanny X-Men*. This first part, written by Walter Simonson, with art by Jackson Guice, marked the debut of Ahab, a denizen from the alternate future, preparing to travel back in time to the present in pursuit of the missing Rachel Summers.

1991

FLASH VERSUS SUBSTANCE

By 1991, story was becoming secondary. Variant covers and sealed issues were on the upswing, inspiring some to not even read the comics they purchased and store them away as investments. In an era where flashy splash pages and characters wielding large weapons were selling comics, the few gems of storytelling were almost overlooked. Among them was writer and artist Frank Miller's *Elektra Lives Again*, a graphic novel as innovative as it was retrospective, while storyteller Barry Windsor-Smith created what some consider the ultimate Wolverine story in the otherwise quiet anthology *Marvel Comics Presents*.

JANUARY

THE NEW FANTASTIC FOUR GO INTO ACTION

• *Fantastic Four* #348

January saw the formation of a new Fantastic Four. When the alien Skrull rebel De'Lila incapacitated the current FF in their own headquarters, Spider-Man, the Hulk, Wolverine, and Ghost Rider were tricked into forming a new Fantastic Four and helping her in her quest to slay the Skrull emperor. Written by Walter Simonson with art by Arthur Adams, this new FF found themselves locked in battle with the Mole Man before bringing De'Lila to justice.

FEBRUARY

DEADPOOL, DOMINO, AND GIDEON

• *The New Mutants* #98

Continuing to hook readers and gather steam, artist Rob Liefeld, along with writer Fabian Nicieza, introduced Deadpool, the slightly unbalanced assassin dispatched to kill the mutant Cable. Though unsuccessful at the task, Deadpool never lost his sense of humor, despite being quite literally stabbed in the back by another character to debut in this issue, the femme fatale Domino. This comic also featured the debut of a future thorn in the New Mutants' side, the mysterious Gideon.

MARCH

WEAPON X

"Everybody's got one. Or two, maybe. Secrets, I mean. I got a doozie. It's a serious motherload. Hard hidin' it, sometimes. But I get by."

• *Marvel Comics Presents* #72

A successful anthology title, *Marvel Comics Presents* had been headlining an X-Men related story since its conception, with Wolverine receiving more than his fair share of the spotlight. But it was not until Barry Windsor-Smith wrote and illustrated the thirteen-chapter *Weapon X* serial, that fans really sat up and paid attention. The serial displayed a mature approach to comic book storytelling complimented by equally sophisticated artwork. In it,

Windsor-Smith set out to tell one of the most anticipated X-Men stories ever told: the secret of Wolverine's adamantium skeleton.

Weapon X, a secret Canadian government program run by Professor Thorton, took Wolverine captive and placed him into a special tank. Here, he became the victim of experiments that took advantage of his mutant healing factor in an attempt to create the ultimate human weapon. Coating his bones with adamantium, an unbreakable metal alloy, the technical experts of the Weapon X program monitored Logan's thoughts and watched as he reverted to his primitive, violent instincts. Using technology to control his functions, Thorton and his crew pit Wolverine against wild wolves and bears, before Logan managed to escape in a fit of rage. However, in a twist, Wolverine's escape was actually a computer-generated fantasy of his mind's eye, and the real Wolverine was still under the control of Weapon X personnel. Now with a taste of freedom, Wolverine acted out his fantasy, freeing himself and escaping into the wild, and was left to wonder if he was still more man than animal.

DARKHAWK MAKES HIS DEBUT

• *Darkhawk* #1

Darkhawk was created by editor Tom DeFalco and artist Mike Manley with scripts by Danny Fingeroth. It was the latest creation in the movement toward darker vigilantes, waging a hard war on crime, but was seen through the mind set of Darkhawk's alter ego, high school student Chris Powell.

Powell had followed his brothers into an amusement park fun house after closing, and saw his police officer father taking a bribe from some gangsters. As the deal went sour, Chris stumbled upon an odd amulet that transformed him into the adult Darkhawk, letting him fight the noble battle his father could not.

OUT WITH THE OLD, IN WITH THE NEW

• *The New Mutants* #99

Solar-powered Sunspot may have quit the New Mutants, but it was not long before he was replaced. Feral, a female mutant, found her way to the New Mutant's bunker hideout, courtesy of writer Fabian Nicieza, with art and plot by Rob Liefeld. This issue also saw the first cameo of future member Shatterstar.

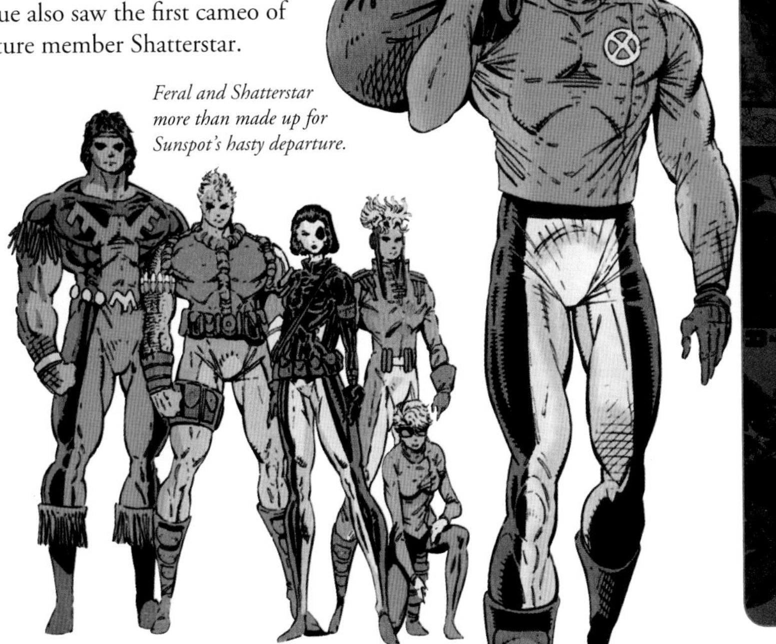

Feral and Shatterstar more than made up for Sunspot's hasty departure.

MARCH

ELEKTRA LIVES AGAIN

"The fire—even across the street it's blistering. But she's cold. She's someplace cold."

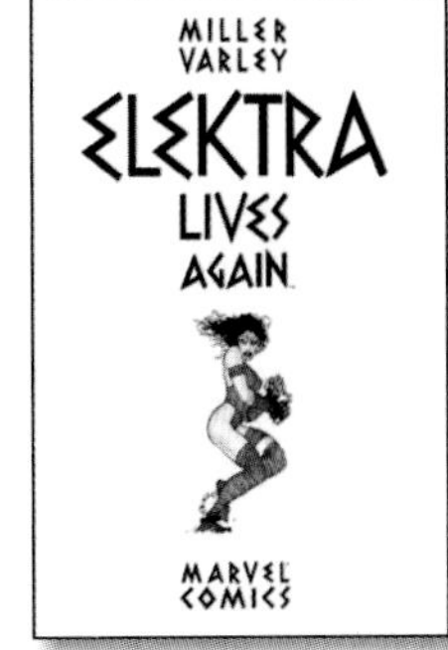

Frank Miller made a triumphant return to Elektra, the character he breathed life into and then subsequently snuffed out, with the graphic novel *Elektra Lives Again*. Miller both wrote and drew this deluxe oversized hardcover, with breathtaking painted coloring from his wife, Lynn Varley. The pair had already perfected their craft on the highly acclaimed miniseries for DC Comics, *Batman: The Dark Knight Returns*.

The story featured an obsessed Matt Murdock (Daredevil's alter ego), who was questioning his own reality, as Elektra, his former lover, returned from the dead. Elektra was being pursued by dozens of reanimated corpses created by the ninja clan, the Hand. To make matters worse, the newly deceased body of Daredevil's arch foe Bullseye went missing from a morgue. Catching up with the ninja clan, Murdock realized he was too late, as Bullseye had already been resurrected and had succeeded in killing Elektra for the second time. However, with her dying breath, Elektra managed to decapitate the villain, and say farewell to Daredevil, dying again in his arms.

Elektra Lives Again was removed from cannon Marvel continuity due to the death of Bullseye and this version of Elektra's resurrection. Nonetheless, the graphic novel was a critical success. Published under the Epic Comics label, *Elektra Lives Again* featured mature ultra-violence and nudity, a rarity for stories featuring mainstream Marvel Super Heroes.

MAY

AGAMEMNON APPEARS

• *The Incredible Hulk* #381

The Hulk first met Agamemnon, the leader of the Pantheon team, in a story written by Peter David with art by Dale Keown. After describing his team's daring method of operations to help mankind, Agamemnon successfully recruited the Hulk to his cause.

The Pantheon initially held the angry Hulk captive to try to reason with him.

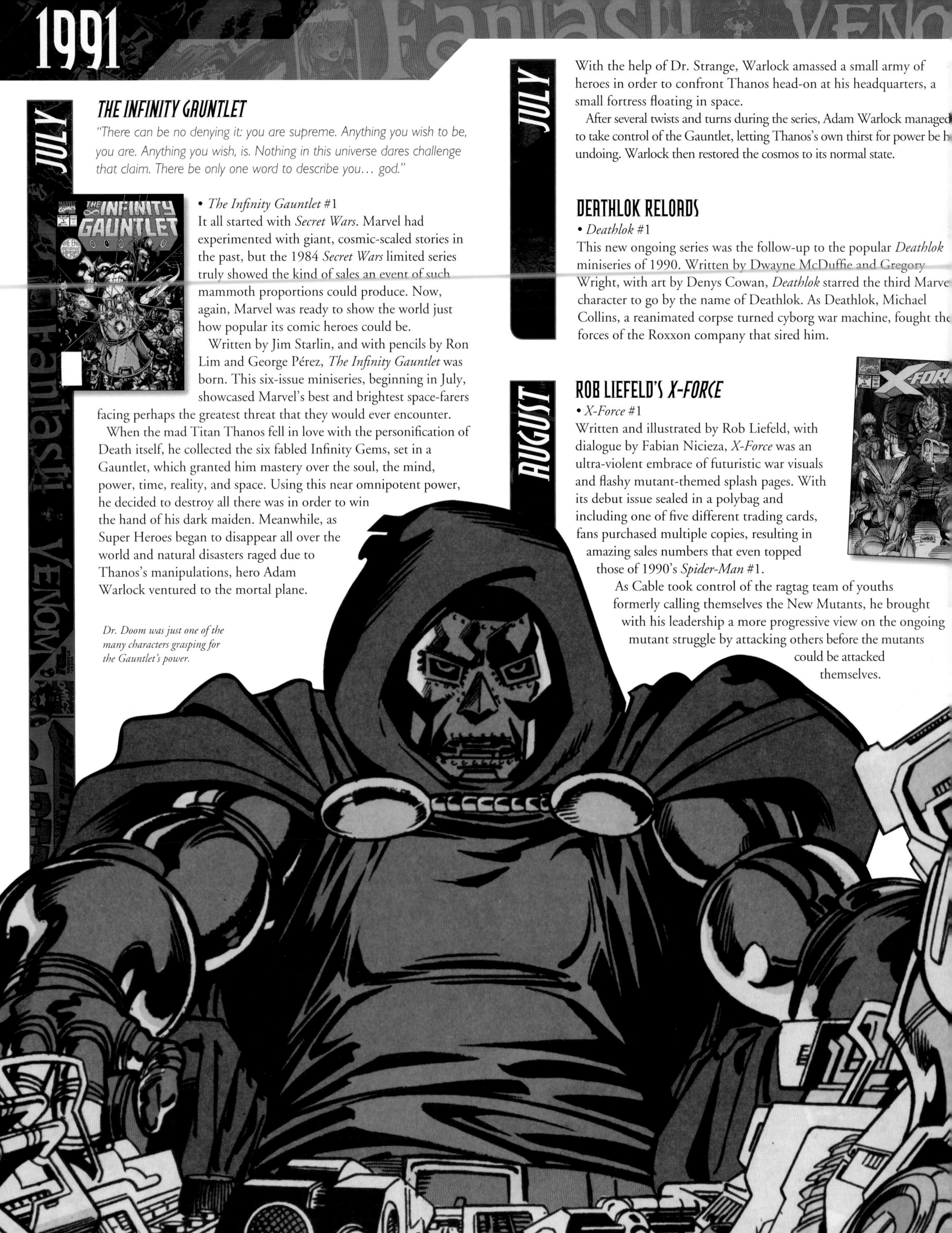

JULY

THE INFINITY GAUNTLET

"There can be no denying it: you are supreme. Anything you wish to be, you are. Anything you wish, is. Nothing in this universe dares challenge that claim. There be only one word to describe you… god."

• *The Infinity Gauntlet* #1

It all started with *Secret Wars*. Marvel had experimented with giant, cosmic-scaled stories in the past, but the 1984 *Secret Wars* limited series truly showed the kind of sales an event of such mammoth proportions could produce. Now, again, Marvel was ready to show the world just how popular its comic heroes could be.

Written by Jim Starlin, and with pencils by Ron Lim and George Pérez, *The Infinity Gauntlet* was born. This six-issue miniseries, beginning in July, showcased Marvel's best and brightest space-farers facing perhaps the greatest threat that they would ever encounter.

When the mad Titan Thanos fell in love with the personification of Death itself, he collected the six fabled Infinity Gems, set in a Gauntlet, which granted him mastery over the soul, the mind, power, time, reality, and space. Using this near omnipotent power, he decided to destroy all there was in order to win the hand of his dark maiden. Meanwhile, as Super Heroes began to disappear all over the world and natural disasters raged due to Thanos's manipulations, hero Adam Warlock ventured to the mortal plane.

Dr. Doom was just one of the many characters grasping for the Gauntlet's power.

JULY

With the help of Dr. Strange, Warlock amassed a small army of heroes in order to confront Thanos head-on at his headquarters, a small fortress floating in space.

After several twists and turns during the series, Adam Warlock managed to take control of the Gauntlet, letting Thanos's own thirst for power be his undoing. Warlock then restored the cosmos to its normal state.

DEATHLOK RELOADS

• *Deathlok* #1

This new ongoing series was the follow-up to the popular *Deathlok* miniseries of 1990. Written by Dwayne McDuffie and Gregory Wright, with art by Denys Cowan, *Deathlok* starred the third Marvel character to go by the name of Deathlok. As Deathlok, Michael Collins, a reanimated corpse turned cyborg war machine, fought the forces of the Roxxon company that sired him.

AUGUST

ROB LIEFELD'S *X-FORCE*

• *X-Force* #1

Written and illustrated by Rob Liefeld, with dialogue by Fabian Nicieza, *X-Force* was an ultra-violent embrace of futuristic war visuals and flashy mutant-themed splash pages. With its debut issue sealed in a polybag and including one of five different trading cards, fans purchased multiple copies, resulting in amazing sales numbers that even topped those of 1990's *Spider-Man* #1.

As Cable took control of the ragtag team of youths formerly calling themselves the New Mutants, he brought with his leadership a more progressive view on the ongoing mutant struggle by attacking others before the mutants could be attacked themselves.

OCTOBER

CLAREMONT AND LEE'S RECORD-BREAKING *X-MEN*

"Gotta say this for the man—he knows how to make an exit."

• *X-Men* #1

It was a simple matter of addition. Take Chris Claremont, the writer who had made *The Uncanny X-Men* the continual hit that it was, and add Jim Lee, the artist who had reinvigorated the title's popularity in recent months. Add the original founding members of Cyclops, Jean Grey, Beast, Iceman, and Archangel to newer fan favorites Wolverine, Storm, Gambit, Colossus, Forge, Banshee, Psylocke, and Rogue. Increase that impressive roster with the ultimate X-villain Magneto, and add in a new ongoing comic title with five variant covers for its first issue. The sum of all these parts was *X-Men* #1, the best selling comic book in the history of the medium, selling well over eight million copies.

When Magneto set up camp on Asteroid M, a floating fortress in Earth's orbit, the X-Men were called into duty by SHIELD Director Nick Fury. They soon confronted Magneto's acolytes in Genosha, where they were wreaking havoc on the country due to its unjust treatment of mutants. Finally gathering their forces, the X-Men headed into space and confronted Magneto in a violent battle of mutant abilities. In the end, when one of Magneto's supposedly loyal supporters fired a plasma cannon at Asteroid M from a shuttle located a safe distance away, Magneto chose redemption. He opted to save the life of his good friend Charles Xavier, sacrificing himself in the process.

This story, concluding in issue #3 of the series, also served as the end of Chris Claremont's association with the X-Men titles for nearly ten years. Claremont cited creative differences with the editorial staff as his reason for departing the X-Universe.

Magneto considered himself the savior of mutantkind, but the X-Men didn't agree.

Four of the five X-Men *#1 covers combined to reveal this large panoramic image, containing probably the most impressive roster of X-Men ever assembled.*

MEANWHILE IN 1991...

OPERATION DESERT STORM
The six-week Gulf War begins with air strikes against Iraq after the UN deadline for Iraq to withdraw from Kuwait expires.

AN END TO THE SOVIET UNION
The USSR officially ceases to exist. Throughout 1990 and 1991 Lithuania, Latvia, Belarus, Georgia, Estonia, Ukraine, Moldova, Azerbaijan, Kyrgyzstan, Uzbekistan, Tajikistan, and Armenia declare their independence. Boris Yeltsin is elected President of Russia.

PRESIDENT TAYLOR EXHUMED
Zachary Taylor, 12th President of the US, is exhumed to determine whether he died from arsenic poisoning, but no arsenic is found.

SONIC THE HEDGEHOG
The first computer game starring the blue hedgehog is released by Sega to rival Nintendo's Mario. The early 1990s see an explosion of home video-gaming.

FREDDIE MERCURY DIES
The solo musician and lead singer of Queen dies of bronchopneumonia resulting from AIDS.

THE RISE OF 24-HOUR MEDIA
Constant coverage of the Gulf War leads to 24/7 news reporting and increased awareness of world events.

THE GRUNGE ERA
Nirvana releases Smells Like Teen Spirit, *part of the grunge movement, famous for distorted electric guitars and angst-ridden vocals.*

MILES DAVIS DIES
Jazz trumpeter Miles Davis dies at the age of sixty-five. Famed for his development of the "cool" jazz style, Davis received the Grammy Lifetime Achievement Award the previous year.

GENERATION X
Douglas Coupland's book Generation X: Tales for an Accelerated Culture, *publishes, referring to the generation born in the late 1960s and early 1970s, which is now adult age.*

ROYAL SPLIT
It is announced that the Prince and Princess of Wales have decided to separate. They have no intention to divorce and will both continue to have an active role in their boys' lives.

AND AT THE MOVIES...
The Silence of the Lambs, *Jonathan Demme's disturbing horror introduces a new kind of psychopathic but cultured anti-hero in Anthony Hopkins' cannibalistic Hannibal Lecter;* Thelma & Louise, *Ridley Scott's groundbreaking feminist road movie follows two women outlaws on the run across America's southwest after shooting a would-be rapist;* JFK, *Kevin Costner's New Orleans DA discovers there is more to the Kennedy assassination than the official story in Oliver Stone's political tale.*

NOVEMBER

BISHOP BURSTS ONTO THE SCENE

• *The Uncanny X-Men* #282

Created by writer John Byrne and artist Whilce Portacio, Bishop found himself traveling back in time to the 20th century, and coming face to face with the X-Men, as the team faced off against Trevor Fitzroy, a mutant able to open portals to the past. Bishop discovered that there was a traitor within the X-Men's ranks and joined their roster, using his energy-absorbing powers to aid the mutant cause until he could deduce the turncoat in their midst.

REST AND RELAXATION

Artist Jim Lee, master of the dynamic splash page, created this pin-up image of the X-Men taking a little well-earned "R and R" time as an extra bonus for the *X-Men*'s debut issue, a double-sized forty-eight-page giant, in October, 1991. These kinds of swimsuit scenes proved popular with the readers, resulting in the series *Marvel Swimsuit Special*, an annual publication that lasted for five consecutive years. Other gallery splashes in this issue of *X-Men* included a parade of X-Men villains, a shot of the X-Men's training facility known as the Danger Room, and a preview of "Things to Come," featuring the ominous villain Omega Red.

Wish you were here!

1992

THE UNIVERSE DARKENS

Sales never again saw the spike that they had in 1991, and many of the biggest names in the comic world began to depart for a bigger slice of the proverbial pie. Despite all this, 1992 saw a continued effort on Marvel's part to launch new titles, most with an emphasis on the dark and the violent. During this era, the antihero became the new hero, perhaps following in the footsteps of the popular *Punisher* and *X-Force* series. These series had caught such favor in the eyes of an audience that was clamoring to the theaters to see the next *Terminator* or *Robocop* film.

Though the hero himself was not getting darker, his world surely was. Villains were growing more bloodthirsty and were no longer content to merely plunder and scheme. The future certainly seemed grim, as showcased in its newest line of *2099* books set in a bleak, corporate-run vision of tomorrow.

JANUARY

THE NEW SWORDSMAN

• *Avengers* #343

Written by Bob Harras with pencils by Steve Epting, the Avengers faced the menace of a mysterious man calling himself the Swordsman, the second one to do so. Later, the Swordsman and his partner Magdalene became honorary Avengers, once the smoke of battle had cleared.

JANUARY

THE FALL OF THE KINGPIN

• *Daredevil* #300

Culminating in the anniversary 300th issue, Daredevil would finally gain the upper hand against longtime foe Wilson Fisk (the Kingpin) in this moody tale by writer D.G. Chichester and penciller Lee Weeks. Serving as an almost sequel to Frank Miller's classic Born Again story line, The Fall of the Kingpin story line began as Daredevil took away Fisk's prized possession, Typhoid Mary. Matthew Murdock, Daredevil's alter ego, then set Kingpin against his former allies, the terrorist organization HYDRA, resulting in the Kingpin losing his home. Finally, Daredevil bested Fisk, leaving the Kingpin a homeless vagr

FEBRUARY

MAVERICK MAKES HIS MOVE

• *X-Men* #5

Jim Lee continued to plot and draw the *X-Men* series and was joined by scripter John Byrne. In the fifth issue, the pair introduced Maverick, an old ally of Wolverine's who had fought alongside him as a fellow CIA operative.

MARCH

PUNISHER ENTERS THE WAR ZONE

• *The Punisher: War Zone* #1

The third ongoing series to star vigilante Frank Castle was *The Punisher: War Zone*, written by Chuck Dixon and with art by John Romita Jr. and Klaus Janson. Though focusing on the Punisher's tough form of vigilante justice, the comic relied on solid storytelling and craft to give the series more appeal to fans than other ultra-violent titles. The comic put a fast-paced spin on the Punisher's usu war on drug runners, and sprouted some memorable moments, including one involving the Punisher interrogating a thug with a popsicle. This scene found its way into the first Punisher movie.

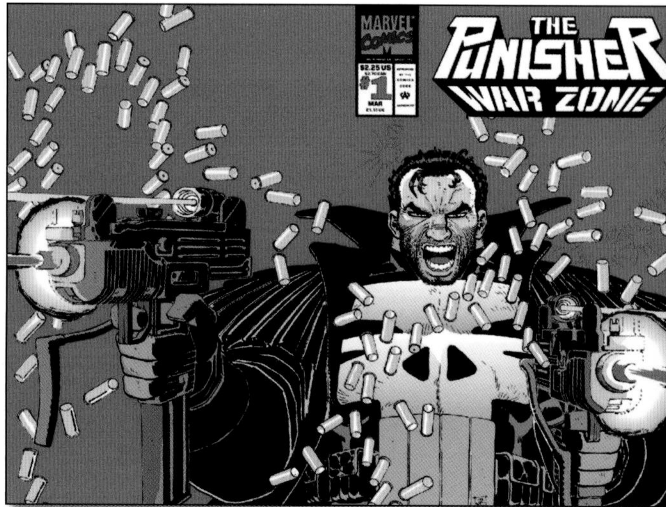

OPERATION: GALACTIC STORM

• *Captain America* #398

The major Avengers crossover story line, Operation: Galactic Storm, began in *Captain America*. It told the story of the Avengers intervening in a battle between the Kree and the Shi'ar. This first episode was written by Mark Gruenwald, with pencils by Rik Levins.

FIRST APPEARANCE OF CARNAGE

"Why am I killin' you…? That's easy. I'm killin' you… 'cause I can."

• *The Amazing Spider-Man* #361

In a genre that was slowly watching its heroes walk a darker path, it simply stood to reason that the villains would have to trump them in that respect. Enter Carnage, the brainchild of writer David Michelinie and penciller Mark Bagley. Carnage was a crueler, more terrible form of the already dark Venom, a symbiote whose fantastic powers were only surpassed by his fanatical blood lust.

After a dozen brutal murders had taken place over the course of a week in Manhattan, Spider-Man finally got a lead on the case when a good friend of his from Empire State University was slaughtered "like a pig on a spit." Peter Parker realized that the villain shared common traits with his old foe Venom and decided to research the prison records of Venom's alter ego, Eddie Brock. In doing so, Parker discovered that Brock had shared a prison cell with unrepentant mass murderer Cletus Kasady. Investigating Kasady's bizarre past history, Spider-Man eventually chanced upon him in an abandoned old orphanage, the only place Kasady ever truly called home. There, Spider-Man caught his first true glimpse of Carnage, the blood-red, souped-up version of Venom's alien symbiote.

Carnage was given life when Brock's symbiote had freed Brock from his jail cell, unwittingly leaving a spawn of itself behind in the chaos. That small slither of the alien symbiote formed so completely with cell mate Kasady that the two considered themselves to be a singular entity, a creature whose only desire was to kill and bring chaos to the world.

A geek at heart, Peter Parker was never above doing a little computer research.

Carnage often caught Spider-Man by surprise, as Peter's spider-sense could not detect the villain.

M The Fantastic Four's favorite blue-eyed monster received his own four-issue miniseries, beginning in April. *The Adventures of the Thing* reprinted some of the Thing's most important stories.

MAY

ENTER THE EXTERNALS

• *X-Force* #10

The Externals, a secret group of immortal mutants, had been mentioned earlier in *X-Force* but were finally seen in issue #10 as frequent X-Force adversary, Gideon, ventured to their secret mountaintop retreat in the Swiss Alps. The series was plotted by Rob Liefeld, scripted by Fabian Nicieza, and penciled by Mark Pacella.

Carnage was a violent sociopath who was said to be loosely modeled after Batman's archenemy, the Joker, of DC Comics fame.

JUNE

SILVER SABLE'S SPOTLIGHT

Silver Sable & The Wild Pack #1

A frequent nemesis of Spider-Man, Silver Sable finally netted her own series thanks to writer Gregory Wright and penciller Steven Butler. Silver Sable teamed with reformed Spidey-foe Sandman and the rest of her cut-throat Wild Pack for a new set of adventures.

OCTOBER

THE X-MEN GET ANIMATED

The new *X-Men* cartoon debuted on October 31st as part of Fox Kids' Saturday morning programming. Featuring the voices of such actors as Tara Strong, Christopher Jay Potter, and Melissa Sue Anderson, and the scripts of known comic book writers like Len Wein and Elliot S. Maggin, the *X-Men* cartoon consisted of seventy-six episodes divided into five seasons. The series held the record for the longest lasting Marvel animated program.

CABLE'S FIRST ROUNDS

• *Cable: Blood & Metal* #1

Mutant Cable's first turn at a starring role was this two-issue limited series from writer Fabian Nicieza and artist John Romita Jr. Detailing Cable's time with his Six Pack mercenary group, the series included members Domino and Cable's later adversary, Garrison Kane.

NOVEMBER

SPIDEY TURNS 2099

"I have respect for the system.... Just none for you."

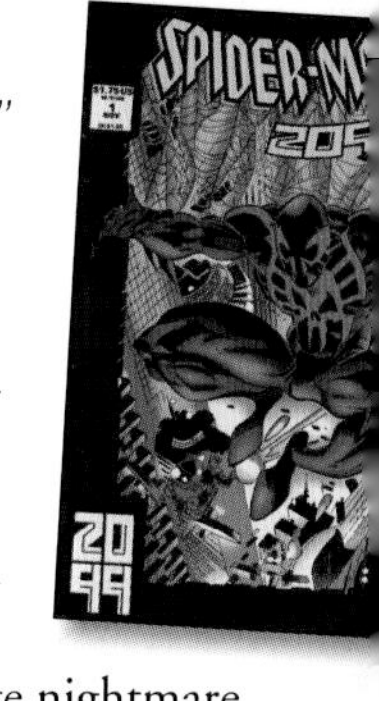

• *Spider-Man 2099* #1

Writer Peter David and artist Rick Leonardi's *Spider-Man 2099* character was first glimpsed in a sneak preview in the pages of *The Amazing Spider-Man* #365 in August 1992. The comic showed a dark vision of the future of the Marvel Universe, and would be the flagship title for a new line of comics set in this dystopian corporate nightmare.

Opening on a new Spider-Man on the run from the police, *Spider-Man 2099* chronicled the life of Miguel O'Hara. O'Hara ha just quit his position as head of the genetics program at the large corporation Alchemax when an experiment was rushed without his permission, permanently mutating a willing test subject. Not takin his resignation lying down, the corrupt head of the company, Tyle Stone, infected Miguel with a designer drug known as Rapture. Th forced O'Hara to subject himself to the genetic experimental proce he had been working on, in order to release the toxic drug from his system. When a jealous coworker noticed Miguel's late night experiment and sabotaged it, Miguel was caught in an accidental explosion that he barely survived. Weakly emerging from the test chamber, O'Hara soon discovered that he now possessed spider-lik powers, including fangs and spiked fingers that allowed him to adh to surfaces. Like the Spider-Man of generations past, Miguel donne a blue and red costume, but this one bore an ominous "death's hea logo, and a web-like "light byte" cloth that allowed him to glide on wind currents. His one goal: to right the corporate wrongdoings th he was powerless to oppose in his civilian identity.

Just like his present day counterpart, the Spider-Man of the year 2099 often found himself at odds with the authorities.

CHOOM

CHOOM

Stryfe shook the X-Men to their core when he nearly assassinated their mentor and friend, Professor Charles Xavier.

X-CUTIONER'S SONG

• *The Uncanny X-Men* #294

The creators of the X-Men books had something to prove. Now that their big name artists had left the company, they needed to show a demanding fan base that they could still deliver the kind of giant comic blockbusters that had made the X-titles the current sensations that they were. So, writers Scott Lobdell, Peter David, and Fabian Nicieza, along with artists Brandon Peterson, Jae Lee, Andy Kubert, and Greg Capullo crafted the X-Cutioner's Song, an epic twelve-part crossover showcasing the various X-teams' battle with the Cable-clone Stryfe. The crossover also contained the stunning revelation that Cable was actually the long lost son of Cyclops and his former lover Madelyn Pryor.

DECEMBER

STAN LEE IS RAVAGED

• *Ravage 2099* #1

Stan Lee returned to his rightful place behind the typewriter with this new series pencilled by Paul Ryan. *Ravage 2099* detailed the struggle of the betrayed head of Eco Central, who had to retire his corporate suit in favor of his primitive instincts as the vigilante Ravage.

Ravage was framed when a Mutroid was paid to burst into his office, claiming that Ravage had betrayed his own company.

MEANWHILE IN 1992...

RACE RIOTS IN LOS ANGELES

Six days of race riots are sparked in Los Angeles after four police officers are acquitted in the trial of the videotaped beating of African-American Rodney King.

QUAYLE GIVES "MURPHY BROWN" SPEECH

Vice President Dan Quayle blames the violence of the Los Angeles riots on a breakdown of society's values and family structure, which he claims is perpetuated by television shows like Murphy Brown.

FIRE AT WINDSOR CASTLE

A spotlight and curtain cause a fire that destroys part of the royal palace Windsor Castle in England.

EARTH SUMMIT

The United Nations Conference on Environment and Development marks a significant step in 172 nations addressing environmental issues such as global climate change.

REALITY TV BEGINS

The Real World *is broadcast and spawns the highly popular reality television genre.*

CDS OUTSELL CASSETTE TAPES

For the first time compact discs are more popular than cassette tapes for recorded music.

PUNCH MAGAZINE FOLDS

The popular illustrated British satirical magazine, Punch, *closes after 150 years of publication.*

EROTICA CONTROVERSY

Madonna releases the music album Erotica. *Its sexual themes are deemed highly controversial and her concerts are banned from Vatican City.*

BIGGEST MALL CONSTRUCTED

Minnesota's Mall of America opens and covers seventy-eight acres and has the largest indoor amusement park.

THE SILENCE OF THE LAMBS DOMINATES THE OSCARS

Based on the novel by Thomas Harris, The Silence of the Lambs *wins five Academy Awards, including Best Actress for Jodie Foster, Best Actor for Anthony Hopkins, and Best Picture.*

AND AT THE MOVIES...

Wayne's World, *Penelope Spheeris' knowing comedy, full of most excellent lines and set pieces, about two slackers running a public-access TV channel;* Unforgiven, *Clint Eastwood's complex western revives the genre by debunking its bloody heroics;* Reservoir Dogs, *Quentin Tarantino's first film, an original take on a heist gone wrong, is packed with memorable characters, dialogue, and soundtrack;* Batman Returns, *Tim Burton's dark imagining of the Batman franchise featuring the Penguin and Catwoman.*

HEY! WE HAVE COMPANY!

1993

THE MORE THE MERRIER

The number of Marvel titles continued to expand in 1993, while Marvel talent continued to be spread thinner and thinner. But it wasn't just Marvel's library that was growing, it was also the number of characters in each story.

It seemed heroes couldn't be bothered to stick to their own titles anymore. Characters like Punisher and Venom were popping up in almost every comic on the shelves. And the larger the story, the more heroes were needed to team-up in it. This emphasis on the idea of the super-team combating a larger threat was illustrated in such stories as Spider-Man's Maximum Carnage and the Midnight Sons' Siege of Darkness epic that crossed through the magic corners of the Marvel Universe. This change of direction culminated in *The Secret Defenders*, where, as well as frequent guest appearances, a different roster of heroes were formed for each new adventure.

JANUARY

THE FUTURE IS DOOMED

• *Doom 2099* #1

Writer John Francis Moore and artist Pat Broderick transported Dr. Doom home to Latveria in this new series. To Doom's surprise, the year was now 2099, and his castle was in ruins. As he donned a new costume, the readers were left wondering if this was the Doom they knew, or a disturbed newcomer.

FEBRUARY

VENOM VEERS WEST

• *Venom: Lethal Protector* #1

This six-issue miniseries was created by Venor veterans writer David Michelir and artist Mark Bagley, and w the first comic in which Veno was the main character. Settin up camp in his new home bas of San Francisco, Venom deal out his fatal form of justice.

THE PUNISHER OF TOMORROW

• *The Punisher 2099* #1

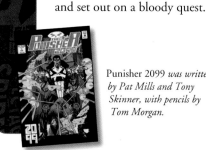

The 2099 alternate reality saw a world where the innocent were only guarded if they had paid up on their police protection plan, and organ harvesting street gangs ran wild through the back alleys of Manhattan, untouched by authority. It was clear that a Punisher was needed more than ever. After seeing his family gunned down while on a trip to the zoo, Jake Gallows donned a uniform similar to that of the original Punisher, Frank Castle, and set out on a bloody quest.

Punisher 2099 *was written by Pat Mills and Tony Skinner, with pencils by Tom Morgan.*

MARCH

DR. STRANGE'S SECRET DEFENDERS

• *The Secret Defenders* #1

Writer Roy Thomas and penciller Andre Coates created this new series that ran until 1995. Using a set of magic and tarot cards, Dr. Strange picked teammates appropriate to the crisis at hand. The first team included Wolverine, Spider-Woman, Nighthawk, and Nomad.

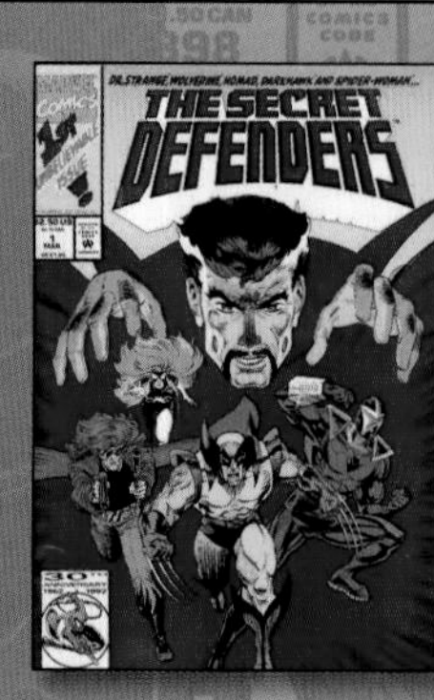

MAY

CABLE CUTS LOOSE

• *Cable* #1

Due to the popularity of *Cable: Blood & Metal*, Cable received his own ongoing series courtesy of writer Fabian Nicieza and artist Art Thibert. The saga opened on Cable's grim future as Garrison Kane, stuck in a time not his own, researched the mysterious Cable to discover that he had a wife and son. On the run due to his snooping into public history files, Kane's life was spared by the arrival of Cabl

Maximum Carnage

"Here comes the bride! All dressed in white! I wish it was red! Then you'd all be dead!"

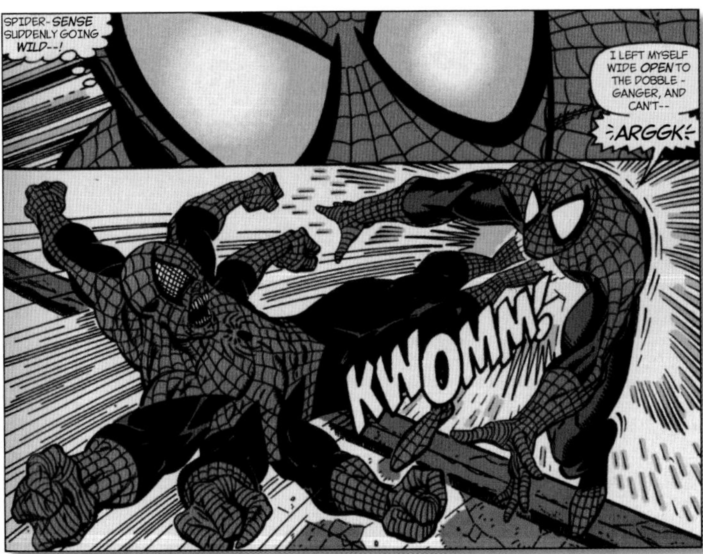

• *Spider-Man Unlimited* #1

Spider-Man's Maximum Carnage story line was an attempt to explore the darkest side of evil. The mammoth fourteen-part story began in the new title *Spider-Man Unlimited*, and continued throughout the Spider-Man line of books, crossing into *The Amazing Spider-Man, Spider-Man, The Spectacular Spider-Man*, and *Web Of Spider-Man*. Writers J.M. DeMatteis, Tom DeFalco, Terry Kavanagh, and David Michelinie and artists Mark Bagley, Sal Buscema, Ron Lim, Tom Lyle, and Alex Saviuk all brought their talents to this key story line.

The story began as Cletus Kasady, the deranged killer also known as Carnage, summoned his alien symbiote while being transferred from the Ravencroft maximum security institution for the criminally insane. Slaughtering the guards, Carnage escaped from captivity after meeting Shriek, a psychotic prisoner who shared his appetite for death. The two began to carve a swath of terror through Manhattan, accepting others to join their cause of chaos, including the evil Spidey duplicate Spider-Doppelganger, demonic Demogoblin, and clone Carrion. Meanwhile, Spider-Man formed an army to confront these villains, including Venom, Cloak and Dagger, the Black Cat, Morbius, Deathlok, Iron Fist, and Captain America himself.

The story line ended when Spider-Man confronted Carnage in Central Park, after Spidey's team took down Kasady's various partners. With help from the unlikely source of Venom, Spider-Man chased Carnage to a graveyard, where Venom knocked Carnage into a generator, causing an explosion that seemingly destroyed the disturbed killer once and for all.

The Death of Harry Osborn

• *The Spectacular Spider-Man* #200

The 200th issue of *The Spectacular Spider-Man*, written by J.M. DeMatteis and with art by Sal Buscema, featured the shocking death of Spider-Man's close friend Harry Osborn. Peter Parker had been dealing with Harry's insanity since Harry's father's death as the original Green Goblin. But their relationship came to a head when Harry kidnapped Peter's wife, Mary Jane. As Spidey faced off against Harry, the tormented Osborn began to have second thoughts, and rescued his son Normie, Mary Jane, and Peter from bombs he had set earlier as the Green Goblin. However, in one last twist, Harry died, poisoned by the goblin formula he had finally willingly rejected.

Deadpool Miniseries Begins

• *Deadpool* #1

The mentally unstable Wade Wilson scored his own four-issue miniseries written by Fabian Nicieza with art by Joe Madureira in August. Throughout the series, Deadpool faced some serious opposition in the forms of Garrison Kane as Weapon X, mutant Black Tom Cassidy, and the unstoppable Juggernaut.

Deadpool, with his carefree attitude, can be his own worst enemy.

Fall From Grace

• *Daredevil* #319

The seven-part Fall From Grace epic story line began in issue #319 of *Daredevil*. When a powerful chemical weapon was lost in the New York City subways, Daredevil found himself in the fight of his life versus the Hand, Silver Sable, Venom, Morbius, SHIELD cyborg John Garrett, the living killing spirit of Elektra, and a literal demon Hellspawn. Daredevil donned a new black costume made of experimental biomimetic material and paired up with Elektra, who was back from the grave. The pair managed to destroy the chemical agent and Hellspawn. However, the resultant battle merged Elektra with the murderous side of her personality that she'd worked so hard to escape from.

Fall From Grace was written by D.G. Chichester, with art by Scott McDaniel.

SEPTEMBER

M Filmmaker Clive Barker's dark vision found its way into comic shops with *Razorline: First Cut*, a special preview edition of his new line of ongoing Super Hero comics for Marvel.

OCTOBER

THE NEXT GENERATION OF X-MEN

• *X-Men 2099* #1

Writer John Francis Moore and artist Ron Lim birthed a new team of mutants adopting Charles Xavier's dream in this uncertain future. The team included leader Xi'an Chi Xan, superspeedster Meanstreak, the self-explanatory Junkpile, and the mineral-condensing Krystalin.

Bloodhawk, Krystalin, Xi'an Chi Xan, Skullfire, Metalhead, Cerebra, and Meanstreak race to the rescue!

DAREDEVIL'S ORIGIN RETOLD

"The costume is probably a good idea. Sewed it myself. God only knows what it looks like."

• *Daredevil: The Man Without Fear* #1

Comic legends Frank Miller and John Romita Jr. united to tell a new version of Daredevil's origin in this carefully crafted five-issue miniseries. Though considered mostly out of the canon of continuity due to a few minor conflicting details with past and future stories, *Daredevil: The Man Without Fear* detailed the tragedy of the life of Matt Murdock and the obstacles he had to overcome to become the just vigilante of the present.

Young Matt's father was a boxer and an unwilling enforcer for local mobsters, so Matt grew up being told to solve his problems with his head, not his fists. He was forced to adopt this attitude when he was blinded by chemicals splashed into his eyes as he saved the life of an elderly man in the path of a runaway truck carrying hazardous materials. Trained by the mysterious martial artist Stick, Matt grew adept at triumphing over his handicap, only to discover further hardships when his father was murdered after refusing to take a dive in one of his fights. Young Matt donned a ski mask and utilized his training to beat his revenge into the men responsible for his father's death. He continued in this manner until a stray fist accidentally knocked an innocent woman out of a window, killing her, and further torturing Matt Murdock's already troubled mind.

Considered a failure by Stick, Murdock later attended college at Columbia University, where he met best friend Foggy Nelson and femme fatale Elektra. Parting ways with Elektra after her father was murdered, Murdock returned to New York, where a kidnapping led to his first costumed caper as Daredevil, and a lifetime of animosity towards Manhattan's king of crime, the Kingpin.

OCTOBER

M Distancing himself from his former identity as Thor, Eric Masterson earned his own ongoing series by Tom DeFalco and Ron Frenz in *Thunderstrike* #1.

Battlin' Jack Murdock's death set the direction of Matthew's life.

OCTOBER

THE DEATH OF MR. FANTASTIC

• *Fantastic Four* #381

The Fantastic Four battled a mysterious demon-like creature in this issue penned by Tom DeFalco and pencilled by Paul Ryan. Dr. Doom had to step in to protect his native country, and nearly died before teleporting the monster away. Doom then managed to lure Reed Richards to him and seemingly ended both of their lives.

In a final deadly act of betrayal, Doom tricked Reed Richards into taking his hand.

NOVEMBER

THE DEATH OF MOCKINGBIRD

• *Avengers West Coast* #100

In a story by writer Roy Thomas and artist David Ross, marksman Hawkeye and his teammates faced off against the demons Satannish and Mephisto in hell. They finally escaped just as a stray fireball struck Hawkeye's wife, Mockingbird, killing her in Hawkeye's arms.

FATAL ATTRACTIONS

• *Wolverine* #75

Beginning with *X-Factor* #92 in July 1993, the Fatal Attractions story line was meant to celebrate the 30th anniversary of the X-Men and crossed over into all the X-titles. The X-Men once again faced off against Magneto, but this time with disastrous results. After Magneto literally ripped the adamantium out of Wolverine's body in the pages of *X-Men* #25, Charles Xavier did the unthinkable and took away Magneto's mind. In *Wolverine* #75, Wolverine was left a shell of his former self, barely surviving Magneto's attack, and now brandishing claws made of solid bone, thanks to writer Larry Hama and penciller Adam Kubert.

DECEMBER

GAMBIT PLAYS SOLITAIRE

• *Gambit* #1

Everyone's favorite smooth-talking Cajun, Gambit, made his way into his first miniseries by writer Howard Mackie and artist Lee Weeks. The miniseries' story revolved around Gambit's ex-wife, Bella Donna, his old clan of thieves, his partnership with Rogue, and a mysterious figure known as the Tithe Collector.

ALSO PUBLISHED

CAPTAIN MARVEL'S LEGACY

• *The Silver Surfer Annual* #6

Writer Ron Marz and penciller Joe Phillips created Genis-Vell, whose cosmic abilities kicked in during the sixth *Silver Surfer Annual*. Originally going under the code name Legacy, Genis-Vell was the son of Mar-Vell of the Kree Empire and helped the Silver Surfer in a battle against Ronan the Accuser. He was later known as Captain Marvel, like his father, and, even later, as Photon. Genis-Vell also became a member of the Thunderbolts.

MEANWHILE IN 1993...

CLINTON IS PRESIDENT
Bill Clinton succeeds George H.W. Bush and is sworn in as the 42nd President of the United States.

WORLD TRADE CENTER BOMBING
A car bomb explodes in the underground car park of Tower One of the World Trade Center in New York, injuring 1,042 people and killing six.

WACO MASSACRE
Agents raid the compound of the Branch Davidians at Mount Carmel near Waco, Texas. After a fifty-one-day standoff, a fire kills over seventy people, including the Branch Davidian leader David Koresh.

CZECHOSLOVAKIA SPLITS
Czechoslovakia is officially dissolved and becomes two countries: the Czech Republic and Slovakia.

THE BEGINNING OF THE INTERNET
A text-based World Wide Web browser is put in the public domain, revolutionizing the way information is used and shared.

***BEAVIS AND BUTT-HEAD* AIRS**
The animation Beavis and Butt-Head *debuts and becomes a classic of 1990s youth culture and the MTV generation, with its lewd humor and social criticism.*

MAASTRICHT TREATY
The Maastricht Treaty takes effect, creating the European Union. It covers both the political and monetary union of many European countries.

ESCOBAR KILLED
In the war on drugs, Colombian drug baron Pablo Escobar is finally tracked down and is killed by police.

FIRST BIONIC ARM
A team of Scottish scientists create the first bionic arm, which uses microchips and sensors to interpret electrical pulses from the brain and move the artificial arm accordingly.

MIDWEST FLOODS
The Mississippi and Missouri Rivers flood the American midwest and cause $15 billion worth of damage.

AND AT THE MOVIES...
Jurassic Park, *CGI predators on the loose in a remote theme park provide plenty of thrills in this monster movie;* Groundhog Day, *Bill Murray's grumpy weatherman finds himself doomed to replay the same day for the rest of his life in this charming comedy;* Schindler's List, *Steven Spielberg's biographical film of Oskar Schindler, a German businessman who saved the lives of more than 1,000 Polish Jews during the Holocaust.*

MAXIMUM CARNAGE

When writer J.M. DeMatteis was first offered the job to write for the Maximum Carnage story line of 1993 by group editor Danny Fingeroth, he was at first adverse to the idea. Not a fan of Spider-Man foes Venom and Carnage, or the trend of mass murdering Super Villains, DeMatteis did not accept the job until he realized that the series would be his chance to air these opinions on a grand scale, pitting the relatively innocent Peter Parker against the darkest corners of the human psyche in the form of these twisted adversaries. While Spider-Man was tempted to sink to his foes' level in the pages of this crossover, he nevertheless managed to cling to a more heroic path.

the AMAZING SPIDER-MAN
THINGS GET EVEN WILDER!
SPIDER-MAN
$1.25 US
202
JUL
WEB OF SPIDER-MAN
$1.25 US
$1.60 CAN
103
AUG
UK 95p
INSIDE: VENOM AT THE MERCY OF CARNAGE!
MARVEL COMICS
MAXIMUM CARNAGE
PART 8 OF 14
SPIDER-MAN
36
JUL
NO MORE MISTER NICE VENOM!
MAXIMUM CARNAGE
PART 11 OF 14
the AMAZING SPIDER-MAN
THINGS LOOK BLEAK FOR VENOM AND HIS PALS--
MAXIMUM CARNAGE
the SPECTACULAR SPIDER-MAN
PART 6 OF 14
MARVEL COMICS
MAXIMUM CARNAGE
PART 12 OF 14
SPIDER-MAN
INSIDE: VENOM!
$1.75 US
37
AUG
THE EXPLOSIVE FINALE TO MARVEL'S WILDEST
GUEST-STARRING MARVEL'S GREATEST ACTION HEROES!

1994

CLONES AND MARVELS

The year 1994 was one that sparked conversation, acclaim, and debate. Marvel continued to introduce new titles that drew on what had connected with their readers in years past, influenced by the success of the heavily armored heroes of the beginning of the decade. *War Machine* birthed a more gun-friendly version of Iron Man; *Fantastic Force* saw a tech-garbed version of Marvel's first family; and *Force Works* let its title speak for itself.

However, it was a very different kind of clone story that would spark controversy in the eyes of the fans for years to come when Marvel decided to spice up the life of their resident icon, Spider-Man. They reintroduced Spider-Man's clone that was last glimpsed in the 1970s, and created the Clone Saga. This giant event crossover seemed to almost spin out of the control of those that orchestrated it, making Peter Parker, and an increasingly discontented fan base, wonder exactly which Spider-Man was the original, and which was the clone.

Through it all shined *Marvels*, written by Kurt Busiek and painted by Alex Ross. This limited series reinvigorated painted comics as a genre, went on to become an acclaimed masterpiece, and spawned more than its own fair share of imitators.

JANUARY

MARVELS

"It was life or death—it was grand opera—it was the greatest show on Earth—and we—every single one of us —we had the best seat in the house."

• *Marvels* #1

Marvels was a four-issue prestige-format graphic novel, written by Kurt Busiek, illustriously painted by then relative newcomer Alex Ross, and printed on high-quality paper. The limited series utilized realistic style in narrative as well as in artwork, a style seldom seen before in mainstream comic books, and was both a critical and financial success. *Marvels* also took the unusual viewpoint of an outsider, of a civilian witnessing firsthand the greatest events in human history.

The series chronicled the life of photojournalist Phil Sheldon from a young man at the dawn of World War II, to his retirement in the 1970s. From the public unveiling of the original android Human Torch, to the flooding of Manhattan by the Sub-Mariner, from the anti-mutant hysteria that evolved with the X-Men, to the coming of the world-eater Galactus, and on to the death of a lone innocent girl named Gwen Stacy, Phil Sheldon saw it all, and recorded it for the rest of his world to see. He called these super-powered figures Marvels, and his affection for these amazing men and women would drive his very existence. But what the world didn't see, the picture Sheldon's photos couldn't paint, was of the death of his optimism, the story behind the scenes of a man mad at the world for not lauding its fantastic protectors, and then furious at that same world for not noticing the little people that were there all along.

Alongside other struggling journalists like J. Jonah Jameson, Phil Sheldon attended the press conference of scientist Phineas Thomas Horton as he unveiled his creation.

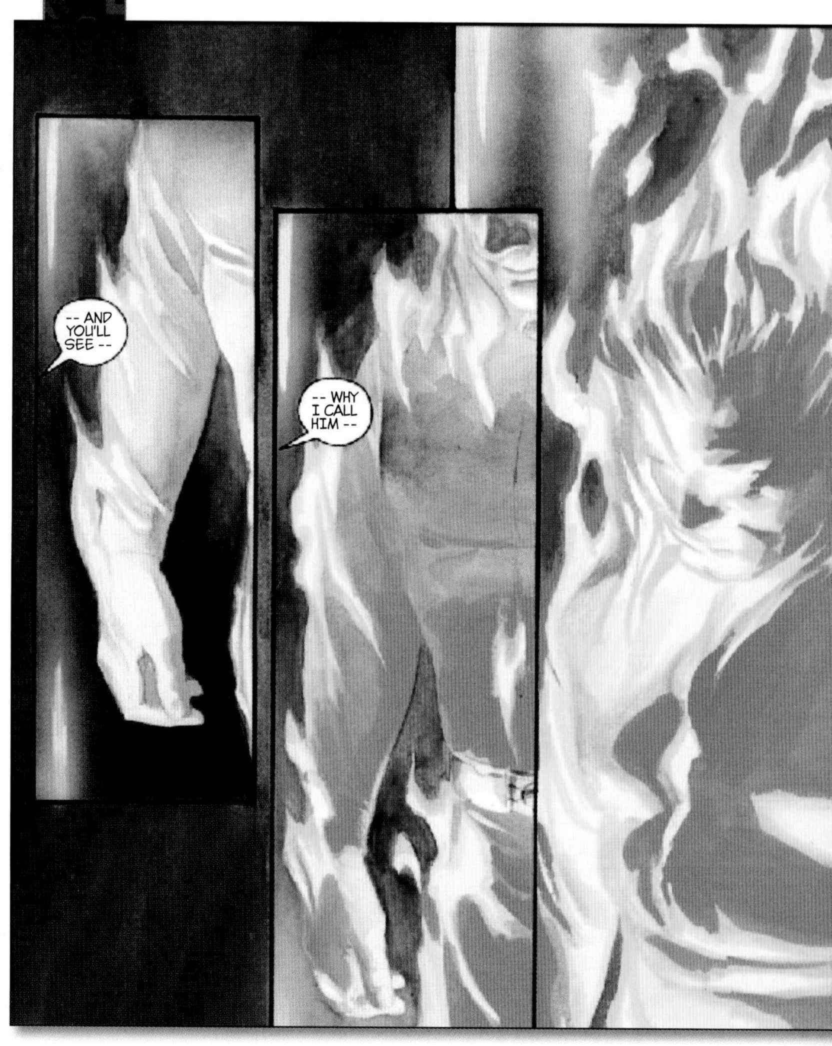

MARCH

HUSK'S HERALDING

• *X-Force* #32

Husk, the skin-shedding future Generation X member and little sister of X-Force's Cannonball, had appeared in comics as early as 1986 but never as a mutant. Her character and mutant abilities, which enabled her to change into various substances, emerged in issue 32 of *X-Force*, thanks to writer Fabian Nicieza and penciller Tony Daniel.

THE WEDDING OF PHOENIX AND CYCLOPS

• *X-Men* #30

X-Men founders Scott Summers and Jean Grey finally got hitched thanks to writer Fabian Nicieza and artist Andy Kubert, amidst all their friends and loved ones. Even Wolverine attended, although he watched from a distance, ever the loner.

The story revealed some benefits to a mutant marriage: The bride could tell if her guests were having a good time just by being near them; some of the attendees could dance on air; and the maid of honor could literally guarantee that there would be no rain.

APRIL

WAR MACHINE FLIES SOLO

• *War Machine* #1

Jim Rhodes, Iron Man's friend turned ex-employee, piloted his War Machine silver armor into his own ongoing series. Written by Scott Benson and Len Kaminski, with pencils by Gabriel Gecko, the series saw a battle with fellow heavily-armed Cable and Deathlok.

MAY

THE RESURRECTION OF GHOST RIDER

• *Ghost Rider 2099* #1

Under the Marvel 2099 imprint, this story was written by Len Kaminski, with art by Chris Bachalo and Mark Buckingham. In it, Kenshiro Cochrane traveled to another dimension to become a superstrong, robotic Ghost Rider.

JULY

FORCE WORKS PREMIERS

• *Force Works* #1

When the West Coast Avengers disbanded, some of its members, led by Iron Man, went on to form a new team, Force Works, which took a more aggressive stance toward superheroics. Writers Dan Abnett and Andy Lanning, alongside penciller Tom Tenney, showcased the team with a unique pop-up, folding cover in its debut issue.

THE BLACK CAT CROSSES PATHS

• *Felicia Hardy: The Black Cat* #1

Anti-hero the Black Cat was given her first miniseries in July. Written by Terry Kavanagh and Joey Cavalieri, with art by penciller Andrew Wildman, the series lasted for four issues. The series saw the Black Cat fight Cardiac and Spider-Man and undergo a search for a mysterious resource referred to as the Chimera.

Black Cat was hired by the Morelle company to steal the Chimera.

OCTOBER

THE CLONE SAGA BEGINS

• *Web Of Spider-Man* #117

The 117th issue of *Web Of Spider-Man* was considered the start of the mammoth crossover known as the Clone Saga, although the story had roots stemming back to the 1970s, when Peter Parker and Gwen Stacy were both cloned by the villainous Jackal.

The beginning of the saga saw Spider-Man come face to face with Peter Parker. Written by Terry Kavanagh and pencilled by Steven Butler, this issue was available in flip book format.

Besides chronicling the return of Spider-Man's original clone, Web Of Spider-Man *#117 also marked the first appearance of Dr. Judas Traveller, a new Spidey foe obsessed with studying the criminal mind.*

TALES TO ASTONISH MAKES A RETURN

• *Tales To Astonish*

Fan-favorite Hulk writer Peter David teamed with painter John Estes for this one-shot that began a series of retro-titled prestige-format specials, including *Strange Tales* and *Tales Of Suspense*. The *Tales To Astonish* special continued the trend, popularized in *Marvels*, of painted comics wrapped in an acetate cover.

When a madman named Knut Caine shot a police officer in broad daylight, Janet Van Dyne (the Wasp) and Hank Pym's peaceful visit to Norway suddenly transformed into a team-up battle with the Hulk versus the forces of the trickster god, Loki. Luckily the heroic trio triumphed, but only after Hulk resisted the temptation for power.

NOVEMBER

GENERATION X MAKES ITS MARK

• *Generation X* #1

Writer Scott Lobdell and artist Chris Bachalo introduced Generation X, the new team of mutants first glimpsed in this month's *The Uncanny X-Men* #318, to their own ongoing series with this deluxe first issue.

Taking place at Xavier's School For Gifted Youngsters, *Generation X* focused on a group of fresh-faced, untrained mutants just as the original *X-Men* series of the 1960s, and *The New Mutants* series of the 1980s, did before it. Brimming with teen angst and the cynical attitude of teenagers of the 1990s, *Generation X* starred Jubilee, Husk, M, Skin and Synch, under the tutelage of Banshee and the White Queen, and debuted new members Chamber, Mondo, and Penance.

Ben Reilly's costume was composed of a pair of red tights, some old web-shooters, and an altered blue Spider-Man sweatshirt he had noticed in a store window.

THE SCARLET SPIDER

"He goes by the name of Ben Reilly, in honor of lost family... but not his family. Not his world, not his memories. Not his life."

• *Web Of Spider-Man* #118

After a supposed death at the hands of the demented geneticist the Jackal in Gerry Conway's classic original clone saga of the 1970s, Peter Parker's clone had recently reemerged in Spider-Man's life, calling himself Ben Reilly. Not wanting to step on the true Spider-Man's toes, but unable to shake his sense of power and responsibility, Ben Reilly could no longer deny his role when he heard that the symbiotic Venom was loose in New York City and causing havoc and mayhem. So, he donned a costume and was dubbed the Scarlet Spider by the press—and by writer Terry Kavanagh and penciller Steven Butler.

This Clone Saga story line continued through the Spider-Man range of books for the next two years. Meanwhile, Ben Reilly learned from the Jackal that he was actually the true Spider-Man, and not the clone as he had always suspected. He even ended up taking over for Peter Parker as Spider-Man, when Peter briefly retired in order to raise the child that he and his wife, Mary Jane, had been expecting.

FORGING THE FANTASTIC FORCE

• *Fantastic Force* #1

Created by writers Tom Brevoort and Mike Kanterovich, the Fantastic Force was a spin-off of the Fantastic Four. The team comprised members Vibraxas, a Wakanda native; Devlor, a boy turned beast; the savage Huntara; and Psi-Lord, the son of Mr. Fantastic and the Invisible Woman.

M Following the continued success of the *X-Men* cartoon, Fox Kids debuted Peter Parker's newly animated adventures, beginning a series that lasted five seasons with sixty-five episodes to its credit.

MEANWHILE IN 1994...

NAFTA TAKES EFFECT
The North American Free Trade Agreement comes into force, phasing out trade barriers between the US, Mexico, and Canada.

***THE SCREAM* IS STOLEN**
Edvard Munch's iconic painting The Scream *is stolen in Oslo, but is then recovered three months later.*

CHANNEL TUNNEL OPENS
After seven years of work, the tunnel linking Britain and France opens, allowing passengers to travel between the two countries in just thirty-five minutes.

NELSON MANDELA IS PRESIDENT
Nelson Mandela is sworn in as the first black President of South Africa.

O.J. SIMPSON ARRESTED
O.J. Simpson surrenders to police after a live televised car chase and is arrested for the murders of Nicole Brown Simpson and Ronald Goldman. He is later acquitted but is found liable in a civil suit.

"SPAMMING"
The term "spamming" enters computer vocabulary as mass marketing campaigns are launched by email, following an explosion in email and commercial Internet sites.

THE ERA OF GENETICALLY MODIFIED FOOD
The Food and Drug Administration approves the Flavr Savr tomato, the first genetically modified food.

PROGRAMS AIMED AT TWENTYSOMETHINGS
Friends *debuts, part of a trend of television networks aiming at twentysomethings. Other programs of this period include* Beverly Hills 90210, Melrose Place, *and* Ally McBeal.

KURT COBAIN FOUND DEAD
The lead singer of rock band Nirvana, *Kurt Cobain, is found after committing suicide in his Seattle home.*

BLACK HOLES ARE REAL
The Hubble Telescope reveals conclusive evidence of the existence of black holes.

AND AT THE MOVIES...
Forrest Gump, *a brisk trot through US cultural history from the 1950s onwards through the life of Tom Hanks' simple man;* Pulp Fiction, *cracking dialogue, superb cast, and countless pop culture allusions characterize Quentin Tarantino's violent, interlocking tales of petty hustlers, hoods, and hit men;* The Shawshank Redemption, *decade-spanning drama based on a Stephen King story, starring Tim Robbins and Morgan Freeman as two inmates experiencing cruelty inside a fictional penitentiary in Maine.*

BUT DON'T OUR MEMORIES DEFINE US? MAKE US WHO AND WHAT WE ARE?

1995
APOCALYPSE NOW

There was no question about it. The X-Men books were back in the spotlight, and were the first line of defense in Marvel's ongoing battle for sales.

As Spider-Man's Clone Saga story line continued, some fans and critics grew tired of the multiple shifts in the story's direction. However, the unified feel created in the Age of Apocalypse X-Men event would attract some of those same disgruntled fans. This story line dominated the many miniseries that appeared in 1995, including *The Astonishing X-Men*, *Generation Next*, *X-Calibre*, *The Amazing X-Men*, *Weapon X*, and *Gambit And The X-Ternals*. The event was also significant for the roster of writers and artists that it showcased. Creatives working on this story line included Warren Ellis, Jeph Loeb, Mark Waid, Joe Madureira, Chris Bachalo, and Andy and Adam Kubert, who were destined to be some of the biggest names in comics.

FEBRUARY

THE AGE OF APOCALYPSE

"His name is Erik Lehnsherr, called Magneto by some... and how he continues to stand is anyone's guess."

• *X-Men: Alpha* (Age Of Apocalypse)
The Age Of Apocalypse was a major crossover event that drastically changed the landscape of the universe that the X-Men existed in. The story began in this *X-Men: Alpha* special by writers Scott Lobdell and Mark Waid and pencillers Roger Cruz and Steve Epting.

Charles Xavier had died and Magneto now headed Xavier's freedom force of mutants, still struggling for Xavier's dream of a peaceful human/mutant coexistence. As the regular line of X-Men books suspended publication for four months in order to make way for a group of various new miniseries, fans were introduced to a world now ruled by the mutant overlord Apocalypse. Under his rule, humans were slaughtered en mass in routine "cullings" and the X-Men were considered traitors to their own species. It was a world where Wolverine, called only Weapon X, had lost a hand in a battle with Cyclops, and where Angel ran a swanky nightclub, more interested in saving his own skin than fighting the good fight.

Fueled by their introduction to the time-traveling Bishop, who remembered how things were before this shift in reality, the X-Men organized a strike to overthrow Apocalypse's rule. At the same time, the humans attacked America from their safe base of resistance in Europe to try to ruin Apocalypse. Magneto and his X-Men triumphed by the end of the story line. They destroyed Apocalypse and sent Bishop back in time to save Xavier's life and change history, just as the humans' bombs began to fall across North America.

Some of the X-Men in this alternate reality included Morph, Rogue, Magneto, Quicksilver, Storm, Iceman, and Nightcrawler.

JANUARY

ROGUE'S RECKONING

• *Rogue* #1
X-Men member Rogue finally starred in her own four-issue miniseries, beginning in January. Written by Howard Mackie with art by Mike Wieringo, *Rogue* told a tale of the Assassin's Guild, which rivaled the guild of thieves that mutant Gambit had belonged to; Gambit's dedication to his "chere" (as he referred to Rogue); and Rogue's first love, Cody, who fell into a coma after a kiss with Rogue sapped him of his energy.

MARCH

ASTONISHING ASSAULT

• *The Astonishing X-Men* #1 (Age of Apocalypse)
In this four-issue miniseries by writers Scott Lobdell and Jeph Loeb and artist Joe Madureira, Magneto divided his troops in order to organize a severe strike against mutant overlord Apocalypse. The miniseries chronicled the adventures of the X-Men as they shut down Apocalypse's Infinites processing plant, a facility used to manufacture soldiers to serve the overlord.

X-MAN ESCAPES

• *X-Man* #1 (Age Of Apocalypse)
Created by writer Jeph Loeb and artist Steve Skroce, X-Man was perhaps the most popular character to emerge out of the Age of Apocalypse event. Nate Grey, X-Man's alter ego, was grown in a lab by evil genius Mr. Sinister. Sinister was planning a revolution against his master, Apocalypse, by combining the DNA of mutant prelate Scott Summers and rebel Jean Grey to create a mutant strong enough to overthrow Apocalypse. Nate fled from Sinister's lab and joined a traveling band of actors, led by the rebel Forge. As his telepathic powers matured, Nate used them to shut down the experiments of the Dark Beast, and to battle the evil Holocaust.

X-Man's troupe of traveling "actors" included familiar faces Toad, Soaron, Brute, Mastermind, and Forge.

MARCH

THE CYCLOPS FACTOR

• *Factor X* #1 (Age Of Apocalypse)
One-eyed prelate Scott Summers rebelled against his master Apocalypse and his jealous brother Havok, siding with Jean Grey's cause in this four-issue miniseries by writer John Francis Moore and artists Steve Epting and Terry Dodson.

X-TERNAL QUEST

• *Gambit And The X-Ternals* #1 (Age Of Apocalypse)
X-Men member Gambit, alongside a team of familiar mutants including Sunspot, Jubilee, Strong Guy, and Lila Cheney, set off on a space-faring adventure in search of the legendary M'Kraan Crystal, which could glimpse into the different realities, including the one that Bishop claimed was the X-Men's true universe.

COLOSSUS' GENERATION

• *Generation Next* #1 (Age Of Apocalypse)
Artist Chris Bachalo and writer Scott Lobdell crafted this four-issue miniseries, beginning in March, detailing the first appearance of super-strong Colossus's team of young mutants and their attack on a slave-run energy factory owned by Apocalypse.

NAVIGATING NIGHTCRAWLER

• *X-Calibre* #1 (Age Of Apocalypse)
With his X-Calibre team, Nightcrawler traveled to Avalon in order to find the clairvoyant Destiny to help prove Bishop's theories about an alternate reality, in this four-issue miniseries by writer Warren Ellis and artists Roger Cruz, Ken Lashley, and Renato Arlem.

AMAZING AGENDA

• *The Amazing X-Men* #1 (Age Of Apocalypse)
Written by Fabian Nicieza with art by Andy Kubert, this four-issue miniseries focused on Quicksilver, Banshee, Iceman, Storm, Dazzler, and Exodus as they tried to aid humans escape from America to a safer Europe.

SECRET WEAPON

• *Weapon X* #1 (Age Of Apocalypse)
Mutant rebels Logan and Jean Grey helped the human attack on America before parting ways when Jean became concerned about the amount of casualties in this four-issue tale by writer Larry Hama, with art by Adam Kubert.

APRIL

THE DEATH OF AUNT MAY

• *The Amazing Spider-Man* #400
Amidst the chaos of the ongoing Clone Saga, Peter Parker's aunt May had suffered a stroke. However, in the opening of the 400th anniversary issue of *The Amazing Spider-Man*, written by J.M. DeMatteis and penciled by Mark Bagley, she seemed to be completely recovered as she checked herself out of hospital. A week later, May revealed that she had known about Peter's dual life for years, before she collapsed weakly into his arms. Peter took May home, and she passed away after saying her final goodbyes to her treasured nephew.

Though Aunt May's death would later be revealed as an elaborate hoax perpetrated by Norman Osborn, her death seemed very real to Peter Parker.

DR. DRUID GETS SURGERY

• *Druid* #1

Writer Warren Ellis had developed his distinctly dark and morbid vision in the pages of *Hellstorm*. Beginning in May, he took supernatural monster-hunter Dr. Druid to new depths in this dark series. With art by Leonardo Manco, the series saw the good doctor truly earn the sinister title of Druid.

JULY

THE X-MEN REOPEN FOR BUSINESS

• *X-Men: Prime*

With their world restored to normal after the Age of Apocalypse, the X-Men returned to business as usual in this extra-sized special by writers Scott Lobdell and Fabian Nicieza and artists Bryan Hitch, Jeff Matsuda, Gary Frank, Mike McKone, Terry Dodson, Ben Herrera, and Paul Pelletier.

MARVELS GETS RUINED

• *Ruins* #1

Labeled a Marvel Alterniverse story, this two-issue prestige-format limited series was written by Warren Ellis and painted by Cliff and Terese Nielsen and Chris Moeller. It showed a morbid vision of the Marvel Universe, a "what if" tale that was an antithesis to Kurt Busiek and Alex Ross's *Marvels*. *Ruins* examined the life of photojournalist Phil Sheldon, as did *Marvels*, but this miniseries saw Sheldon witness an Avengers Quinjet exploding and later die from radiation spread to him by Peter Parker.

DEATH OF THE JACKAL

• *Spider-Man Maximum Clonage: Omega*

Continuing the epic Clone Saga, the team of artists Tom Lyle, Robert Brown, Roy Burdine, and Mark Bagley revealed the supposed final fate of the genius Jackal. Facing Spider-Man and the Scarlet Spider on the rooftop of the *Daily Bugle*, the Jackal was intent on setting off a deadly virus bomb. However, after plaguing Spider-Men with his machinations and other clones, the Jackal fell to his death while trying to rescue the clone of Gwen Stacy.

SEPTEMBER

SECRETS OF SPIDEY'S PAST

• *Untold Tales Of Spider-Man* #1

With all the confusion going on in Peter Parker's life in his other books, writer Kurt Busiek and artist Pat Olliffe stepped in to fill the void for the kind of classic Spider-Man stories that Stan Lee and Steve Ditko had imagined at the character's inception.

Telling stories set in Peter's high school days, *Untold Tales Of Spider-Man* still managed to create a host of new characters, including the flame-wielding Scorcher and the misunderstood monster Batwing. And to further contrast with the other Spider-Man titles of its day, this series also strived to tell easily accessible one-part stories, much like the original comics that inspired it.

Each issue of Untold Tales Of Spider-Man *was priced at only ninety-nine cents to try to gain a new and wider readership.*

1995

MEANWHILE IN 1995...

OKLAHOMA CITY BOMBING
In Oklahoma, 168 people are killed and over 800 are injured in a terrorist attack on an office complex by Timothy McVeigh and Terry Nichols.

MILLIONS WATCH THE LIVE O.J. SIMPSON TRIAL
More than half of the US population watches the verdict of the actor and American football player O.J. Simpson trial as he is declared not guilty. The "trial of the century" is one of the most watched moments in the history of American television.

SARIN ATTACK ON THE TOKYO SUBWAY
Members of the Aum Shinrikyo religious movement release sarin gas on five trains, killing twelve, seriously harming fifty-four, and affecting hundreds more.

WINDOWS 95 RELEASED
This new operating system goes on sale with a revolutionary graphical user interface that is highly consumer-orientated.

AMAZON.COM GOES LIVE
The commercial website amazon.com starts trading and grows steadily over the next few years, rather than at the fast—but unstable—rate at which many of the internet companies appear to grow.

NEW EUROPEAN UNION MEMBERS
Sweden, Austria, and Finland join the European Union.

FIRST SOLO PACIFIC BALLOON FLIGHT
Steve Fossett becomes the first person to cross the Pacific in a solo hot air balloon flight.

RABIN ASSASSINATED
Israeli Prime Minister Yitzhak Rabin is assassinated at a Tel-Aviv peace rally, two years after shaking hands with PLO leader Yasser Arafat in Washington DC.

EXTREME SPORTS ARE BIG
Thanks to an explosion in their popularity, extreme sports are given their own tournament on EXPN's The X-Games.

AND AT THE MOVIES...
Toy Story, *Pixar's groundbreaking CGI "buddy" movie about toys coming to life is the first CGI animation feature;* The Usual Suspects, *Bryan Singer's purposefully confusing con-trick film is full of misdirection, convoluted plotting, and macho repartee;* Heat, *Michael Mann's gripping account of a symbiotic relationship between a cop and a criminal and the dangers of bonding with other people;* Apollo 13, *Ron Howard's dramatization of the ill-fated Apollo 13 mission to the moon in 1970.*

Tales To Astonish ***(Dec., 1994)***
John Estes, an artist also known for his work on the Fleer Ultra X-Men *trading card series from 1994 and the* Marvel Masterpiece *trading cards from 1993, painted this one-shot. The script was by Peter David, who also was no stranger to the Hulk, having scripted the brute's adventures for several years.*

WE'RE NOT FINISHED YET... EVERYONE GET TO THE ESCAPE PODS!

1996

CROSSOVERS TAKE OVER

The crossover had gone from being a clever way to attract new readers to a particular title to a necessary industry standard. With the Onslaught and Heroes Reborn events starting in this year, and the Clone Saga finally dragging itself to a halt, Marvel set out for the ultimate crossover—one with DC Comics.

Having produced joint ventures in the forms of stand alone specials dating back to *MGM's Marvelous Wizard Of Oz* comic adaptation of 1975, Marvel and DC set out to accomplish something on a larger scale, and the result was *Marvel Versus DC* (or *DC Versus Marvel*, depending on which issue of the series you were reading), a miniseries that would spin off into not just two sequels, but also the creation of a third fictional comic company, Amalgam. Under the Amalgam label, Marvel and DC produced two waves of twelve specials that featured combined versions of their characters, creating the illusion of a long-standing merged company, and going so far as to include fake letters columns and footnotes within the issues, referring to other comics that never actually existed.

But despite the popularity of all the events of 1996, at the end of the year Marvel made the most drastic crossover of its publishing history—into bankruptcy.

JANUARY

THE FUTURE OF THE FF

• *Fantastic Four 2099* #1
After an accident in the Negative Zone landed the Fantastic Four in the dystopian 2099 future, they finally saw what life was like without constant accolades and admiration. This eight-issue series was written by Karl Kesel with art by *2099* veteran penciller Rick Leonardi.

FEBRUARY

MARVEL TAKES ON THE COMPETITION

"The showdown of the century! Who will win? You decide!"

Marvel Comics Versus DC *pitted each company's iconic characters against each other. also introduced the first character to be shared by both comic companies—Axel Asher. Al known as Access, Axel Asher was the guardian of the gateway between worlds.*

• *Marvel Comics Versus DC* #1
Marvel and DC heroes had faced each other before. Some had even teamed up on that rare, special occasion. But finally, in this deluxe four-issue miniseries by writers Ron Marz and Peter David and pencillers Dan Jurgens and Claudio Castellini, with two issues published by Marvel and two by DC, comic fans got to see their favorite heroes from both Marvel and DC Comics battle it out in fights with actual definitive outcomes. And better yet, the fans got t vote for the victor of each bout.

Using ballots sent in advance to their local comic store, fans were able to vote for who they wanted to win in five different battles. Along with their ballot, readers received a free preview of the miniseries itself, along with a promotional trading card, advertising the upcoming 100-card set from SkyBox International, also a joint venture between the two comic book publishing houses.

In the series, two cosmic entities became aware of the other's existence, and decided to have a duel for supremacy, each choosing powerful representatives from his world to wage his private war for him. After a few preliminary fights, Wolverine defeated the alien powerhouse Lobo in a barroom brawl; Storm bested Wonder Wom using the power of the elements; Spider-Man used his years of experience to take down the Superman-clone Superboy; Superman showed Hulk who truly was the strongest one; and Batman KOed Captain America with a batarang to the head. After the fights, the cosmic entities merged their worlds into one whole, creating the ne and unique universe, and thereby spinning the story off into a serie of joint one-shots published under the label Amalgam Comics.

APRIL

JUSTICE HAS A NEW NAME

• *JLX* #1

Combining DC's Justice League and Marvel's X-Men, this Amalgam special was written by Gerard Jones and Mark Waid, with pencils by Howard Porter. The one-off featured combined characters like Mariner (Namor and Aquaman) and Night-Creeper (Nightcrawler and the Creeper).

JLX also included J'onn J'onzz, the last survivor of the Martian race known as the Skrulls.

APRIL

THE DARK CLAW DETECTIVE

• *Legends Of The Dark Claw* #1

Dark Claw, a combination of Wolverine and Batman, cut his way into his own Amalgam special, thanks to writer Larry Hama and penciller Jim Balent. Also featured in the issue was Dark Claw's sidekick, Sparrow, a mix of Jubilee and Robin.

AMERICA'S MAN OF STEEL

• *Super-Soldier* #1

Amalgam's Super-Soldier emerged in the days of World War II and was a cross between classic patriots Captain America and Superman. Super-Soldier fought such foes as Amalgam's Ultra-Metallo and the green skulled Lex Luthor, as chronicled by writer Mark Waid and artist Dave Gibbons.

A NEW CLONE

• *Spider-Boy* #1

Written by Karl Kesel with pencils by Mike Wieringo, the "awesome arach-kid" Amalgam hero Spider-Boy faced the likes of Bizarnage (Carnage and Bizarro), with the help of the Challengers of Fantastic (the Fantastic Four and the Challengers of the Unknown).

THE STORMING OF THE AMAZONS

• *Amazon* #1

In her own Amalgam special by writer/artist John Byrne, Princess Ororo of the hidden island Themyscira, a combination of Wonder Woman and Storm, fought the very gods themselves and reminisced about her childhood among the Amazons and her old friend Diana.

JUNE

THE ONSLAUGHT EPIC

• *X-Men* #53

Jean Grey was the first to encounter the mysterious entity calling himself Onslaught, as he tried to recruit her for his war. After a tour through the psyche of her mentor, Professor X, Jean rejected the ominous being's offer, scarred by witnessing the dark side of her teacher's mind. First appearing in this issue by writer Mark Waid with pencils by Andy Kubert, Onslaught's emergence would spell doom for many of the Marvel heroes.

Onslaught left Jean Grey with a warning: his name literally written across her forehead.

OCTOBER

ONSLAUGHT EPIC ENDS

"It was an age unlike any other. And this is the story of its end..."

• *Onslaught: Marvel Universe*

Labeled "Marvel's latest rage" in its house ads, the Onslaught epic story line had been crossing over through many of the publisher's various titles since power-mad villain Onslaught's formal debut in the pages of *X-Men* #53 in June of this year. Tying into all of the X-Men titles, as well as comics starring the Avengers, Ghost Rider, Daredevil, Spider-Man, the Fantastic Four, and the Hulk, this gigantic story filled six volumes when it was originally reprinted in trade paperback form.

A manifestation of the dark halves of Charles Xavier's and Magneto's psyche, Onslaught truly rose to power in the *Onslaught: X-Men* special (August) by writers Mark Waid and Scott Lobdell and artist Adam Kubert. Quickly besting the X-Men after failing to recruit them to his cause, Onslaught began to battle other heroes as the Avengers and Fantastic Four were alerted to his presence.

Although there were many artists and writers who contributed to Onslaught's attack on mankind, it was again the three main masterminds behind the event, Waid, Lobdell, and Kubert, who would craft the *Onslaught: Marvel Universe* special, the final chapter in this dramatic tale that saw a plethora of heroes engaged in one final battle with Onslaught, now evolved into a state of pure psionic energy. The heroes realized that if enough of them threw themselves into this energy void, making the ultimate sacrifice, Onslaught was affected, and would be defeated. Therefore the Avengers and the Fantastic Four leaped into the unknown as the X-Men attacked one last time, finally destroying the psychic beast.

NOVEMBER

ELEKTRA CARVES HER NICHE

• *Elektra* #1

Finally given her own ongoing series by writer Peter Milligan and artist Mike Deodato Jr., Elektra found a new use for her grace and skill after defeating a group of ninjas robbing a theater company. Taking a job as a dancer to help fund the martial arts training center she'd invested herself into, Elektra soon realized she was being stalked by psychopathic assassin Bullseye. The two later had a vicious battle in a back alley but Elektra managed to avenge her earlier death at Bullseye's hands by besting him.

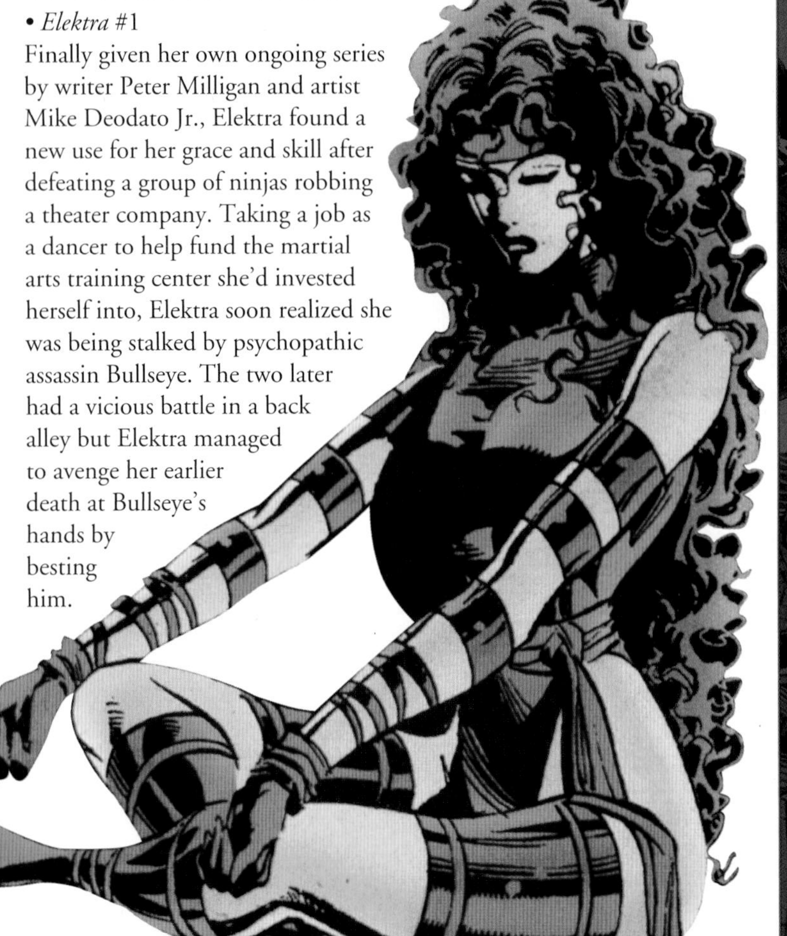

NOVEMBER

JIM LEE'S IRON MAN

Iron Man #1

Part of the Heroes Reborn event, Iron Man was relaunched into a new universe courtesy of writers Scott Lobdell and Jim Lee, with pencils by Whilce Portacio. In this new world birthed through Onslaught's death, Tony Stark squared off against the Hulk.

JIM LEE'S FANTASTIC FOUR

• *Fantastic Four* #1

Jim Lee both wrote and drew this Heroes Reborn relaunch title with the help of fellow scripter Brandon Choi. This issue retold the origin of the Fantastic Four and their fateful space mission that granted them superpowers. It also saw the introduction of the Mole Man.

ROB LIEFELD'S CAPTAIN AMERICA

• *Captain America* #1

Steve Rogers earned a fresh start in the Heroes Reborn universe by writer Jeph Loeb and artist Rob Liefeld. This creative team portrayed Rogers as a regular suburban family man who slowly began to remember his previous life as war hero Captain America.

Liefeld's Captain America retained the same costume as the original, with only the trademark "A" missing from Cap's forehead, replaced by a winged symbol.

ROB LIEFELD'S AVENGERS

• *The Avengers* #1

Another Heroes Reborn title, *The Avengers* was plotted and drawn by Rob Liefeld with a script by Jim Valentino and additional pencils by Chap Yaep. This issue saw Thor, Scarlet Witch, Swordsman, Captain America, the Vision, and Hellcat face off against the villain Loki. Along with the three other Heroes Reborn titles, this new series marked the return to Marvel for several of Image Comics' hottest creators, including Liefeld and Valentino, giving them free reign in this new universe.

MARVEL AND DC GRANT FANS ACCESS

• *DC/Marvel: All Access* #1

In this sequel to the hit *Marvel Versus DC* miniseries, Access, the hero shared by both comic companies, began to notice characters appearing in the wrong universes. In this four-issue miniseries, writer Ron Marz and artists Jackson Guice and Josef Rubinstein featured interesting pairings, such as Venom battling Superman, the Scorpion being bested by Batman, and the X-Men fighting the JLA. The series also saw a return of several of the fan-favorite Amalgam heroes, including the powerful Dr. Strangefate and mutant Dark Claw.

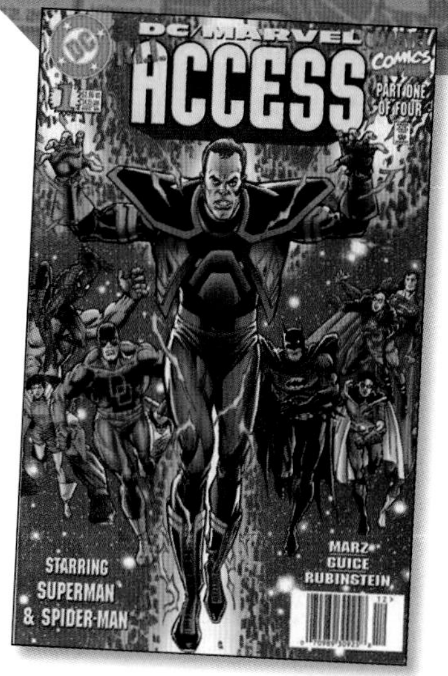

THE DEATH OF BEN REILLY

• *Spider-Man* #75

The Clone Saga finally came to a dramatic close thanks to the team of writer Howard Mackie and artist John Romita Jr. The original Green Goblin, Norman Osborn, was revealed to be alive and the ultimate mastermind behind all of Spidey's clone troubles. Peter Parker also discovered that he was not a clone, and that Ben Reilly was, forcing Peter back into action as Spider-Man after Osborn caused the death of Spidey's unborn daughter, and then that of Ben Reilly himself.

Ben Reilly died the same way that Norman Osborn had seemingly perished all those years ago, speared by the Green Goblin's glider.

After Spider-Man defeated the Goblin, he watched Ben Reilly's body turn to dust, proving Peter Parker to be the genuine article.

MARVEL FILES FOR BANKRUPTCY

After businessman Ron Perelman purchased Marvel Entertainment Group, the parent company of Marvel Comics, he attempted to expand the business by purchasing ToyBiz, Fleer/Skybox, and Malibu Comics. This culminated in a debt Marvel could not pay off, forcing the company to file for bankruptcy.

MEANWHILE IN 1996...

UNABOMBER ARRESTED

Theodore Kaczynski is arrested on suspicion of being the "Unabomber" terrorist, who caused a series of bombings across the US during the 1970s, 1980s, and 1990s.

DOLLY THE SHEEP IS BORN

In a landmark step for genetic cloning, the first mammal to be cloned from an adult cell is born in Scotland. This breakthrough establishes that a cell from a particular body part can be used to create an entire individual.

CENTENNIAL OLYMPIC PARK BOMBING

Two are killed when a bomb explodes during a rock concert in a park developed by the Atlanta Olympic Committee.

A ROYAL DIVORCE

The Prince and Princess of Wales are officially divorced after marrying in 1981.

THE TALIBAN TAKE KABUL

The Taliban take control of Afghanistan's capital, Kabul, and overthrow the existing regime of President Burhanuddin Rabbani.

FIRST US WOMAN SECRETARY OF STATE

Madeleine Albright becomes the first women to be the US Secretary of State. She is nominated by President Clinton and then confirmed by the US Senate 99-0.

THE MYSTERY OF JONBENET RAMSEY

The six-year-old beauty-pageant contestant is found dead in the basement of her parents' home in Boulder, Colorado, drawing immense media coverage and national interest.

"POSSIBLE LIFE ON MARS"

Scientists who have been studying an ancient Martian meteorite announce that a primitive type of microscopic life may have been present on Mars around four billion years ago.

POKÉMON CRAZE BEGINS

The first Pokémon video games are released in Japan. The characters become a worldwide phenomenon, popularized in video games, a television cartoon series, trading cards, and other merchandise.

NINTENDO 64 RELEASED

The Nintendo 64 is released. Gamers rejoice.

AND AT THE MOVIES...

Fargo, *this tragic-comic murder investigation is a flamboyant confection of genres given a modern twist by the quirky Coen brothers;* Mission: Impossible, *Brian De Palma's glossy, fast-paced, high-octane version of the TV series has Tom Cruise racing against time to save his name;* Scream, *a psychopathic serial killer is stalking a group of teens in Wes Craven's postmodern horror movie.*

BUT I AM SANE ENOUGH TO KNOW THIS... IN A WAR BETWEEN MAN AND MUTANTKIND... NO ONE WINS.

1997

MANY HAPPY RETURNS

Despite the ongoing legal battles for control of the company, and the uncertain fate of the Marvel Universe in the real world, the fictional world was following a definitive course. Although the flashy excitement of the Heroes Reborn event had given fans a nostalgic visit to the early part of the decade, by the end of the year, Marvel had set the stage for a return to its time-honored classic lineup, not wanting to lose readers who were put off by the change.

Also returning was Marvel's crystallized working relationship with DC Comics. Another wave of Amalgam specials debuted in the summer, and a third and final sequel to the popular *Marvel Comics Versus DC* miniseries hit the stands before the end of 1997.

As the X-Men comics returned to their tried and true method of netting sales—the crossover event—writer Kurt Busiek returned to what he did best, creating innovative story concepts. This was evidenced in his new series, *Thunderbolts*. Marvel's marketing division prevented advance information from being leaked, returning comic book fandom to the unsuspecting audience they were in days gone by.

JANUARY

DEADPOOL GETS A LIFE

• *Deadpool* #1

Marvel's Merc with a Mouth landed his own title in the form of this monthly series by writer Joe Kelly and artist Ed McGuinness. In this debut issue, Deadpool took an assignment to disrupt gamma testing in Antarctica, a mission that brought him face to face with Alpha Flight's Sasquatch, who was performing experiments under his alter ego of Walter Langkowski. After being told about the damage he would c to the southern hemisphere if the testing plant were to reach critica mass, Deadpool saved the plant from a meltdown of his own desig

DOMINO BRANCHES OUT

• *Domino* #1

Writer Ben Raab and penciller David Perrin gave X-Force member Domino her own three-issue miniseries. Domino's Carnaval vacation was interrupted when she ran into Alpha Flight's Puck, and discovered Lady Deathstrike had kidnapped one of Domino's old flames.

THE THUNDERBOLTS DEBUT

• *The Incredible Hulk* #449

Writer Peter David and artist Mike Deodato Jr. debuted Marvel's newest superteam, the Thunderbolts, in issue 449 of *The Incredible Hulk*. This was an attempt to make the public aware of this fledgling group before they got their own comic. When the Hulk was literally shot out of the sky by a missile, he found himself locked in battle with these mysterious heroes, who were intent on bringing him to justice.

APRIL

THE THUNDERBOLTS' BIG CON

"The world will discover what a viper it has clasped to its breast, but by then it will be too late—far too late!"

• *Thunderbolts* #1

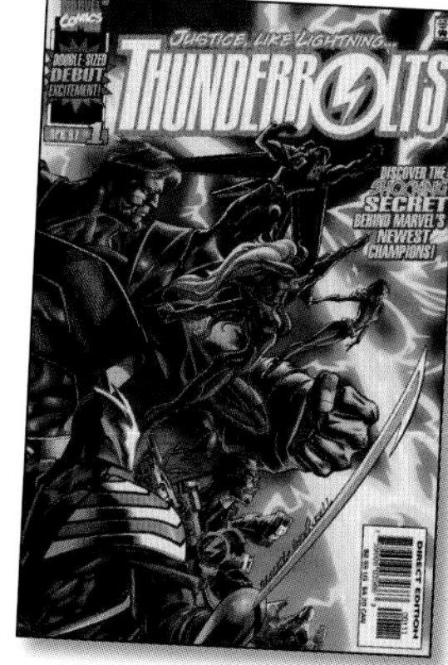

Onslaught had taken the heroes and America was left with quite a void to fill. So when the Thunderbolts first appeared on the scene and stopped a group of thieves from looting the rubble from what was once a pleasant New York neighborhood, the public was quick to embrace them as the next generation of Super Heroes. But what the world didn't know was that the Thunderbolts were secretly the old Avengers foes, the Masters of Evil, masquerading as heroes. Baron Zemo was posing as Citizen V, the Beetle was disguised as Mach-I, Moonstone had dubbed herself Meteorite, Screaming Mimi had transformed herself into Songbird, Fixer had become Techno, and Goliath was calling himself Atlas.

Writer Kurt Busiek had pitched his idea just before the Onslaught crossover had rocked the Marvel landscape. Realizing that the only heroes left to fight crime in their universe were shadowy figures like Spider-Man and Daredevil, Busiek thought that some of the villains might use this to their advantage, gaining the public's trust in order to slowly take over the world. So, along with penciller Mark Bagley, Busiek set out to create the Thunderbolts, realizing that the tricky part would be to keep this secret from the readers.

Busiek and company ignored the pleas from Marvel's marketing division who thought that sales would be affected by not revealing the comics' twist. They managed to conceal their comic's confidential ending until the release of the first issue, and indeed shocked their entire fan base with their dramatic reveal.

JUNE

OPERATION: ZERO TOLERANCE

"I wanted you to see this, Charles. But more than that… I wanted you to understand. Your goal? Your crusade? Your sacred dream? It's over."

• *X-Men* #65

The Operation: Zero Tolerance event was the brainchild of writer Scott Lobdell. This massive X-Men crossover had been foreshadowed for some time, its roots planted in the pages of various comics even before the Onslaught event. In an attempt to give the anti-mutant cause a face as iconic and recognizable as Magneto, Lobdell created Bastion, a super-powered individual whose secrets were embedded in the history of the X-Men themselves. Bastion had been worming his way through the government machine, and was now in a position of power to unleash his desire to destroy all mutants on an unsuspecting public.

Operation: Zero Tolerance truly began in the prologue within *X-Men* #65 as the government blasted the X-Men's blackbird plane out of the sky. Written by Scott Lobdell and drawn by Carlos Pacheco, the story sprang from there into all the other X-titles of the time, and featured the work of writers James Robinson, John Francis Moore, Larry Hama, Steve Seagle, and Joe Kelly, and artists Randy Green, Chris Bachalo, Adam Pollina, Leinil Francis Yu, Pop Mahn, Pascual Ferry, Rob Haynes, and Salvador Larroca.

As the story line continued, Bastion took the most powerful X-Men hostage, backed by a US government that had given up on mutantkind after the Onslaught disaster and the Legacy virus. Meanwhile, Iceman amassed a team of unlikely heroes to oppose Bastion and his army of Prime Sentinels, humans turned powerful cybernetic killing machines. He succeeded with a little help from SHIELD, and the ever shifting opinion of the fickle public.

When activated, the human carrier of the Prime Sentinel ceased to be, taken over by the Prime Sentinel's computerized programming.

Bat-Thing was actually scientist Kurt Sallis who experimented on himself with gene splicing in order to stage off a terminal illness.

BAT-THING FLIES HIGH

• *Bat-Thing* #1

In this Amalgam special written by Larry Hama with pencils by Rodolfo Damaggio, Gotham City was patrolled by Bat-Thing. A combination of Marvel's Man-Thing and DC's Man-Bat, Bat-Thing subdued criminals with his acid touch and bestial nature.

JUNE

LANTERN LIGHTS UP

• *Iron Lantern* #1

Writer Kurt Busiek and artist Paul Smith created Iron Lantern, the Amalgam of Marvel's Iron Man and DC's Green Lantern, for this special. By day, Iron Lantern was the millionaire Hal Stark, and by night he was a hero who fought Madame Sapphire and Great White.

THE MAIN DUCK

• *Lobo The Duck* #1

A combination of Howard the Duck and ultra-violent alien Lobo, this Amalgam special was written by Alan Grant with pencils by Val Semeiks. The special centered around a foul-mouthed fowl as he explored a New York City that lay in ruins.

MARVEL'S METAL MEN

• *The Magnetic Men Featuring Magneto* #1

Magneto (a combination of Magneto and Will Magnus) returned in his second Amalgam special, care of writer Tom Peyer and artist Barry Kitson. This special featured Magneto's Magnetic Men (an amalgam of Brotherhood of Evil Mutants and Metal Men).

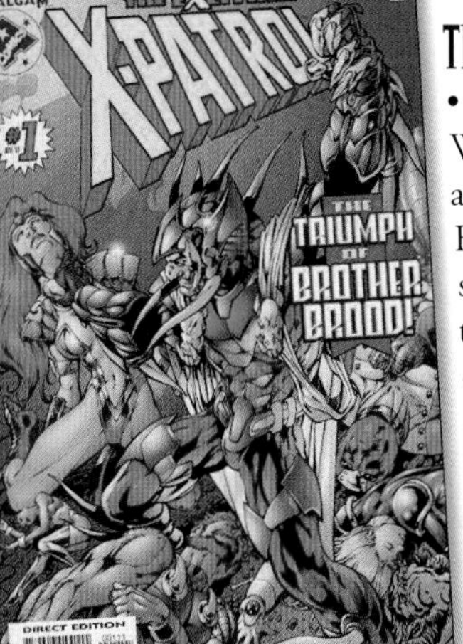

THE DOOM OF X-FORCE

• *The Exciting X-Patrol* #1

Writer Barbara Kesel, along with penciller Bryan Hitch, created this second Amalgam special to feature the X-Patrol. A combination of X-Force and Doom Patrol, the team included members Shatterstarfire (Shatterstar and Starfire) and Beastling (Beast and Changeling).

NOVEMBER

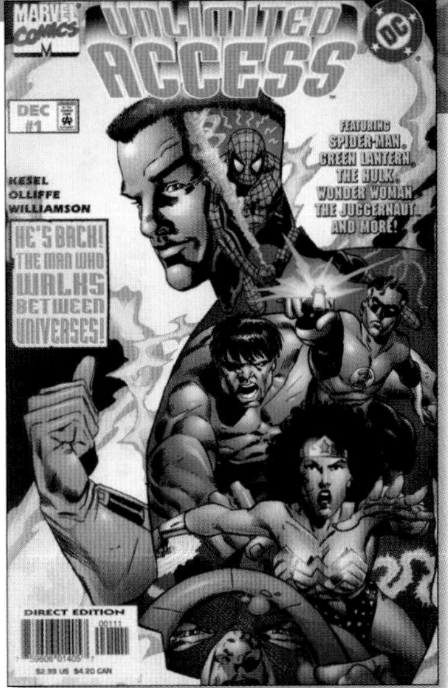

ACCESS THROUGH THE AGES

• *Marvel/DC: Unlimited Access* #1

Unlimited Access was the third and final major intercompany four-issue miniseries of the late 1990s. The series continued the adventures of Access, the "cosmic hall monitor" who policed the DC and Marvel Universe to prevent another Amalgam event from happening. This series, by writer Karl Kesel and artist Pat Olliffe, featured such momentous bouts as the Hulk versus Green Lantern, the Sentinels hunting the Legion of Super-Heroes, and the classic Avengers battling the original JLA.

SPIDER-MAN TURNS JAPANESE

• *Spider-Man: The Manga* #1

The black and white Japanese Spider-Man comics of the late 1970s were published for an American audience that now embraced the style of Manga storytelling. Written and drawn by Ryoichi Ikegami, with English translation by Mutsumi Masuda and C.B. Cebulski, the series ran until April 1999.

BORN AGAIN HEROES

"And with the explosive force of air rushing to fill a vacuum, the travelers are drawn back into their homeworld, leaping into existence all over the world… or… to put it simply… the heroes… return."

• *Heroes Reborn: The Return* #1

Sales were high for the four different 1996 *Heroes Reborn* series that were born out of the ashes of the Onslaught event. However, the drastic changes to the origins and continuity of the main characters proved quite controversial with the fans, many of whom had invested years of their lives reading about the personal history of these heroes. While the change to these reimagined versions of the Marvel icons was never intended to be permanent, the return of their old favorites could not come soon enough for many readers. That was where legendary scribe Peter David and artist Salvador Larroca came in.

Creating a four-issue miniseries that tied up the loose threads left hanging in the *Heroes Reborn* universe, David and Larroca cast Franklin Richards, son of the FF's Mr. Fantastic and Invisible Woman, in a starring role, as he became aware of his parents living in this newly imagined universe. With the help of Man-Thing, and the coldly distant Celestial Ashema, Franklin was able to help lead his heroes home, despite losing Thor and Dr. Doom in the tumultuous journey.

To attract new readers to this series, each extra-sized issue featured four pages of summary text, giving the audience an update on the recent history of the major players in the saga. The readers also got sneak peaks into the four new ongoing titles, including *The Avengers*, that Marvel was launching to coincide with the return of their icons to the mainstream Marvel Universe.

MEANWHILE IN 1997…

THE "WORLD'S FASTEST MAN"

Olympic champions Donovan Bailey and Michael Johnson compete in the "World's Fastest Man" title in a 164-yard (150-meter) race. Bailey wins when Johnson suffers injury.

NEW LABOUR PRIME MINISTER

Tony Blair is Britain's Labour Prime Minister after eighteen years of Conservative rule.

A BOY WIZARD CALLED HARRY

The first Harry Potter book, Harry Potter and the Philosopher's Stone, *publishes in the UK. It is released the following year in the US as* Harry Potter and the Sorcerer's Stone.

THE "PEOPLE'S PRINCESS" DIES

Princess Diana is killed in a car crash in Paris, prompting a mass outpouring of public grief. Over two billion people watch her funeral on TV.

CLONING MILESTONE

Scientists at Oregon Regional Primate Research Center create two monkeys using DNA taken from cells of developing monkey embryos. These are the first primates to be cloned.

RISE IN MEDIA VIOLENCE

The late 1990s see an increase in violently and sexually explicit television programs and video games. Due to complaints, a parental rating system for television is established in 1997.

BUFFY SLAYS VAMPIRES

The science fiction genre is renewed with Buffy the Vampire Slayer, *a series that is both a hit in the mainstream and garners cult following. It is notable in the fantasy genre for the theme of superheroes struggling with real life.*

AND AT THE MOVIES…

LA Confidential, *three LA policemen with very different personalities investigate a shooting at an all-night diner in this adaptation of crime writer James Ellroy's novel;* Titanic, *Leonardo DiCaprio and Kate Winslet star in James Cameron's highest grossing film of all time;* Men In Black, *Will Smith and Tommy Lee Jones play wisecracking, black-suited, polarized agents employed to defend Earth from illegal aliens;* Tomorrow Never Dies, *the eighteenth spy film in the Bond franchise and the second to star Pierce Brosnan.*

"The SPACE ROCKET landed in 1938.
" -- and -- by the time WORLD WAR TWO began -- ADDED them to their experimental 'SUPER-SOLDIER' formula, hoping to create a champion of LIBERTY.
"They INJECTED formula into a VOLUNTEER -- one name I cannot REVEAL --
" -- and exposed him to a MASSIVE jolt of SOLAR RADIATION. Given what they KNEW of the alien cells, the scientists had SOME clue as to how this might AFFECT the test subject --
" -- but NO one expected him to be granted POWERS and ABILITIES --
" -- so FAR BEYOND those of MORTAL MEN."

SUPER-SOLDIER LEADS THE FIGHT

In 1996, writer Mark Waid and artist Dave Gibbons collaborated on *Super-Soldier* (April), an Amalgam one-shot that featured the combination of Marvel's Captain America with DC's Superman. When Marvel and DC released a second wave of Amalgam specials, super-strong Super-Soldier was one of the few characters, along with Dark Claw and the Magnetic Men, to garner a second special, this time entitled *Super-Soldier: Man Of War* (June, 1997). In this second one-shot, Dave Gibbons took a more active role, and not only drew the issue, but also co-plotted the story with Mark Waid.

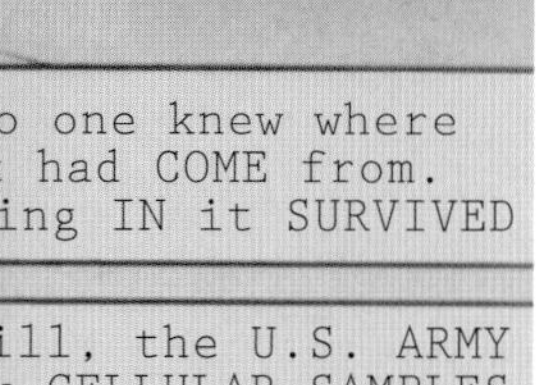

o one knew where
had COME from.
ing IN it SURVIVED

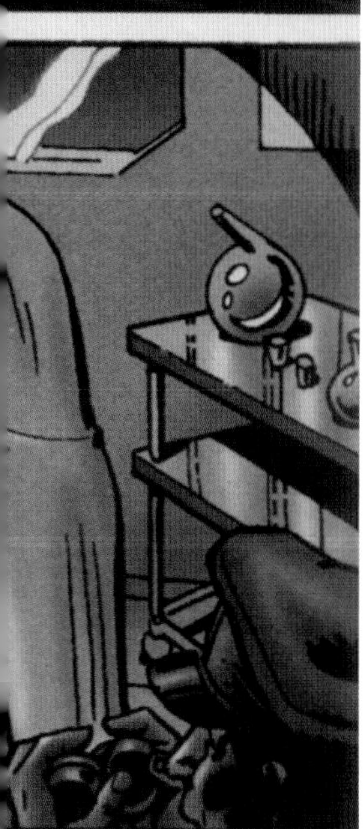

ill, the U.S. ARMY
k CELLULAR SAMPLES
from the corpse
IN -- EXPERIMENTED
with them --

"That wasn't their ONLY surprise.

"They found ME in the SHADOWS, eager to make my MARK as a CUB REPORTER.

"Fortunately, we Olsens talk FAST. I struck a DEAL.

"I wouldn't rat out the PROJECT -- IF the government made me the OFFICIAL PRESS FLAK --

" -- of SUPER-SOLDIER.

"With MY HELP, ALLIED TROOPERS and NAZI WARMONGERS alike read of Super-Soldier's EVERY MOVE -- witnessed his EVERY VICTORY.

"By MARCH of 1942, Super-Soldier had the war all but WON nearly SINGLE-HANDEDLY -- "

YOU WANT A SPIDER-PERSON...? FACE IT, TIGER... YOU JUST HIT THE JACKPOT!

1998

NEW DAYS AND NEW KNIGHTS

By 1998, Marvel's bankruptcy issues had been settled in court, and ToyBiz, a large toy manufacturer and former subsidiary of Marvel Comics, was now running the show. And with a secure rock to stand on, Editor-in-Chief Bob Harras, along with publisher Bill Jemas, set out to bring Marvel's stable of well-known characters back out of the shadows and into the black.

Attracting new readers was at the forefront of the company's game plan. With the Heroes Return event, many classic characters saw their comic restarted and brandishing a new first issue, including Captain America and Iron Man. Making the most of these revamps, Marvel began to add a gatefold cover to many of their comics, a trend which had started at the end of the previous year. These fold-out covers were packed with information that would bring new readers up-to-speed instantly with the recent happenings and history of each comic's title character, making each issue that much more accessible to Marvel's audience.

It was this kind of thinking that led to the creation of the Marvel Knights imprint, a line of comics exploring the darker side of the Marvel Universe by the hottest name talents of the day, including writer/director Kevin Smith and artist and editor Joe Quesada.

JANUARY

FANTASTIC FOUR'S FRESH START

• *Fantastic Four* #1

Writer Scott Lobdell rearranged his X-schedule to try his hand at writing a different team of Marvel heroes in this new *Heroes Return* series. It was drawn by Alan Davis, and featured the debut of a new team of villains called the Ruined.

CAPTAIN AMERICA FIGHTS BACK

• *Captain America* #1

Writer Mark Waid began what many fans still consider to be the ultimate run on the *Captain America* title with this new series penciled by Ron Garney. This issue featured a disoriented Cap returning from the *Heroes Reborn* universe, and finding himself mysteriously in Japan. At the back of the comic was an interview with Garney, discussing the creation of his dynamic cover. Besides showcasing Cap's battle with Lady Deathstrike, this issue also saw the return of Kang the Conqueror.

Cap was floored to discover that a blockbuster movie had been made about him during his absence.

The Avengers reunited to battle Mordred and his powerful aunt Morgan Le Fay.

George Pérez was known for his attention to detail and often drew large team spreads.

BUSIEK'S AVENGERS ASSEMBLE

"And the crowd goes wild --!"

• *The Avengers* #1

After the sales boost *The Avengers* received during the Heroes Reborn event, the powers that be at Marvel wanted to make an equally impressive splash when they returned their heroes to the Marvel Universe proper. And at the top of their short list of dream artists for the Heroes Return project was George Pérez, who'd left his mark on the team in the 1970s, before going on to collect hoards of DC fans as well. He drew two of their mega-hits, *Crisis On Infinite Earths* and *The New Teen Titans*, among scores of other projects for both publishers. But when asked to both write and draw the title, Pérez declined the invitation, stating he would rather just pencil the book, as he felt he was not well-versed enough in the team's recent adventures and developments. He did, however, suggest a writer that he wanted to work with—Kurt Busiek.

Making small waves with *Thunderbolts* and *The Untold Tales Of Spider-Man*, Busiek had recently made a successful play to scribe the newly relaunched *Iron Man* series, but he was blown away when offered the seat at the helm of *The Avengers*. He quickly jumped at the opportunity to work on his dream project with his dream collaborator. With the debut issue, he reintroduced the classic team, now consisting of members Captain America, Iron Man, Hawkeye, Scarlet Witch, Thor, Vision, Iron Man, Warbird with new members, the former New Warriors Justice and Firestar, alongside cameo appearances by nearly every single former Avenger in the team's long and varied history.

FEBRUARY

SPIDER-GIRL

What If...? #105

What if the daughter of Peter Parker and Mary Jane Watson had survived the Clone Saga? That was the question that writer Tom DeFalco and artist Ron Frenz posed in this stand-alone issue that starred the teenager May Parker. It focused on her coming to terms with the spider-powers she inherited from her father, who had now retired from a life of fighting crime to become a police scientist. Proving popular, Spider-Girl not only spun off into her own long-lasting title, but helped establish this new possible future of the Marvel Universe, referred to as the MC2 Universe.

IRON MAN REINVENTS HIMSELF

• *The Invincible Iron Man* #1

Tony Stark returned in style, opening a new branch of his company called Stark Solutions, in this new ongoing series by writer Kurt Busiek and artist Sean Chen.

MARCH

X-MEN HIT THE ORIENT

• *X-Men: The Manga* #1

Under the Marvel Imports label, writer/artist Hiroshi Higuchi chronicled the black-and-white newsprint tales of the X-Men as translated by Mutsumi Masuda. This title showed the X-Men struggling against familiar foes in stories similar to that of the X-Men animated cartoon.

JULY

THOR GETS IN TOUCH WITH HIS HUMANITY

• *The Mighty Thor* #1

Thor thundered into his new ongoing series by writer Dan Jurgens and artist John Romita Jr. Thor returned to the fabled Asgard to find this once majestic home of the Norse Gods now lying in ruins. He headed back to the mortal plane only to meet Jake Olson, a human paramedic whose life would be forever intertwined with that of the thunder god.

AUGUST

Blade was released on August 21 and starred Wesley Snipes as Marvel's resident half-vampire/half-human, as well as actors Kris Kristofferson and Stephen Dorff. The film was directed by Stephen Norrington and written by David S. Goyer.

OCTOBER

SPIDER-GIRL WEBS HER OWN SERIES

• *Spider-Girl* #1

Spider-Man's daughter May Parker swung to new heights in her own ongoing series. Written by Tom DeFalco and drawn by artist Pat Olliffe, she faced such threats as Crazy Eight and Mr. Nobody. The series followed a zero issue, also in October, that reprinted her origin from *What If...?* #105.

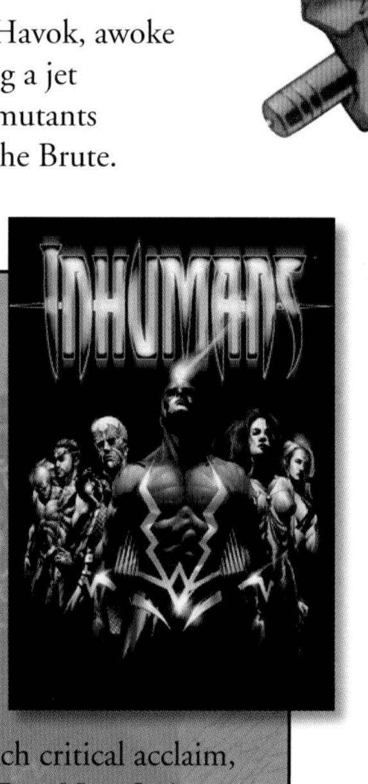

MAKING MUTANT X

Mutant X #1

Written by Howard Mackie and artist Tom Raney. Alex Summers, the mutant known as Havok, awoke in a world not his own after narrowly surviving a jet explosion. He joined ranks with strange new mutants including Marvel Woman, Bloodstorm, and the Brute.

NOVEMBER

THE INHUMAN STRUGGLE

• *Inhumans* #1

In this twelve-issue Marvel Knights limited series, writer Paul Jenkins and artist Jae Lee put a realistic face on the denizens of the mystical city Attilan. It detailed the Inhumans' conflicts with the easily threatened human population and showcased the tragic lives of King Black Bolt, his Queen Medusa, and their royal court. This new title earned much critical acclaim, including the prestigious Eisner award for Best New Series.

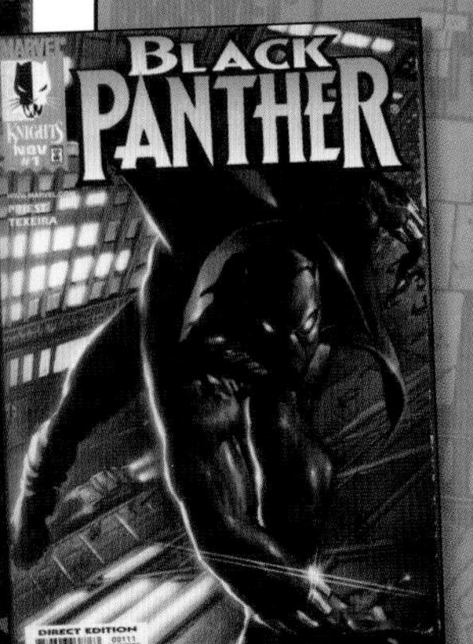

BLACK PANTHER HITS THE STREETS

• *Black Panther* #1

Writer Christopher Priest, and artists Mark Texeira and Joe Quesada put a new spin on the life of Wakanda Warrior King, Black Panther as he ventured to the concrete jungle of New York City. This quirky Marvel Knights title was known for its innovative storytelling, including its use of titles before each scene.

NOVEMBER

DAREDEVIL GETS KNIGHTED

"When it rains, it pours."

• *Daredevil* #1

It was a dream come true for many comic fans. Kevin Smith, the writer/director of such cult films as *Clerks, Mallrats,* and *Chasing Amy*, which had taken the comic book world by storm mostly due their Super Hero in-jokes and *Star Wars* debates, had been hired by Marvel to write for *Daredevil*, a character whose title many thought could use a major facelift. To top it all off, fan-favorite artist Joe Quesada was not only going to draw the comic, but would also be at the helm of its creative direction as the editor.

Viewed as the flagship title for the new Marvel Knights imprint, *Daredevil*, along with fellow titles *Inhumans, Black Panther,* and *The Punisher*, was the result of Marvel outsourcing these darker titles to Joe Quesada and Jimmy Palmiotti's company, Event Comics, in an effort to create a line of books that dealt with more sophisticated and mature themes. And with Kevin Smith writing the first eight issues of this series, *Daredevil*, was an instant hit, and helped start the trend of comic companies recruiting writers from other media besides merely the close-knit world of comic books.

In this epic story, Matt Murdock saw his life turned upside down as he found himself the unwilling caretaker of a baby supposedly born by immaculate conception. He also discovered that his former love Karen Page had been diagnosed with HIV and then saw her die at the hands of Bullseye. He finally deduced it was all a ploy of a revenge-seeking Mysterio whom Daredevil had bested in a previous battle.

Matthew Murdock became a "guardian devil" when a young girl showed up at his offices and handed him her baby, telling him an angel had commanded her to do so.

At 5:26 p.m., the savior was left in the devil's care.
HEY! WAIT A SECOND!
End of Issue One

MEANWHILE IN 1998...

MONICA LEWINSKY SCANDAL
After allegations of an affair with a 24-year-old White House intern, President Clinton states that he "did not have sexual relations with that woman."

US EMBASSY BOMBINGS
Simultaneous attacks hit US embassies in Dar es Salaam, Tanzania and Nairobi, Kenya. The explosions kill hundreds and are linked to terrorist group al-Qaeda.

SMOKING BAN IN CALIFORNIA
Smoking is outlawed in all Californian bars and restaurants.

GOOD FRIDAY AGREEMENT
The British and Irish Governments sign a landmark agreement, endorsed by most Northern Ireland political parties. It is a major political development in the peace process in which all parties agree to use "extensively peaceful and democratic means."

THE iMAC IS UNVEILED
Apple launches its first "all-in-one" desktop computer. The brightly colored translucent computers, inspired by gumdrops, become a design classic of all time.

GOOGLE IS BORN
Google, Inc. is founded in California by Larry Page and Sergey Brin, who are Ph.D. students at Stanford University.

MATTHEW SHEPARD KILLED IN "GAY-BASHING" ATTACK
The 21-year-old student's death brought national attention to the issue of hate crime legislation at both the state and federal levels and sparked public reflection on homophobia.

CLINTON IMPEACHED
Impeachment hearings against President Clinton for perjury and obstruction of justice, begin over claims he lied about his sexual relationship with White House intern Monica Lewinsky.

INDIA GOES NUCLEAR
India resumes nuclear testing on May 12, violating a worldwide ban on nuclear testing.

ARKANSAS SCHOOL MASSACRE
Two young boys kill five people at an Arkansas middle school after a hoax fire alarm.

AND AT THE MOVIES...
Saving Private Ryan, *from the opening visceral scenes of the D-Day landings, Steven Spielberg brings an intensity missing from earlier war films;* A Bug's Life, *Pixar's inspired recreation of* The Seven Samurai *with a misfit ant recruiting a gang of insect mercenaries to defend his colony from marauding grasshoppers;* Ring, *Japanese horror, reliant on sound and atmosphere, about a cursed videotape that kills anyone who watches it.*

DECEMBER

REWRITING SPIDER-MAN'S HISTORY
• *Spider-Man: Chapter One* #1

John Byrne tried his hand at writing and drawing this thirteen-part retelling of Peter Parker's past, which sparked much controversy with the fans, and is now generally considered outside the realm of canon Spider-Man continuity.

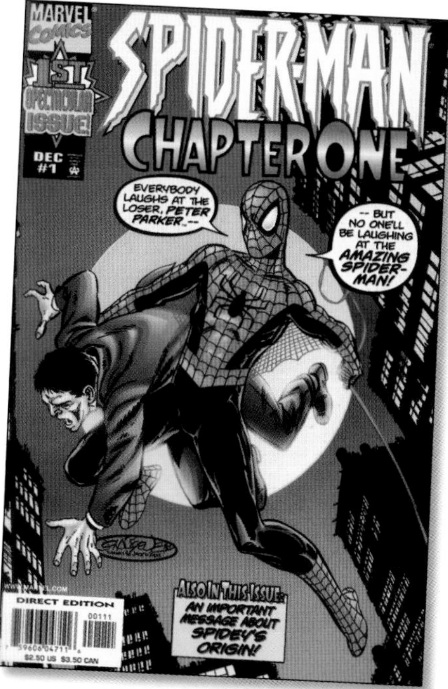

M Kurt Busiek and Carlos Pacheco teamed together to tell a time-spanning adventure in the twelve-issue limited series *Avengers Forever*. They pitted various teams of heroes against Kang the Conqueror, Immortus, and the Kree Supreme Intelligence.

ALSO...

THE SLINGERS SURFACE
• *Slingers* #0

The young Slingers team consisted of Prodigy, Hornet, Ricochet, and Dusk. They debuted in a preview zero issue available only through *Wizard Magazine*, written by Joseph Harris with art by Adam Pollina.

1999

SEEING WHAT WOULD STICK

Marvel was throwing everything against the wall. After the successful revamps of most of their major iconic characters, Marvel had still been unable to find a stable foothold for Spider-Man, as most fans were still put off a bit from the elaborate continuity originating in the Clone Saga. As the maxi-series *Spider-Man: Chapter One* continued to instigate much debate with the fans, while still becoming a modest success, Marvel decided to try their hand at restarting Spider-Man's monthly comics, weeding the many books down to a manageable two main titles—*The Amazing Spider-Man* and *Peter Parker: Spider-Man*. All in all, despite John Byrne and company's best efforts, Spider-Man still wouldn't find his footing until the arrival of J. Michael Staczynski in 2001.

The year 1999 also saw other concepts being tossed up for the fans to judge. A new Black Widow debuted in the pages of *Inhumans,* The New Warriors were granted another chance at a monthly comic, and the untold past of the X-Men was explored in *X-Men: The Hidden Years*, but none of these ideas really took a hold of the readers. However, things were changing, and an editorial shuffle was about to take place, one that would see a familiar face be promoted to Editor-In-Chief the following year.

JANUARY

A NEW SPIN ON SPIDEY

"I did my time. I had the power and I acted responsibly. It's time for Peter Parker to live."

• *The Amazing Spider-Man* #1
Peter Parker's life as Spider-Man was over. After his last confrontation with the Green Goblin, Peter had burned his costume, wanting a chance at a normal existence. His Aunt May was back in his life, her death proven to be merely an elaborate hoax. This new first issue was written by Howard Mackie with art by John Byrne. In it, the deadly Scorpion attacked Peter Parker's new employer, the Tri Corp Research Foundation, and Spider-Man showed up to confront him. This would hardly be unusual if it weren't for the fact that Peter Parker wasn't the one wearing the webs.

As the story progressed in later issues, and also in the pages of *Peter Parker: Spider-Man*, it was revealed that the Spider-Man impersonator that forced Peter Parker to resume his role as resident web-slinger wasn't a Spider-Man at all, but rather the new Spider-Woman, Mattie Franklin. Mattie had gained her superpowers in the bizarre Gathering of the Five ceremony that had taken place in the last issue of the first volume of *The Amazing Spider-Man* (November, 1998).

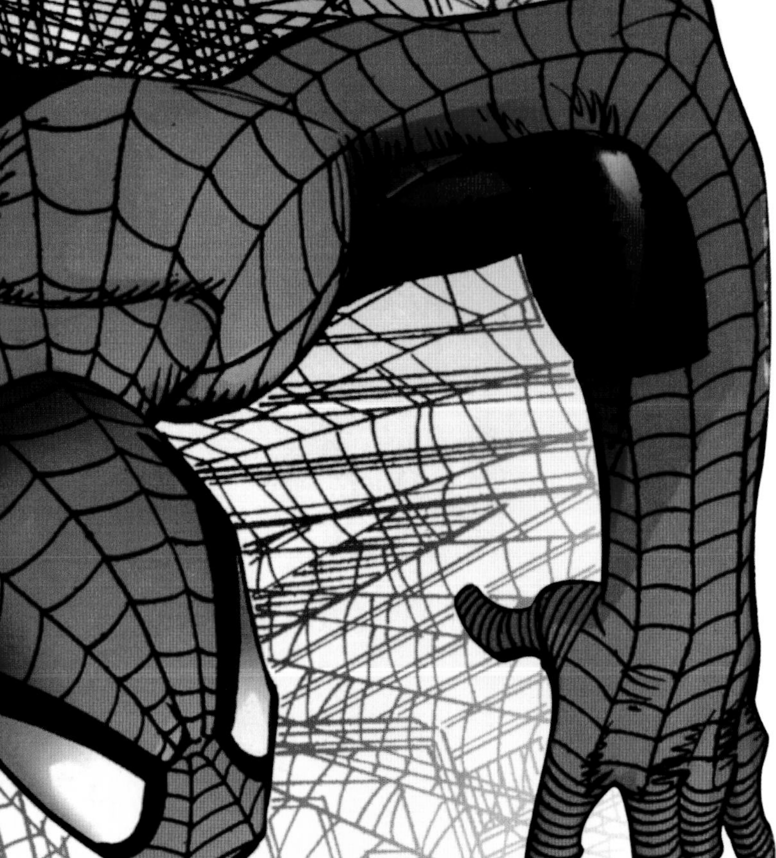

JANUARY

Besides launching this new storyline, and featuring an impressive roster of guest stars, including the Fantastic Four, the Avengers and Daredevil, this introductory issue also featured a wrap-around, gatefold cover, a back-up story drawn by Rafael Kayanan, and an extra comic story written and drawn by Byrne that detailed Peter Parker's many powers, and harkened back to the Stan Lee and Steve Ditko bonus stories that appeared as early as the first Spider-Man annual of 1964.

PETER PARKER CAN'T LOSE

• *Peter Parker: Spider-Man* #1

Peter Parker tried to stay retired as his replacement tackled a new foe called the Ranger in this story written by Howard Mackie with art by John Romita Jr. This issue also featured a backup story from Peter's childhood, and Romita Jr. model sheets that artists could use as reference.

FEBRUARY

GAMBIT GOES MONTHLY

• *Gambit* #1

Scribe Fabian Nicieza, along with penciller Steve Skroce, chronicled Gambit's first ongoing series. They had him pilfering an ancient tomb guarded with the latest technology, battling the X-Cutioner, and charming a score of ladies, including his longtime flame, fellow X-Men member Rogue.

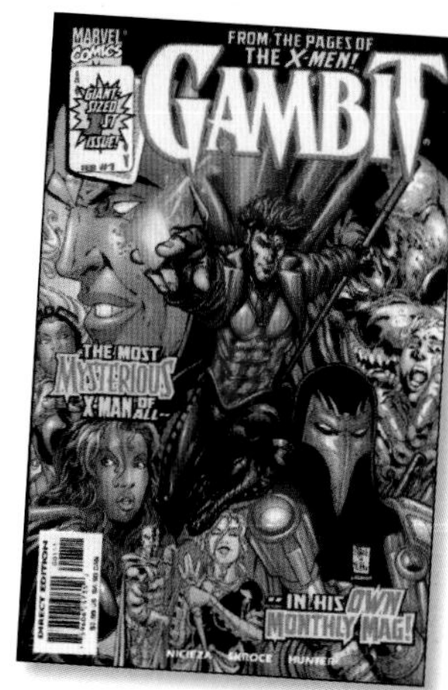

MARCH

THE NEW BLACK WIDOW

• *Inhumans* #5

As writer Paul Jenkins and artist Jae Lee continued their award-winning Marvel Knights limited series, they introduced Yelena Belova, the second Soviet super spy to go by the moniker Black Widow. The story followed Belova as she arranged to undermine the Inhumans' vaunted security system.

X MARKS THE SPOT

• *Earth X* #0

After his success detailing the future of the DC Universe in his epic painted miniseries *Kingdom Come*, Alex Ross took a turn playing fortune-teller for the Marvel stable of heroes. He wrote this fourteen-part saga alongside Jim Krueger, with pencils by John Paul Leon. Ross painted each lavish cover himself and told this epic tale through the eyes of Machine Man as he took the place of the Watcher, recording the future of the Marvel Universe. This was a world where everyone had superpowers, and an aged Captain America fought alongside his partner Redwing against the forces of the brainless parasites known as HYDRA.

APRIL

THE HULK UNLEASHED

• *Hulk* #1

Bruce Banner took to the road in an attempt to escape his past in this new series by writer John Byrne and artist Ron Garney. This debut issue saw Banner arrive in the small town of Faulkner and rent a vacant room. Suffering from nightmares, Bruce awoke to discover that the town had almost destroyed as the Hulk refused to give Banner a moment's peace.

MAY

MARVEL SUPER HERO ISLAND

When the Universal Studios theme park in Orlando, Florida opened up a sister park called Universal's Islands of Adventure, Marvelites young and old got the chance to walk into the pages of their favorite comic books at Marvel Super Hero Island, one of the five new islands that made up the park. The Marvel Island included such rides as the Incredible Hulk Coaster, Doctor Doom's Fearfall, the scrambler-like Storm Force Accelatron, and perhaps the gem of the bunch, the Amazing Adventures of Spider-Man, a 3-D romp through the rooftops that began in the heart of the *Daily Bugle* itself.

In Hulk *#1, Bruce Banner spent his days trying to repair the damage that the Hulk caused at night.*

JUNE

BLACK WIDOW VS. BLACK WIDOW

• *Black Widow* #1

Devin Grayson, a writer who had demonstrated her ability to craft strong women a few years earlier at the helm of DC's *Catwoman*, made the switch to Marvel in order to orchestrate the first Black Widow miniseries alongside artist J.G. Jones. This new three-issue series pitted Yelena Belova, the new cutthro heir to the Black Widow title who'd debut a few months prior in the pages of *Inhumans*, against Natasha Romanov, the defender and originator of the Black Wido name. It saw the two femme fatales battlin it out over an experimental military drug that reduced its users into frenzied, feral madmen.

OCTOBER

THE NEWER WARRIORS

The New Warriors #1

In an attempt to garner the same warm reception they received at the decade's start, the New Warriors were given a new ongoing series by writer Jay Faerber and penciler Steve Scott, starring a few familiar faces, including Speedball, Nova, and Namorita.

The New Warriors *only lasted eleven issues, perhaps due to the absence of popular members like Firestar and Night Thrasher.*

NOVEMBER

ORIGINS OF THE X-MEN

• *X-Men: Children Of The Atom* #1

Feeling that the legacy of the X-Men lacked a true origin story, writer Joe Casey joined with pencillers Steve Rude, Paul Smith, Essad Ribic, and Michael Ryan to create this six-part miniseries in the same vein as the hit *Batman: Year One* saga, with which writer Frank Miller and artist David Mazzucchelli had taken the comic world by storm in the 1980s. The tragic events of the school shooting in Columbine, Colorado, that occurred while Casey was crafting the book's second issue affected the tone of the series, which was rife with race metaphors and coming-of-age drama.

Chronicling Professor X's initial recruitment of the X-Men, Children of the Atom *introduced Angel as a shadowy crime fighter.*

DECEMBER

THE X-MEN'S LOST ADVENTURES

• *X-Men: The Hidden Years* #1

In 1970, with the arrival of the 67th issue of the original *X-Men* comic, the title began to reprint old material, and wouldn't be revitalized until the *Giant-Size X-Men* special of 1975 that launched the comic to new heights of popularity. This left fans to wonder what the originals were up to in all that time, a question that writer/artist John Byrne decided to answer in this new ongoing series. Set in those mysterious in-between years, decades-old loose ends were tied up as the X-Men faced teenaged infighting, journeys to the Savage Land, and even a rematch bout with Magneto.

MEANWHILE IN 1999...

CLINTON ACQUITTED

President Clinton is cleared of the perjury and obstruction of justice charges brought against him over allegations he lied about his relationship with White House intern Monica Lewinsky.

COLUMBINE HIGH SCHOOL MASSACRE

Two students open fire at school, killing thirteen others, before turning their guns on themselves. The event stirs public debate about gun control laws and youth culture.

MILOSEVIC INDICTED FOR WAR CRIMES IN THE HAGUE

The former President of Yugoslavia is indicted by the UN's International Criminal Tribunal for the Former Yugoslavia for crimes against humanity in Kosovo. Charges are added later for war crimes and genocide in Bosnia and Croatia.

KOSOVO PEACE TREATY SIGNED

NATO and Yugoslavia sign a peace treaty and UN Resolution 1244 places Kosovo under interim UN administration.

HEROIC FEAT IN A ROWBOAT

After eighty-one days at sea, Tori Murden becomes the first woman to cross the Atlantic in a rowboat.

YELTSIN RESIGNS

In Russia, President Yeltsin resigns and is succeeded by former KGB official Vladimir Putin.

PRINCE EDWARD AND SOPHIE MARRY

On June 19, the wedding of England's Prince Edward and his long-time girlfriend Sophie Rhys-Jones takes place.

ALPS TUNNEL FIRE

A fire in the Mont Blanc Tunnel kills 39 people, closing the tunnel for nearly three years.

Y2K BUG

The world braces itself for the Y2K bug, as it is believed that there may be havoc on computer systems when the date reaches January 1, 2000.

AND AT THE MOVIES...

Star Wars: Episode I—The Phantom Menace, *George Lucas revisits his galaxy far, far away in the prequel movie exploring the childhood years of future Sith Lord, Anakin Skywalker;* The Sixth Sense, *M. Night Shyamalan's complex tale of a paranormal child virtually reinvents the supernatural thriller with its twist ending;* The Matrix, *imaginative fusion of virtual reality philosophy, martial arts, SFX, and innovatively choreographed action sequences create a sci-fi spectacular;* Fight Club, *David Fincher's subversive, masculine cult fantasy about a secret cell of frustrated white-collar workers.*

BACK AND FORTH

Jim Krueger and Alex Ross, the writing team who later collaborated on DC's *Justice* miniseries, kicked off their epic fourteen-part *Earth X* saga with a special #0 issue in March, 1999, that explained just how robot Machine Man became the eyes and ears for the blind Uatu the Watcher. Just as each issue of the ensuing series revealed a bit of the future of the Marvel Universe, it also delved back into Marvel's rich history, as shown in this double-page splash image by interior artist John Paul Leon. Ross himself painted the series' covers, as well as those of its two sequel series, *Universe X* and *Paradise X*, after *Earth X* proved to be a hit with the readers.

'E BEEN
E NOBILITY
' OF EARTH'S
1. BUT WE
SE SIGHT
'E HERE."
"MANKIND RESENTS ITS NEED FOR AUTHORITY.
"THEY WISH TO BE THEIR OWN AUTHORITY, X-51. THEY WOULD BE GODS THEMSELVES.
'HEY ARE
ND HOUNDED...
T OF NOTHING
N THE NEED
IMANITY TO
SOMETHING.
"THE HEROES ARE HATED BECAUSE THEY THREATEN THE VERY EXISTENCE OF THE PEOPLE THEY FEEL COMPELLED TO PROTECT."

2000s

Marvel was heading into the future. Starting on shaky ground as it attempted to bounce back from its recent brush with bankruptcy, Marvel made radical changes, and rarely looked both ways before leaping toward new horizons. The editorial staff was overhauled, and an emphasis on quality storytelling returned to the forefront. Novelists, screenwriters, and playwrights were recruited to give Marvel's stable of characters a contemporary voice, and the quality of the hired artistic draftsmen continued to rise. As the direct comic book store market dwindled, Marvel adapted by renewing its interest in collecting multiple issues into paperback form. And perhaps most importantly, Marvel began its assault on Hollywood, releasing a steady stream of film projects, and seeing massive returns for its efforts. The stigma of the 1990s had been lifted, and things continued to look up.

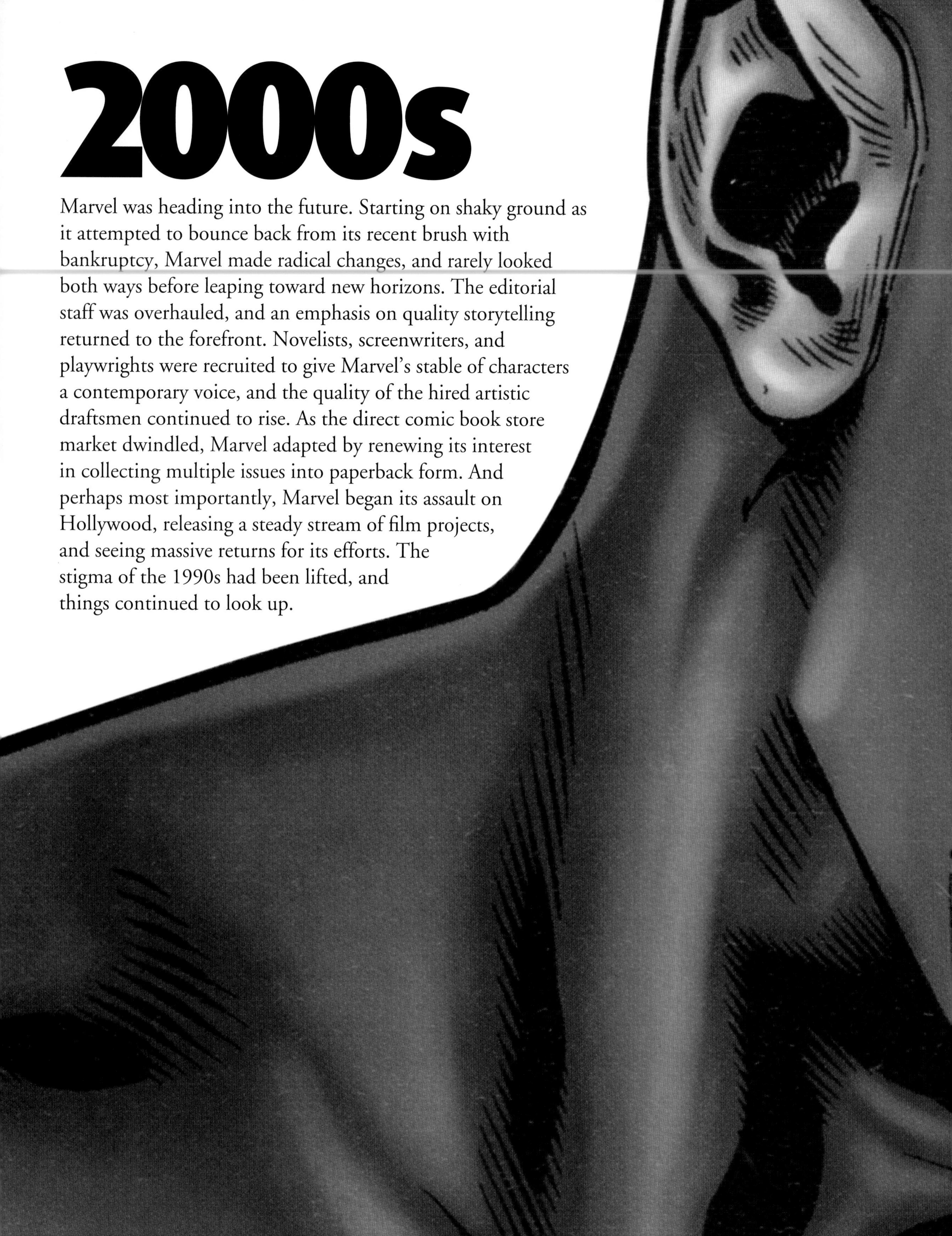

WHAT'S HAPPENED TO YOU...? YOU SHOULDN'T HAVE STAYED THIS WAY--YOU SHOULD'VE EVOLVED BY NOW.

2000

NEW KIDS IN TOWN

Bill Jemas became the new President of Marvel Comics and he quickly promoted Joe Quesada—a superstar comic artist who had done wonders in recent years with his Marvel Knights imprint—into the position of Editor-in-Chief. They seemed to have the magic touch. Through a combination of brainstorming and butting heads, these two set out to recreate Marvel Comics into the thriving company that it is today.

And they didn't do it quietly. Among many of the changes Quesada and Jemas brought about was hiring new editors like Axel Alonso and Stuart Moore, both formerly of DC/Vertigo Comics, who applied their success and connections to their new Marvel assignments. Quesada also created a few editorial mandates, instructing his staff to stop bringing characters back to life in order to up the drama and consequence when they die in the first place, as well as to cease the constant nostalgia and self-referential elements that seemed to plague a majority of Marvel's books at the time.

The Marvel Knights line continued its success, Jemas and Quesada went one better, and created the Ultimate imprint—a long-lasting line of blockbuster comics that would remain at the top of the sales charts for years.

APRIL

Having witnessed his family die before his eyes as innocent bystanders caught in the crossfire of a mob dispute, Frank Castle set off down a lonely path as the Punisher. Writer Garth Ennis, no stranger to chronicling the adventures of cut-throat anti-heroes after writing the series Hitman *for DC Comics, was drawn to Punisher due to the character's twisted nature as the only serial killer who was also a Super Hero.*

ELCOMING THE PUNISHER BACK

unfight in a morgue, rule one: don't hide ind the thin guy."

The Punisher #1

e team of writer Garth Ennis and artist eve Dillon, best known for their award-nning series *Preacher* for DC/Vertigo mics, took a shot at the Punisher in s twelve-issue series that was then llowed up by an ongoing volume. ith the last Marvel Knights *Punisher* niseries taking more of a supernatural proach to Frank Castle's obsessive war crime, Ennis returned the Punisher his roots, reinstating him as a near-otionless killing machine in this ody black comedy adventure that stantly won over the readers. In fact, the first issue of this new Punisher series buted fifth in sales out of all the comics released that month, only bested by ur X-Men titles.

As the Punisher waged a gory war on mob boss Ma Gnucci, reducing her to a adriplegic before later killing her altogether, he was pursued by the hapless etective Soap, a down-on-his-luck cop given the near-impossible task of taking e Punisher in for his crimes. Attempting to ignore a supporting cast of ighbors living in his rundown apartment building, including the obscenely ese Mr. Bumpo, and the overly excited Spacker Dave, the Punisher set up a e for himself under the transparent alias of John Smith.

As the series progressed, the Punisher took on the overly tough and aloof sassin the Russian, bested Daredevil, and became the inspiration for a league of llers called the Vigilante Squad, a murderous group that Frank Castle put an d to in true Punisher fashion.

After the initial twelve-issue series, Ennis and Dillon paired up again on Punisher's ongoing series, with Dillon leaving the title after seven issues. Ennis himself took a brief hiatus at the same time, before returning to the comic with issue thirteen and staying until its conclusion at issue #37.

MAY

GENERAL RYKER

• *The Incredible Hulk* #14

Hulk was once again plagued by the military thanks to writer Paul Jenkins and artist Ron Garney. As Bruce Banner mourned his wife, General Ryker, a military mastermind who wanted to recreate the Hulk, slowly unearthed his trail.

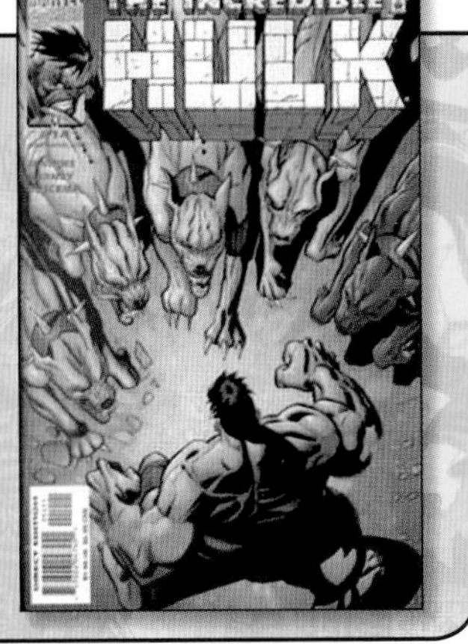

JULY

THE X-MEN COME TO LIFE

• *X-Men: The Movie*

In July, the X-Men exploded into theaters. A comic-book adaptation was published to coincide with the movie release and carried a cover date of September. Featuring a script by Ralph Macchio, with pencils by Anthony Williams and inks by Andy Lanning, it told the story of Wolverine and Rogue's first meeting with Charles Xavier's X-Men. This first X-Men feature film was directed by Bryan Singer, with a screenplay by David Hayter and Tom DeSanto, and starred Patrick Stewart as Professor X, Halle Berry as Storm, Ian McKellen as Magneto, James Marsden as Cyclops, Famke Janssen as Jean Grey, Anna Paquin as Rogue, and Hugh Jackman as Wolverine.

BEFORE THE THING

• *Before The Fantastic 4: Ben Grimm And Logan* #1

Beginning in July, this three-issue miniseries, written by Larry Hama and with art by Kaare Andrews, detailed an early team-up of the Thing and Wolverine, before they each earned their respective monikers, as the two participated in a government mission together. It also featured Carol Danvers, the heroine who would later become Ms. Marvel, as well as an appearance by the future Black Widow.

AUGUST

MARVEL BOY MAKES THE SCENE

• *Marvel Boy* #1

Writer Grant Morrison and artist J.G. Jones introduced a new Marvel Boy in this six-issue Marvel Knights miniseries, as the space-faring anti-establishment alien Kree adventurer crash-landed on Earth and found himself the captive of the villainous Dr. Midas.

SEPTEMBER

THE SECRET OF THE SENTRY'S SUCCESS

"The other people on the train... you're making them nervous now... Maybe it's because you look like hell. Or maybe it's because now that you're beginning to remember... you're no longer casting a shadow."

• *The Sentry* #1

Some felt it was a big con, while others saw it as an inspired marketing strategy. The team of writer Paul Jenkins and artist Jae Lee had already proven themselves with their award-winning earlier collaboration on the *Inhumans* series for the Marvel Knights imprint. So, when they re-teamed on a new limited series entitled *The Sentry*, Editor-in-Chief Joe Quesada knew he was sitting on a winner. The only real question was how to get the public as excited about this brand new character as he was.

So Quesada called *Wizard* magazine. Long established as the go-to guide for comic teasers and inside scoops, *Wizard* was covering new and upcoming comic releases for an ever-increasing audience. But Quesada didn't want a simple plug, or even an in-depth article. He wanted to try something different.

Inspired by the Orson Welles *War of the Worlds* radio hoax from 1938, Quesada had *Wizard* run a fake obituary for a fictional comic book artist named Artie Rosen. Later, a follow-up article was printed, stating that a secret cache of Rosen's artwork had been discovered by his family, and included drawings of the hero the Sentry, a tormented character that Stan Lee and Rosen had created prior to *Fantastic Four* #1, the comic that was recognized as kicking off the Marvel era.

With this fictional groundwork properly laid, the Sentry's five-issue miniseries was released, along with five tie-in one-shot specials, to the now eagerly anticipatory masses, showcasing the hero's fight with the dark half of his personality, an entity known as the Void.

The Sentry battled the Void through the pages of his own title. He continued the fight through a series of specials, drawn by Phil Winslade, Mark Texeira, Rick Leonardi, and Bill Sienkiewicz, as the heroes of the Marvel Universe began to slowly remember him.

BEFORE MR. FANTASTIC

• *Before The Fantastic 4: Reed Richards* #1

Continuing the trilogy of pre-Fantastic Four adventures, the man who would become Mr. Fantastic starred in a three-issue miniseries. Courtesy of writer Peter David and artist Duncan Fergredo, it was an Indiana Jones-like adventure, opposite Victor Von Doom.

PATSY WALKER GOES TO HELLCAT

• *Hellcat* #1

Longtime Marvel mainstay Patsy Walker stole a brief moment in the sun in this three-issue miniseries by writer Steve Englehart and artist Norm Breyfogle. It delved into Pasty's past as a romance comics star, and her present, fighting the evil sorcerer Dormammu as Hellcat.

SPIDER-MAN REACHES THE ULTIMATE

"Great things are going to happen to you and your life, Peter. Great things. And with that will come great responsibility."

• *Ultimate Spider-Man* #1

It had been attempted before, and had failed miserably. There was just no re-imagining Spider-Man's origin story. The fans liked him the way he was, and projects that tweaked, revamped, or dramatically altered Peter Parker's past, like John Byrne's *Spider-Man: Chapter One* limited series, had fallen by the wayside and were forgotten almost as soon as they were created. So, everyone said it couldn't be done.

But Bill Jemas and Joe Quesada weren't about to believe that for a second. With Quesada ordering a new forward-looking policy, rather than falling back on what had been done in the past, Jemas decided to recreate a Spider-Man that would capture the energy and vitality of today's youth, and would speak to a contemporary audience, rather than one young in the 1960s. To reach that goal, he hired indy-comic rising star Brian Michael Bendis to co-write the series with him, and popular Spider-Man veteran artist Mark Bagley to serve as the book's penciller. Soon, *Ultimate Spider-Man* was released, stunning the masses and sparking the red-hot fire that would launch an entire line of comics based in this newly formed Ultimate universe's reality.

After the initial origin arc, which saw Peter Parker first don his webs when inspired by the death of his uncle Ben, Bendis took the writing chores over completely. He slowly departed from the basic storyline that Stan Lee and Steve Ditko had crafted all those years ago, and headed in a brave new direction to create Marvel's newest consistent best-seller. In this new universe, Peter Parker was reborn as a troubled teenager, balancing his life as a website technician for the *Daily Bugle*, typical high school angst, and tumultuous friendships with Gwen Stacy, Harry Osborn (Hobgoblin), and even Eddie Brock (Venom).

The Peter Parker that starred in Ultimate Spider-Man *wasn't an adult, but a struggling high school student who quickly confided his secret identity to his girlfriend, Mary Jane Watson.*

X-Men: Evolution, an animated series, debuted on Kids WB on November 4th. It lasted four seasons, and amassed fifty-two episodes. Dealing with core X-Men members Professor X, Wolverine, Jean Grey, Cyclops, Storm, Nightcrawler, Rogue, and Shadowcat, *X-Men: Evolution* also debuted new member Spyke.

A STORM COMING

• *Before The Fantastic 4: The Storms* #1

Written by Terry Kavanagh and drawn by Charlie Adlard, this final three-issue installment of stories reaching into the Fantastic Four's past detailed an early adventure of siblings Johnny and Sue Storm as they uncovered the secret of an ancient amulet.

MEANWHILE IN 2000...

Y2K
The new millennium begins and the world braces itself for computer havoc when computers hit January 1, 2000, but the feared havoc does not materialize.

THE FIRST FIRST-LADY SENATOR
Hillary Clinton becomes the first First Lady to win office when she is elected to the US Senate.

GEORGE W. BUSH ELECTED PRESIDENT
The Florida presidential recount is halted and so victory goes to George W. Bush.

CIVIL UNION FOR SAME-SEX COUPLES
The state of Vermont legalizes civil union for same-sex couples.

REFORMISTS IN IRAN
Reformists win control of the Iranian parliament for the first time since the 1979 Islamic revolution.

ANTI-GLOBALIZATION PROTESTS TURN VIOLENT
The era of globalization is accompanied by regular anti-globalization demonstrations. Violence breaks out during protests at the IMF and World Bank summits in Prague.

WORLDWIDE COMPUTER DISRUPTION
The "I love you" virus wreaks havoc on computers.

DIGITAL MOVIE DISTRIBUTION
The short film 405 is the first movie to be distributed on the Internet.

THE HUMAN GENOME DECIPHERED
A working draft of the genome (DNA) is published as part of the Human Genome Project.

FIRST DOUBLE ARM OP
A team of international surgeons conduct the first double arm transplant in France in a seventeen-hour operation.

NEW GALLERY FOR MODERN ART
The Tate Modern gallery opens in London in a former power station on the River Thames.

AND AT THE MOVIES...
X-Men, *when embittered mutant Magneto declares war on humanity, the X-Men are charged with saving the world in this story of Marvel's popular team;* Gladiator, *Hollywood's first classical epic for thirty years tells the story of Maximus, an exiled Roman General turned gladiator, played by Russell Crowe;* Crouching Tiger, Hidden Dragon, *Ang Lee's sweeping, romantic, gravity-defying take on the martial arts genre;* Mission: Impossible II, *Tom Cruise reprises his role as Ethan Hunt, trying to stop a virus being released by a former agent.*

THIS BLADE I AM HOLDING.
I HAVE DIED AT THE END OF IT.

2001

THE HERO IS BACK

It was a whole new ballgame. Now firmly behind the wheel as Marvel's Editor-in-Chief, Joe Quesada brought to mainstream Marvel all he had learned in the Marvel Knights corner of the universe. Big-name creators and innovative storytelling were at the forefront of his new direction. Several of the company's icons were about to get a facelift, and not through gimmicky, ad-driven events, but through solid writing and art, with the emphasis firmly on character development. Established pros like Grant Morrison and Peter Milligan mixed with relative newcomers like Brian Michael Bendis and Judd Winick. What's more, Quesada had learned from movie writer and director Kevin Smith's run on *Daredevil* that looking outside the comic book writer pool to other media had its rewards, so he recruited creator of TV's *Babylon 5,* J. Michael Straczynski, who had recently made a splash with Top Cow's *Rising Stars* comic series, to take over the writing on Spider-Man's flagship title. Marvel's characters were returning to their roots, and good stories were once again at the forefront.

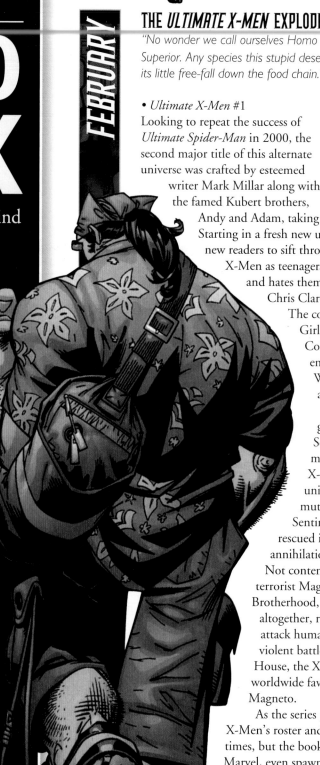

JANUARY

BLACK WIDOW TIMES TWO

• *Black Widow* #1

Devin Grayson returned to scribe the adventures of Natasha Romanov and her would-be successor Yelena Belova, this time joined by co-writer Greg Rucka and painter Scott Hampton. This three-issue miniseries saw the two Black Widows switch identities.

FEBRUARY

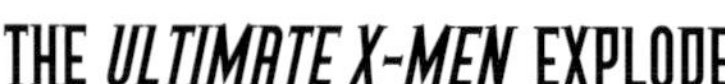

THE *ULTIMATE X-MEN* EXPLODE

"No wonder we call ourselves Homo Superior. Any species this stupid deserves its little free-fall down the food chain."

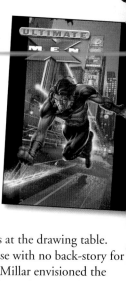

• *Ultimate X-Men* #1

Looking to repeat the success of *Ultimate Spider-Man* in 2000, the second major title of this alternate universe was crafted by esteemed writer Mark Millar along with the famed Kubert brothers, Andy and Adam, taking turns at the drawing table. Starting in a fresh new universe with no back-story for new readers to sift through, Millar envisioned the X-Men as teenagers, fighting for a world that fear and hates them, much as writers Stan Lee and Chris Claremont had done before him. The core team was made up of Marv Girl, Cyclops, Beast, Storm, and Colossus, but by the second issue end, new recruits Iceman and Wolverine had already been added to their ranks.

In a world where the US government had created giant Sentinel robots to rid the Earth mutantkind, the Ultimate X-Men wore black leather uniforms that shielded their mutant physiology from the Sentinel's detection equipment, and rescued innocent mutants from annihilation at the robots' gigantic hand Not content at mere survival, the mutant terrorist Magneto, along with his villainous Brotherhood, set out to conquer the nation altogether, reprogramming the Sentinels to attack humans instead of mutants. After a violent battle on the lawn of the White House, the X-Men prevailed, winning worldwide favor and seemingly killing Magneto.

As the series progressed further, the X-Men's roster and creative teams changed a few times, but the book remained a solid seller for Marvel, even spawning a crossover with the Ultimate Universe equivalent of the Avengers in a miniseries entitled *Ultimate War.*

Much like in the original X-Men comics of the 1960s, Henry McCoy, the X-Men's Beast, had a human look when he first debuted in the pag of Ultimate X-Men. *And much like his mainstream Marvel Unive counterpart, Beast soon developed a familiar blue hue.*

FEBRUARY

THE DEATH OF COLOSSUS

• *Uncanny X-Men* #390

Beast was elated to find a cure for the Legacy Virus that had been killing mutants for the last few years. However, in order to be released into the air where it could harmlessly cure all those infected, the antivirus had to be injected into a single carrier, causing that person's death. In a story by Scott Lobdell with art by Salvador Larroca, Colossus valiantly sacrificied himself so that mutantkind would survive.

MARCH

BLINKING IN

• *Blink* #1

Written by Scott Lobdell and Judd Winick with pencils by Trevor McCarthy, the four-issue *Blink* miniseries chronicled the teleporting mutant Blink's travels as she left the Age of Apocalypse, journeyed to the Negative Zone, and discovered the dimension-hopping Exiles.

MAY

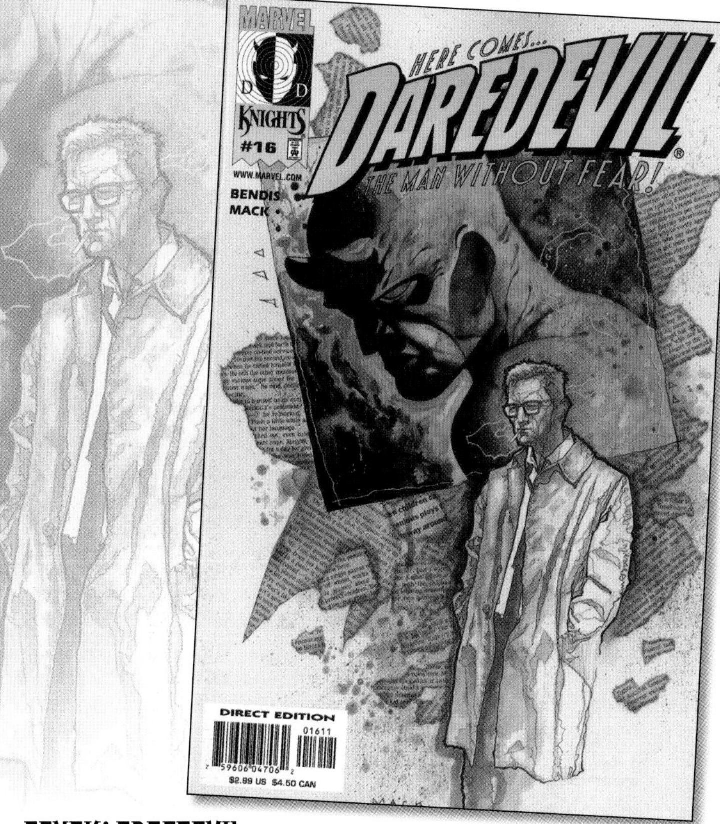

BENDIS' DAREDEVIL

• *Daredevil* #16

Writer Brian Michael Bendis began his impressive run on the *Daredevil* title with a small character-driven four-part story, teaming with his old friend David Mack. Mack had just written the previous story line, which debuted the character Echo, and his partnership with Bendis served as a great transition to Bendis' monumental fling with the Man Without Fear. Very early in his run, Bendis outed Daredevil's secret identity to the press, exposing Matt Murdock to a different kind of danger. Bendis would go on to have Daredevil declare himself Kingpin, get married, and, most shockingly of all, be sent to prison for his illegal vigilante acts.

MAY

MARVEL ABANDONS THE COMICS CODE

Fearing that the Comics Code Authority rating system misled the public into believing all comics were merely for children, Joe Quesada finally ended Marvel's longstanding relationship with the Code. Instead he implemented a new ratings system similar to that of the Motion Picture Association.

JUNE

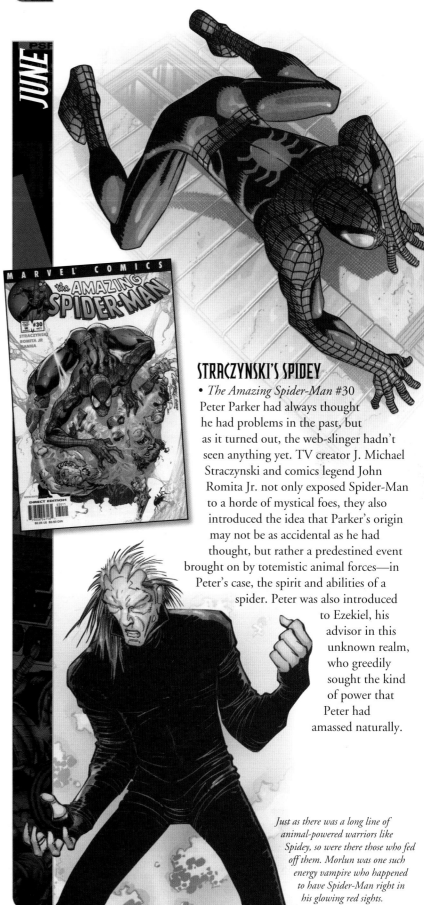

STRACZYNSKI'S SPIDEY

• *The Amazing Spider-Man* #30

Peter Parker had always thought he had problems in the past, but as it turned out, the web-slinger hadn't seen anything yet. TV creator J. Michael Straczynski and comics legend John Romita Jr. not only exposed Spider-Man to a horde of mystical foes, they also introduced the idea that Parker's origin may not be as accidental as he had thought, but rather a predestined event brought on by totemistic animal forces—in Peter's case, the spirit and abilities of a spider. Peter was also introduced to Ezekiel, his advisor in this unknown realm, who greedily sought the kind of power that Peter had amassed naturally.

Just as there was a long line of animal-powered warriors like Spidey, so were there those who fed off them. Morlun was one such energy vampire who happened to have Spider-Man right in his glowing red sights.

JULY

X-MEN BECOMES *NEW X-MEN*

"Forget your dental practice. Your future lies in genocide."'

• *New X-Men* #114

Despite the success and mainstream attention from the blockbuster *X-Men* movie of the previous summer, the mainstream *X-Men* comics themselves seemed to lack the innovation and creative direction that had given the team such staying power. That all changed when respected writer Grant Morrison and talented artist Frank Quitely took center stage. Morrison was no stranger to reinvigorating franchises, having relaunched the Justice League a few years prior for DC Comics in 1997's *JLA*. With that series, Morrison had stripped the title down to its bare essence and examined what made it popular and exciting in the first place. This, too, was his approach when brought on board for the X-Men.

Renaming the *X-Men* comic *New X-Men*, Morrison ignored the convoluted plot threads that had seemed to plague the X-family of books for years, and instead focused on the original idea of a mutant school run out of Charles Xavier's mansion. The roster was simplified to focus on the mainstay stars of the book: Cyclops, Beast, Jean Grey, Wolverine, and the classic former villain Emma Frost (aka the White Queen), who was thrown in for a touch of new blood and diversity. The characters all received a visual makeover as well, now wearing black leather uniforms, similar to the costumes seen in the feature film. This trend would be carried over to the other X-titles of the time, including *X-Treme X-Men* and *Uncanny X-Men*. Morrison also introduced a new villain for the team, Cassandra Nova, a bodiless parasite and the evil twin of Xavier, who had a vendetta toward mutants and humans alike.

Used to battling traditional giant Sentinels, the X-Men were unprepared to face Cassandra Nova's army of Wild Sentinels. These self-replicating robots used spare parts to evolve into more effective forms, allowing Nova to destroy the mutant nation of Genosha.

JULY

X-FORCE OVERHAUL

• *X-Force* #116

X-Force, an X-Men spinoff, received a makeover in July thanks to writer Peter Milligan and artist Mike Allred. A mixture of dark comedy and underground heroics, *X-Force* received critical acclaim, but a mixed reaction from fans. This all-new X-Force roster included the teleporting U-Go Girl, the alienated Orphan, the easily angered Anarchist, the exhaustively trendy Phat, the brutal bookworm Vivisector, and Doop—an alien sidekick.

AUGUST

DAREDEVIL'S TRUE COLORS

• *Daredevil: Yellow* #1

The creative team of writer Jeph Loeb and artist Tim Sale, known for their best-selling DC Comics miniseries *Batman: The Long Halloween* and *Batman: Dark Victory*, examined the early life of some of Marvel's iconic characters. First they tackled Daredevil in this six-issue miniseries, beginning in August, which focused on Matthew Murdock's time in his original yellow costume, and his relationship with Karen Page.

ENTER EXILES

• *Exiles* #1

Writer Judd Winick and artist Mike McKone told the story of a familiar band of dimension-hopping mutant heroes, including Sabretooth and Morph, as they traveled to different timelines to mend ripples in the time stream.

SEPTEMBER

ELEKTRA'S SECOND CHANCE

• *Elektra* #1

The favorite female assassin of the Marvel Universe returned for her second ongoing series in September thanks to writer Brian Michael Bendi and artist Chuck Austen. Elektra faced off against the organizations of HYDRA and SHIELD, among other takers, before the new creative team c writer Greg Rucka and artist Carlo Pagulayan eventually took over.

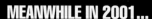

OCTOBER

WOLVERINE'S PAST REVEALED

"What's the matter, Jamey-Boy… forget where you came from?"

• *Origin* #1

Ever since his debut in the 1970s, Wolverine had been a character whose past was shrouded in mystery. But after the success of the first X-Men feature film, Editor-in-Chief Joe Quesada realized that sooner or later, the film franchise was going to want to examine Wolverine's enigmatic past. Rather than adapting what Hollywood envisioned for Logan's beginnings, Quesada, along with writer Bill Jemas, scripter Paul Jenkins, and artist Andy Kubert, decided to beat them to it with *Origin*, a six-issue miniseries, beginning in October, which told the story of Wolverine's early years. And sure enough eight years after *Origin*, Hollywood will release its own version with *X-Men Origins: Wolverine.*

After a couple of red herrings were planted to keep the fans guessing, Wolverine's real identity was revealed as James Howlett, the son of a self-made millionaire and his depressed wife. The story chronicled James' early life. A sickly child, his mutant powers manifested themselves when he witnessed his father's death at the hands of their groundskeeper, Logan, and his son, a boy known only as Dog. Thrown out by his family, James traveled to a remote part of Canada with his childhood sweetheart, Rose. Adopting the name Logan, James grew to manhood, but with little recollection of what had passed. When Dog reentered their lives, James accidentally killed Rose during the resulting combat. James then retreated into the woods away from society, and Wolverine was truly born.

Rose and James shared a life of privilege, while Dog had to endure a hard existence with an abusive alcoholic father. This made the troubled boy bitter and vengeful.

NOVEMBER

INTRODUCING *ALIAS*

• *Alias* #1

The herald to the start of Marvel's adult imprint, MAX, *Alias* was the first of a new comic series that was targeted specifically for a mature audience. Written by Brian Michael Bendis and featuring the art of Michael Gaydos and covers by David Mack, *Alias* explored the life of cynical private investigator Jessica Jones, who just happened to be a former Super Hero named Jewel. Armed with a realistic approach to the fantastic, the series chronicled Jessica's adventures as she protected Captain America's secret identity, dated and fell in love with Luke Cage, and even faced her past demons in the form of the villainous Purple Man—who had brainwashed her when she was known as Jewel.

DECEMBER

THE BLACK ISSUE

• *The Amazing Spider-Man* #36

Writer J. Michael Straczynski and penciller John Romita Jr. paid tribute to those who died during the real-life terror attacks on the World Trade Center on September 11. A full-page splash saw "real life" heroes standing in front of Marvel Super Heroes.

MEANWHILE IN 2001…

PRESIDENT BUSH SWORN IN

George W. Bush succeeds Bill Clinton and becomes 43rd President of the US.

9/11

Al-Qaeda terrorists hi-jack planes and destroy the World Trade Center, attack the Pentagon, and crash in Pennsylvania killing more than 3,000 people.

BUSH: "WAR ON TERROR"

President Bush declares that the US is at war against terror after the 9/11 attacks on the US.

ANTHRAX ATTACKS

Letters containing anthrax are posted to media offices and two US senators, killing five people.

2001 CINCINNATI RIOTS

African-American Timothy Thomas is shot dead by a police officer in Cincinnati. The event sparks three days of riots in the city.

OPERATION "ENDURING FREEDOM"

As part of the War on Terror, US and UK forces invade Afghanistan to overthrow the Taliban.

9/11 BENEFIT CONCERTS

The Concert for New York City *and the* United We Stand *concert in Washington take place to pay tribute to the victims and heroes of the 9/11 terrorist attacks.*

THE USA PATRIOT ACT

The USA PATRIOT—Uniting and Strengthening America by Providing the Appropriate Tools to Intercept and Obstruct Terrorism—Act becomes law to strengthen the US's armory in the War on Terror, but sparks debate on civil liberties.

FIRST "SPACE TOURIST"

Multimillionaire Dennis Tito is the first person to pay for his ticket to travel to outer space.

CONTROVERSY OVER STEM CELL RESEARCH

Embryos are created for the harvest of stem cells, sparking strong ethical debate.

A PATENT FOR GOOGLE

Google is awarded a patent for the search algorithm used by its search engine.

WIKIPEDIA.ORG

The free, online encyclopedia goes live, and transforms the way people share information.

AND AT THE MOVIES…

Spirited Away, *Hayao Miyazaki's fantastical anime about a sullen girl lost in the spirit world who must find her way back to reality;* Lord of the Rings: The Fellowship of the Ring, *director Peter Jackson's special effects-laden tale of Hobbit Frodo's epic quest, adapted from J.R.R. Tolkien's classic fantasy;* Shrek, *DreamWorks hits the big time in this irresistibly witty animation about a giant green monster and his donkey friend.*

New X-Men Annual ***(2001)***

Writer Grant Morrison and artist Leinil Francis Yu helped launch a new approach to Super Hero storytelling, turning the comics world on end, literally. Dubbed "Marvelscope," by Editor-in-Chief Joe Quesada, this extra-sized issue had to be held on its side in order to be read, creating a widescreen, cinematic effect for its readers. This comic also marked the first appearance of Xorn, a new X-Men member. Xorn later went insane, and attacked the team who had treated him like family.

YOU HAVE A NEW MASTER NOW.

2002

HITTING THEIR STRIDE

Marvel seemed to have it figured out. The plan of attracting big name creators to big name projects had slipped into cruise control. As if a continuation of the last two years, 2002 stayed the course—and fans stuck around for the ride.

Continuing the success of the Ultimate titles, *The Ultimates* did not disappoint fans, or the Marvel sales division. Continuing the trend of modern, cinematic storytelling, writer Bruce Jones took over *The Incredible Hulk*, breathing new life into the title that it hadn't seen since Peter David's innovative rollercoaster scripts. Continuing the string of X-Men related revamps, *Cable, Deadpool,* and *X-Force* all underwent title changes in an attempt to attract the multitudes of readers who jumped onboard when *X-Men* began calling itself *New X-Men*. As *Spider-Man: Blue* continued the string of colorful hits by Jeph Loeb and Tim Sale, Captain America continued to fight for his country in the pages of his own new title. And continuing the idea of big-budget Marvel movie blockbusters, *Spider-Man* hit theaters, finally giving everyone's favorite wall-crawler a movie worthy of his iconic status. Even the toy company ToyBiz found success with their new action figure line called Marvel Legends.

JANUARY

JONES' HULK

"And what're you runnin' from... mister...?"
"Myself."

• *The Incredible Hulk* #34

Creating a lengthy run to rival that of J. Michael Straczynski over on *The Amazing Spider-Man* and Brian Michael Bendis on *Daredevil*, writer Bruce Jones reinvented the green goliath with a modern, cinematic approach. Starting with artist John Romita Jr., and later pairing with other impressive artists including Lee Weeks, Stuart Immonen, and Mike Deodato Jr., Bruce Jones told the simple human story of a man on the run, a man who just happened to be able to turn into a monster whenever he got angry.

When the Hulk was framed for the murder of a little boy by a secret organization calling itself Home Base, Bruce Banner found himself hunted by local law enforcement, as well as by the clandestine organization itself. Roaming from state to state and in constant contact with a mysterious Mr. Blue—later revealed to be the resuscitated Betty Ross Banner—the Hulk fought perverted clones of himself, undead double agents, the robotic blood-thirsty Krill, an his old foes the Abomination and the Absorbing Man, before getting to the bottom of the giant conspiracy. With the help of Doc Samson, Bett Ross Banner, and new love interest Nadia Dornova, the Hulk finally uncovered the man behind his recent trouble and Home Base itself. It was the the Leader—his old mind-manipulating enemy—now reduced to little more than a brain in a jar. Eventually Hull defeated the Leader, but when shattering his foe's encasemen an unchecked shard of glass accidentally pierced Nadia's heart, killing her and sending the Hulk back into a life of isolation and loneliness.

Shaving his head to conceal his identity, Bruce Banner often holed up in seedy motels, trying to avoid prying eyes whenever possible.

MARCH

SECOND INSTALLMENT FOR BLADE

• *Blade II: Bloodhunt—The Official Comic Adaptation*

The March 22nd movie release of the sequel to the original *Blade* film was accompanied by a comic-book adaptation, coverdated April. The comic was adapted by Steve Gerber and David S. Goyer and the pencils were by Alberto Ponticelli.

THE ULTIMATE TEAM

"At ease, boys. Go get yourselves a glass of champagne, huh? Ain't every day we save the world."

• *The Ultimates* #1

With *Ultimate Spider-Man* and *Ultimate X-Men* serving as two of Marvel's most consecutive best sellers, it was only a matter of time before the decision was made to reinvent one of the most popular teams of heroes, the Avengers, into this fresh new universe. And writer Mark Millar and artist Bryan Hitch were up to the challenge.

As this new thirteen-issue limited series began, Nick Fury, now a man of African descent, was shown as the driving force behind a new government-sponsored team of super soldiers, called, simply, the Ultimates. Reacting to a fight between the Hulk and Spider-Man, shown in *Ultimate Spider-Man*'s companion title *Ultimate Marvel Team-Up*, Fury recruited Iron Man, Giant Man, the Wasp, and Bruce Banner himself onto his new private army. But the team wouldn't gel until World War II hero Captain America was discovered in the Arctic Ocean, perfectly preserved in a block of ice.

Joined by Thor later in the series, the team found that its first major challenge was to stop the rampage of one of its own, when Bruce Banner had a heart attack and lost control of his faculties, changing into the Hulk in the middle of Manhattan. More infighting occurred later as Captain America discovered that the Wasp had fallen victim to the spousal abuse of her husband, Hank Pym, and Captain America took down Giant Man in a ruthless battle. Finally, as new members Hawkeye, Black Widow, Quicksilver, and Scarlet Witch joined the team, the Ultimates found their place among their world's national heroes as they managed to stave off a massive alien invasion.

Climbing Mount Everest purely for the inspiration, Tony Stark, the head of the third largest company in America, Stark International, found the resolve to start a new chapter in his life as Iron Man.

The heart and soul of the team, the Ultimate version of Captain America possessed enough strength to rival that of the Hulk, but at his core he remained a loyal soldier to his country.

SPIDER-MAN CASTS HIS WEB FAR AND WIDE

• *Spider-Man: The Official Movie Adaptation*

Marvel released an official forty-eight-page adaptation of the *Spider-Man* movie that hit the screens on May 3. With a coverdate of June, the script was written by Stan Lee with art by Alan Davis, Mark Farmer, and Dave Kemp. A trade paperback was also released to tie in with the film release. Cult movie director Sam Raimi and screenwriter David Koepp's presented an interpretation Peter Parker's origin story in the movie and it starred Tobey Maguire as Peter Parker, Willem Dafoe as the Green Goblin, and Kirsten Dunst as Mary Jane Watson.

JUNE

CAPTAIN AMERICA SOLDIERS ON

• *Captain America* #1

The darker Marvel Knights line of books accepted Steve Rogers under their umbrella as writer John Ney Rieber and artist John Cassaday restarted the series with a new first issue, showing how Captain America would exist in the post-9/11 world.

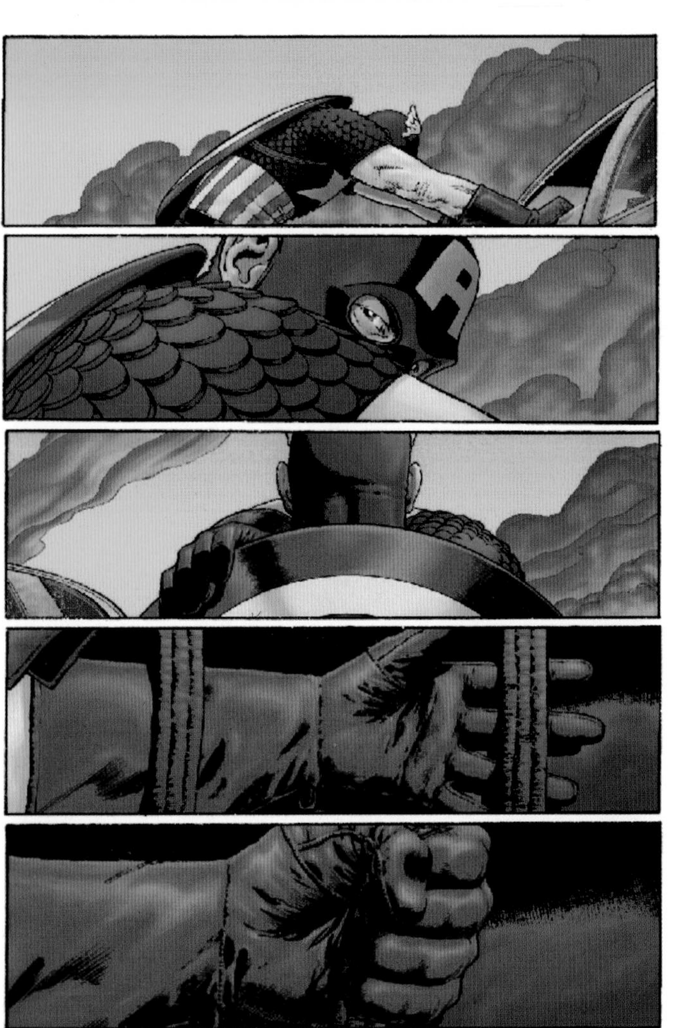

This new series began showing Steve Rogers working in the wreckage of the Twin Towers, angry at the world for the events of September 11, but never giving up his faith that humanity is also capable of good.

JULY

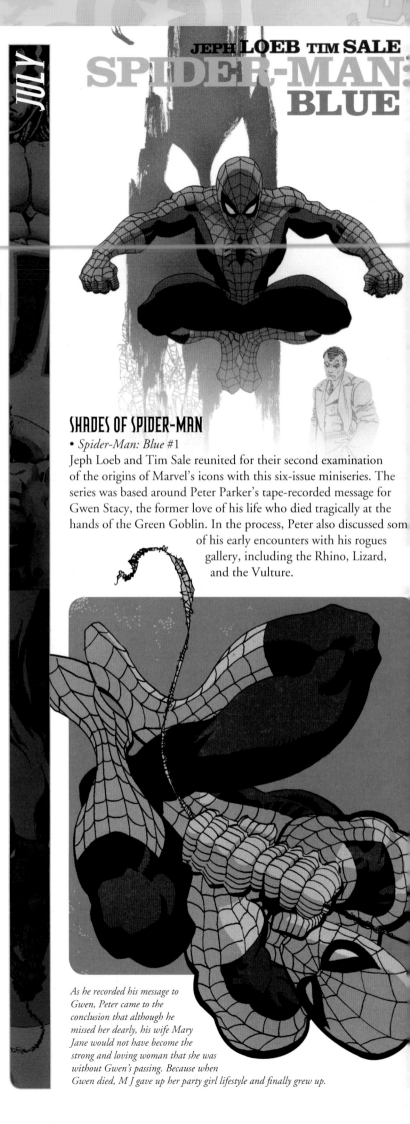

JEPH LOEB TIM SALE SPIDER-MAN: BLUE

SHADES OF SPIDER-MAN

• *Spider-Man: Blue* #1

Jeph Loeb and Tim Sale reunited for their second examination of the origins of Marvel's icons with this six-issue miniseries. The series was based around Peter Parker's tape-recorded message for Gwen Stacy, the former love of his life who died tragically at the hands of the Green Goblin. In the process, Peter also discussed some of his early encounters with his rogues gallery, including the Rhino, Lizard, and the Vulture.

As he recorded his message to Gwen, Peter came to the conclusion that although he missed her dearly, his wife Mary Jane would not have become the strong and loving woman that she was without Gwen's passing. Because when Gwen died, M J gave up her party girl lifestyle and finally grew up.

AUGUST

THE EVIL THAT MEN DO

• *Spider-Man And The Black Cat* #1

Movie writer and director Kevin Smith returned to play in the Marvel sandbox alongside artist Terry Dodson for a six-issue miniseries. It pitted Spider-Man and the Black Cat against a new villain named Mr. Brownstone, a criminal with the ability to teleport drugs into his clients' systems. With the help of Daredevil and Nightcrawler, the duo put an end to Brownstone, accidentally helping create a new Mysterio in the process, in the form of Brownstone's brother, Francis Klum.

SEPTEMBER

EX-X-FORCE

• *X-Statix* #1

With a voice clearly its own, the further adventures of Peter Milligan's and Mike Allred's version of *X-Force*, now received a name—*X-Statix*. It featured a few roster changes here and there, including new members Dead Girl and Venus Dee Milo.

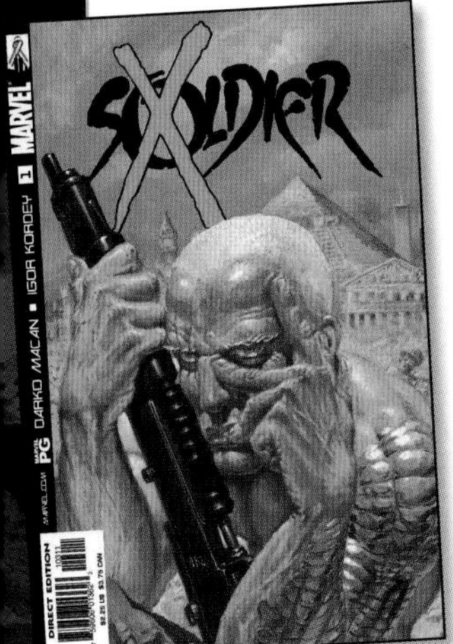

EX-CABLE

• *Soldier X* #1

Following the popular changes to the other X-titles, Cable received his own facelift courtesy of writer Darko Macan and artist Igor Kordey. The pair examined Cable's life after he had purged the Techno-Organic virus from his body.

SEPTEMBER

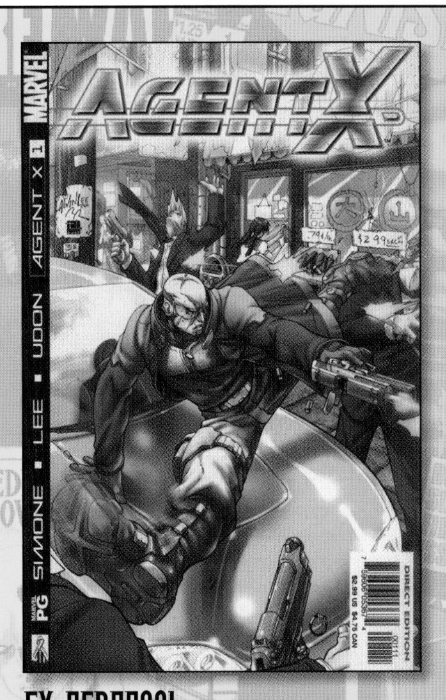

EX-DEADPOOL

• *Agent X* #1

Always in need of a makeover, Deadpool found something close in the pages of *Agent X*, thanks to writer Gail Simone and art team UDON Studios. This series kept fans guessing as to its protagonist's secret identity, finally revealing him to be Deadpool's enemy, Nijo Minamiyori.

MEANWHILE IN 2002...

DANIEL PEARL KIDNAPPED
American journalist, Daniel Pearl, is kidnapped and then murdered in Pakistan while investigating links between al-Qaeda and Pakistan's Inter-Services Intelligence.

BALI BOMBINGS
Over 200 people are killed when al-Qaeda linked suicide bombers hit two nightclubs on the Indonesian island of Bali.

MOSCOW THEATER SIEGE
Chechen militants take over 800 people hostage in a theater. After a three-day standoff, Russian forces end the crisis using chemical gas, which kills at least 129 civilians.

RESOLUTION 1441
The UN Security Council approves Resolution 1441, which gives Saddam Hussein a final chance to comply with the disarmament demands of previous resolutions and UN weapons inspectors enter Iraq.

DEPARTMENT FOR HOMELAND SECURITY
The United States Department for Homeland Security is created and is tasked with protecting the US from terrorist activity and responding to natural disasters.

MILOSEVIC ON TRIAL
The trial of Slobodan Milosevic, the former President of Serbia and Yugoslavia, begins at the UN war crimes tribunal. He is charged with crimes against humanity, breaching the Geneva convention, and genocide.

THE QUEEN MOTHER DIES
Queen Elizabeth, The Queen Mother dies peacefully in her sleep at Windsor Castle aged 101.

SINGLE CURRENCY IN EUROLAND
Twelve European countries formally adopt the Euro as a common currency.

GOLDEN JUBILEE
After fifty years on the British throne, Queen Elizabeth II celebrates her golden jubilee with celebrations in the UK and a tour of the Commonwealth nations.

SPIDEY ON THE BIG SCREEN
The movie Spider-Man *is the box-office blockbuster of the year and grosses more than $400 million dollars.*

AND AT THE MOVIES...
City of God, *Fernando Meirelles' frenetic film set in Rio's slums borrows a boxload of exciting cinematic tricks to present a bleak tale of rival juvenile gangs;* Minority Report, *visionary sci-fi movie based on a Philip K. Dick story set in a society where criminals are caught before they can commit a crime;* The Lord of the Rings: The Two Towers, *second installment of Peter Jackson's high-concept adaptation of J.R.R. Tolkien's fantasy epic.*

IS THAT ALL YOU BOYS ARE INTERESTED IN, CELEBRITIES?

2003

MOVIES AND SHAKERS

Some people saw it as the next stage in the evolution of the medium: Marvel was hoping to bring its characters into the lives and homes of mainstream audiences. And the company was armed with two relatively new weapons in this ambitious battle—the Super Hero movie and the trade paperback.

Marvel had already reintroduced the Super Hero film for the next generation. From 2000 to 2002, moviegoers had enjoyed blockbuster movies featuring their favorite characters: *Blade*, *X-Men*, and *Spider-Man*. In 2003, three new Marvel movies burst onto the big screen, and the future would see at least one Marvel movie released every year.

Meanwhile, Marvel began to slowly discover the trade paperback market, an area that it had merely dabbled in before. More and more, comics became arc-based, telling five or six-part stories that transferred perfectly to trade form. The graphic novel section in bookstores had begun to grow, and it appeared that comics were no longer just for the "Wednesday crowd" anymore. Many of the diehard collectors had switched to the convenience of collected reprint editions, and the phrase "wait for the trade" became a permanent part of the average comic fan's vernacular.

JANUARY

THE TRUTH BEHIND CAPTAIN AMERICA

• *Truth: Red, White & Black* #1

This seven-issue miniseries from writer Robert Morales and illustrator Kyle Baker delved into the previously untold story of the original Captain America, Isaiah Bradley, a black serviceman of the US Army's Camp Cathcart. Bradley became an unwitting test subject of the government after the bombing of Pearl Harbor. As a result he gained super powers and donned a shield and uniform in service of his country.

MARCH

DAREDEVIL ADAPTATION

• *Daredevil: The Official Adaptation Of The Hit Movie!*

With the movie release of *Daredevil* on February 14, Marvel produced a comic-book adaptation. The comic was adapted by Bruce Jones from the script by director Mark Steven Johnson, and featured a lone Daredevil on the cover, painted by Brian Stelfreeze. The movie starred Ben Affleck as Daredevil.

APRIL

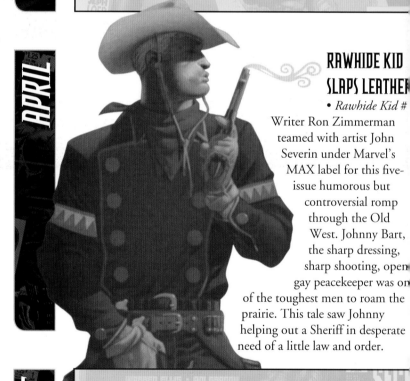

RAWHIDE KID SLAPS LEATHE

• *Rawhide Kid #*

Writer Ron Zimmerman teamed with artist John Severin under Marvel's MAX label for this five-issue humorous but controversial romp through the Old West. Johnny Bart, the sharp dressing, sharp shooting, open gay peacekeeper was o of the toughest men to roam the prairie. This tale saw Johnny helping out a Sheriff in desperate need of a little law and order.

JUNE

X-MEN TRIUMPH AGAIN

• *X-Men 2*

In May, the second X-Men movie was released entitled *X2: X-Men United.* Marvel's comic-book adaptation of the movie carried a date of June and featured Lady Deathstrike, Storm, and Mystique on the cover. The screenplay's script, written by Bryan Singer, David Hayter, and Zak Penn, was adapted by Chuck Austen while Patrick Zircher, Larry Strucker, and Ian Hannin all worked on the art. As well as the characters featured in the original movie, this second installment also saw the inclusion of a few new X-characters, including Nightcrawler, portrayed in the movie by Alan Cumming.

JUNE

HULK HITS HOLLYWOOD

• *Hulk: The Official Movie Adaptation*

In June, director Ang Lee brought Bruce Banner to the silver screen with the help of screenwriters John Turman, Michael France, and James Schamus. Marvel continued their trend of bringing out a comic-book adaptation of the movie, this time with pencils by Mark Bagley, inks by Scott Hanna, and a script by Bruce Jones. The cover art featured an angry Hulk reaching out to the reader and the story told how Bruce Banner transformed into the Incredible Hulk. Eric Bana starred in the film's title role alongside love interest Betty Ross, played by Jennifer Connelly. The movie also featured cameos from Stan Lee and Lou Ferrigno, the TV Hulk.

THE VENGEANCE OF VENOM

• *Venom* #1

Surprisingly Venom did not net his own ongoing series until over ten years after the height of his popularity. Even this thriller title by writer Daniel Way and artist Francisco Herrera actually starred a clone of the symbiote more than Eddie Brock himself!

PUNISHER: BORN

• *Born* #1

Garth Ennis and Darick Robertson teamed to tell the story of how Frank Castle came to possess the mindset of the unfeeling Punisher in this four-issue miniseries for Marvel's mature MAX line. Set on the Cambodian border in the closing days of the Vietnam War, *Born* detailed Frank's merciless killing of not just enemy soldiers, but also of American men who crossed a moral line that Frank found unacceptable. The miniseries ended with Frank agreeing to wage a war with no end.

JULY

RUCKA'S WOLVERINE

• *Wolverine* #1

Novelist Greg Rucka restarted Wolverine's title and stayed on for a nineteen-issue run, pairing at first with artist Darick Robertson. During this time, Rucka set Logan out to avenge waitress Lucy Braddock, had him obsessed over by ATF agent Cassie Lathrop, forced him into a battle royal with Sabretooth, and introduced him to the Native, a female Weapon X survivor (and his forgotten former lover) before relinquishing the reins of the title over to writer Mark Millar.

JULY

MARVEL'S RUNAWAY HIT

"I've known our parents were evil since age five. This perverted little gathering just confirms it."

• *Runaways* #1

The kids thought it was all for charity. Once every year, teenager Alex Wilder's parents had a quiet little get-together in their suburban home with five other married couples. And every year, their children were forced to have awkward conversations as they attempted to hang out while their parents were conducting whatever kind of business it was they conducted. The problem with this scenario was, there were teenagers involved. And teenagers get bored.

Exploring a secret passageway Alex had discovered months earlier while hunting for Christmas presents, the seven kids decided to spy on their parents, and see what they were really like behind closed doors. Unfortunately, they weren't prepared for what they would see next. Their parents were actually members of a team of Super Villains known as the Pride, and their children watched in secret as the men and women that raised them killed an innocent girl in some sort of ritual sacrifice. So they did what any normal kids would do in their situation. They ran away from home.

Writer Brian K. Vaughan and artist Adrian Alphona crafted this ingenious premise, introducing this band of Runaways to the Marvel Universe and slowly, as each teammate gained powers or learned to harness their natural aptitudes, to the role of Super Heroes as well. Setting up camp in the "Hostel," the remains of an earthquake-destroyed home in California, the Runaways finally managed to halt their parents' plans for world domination, despite team member Alex showing his true colors as a traitor to their heroic cause.

The Runaways included teammates Arsenic and her telepathically linked dinosaur Old Lace, the sorceress Sister Grimm, the solar-powered Lucy in the Sky, heir to technological gadgets Talkback, and the aptly named Bruiser.

SEPTEMBER

SPECTACULAR AGAIN

• *The Spectacular Spider-Man* #1
With *Peter Parker: Spider-Man* coming to a close in August, writer Paul Jenkins once again took up his seat behind the computer to document Spider-Man's life in the pages of this new series, aided by popular artist Humberto Ramos. Starting with Venom sliming his way back into Spider-Man's life, this book would go on to debut Spidey's organic web-shooters, a result of his battle with the insect-like Queen, and an innovation inspired by the first *Spider-Man* film.

SEPTEMBER

JUSTICE FOR THE AVENGERS

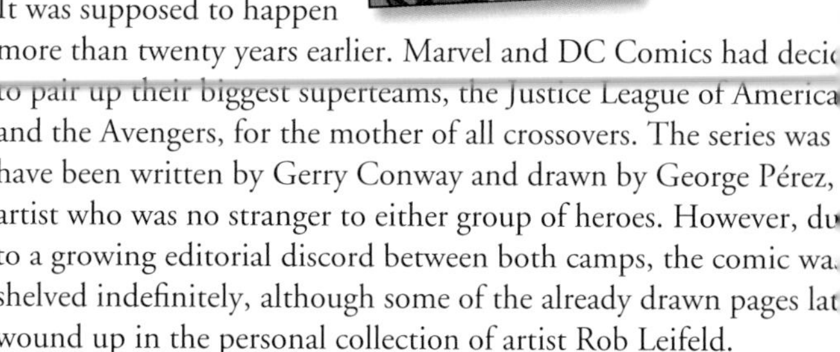

"In the nothingness of the trans-dimensional void, two worlds—two universes—convulse. And shudder. And begin to crumble."

• *JLA/Avengers* #1
It was supposed to happen more than twenty years earlier. Marvel and DC Comics had deci to pair up their biggest superteams, the Justice League of America and the Avengers, for the mother of all crossovers. The series was have been written by Gerry Conway and drawn by George Pérez, artist who was no stranger to either group of heroes. However, du to a growing editorial discord between both camps, the comic wa shelved indefinitely, although some of the already drawn pages lat wound up in the personal collection of artist Rob Leifeld.

Years passed and so did dozens of other collaborative comics between the two publishing houses, including the popular *Marvel Versus DC/DC Versus Marvel* miniseries. But while the Just League and the Avengers did get a chance to square off a few time in these various specials and limited series, the fans always lament the death of what would have been the ultimate in team-ups, pitti the iconic versions of each team versus the other.

But as 2003 rolled around, both Marvel and DC had spent yea reestablishing their characters, and a classic feel was once again prevalent in the majority of their titles. The timing seemed perfec to give the fans what they wanted. So George Pérez returned, teaming with writer Kurt Busiek to create this four-issue prestige format limited series, to tell the story of the DC villain Krona breaching the barrier of the Marvel Universe, and Marvel's Grandmaster, pitting the unwitting Justice League against the Avengers in a contest meant to challenge this new threat.

OCTOBER

SUPREME POWER PREMIERS

• *Supreme Power* #1
Writer J. Michael Straczynski and artist Gary Frank took a surprisingly dark reassessment of the Squadron Supreme, Marvel's version of the most iconic DC heroes, in this new mature ongoing series under the MAX imprint. Telling the familiar story of an innocent married farm couple chancing upon a baby abandoned in the wreckage of a rocket ship from outer space, *Supreme Power* gave the story a cynical twist as the government then forcibly removed the child from the young couples' custody. The baby grew up to become Hyperion, the first of his new super-powered ilk, and one who was not quite content with the state of his world.

Hyperion had all the powers of DC's Superman, but a more rebellious attitude. He soon joined forces with other dark heroes including Dr. Spectrum, Nighthawk, and Blur.

MARVEL'S SWEET 1602

• *1602* #1

Neil Gaiman, the *New York Times* best-selling novelist and legendary writer of DC/Vertigo's acclaimed *Sandman* series, took his creative vision and penchant for times past to Marvel, crafting this eight-issue miniseries alongside fan-favorite artist Andy Kubert. Digitally painted by Richard Isanove, with woodcut-like covers by Scott McKowen, this series took an alternative look at what the classic Marvel pantheon would be like if they had existed in the 17th Century. Set in England as well as in the newly colonized America, *1602* featured the adventures of British intelligence agent Sir Nicholas Fury, his assistant Peter Parquagh, and the mysterious Virginia Dare.

Just as in modern times, in the alternate universe of 1602*, mutants were hated and feared. At the story's start, original X-Men Angel was set to be executed by the ruling government of Spain.*

X-23 AND THE NYX

• *NYX* #1

Taking a realistic approach to a group of New York City gutterpunks similar to the no-holds-barred film *Kids*, Joe Quesada wrote this seven-issue miniseries, teaming with artists Joshua Middleton and Robert Teranishi. *NYX* focused on the daily lives of a few teens with mutant powers, and in its third issue, debuted X-23 (left), a female clone of Wolverine whose origins dated back to the *X-Men: Evolution* animated series.

SPIDER-MAN HITS 500

• *The Amazing Spider-Man* #500

After issue # 58 of the second volume of *The Amazing Spider-Man*, writer J. Michael Straczynski and artist John Romita Jr. returned the title to its original numbering just in time for this landmark anniversary issue. In this third chapter of a story entitled "Happy Birthday," Spider-Man found himself witnessing his future and revisiting some of the most memorable moments in his career, as he and Dr. Strange fell victim to a magic spell while battling the evil Dormammu. Revisited memories included the death of Gwen Stacy and a ferocious bout with the Hulk.

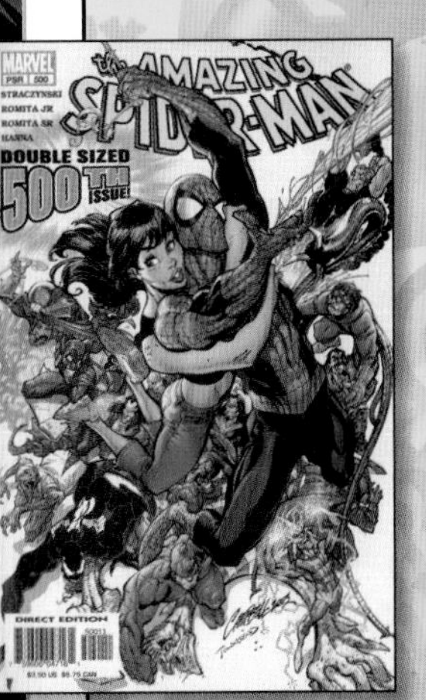

Bruce Banner recounted his days as the gray Hulk to his old psychiatrist friend Dr. Samson, as he mourned the loss of Betty Ross.

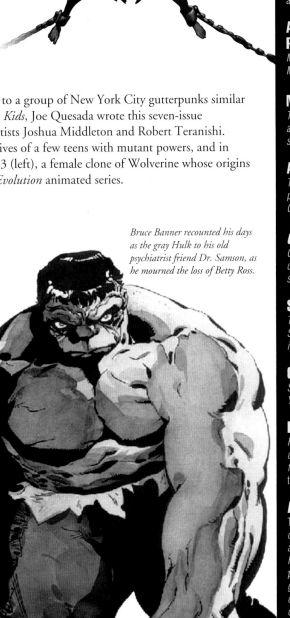

HULK'S GRAY MATTERS

• *Hulk: Gray* #1

The team of writer Jeph Loeb and artist Tim Sale united once again for this six-issue mini series retelling the Hulk's origin and dealing with the relatively short period in his first adventures when his skin hadn't developed its green hue.

MEANWHILE IN 2003...

AN ULTIMATUM FOR SADDAM
President Bush presents Saddam Hussein with an ultimatum: leave Iraq or face military action.

OPERATION IRAQI FREEDOM
The Second Gulf War begins when US and British coalition forces attack Iraq after Saddam Hussein fails to meet their demands regarding disarmament. Although combat operations officially end on May 1, the conflict continues.

SADDAM HUSSEIN FOUND
More than nine months after the US invasion, the former leader of Iraq is found in hiding and is taken into custody to await trial.

A PRIME MINISTER FOR PALESTINE
Mahmoud Abbas is sworn in as the first Prime Minister of Palestine.

NORTHEAST BLACKOUT
The biggest power outage in US history brings a blackout to Ontario, Canada, and to eight states in Northeastern and Midwestern America.

ARNOLD IS BACK
The actor Arnold Schwarzenegger goes into politics and is elected the 38th Governor of California.

***COLUMBIA* EXPLODES**
On its 28th mission, the space shuttle Columbia *disintegrates on re-entry over Texas, killing all seven astronauts on board.*

SARS
The first known case of the disease SARS—Severe Acute Respiratory Disease—is identified in Vietnam.

GENETICS BREAKTHROUGH
Scientists discover the genetic code of the Y chromosome.

HARRY POTTER #5
Harry Potter fans line up outside book stores until after midnight for the release of the fifth book, Harry Potter and the Order of the Phoenix.

AND AT THE MOVIES...
The Lord of the Rings: The Return of the King, *culmination of Peter Jackson's stunning adaptation of J.R.R. Tolkien's trilogy, about Frodo's quest to destroy a ring with magic powers;* Finding Nemo, *a sophisticated Pixar gem about a worried clownfish who swims the ocean looking for his son, trapped inside a dentist's aquarium;* School of Rock, *a manic Jack Black teaches a group of schoolchildren how to rock, in Richard Linklater's feelgood comedy;* Pirates Of The Caribbean: The Curse Of The Black Pearl, *a Disneyland ride proves the surprise inspiration for this tongue-in-cheek swashbuckling extravaganza featuring Johnny Depp's memorable rock-star pirate.*

LOGAN'S GONE FERAL!
AAAUUUUUUUUU
Jean, I'm so sorry about everything.
I...I didn't ever mean to hurt you.
Shh!
Shh!
The Phoenix understands...
I haven't seen you so alive for a long time Scott...
...my best friend...
...have to go now...

New X-Men *#150 (Feb., 2004)*
Scott Summers, the X-Man known as Cyclops, and his wife Jean Grey had always had a tumultuous relationship, even at the best of times. With the otherworldly Phoenix Force haunting Jean's life due to her mutant prowess as a telepath, Cyclops had seen Jean die in his arms before, only to have her rise from the ashes like her Phoenix namesake. And even though they'd grown apart in recent months due to his involvement with Emma Frost, Jean's death truly affected Scott.

THIS IS A NEW LOW.
AN UNDERWEAR MODEL THINKS I NEED DEPTH.

2004

PLANTING THE SEEDS

Marvel watched the fruits of its labor grow and mature. Its new Ultimate and MAX lines had amassed fan and critical success, but Marvel refused to rest on its laurels and instead began to plant new ideas and concepts, hoping to harvest an equally successful crop in the future. It was this attitude and willingness to experiment that sprouted Icon, a new Marvel imprint that would publish creator-owned properties. With this new label, creators like Brian Michael Bendis and Michael Avon Oeming were able to move their popular *Powers* series from Image Comics to Marvel, gaining increased distribution. David Mack did likewise with his title *Kabuki*, and later, other major name talent would create original properties for the imprint, including writers like J. Michael Straczynski, Ed Brubaker and Mark Millar.

Simultaneously, Marvel was planting story seeds as well. Brian Michael Bendis ended the *Avengers* series, paving the way for a replacement title, as well as the upcoming *House of M* event. These new books, along with the *Secret War* miniseries that chronicled the fall of one of Marvel's oldest heroes and set the stage for an underground rebellion, helped form the roots of 2006's *Civil War*, and even 2008's *Secret Invasion.*

FEBRUARY

FANTASTIC FOUR GET THE ULTIMATE TREATMENT

• *Ultimate Fantastic Four* #1

Ultimate veterans Brian Michael Bendis, Mark Millar, and Adam Kubert reexamined Marvel's first family, creating this alternate version of the Fantastic Four. In it, genius Reed Richards develops a teleportation device as a young teen, which led to him getting drafted into a special school for gifted students run out of the Baxter Building in Manhattan. There Reed met Sue and Johnny Storm, and developed a larger scale version of his device. This was tampered with by fellow student Victor Van Damme, causing an accident that granted the four super powers, along with Reed's visiting boyhood friend, Ben Grimm.

Fighting such villains as their former friend Dr. Doom and their former teacher the Mole Man, this new FF even found time to travel to the Negative Zone.

THE DEATH OF JEAN GREY

• *New X-Men* #150

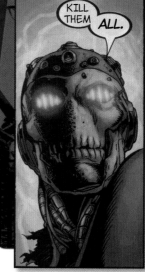

Writer Grant Morrison and artist Phil Jimenez combined to put an end to Jean Grey. Xorn, a mutant posing as the villain Magneto, trapped Jean and Wolverine on Asteroid M and hurled it toward the sun. With no chance of escape, and with Jean dying before his eyes, Logan ran her through with his claws in order to spare her further suffering. This act released the Phoenix Force insider her, which she ultimately used to save both their lives and return them to Earth.

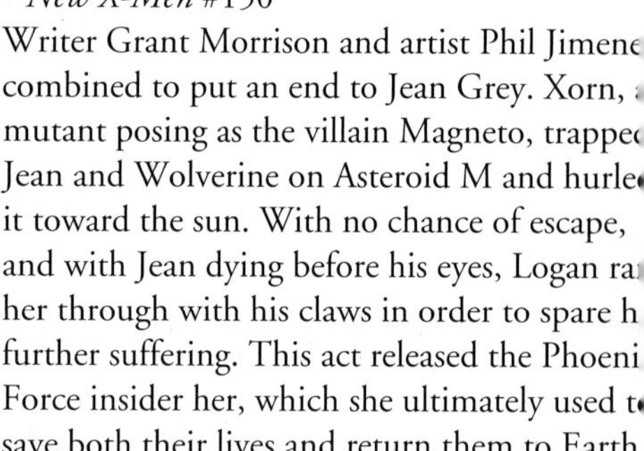

Thought defeated by Jean's Phoenix powers, Xorn had enough strength left to give Jean a lethal electromagnetic pulse, killing her before he in turn was beheaded by a feral Wolverine.

MARCH

PUNISHER GOES TO THE MAX

• *The Punisher* #1

When *The Punisher* was restarted to fall under the mature reader MAX label, longtime *Punisher* scribe Garth Ennis, alongside artist Lewis Larosa, was finally able to cut loose with all the trademark ultra-violence and adult-oriented black comedy that made his legendary *Preacher* run for DC/Vertigo such a smash hit.

As the Punisher continued his war on the gangs of New York, he was kidnapped by his old sidekick Microchip in an attempt to get the Punisher to kill enemies of America on the government's dime. Castle rejected the offer in true Punisher fashion, and even killed his old ally for selling him down the river.

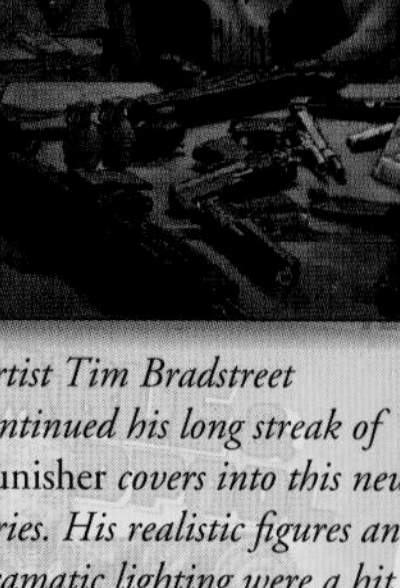

Artist Tim Bradstreet continued his long streak of Punisher *covers into this new series. His realistic figures and dramatic lighting were a hit with the fans.*

JUNE

A NEW 4

• *Marvel Knights 4* #1

Playwright Roberto Aguirre-Sacasa and artist Steve McNiven focused on the family dynamic that holds the Fantastic Four together in this new ongoing series. As the Four discovered that their money manager had stolen their fortune, the family was forced to grow closer together as they each entered the work force. The Invisible Woman became a teacher, the Thing became a construction worker, the Human Torch a fireman, and Mr. Fantastic took a job at a law firm.

FURY'S PRIVATE WAR

• *Secret War* #1

The top secret world of espionage and intrigue behind Marvel's super spy organization SHIELD met the world of spandex and Super Heroes in this five-issue painted miniseries by writer Brian Michael Bendis and artist Gabriele Dell'Otto. When it was discovered that Super Villains were being bankrolled by foreign Prime Minister Lucia Von Bardas, Nick Fury organized a covert strike force in order to do what America's government was unwilling to do—invade Latveria. The result was a retaliatory battle in the streets of Manhattan, and Nick Fury being removed from his position as Director of SHIELD and given the new title of wanted war criminal.

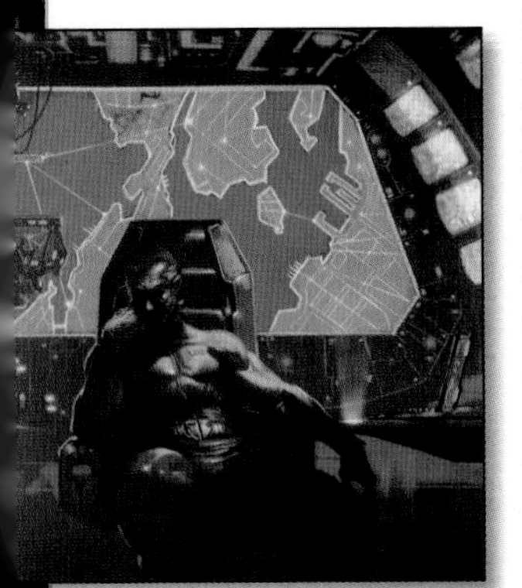

M On April 16, The Punisher hit theaters. Directed by Jonathan Hensleigh, the film starred Thomas Jane as Frank Castle opposite mob boss Howard Saint, portrayed by John Travolta.

MARVEL'S MERCENARIES TEAM UP

• *Cable & Deadpool* #1

Writer Fabian Nicieza returned to pair up two of his favorite creations. With artist Mark Brooks plus a few covers by *X-Force* alum Rob Liefeld, this ongoing series began with Cable and Deadpool on the hunt for the same dangerous biotoxin.

SHE-HULK GOES TO WORK

• *She-Hulk* #1

Fired from her law firm and kicked out of the Avengers Mansion for her rowdy behavior, She-Hulk (aka Jennifer Walters) started a new chapter in her life as chronicled by writer Dan Slott and artist Juan Bobillo. Finding employment with the most prestigious law firm in Manhattan, Goodman, Lieber, Kurtzberg, and Holliway, She-Hulk realized that her dream job might not be all that she had originally hoped for, as she found herself reduced to working on the firm's Superhuman Law division.

One of the stipulations of She-Hulk's new job was that she had to work as the shy Jennifer Walters, not the boisterous and confident She-Hulk.

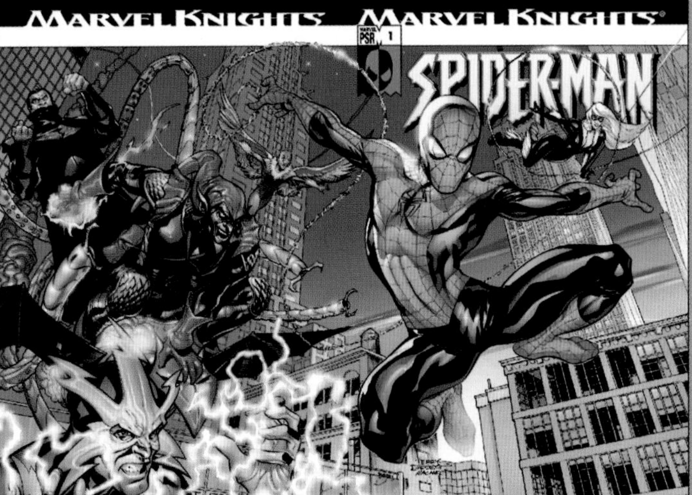

Viewed together, the front and back covers of this first issue made a complete action-packed image. Penciller Terry Dodson's wife, Rachel Dodson, inked this Spider-Man series.

MARVEL KNIGHTS SPIDER-MAN

• *Spider-Man* #1

Now secured in his superstar status due to the success of his mega-hit *The Ultimates*, Mark Millar decided to try his hand at writing the life of Peter Parker in this all-new ongoing series drawn by fan favorite penciller Terry Dodson. Together, the pair crafted a large-scale twelve-part story that saw Spider-Man's life being plagued yet again by the Green Goblin, as Osborn funded an elaborate plan against the web-slinger, financing power enhancements for Peter's old foes, kidnapping his aunt May, and even forming a Sinister Twelve. The series also saw the villainous Scorpion take up Eddie Brock's old mantle as the new Venom.

With a little help from some of the other heroes of the Marvel Universe, Spider-Man finally managed to defeat the Green Goblin and rescue his aunt.

M The sequel to the 2002 movie, *Spider-Man 2* was released on June 30. The film saw the introduction of classic Spider-Man foe Dr. Octopus, portrayed by Alfred Molina, as well as the return of many of the supporting players from the previous film.

JULY

X-MEN ASTONISHES FANS

"Sorry, Logan. Super Heroes wear costumes. And quite frankly, all the black leather is making people nervous."

• *Astonishing X-Men* #1

Joss Whedon had already built himself quite an audience. Due to his creation of the popular *Buffy the Vampire Slayer* television series, as well as the sci-fi cult favorite *Firefly*, Whedon was given his own X-Men title, which quickly became a smash hit. Drawn by popular artist John Cassaday, whose realistic rendering had previously helped *Captain America* climb sales charts, *Astonishing X-Men* premiered, officially marking the end of the era of the *New X-Men* by doing away with the leather uniforms that had been the trademark of that period in the super heroes' lives.

Returning Kitty Pryde—a mutant with a hip and sarcastic nature—to Xavier's School, Whedon also resurrected her old flame, Colossus, revealing that the hero had been somehow revived after his death from the Legacy Virus. Whedon also continued to examine the friendship as well as the animosity between Cyclops and Wolverine, who were both still mourning the loss of fellow X-Men member Jean Grey.

As Whedon and Cassaday's run continued, they introduced a sub-division of SHIELD called SWORD (Sentient Worlds Observation and Response Department), as well as a new villain named Danger, the living personification of the X-Men's high-tech danger room training facility. The team also orchestrated an invasion of Xavier's School by a band of heavy-hitting villains and a treacherous Emma Frost. However, in actuality this was all the result of the mind manipulations of the imprisoned Cassandra Nova, the disembodied twin sister of Professor Charles Xavier.

When Wolverine returned from one of his extended absences, he found Cyclops in bed with the White Queen. Wolverine didn't approve of Cyclop's choice, and the two battled on the front lawn of the school.

AUGUST

ARAÑA AUDITIONS

• *Amazing Fantasy* #1

Thanks to writer Fiona Avery and artist Mark Brooks, average Brookly high schooler Anya Corazon began developing super powers and was recruited by the mystical secret Spid Society to fight against the Sisterhoc of the Wasp. Named Araña, her stor helped kick off the new *Amazing Fantasy* series, which focused on nev characters by rotating creative teams

SINS PAST

• *The Amazing Spider-Man* #509

In this storyline by writer J. Michael Straczynski and artist Mike Deodato Jr., Peter Parker was shocked when he encountered a woman who was the spitting image of Gwen Stacy. Spider-Man soon discovered that this Gwen look-alike was one of a pair of siblings who were the result of an affair that Gwen had had with Norman Osborn years ago. The two children had been aged by their father and given super powers in a plan to destroy Peter Parker for good.

First encountering the young duo of Gabe and Sarah Stacy while visiting Gwen Stacy's grave, Peter Parker realized that his attackers had powers similar to his own. It was thes abilities that Gabe would later exploit, as the misguided Gray Goblin.

SEPTEMBER

CARNAGE'S KID

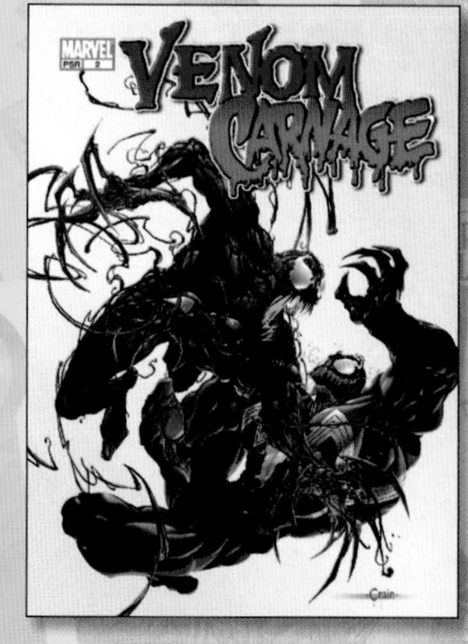

• *Venom VS. Carnage* #1

Writer Peter Milligan jointed artist Clayton Crain in this four-issue miniseries which told the story of Carnage giving birth to a new symbiote. Police officer Patrick Mulligan became the creature's reluctant host, calling himself Toxin, as the creature's base instincts wrestled with his own good judgment.

SEPTEMBER

AVENGERS DISASSEMBLED

"If I told you a story like this, you'd say to yourself, this sounds like a person who has lost control of themselves on a deep psychological level. You'd say this sounds like a disturbed person."

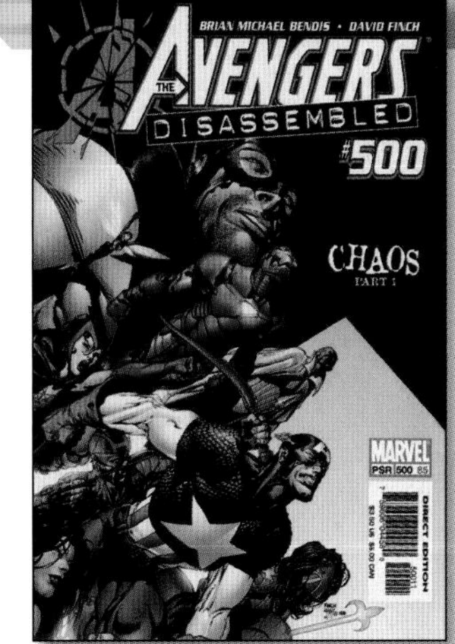

• *The Avengers* #500

It started with a bang. Literally. Jack of Hearts, a former Avenger who had died in space on an earlier mission, returned to the Avenger's Mansion, a walking corpse. As Ant-Man Scott Lang rushed outside to greet his friend, Jack exploded, killing Scott and taking most of the mansion with him. And that was just the beginning.

Writer Brian Michael Bendis would turn the Avengers' world on its end with this shocking new crossover event drawn by artist David Finch. Originating in the pages of *The Avengers*, and crossing into *Captain America*, *The Invincible Iron Man*, *The Mighty Thor*, *Fantastic Four*, and *The Spectacular Spider-Man*, this mammoth story was constructed so that each title's adventure could be enjoyed separately, or the reader could choose to read all the various comics and get a thorough account of exactly how this storyline affected the entire Marvel Universe.

As the tale continued, the Avengers lost Thor, the Vision, and Hawkeye to various, seemingly random battles. After uniting the remaining Avengers past and present, the team discovered that the cause of all their recent problems was in reality their teammate the Scarlet Witch. Having relied on her mutant ability to access what she called "chaos magic" to fight alongside the Avengers for years, the Scarlet Witch, aka Wanda Maximoff, had been slowly slipping into insanity, eventually losing her struggle with reality. Only with the help of Dr. Strange did the Avengers finally triumph over Wanda, delivering the disturbed shell of a woman into her father Magneto's custody.

The Scarlet Witch warped reality so it appeared as if five Ultron androids were attacking the Avengers. She-Hulk lost control under Wanda's influence and literally ripped the Vision in two. Shortly after, Hawkeye died fighting a Kree battleship that Wanda had also conjured up.

OCTOBER

ULTIMATE GALACTUS

• *Ultimate Nightmare* #1

Beginning the *Ultimate Galactus Trilogy*, a trio of miniseries that introduced the Ultimate Universe to the world-killing Gah Lak Tus, *Ultimate Nightmare* was a five-issue limited series by writer Warren Ellis and artists Trevor Hairsine and Steve Epting, which teamed the Ultimates with the X-Men.

Ultimate Secret, *the four-issue sequel, debuted Captain Marvel and the five-issue* Ultimate Extinction *showed what happened as Gah Lak Tus finally made his way to Earth.*

NOVEMBER

STRANGE ORIGINS

• *Strange* #1

Scribes J. Michael Straczynski and Samm Barnes, with artist Brandon Peterson, retold Dr. Stephen Strange's mystical origin for a new generation of fans in this six-issue limited series. Given a new costume by artist Joe Quesada, this modernized version of Strange's beginnings showed him involved in a skiing accident that mangled his surgical fingers, discovering magic in an elaborate mansion hidden in a back alley, and fighting Dormammu for the first time.

DECEMBER

M Written and directed by David Goyer, *Blade: Trinity*, the third installment of the Blade films, once again starred Wesley Snipes as the Daywalker vampire hunter, alongside Kris Kristofferson as Blade's mentor, Abraham Whistler.

MEANWHILE IN 2004...

EU SWELLS TO TWENTY-FIVE
Ten new countries join the European Union, bringing the number of member states to twenty-five.

MADRID TRAIN BOMBINGS
Al-Qaeda terrorist bombs explode on commuter trains in Madrid, injuring over 1,500 and killing nearly 191.

ABU GHRAIB SCANDAL
The television program 60 Minutes II *reveals the torture and abuse of prisoners by US forces at the Abu Ghraib prison in Iraq.*

CHECHEN PRESIDENT ASSASSINATED
Akhmad Kadyrov is killed by an explosion in Grozny during a World War II memorial parade, dashing the Kremlin's hopes he would be able to bring stability to war-torn Chechnya.

SAME SEX MARRIAGE
Massachusetts is the first US state to legalize same-sex marriage.

BESLAN HOSTAGE CRISIS
Chechen separatists raid a school and take 1,200 children and adults hostage. Chaos reigns when Russian special forces storm the school on the third day and 334 civilians are killed, including 186 children.

AN ELECTED PRESIDENT FOR AFGHANISTAN
Hamid Karzai becomes the first democratically elected President of Afghanistan.

THE BOXING DAY TSUNAMI
An undersea earthquake in the Indian Ocean causes the worst tsunami on record, killing more than 225,000 people in eleven countries.

SEDNA DISCOVERED
Astronomers find Sedna, a trans-Neptunian object and the most distant object ever identified in our solar system.

WORLD'S TALLEST BUILDING
Taipei 101, a 101-floor skyscraper built in Taiwan, opens as the structurally tallest building in the world.

AND AT THE MOVIES...
Spider-Man 2, *Sam Raimi's tour-de-force, SFX Super Hero sequel keeps the soul of the original Marvel story without sacrificing any of the excitement;* The Incredibles, *Pixar's original animation imagines a suburban family of undercover Super Heroes forced into action to save the world from rampaging robots;* Harry Potter and the Prisoner of Azkaban, *Alfonso Cuarón's dark, understated vision of J.K. Rowling's fantasy world captures a sense of the magic beneath the mundane.*

HARD TO BELIEVE I USED TO BE ABLE TO FIT THIS INTO A BRIEFCASE.

2005

THE RETURN OF THE EVENT

By 2005, Marvel had reestablished its properties by returning many characters to their roots with cutting-edge storytelling from hot creators. Now, Marvel was ready to reestablish another of its honored traditions—the crossover. With hints of major universe-spanning events in 2004's *Avengers Disassembled* and *Secret War* story lines, and with their main competitor DC Comics finding success in their major event crossovers like *Identity Crisis* and *Infinite Crisis*, Marvel and the marketplace seemed primed for larger, multi-part stories.

Having established himself as a major player in the world of comics with his fan-favorite titles *Ultimate Spider-Man* and *Daredevil*, writer Brian Michael Bendis made the *House of M* miniseries branch out past its own pages. Much like the X-Men story arc Age Of Apocalypse before it, *House of M* birthed a new reality with miniseries spin-offs starring the characters from the flagship title. Spider-Man, Iron Man, and the Fantastic Four were among those characters whose alternate realities were explored in this fashion.

At the end of the year, another crossover event began, though it was limited to the pages of Spider-Man's core titles. The Other storyline altered Peter Parker's life forever, and paved the way for the changes that Spider-Man was to endure in the future.

JANUARY

AVENGERS ASSEMBLE AGAIN

"We'll find out who our enemies are. We'll find out who did this. And then we'll avenge it."

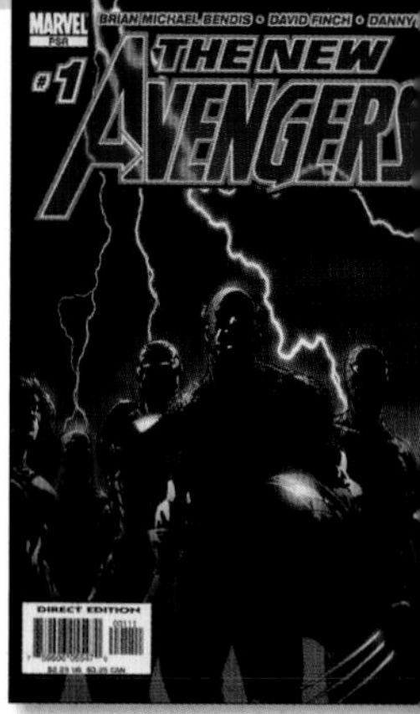

The cover for The New Aveng *#1 was available in this standar version, as well as in three varia cover editions.*

• *The New Avengers* #1

In the aftermath of the *Avengers Disassembled* storyline, the Marvel Universe was purposely left without its mightiest team of heroes. This would all change as superstars writer Brian Michael Bendis and artist David Finch relaunched the title under the name *The New Avengers*. The comic focused more on Marvel's arguably most popular Super Heroes, including Spider-Man, Captain America, Iron Man, Wolverine, Spider-Woman, and Luke Cage.

Much like the original team of the 1960s, the New Avengers' orig was born by circumstance. The members were drawn together by a massive breakout attempt at the Raft, New York City's maximum-security installation. Meeting on the scene, the unofficial team managed to curb the riots, and together set out to discover the mastermind behind the escape attempt. Following a trail that led to the Savage Land, a time-lost island inhabited by dinosaurs and oth primitive forms of life, the fledging group of heroes eventually discovered that the prison breakout was actually just part of a cove up for a deeply rooted government conspiracy involving a rogue faction of SHIELD and an illegal slave-labor vibranium mine run b the second Black Widow.

As the series progressed, the mentally tormented powerhouse known as the Sentry and a mysterious ninja named Ronin (former Daredevil's ally Echo) both joined the team. The New Avengers announced themselves to the world, and based themselves in their new headquarters located atop Manhattan's Stark Tower.

Merely a hired gun, Spider-Man's old foe Electro used his electric powers to cause a blackout in the Raft prison, causing a riot that freed forty-two super-powered villains.

ELEKTRA MAKES IT BIG

• *Elektra: The Official Movie Adaptation*

To tie in with the January movie release of *Elektra*, Marvel brought out a comic-book adaptation, coverdated February. The movie was a spin-off from 2003's *Daredevil* and Jennifer Garner reprised her role as the assassin antihero.

January

IRON MAN'S NEW ARMOR

• *The Invincible Iron Man* #1

Writer Warren Ellis teamed up with illustrator Adi Granov to create a new spin on Iron Man that would have long-lasting effects. When a face from Tony Stark's past, Maya Hansen, injected an experimental electronic super-soldier serum known as the Extremis solution into a test subject, Iron Man was forced to undergo a drastic transformation in order to stop the resulting violent renegade. Critically injured, Iron Man injected himself with the same solution in order to interface with his armor on a biological level. Now able to control his armor with a mere thought, Iron Man became the ultimate blend of man and machine.

Stark also soared to new professional heights as Director of SHIELD.

CAP'S BACK

• *Captain America* #1

When acclaimed writer Ed Brubaker made the switch from DC to Marvel, he brought with him yet another relaunch for Steve Rogers. A critical and financial hit, this new *Captain America* series featured the art of realistic draftsman Steve Epting, and saw the supposed death of Cap's main adversary, the Red Skull. Later on in the series, Cap's former sidekick Bucky Barnes made his shocking return, his death apparently just as exaggerated as Cap's was at the end of World War II.

February

THE ULTIMATE SEQUEL

• *Ultimates 2* #1

Following the success of the original *Ultimates* maxiseries, Mark Millar and Bryan Hitch teamed up again for the thirteen-issue sequel. The series saw the creation of a multi-national Super Hero force, the redemption of the Hulk, and an attack by Thor's brother Loki on a level never before witnessed in the Ultimate universe. The series ended with Captain America proved innocent, but his team deciding to sever all government ties.

When Loki made the world believe that Captain America was a murderer, Cap went on the run from his own government.

April

RUNAWAYS RENEWED

• *Runaways* #1

Picking up where the first series left off, writer Brian K. Vaughan's *Runaways* was granted a new first issue, a rare move for Marvel. As the young band of misfit heroes were joined by new teammate Victor Mancha, they found themselves pursued by a team of former child Super Heroes and battling for their lives against the robot Ultron. Later on in the series, another fan favorite, Joss Whedon, replaced Vaughan.

April

YOUNG AVENGERS COME OF AGE

"They're not going to approve . . . but since when has that ever stopped us?"

• *Young Avengers* #1

In 2005, television writer and producer Allan Heinberg (*Grey's Anatomy*, *The OC*, *Sex and the City*) and penciller Jim Cheung teamed together to create a comic title that focused on younger counterparts to the Earth's Mightiest Heroes. Originally consisting of junior versions of Captain America, Iron Man, Hulk, and Thor (Patriot, Iron Lad, Hulkling, and Wiccan respectively), the Young Avengers instantly collected a sizable following of fans, all eagerly anticipating discovering the origins of the enigmatic young team.

Patriot, the Young Avengers' leader, was actually the grandson of the original Captain America born in the miniseries Truth: Red, White and Black *(Jan., 2003).*

As the the series progressed, Iron Lad was revealed to be in actuality a young version of the time-traveling Avengers foe, Kang the Conqueror. Rallying other young heroes to aid him in his fight against his future self, the young version of Kang formed the Young Avengers, despite the disapproval of the teams' older namesakes. Soon joined by Cassie Lang, daughter of the second Ant-Man calling herself Stature, and a new female Hawkeye, the team fought and defeated Kang's adult form, before Kang's younger self was forced to return back to his normal era of the future, to keep the time stream safe.

With a little funding from Hawkeye's father, the rest of the Young Avengers decided to stay together as a team. They reemerged with a new hideout and costumes more fitting to their individuality, which allowed them to step out of the Avengers' shadow.

Shown his fate by his evil future self, Iron Lad traveled back in time to enlist some 21st Century help.

May

PUMPING ULTIMATE IRON

• *Ultimate Iron Man* #1

Acclaimed sci-fi novelist Orson Scott Card, with Marvel artists Andy Kubert and Mark Bagley, delved into Tony Stark's past in the five-issue miniseries *Ultimate Iron Man*, inventing a bizarre skin condition for the young hero.

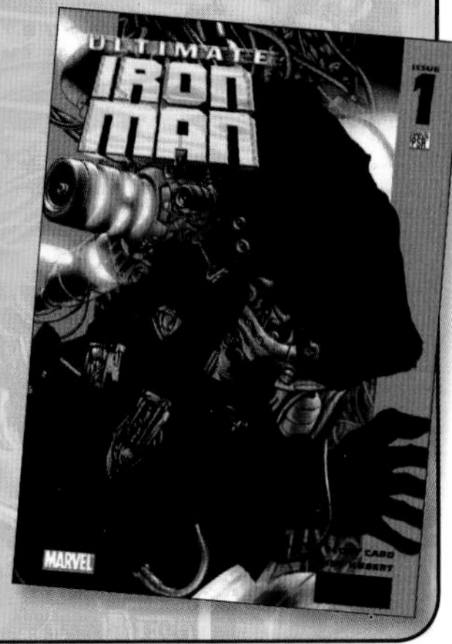

Ultimate Iron Man's body was mostly neural tissue, giving him superhuman intelligence but causing him constant pain.

JULY

THE FANTASTIC FOUR IN ACTION

• *Fantastic Four: The Movie*

In 2005, Marvel published an official comic adaptation of the *Fantastic Four* movie, which hit theaters on July 8. Adapted by Mike Carey, with art by Dan Jurgens and Sandu Florea, the trade paperback included a selection of classic Fantastic Four stories that inspired the movie as well as the movie adaptation itself. The movie was directed by Tim Story, written by Mark Frost and Michael France, and starred Jessica Alba as the Invisible Woman, Ioan Gruffudd as Mr. Fantastic, Chris Evans as the Human Torch, Michael Chiklis as the Thing, and Julian McMahon as Dr. Doom.

AUGUST

WORLD OF M

"No more mutants."

• *House Of M* #1

After successfully disassembling the Avengers, the tormented Scarlet Witch still wasn't finished tampering with the lives of the men and women she'd fought beside for so many years. And writer Brian Michael Bendis certainly wasn't finished with her, either. Teaming with artist Olivier Coipel, Bendis created *The House of M*, a major Marvel crossover event centered around an eight-issue miniseries, beginning in August, that would have lasting repercussions to the entire universe the heroes populated.

At the insistence of her brother Quicksilver, the Scarlet Witch literally rewrote history, unleashing the full extent of her magic abilities to change the world in her own image. Where once mutants were a minority on Earth, now they were the vast majority. Humans were now the outcasts, dwindling few on the verge of extinction. The planet was ruled by Magneto and his royal family—the House of Magnus. They governed a brave new world. It was a world where Spider-Man wa adored by the public and married to Gwen Stacy. A world where Hulk ruled over all of Australia, and Wolverine served dutifully as agent of SHIELD. And it would have stayed that way, if not for a little girl named Layla Miller, a mutant with the ability to restore people's minds to the way they were before the Scarlet Witch's tampering. Soon, a ragtag team of enlightened heroes took their fight to Magneto, showing him the way the world was supposed t be. Enraged by his son's presumptuous ambition, Magneto viciou attacked Quicksilver, until the Scarlet Witch was forced to return the world to normal. Or so the heroes thought.

The House Of M *miniseries featured painted covers by artist Esad Ribic.*

The X-Men were among the heroes who gathered to discuss what punishment was to be given to the Scarlet Witch after she disassembled the Avengers.

SEPTEMBER

DAREDEVIL'S PUNISHMENT

• *Daredevil Vs Punisher* #1

Crime writer David Lapham, who made a name for himself writing and drawing the independent hit *Stray Bullets*, set his sights on the Marvel Universe and crafted the six-issue miniseries *Daredevil Vs Punisher*, pitting the two vigilantes against each other.

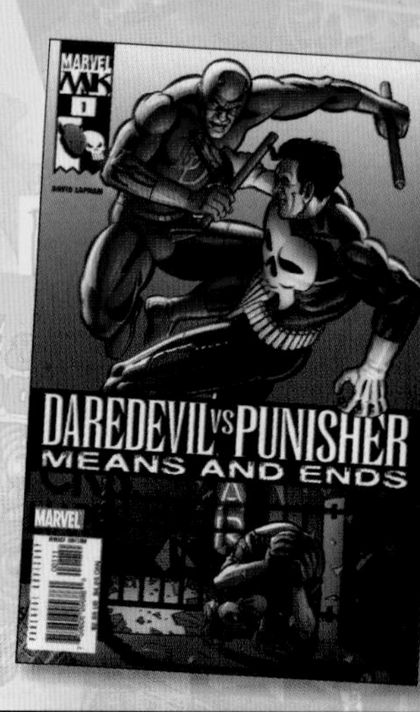

Daredevil Vs Punisher *marked the return of the classic Spider-Man foe, the Jackal, who ran his criminal organization from a jail cell.*

SPIDER-MAN: THE OTHER

"You're a good man who's led a good life. Prepare to die."

• *Friendly Neighborhood Spider-Man* #1

Beginning in the pages of the new title, *Friendly Neighborhood Spider-Man*, the Other storyline crossed over with all the current Spider-Man books, chronicling the supernatural tale of Peter Parker's death and evolution. From a story orchestrated by writer J. Michael Straczynski, writers Peter David and Reginald Hudlin teamed with artists Mike Wieringo, Pat Lee, and Mike Deodato Jr. to tell this epic tale that altered Spider-Man's powers and proved quite controversial with the fans. Serving as a prelude to Spider-Man's future wardrobe change, each issue in the series was also available in a variant edition that showcased a different costume that Spidey had worn in the course of his long career.

An energy vampire who wanted to feast on Parker's spider-based energies, Morlun had the ability to track Spider-Man wherever he went.

The story began as Spider-Man was diagnosed with an unknown terminal illness while simultaneously being stalked by his mystical adversary, Morlun. After a furious battle with his hunter, Spider-Man was defeated and hospitalized, his face swollen past recognition. But as Morlun crept into the hospital to feed off Peter's powers, Spider-Man managed one last burst of animalistic energy, viciously beating Morlun, and magically devouring him. Returning to normal, Peter Parker managed a soft farewell to his loving wife before dying in her arms. But days later, Spider-Man would return, his body somehow regenerated anew after spending time in a giant cocoon. Now with new powers, including enhanced sensitivity and spike-like stingers that protruded from his forearms in times of danger, Spider-Man cautiously renewed his fight against crime, knowing he would never survive another such brush with death.

The main artist of Friendly Neighborhood Spider-Man, *Mike Wieringo, had earned a strong following working with writer Mark Waid on their noted* Flash *run for DC Comics, as well as their historic stint on Marvel's own* Fantastic Four *in the late 2000s.*

MEANWHILE IN 2005...

HURRICANE KATRINA
One of the five deadliest hurricanes in US history hits Louisiana and Mississippi, killing nearly 2,000 and creating economic disaster.

7/7 HORROR ATTACK
In the first suicide attack in Britain, four "homegrown" suicide bombers detonate themselves on the London Underground and bus system, killing fifty-six and injuring over 700.

"DEEP THROAT" REVEALED
Thirty years on from Watergate, the Washington Post *reveals that the mystery source "Deep Throat" was deputy head of the FBI, Mark Felt.*

PROTESTS AGAINST WAR IN IRAQ
Demonstrations against the war in Iraq take place around the world, with over 150,000 protestors gathering in Washington.

ISRAEL LEAVES GAZA STRIP
After thirty-eight years of occupation, Israel withdraws settlers and military forces from the Gaza Strip, leaving the territory under the control of the Palestinian Authority.

"ORANGE REVOLUTION"
Victor Yushchenko is sworn in as President of the Ukraine, bringing an end to the "Orange Revolution"—the upheaval that followed the corruption of the 2004 election.

A ROYAL WEDDING
His Royal Highness Prince Charles marries Camilla Parker Bowles at Windsor Castle.

LIVE 8
Twenty years after Live Aid, the Live 8 benefit concerts take place in nine countries as part of the "Make Poverty History" campaign, which coincides with the G8 Conference and Summit.

KYOTO PROTOCOL TAKES EFFECT
The Kyoto Protocol on climate change becomes law. Signatories are legally bound to lower worldwide greenhouse gas emissions, but the US and Australia are not included.

DEMOCRACY IN HONG KONG?
A quarter of a million people gather in Hong Kong to protest for democracy.

MISSION TO MARS
NASA launches the Mars Reconnaissance Orbiter to research the planet from its orbit.

AND AT THE MOVIES...
Batman Begins, *Christopher Nolan's prequel looks behind the shadows to show how orphaned Bruce Wayne became a masked Super Hero;* Sin City, *Robert Rodriguez's distinctive monochrome vision of Frank Miller's popular graphic novel about the sleazy goings-on in Basin City;* Corpse Bride, *Tim Burton's sweetly macabre stop-motion masterpiece features the voice talent of Johnny Depp and Helena Bonham Carter.*

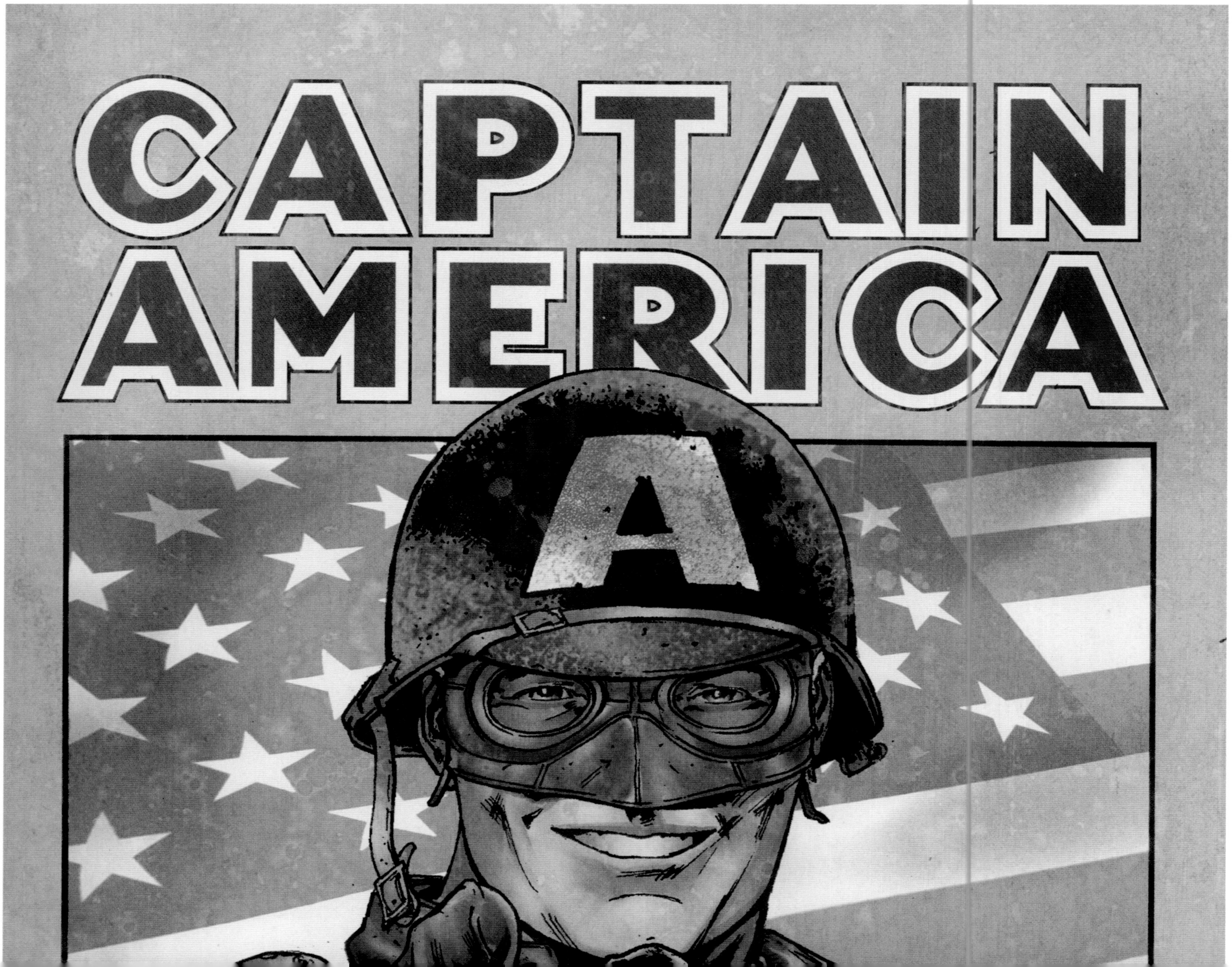

CAPTAIN AMERICA

The Ultimates: Super-Human *(2005)*
Writer Mark Millar and artist Bryan Hitch were at the top of their respective games when they crafted the first Ultimates maxiseries. Both had attracted much attention on the Wildstorm title The Authority *and with related JLA projects for DC Comics. With both men's past works rooted in books of blockbuster proportion, Millar and Hitch were the obvious team to recruit when Marvel decided it was time to revamp the Avengers and birth them into an Ultimate, more mature universe. And one of the pair's boldest reimaginings was Captain America, who traded in his mask's trademark wings for a painted Army helmet.*

I DO THIS FOR FUN. MY MOM SAID IT WAS THIS OR A NEWSPAPER ROUTE...

2006

MARVEL GOES TO WAR

The entire universe had been drafted. As Tony Stark went to speak about the Super Hero Registration Act before a terrified congress, the hero community found itself split down the middle. Some heroes were siding with Iron Man, in favor of registering their powers with the government, and others were in Captain America's camp, choosing to help form an underground rebellion. But despite the split in their fictional universe, the editorial direction of Marvel Comics had rarely been more unified.

And that unity led to the *Civil War*, an epic miniseries event that garnered much media attention from various major newspapers, even prompting a visit by Editor-in-Chief Joe Quesada to Comedy Central's *Colbert Report*. Each comic that tied into the main storyline of the ongoing war sported a split-screen cover image, allowing the titles to be easily recognizable to a hungry fan base that was desperately seeking out every battle-hardened adventure.

And while the war at home racked up casualty after casualty, Marvel's space-faring heroes entered their own private war in the pages of *Annihilation*, a crossover event spotlighting lesser-used cosmic heroes like the Silver Surfer and Drax the Destroyer. War was everywhere, and Marvel was truly reaping the benefits.

JANUARY

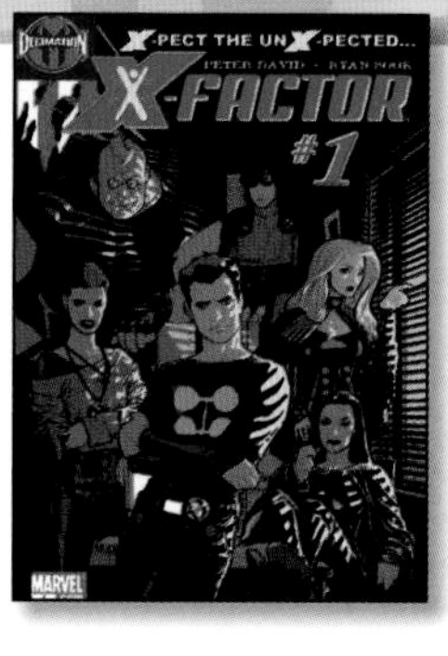
X-PECT THE UN-X-PECTED...
X-FACTOR
#1

X-FACTOR INVESTIGATIONS

• *X-Factor* #1

Writer Peter David returned to the team he popularized in the early 1990s, this time wi artist Ryan Sook. Taking a noir approach, Jamie Madrox opened X-Factor Investigatio a private detective agency employing other mutants including Siryn, M, and Strong G

VULCAN'S VENGEANCE

• *X-Men: Deadly Genesis* #1

A modern-day story revealing dark secrets of a supergroup's past, this six-issue miniseries by acclaimed writer Ed Brubaker and artist Trevor Hairsine delved into the hidden story behind the famous *Giant-Size X-Men* #1 of the mid 1970s. It told the story of anothe team of X-Men that Professor X had organized to invade the islan of Krakoa, a team that had seemingly perished in battle.

AHHH!

As the X-Men began to experience strange visions, Cyclops and Marvel Girl were kidnapped, and Banshee was killed. Later, their enemy was revealed to be a mutant nar Vulcan, a survivor of the first storm on Krakoa, and the brother of Scott and Alex Summ

X-MEN FACE DECIMATION

• *House Of M: The Day After*

In this Decimation story line tie-in one-shot by Chris Claremont, Randy Green, and Aaron Lopresti, most of the mutant population awoke to discover that their abilities were gone thanks to the Scarlet Witch, with only an estimated 198 individuals unaffected.

HOUSE OF
THE DAY AFTER

FEBRUARY

BENDIS · REED · LUNA BROTHERS
SPIDER-WOMAN
ORIGIN
FROM THE PAGES OF THE NEW AVENGERS

SPIDER-WOMAN'S SECRETS

• *Spider-Woman: Origin* #1

With her popularity increased due to her inclusion on the roster of the New Avengers, Jessica Drew, the original Spider-Woman, had her orig updated in this five-issue limited series by writers Briar Michael Bendis and Brian Reed, and artists Jonathan ar Joshua Luna. After a lab experiment on Wundagore Mountain altered her DNA in her mother's womb, Jessi Drew was born, developing superpowers at a very young age. Kept in a coma for years by HYDRA forces, Jessica was traine to be an agent of the evil spy organization, before later seeing the error of her ways and joining forces with SHIELD.

QUICKSILVER'S QUEST

• *Son Of M* #1

Tying into the Decimation fall-out from the *House Of M* miniseries, a de-powered Quicksilver traveled to Attilan and stole a portion of the Terrigen Mists (the source of the Inhumans' powers) in this six-issue limited series by writer David Hine and artist Roy Allan Martinez. Now with new time-leaping abilities, Quicksilver's heroic nature slowly began to fade away.

THE IRON SPIDER

"Not to put too fine a point on it... I need your help. And your word, that you'll stick with me through what's coming, no matter what."

• *The Amazing Spider-Man* #529

They were on the road to a civil war, but they just didn't know it yet. With a new lease on life after the Other story line, Peter Parker had become Iron Man's right-hand man, the two growing close as members of the New Avengers team. Tony Stark designed a new uniform for Spider-Man, with an array of new gadgets to help him in his crusade against crime. He also seemed to be trying to buy Peter's favor by creating a home for the Parker family in the illustrious Stark Tower, after their old home burned to the ground, But all these favors would come back to bite Parker harder than a radioactive spider, when Stark later asked Spider-Man to side with him over the controversial Super Hero Registration Act that the government was considering passing.

Written by J. Michael Straczynski with pencils by Ron Garney and a cover by Bryan Hitch, plus a variant cover by Mike Wieringo, *The Amazing Spider-Man* #529 was the issue that debuted Spidey's new look. Spider-Man's new costume could allow him to glide for short distances, deflect small caliber bullets, listen to police and emergency bands, view the infrared and ultra-violet spectrums, and even breathe under water for a brief amount of time. The costume also included three arm-like waldoes at the back, and could camouflage itself at will so as to appear invisible to the naked eye or resemble Spider-Man's traditional blue and red uniform.

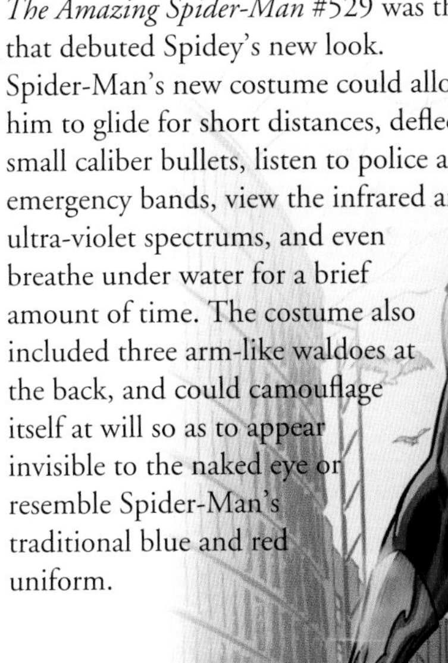

After the events of the Civil War, Peter Parker would abandon his new iron spider look in favor of his old duds. This costume was then used to arm Stark's Scarlet Spiders.

PLANET HULK

• *The Incredible Hulk* #92

Writer Greg Pak, along with artist Carlo Pagulayan, sent the Hulk into space where he crash-landed on the primitive planet of Sakaar, a world of gladiators and cruel kings. His powers severely reduced during the journey, Hulk was taken captive and sold as a slave. He met an army of alien allies in the gladiatorial arenas, and soon joined in the brotherhood pact of Warbound with them, before instigating a revolution against Sakaar's Red King. Called the Green Scar by a doting populace, the Hulk finally became emperor and even took a warrior queen Caiera, who soon became pregnant with his child.

The Hulk had seemed to find peace at last on Sakaar, until his spaceship, one crafted by the elite of Earth's heroes, exploded and tragically killed his wife and unborn child.

BRUBAKER'S DAREDEVIL

• *Daredevil* #82

Writer Ed Brubaker and artist Michael Lark had quite a challenge ahead of them when they took over the reins of *Daredevil* from the popular team of writer Brian Michael Bendis and artist Alex Maleev. Already forming a strong working relationship in the pages of DC Comics' *Gotham Central*, Brubaker and Lark began their run with Matthew Murdock in jail, as a Daredevil impersonator ran free around the rooftops of New York City. As their dark and moody tale progressed in later issues, Daredevil saw his best friend fake his death and then enroll in the witness protection plan, before he himself escaped prison and fled the country.

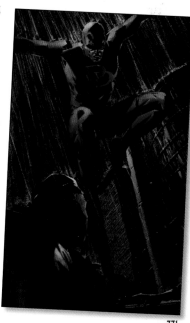

Although Matt Murdock was locked away in prison, "Daredevil" continued to fight crime. After Murdock escaped his jail cell, he confronted this imposter to discover he was in reality the hero Iron Fist.

MAY

MEETING OF THE MINDS

In another of their meetings, the Illuminati decided to exile the Hulk into space to finally end his unpredictable rampages on Earth.

• *The New Avengers: Illuminati*
In this momentous special that would birth both the beginnings of *Civil War* and *Planet Hulk*, writer Brian Michael Bendis and artist Alex Maleev crafted the untold story of an elite group of Marvel heroes deciding to meet regularly in order to maintain a flow of information between their various Super Hero groups. Comprising Iron Man, Dr. Strange, Professor X, Mr. Fantastic, Black Bolt, and Namor the Submariner—with the Black Panther refusing his invitation—this new Illuminati met several times during the course of this special, once to discuss the Super Hero Registration Act that was about to be passed by congress.

X-MEN: THE LAST STAND

The powerhouse cast of the original X-Men movies reunited to create this third installment, under the guidance of director Brett Ratner and screenwriters Zak Penn and Simon Kinberg. Released on May 26th, this film saw the screen debuts of Beast, brought to life by Kelsey Grammer, and Angel, portrayed by Ben Foster. Ellen Page also joined the cast as Kitty Pryde, a character who had previously only been glimpsed in cameo roles in the other X-films.

JULY

DECLARING WAR

"Congratulations, children. You just joined the resistance."

Originally aligning with his mentor Iron Man, Spider-Man soon realized he'd been misguided, and changed his allegiance to Captain America's side. He continued to fight for the rebellion even after Cap turned himself over to the authorities.

• *Civil War* #1
Accompanied by an advertising campaign challenging readers with the question, "Whose side are you on?" writer Mark Millar and artist Steve McNiven unleashed *Civil War* on the public, an epic seven-issue limited series that sparked some of the most heated fan debate in the history of Marvel Comics. Selling over 300,000 copies for its debut issue, a feat rarely seen in the marketplace of the 2000s, each issue of *Civil War* also came in a variant edition with a cover by Michael Turner, as well as in a sketch variant version featuring Turner's pencil art. The events of this tumultuous story crossed over into nearly every Marvel title of the time, and severely impacted the lives of nearly every major hero in its legendary stable.

As the government passed the Super Hero Registration Act, a new bill that required every superpowered individual to register his or her identity with the government, Iron Man became the Act's spokesman, promoting the idea of an organized and unified sect of superhumans. Captain America, however, found the Act unconstitutional, and an invasion of privacy for those heroes requiring secret lives in order to protect their loved ones, and form an underground militia intent on combating Stark's forces.

As the series progressed, heroes chose sides and lines were drawn the sand, Iron Man and his band of registered heroes began arresti any unlicensed vigilantes. After the death of the hero Goliath, and fierce battle through the streets of Manhattan, Captain America surrendered to Stark's forces, disgusted at what both sides had been reduced to. Cap's team went into hiding, choosing not to give up their fight, as Captain America was led away to a maximum securit cell. Meanwhile, Iron Man took over as the director of SHIELD, ushering in a new age for the heroes of the Marvel Universe.

...YOU'RE PLAYING WITH THE BIG BOYS NOW.

In a conflict with the New Warriors in Stamford, Connecticut, the villain Nitro explode killing hundreds of innocent men, women, and children and inspiring a grieving U.S. government to retaliate with the Super Hero Registration Act.

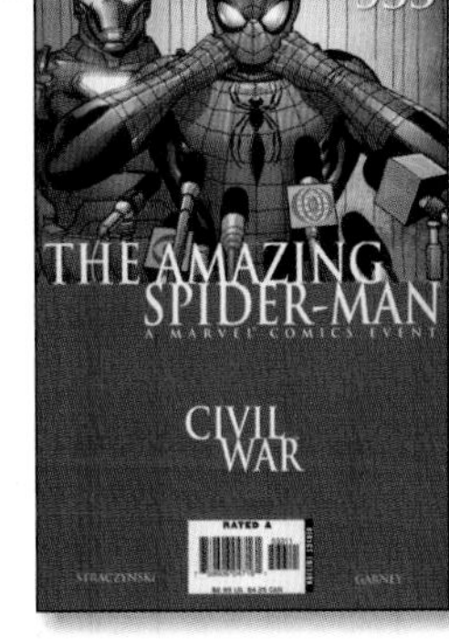

SPIDER-MAN UNMASKS

• *The Amazing Spider-Man* #533

With the welfare of his family always at the forefront of his mind, Peter Parker's identity was a well-guarded secret. So, he was forced to make a hard decision when asked to publicly unmask alongside his friend and mentor Iron Man, to show his support for the Super Hero Registration Act. In this story by writer J. Michael Straczynski and artist Ron Garney, Spider-Man decided to finally reveal his identity to a stunned world.

WAR ON THE FRONT LINES

• *Civil War: Frontline* #1

In this eleven-issue limited series, writer Paul Jenkins revealed the humanity behind the Civil War. Through a collection of short stories and multi-part serials he chronicled the conflict from the point of view of reporters Ben Urich and Sally Floyd. The series featured stories by artists Ramon Bachs, Steve Lieber, Leandro Fernandez, Lee Weeks, and a host of other creators including cover artist John Watson, and also detailed the hero Speedball's metamorphosis into the dark Penance.

X-MEN GO TO WAR

• *Civil War: X-Men* #1

Writer David Hine and artists Yanick Paquette and Aaron Lopresti chronicled the adventures of the 198 surviving mutants, as they escaped their lives of captivity in the refugee camps set up for them by a controlling government in this four-issue miniseries.

SEPTEMBER

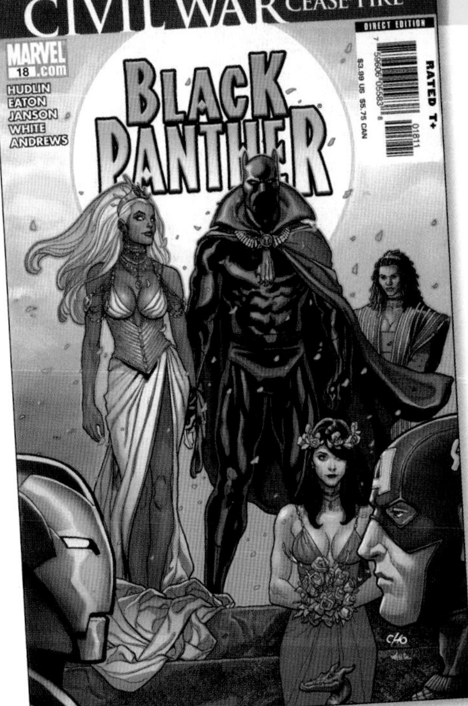

BLACK PANTHER TAKES A QUEEN

• *Black Panther* #18

After a lengthy courtship, Ororo Munroe, Storm of the X-Men, and King T'Challa of Wakanda, gathered their friends together for a brief interlude from the ongoing Super Hero Civil War—a wedding ceremony. In a story written by Reginald Hudlin with pencils by Scot Eaton and additional art by Kaare Andrews, Storm walked down the aisle in a dress designed especially for her by the costume designer of TV's *Guiding Light*, Shawn Dudley.

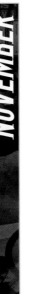

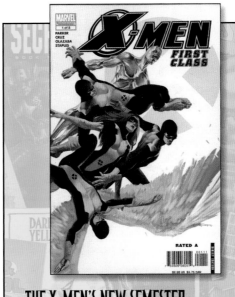

THE X-MEN'S NEW SEMESTER

• *X-Men: First Class* #1

In this eight-issue miniseries that later sparked its own ongoing title, writer Jeff Parker and artists Roger Cruz and Paul Smith united to tell the early adventures of the original five X-Men as they adjusted to life at Xavier's School for Gifted Youngsters.

MEANWHILE IN 2006...

MISSION TO PLUTO
The space craft New Horizons *sets off on a nine-year journey to gather information on Pluto.*

SADDAM EXECUTED
Former Iraqi premier Saddam Hussein is executed for crimes against humanity in Baghdad.

CONFLICT IN IRAQ CONTINUES
The US death toll in Iraq reaches 3,000.

HAMAS IS ELECTED IN PALESTINE
The Islamic militant organization Hamas wins democratic control of the government of the Palestinian Authority.

ONE BILLIONTH SONG ON iTUNES
The popularity of buying music downloads on MP3 is clear by the success of iTunes.

MILOSEVIC DIES
The former Yugoslavian leader, Slobodan Milosevic dies of a heart attack in his cell while still on trial at the Hague for war crimes.

2006 LEBANON WAR
Lebanon sees thirty-three days of conflict, largely between Hezbollah paramilitary forces and the Israeli military.

NATASCHA KAMPUSCH ESCAPES
The eighteen-year-old Austrian girl, who was kidnapped aged ten, flees from the house cellar where she was held captive for eight years.

NINTENDO RELEASES THE Wii
A new generation of gaming is launched with the Wii, a new console targeted at a broader demographic than previous video games.

ECHOES OF COLD-WAR SPY GAMES
In a plot reminiscent of the Cold War, the former KGB agent Alexander Litvinenko is poisoned with a radioactive substance in a London sushi bar.

SOCIAL NETWORKING GOES INTO CYBERSPACE
People bond with each other on the Internet as social networking sites like MySpace, YouTube, and Facebook become popular.

AND AT THE MOVIES...
Pan's Labyrinth, *a young girl forgets her brutal fascist stepfather by escaping into an eerie fantasy world in Guillermo del Toro's surreal film;* Casino Royale, *Daniel Craig's edgy 007 takes on a terrorist banker in his first mission;* The Departed, *Martin Scorsese's tale of Leonardo DiCaprio's cop who goes undercover as a gangster and Matt Damon's gangster who goes undercover as a cop.*

2007

NEW WORLD ORDER

After the huge success of the *Civil War* miniseries, Marvel had once again realized the potential of the blockbuster crossover event to generate sales. With even *Civil War* reprints selling above and beyond expectations, it was only a matter of time before the powers that be at Marvel decided to see if lightning could strike twice for them. And with the natural procession of events set up back in the original *Illuminati* special of 2006, World War Hulk soon reared its monstrous head, creating shockwaves once again in the comic marketplace.

Meanwhile, the war had impacted on the fictional residents of the Marvel Universe as well. Despite Captain America's surrender, many of his underground forces refused to give in, and for the first time in history, the Avengers saw themselves split into two factions with each refusing to acknowledge the other as the genuine article. Spider-Man found out just why he'd been wise to fight to keep his identity hidden from the rest of the world for so long, and Captain America became a casualty of the fallout of war. But through all the carnage, familiar heroes would return, ensuring that Marvel had plenty of new surprises up its sleeve.

JANUARY

IRON FIST BREAKS THROUGH

• *The Immortal Iron Fist* #1

Already amassing much acclaim for his work on *The Uncanny X-Men, Captain America,* and *Daredevil*, Ed Brubaker teamed with co-writer Matt Fraction and artist David Aja to give Iron Fist another shot at an ongoing title.

FEBRUARY

M *Daredevil* writer/director Mark Steven Johnson wrote and directed Ghost Rider's first feature film. The film opened on February 16, and starred Nicholas Cage in the title role, alongside Eva Mendes, Peter Fonda, and Wes Bentley.

MARCH

THE RETURN OF CAPTAIN MARVEL

• *Civil War: The Return*

The original Captain Marvel returned with the help of writer Paul Jenkins and artist Tom Raney in this one-shot special. He had reached out to touch a crease in the fabric of existence, only to be teleported to our conflicted present.

THUNDERBOLTS IN NEW HANDS

• *Thunderbolts* #110

Reimagined by Warren Ellis and Mike Deodato J after *Civil War*, the Thunderbolts became a government-sponsored strike force bent on taking down unregistered heroes. Led by the Green Goblin, the team included returning members Songbird, Moonstone, and Radioactive Man, alo with new blood Penance (formerly Speedball), Venom, Bullseye, and a new Swordsman.

APRIL

SPIDER-MAN: BACK IN BLACK

• *The Amazing Spider-Man* #539

With Spider-Man's secret identity now public, the Kingpin had hired a sniper to assassinate him. However, the bullet found its way to Aunt May instead, putting her in a coma. Infuriated by the attack, Peter donned his old black costume (first seen in *Marvel Super Heroes Secret Wars* #8, Dec., 1984) to reflect his no-holds-barred attitude. He ruthlessly followed a trail of clues back to the Kingpin, before giving his old foe a vicio beating. In this story, written by J. Michael Straczynski with pencils by Ron Garney, a vengeful Spider-Man served up a lesson to al those that would endanger his family.

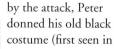

Spider-Man had originally abandoned his black costume because he felt it conveyed the wrong message. But once he s his aunt in a coma, he decided that the gloves were off, and that a darker message was appropriate.

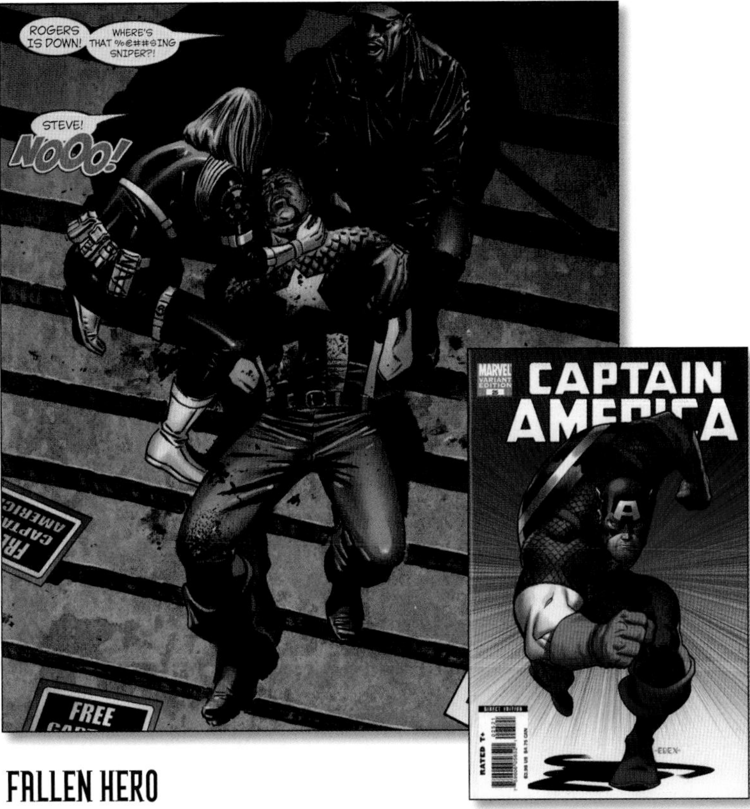

FALLEN HERO

"He was supposed to be the first of an army... an army of super soldiers... but it all went wrong."

• *Captain America* #25

America had never been more defeated. The Civil War was over, and the freedom fighters had lost. Captain America had turned himself over to police custody after seeing the damage that the war between these two groups of "heroes" had brought to the country he loved so much. But writer Ed Brubaker and artist Steve Epting had one final nail to put in Cap's coffin, and maybe in the coffin of the American Dream as well.

As Captain America was led in shackles up the stairs to the Federal Courthouse in Manhattan, a shot rang out. A sniper's bullet from across the street felled the hero, and chaos erupted as hundreds of spectators and reporters ran for their lives. As distraught government agent, Sharon Carter, rushed to be by the side of the man she loved, three more shots were fired by a mysterious source, ensuring Steve Roger's death. And it wasn't until much later, after Cap's pals Bucky Barnes and the Falcon had tracked down the sniper, Crossbones, and brought him to justice, that Sharon realized the truth. The second gunman, the one who'd fired those three mystery shots, had been her, albeit under Dr. Faustus' control. The whole tragic mess had been orchestrated by Cap's arch foe, the Red Skull, but Sharon Carter had done the deed. Agent 13 had killed Captain America. Surprising an unsuspecting fan base who thought the worst was over for Steve Rogers, Captain America's death captured worldwide media attention, and spawned several reprint editions.

THE SPOILS OF WAR

• *Civil War: The Initiative*

Written by Brian Michael Bendis and Warren Ellis, with art by Marc Silvestri, this one-shot special served as an introduction to the post-Civil War Marvel Universe. Debuting new teams like Omega Flight and the new lineup of the Thunderbolts, the issue also had Iron Man deciding who would make the cut in his new Avengers, and Ms. Marvel attempting to recruit Spider-Woman back onto the government's side.

THE AVENGERS EXPAND

"The World needs the Avengers. The best of the best. The best and the brightest. Symbols. Icons."

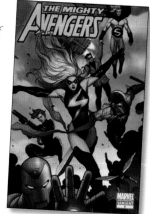

• *The Mighty Avengers* #1

The war was over. It was a time of healing and rebirth. And who better to lead the way in this brave new world than one of the architects of its design, Brian Michael Bendis. With the help of artist Frank Cho, Bendis created the Mighty Avengers, a government-sponsored team that would serve as the antithesis to the still-underground New Avengers. While Spider-Man, Luke Cage, Spider-Woman, Dr. Strange, Iron Fist, Wolverine, and the second Ronin (the newly adopted identity of the resurrected Hawkeye) all hid from the law, the Mighty Avengers were in place to enforce it. With Ms. Marvel serving as the team's leader, the Mighty Avengers were handpicked by the newly appointed Director of SHIELD, Tony Stark, aka Iron Man. The Sentry, Wonder Man, Black Widow, and the Wasp all renewed their Avengers memberships in this core team, along with newcomer, Ares, the angry god of war, and brother of the former Avenger, Hercules.

Besides existing as the first line of defense for their country and even the world, the Mighty Avengers also served as the figurehead for the newly divided American people. They stood as a team for others to look up to, and for the other Avengers teams in Iron Man's new program to base themselves on. For in the wake of the Civil War, Tony Stark had devised a fifty-state Initiative program, in which every state would get its own trained and licensed team of Super Heroes to defend it, in order to prevent future tragedies like the explosion in Stamford, Connecticut.

The first challenge the Mighty Avengers faced was an attack on Manhattan by the Mole Man and longtime Avengers' foe, Ultron.

M Peter Parker returned to the silver screen on May 4 in Sam Raimi's third installment. Tobey Maguire reprised the title role, and Kirsten Dunst and James Franco returned as supporting characters Mary Jane Watson and Harry Osborn, with Franco also adopting the new identity of Spidey adversary, New Goblin.

JUNE

THE AVENGERS TAKE THE INITIATIVE

• *Avengers: The Initiative* #1

Using the *Civil War: The Initiative* special as a springboard, writer Dan Slott along with artist Stefano Caselli created this new series to spotlight the government's training program for newly registered superhuman agents. Under the tutelage of Yellowjacket, War Machine, Justice, and drill instructor the Gauntlet, new heroes were trained at the Camp Hammond military base in Stamford, Connecticut, each with the hopes of filling a slot in one of the fifty new state Avengers teams.

ALPHA MEETS OMEGA

• *Omega Flight: The Initiative* #1

When the majority of Canada's Super Hero team Alpha Flight was killed due to fallout from the House of M event, writer Michael Avon Oeming and penciller Scott Kolins filled the gap they'd left behind with *Omega Flight*, a five-issue miniseries spotlighting a new team of heroes based in Canada.

June 15 saw the release of *4: The Rise Of The Silver Surfer*, the second Fantastic Four feature film. The movie showcased the computer generated Silver Surfer character and the mysterious Galactus.

COPING WITHOUT CAPTAIN AMERICA

• *Fallen Son: Wolverine* #1

After the death of Captain America, a series of one-shots were released showing how various heroes were dealing with the tragedy. Written by Jeph Loeb with art by Leinil Yu, Ed McGuinness, John Romita Jr., David Finch, and John Cassaday, the specials dealt with the five stages of grieving: denial, anger, bargaining, depression, and acceptance.

Wolverine starred in the first of five one-shots, all spotlighting different characters including the Avengers, Spider-Man, Iron Man, and Captain America himself.

AUGUST

THE HULK DECLARES WAR

"They thought he was finally dead. But he survived. Because he is the Green Scar... the Worldbreaker... the eye of anger... The Hulk. And now he's coming home."

• *World War Hulk* #1

Fresh off exiling the Hulk into outer space in the pages of his own title, writer Greg Pak teamed up with legendary artists John Romita and Klaus Janson for the largest crossover event of 2007, *World War Hu* This five-issue miniseries spawned severa spin-off titles and specials, and showcased more powerful Green Goliath than anyone had ever seen before.

When his newly adopted plar of Sakaar was mostly destroyec by the explosion of a spaceshi Hulk naturally blamed the creators of th ship for t tragic dea of h new wife Caiera, and the en of his dream of a peaceful existence. Heading back to Earth to seek out vengeance on the heroes who isolated him into space in the first place, Hulk attacked the members of the elite Illuminati one by one, until they we all his captives. Along with his loyal Warbound followers, Hulk later forced h prisoners to do battle against one another converting Madison Square Garden into a gladiatorial arena of sorts. Finally, the time arrival of the Hulk's former sidekick Rick Jones and his former ally the Sentry, succeeded in knocking some sense into the brute. That is until Hulk's alien comrade Mie seemingly killed Jones, revealing that it was Miek himself who h rigged Hulk's spaceship to explode, killing millions of innocents. Hulk then began an uncontrollable destructive rampage that was only ended when Iron Man unleashed a satellite laser attack on him, finally returning the Hulk to his meek Bruce Banner form.

HULK FACES FRONT

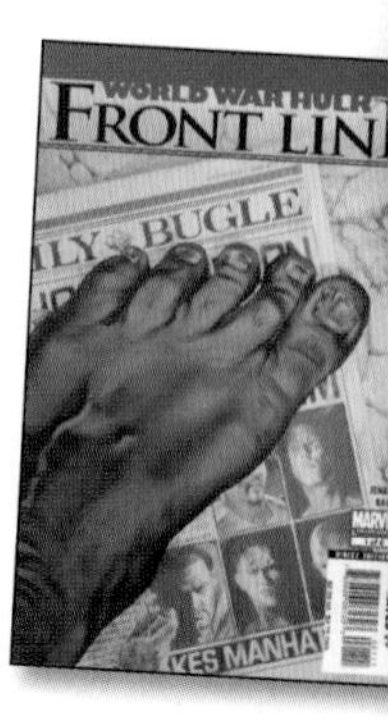

• *World War Hulk: Front Line* #1

This six-issue miniseries written by Paul Jenkins with art by Ramon Bachs looked at World War Hulk from the perspective of newspaper journalists Ben Urich and Sally Floyd as they attempted to chronicle the chaos that Manhattan had birthed.

THOR THUNDERS ON

• *Thor* #1

With his impressive run ending on *The Amazing Spider-Man*, writer J. Michael Straczynski decided to tackle another of Marvel's iconic pantheon—Thor. Thought dead since the Avengers Disassembled story line, Thor returned to Earth after struggling with his inner demons. Aided by fan-favorite artist Olivier Coipel, Thor ventured to the mortal plane and reestablished his old secret identity of Dr. Donald Blake.

ONE MORE DAY

"You will not consciously remember this bargain, or this moment, or the life you lived to this point. But there will be a very small part of your soul that will remember, that will know what you lost. And my joy will be in listening to that part of your soul screaming throughout eternity."

• *The Amazing Spider-Man* #544

When the powers that be thought it was time to reinvigorate the Spider-Man franchise by restoring some of the elements to Peter Parker's life that made Spider-Man a hit in the first place, they realized that a few of those components would prove challenging to restore. After all, Peter Parker was no longer the swinging bachelor he'd been in the past, as he was married to Mary Jane Watson. Also, during the events of Marvel's Civil War, Peter had outed his secret identity to the public, effectively changing all of his current relationships and making him a fugitive.

Editor-in-Chief Joe Quesada sought to change all that, and began to conspire just how to put those genies back in their respective bottles. His solution was One More Day, a four-issue series spanning all three Spider-Man books. J. Michael Straczynski took up the writing chores over Quesada's plot, and Quesada himself pencilled the story.

As Spider-Man's Aunt May lay dying in a hospital bed from a sniper's bullet meant for Peter, the Parkers were forced to answer the toughest question ever put to them. The demon Mephisto had taken an interest in their hopeless situation, and smelled an opportunity. Accepting Mephisto's offer of the life of their aunt in exchange for the love that Peter and Mary Jane shared, the young couple woke up alone in a world they no longer recognized. A world in which the two of them could never be together again, and never even remembered being together in the first place.

Spider-Man first turned to billionaire Tony Stark in order to obtain funds to keep his Aunt May alive. And after a violent conflict, ending with Iron Man encased in a webbing cocoon, Iron Man agreed to do just that, but in his own secretive way.

MEANWHILE IN 2007...

VIRGINIA TECH MASSACRE
In the deadliest school shooting in US history, thirty-two people are killed on a university campus when a student goes on a shooting rampage before turning the gun on himself.

FEMALE SPEAKER OF THE HOUSE
Nancy Pelosi becomes the first female speaker of the House of Representatives.

NEW PRIME MINISTER FOR BRITAIN
After ten years in power, Tony Blair resigns as Prime Minister and is succeeded by the Labour Chancellor Gordon Brown.

BENAZIR BHUTTO ASSASSINATED
After returning from exile to stand for office, former Pakistani Prime Minister Benazir Bhutto is assassinated at an election rally.

DARK PROTEST AGAINST CLIMATE CHANGE
Sydney, Australia switches off all the lights in the city from 7.30pm to 8.30pm in a statement on global climate change.

APPLE RELEASES THE iPHONE
Following the success of its iPod, Apple produces its version of the mobile phone and MP3 player in one.

SCOUT MOVEMENT CELEBRATES
The World Organization of the Scout Movement celebrates the centenary of its founding and of Lord Baden Powell's first scout camp.

A CONCERT FOR DIANA
Ten years after her death, a concert takes place at Wembley Stadium in London in honor of the former Princess of Wales.

BRIDGE STRETCHES INTO HISTORY BOOKS
The second span of the Tacoma Narrows Bridge opens in Washington, and is the longest twin suspension bridge in the world.

THE FINAL INSTALLMENT OF HARRY POTTER
The seventh and final Harry Potter book, The Deathly Hallows, *makes publishing history when it sells over eleven million copies worldwide in the first twenty-four hours of being released.*

AND AT THE MOVIES...
No Country for Old Men, *the Coen brothers tell this violent tale of greed and a sociopathic hit man hunting down a missing $2 million;* Enchanted, *real and animated worlds collide in Disney's comic fairytale about a princess seeking her Prince Charming in modern-day New York;* The Bourne Ultimatum, *the last in this exciting trilogy has Matt Damon's Bourne dodging new assassins while he searches for his unknown past.*

PRISONERS OF WAR

As writer Mark Millar and artist Steve McNiven's *Civil War* miniseries continued to shake the foundations of the Marvel Universe, both sides began to up the ante. Iron Man and his team of pro-registration Super Heroes were capturing unlicensed heroes by the truckload and dragging them to their impenetrable maximum security prison, designed by Mr. Fantastic and located in the removed dimension of the Negative Zone. It was here that the heroes of the resistance staged a massive attack with the help of the Invisible Woman, who had broken allegiances with her own husband. This contained fight bled out into the streets of New York City, where the rebel Cloak teleported everyone in order to escape imprisonment at the hands of Stark's team.

"You want some of this?...
And we're not just drinking...
we're paying tribute."

2008

BRAND NEW BRAND

It was a brand new day. And not just in the pages of *Amazing Spider-Man* comic books. Bruce Banner had been incarcerated, and there was a new and mysterious Red Hulk roaming the Russian countryside. Captain America had returned, even if the man beneath the mask had not; the X-Men had been rocked by the events of the "Messiah Complex" story line that had ended the previous year, spawning brand new *X-Force* and *Young X-Men* titles.

However, the main focus was on Spider-Man, as new editor Stephen Wacker arrived at the helm of flagship title *The Amazing Spider-Man*. Fresh off the weekly hit comic for DC Comics entitled *52*, Wacker utilized his expertise at working under tight deadliness to revitalize Spider-Man's comic by releasing it three times a month, with a rotating staff of creators. Hiring his Spidey "brain trust," consisting of writers Dan Slott, Zeb Wells, Marc Guggenheim, and Bob Gale, Wacker set out to create a fresh start for Peter Parker in this newly streamlined reality.

The result was a fresh world of possibility for the wall-crawler, and an infectious excitement that seemed to spread throughout the entire Marvel Universe.

JANUARY

WORLD'S GREATEST

• *Fantastic Four* #554

Mark Millar returned to the family he'd helped put through the ringer in the pages of *Civil War* as the newest writer of *The Fantastic Four.* Accompanied by one of his regular partners in crime, penciler Bryan Hitch, Millar crafted a story that saw the return of Reed Richard's ex, Alyssa Moy.

THE INCREDIBLE HERCULES

• *The Incredible Herc* #112

With Bruce Banner safely locked away in a government installation after the events of *World War Hulk*, the demi-god and former Avenger Hercules stepped up to fill the brute's massive shoes and prompt a title change to *The Incredible Hulk* comic. Written by Greg Pak and Fred Van Lente and drawn by Khoi Pham, *The Incredible Herc* followed the adventures of Hercules and boy genius Amadeus Cho as they set out to destroy the government agency SHIELD.

FEBRUARY

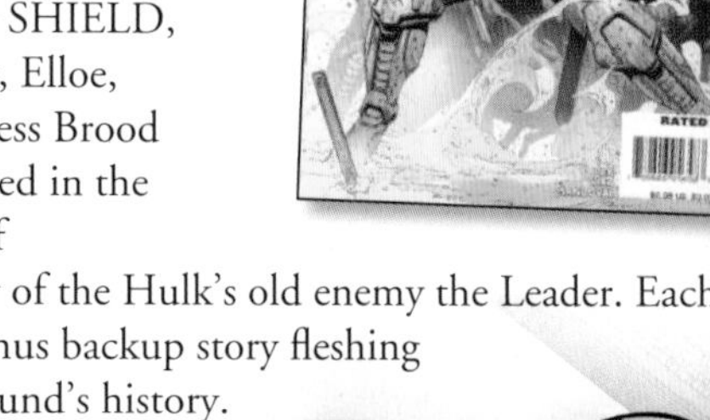

THE AFTERSMASH OF WAR

• *Warbound* #1

Hulk's inner circle earned its own five-issue miniseries in this *World War Hulk: Aftersmash!* tie-in by writer Greg Pak and artists Leonard Kirk and Rafa Sandoval. On the run from the government agency SHIELD, Hulk's alien allies Korg, Elloe, Hiroim, and the nameless Brood found themselves trapped in the sealed-off small town of Gammaworld, courtesy of the Hulk's old enemy the Leader. Each issue also featured a bonus backup story fleshing out more of the Warbound's history.

BRAND NEW DAY

• *The Amazing Spider-Man* #546

With his many titles whittled down to just his flagship book, Spider-Man began a new chapter, thanks to a rotating creative team, kick-started by writer Dan Slott and penciler Steve McNiven. With his marriage to Mary Jane Watson now no more than a fading dream, Peter Parker's life began anew as he lived with Aunt May, now perfectly healthy thanks to the machinations of the demon Mephisto.

MARCH

THE NEW CAPTAIN AMERICA

• *Captain America* #34

Former sidekick Bucky Barnes donned a new costume designed by superstar painter Alex Ross in this second act of writer Ed Brubaker's and penciler Steve Epting's epic storyline "The Death of Captain America." With the mystery of the new Cap finally revealed to the hordes of fans who joined the book after Steve Rogers' surprise death, the plot thickened as the Red Skull's evil influence seemed to extend to every corner of America, causing an economic crisis.

THE TWO-FISTED TWELVE

• *The Twelve* #1

Set in the closing days of World War II, when the Super Heroes finally invaded Germany en masse, this twelve-issue limited series focused on a mostly forgotten band of heroes who had been subdued by Nazi scientists and trapped in time, until they were unearthed, in a state of cryogenic suspension, at a construction site in the present. The twelve consisted of Dynamic Man, Mister E, Master Mind Excello, Rockman, Black Widow, Captain Wonder, Fiery Mask, Blue Blade, Laughing Mask, the Witness, Electro, and the Phantom Reporter. Giving this dozing dozen the culture shock of a lifetime were writer J. Michael Straczynski and artist Chris Weston.

THE RED HULK

• *Hulk* #1

With Hercules stealing the spotlight in his old title, the Hulk's adventures began anew in this ongoing series by the team of Jeph Loeb and Ed McGuinness. Debuting a new, crimson-hued Hulk with a mysterious secret identity that both a team of heroes led by Doc Samson and the readers were left to deduce, *Hulk* began with the apparent death of classic foe the Abomination.

Readers were faced with a tantalizing mystery: the real human identity of the Red Hulk.

M March 8 saw Peter Parker's return to television with the new Kids WB animated series, *The Spectacular Spider-Man*, featuring the combined efforts of *Gargoyles* creator Greg Weisman, director Victor Cook, and character designer Sean Galloway.

APRIL

X-FORCE FIGHTS BACK

• *X-Force* #1

After the events of the "Messiah Complex" crossover of late 2007, where the mutant Caliban tragically lost his life, Cyclops formed a new deadly strike force to do the dirty work that the X-Men wouldn't lower themselves to do. Featuring the team of Wolverine, X-23, Warpath and Wolfsbane, this new X-Force set out to put a permanent end to extremist group the Purifiers, thanks to writers Craig Kyle and Christopher Yost, and artist Clayton Crain.

It took the combined might of some of the X-Men's most ferocious alumni to tackle the reborn threat of their old foe Bastion.

MAY

M Director Jon Favreau, along with screenwriters Mark Fergus, Hawk Ostby, Art Marcum, and Matt Holloway blasted Iron Man off on his first big screen adventure on May 2, starring Robert Downey Jr. in the lead role, alongside an impressive supporting cast.

JUNE

Edward Norton both co-wrote and starred in *The Incredible Hulk*, the semi-sequel to 2003's *Hulk* film. Directed by Louis Leterrier and also written by Zak Penn, this June 13 release also starred Liv Tyler, Tim Roth, and William Hurt.

THE SECRET IS OUT

"...I know who I am... but who are you guys supposed to be, exactly?"

• *Secret Invasion* #1
With plot elements planted years earlier in the pages of comics written by Brian Michael Bendis, the infiltration of Earth by the alien race of shapeshifters the Skrulls first surfaced in the pages of *New Avengers* #31, when a dying Elektra transformed to reveal herself as one of these chameleon-like aliens. Emerging from the imagination of writer Brian Michael Bendis and artist Leinil Francis Yu, this epic miniseries began with every hero and villain's authenticity in question, and ended with a bang that shifted the entire power structure of the Marvel Universe.

Secret Invasion consisted of eight issues of heroes struggling against a barrage of alien attacks, and tied into many spinoff comics focusing on those battles in detail. By the miniseries' final issue, the invasion was ended by the unlikely heroism of Norman Osborn, formerly the renowned Spider-Man enemy the Green Goblin. During a climactic fight that saw the apparent death of longtime Avenger Wasp, Osborn fired the shot heard around the world, killing the Skrull queen and helping Earth defeat the Skrulls. This seemingly valiant act maneuvered Osborn into an extremely powerful position: he became the head of the Avengers, the Fifty-State Initiative and assumed all the powers that used to belong to the superspy agency SHIELD.

As both the Mighty Avengers and the New Avengers followed a crash-landing Skrull spaceship to the Savage Land, Dr. Hank Pym and Reed Richards examined the body of the deceased Skrull who impersonated Elektra. However, just as Mr. Fantastic let his guard down, Pym showed his true colors and attacked his friend, revealing that he was a Skrull in disguise.

JULY

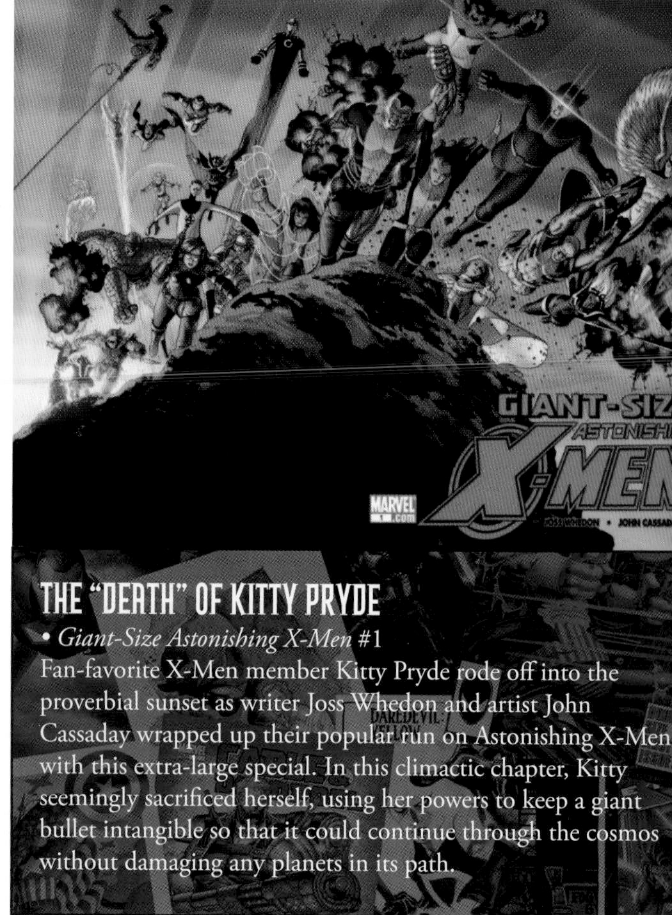

THE "DEATH" OF KITTY PRYDE

• *Giant-Size Astonishing X-Men* #1
Fan-favorite X-Men member Kitty Pryde rode off into the proverbial sunset as writer Joss Whedon and artist John Cassaday wrapped up their popular run on Astonishing X-Men with this extra-large special. In this climactic chapter, Kitty seemingly sacrificed herself, using her powers to keep a giant bullet intangible so that it could continue through the cosmos without damaging any planets in its path.

UPGRADING IRON MAN

• *The Invincible Iron Man* #1
The *Iron Man* film was a smash hit at the box office, and the start of the largest and most successful Marvel movie initiative in the history of the company. Capitalizing on that popularity, Iron Man soon received a new comic book series, *The Invincible Iron Man*, courtesy of writer Matt Fraction and artist Salvador Larroca. This new title not only granted Tony Stark a powerful foe with the return of genius Ezekiel Stane, it also entranced audiences with a high-octane revitalization of the Iron Man character, endowing the hero with touches of the trademark wit that had helped make the movie such a worldwide success.

THE ULTIMATE COVER UP

• *Ultimate Origins* #1
Brian Michael Bendis delved a bit more into the backstory of the Ultimate Universe he helped create when he penned this five-issue series with artist Butch Guice. Flashing back to the days of World War II, the series revealed that mutants of the Ultimate world were not a natural genetic evolution, but the result of the government's super-soldier program.

OLD MAN LOGAN

"Get ready for the ride of your **life***."*

• *Wolverine* #66

In the modern landscape of Super Hero comic books, future tales, flashback origins or "what if?"-style epics are rare in the pages of a character's regular title. While these self-contained, multi-part stories were often included within the main titles of the 1980s, comic companies subsequently preferred to spotlight these special tales as miniseries or graphic novels. However, when writer Mark Millar and artist Steve McNiven crafted the eight-part future tale known as "Old Man Logan," Marvel decided to include the series in its regular *Wolverine* title. The result was revitalized sales for the monthly comic, and an unexpected treat for regular readers.

One part glimpse into the dystopian future of the Marvel Universe, and one part buddy comedy, "Old Man Logan" was a fast-paced, violent romp starring an aged Wolverine embarking on a cross-country road trip with an equally time-weathered Hawkeye. When his family was threatened by the corrupt descendants of the incredible Hulk, Wolverine traveled over 3000 miles in Spider-Man's old buggy, the Spider-Mobile, battling Moloids, a Venom/dinosaur hybrid, and other twisted and deadly threats, culminating in a bloody battle as fierce as any Logan had ever experienced.

At the start of "Old Man Logan," Wolverine was retired from a life of crime fighting, living in poverty with his wife and two kids.

MEANWHILE IN 2008...

RECESSION STARTS TO BITE
The previous year's subprime mortgage crisis sparks a downturn in the US economy signaling worldwide recession. Lehman Brothers files for bankruptcy, the largest in US history.

CASTRO STANDS DOWN
Fidel Castro announces his resignation as President of Cuba, a post he has held since 1976. His younger brother Raul is elected President.

THE FIRST BIONIC EYES
At London's Moorfields Eye Hospital, two blind patients become the first people to receive bionic eyes.

CYCLONE DEATH TOLL
More than 138,000 people lose their lives in the catastrophic destruction caused by Cyclone Nargis, Burma's worst natural disaster.

ARTHUR C. CLARKE DIES
Sir Arthur C. Clark, the author of 2001: A Space Odyssey *and the host of TV shows about mysterious phenomena, dies aged 90. Known, with Robert Heinlein and Isaac Asimov, as one of the "big three" science-fiction writers.*

NEW RUSSIAN PRESIDENT
Dmitry Medvedev becomes President of Russia, replacing Vladimir Putin.

US PRESIDENTIAL ELECTION
The first African American candidate to be nominated by either party, Democrat Barack Obama defeats Republican John McCain to become the 44th President of the United States.

MUMBAI TERROR ATTACKS
Pakistani-based Islamist extremists stage terrorist attacks in Mumbai, India, in which 164 people are killed and over 300 injured.

MADONNA'S MILLIONS
In the year of her 50th birthday, Madonna's Sticky and Sweet world tour is the highest-grossing by a solo artist, with ticket sales of $280 million.

AND AT THE MOVIES...

In Indiana Jones and the Crystal Skull, *Indy battles Soviet agents; Christopher Nolan's* The Dark Knight *pits Batman against The Joker; James Bond embarks on a vengeful quest in* Quantum of Solace; *former Bond Pierce Brosnan sings in the Abba musical* Mamma Mia!; *Kathryn Bigelow's* The Hurt Locker *follows a US Army bomb disposal squad in the Iraq War; sleeper hit is* Slumdog Millionaire, *about a young quiz show winner from the slums of Mumbai.*

When Marvel revamped the Spider-Man franchise, they knew they were treading on dangerous ground. Peter Parker had such a rich history, Marvel didn't want to alienate fans by altering too much of his backstory. However, the company felt Spider-Man was in need of a fresh start, so they erased his marriage to Mary Jane Watson from continuity and brought back his old friend and sometime enemy, Harry Osborn. Fans quickly embraced this "Brand New Day" that saw Spidey return to his roots as an everyman down on his luck, in a now thrice-monthly flagship title.

"It's a new day. So listen carefully. This is how it's going to be."

2009

DARK REIGN

It was always darkest before the dawn. Or at least that was what the heroes of the Marvel Universe had to keep telling themselves. When the corrupt Norman Osborn fired the bullet that ended the Skrull threat of *Secret Invasion*, the power structure of the entire world began to shift. Tony Stark was ousted as head of SHIELD, and Osborn renamed the organization HAMMER, even taking control of the Avengers team. Heroes already alienated by the Super Human Registration Act and the events of the *Civil War* series were now hunted by Osborn's men.

This was the status quo of "Dark Reign," a crossover event felt in the majority of Marvel's titles. While not linked by a main series or miniseries, the events of "Dark Reign" were widespread and nearly as ambitious as the world-changing battles waged in 2006-7's *Civil War*. An ominous shadow had fallen over the Marvel Universe, and the result was a refreshing batch of stories dealing with rebellion, corrupt governments, and the manipulation of public perception.

JANUARY

A SHOCK TO THE SENSES

• *The Amazing Spider-Man* #578

Fan-favorite writer Mark Waid stopped b the Spider-Man offices to pen an acclaim story alongside brilliant comic artist Marcos Martin. In only two issues, the d wove a tale full of tension as Spidey battl the Shocker in the New York City subwa tunnels. Waid and Martin also introduce a major new character into Peter Parker's world, J. Jonah Jameson S the father of *The Daily Bugle*'s most infamous publisher.

> M The newly formed production company Marvel Animation debuted the *Wolverine and the X-Men* animated series on January 23. The series lasted for one season and consisted of 26 episodes.

THE ULTIMATE PRICE

• *Ultimatum* #1

The Ultimate Comics Universe was in need of a shakeup, and writer Jeph Loeb and artist David Finch instigated a thorough reboot of the Ultimate titles in the pages of this five-issue, crossover miniseries. As the home of Spider-Man, the Fantastic Four, and the Ultimates, New York City played an important role in the Ultimate Universe. So when the mutant villain Magneto used his abilities to drown the city in the biggest flood it had ever seen, the damage and loss of life was tremendous—many heroes and villains wouldn't survive to see the birth of the new status quo, including mainstays like Wolverine, Professor X, Cyclops, Hank Pym, the Wasp, Doctor Doom, and even Magneto himself.

THE FINAL IRON CURTAIN

• *Iron Man: The End* #1

The classic team of David Michelinie and Bob Layton reunited on the character they had revolutionized years earlier to give Iron Man his swan song in the pages of *Iron Man: The End* special. Plotted by the legendary duo and drawn by artist Bernard Chang, this one-shot saw Tony Stark pass on his heroic mantle to young scientis Nick Travis, while focusing on his latest scientifi breakthrough, an elevator into outer space.

FEBRUARY

WAR AND PIECES

• *War Machine* (2nd series) #1

Spinning out of the pages of the *Dark Reign: New Nation* one-shot, former Iron Man James Rhodes received his own title once again, this time with the help of writer Greg Pak and artist Leonardo Manco. This gritty series saw the now half-human cyborg that was Rhodey take on high-profile threats, including the Ultimo virus.

SCARED OF THE DARK

"I want an army of men and women ready to take back the world. And those who are not ready will be replaced."

• *Dark Avengers #1*

At the end of writer Brian Michael Bendis' *Secret Invasion* event, former Green Goblin Norman Osborn was shown talking with a clandestine alliance of elite Super Villains dubbed the Cabal. Made up of tried and true villains, including Osborn, Loki, Doctor Doom, and the Hood, along with the morally ambiguous White Queen and Namor, the Sub-Mariner, the Cabal was the secret power structure behind the post-Invasion world. As Bendis and artist Mike Deodato launched *Dark Avengers*, readers quickly realized just how drastic the landscape of that world had become.

Norman Osborn was in charge. Given power over the now-dissolved agency that was SHIELD, Osborn usurped Tony Stark's position to create HAMMER and legally hunt down all the heroes he had despised for most of his adult life. With public opinion on his side, Osborn donned the identity of the Iron Patriot, a perverse amalgam of the uniforms of his enemies Iron Man and Captain America, and recruited his own team of Avengers to help enforce his iron-fist rule. Osborn conned the Sentry and the god of war Ares into fighting by his side, as well as Marvel Boy (renaming him Captain Marvel). He filled out the rest of the team's ranks by disguising Super Villains in heroic garb. The assassin Bullseye became the new Hawkeye, Venom passed himself off as Spider-Man, and Moonstone dubbed herself Ms. Marvel. Even Wolverine's corrupt son Daken joined Osborn's cause, taking his father's moniker and wearing Wolverine's old costume. The villains had become the heroes and the heroes had become the villains. And just like that, the Avengers legacy was tainted, seemingly forever.

SPIDEY MEETS THE PRESIDENT

• *The Amazing Spider-Man* #583

While the main story of this issue, by writer Mark Waid and artist Barry Kitson, was an interesting examination of Peter Parker's relationship with his former girlfriend Betty Brant, this self-contained tale wasn't the reason readers flocked to comic stores (persuading Marvel into publishing multiple reprints). The real reason for the issue's popularity was evident on its cover, which showed Spider-Man snapping a photo of the newly elected President of the United States, Barack Obama. Besides its main tale, this landmark issue featured a backup tale by writer Zeb Wells and artist Todd Nauck, that teamed Spidey with the President in order to stop the masquerading Chameleon from being sworn in as the new Commander-in-Chief.

LIVING IN DARKNESS

• *Punisher* #1

Writer Rick Remender and artist Jerome Opena showed readers what life was like for Frank Castle in a world under Norman Osborn's thumb. In this first issue of his new, ongoing series, Punisher took on the all-powerful Sentry in a fight the vigilante actually managed to walk away from.

Norman Osborn altered Venom's form in order to make him seem presentable to the public as Spider-Man.

MAY

"War of Kings starred many familiar faces to longtime Marvel readers, including Darkhawk, Gladiator, and Black Bolt.

COSMIC WARS

• *War of Kings* #1

Writers Dan Abnett and Andy Lanning, along with penciler Paul Pelletier, set the cosmic stage for war with this epic five-issue miniseries, which set up an interstellar battle between the alien races of the Shi'ar and the Kree, with many of Earth's heroes caught in the middle.

LOVE AND DEATH

• *New Avengers: The Reunion* #1

Death and rebirth was a concept not foreign to Super Heroes in general, and certainly not to Avengers Ronin and Mockingbird. Mockingbird had just returned to Earth from the seeming dead in the pages of *Secret Invasion*, and Ronin (formerly Hawkeye) had been granted a new lease on life by the deeds of the Scarlet Witch. In this four-issue series by writer Jim McCann and artist David Lopez, the rocky relationship between the two formerly dead and formerly married crime fighters was more stable, even if the tender moments were shared only during pauses in gunfire.

AUGUST

THE NEW WOLVERINE

• *Dark Wolverine* #75

Wolverine's misguided, cruel son Daken had made his debut in the pages of *Wolverine: Origins*, penned by Daniel Way, an intriguing series that delved into the previously mysterious past of the feral mutant. So it made sense that when Daken graduated to his father's mantle and usurped his comic book title, Daniel Way should be the pilot guide the adventures of this Dark Wolverine. With him was co-writer Marjorie Liu and penciler Guiseppe Camuncoli, who helpe chronicle Daken's machinations in the "service" of Norman Osbor

CAPTAIN AMERICA: ALIVE AND WELL

• *Captain America* #600

Just in time for the title's 600th issue, Captain America returned to its original numbering with this oversized, blockbuste installment. Included in this issue was a feature story written by Ed Brubaker and drawn by Butch Guice, Howard Chaykin, Rafael Albuquerque, David Aja, and Mitc Breitweiser, that hinted at the possibility that Steve Rogers might still be alive, despite Captain America's recent "death." The issue also featured tv shorter tales (by Roger Stern and Kalman Andrasofszky, as well as Mark Waid and Dale Eaglesham) that remembered the hero's impressive legacy, as well as a reprint of a classic Captain America/ Red Skull battle from 1942 by Stan Lee and Al Avison. If that was enough for every fan of the red, white, and blue hero, this issue contained a two-page origin story by Paul Dini and Alex Ross, and column by Captain America co-creator Joe Simon.

SEPTEMBER

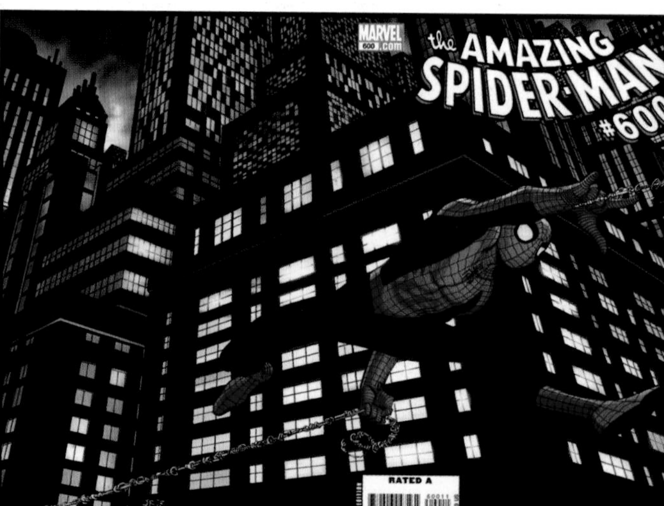

SPIDEY'S 600TH

• *The Amazing Spider-Man* #600

Hard on the heels of Captain America's anniversary, owing to its thrice-monthly release schedule, *The Amazing Spider-Man* reached its 600th issue with the largest collection of all-new material in the title's history. Writer Dan Slott and penciler John Romita Jr. handled the issue's main story, which saw the return of Doctor Octopus and the momentous wedding of Peter Parker's Aunt May to J. Jonah Jameson, Sr. The comic also featured a story by Spidey's legendary creator, Stan Lee, paired with artist Marcos Martin, as well as contributions from many other members of the Spider-Man brain trust.

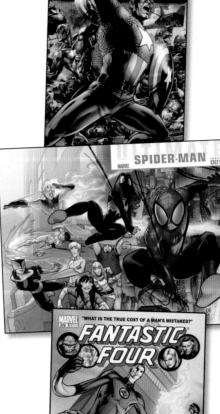

SEPTEMBER

THE RETURN OF THE CAPTAIN

• *Captain America: Reborn* #1

Steve Rogers borrowed a page from Kurt Vonnegut's classic novel *Slaughterhouse-Five* when he became unstuck in time in this new, six-issue, time-spanning miniseries. Written by Cap's regular scribe Ed Brubaker, and featuring the realistic artwork of Bryan Hitch and Butch Guice, this series started where *Captain America* #600 left off, revealing that everyone's favorite star-spangled hero was alive, but lost in the timestream. While the world believed Cap had been shot dead on the steps of the courthouse, an investigation by Agent 13 and a team of Cap's other allies proved otherwise in this adventure, which returned Steve Rogers to his proper place in the present-day Marvel Universe.

OCTOBER

ULTIMATE REBOOT

• *Ultimate Comics Spider-Man* #1

Briefly thought dead after the tragic events of Ultimatum, Spider-Man swung back into a new series, by longtime scribe Brian Michael Bendis and new series artist, David Lafuente. As Peter Parker tried to balance high-school drama, a job at the Burger Frog, and the chaos of life as Spider-Man, things got even crazier when his Aunt May let Johnny Storm of the Fantastic Four live at Peter's home. As the series continued, May would take in more of Peter's amazing friends, including the former X-Men member Iceman.

FANTASTIC FORAY

• *Fantastic Four* #570

New writer Jonathan Hickman began what would become a critically acclaimed run on Marvel's first family of Super Heroes with this issue, paired with artist Dale Eaglesham. In this initial issue of Hickman's time on the title, Reed Richards joined forces with many different Reeds from parallel dimensions.

NOVEMBER

SOMETHING IN THE WAY SHE MOVES

• *Spider-Woman* #1

When the long-awaited collaboration of writer Brian Michael Bendis and artist Alex Maleev on Spider-Woman's new series hit comic stores, it wasn't the only way readers could experience the post-Secret Invasion adventures of Jessica Drew. Also presented online as the first attempted, ongoing, in-continuity motion comic, Spider-Woman came to life on readers' screens, providing a new experience for fans curious to see Drew in action as an alien hunter in the service of the agency SWORD. Despite fan demand and a positive reception, the series lasted only seven issues, due to the extremely time-consuming workload on artist Alex Maleev.

Red She-Hulk was later revealed to be the Hulk's love interest, Betty Ross.

LADY IN RED

• *Hulk* #15

The world of the incredible Hulk gained a new super-strong player with the introduction of Red She-Hulk, the female equivalent of the title's mysterious protagonist. Written by Jeph Loeb and drawn by Ian Churchill, this issue saw Red She-Hulk's surprising debut during a hectic brawl between the Red Hulk's forces and the members of X-Force.

MEANWHILE IN 2009...

J.G. BALLARD DIES

British science-fiction writer J.G. Ballard, famous for his dystopian visions of modern life, dies aged 78.

BLACK SATURDAY

Wildfires, dubbed the Black Saturday bushfires, devastate the Australian state of Victoria. Some of the fires are deliberately started.

THE KING OF POP IS DEAD

News of the death of recording artist Michael Jackson triggers a worldwide outpouring of grief. Jackson's physician, Conrad Murray, is later charged with involuntary manslaughter.

TOTAL ECLIPSE

The longest-lasting solar eclipse of the century—lasting over six-and-a-half minutes—occurs over parts of Asia and the Pacific.

LES PAUL DIES

A pioneer of the electric guitar and a hugely influential guitarist, Les Paul dies aged ninety-three.

WORLD'S FASTEST MAN

Jamaican sprinter Usain Bolt runs 100 metres in 9.58 seconds, a new world record. Bolt also achieves a world record in the 200 metres, becoming the first man to hold both records at the same time.

LOCKERBIE BOMBER FREED

The Scottish government releases Libyan Abdelbaset al-Megrahi, convicted of the 1988 Lockerbie bombing of Pan Am flight 103, on the grounds that he has terminal cancer.

A DREAM COMES TRUE

Susan Boyle, winner of British television's Britain's Got Talent *show, sees her debut album,* I Dreamed A Dream, *top world album sales.*

WATER ON THE MOON

NASA announces the discovery of "significant" amounts of water in the Cabeus crater on the Moon.

AND AT THE MOVIES...

James Cameron's sci-fi fantasy Avatar *smashes box-office records and starts a 3D craze; Harry Potter falls in love in* Harry Potter and the Half-Blood Prince; *vampire Robert Pattinson abandons human Kristen Stewart in* The Twilight Saga: New Moon; *in* Star Trek, *Captain Kirk and Spock battle the Romulans; Guy Ritchie's* Sherlock *updates Sherlock Holmes; Quentin Tarantino's* Inglourious Basterds *tells a black-comic World War II tale of a Jewish resistance group's attempt to assassinate Nazi leaders.*

Dark Avengers ***#1 (March, 2009)***
Writer Brian Michael Bendis navigated his way through the darkest territories of the Marvel Universe, with the help of Mike Deodato, when the pair let a band of villains borrow the heroic name of the Avengers for their own nefarious purposes. The Marvel Universe had become a world controlled by former Green Goblin Norman Osborn through the use of smoke and mirrors on a grand scale. Dark Avengers *explored that fascinating reality through the adventures of its "protectors," villains disguised as some of the noblest faces in the history of super heroics. The infamous team was led by the Iron Patriot, Osborn's new identity that managed to insult two legends simultaneously: the icons Captain America and Iron Man.*

2010s

In the spring of 2008, the business side of Marvel Comics changed forever. While the company had successfully licensed its properties to movie studios, resulting in blockbuster films starring the likes of Spider-Man and the X-Men, Marvel now took direct control of movie adaptations, with the debut of the hit *Iron Man*. Followed shortly by *The Incredible Hulk*, *Iron Man* introduced the world to Marvel Studios, a powerful player on the Hollywood scene able to self-finance its own films. Marvel Studios began to pump out hit after hit at the box office, leading to the release of *The Avengers* in 2012 and the establishment of a cinematic Super Hero universe.

Meanwhile, Marvel Comics decided to revitalize its own universe. Once more celebrating the iconic nature of its characters, Marvel initiated the "Heroic Age." By the end of 2010, five writers had been chosen to pilot this era of comics as the company's "architects." Writers Brian Michael Bendis, Jason Aaron, Ed Brubaker, Matt Fraction, and Jonathan Hickman were handed the keys to the Marvel Universe, promising readers an exciting ride in the years to come.

"... I'm going to need all of you for what comes next."

2010

THE AGE OF HEROES

It all ended with a punch in the face. Norman Osborn's corrupt empire finally fell during the events of the *Siege* miniseries, when Spider-Man socked his longtime foe on the jaw. The good guys reclaimed their Super Hero status, and fans saw the return of the traditional Marvel Universe, one they hadn't really witnessed since the *Civil War* series in 2006.

While many readers had enjoyed the turmoil and unrest of the dark landscape of the last four years of storytelling, Marvel understood that the majority of fans were now ready for a return to the familiar. So Marvel introduced the "The Heroic Age," an official return to the traditional status quo. This event, celebrating the return of Super Heroes to the forefront, was ushered in by a series of banners that ran along the top of many new comic book titles. Marvel also issued many variant covers that featured iconic representations of their most classic crime fighters. The wars were over and the heroes had won.

At least, for now...

JANUARY

RUNNING THE GAUNTLET

• *The Amazing Spider-Man* #612

Spider-Man's classic rogues were back, updated for his Brand New Day relaunch, in "The Gauntlet," a twenty-two-part saga that began with this issue by writer Mark Waid and artist Paul Azaceta. Before Peter Parker could get a breather, he'd face Electro, Sandman, Mysterio, Morbius, the Juggernaut, the Lizard, a new Rhino, and Vulture.

MAXIMUM KINGPIN

• *PunisherMAX* #1

The adventures of Frank Castle were once again taken to the max with this new series by writer Jason Aaron and artist Steve Dillon. Featuring all the violence and disturbing themes the MAX imprint was known for, this bloody series saw a new take on the origin of the Kingpin.

MARCH

UNDER SIEGE

"It's time to take back this country."

• *Siege* #1

Norman Osborn had gone too far. It was time for his "Dark Reign" to come to an end. Almost two years had elapsed since the end of the Secret Invasion event and Osborn's rise to power. The heroes of the Marvel Universe had been forced to operate as outlaws against a corrupt, overbearing system. They had been waiting for a chance to reassert the proper status quo, and in this four-issue series by writer Brian Michael Bendis and artist Olivier Coipel, they would finally be given that opportunity.

Manipulated by the nefarious Norse god Loki, Osborn staged an attack on the home of the gods, Asgard, which had recently relocated to the airspace above Broxton, Oklahoma. Despite being ordered to stand down by the President of the United States, Osborn went ahead with the attack, which led to a brutal battle between Captain America's Avengers and Osborn's Dark Avengers. The resulting death toll was high, and included such powerhouses as Ares, Sentry, and even, seemingly, Loki himself. When the dust settled, the heroes were still standing, and a new Heroic Age had dawned in the Marvel Universe.

The Ave... triumph... machi... Norma... an...

MAY

ULTIMATE UPGRADES

• *Ultimate New Ultimates* #1

Jeph Loeb returned to the Ultimate Universe to script this five-issue miniseries alongside artist Frank Cho. This series not only returned Thor to the land of the living, it also featured a now super-powered version of the Ultimate Defenders.

On May 7, director Jon Favreau and actor Robert Downey Jr. returned to pilot Iron Man back into theaters with *Iron Man 2*, featuring a screenplay by Justin Theroux.

JUNE

THE DEATH OF NIGHTCRAWLER

• *X-Force* #26

The fan-favorite mutant Nightcrawler paid the ultimate price for his adventures with the X-Force in this tragic tale by writers Christopher Yost and Craig Kyle, and artist Mike Choi. In this chapter of the "Second Coming" storyline, Nightcrawler sacrificed himself in order to save the life of Hope Summers.

CAGE FIGHT

The New Avengers: Luke Cage #1

Luke Cage stepped into the spotlight with his own three-issue miniseries, by writer John Arcudi and artist Eric Canete. Set in the final days of Norman Osborn's "Dark Reign," the story saw Cage square off with Spider-Man's foe Hammerhead, as well as one of his own old enemies, Lionfang

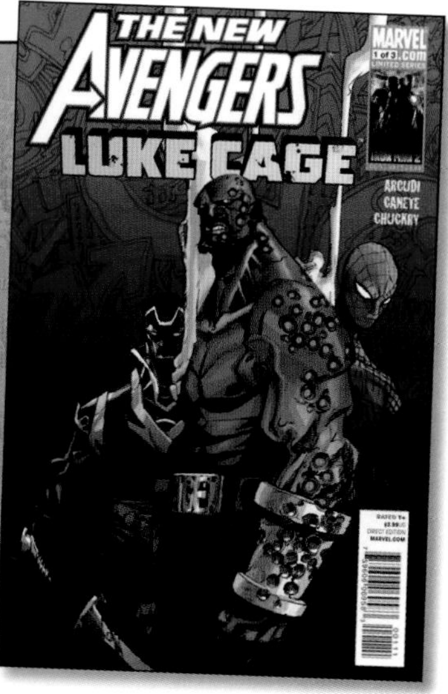

JULY

LOGAN AND PETER'S EXCELLENT ADVENTURE

• *Astonishing Spider-Man & Wolverine* #1

Spider-Man and Wolverine had shared many classic team-up stories over the years, and even served side by side on teams like the New Fantastic Four and the New Avengers. However, the two had never really seen eye to eye. In this six-issue series, writer Jason Aaron and artist Adam Kubert examined the duo's complex relationship in an offbeat story that saw them time-travel to the cretaceous period, the far-flung future, and the Old West. In what turned out to be a bizarre reality TV show produced by the infamous Mojo, the two heroes found some common ground.

JULY

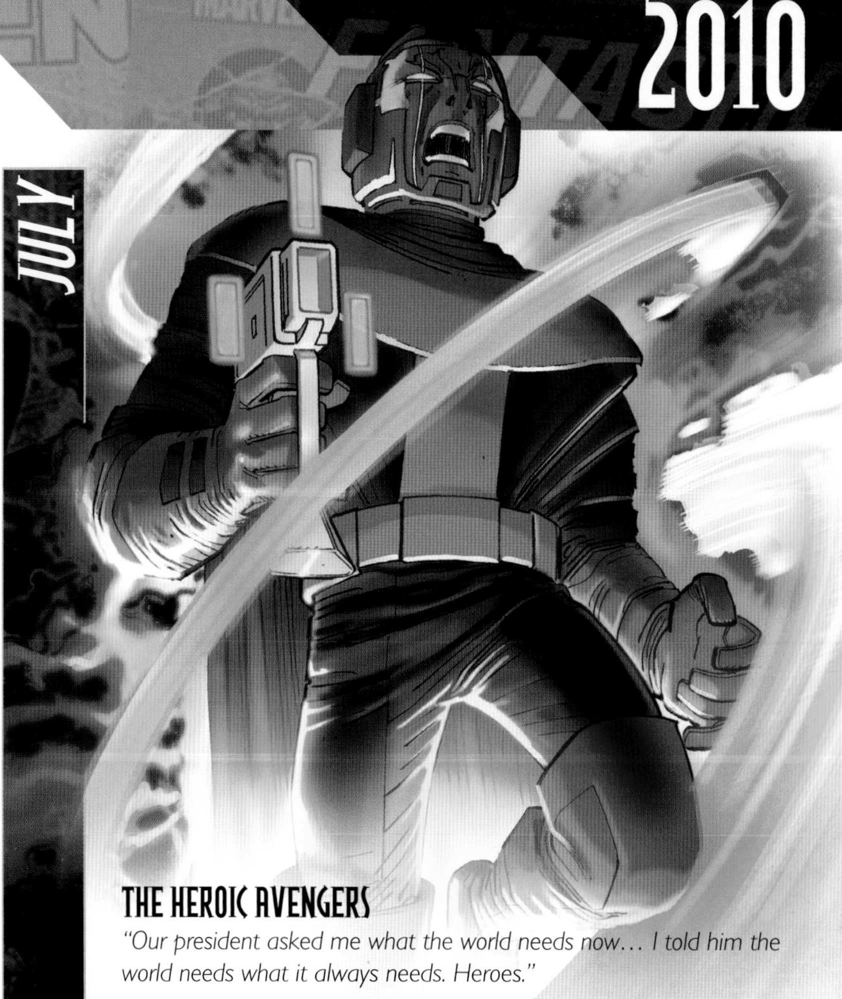

THE HEROIC AVENGERS

"Our president asked me what the world needs now… I told him the world needs what it always needs. Heroes."

• *The Avengers* #1

Norman Osborn was out and Steve Rogers was in. Handpicked by the US President, the former Captain America was charged with creating the Super Hero landscape in the aftermath of the dramatic *Siege* event on Asgard. Central to this new Heroic Age were Rogers' choices for the primary branch of the Avengers. With nearly every Super Hero to choose from, Rogers chose the best of the best, under the guidance of his right-hand woman, Maria Hill: Thor, Hawkeye (returning to his classic mantle after giving up the role of Ronin), Spider-Man, Wolverine, Captain America (James Barnes), Spider-Woman, and Iron Man. The team immediately faced the threat of Kang, and were forced to recruit the former Marvel Boy, now called the Protector, to embark on a time-spanning adventure.

In this new, ongoing series by writer Brian Michael Bendis and artist John Romita Jr., the Avengers were rocked by threat after threat, forced to fight their old teammate Wonder Man. They also faced former crime boss the Hood, who had undergone a quest to retrieve the gems of the fabled, all-powerful Infinity Gauntlet. The Avengers triumphed over these challenges and, with the recruitement of the Red Hulk, it was clear that the Avengers were once again the most powerful team in the Marvel Universe.

STEVE ROGERS' SECRET

• *Secret Avengers* #1

As the newly appointed "top cop of the world" one of Steve Rogers' first decisions was to form a team of Secret Avengers in this new series by longtime Captain America writer Ed Brubaker and artist Mike Deodato. This clandestine strike force of black-ops experts included Valkyrie, Black Widow, Agent 13, War Machine, Beast, Moon Knight, Ant-Man (Eric O'Grady), and Nova (Richard Rider).

AUGUST

THE NEW NEW AVENGERS

• *The New Avengers* #1

The New Avengers had been a force for the underground resistance since the beginning of the Super Hero Civil War. But now, in the wake of Steve Rogers' promotion to head of the Avengers, the team was finally made legitimate in this series by writer Brian Michael Bendis and penciler Stuart Immonen. To make room for this title, as well as the other new "Heroic Age" Avengers comics including *Secret Avengers*, *The Avengers*, and the youth-based new title *Avengers Academy*, the former four Avengers titles (*Dark Avengers*, *The Mighty Avengers*, *The New Avengers*, and *Avengers: The Initiative*) were cancelled, making it apparent to readers that this was indeed the start of a bold new era.

As the series began, Luke Cage was put in charge of the team, having proved himself during the New Avengers' previous incarnation. Ms. Marvel, Spider-Man, Wolverine, the Thing, Jessica Jones Cage, Mockingbird, Iron Fist, and Hawkeye helped round out the rest of the roster, although Hawkeye would soon depart to focus on his adventures with the main branch of the Avengers. Norman Osborn's former first in command Victoria Hand was also brought into the fold as the team settled in at the Avengers Mansion, leaving the main Avengers branch to establish Avengers Tower as their home base. The Avengers franchise was renewed and, as usual, more than ready for action.

THE GRIM HUNT

• *The Amazing Spider-Man* #634

Sick and exhausted from running a gauntlet of his fiercest foes, Peter Parker was in no condition to be hunted by the Kraven family. But in this four-part storyline by writers Joe Kelly and Zeb Wells and artists Michael Lark, Marco Checchetto, and Stefano Gaudiano, Spider-Man was nearly killed so that the original Kraven the Hunter could be resurrected.

THE YOUNG AND THE RESTLESS

• *Young Allies* #1

When a group of young villains attacked New York City, veteran hero Firestar partnered with Gravity, the new Nomad and Toro, and Arana (now calling herself Spider-Girl after her predecessor was killed during the events of the "Grim Hunt") to combat the threat as a group of Young Allies in this six-issue series by writer Sean McKeever and penciler David Baldeón.

SEPTEMBER

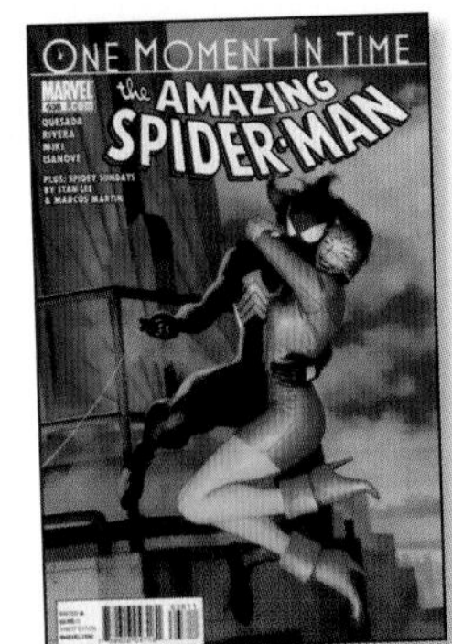

ONE MOMENT IN TIME

• *The Amazing Spider-Man* #638

Editor-in-Chief Joe Quesada returned to Spider-Man's world to answer some of th continuity questions fans had been wondering about since the "One More Day" event of 2007. This emotional, four-part story scripted by Quesada and illustrated by Paolo Rivera explained that Peter Parker and Mary Jane Watson date in the past, but never married.

TWILIGHT OF THE X-MEN

• *X-Men* #1

If box-office returns and book sales were any indication, vampires were a hot commodity. So it was only a matter of time before the mutants of the X-Men found themselves fighting off a plague of the infamous bloodsuckers. The bloody battle began in this newly relaunched title featuring a script by Victor Gischler and pencils by Paco Medina.

DISAPPEARING INTO SHADOWS

• *Shadowland* #1

Usually the star of solo adventures, Daredevil was thrown into the crossover spotlight thanks to this five-issue miniseries event written by Andy Diggle and drawn by Billy Tan. After accepting leadership of notorious ninja clan the Hand, Daredevil built his own kingdom of sorts in New York City's Hell's Kitchen, calling the fortress Shadowland. As Daredevil's personality darkened (as did his uniform, changing from red to black), many of his allies began to suspect that there was something wrong with the Man Without Fear. They discovered that Daredevil had been possessed by a force of evil known as the Beast of the Hand. After a battle with a host of Super Heroes, Daredevil bested his inner demon and disappeared into the darkness.

Matt Murdock lost his mor compass, corrupted by the dark forces he surrounded himself with.

OCT

Marvel Animation debuted the critically acclaimed animated series, *The Avengers: Earth's Mightiest Heroes*, on October 20, beginning a series of fifty-two episodes.

NOVEMBER

WOLVERINE GOES TO HELL

• *Wolverine* #1

Popular Wolverine scribe Jason Aaron took another stab at the character with the help of artist Renato Guedes in this debut issue that saw the start of a new storyline crossover event entitled "Wolverine Goes to Hell." The issue also featured a backup tale, starring the Silver Samurai, by Aaron and Jason Latour.

ALL IN THE FAMILY

• *Daken: Dark Wolverine* #1

Writers Daniel Way and Marjorie Liu continued the adventures of Wolverine's wayward son Daken in this series illustrated by Giuseppe Camuncoli. This new ongoing comic, along with the new *Wolverine* relaunch and another fledgling title *X-23*, helped carve Wolverine out his own family of comics in Marvel's lineup.

DECEMBER

FROST AND THE FÜHRER

• *Ultimate Thor* #1

The ultimate God of Thunder received his own four-issue miniseries, thanks to writer Jonathan Hickman and artist Carlos Pacheco. In this time-spanning story, Asgard faced the threat of a deadly alliance between Frost Giants and Nazi forces.

FACING APOCALYPSE

• *Uncanny X-Force* #1

When a secret society attempted to jumpstart the Age of Apocalypse in the X-Men's reality, Wolverine joined forces with Deadpool, Psylocke, Fantomex, and Archangel for this newest incarnation of the X-Force, written by Rick Remender and illustrated by Jerome Opeña.

THE RETURN OF CARNAGE

• *Carnage* #1

Thought dead since the beginning of the original New Avengers series of 2005, Carnage made his disturbing return in a five-issue miniseries by writer Zeb Wells and artist Clayton Crain. As Spider-Man and Iron Man did their best to handle the deadly menace of the old Spider-Man foe, readers glimpsed the first appearance of a new symbiote-powered character, Scorn.

MEANWHILE IN 2010...

AL-QAEDA THREAT

The US and UK close Yemen embassies in the face of threatened attacks by groups linked to terrorist organization al-Qaeda.

J.D. SALINGER DIES

J.D. Salinger, famously reclusive author of controversial, rite-of-passage novel The Catcher in the Rye, *dies aged 91.*

TALLEST BUILDING

The Burj Khalifa tower, a skyscraper in Dubai, UAE, is the tallest building in the world.

HAITI EARTHQUAKE

An earthquake measuring 7.0 on the Richter scale devastates Port-au-Prince, killing over 230,000 people. Many countries pledge aid.

CHART TOPPER

Lady Gaga scores her sixth consecutive US number one with "Telephone." She later accepts MTV's Video of the Year, for "Bad Romance," wearing a dress made of meat.

FLYING BLIND

Clouds of ash from Iceland's erupting Eyjafjallajökull volcano disrupts flights across northern and western Europe for several days.

DENNIS HOPPER DIES

Resolutely unconventional filmmaker, actor, photographer, and painter Dennis Hopper dies aged 74.

GOING, GOING...

Picasso's Nude, Green Leaves and Bust *sells for $106.5 million at auction—a new world record for a work of art.*

SUN POWER

Solar Impulse *completes the first 24-hour flight by a solar-powered aircraft.*

US SECRETS REVEALED

Reports concerning US involvement in the war against the Taliban in Afghanistan as well as over a quarter of a million diplomatic cables appear on Wikileaks, an internet site specializing in publishing confidential material.

EIRE BAIL OUT

The European Union agrees an $85 billion rescue deal to save Eire defaulting on its international debts.

AND AT THE MOVIES...

Disney/Pixar's Toy Story 3 *is the highest-grossing picture, followed by Tim Burton's* Alice in Wonderland; *The Twilight and Harry Potter franchises meet continued success with* The Twilight Saga: Eclipse *and* Harry Potter and the Deathly Hallows: Part 1; *Christopher Nolan's* Inception *baffles and enthralls audiences; a ballerina loses her mind in Darren Aronofsky's Black Swan; a cop uncovers mystery and madness in Martin Scorsese's* Shutter Island.

The Avengers ***#1 (July, 2010)***

When it came to revitalizing one of Marvel's largest team franchises, writer Brian Michael Bendis pulled out all the stops. Teamed with powerhouse artist John Romita Jr., Bendis pulled together some of the biggest icons in the Marvel pantheon to form the Avengers, and immediately had them face some of their most daunting foes. In fact, in the first six issues of the title, the Avengers faced Apocalypse, Ultron, Galactus and even a future version of the Hulk, any one of whom would be regarded as a major level threat all on his own. The overall effect was truly a blockbuster return for Marvel's greatest heroes.

"I got news for you, buddy: we're all Avengers now."

2011

TO THE POINT

One of the things that makes Super Hero comics so unique is the fact that, from nearly the very beginning of the history of the industry, each tale set in a particular comic book universe built on the stories that preceded it. The Marvel Universe has been expanding and evolving since the late 1930s; for this reason, it can be difficult for new readers to find good entry points to begin their comic book reading. Over the years, Marvel has tried many different methods to attract new readers. One way is to restart a series with a new first issue. Another is to release a zero issue that details the title character's origin. In 2011, Marvel tried a new initiative, calling it Point One.

With *The Invincible Iron Man #500.1*, the subsequent issue to that hero's oversized 500th anniversary special, Marvel began to release Point One stand-alone specials that could be easily understood by new readers. Point One issues were the perfect place for teasing new storylines—*The Amazing Spider-Man #654.1* showcased the newest incarnation of Venom for the first time—or ushering in bold new eras for some of Marvel's biggest characters.

JANUARY

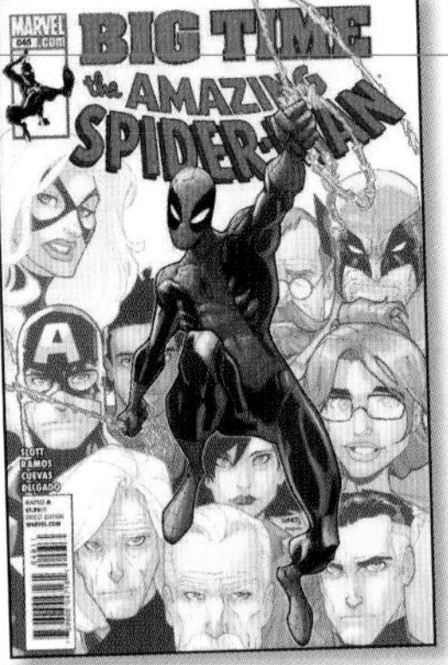

BIG TIME

• *The Amazing Spider-Man* #648

Spider-Man's "Brand New Day" had co to a close after more than a hundred issues, clearing the way for the series' n regular writer, Dan Slott, and a new direction for Spider-Man's flagship titl With the assistance of artist Humberto Ramos, this issue saw Peter Parker fina achieve his dream job: a high-paying gi developing new technology for the innovative company Horizon Labs.

WORLDWIDE SPIDER WEB

• *Spider-Girl* #1

Writer Paul Tobin and penciler Clayton Henry helped the teenage heroine formerly known as Araña into her new role as Spider-Girl in this eight-issue series. Using the innovative device of Spider-Girl's Twitter feed for captions, Spider-Girl was updated for a new generation of readers.

MARCH

THE DEATH OF THE HUMAN TORCH

• *Fantastic Four* #587

Wrapped in an ominous black polybag with a large "3" printed on the conclusion to the five-part "Three" storyline in *Fantastic Four* prepared fans for the worst from the get-go. Written by Jonathan Hickman and illustrated by Steve Epting, this issue saw founding Fantastic Four member Johnny Storm, the Human Torch, sacrific himself so that the world would be spared an invasion by Annihilu insectoid hordes. The issue's ending was poignant and powerful, as the Thing did his best to comfort Johnny's niece and nephew duri the aftermath of the battle. Happily, the Human Torch's death wou not prove to be permanent...

While the team did everything in its power to stop the forces of Annihilus, only Johnny Storm's sacrifice could save the day.

MAY

LOOKING TO THE FUTURE

• *FF* #1

The famous initials of Marvel's first family, the Fantastic Four, took on new meaning when the team adopted the name of the Future Foundation, in this ongoing series by writer Jonathan Hickman and artist Steve Epting.

In the wake of the death of Johnny Storm, the Human Torch, the Fantastic Four was no more. But Johnny Storm was a never-say-die type of person, and in his holographic will, he requested that the Fantastic Four continue without him. Johnny even had a replacement in mind, his old friend and sometime rival, Peter Parker, the Amazing Spider-Man.

While Spider-Man quickly accepted the position on the team, despite his other commitments to two different teams of Avengers and his work at Horizon Labs, he soon realized that the Fantastic Four he'd signed up for was a thing of the past. The team had become the Future Foundation, an organization dedicated to changing the world for the better. Not only did the team now wear white and black uniforms rather than their traditional blue costumes, but it also consisted of a think tank of some of the world's brightest—and youngest—shining stars. The Fantastic Four had evolved, and Spider-Man was along for the ride.

M The Mighty Thor received the blockbuster treatment in his first feature film, which hit screens on May 6. *Thor,* starring Chris Hemsworth as the title character, was directed by Kenneth Branagh and featured a screenplay by Ashley Miller, Zack Stentz and Don Payne, based on a story by Mark Protosevich and J. Michael Straczynski.

VEINS OF VENOM

• *Venom* #1

Peter Parker's former high-school bully Flash Thompson took center stage in his first-ever ongoing series as the new Venom. Wearing the symbiote suit at the behest of the US government's Project Rebirth, Flash was finally able to imitate his hero Spider-Man, in this debut issue by writer Rick Remender and artist Tony Moore.

JUNE

M Marvel made its way to Broadway with the musical *Spider-Man: Turn Off The Dark*. Despite some hiccups, a revised and improved version of the show debuted on June 14.

M The X-Men movie franchise saw a revitalization on June 3 at the hands of director Matthew Vaughn with the release of the film *X-Men: First Class*. Vaughn co-wrote the screenplay along with Ashley Miller, Zack Stentz and Jane Goldman, with additional story credits going to Sheldon Turner and Bryan Singer.

NOTHING TO FEAR

• *Fear Itself* #1

With Marvel Studios debuting two more pieces of their Avengers franchise with the release of *Thor* and *Captain America: The First Avenger,* it made sense for Marvel Comics to capitalize on the mainstream attention given to these two heroes with a blockbuster event. Enter *Fear Itself,* a seven-issue miniseries on a grand scale. Placing both Cap and Thor at the forefront of this crossover was writer Matt Fraction and artist Stuart Immonen.

The story began when the Red Skull's daughter, Sin, released an evil force on Earth by uncovering a powerful mystic hammer. Unleashing a chain of events that freed the corrupt brother of the Norse god Odin—a being calling himself by Odin's title, the All-Father—Sin received a power upgrade, as did many of Marvel's already powerful heavy hitters. With mind-controlled servants, including Hulk and Juggernaut, at his side, the evil All-Father sought to instill fear in the people of Earth, thereby boosting his own power. In the end, an army led by Captain America bested the villains, although it cost the heroes dearly. When the smoke cleared, it seemed that both Thor and Captain America's old sidekick, James Barnes, were among the dead.

A MIGHTY QUEST

• *The Mighty Thor* #1

The religious and philosophical ramifications of gods living among humans were explored by writer Matt Fraction and artist Olivier Coipel in this new series starring Thor. This debut issue also featured Thor, Sif, and Loki on an adventure in search of the mystical Worldheart, as well as an ominous appearance by the Silver Surfer.

JULY

M Director Joe Johnston took audiences back to World War II for the July 22 release of *Captain America: The First Avenger.* Starring Chris Evans as the patriotic title hero, and written by Christopher Markus and Stephen McFeely, this film helped complete Marvel's cinematic movie universe, and pave the way for an upcoming Avengers film.

MOON KNIGHT MAKEOVER

• *Moon Knight* #1

The critically acclaimed team of writer Brian Michael Bendis and artist Alex Maleev, who revitalized Daredevil and Spider-Woman, took on their next vigilante in Moon Knight. Bendis and Maleev moved the hero to the streets of Los Angeles and examined his multiple personalities, forcing Moon Knight to live with the conflicting personalities of Spider-Man, Wolverine, and Captain America inside his head.

AUGUST

THE DEATH OF SPIDER-MAN

• *Ultimate Comics Spider-Man* #160

When the Ultimate Comics imprint was first created by Marvel in 2000, the idea behind it was to attract new readers to their most popular characters, without the heavy burden of decades' worth of continuity. Marvel re-envisioned Spider-Man, X-Men, and the Avengers (as the Ultimates) as brand-new heroes just starting their adventures. With the extra incentive of top-drawer, exciting talent, the imprint was a hit, doing exactly what it set out to do.

But ten years later, the Ultimate line had built up its own complex continuity. The imprint wasn't quite as easy to jump into, and needed something to set it apart from the mainstream Marvel Universe. To accomplish that goal, writer Brian Michael Bendis did the unthinkable and killed the character he had done so much to bring to life. Bendis, along with returning penciler Mark Bagley, killed Peter Parker.

When the Green Goblin escaped from the Triskelion, he took his own team of powerhouse Super Villains with him: Electro, Doctor Octopus, Sandman, the Vulture and Kraven. After taking a bullet for Captain America in a related conflict, Spider-Man was then forced to face this lineup of his most dangerous foes, as the Goblin brought the fight to Peter's neighborhood and the home of his beloved Aunt May. Peter finally defeated the villains with the help of Iceman and the Human Torch, but his injuries proved too great and he died in the arms of Mary Jane Watson.

SPIDER-ISLAND

• *The Amazing Spider-Man* #666

New York City has always featured prominently in Spider-Man's life—so writer Dan Slott decided to give the Big Apple an upgrade. Virtually the entire population of Manhattan gained spider powers, thanks to the machinations of the villainous Jackal and his partner in crime, the Queen. While this prologue chapter by artist Stefano Caselli (who also drew the epilogue chapter in *The Amazing Spider-Man* #673) only hinted at the dangers to come, the following six issues—drawn by Humberto Ramos—threw Peter Parker into a world where his exceptional abilities no longer made him that special. By the end of this mammoth crossover event, Peter would learn that it was the man rather than the spider than had made him a hero for all these years.

BRAVO FOR CAPTAIN AMERICA

• *Captain America* #1

Acclaimed writer Ed Brubaker was back to chronicle yet another chapter of Captain America's life, this time with the help of penciler Steve McNiven, in this new series that pitted the hero against a mysterious face from his past, a covert agent dubbed Codename: Bravo.

CYCLOPS VS. WOLVERINE

• *X-Men: Schism* #1

Allies and brothers-in-arms for year Wolverine and Cyclops reached th breaking point of their relationship in this five-issue miniseries by write Jason Aaron and pencilers Carlos Pacheco, Frank Cho, Daniel Acuñ Alan Davis, and Adam Kubert. When Wolverine witnessed mutan teenagers being treated like soldiers he took many of Cyclops' forces away from his stronghold in Utop to rediscover the peaceful dream o Charles Xavier back in New York.

DERRING-DO

• *Daredevil* #1

Blind swashbuckling lawyer Matt Murdock returned to his somewhat lighter roots thanks to the brilliant combination of writer Mark Waid and artist Paolo Rivera (with the equally talented Marcos Martin penciling later issues) for this new ongoing series. With an emphasis on visual storytelling and exploring the details of Daredevil's hypersensitive powers, Murdock was taken in a less gritty direction, facing threats from Marvel's Super Villain community, as well as realistic challenges, such as issue seven's powerful story of Murdock leading a troop of blind children through a snowstorm.

ANOTHER ROUND OF PUNISHMENT

• *The Punisher* #1

Writer Greg Rucka and artist Marco Checchetto started a new chapter of Frank Castle's life with a bang as his new series began with a violent gun battle at a wedding reception. Realistic and as violent as Punisher readers would expect, this new series examined the Punisher's life from his point of view as well as from that of local law-enforcement officers.

THE SOUND AND THE FURY

• *Ultimate Comics: The Ultimates* #1

The newest take on the extremely busy world of Nick Fury and the Ultimates arrived in the form of this ongoing series by writer Jonathan Hickman and artist Esad Ribic, showcasing Fury juggling the many crises that face the Ultimate Universe.

NOVEMBER

THE NEW SPIDER-MAN

• *Ultimate Comics Spider-Man* #1

Ultimate Spider-Man was dead. Long live Ultimate Spider-Man.

While Peter Parker had met his demise at the end of the first volume of *Ultimate Comics Spider-Man*, a replacement soon stood up to accept his mantle in the form of young Miles Morales. While fans first glimpsed Miles in action in Spider-Man's traditional costume in the fourth issue of the six-issue *Ultimate Comics Fallout* miniseries (October, 2011) in a short story by writer Brian Michael Bendis and artist Sara Pichelli, they didn't discover the origin of the new hero until this debut issue by the same writer/artist team.

This series began in a flashback set eleven months prior. When a test subject spider escaped the confines of Osborn Industries and bit the hand of Miles Morales, Miles discovered that he could adhere to walls, sting opponents, and blend in with his environment so as to become virtually invisible. But seeing the way mutants are treated in the modern world, Miles was reluctant to accept his new legacy. When Peter Parker died, Miles discovered that with great power comes great responsibility and, after an impressive fight with Electro, the young man soon donned a black and red version of the world-famous Spider-Man suit.

Following increased reader interest due to real-world news coverage, the Ultimate Comics imprint had finally gone back to its roots. Just like a decade ago, *Ultimate Comics Spider-Man* was a fresh and inviting version of the longtime Marvel character, easily accessible for new readers.

ULTIMATE AND AMAZING FRIENDS

• *Ultimate Comics X-Men* #1

Writer Nick Spencer and artist Paco Medina helped to launch this ongoing series, starring new and established mutant characters, as well as recent Spider-Man supporting characters such as Kitty Pryde, the Human Torch, and Iceman.

DECEMBER

HEADMASTER WOLVERINE

• *Wolverine and the X-Men* #1

Writer Jason Aaron and Chris Bachalo chronicled the challenges Wolverine faced as headmaster of the newly established Jean Grey School For Higher Learning in Westchester County, New York, in this new, ongoing title that dealt with the fallout from the *X-Men: Schism* miniseries. Previous headmaster Cyclops would subsequently continue fighting for mutantkind in the pages of the newly relaunched *Uncanny X-Men* series by writer Kieron Gillen and penciler Carlos Pacheco that would debut in January 2012.

Wolverine and Beast were just a few of the faculty members at the Jean Grey School.

MEANWHILE IN 2011...

THE ARAB SPRING
Anti-government demonstrations throughout the Arab world lead to regime change in Tunisia, Egypt, and Yemen. Tensions persist in other Arab nations.

ELIZABETH TAYLOR DIES
Film star Elizabeth Taylor, the epitome of Hollywood glamour, dies aged 79.

ROYAL WEDDING
The British royal family's Prince William, Duke of Cambridge, marries Catherine Middleton. More than two billion people watch the ceremony on television.

BIN LADEN KILLED
A US commando raid in Pakistan results in the death of Osama bin Laden, leader of terrorist organization al-Qaeda.

FANTASY RULES
Big-budget fantasy series Game of Thrones*—a future worldwide hit—premieres on the HBO TV channel.*

MLADIC ARRESTED
Bosnian Serb commander Ratko Mladic, wanted for genocide during the Bosnian War, is arrested in Serbia.

AMY WINEHOUSE DIES
Troubled British singer and songwriter Amy Winehouse dies, aged 27.

MASSACRE IN NORWAY
Anders Breivik bombs government buildings and kills 77 people at a socialist youth camp.

THE OCCUPY MOVEMENT
In protest at social and economic inequality, protestors occupy New York's Wall Street. The Occupy Movement spreads to more than 80 countries.

STEVE JOBS DIES
"Father of the Digital Revolution" Steve Jobs, founder of Apple Inc. and pioneer of the personal computer, dies aged 56.

GADDAFI OVERTHROWN
In Libya, rebel forces, aided by NATO airstrikes, overthrow dictator Muammar Gaddafi's regime, which has lasted more than 40 years. Gaddafi is killed.

JOE SIMON DIES
The first editor of Timely (later Marvel) Comics, Joe Simon, dies aged 98.

AND AT THE MOVIES...

Established franchises dominate the box-office: Harry Potter and the Deathly Hallows—Part 2, Transformers: Dark of the Moon, Pirates of the Caribbean: On Stranger Tides, The Twilight Saga: Breaking Dawn: Part 1; *Hollywood buys into a fashion for Scandinavian thrillers with an English-language version of* The Girl With the Dragon Tattoo; The Artist, *set in Hollywood as "talkies" replace silent pictures, becomes a massive international hit—despite being French, silent, and shot in black-and-white.*

Daredevil *#4 (Dec., 2011)*

When Daredevil originally debuted in the pages of the original Daredevil # 1 (April 1964), the character wasn't the grim avenger of the night he later became. Over the years, the hero darkened in personality, as did the world he inhabited. In fact, many of the artists and writers associated with DC Comics' grim and gritty Batman franchise were equally associated with the history of Marvel's Man Without Fear. However writer Mark Waid and artists Paolo Rivera and Marcos Martin decided to return to Stan Lee's original tone for Daredevil in this revamp, bringing a bit of light back into the blind world of Matt Murdock. This new team used innovative storytelling techniques to give a fresh perspective to the decades-old hero.

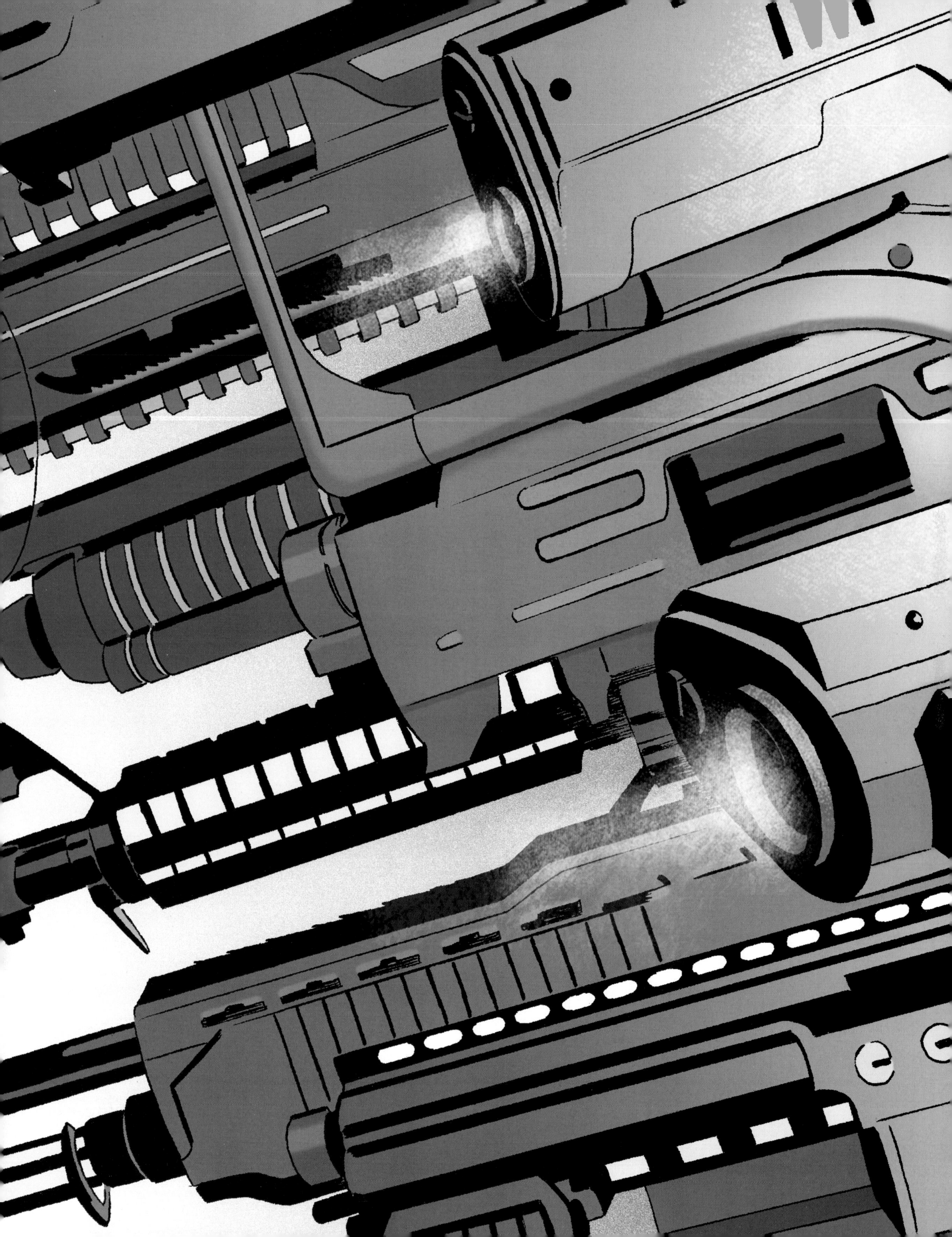

"There always has to be destruction... before the rebirth."

2012

INFINITY AND BEYOND

Over the last few years, the digital comics market had started to grow exponentially. With the rise in popularity of handheld devices like iPads and Kindles, comic book companies recognized the potential for digital comics to be the "new newsstand." Comics could once again become impulse buys for new readers unwilling to hunt down a local comic book store.

Marvel was quick to recognize this growing market, and began offering a free digital download with purchase of their titles. With the release of *Avengers Vs. X-Men*, their biggest event of 2012, Marvel further raised the bar on digital interaction. On many pages of that series, an AR symbol could be found. This new Augmented Reality feature allowed readers to see characters come alive and view other bonus content simply by scanning the image into their mobile devices. In addition, Marvel released Infinite Comics, with the help of renowned writer Mark Waid. These digital-first comics used moment-to-moment story beats to control the pacing of a tale in a way traditional print comics simply could not. If the future of the comic book industry was indeed the digital marketplace, Marvel was going to great lengths to make sure that it not only kept up with the trends, but helped create them.

JANUARY

AMAZING AND AVENGING

• *Avenging Spider-Man* #1

Spider-Man's life as a team player was explored in this new ongoing series that paired the web-slinger with his Avengers teammates. The series began with a three-part story that cast the web-slinger alongside the Red Hulk in a battle to free the Mole Man, by writer Zeb Wells and artist Joe Madureira.

FOUR ONCE MORE

• *Fantastic Four* #600

The Human Torch returned to the Fantastic Four just in time to see the te reach a new milestone. By writer Jonat Hickman and artists Steve Epting, Carmine Di Giandomenico, Ming Do Leinil Francis Yu, and Farel Dalrymple this oversized issue revealed that Johnn Storm had been resurrected by the forc of Annihilus.

Actor Nicolas Cage drove Ghost Rider back into theaters with the February 17 release of *Ghost Rider: Spirit of Vengeance*, directed by Mark Neveldine and Brian Taylor, and written by Scott Gimple, Seth Hoffman, and David S. Goyer.

THE ARRIVAL OF WINTER

• *Winter Soldier* #1

After the events of *Fear Itself*, the world believed James Barnes was dead. And that's exactly the way the hero preferred it as he began a new string of top-secret adventures as the Winter Soldier, in this series by writer Ed Brubaker and Butch Guice.

Marvel Animation reignited the animated Spider-Man franchise with a new cartoon based on the highly acclaimed Ultimate Spider-Man series. Also called *Ultimate Spider-Man*, the cartoon debuted on April 1.

READERS ASSEMBLE!

• *Avengers Assemble* #1

Just in time for the debut of Marvel Studios' blockbuster *Avengers* feature film came *Avengers Assemble*, an ongoing series jumpstarted by writer Brian Michael Bendis and artist Mark Bagley that pitted the Avengers against the now-upgraded Zodiac. The cover of this first issue featured Iron Man, Thor, Hawkeye, Black Widow, the Hulk, and Captain America—the same team starring in the blockbuster film. This series was meant as a perfect jumping-on point for new readers, a way for th to get in on a title from the start.

MAY

AVX

• *Avengers Vs. X-Men* #0

While Marvel Studios was busy scoring at the box office, Marvel Comics was not to be outdone. With the release of *Avengers Vs. X-Men* #0, Marvel embarked on a thirteen-issue crossover event that would shake up its entire Super Hero universe. Supported by various innovative digital tie-ins, including an ad that, when scanned with a compatible digital device, allowed Marvel's new Editor-in-Chief Axel Alonso to walk onto the pages of each reader's comic, *Avengers Vs. X-Men* promised a battle royal involving nearly every major Marvel hero.

To birth a series with such an epic feel, a large creative team was recruited. Marvel teamed all its world-building "architects" for the project: writers Brian Michael Bendis, Jason Aaron, Ed Brubaker, Jonathan Hickman, and Matt Fraction. Serving as artists for the series were heavy-hitters Frank Cho, John Romita Jr., Olivier Coipel, and Adam Kubert.

With this creative team in place, the series explored the ramifications of the return of the Phoenix Force, a powerful entity familiar to longtime X-Men fans. The Phoenix Force corrupted Cyclops of the X-Men and, when he and his team began to shape the world in their image, the Avengers fought against their former allies. They finally bested Cyclops with the help of the X-Men's own protégée, Hope Summers, although it cost the life of Charles Xavier, Professor X of the X-Men. Aided by the probability-altering powers of the Avengers' Scarlet Witch, Hope shattered the Phoenix Force, creating a new generation of mutants all over the world.

While many characters fought during AVX, two of the most important players turned out to be the Scarlet Witch and Hope Summers.

MAY

Marvel Studios released their biggest hit to date in the form of their highly anticipated film *Marvel's The Avengers* on May 4. The movie was written by director Joss Whedon, alongside screenwriter Zak Penn, and starred Robert Downey Jr., Chris Evans, Mark Ruffalo, Chris Hemsworth, Scarlett Johansson and Jeremy Renner as Super Hero teammates.

JUNE

KNOCK-DOWN, DRAG-OUT

• *AVX: VS.* #1

Fans had been debating battles between their favorite Marvel heroes for decades, so when *Avengers Vs. X-Men* debuted, they rushed to see the results of many of these fantasy bouts. However, with only thirteen-issues to tell a globe-spanning story, the main miniseries didn't have room to delve into the specifics of the epic battles being waged. Enter *AVX: VS.*, a six-issue companion series with shifting creative teams, showcasing at least two big fights per issue. The initial issue of this fast-paced series featured Iron Man triumphing over Magneto in a tale by writer Jason Aaron and artist Adam Kubert, as well as the Thing defeating Namor in a story by writer Kathryn Immonen and artist Stuart Immonen.

JULY

The Amazing Spider-Man, a reboot of the Spider-Man film franchise, premiered on July 3 starring Andrew Garfield as Peter Parker. The aptly-named Marc Webb was the movie's director, with James Vanderbilt, Alvin Sargent, and Steve Kloves tackling the film's screenplay.

AUGUST

DARK THUNDERBOLTS

• *Dark Avengers* #175

Luke Cage went from Thunderbolt to Dark Avenger when he was put in charge of a new team in this issue by writer Jeff Parker and artist Declan Shalvey. Filling out Cage's ranks were: Hulk's son Skaar, cyborg Thor double Ragnarok, Hawkeye's brother Trick Shot, unhinged Scarlet Witch impersonator Toxie Doxie, and the monstrous spider-creature Ai Apaec.

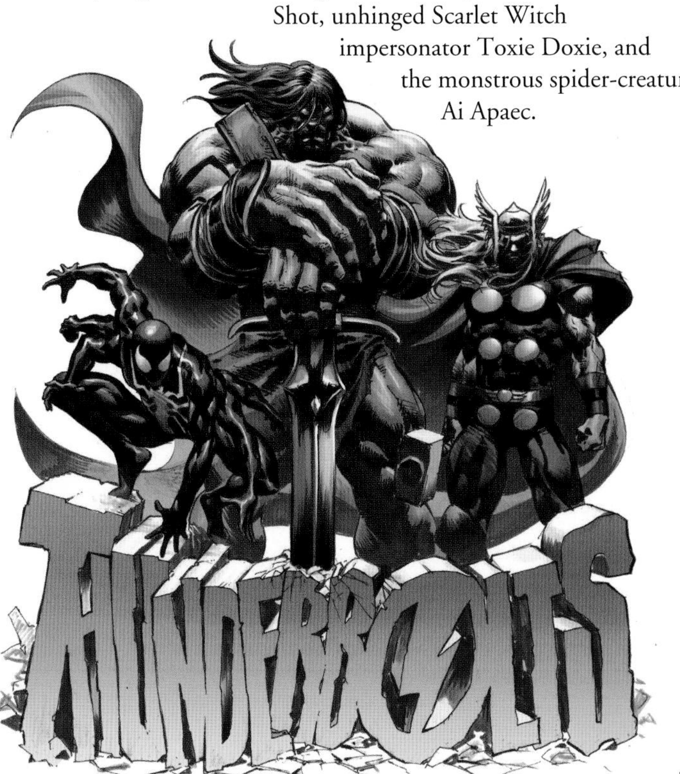

AUGUST

NORTHSTAR'S WEDDING

• *Astonishing X-Men* #51

For decades, Marvel Comics had stood against bigotry and hatred, often using the plight of the X-Men as a metaphor for the struggles faced by minority groups. So when same-sex marriage became legal in New York State in 2011, it didn't take long for Marvel to stand up once again for equal rights by having two of its gay characters marry in Manhattan in classic comic-book fashion. Performing the ceremonies for Northstar and new husband Kyle Jinadu in front of a multitude of X-Men and Alpha Flight members in this heartfelt issue was writer Marjorie Liu and penciler Mike Perkins.

SEPTEMBER

MS. MARVEL GETS A PROMOTION

• *Captain Marvel* #1

A supporting character of the original Captain Marvel, and a longtime fan favorite, Carol Danvers had been through several costume overhauls and name changes over the years. She went from being called Ms. Marvel, to Binary, to Warbird, and back again, but she never fully accepted her role as the official replacement to the alien hero Mar-Vell. In this issue by writer Kelly Sue DeConnick and artist Dexter Soy, Carol finally seized hold of her destiny as the new Captain Marvel, adopting a new costume of impermeable fabric designed by Tony Stark.

OCTOBER

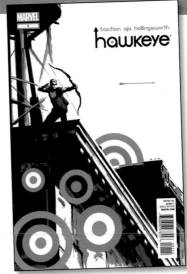

STRAIGHT SHOOTER

• *Hawkeye* #1

Clint Barton's time away from the Avengers was explored in this new series by writer Matt Fraction and artist David Aja. Containing stories far removed from the event-style super-confrontations of the Avengers, this title focused on Clint's more realistic adventures, such as dealing with a corrupt New York City landlord. A brilliant, character-driven piece, *Hawkeye* was immediately gripping, taking full advantage of colorist Matt Hollingsworth's beautiful, muted color palette, which enhanced Aja's artful storytelling. The result was a very different kind of Marvel comic that was every bit as entertaining as its blockbuster companions.

DECEMBER

DEVIL'S END

• *Daredevil: End of Days* #1

Matt Murdock's career was brought to an end in this eight-issue miniseries set in the not-too-distant future. The product of the collected talents of many Daredevil luminaries, including writers Brian Michael Bendis and David Mack, and artists Klaus Janson and Bill Sienkiewicz, this Citizen Kane-like tale followed reporter Ben Urich as he investigated Daredevil's final fight, when the hero was apparently killed by his longtime enemy Bullseye in a brutal battle caught on video.

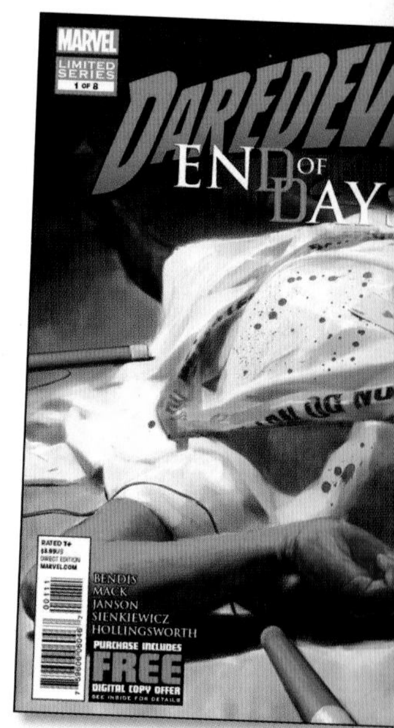

AVENGING XAVIER

• *Uncanny Avengers* #1

In the fallout of the *Avengers Vs. X-Men* event, Captain America found himself in a world that was more anti-mutant than ever. Realizing that the Avengers hadn't done enough to help mutants over the years, Cap set out to create a new breed of Avengers, in this ongoing series by writer Rick Remender and artist John Cassaday. Placing Cyclops' brother Havok in charge of this new group, Cap recruited several other mutants, including Rogue, Wolverine and Scarlet Witch, pairing them with traditional, non-mutant powerhouses like Thor, to create a formidable team. They soon needed every ounce of that strength when the Red Skull stole the powerful mind of deceased Professor X to use as a weapon.

TEAM ADDITIONS

• *A+X* #1

Spinning out of *Avengers Vs. X-Men* was this new title with a shifting creative team. Taking the opposite approach of the conflict of *Avengers Vs. X-Men*, this series focused on two team-up stories in each issue, featuring X-Men and Avengers working alongside one another. The initial issue featured a Captain America/Cable pairing by writer Dan Slott and artist Ron Garney, as well as a Hulk/Wolverine team-up by scripter Jeph Loeb and penciler Dale Keown.

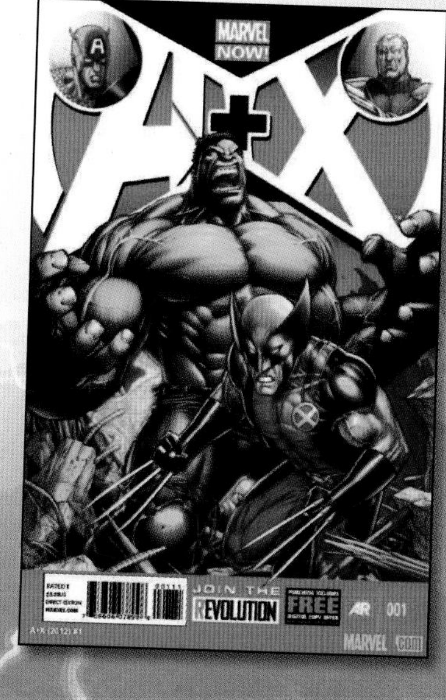

GODS AND MONSTERS

• *Thor: God of Thunder* #1

Writer Jason Aaron and artist Esad Ribic gave Thor more than he bargained for in this ongoing series, in which the hero met the threat of Gorr the God Butcher in a story that spanned Thor's past, present, and future.

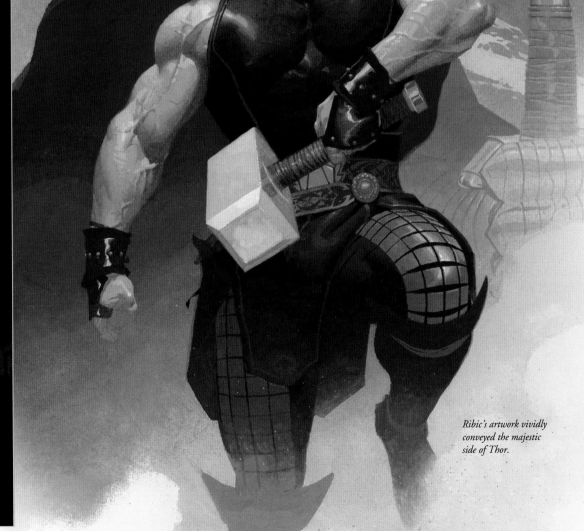

Ribic's artwork vividly conveyed the majestic side of Thor.

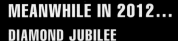

MEANWHILE IN 2012...

DIAMOND JUBILEE
Queen Elizabeth II celebrates her diamond jubilee as queen of the UK, Canada, Australia, and New Zealand.

21 AGAIN...AND AGAIN
British singer Adele wins six Grammy awards for her album 21, which has yielded three US number one singles.

BRITANNICA OUT OF PRINT
After more than 240 years as a set of printed volumes, the Encyclopedia Britannica *is now only available online.*

SCREAMING TO THE BANK
A pastel version of The Scream, *by the Norwegian artist Edvard Munch, sells for $120 million at auction, a record for a work of art.*

INDIA BLACKOUTS
More than 620 million people are without electricity for two days, the largest blackout in India's history.

NEIL ARMSTRONG DIES
Astronaut Neil Armstrong, the first man ever to set foot on the Moon, dies aged 82.

DRUGS CHEAT
Cyclist Lance Armstrong, seven times winner of the Tour de France, admits using performance-enhancing drugs.

MARS LANDING
NASA's Mars Science Laboratory's rover Curiosity *lands on Mars' Gale Crater and commences exploration of the planet.*

A LONG WAY DOWN
Austrian skydiver Felix Baumgartner achieves a record space dive, leaping from a helium balloon 24 miles (39 km) over Roswell, New Mexico.

DOOMSDAY SCENARIO
Mayan calendar predictions that the world will end on December 21, 2012 prove groundless.

AND AT THE MOVIES...

Batman and Bond return in The Dark Knight Rises *and* Skyfall; *Bilbo Baggins joins a group of dwarves in a quest to defeat a dragon in part one of Peter Jackson's epic* The Hobbit *trilogy; Quentin Tarantino's* Django Unchained *is a violent story of slavery in the Deep South; hit musical* Les Misérables *gets the big-screen treatment; Kathryn Bigelow's* Zero Dark Thirty *chronicles the hunt for al-Qaeda leader Osama bin Laden; Ang Lee's* Life of Pi *is praised for its groundbreaking use of 3D and digital technology.*

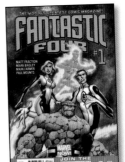

"We have to get bigger."

2013

MARVEL NOW

In the landscape of the modern Super Hero comic book, crossovers and large-scale events have proven to be a tried and true method of generating sales and excitement throughout the readership. Oftentimes the aftermath of these events can spawn an even larger audience, if the changes to the comic book universe are bold enough.

In October 2012, Marvel decided to reinvigorate its titles with a bold move. The company took the success of the *Avengers Vs. X-Men* maxiseries as its springboard, shuffled creative talent around, and restarted many of the highest-profile titles. Dubbed "Marvel NOW!," these books began to hit comic stores near the end of 2012 and were an instant crowd pleaser. With big-name writers and artists tackling properties previously foreign to them, the revamp resulted in fresh takes on classic characters. At the same time, the Marvel NOW! relaunch managed to keep fans excited and positive about the future.

JANUARY

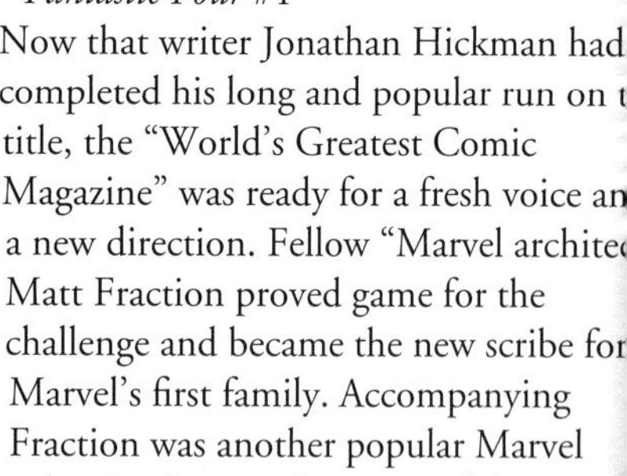

FANTASTIC VOYAGE

• *Fantastic Four* #1

Now that writer Jonathan Hickman had completed his long and popular run on t title, the "World's Greatest Comic Magazine" was ready for a fresh voice an a new direction. Fellow "Marvel architec Matt Fraction proved game for the challenge and became the new scribe for Marvel's first family. Accompanying Fraction was another popular Marvel mainstay, penciler Mark Bagley. In the very first issue of this newly restarted title, Fraction and Bagley created a smooth transition fro Hickman's run by having Mr. Fantastic discover that he and the r of the Fantastic Four seemed to be dying from the long-term effec of the cosmic rays that had first given them their superpowers. To discover a cure, Reed Richards gathered up his family and head on a journey through space and time, charting a bold new path for the heroes.

A STRONG FOUNDATION

• *FF* #1

Already handling the writing chores for *Fantastic Four*, it made sense that Matt Fraction take over writing the rebooted *FF* title as well, this time alongside artist Michael Allred. Together, they informed readers about the activities of the Future Foundation while the Fantastic Four were away exploring the cosmos, spotlighting the Foundation's reluctant new head, Scott Lang, the second man to take up the Ant-Man mantle.

MR. ROGERS' NEW NEIGHBORHO

• *Captain America* #1

Steve Rogers' past and present were examined in this volume of Cap's adventures by writer Rick Remende and artist John Romita Jr. Moving a slightly more off-beat direction than the one taken by writer Ed Brubaker during his long run on th character, this first issue saw Cap fight a villain named the Green Sk before traveling on an abandoned subway train to Arnim Zola's stronghold in Dimension Z.

EXTREMIS CIRCUMSTANCES

• *Iron Man* #1

Writer Kieron Gillen and penciler Greg Land donned their best suit of iron to begin their run charting the adventures of Tony Stark. Clad in black and gold armor, Iron Man found his life haunted once again by the threat of Extremis, following the death of his colleague Maya Hansen.

GET CYCLOPS

• *All-New X-Men* #1

Writer Brian Michael Bendis had finished his time on the Avengers titles, having been one of the main pilots for the Marvel Universe for years. With this new, ongoing series, Bendis shifted his focus to a Marvel franchise that he hadn't had the chance to explore in detail. With penciler Stuart Immonen providing the book's striking visuals, Bendis began his tenure on the X-Men, centering on the team's founding members: Cyclops, Beast, Iceman, Marvel Girl, and Angel. In this engrossing storyline, Beast traveled back in time to visit his younger self and the rest of his original team. Now that the Cyclops of the present had taken the mutant cause to an almost militant extreme, Beast decided that the only way to combat the threat of his old ally was to recruit a Cyclops that was younger, less jaded, and on the right side of the law.

BRUCE BANNER, AGENT OF SHIELD

• *Indestructible Hulk* #1

The Hulk received the Marvel NOW! relaunch treatment in this issue penned by Mark Waid and illustrated by Leinil Francis Yu. Packed with action as the Hulk took down the Mad Thinker, this issue established Bruce Banner as the newest employee of the superspy agency SHIELD.

XAVIER'S LEGACY

• *X-Men Legacy* #1

The many personalities of Legion, the unbalanced son of Charles Xavier, were put in the spotlight in this revamp of the X-Men Legacy title by writer Simon Spurrier and penciler Tan Eng Huat. The series set off at a fast pace when one of Legion's inner demons killed the inhabitants of a Himalayan commune, forcing the rest of the world to view the mutant as a murderous fugitive.

EXPANDING THE AVENGERS

• *Avengers* #1

The latest epic in the continuing saga of the Avengers began in this new Marvel NOW! series by writer Jonathan Hickman and artist Jerome Opeña. Captain America, the Hulk, Thor, Hawkeye, Black Widow, and Iron Man responded to an attack on Earth emanating from Mars. They were shocked to be immediately, and almost effortlessly, overpowered by new foes Ex Nihilo and his allies Aleph and Abyss. Only Captain America made it back to Earth after the battle, and the hero realized that there was just one way to counter such a dire threat: the Avengers had to increase their ranks.

JANUARY

THUNDERBOLT ROSS

• *Thunderbolts* #1

The Red Hulk, aka retired General "Thunderbolt" Ross, recruited an unlikely array of hardened killers into a new breed of Thunderbolts, thanks to writer Daniel Way and artist Steve Dillon. Using leverage when necessary, Ross organized a team including heavy hitters Venom, Deadpool, Elektra, and the Punisher.

THE DEATH OF PETER PARKER

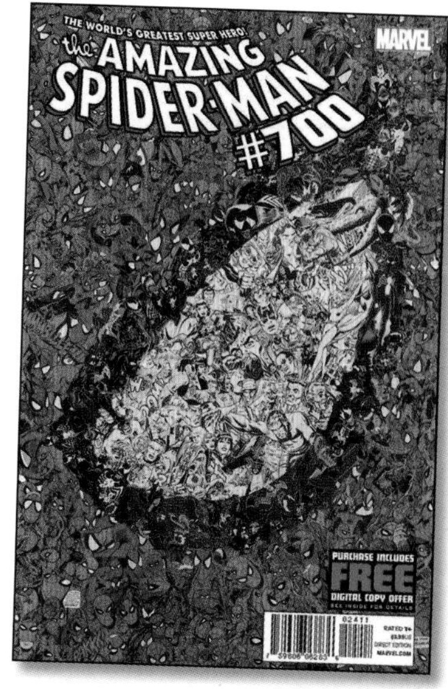

• *The Amazing Spider-Man* #700

It was the end of an era. This issue marked not only the apparent final issue of Spider-Man's flagship title, but also the supposed conclusion of the adventures of Peter Parker as everyone's friendly neighborhood wall-crawler. In this oversized anniversary edition celebrating fifty years of Spider-Man, Doctor Octopus won a battle with the web-slinger after swapping minds with the hero. As a result, Peter Parker's mind seemingly passed away with Doctor Octopus' frail form, while Octopus lived on in the healthy body of Peter Parker. This shocking conclusion to Spider-Man's story was delivered to audiences by writer Dan Slott and penciler Humberto Ramos. The issue also included two other stories, one by writer J. M. DeMatteis and penciler Giuseppe Camuncoli, and the other by writer Jen Van Meter and artist Stephanie Buscema, as well as a letter column moderated by Stan Lee himself.

FEBRUARY

INSIDE THE ILLUMINATI

• *New Avengers* #1

Writer Jonathan Hickman continued his chronicle of the Avengers in this series with penciler Steve Epting. Starring the newest incarnation of the Illuminati, Marvel's most elite team of Super Heroes, this issue began with a spotlight on Black Panther.

SPIDER-MAN 2.0?

• *The Superior Spider-Man* #1

While Doctor Octopus apparently succeeded in killing Peter Parker after swapping minds with the hero, he was unable to destroy Peter's sense of responsibility. Since the two shared the same memories, Peter was able to transfer his greatest life lesson into Doctor Octopus' consciousness before seemingly passing on. This new series by writer Dan Slott and artist Ryan Stegman examined Doc Ock's life as Spider-Man as the villain tried to turn over a new leaf, with the help of the "ghost" of Peter Parker, who still lingered in his mind.

The Amazing Spider-Man *#700*
(Feb., 2013)
Doctor Octopus was dying, but it was against the Super Villain's character merely to accept his dismal fate. By trapping his mind in Spider-Man's healthy body, Doc Ock not only extended his life, but he also condemned his greatest foe to death at the same time. In the apparent final issue of Spidey's longest-running title, Peter Parker managed to claim a hint of victory from defeat, even while trapped in Doc Ock's dying form. Discovering that a link existed between their minds, Parker forced Doctor Octopus to witness all of Spider-Man's greatest tragedies. So while Peter "died" in Doc Ock's body, Uncle Ben's famous maxim, "With great power comes great responsibility," found a home in Doctor Octopus' mind, birthing a new heir to the Spider-Man legacy.

AFTERWORD

Well, here we are, True Believers, the dreaded afterword.

I know, I know, you're bummed; all that great artwork, all those incredible stories, all that colorful history, and now here we are at the end, the very last page and word.

Buy hey, chin up, 'cause your ol' pal, Joey Q is going to slap some knowledge on you and brighten up your day. See, this isn't anywhere near where the Marvel story ends, because this sixty-plus-year overview you're currently holding is merely the beginning of the Marvel story.

So, if it makes you feel any better, let's consider this afterword as a simple introduction to what lies ahead. What you've just read is simply Act I, and we're just getting warmed up. Act II is just beginning and now you've got a front row seat.

Thanks to all the greats like Stan, Jack, Steve, John, and so many others, the foundation was set for what eventually became the greatest fantasy universe in the history of modern civilization. On a par with the likes of Homer and Shakespeare, Stan and company gave us a litany of characters and fables not seen since the stories of the all-powerful Greek and Roman pantheon of deities. The biggest difference is that the Marvel Universe is vastly superior, and given a few thousand years will still be on the tip of everyone's tongues, while Zeus and Hercules will have been as forgotten along with Betamax and Crystal Pepsi.

Now, while I'd love to sit here and tell you how it's all going to pan out millennia from now, let's keep it closer to home and look at where we are today. Not only is Marvel the top publisher of Super Hero and action adventure comics in the world, but our characters and stories grace everything from lunch boxes to video games. So great has grown the iconic appeal of Marvel characters that now Marvel finds itself adding a new feather in its cap of ever-growing entertainment conquests: Hollywood! 2008 marked the release of Marvel Studio's very first movies, and like so many of Marvel's current endeavors, Marvel fans were legion in their support, and the rest of the world came along for the ride as well.

This book notwithstanding, there has been so much written about these last sixty-plus years of Marvel, and rightfully so, but what tickles me pink is that there is so much yet to be written and that, my friends, is what jazzes me to no end. So many have asked about the secret of our success, what's the Marvel formula? To me the answer is simple: stay true to your ideals and stay true to what made Marvel great in the first place. But there is one added ingredient that makes the Marvel secret formula impossible to recreate.

YOU!

There is no reader, no fan, like the Marvel fan and that's part of what makes Marvel as engaging as it's been over the years, you're part of our family. You have a voice and we're always listening. For the uninitiated, this may be a bit tough to grasp at first, but trust me, read a few of our books and you'll quickly understand what living the MarveLife means. Before long you'll find yourself a True Believer in good standing.

Now, while I feel it may be proper etiquette to be bidding you au revoir at this point, I just can't bring myself to say the words with any conviction, as I know there are so many more chapters to be written about the Marvel story, and we'll surely meet here again. So, for now, let's keep it simple, shall we?

See ya in the funnybooks!

Joe Quesada

THE MIGHTY THOR
APPROVED BY THE COMICS CODE AUTHORITY
MARVEL COMICS GROUP
12¢ 148 JAN
DR. STRANGE
MARVEL COMICS GROUP
IS HE ALIVE-- OR DEAD?
BACK, ALL OF YOU-- THE GIRL IS MINE!!
THE BRIDE OF THE SERPENT GOD!
54 SEPT.
10¢
"I UNLEASHED MONSTRO ON THE WORLD!"
BLACK RIDER
SEPT.
BLACK RIDER RIDES AGAIN!
10¢
STARRING THE BLACK RIDER "TREACHERY AT HANGMAN'S BRIDGE!"
MARVEL LIMITED SERIES
1 of 5
PAK ROMITA JR. JANSON STRAIN
WORLD WAR
RATED T+
$3.99 US $4.75 CAN
MARVEL COMICS GROUP
DEATH WITHOUT WARNING!
MARVEL .com
110
RATED T+
ELLIS DEODATO
$2.99 US $3.75 CAN
$1.75 US
1 DEC
2099
TWO-GUN KID
44 OCT.
ALL BRAND-NEW TWO-GUN KID TALES
TWO-GUN KID
CAN THE TWO-GUN KID, SINGLE-HANDED, WIN THE "GUNFIGHT AT RAWHIDE RIDGE!"
10¢
THE KID HASN'T A CHANCE, BOYS! HE'S ALMOST OUTA AMMO! HERE'S WHERE WE GIT 'IM!!!
MARVEL COMICS PRESENTS
BEFORE WOLVERINE THERE WAS
WEAPON X
LOVERS magazine

INDEX

A note on using this index: Where a character's comic is the same as the character's name, these have been indexed together. For example, Black Knight/*Black Knight* lists entries for both the character and comic.

A

B

C

D

E

F

INDEX

K

L

M

INDEX

N

O

Q

R

S

T

W

X

Y

Z

ACKNOWLEDGMENTS

Tom Brevoort: Many thanks to Dr. Michael J. Vassallo, Tom Lammers, and the folks behind the Atlas Tales website (www.atlastales.com) for their research assistance. And always, Jessica, Jarreth, and Torin.

Tom DeFalco: Many thanks to Stan Lee, Jack Kirby, Steve Ditko, Larry Lieber, Don Heck, and the original Marvel Bullpen and the Merry Bullpenners who followed—especially the ones that I had the privilege of working with! HOO-HA and thanks for being there!

Matthew K. Manning: Many thanks to Mark Beazley and Steve Flack for lending me some of the reading material I was missing, to my friends and family for putting up with my absence these last few months, and of course to Dorothy, for her love, support, and her uncanny ability to bring me back into the real world, if only for a moment or two.

Peter Sanderson: My thanks to Roy Thomas, one of the greatest authorities in comics' Golden Age, for his help with my questions about Timely in the 1940s.

Dorling Kindersley would like to thank Stan Lee for the foreword; Joe Quesada for the afterword; Adam Levine, Jeff Poulin, Chris Allo, and Darren Montalbano at Marvel; Dr. Michael J. Vassallo for supplying images; Orbital Comics; Comicana; Gosh!; Elizabeth Dowsett for the real events panels; Nigel Ritchie for the movie information; Leah Lwin for design assistance; Victoria Taylor and Jo Casey for editorial assistance; and Marian Anderson for the index. Also a big thank you to Jim Cheung and Justin Ponsor for the incredible cover art. Thanks to Ian Walker and Oliver and Phoebe Martin.

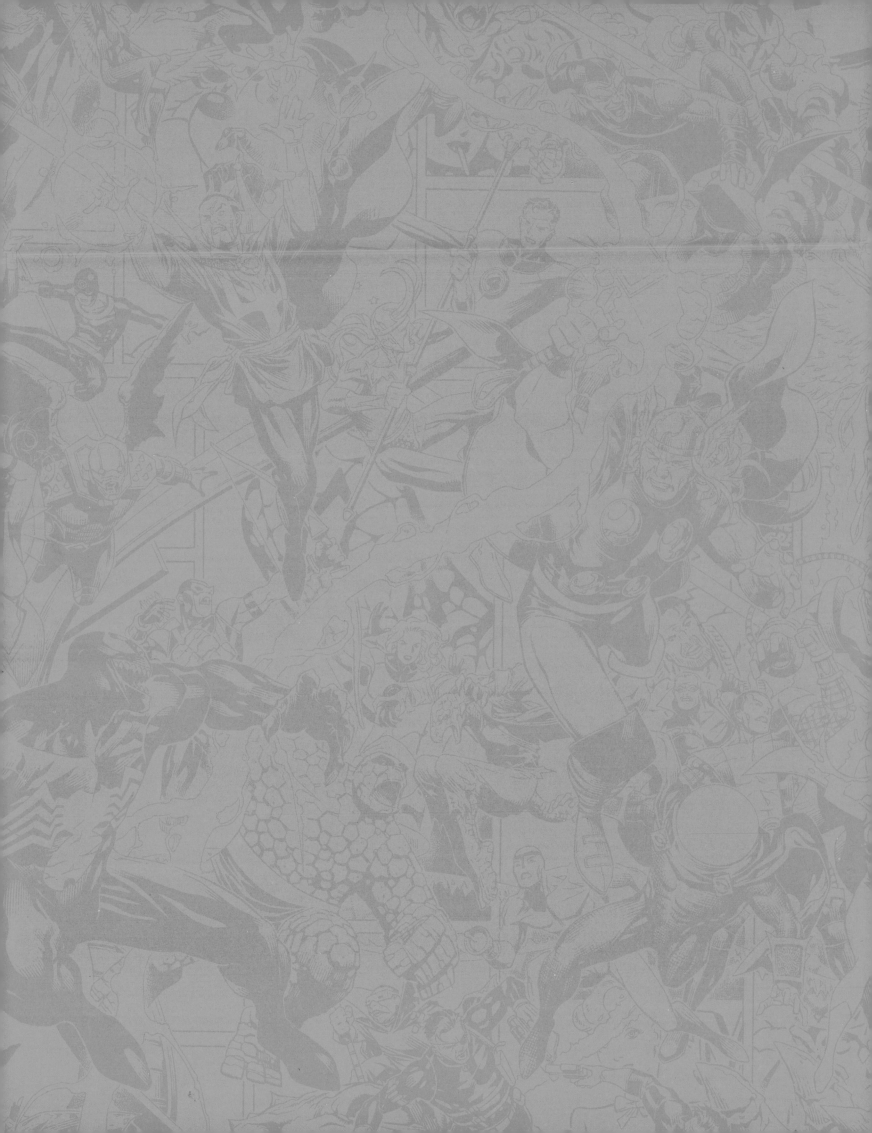